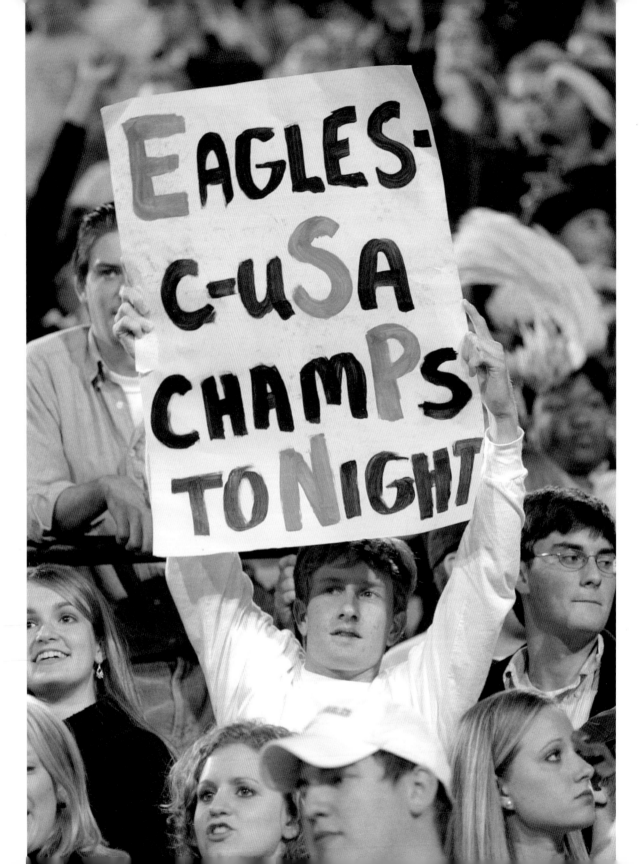

ROCK SOLID

ROCK SOLID
SOUTHERN MISS FOOTBALL

John W. Cox
and Gregg Bennett

University of Southern Mississippi
and University Press of Mississippi

www.upress.state.ms.us

All photographs courtesy of University of Southern Mississippi Athletic Department, University of Southern Mississippi Photo Services, or University of Southern Mississippi Archives unless otherwise noted. Photographs on pages i, ii, iv, vi, and vii courtesy of Bert King Photography

Designed by Todd Lape

The University Press of Mississippi is a member of the Association of American University Presses.

Copyright © 2004 by University of Southern Mississippi
All rights reserved
Printed in Canada

12 11 10 09 08 07 06 05 04   4 3 2 1

∞

Library of Congress Cataloging-in-Publication Data

Cox, John W.
  Rock solid : Southern Miss football / John W. Cox and Gregg Bennett.
    p. cm.
  Includes index.
  ISBN 1-57806-709-X (cloth : alk. paper)
  1. University of Southern Mississippi—Football—History. 2. Football—Mississippi—History. I. Bennett, Gregg. II. Title.
  GV958.U5854C67 2004
  796.332'63'0976218—dc22   2004009470

British Library Cataloging-in-Publication Data available

CONTENTS

[ix] **FOREWORD**

[3] **THE EARLY YEARS**
1912–1922

[12] **STATE TEACHERS COLLEGE AND THE BOBO ERA**
1923–1930

[24] **THE TRANSITION ERA**
1931–1941

[45] **THE POSTWAR ERA**
1946–1949

[64] **THE FABULOUS FIFTIES**
1950–1959

[97] **THE DECADE OF DEFENSE**
1960–1969

[135] **THE BEAR, BOBBY, THE EAGLES, AND ROBERTS STADIUM**
1970–1979

[173] **EAGLE FEVER AND I BELIEVE**
1980–1989

[211] **THE FINAL DAYS AS AN INDEPENDENT AND CONFERENCE USA**
1990–2003

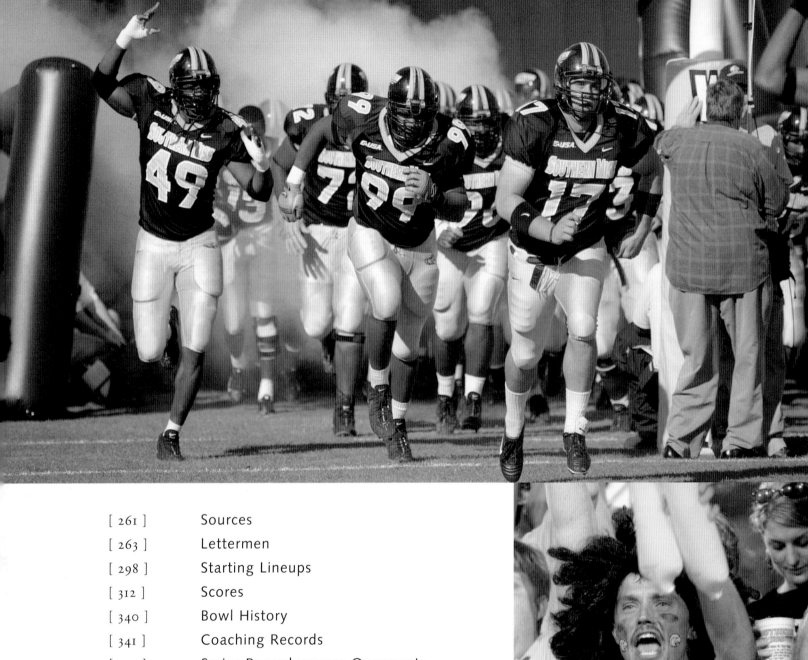

[261]	Sources
[263]	Lettermen
[298]	Starting Lineups
[312]	Scores
[340]	Bowl History
[341]	Coaching Records
[343]	Series Records versus Opponents
[347]	Award Winners and Honors
[353]	Players in the Pros
[359]	Index

FOREWORD

Pride and tradition. Heart and commitment.

That's what Southern Miss football is and always has been about. A collection of players that bonds together into a team, believing in themselves when no one else did. And reaching that final goal, that dream against all odds.

I am proud to have spent four of the most extraordinary years of my life wearing the Black and Gold and being a Golden Eagle. I'll never forget the feeling, that thrill that first time as a seventeen-year old quarterback walking out into Roberts Stadium and then going out each Saturday and putting it all on the line until our team had no more to give. And I remember the final time playing in Roberts Stadium and how I wished it never had to end. I wouldn't trade those four years for anything in the world.

The teams that I was a part of played in two bowl games, the 1988 Independence Bowl and the 1990 All-American Bowl, and recorded victories over teams like Alabama, Auburn, and Florida State. But we always remembered and carried with us that golden tradition of Southern Miss football.

As a part of Southern Miss football, my teammates and I carried the banner of those that had come before us and helped to lay an even stronger foundation for those that would follow, teams that battled in obscurity, never knowing the excitement of the television cameras or a sell-out crowd, never having an opportunity to play for a conference championship, but instead playing like we did, for the love of the game.

I am honored to have a place in the history of Southern Miss football and extremely proud of the contributions I made, and enjoy each week during the season watching and reading about the accomplishments of my Golden Eagles.

As you read *Rock Solid: Southern Miss Football*, you will remember the players who provided the magical moments at Faulkner Field, Roberts Stadium, and other stadiums around the country and the teams that made you proud that you are a Golden Eagle.

Pride and tradition. Heart and commitment. That's Golden Eagle football.

Southern to the top!

—**Brett Favre**
Quarterback, Green Bay Packers

ROCK SOLID

THE EARLY YEARS
1912–1922

> The intercollegiate athletic program is important in the history of any educational institution. It can gain recognition for a school in the regional and national press, stimulate alumni support, be an effective recruiting device, be an entering wedge for increased legislative support, and change the whole tune of life of an institution.
>
> —**William McCain, President,** University of Southern Mississippi

On March 30, 1910, the Mississippi State Legislature passed House Bill 204, which called for the establishment of a two-year institution to qualify teachers for the state's public schools. Hattiesburg and Forrest County offered the college's board of trustees $260,000 and 840 acres of land, beating out the Laurel and Jackson areas for the honor of hosting the new Mississippi Normal College, which opened its doors to its 230 students on September 18, 1912.

Athletics, most notably football, must have been on the minds of both the administration and the students, because less than a month passed before the college's first football game occurred. Also during that first month, approximately

150 students organized an athletic association, with science professor Ronald J. Slay as athletic director, L. S. Venable as president, W. T. Shows as vice president, and Maude McCaleb as secretary-treasurer. At the association's first meeting, held in October 1912, the school colors of black and gold were adopted following the suggestion of Stella McLaurin of Montrose, Mississippi. A group of local male students produced a vaudeville show to provide funds for the first football team and the launching of the intercollegiate sports program. The players on the first team dressed and had access to showers on the first floor of Forrest County Hall.

The major pre–World War I scheduling problem was getting games against other colleges or universities, with most competitions occurring between the Normalites and area high schools or military academies. The football program, like the university, was making an attempt to build a foundation for itself. From those early days forward, football would retain its important role at the University of Southern Mississippi, as evidenced by the fact that with the exception of war years, the school has fielded a football team in every year since.

1912 SEASON

On October 13, 1912, men from the Normal College played the Hattiesburg Boy Scouts, who were coached by Claude Bennett, who would later become president of the Mississippi State Teachers College, the Normal College's second name. This inaugural football contest, which consisted of four eight-minute quarters, was held at Kamper Park, which would remain the football team's home until 1932.

According to Frank D. Montague, one of the team's best players, the squad had only 15 members, and organizers had to work hard to get even that many, since few potential players understood the game. Additional players would join the team later in the season. Slay served as the coach. The team included center H. B. Longest, guards E. J. Riley and Jack Thompson, tackles G. C. Thatch and Eugene Smith, ends P. E. Phillips and J. P. (Shorty) Welborn, quarterback G. B. (Blink) Anderson, right half Benton Holmes, left half L. S. (Strut) Venable, fullback Claude Turner, and substitutes W. G. Edwards and H. V. McRae. Venable and another player, Ernest W. Love, each had only one arm and would mockingly wave their stumps in opponents' faces.

The Normal College team won the game by a score of 30–0 in front of many students who had walked the mile or so to Kamper Park. The Hattiesburg Traction Company had given courtesy rides to the football team. Like many collegiate athletic events both then and now, business support helped make the game possible.

Gulf Coast Military Academy, also beginning its first season of football competition, challenged

Ronald J. Slay was a professor on the Mississippi Normal faculty. He was appointed as athletic director and head football coach of the first football team in 1912.

THE EARLY YEARS

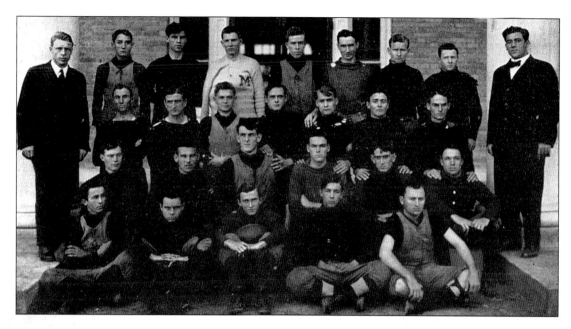

The 1913 Mississippi Normal College football team was coached by former Mississippi A & M star M. J. (Blondie) Williams (back row on left). In Williams's only year as coach the team struggled to a 1–5–1 record.

Normal College to a game at Kamper Park on Saturday, October 19. A campus pep rally was held on October 18, and members of the football team voted to accept the cadets' challenge, "provided they come, irrespective of the weather." The Cadets won the battle 6–0.

On November 5, Normal College hosted Mobile Military Academy and won by a score of 6–0. The team finished its inaugural season with a surprisingly successful 2–1 record.

1913 SEASON

At Slay's request, M. J. (Blondie) Williams, captain of the 1911 Mississippi State football team that had finished 7–2–1, took over as the Normal College head coach in 1913. In the wake of the team's successful inaugural season, 40 men tried out for the 1913 team. Slay announced early in September that the Ole Miss Rebels would travel to Hattiesburg to meet Normal, generating a great deal of interest in and around the city. The Commercial Club of Hattiesburg announced that it would handle all promotional activities, hoping to attract as many fans as possible.

The season did not get off to a good start, as Normal lost 25–0 at Poplarville High School and 19–0 at Gulf Coast Military Academy in Gulfport. The team rebounded with an 11–0 home victory against Mobile Military Academy. A home rematch with Gulf Coast Military Academy produced an 11–6 loss, and a rematch with Mobile Military Academy in Mobile resulted in another loss, this time by a 14–0 score. A home game with Poplarville High School ended in a 0–0 tie.

THE EARLY YEARS

Interest in the November 27 game between Normal and Ole Miss had been high until an unfounded report circulated that the second team would be coming from Oxford. The manager of the Ole Miss squad denied the report, declaring, "It is as much to our advantage to send our varsity as it is to you." Despite the rumors, a large crowd gathered at Kamper Park and witnessed the Rebels, the team from Mississippi's oldest state-supported institution, defeat the squad from the youngest state-supported institution by a score of 13–7. Normal finished the year at 1–5–1.

1914 SEASON

A. B. Dillie, a former star halfback at Mississippi A & M, took over as the Normalites' head football coach in 1914, providing some stability by remaining in the position through the 1916 season. The team included Longest, Jack Thompson, G. R. Touchstone, Roland Cowpart, Carl McLeod, Tommy Rowan, Spicer Furlow, and Wiley Golden. The season opened with a 39–0 loss at Mississippi College, followed by a 24–13 loss on the road at Spring Hill College. The team picked up its first win of the season by shutting out Mobile Military Academy 24–0 at Kamper Park. The team then lost on the road at Gulf Coast Military Academy 22–0 and defeated Perkinston High School 9–0 at home. The squad finished with a 0–0 tie at home against Poplarville High School, giving Normal a 2–3–1 mark on the year.

Dillie was a former star halfback at Mississippi A & M. He spent three seasons as head coach at MNC from 1914 to 1916.

1915 SEASON

Dillie's second Normal squad featured the debuts of two notable players, Clifton C. (Mutt) Campbell and C. R. (Tall) McLeod. The team opened its season by losing its first two games, 6–0 against Poplarville High School at home on October 9 and 3–0 at Gulf Coast Military Academy a week later. A 26–0 win at Kamper Park over Perkinston High School on October 30 gave the team its first win of the season, but a 33–7 loss at Spring Hill on the following week dropped the team's record to 1–3. The team bounced back with a three-game home winning streak, rolling over Copiah-Lincoln High School 55–0 on November 13 and adding 12–0 and 7–6 wins over Poplarville High School on November 20 and Gulf Coast Military Academy on November 25, respectively. A 55–7 loss to Mississippi College left the team with a 4–4 record on the year.

Although the Normal School team had not developed as quickly as fans and coaches had hoped, the upstart program still had made great strides over its first four years of competition. Although both Mississippi College and Spring Hill College had defeated the Normal footballers,

The 1916 Mississippi Normal College football team included M. M. Roberts (first row on right), for whom the current stadium is named.

scheduling such games was very important to the young institution as it continued to try to establish itself as a proven program.

berlain Hunt Academy, and Gulf Coast Military Academy, but no evidence exists to indicate that these games were ever played.

1916 SEASON

The Normalites greatest pre–World War I success came in the form of a 1916 loss to Ole Miss by a score of 13–7 that seemed to show that the school, led by Tom Donahue, R. V. Peacock, M. M. and C. C. Roberts, W. J. (Puny) Davis, and W. C. (Red) Smith, could hold its own with Mississippi's highest-profile university and be a national competitor in football. The squad played three recorded games that season, losing to Meridian High School 31–0, Mississippi College 75–0, and Spring Hill 87–0. Games were also scheduled with Poplarville High School, Cham-

1917–18 SEASONS

The U.S. involvement in World War I had wide repercussions throughout the country, and Mississippi Normal College was no exception. Football was not a part of university life during 1917 and 1918 because the campus was united in an attempt to aid the war effort overseas.

1919 SEASON

Slay, the director of athletics, called the first postwar football practice session for September 16,

The first team fielded by Mississippi Normal College after World War I posted a 4–1–2 record. It was coached by Cephus Anderson, a prominent young lawyer and Hattiesburg native, who had been captain of the Ole Miss football team in 1916. Front row (left to right): Zack Lee, C. C. (Mutt) Campbell, A. H. Parsons, B. B. (Opp) O'Mara, Arthur Hays (mascot), Lynn McCleskey, Dewey Lane, James (Glen) Vinson; Middle row: Johnny Montgomery, R. Williams, Clarence (Red) Holleman, J. R. (Black) Busby; back row: Coach Cephus Anderson, G. G. Evans, Willie Smith, N. H. Cornelius, J. R. Johnson, Pete Downer, Will Wood, Warren McCleskey, V. C. Cagle, and assistant coach Ebel Wilden.

1919. He believed the school had a chance to field one of the state's best teams. Slay had traveled throughout the state and had contacted numerous students who had played football and planned to attend Normal College. The Normalites' new coach was Cephus Anderson, who had played four years of varsity football at Ole Miss and was a prominent young Hattiesburg lawyer. When football returned to the Normal campus in 1919, almost all of the college's students and faculty bought season tickets, eager to see the team play. The 1919 football season would prove to be a breakout year for the young college.

The team opened the season at home, shutting out Perkinston Agricultural High School 12–0 on October 4 and Poplarville Agricultural High School 2–0 on October 18. Coach Anderson was optimistic about his team, which was led by Johnnie Montgomery, Captain B. B. O'Mara, J. R. Busby, C. C. Campbell, and R. M. Williams. The *Hattiesburg American* reported that the Poplarville team was determined to protect its undefeated, untied, and unscored-on record. Anderson declared, "Bring 'em on. The bigger they are, the harder they fall, and the more they talk, the less they play. We are going to lick 'em to a frazzle."

The first real test for the 1919 footballers came on October 25 at Meridian College. Although the game ended in a 6–6 deadlock, the vaunted Normal defense remained perfect as Meridian managed to score only by returning a Normal fumble for a touchdown. Still, the tie upset the young Normal College players, who vowed to make amends in a scheduled rematch with Meridian College later in the season.

Normal was excited about renewing its rivalry with Gulf Coast Military Academy, coached by former Vanderbilt All-American Ray Morrison, which would come to Kamper Park on November 1. The two teams tied 6–6, with Normal's defense, which had quickly become the team's trademark, allowing its first touchdown of the season.

The scheduled home game with Chamberlain-Hunt Academy on November 8 afforded the Normalites a breather before the biggest contest of the season, against Mississippi College. The academy provided little opposition for the Normalites, as the vaunted defense once again pitched a shutout, this one 20–0.

The greatly anticipated November 17 matchup with Mississippi College was pivotal for Normal College. The game featured one of only two college teams on Normal's 1919 schedule (Meridian College was the other), and Mississippi College had solidly beaten the Normalites in previous years. Normal College President Joe Cook called the contest "the greatest athletic event that has been staged in Hattiesburg for several years." Attired in black gowns, students from Hattiesburg's Women's College arrived at the park by streetcar to sit in a special section in the stands and cheer for the Baptist men from Mississippi College. On the opposite side of the field, a section was reserved for the Normal College students who marched from the campus to Kamper Park, with women neatly dressed in white middy blouses and skirts. Going into the fourth quarter, Normal was winning the exciting game, but the celebrated defense uncharacteristically gave up two scores, and the more powerful Mississippi College team won 19–7. Normal's coaches and players protested vehemently when the head linesman called a touchdown pass incomplete but was overruled by the other official. The Normal coaching staff also lodged a protest regarding the eligibility of one of the Mississippi College players, but this protest too was disallowed. The game indicated that Normal could hold its own against a southern power. The close and controversial loss to Mississippi College showed that Normal College was well on its way to establishing a good football program.

The season reached its glorious end with a Thanksgiving rematch in Hattiesburg against Meridian College. Normal's 47–0 victory on November 27 proved to the school's fans that the first Meridian game did not accurately show which team was better. The defense yielded only 31 points all season, and the team finished with a 4–1–2 record.

The season also featured the debut of the training table concept, which Professor Slay introduced to help improve players' morale. The privilege of sitting at a specially designated table for meals in the dining hall became a highly coveted

B. B. O'Mara played at Ole Miss in 1918 and 1921, but coached the MNC football squad in 1920. Ironically one of his losses as head coach was a 54–0 defeat by Ole Miss, the team he would return to play for the following year.

THE EARLY YEARS [9]

honor accorded only to football players who attended all practice sessions.

1920 SEASON

After the 1919 season, hopes were high for a good campaign. The revolving door of coaches continued as fullback B. B. (Opp) O'Mara, one of the team's best athletes, became the player-coach for the 1920 season. Also starring for the team were Mutt Campbell, J. P. Busby, Bob Huff, and Puny Davis.

After whipping Perkinston Agricultural High School 64–0 in the season opener on October 2, Normal learned on October 5 that Ole Miss would be visiting Kamper Park on October 9. Although negotiations for the game had been ongoing for some time, Ole Miss did not agree to include Normal College on the schedule until October 5. The game itself involved less suspense, as Ole Miss clobbered Normal by a score of 54–0. The Rebels were a much better football team in every facet of the game, and the defeat was quite a setback for the Normalites.

Normal next battled Millsaps to a 7–7 tie at home on October 16, then swept a pair of games from Spring Hill College, winning 12–2 in Mobile on October 23 and 32–0 in Hattiesburg on November 6. Normal played Tulane's freshman team, the Yannigans, at Kamper Park the following week. Tulane boasted one of the South's best football programs during this era, and although the game was hard fought, Normal failed to score, losing 19–0 in front of 1,500 spectators. Normal ended the season by defeating Mississippi Industrial Training School of Columbia 27–0 on November 20 and Gulf Coast Military Academy 40–0 on November 25.

Despite the team's 5–2–1 record, it was obvious that the institution was still not quite ready for big-time football, especially the brand played by schools like Ole Miss and Tulane. However, the team was improving and was no longer exclusively playing high schools.

1921 SEASON

The coaching carousel continued as O'Mara left to play for Ole Miss, leaving Normal once again searching for a new head football coach. The choice was O. V. (Spout) Austin, a former baseball and basketball star at Ole Miss. Austin was very knowledgeable and was said to enjoy talking about the game with anyone who would listen—faculty, students, or players in after-practice chalk talks. Only six lettermen returned from the 1920 squad, but Normal gained a new source of players when Hattiesburg High School began a football program.

Normal opened the season on October 7 with a 20–0 win at Ellisville High School, followed by a lopsided October 15 drubbing of Mize High School by the unbelievable score of 113–0. After losing 27–0 at Millsaps

O. V. "Spout" Austin was a former baseball and football player at Ole Miss and the manager of the Rebel football team in 1910. He coached Mississippi Normal College's football team from 1921 to 1923.

on October 21, the team rebounded with a 37–0 win over Jones County High School. The season ended with losses in the final three games, on the road at St. Stanislaus (49–0) and at home to Poplarville High School (40–0) and Loyola University (25–13), for a 3–4 season mark.

Normal was not improving in part because many of the school's better players either had graduated or departed for other schools that took football a little more seriously. Like O'Mara, Johnnie Montgomery was playing for Ole Miss, while Mutt Campbell had gone off to Louisiana State University and both Black and Red Busby were on the roster at Mississippi College. But in keeping with its mission of training teachers, former Normal players Lynn McClesky, Bill Wood, Bob Huff, and Johnnie Potero were coaching high school football.

1922 SEASON

The 1922 season saw basically the same results as the previous year. Sandwiched between a season-opening September 29 win against Jones County High School in Ellisville and a season-ending 19–12 home victory over the Mississippi State freshman team on Thanksgiving Day, the Normalites lost six straight games.

After a 6–0 loss to Purvis High School, Normal suffered a tough 10–7 defeat by Millsaps on October 10 as the feature attraction of the Mississippi State Fair in Jackson. Normal was shut out in its next four games, a 10–0 defeat at St. Stanislaus, a 20–0 home loss to Gulf Coast Military Academy, a 20–0 loss at Loyola University of New Orleans, and a 44–0 thumping at Marion Military Institute.

After the November 11 defeat by Loyola, Coach Austin sent an open letter to New Orleans newspapers in which he charged that an official had displayed no regard for the rules of the game and had cheated Normal: for example, Austin contended, "Mr. Ernst displayed his total disregard of rules, or his ignorance of them, and on the very first play of the game. Loyola kicked to Normal, the ball going out of bounds on the three yard line. Instead of kicking off again, as Rule 13, Section 7, specifies, he forces Normal to put the ball in scrimmage, on their three yard line." Although other observers echoed Austin's charges, there was no changing the fact that the Normalites had failed to score and had lost the game.

The 1922 season marked the beginnings of the debate over whether Normal College should join a collegiate athletic conference. The topic would remain the defining feature of football at the school for most of its existence. Talk of a conference affiliation would have been unthinkable just a few years earlier, but the team's modest success, the school's growth, and the increase in football's popularity had started to earn Mississippi Normal College the respect of other college football teams.

STATE TEACHERS COLLEGE AND THE BOBO ERA
1923–1930

Mississippi Normal College changed its name to the State Teachers College in 1924. Along with the new name came numerous advantageous changes in the school's mission. The college would begin to offer a four-year degree, arguably allowing for the recruitment and retention of better or "more desirable" students. According to the *Normal College News,* attracting these types of students could help the school "maintain higher standards of work as well as social standards." While the institution was going through some positive changes, however, Coach Spout Austin's football program stayed on the course it had traveled during the early 1920s.

The 1923 Mississippi Normal football team finished the season with a record of 2–5. Front row (left to right): E. W. Hester, Rowells, L. E. Gafford (Captain), Eubanks, A. H. Applewhite, Nollie Felts; second row: Warren McCleskey, M. R. Vines, Fred (Coon) Leech, O. E. Cowart, Norton; back row: W. L. Parker, R. H. Tucker, Pigott, L. Busch, Coach O. V. (Spout) Austin.

Nollie Felts (1923–1926) is still regarded as one of the best all-around football players in school history. Primarily an end, he also played quarterback. Following his career at State Teachers College he played three years at Tulane, where he was named All-American in 1931.

1923 SEASON

In keeping with preseason prognostications of a poor 1923 season, Normal finished at 3–3. As in previous campaigns, the schedule featured a mixture of high school and regional college teams. The team began the season on October 5 at Kamper Park against Purvis High School, winning 26–0, then lost 31–0 the following week to Millsaps. After beating Seashore Camp Ground 52–0 on November 3, Normal dropped a hard-fought 7–6 decision to old rival Gulf Coast Military Academy and suffered an embarrassing 66–0 pasting against Southwestern Louisiana Industrial Institute in Lafayette. A 6–0 victory over the Mississippi College freshmen at Kamper Park closed the season.

Teachers College had hoped for a matchup against the Ole Miss freshmen, and after negotiations with R. L. Sullivan, the school's athletic director, a game was scheduled. Hattiesburg's merchants were asked to underwrite the game expenses by purchasing small lots of tickets, which they could dispose of at their discretion. The plan apparently failed, and the game was canceled with no reason given, although both coaches wanted to play.

STC's captain and best player in 1923 and for several subsequent seasons was Nollie Felts, a back who had prepped at Hattiesburg High, where he seemed to do everything. In language common among sportswriters of the day, The *Hattiesburg American* described his contributions: "Nolly Felts is a treasure. Signals—he can call 'em. Place kicks—he can send 'em over the bar and between the posts. His punts sail down the field like they are shot out of a gun and if he sticks his 165 pounds of muscle into a man, that man gets acquainted with Mother Earth. Nolly Felts is captain and at quarter is showing wonderful talent in managing his team and driving them down the field. He is full of the old spirit and never loses his head."

1924 SEASON

The 1924 season brought dramatic changes to the STC football team. William Herschel Bobo replaced Austin as athletic director and head football coach, the schedule was drastically altered and for the first time did not include any high school teams, and the team gained its first consistent nickname, the Yellow Jackets, although the press continued to occasionally refer to the squad as the Pedagogues or Teachers, a far cry from the plethora of names that had previously been used, including the Tigers, Bengals, Huskies, Reds, and Normalites.

The college received more preseason publicity than ever before. The *Jackson Daily News* began to cover the Teachers College football team, and other papers, including the school's publication, the *Teachers College News,* were beginning to emphasize coverage of the school's football team. A lot of this interest resulted from the new head coach, a state and regional media darling. Bobo, "one of the best known athletes in the south," according to the *Jackson Daily News,* had coached a professional baseball team to the Cotton States League championship during the previous spring, and the press believed that this success augured well for his tenure as a football coach. He had been hired to guide STC into a new football era.

One of Bobo's first actions as the Teachers College coach was to recruit some new, more experienced players, among them Losa Crane from Louisiana State University, Bull Talley from Marion Military Institute, and high school all-

Herschel Bobo coached at State Teachers College for four seasons (1924–1927). He was forced to resign because he was also player manager of Hattiesburg's pro baseball team in the Cotton States League. The school at the time was trying to get invited into the Southern Intercollegiate Athletic Association, which prohibited coaches from being under contract to professional organizations.

star quarterback J. M. Tujaque Jr. from Biloxi. Only six of the previous year's players returned, and the newcomers were so good that the *Jackson Daily News* said that Nollie Felts would face "competition for his position" from one of Bobo's recruits.

The debut of the 1924 Yellow Jackets was very successful, as they, in the words of the *Hattiesburg American*, "overwhelmed the Clarke Memorial College eleven in a one-sided game," winning 27–0 on October 4 at Kamper Park. Next up were the Loyola Wolves on October 18, and the high hopes engendered by the opening victory were quickly dashed. The *Hattiesburg American* reported that "everyone connected with Loyola University's varsity football squad except the water boy and student manager was given a chance to do his share towards winning in a listless game from the Mississippi State Teachers' College eleven of Hattiesburg by a score of 32 to 7."

The Yellow Jackets lost the next game against Pearl River Junior College (formerly Poplarville Community College) by a score of 26–6 in front of 1,500 spectators, equaling the largest crowd ever to attend a football game in Hattiesburg. Many STC supporters reacted bitterly to the loss, charging that the Poplarville rivals' motto was "to play dirty is to win." Such sour grapes from an editor of the *Teachers College News* prompted President Cook to write a fiery letter to the paper. "I suppose the sting of defeat prompted the reporter to use such language," President Cook commented. "I am writing to assure the public and the Poplarville Junior College that the State Teachers College entertains no such sentiments.

We got beat. That is all there is to it. We shall hope for better luck next time."

Gulf Coast Military Academy tied the Yellow Jackets 14–14 the following week in Gulfport, and on November 7 STC and the Mississippi State freshmen reached the same result in Starkville. The Teachers then took a long trip to Deland, Florida, to play Stetson University, one of the best college football teams in the South. Stetson's gridders were unbeaten and unscored on when the Yellow Jackets arrived on campus. There was little chance that the Teachers would win, but Coach Bobo optimistically promised that the game would be close. He was wrong—the final score was 48–6—but the result was not indicative of the day's events. Stetson yielded its first touchdown of the year when Felts crossed the goal line on a long pass play, and at halftime STC trailed by only 1 point. Stetson scored 28 points in the fourth quarter against Bobo's outmanned and tired troops.

Fred (Coon) Leech was a versatile player who saw time at end, tackle, and guard from 1922 to 1925. Voted the school's Best Boy Athlete in 1924, he was named a charter member of the school's Sports Hall of Fame in 1965.

The Yellow Jackets rallied to win the final two games of the season, beating Marion Military Institute 7–6 before defeating Louisiana College in a game that featured a fantastic finish. With less than two minutes left in the contest, STC trailed 12–10 and had the ball around midfield. Bull Tally completed a pass to Hi Ferrell, who ran to the 10-yard line as time was running out. The Yellow Jackets ran one play before calling on R. H. Tucker, who had scored all the team's points, to kick the game-winning field goal.

STC finished the toughest schedule in the school's history with a record of 3–3–2. Confidence in the football program reached unprecedented heights, and Bobo took advantage of this optimism to request that the Southern Intercollegiate Athletic Association (SIAA), which at the time included such schools as Millsaps, Mississippi College, Tennessee-Chattanooga, Howard College (later Samford University), and the Citadel, accept Mississippi State Teachers College as a member. Of course, along with the excitement over the team's 1924 success and the possibility of joining the big-time SIAA came unprecedented expectations for on-field success.

1925 SEASON

Predictions for the 1925 season were not positive. The squad bore little resemblance to the team that had finished the previous campaign. Starting quarterback Paul Tally was out for the season with an injury, and ailments felled such other key players as R. H. Tucker. Furthermore, the linemen had little experience. However, Ferrell, whom the *Jackson Daily News* called "without a doubt one of the fastest backfield men in the state" and later a New York Yankees baseball farmhand, returned for the Yellow Jackets, moving from halfback to quarterback to take advantage of his mental and leadership strengths and becoming the team's captain, leader, and star.

Despite Ferrell's play, the Yellow Jackets failed to win a contest and could muster only a 7–7 tie against the freshman team from Mississippi A & M. The team lost its first two games, to Clarke Memorial College 32–0 and to the Ole Miss freshmen 38–6, before Bobo recruited his predecessor as coach, Spout Austin, to help prepare the players for the next game. The results did not change, however, as STC lost to the All-Navy Service Team 32–6, Southwestern Louisiana Institute 40–0, Pearl River Junior College 13–7, and Spring Hill College 40–0. The team's best chance for a win might have come in the fifth game of the season, which was scheduled to be played against old foe Gulf Coast Military Academy, but the contest was canceled when the train bringing the Gulf Coast team to Hattiesburg derailed.

Whatever momentum the 1924 Yellow Jackets had established for STC was quickly halted by the dismal on-field efforts of the 1925 season. All talk of joining the SIAA evaporated, as the team's poor performance shook the foundation of Bobo's plans and disappointed school officials.

1926 SEASON

After opening the 1926 season on September 25 with a 33–6 loss at Southwestern Louisiana, the Yellow Jackets were determined to get revenge against Clarke Memorial College. Hattiesburg residents jumped on the bandwagon, coming out to watch the team's extensive workouts under Coach Bobo. The fans' interest and the players' hard work paid off with a 12–7 victory over Clarke on October 2. Subsequent weeks brought a 27–6 road loss to Spring Hill on October 9, a 14–7 defeat of Louisiana College on October 16 at Kamper Park, and a 26–3 road win over Perkinston Junior College on October 22. The October 30 home game with Gulf Coast Military Academy ended in a 6–6 tie that was marred by an ugly all-out brawl that included the Cadets' coach, who jumped a fence to join the fray. The final two games of the 1926 season were a 20–0 home loss to Pearl River Junior College on November 13 and a 26–7 road defeat administered by Mississippi State's freshmen on November 27. The 3–4–1 season ended on a brighter note when tackle Albert Rogers was named to the 1926 all-state college team.

1927 Yellow Jacket leaders were A. T. Gullett, Albert Rogers, and J. P. (Noonie) Hackney.

1927 SEASON

The 1927 season, Bobo's fourth year as head coach and athletic director, opened on September 24 with STC losing to Southwestern Louisiana Institute 6–0. Two of the Yellow Jackets' best players, fullback Albert Rogers (ear) and wingman S. A. Brasfield (broken arm) were injured in the contest, with Brasfield sidelined for several weeks. The following week's game was a fierce defensive battle with Perkinston Junior College that resulted in a 0–0 tie. STC managed only 108 yards while holding Perkinston to just 47 yards and a pair of first downs. The Yellow Jackets' best chance to win the game came on the first play of the second quarter, when G. H. Russell intercepted a Bulldog pass and raced 40 yards to the end zone. Just before he crossed the goal line, however, a teammate cut down a Perkinston tackler from behind, nullifying the touchdown.

On October 8, STC's first-ever matchup with Hinds Junior College occurred in a cold, steady rain on an increasingly muddy field. The Yellow Jackets scored two touchdowns—the first on a 10-yard pass from quarterback Jack Gay to J. P. (Noonie) Hackney and the second on a 4-yard run by A. T. Gullette—to beat Hinds 12–0. On October 21 the visiting Mississippi State freshmen defeated the Yellow Jackets by a score of 24–0. STC

STATE TEACHERS COLLEGE AND THE BOBO ERA

threatened to score twice in the second quarter, reaching the Bulldog 2-yard line, but the defense held, and Mississippi State scored two fourth-quarter touchdowns to break open what had been a close game. Two more road losses ensued, an 18–0 defeat at Clarke Memorial College on October 29 and a 37–0 whitewashing at Spring Hill a week later.

STC finished the year with a pair of wins. On November 11, the Yellow Jackets defeated Pearl River Junior College 15–0 at Kamper Park. STC capitalized on Pearl River turnovers, jumping out to an early 6–0 lead after a Pearl River fumble was followed two plays later by a Gullette-to-Hackney 50-yard touchdown pass. In the third quarter, Hackney intercepted a Pearl River pass, and Gullette scored moments later on a 10-yard run, making the score 12–0. Albert Rogers added a short field goal for the game's final points. In the last game of the season, against St. Stanislaus in Bay St. Louis on November 18, the Yellow Jackets trailed 13–6 at halftime but fought back, getting a pair of touchdowns from Gullette and another from Hackney to win the game 25–13.

The Yellow Jackets' second straight 3–4–1 season was Bobo's last as head football coach and athletic director. Although the school did not manage a winning season during Bobo's tenure, the gap between STC and the SIAA teams was narrowing. Although Bobo's teams represented an improvement over those of his predecessor, he still faced a problem with retaining players, especially those with talent. During this era, college players commonly transferred among schools, often failing to take classes. Rather than being student-athletes, these players were professionals.

Coach William Saunders (1928–1929) came to STC from Tupelo High School. He had spent two seasons as a player at Mississippi A & M and had also played at Georgia Tech and Auburn. He also assumed the duties of athletic director during his two seasons.

1928 SEASON

Bobo was not the only notable departure from STC after 1927. The college's president, Joe Cook, left and was replaced by Claude Bennett, who had some background in athletics and had

The 1928 STC football team, under Coach Saunders, finished the year with a 4–5 record.

coached the opposition at the Normal College's first football game. Willie B. Saunders became the new football coach and athletic director, and at least initially, he was apparently far less popular than Bobo: newspapers seldom mentioned Saunders as the squad's leader. Saunders had played for two years at Mississippi State before transferring to Georgia Tech and Auburn and then moving into coaching. He came to STC from Tupelo High School.

The first game of the 1928 season represented one of the ugliest defeats in the school's 15 years of football and did little to endear Saunders to the STC faithful. Old nemesis Mississippi College administered an 83–0 shellacking of the Yellow Jackets, who were "outclassed and outplayed in every department of the game," according to the *Student Printz,* the school newspaper. Such an embarrassing loss constituted quite a setback for a school trying to get some recognition by playing other college opponents and was an inauspicious beginning for Saunders.

Remarkably, however, the Yellow Jackets bounced back during the next three weeks by beating Perkinston Junior College 12–2, the Newton Aggies 7–0, and, in the season's highlight, "ancient rival" Pearl River 6–0, "taking to the air in a last minute frantic attempt to score." Hattiesburg went wild. Ecstatic STC students "staged a pajama parade in celebration of the second STC victory in the eleventh annual contest played between the two schools."

The winning streak ended on October 27, when the team traveled to Lafayette and once again lost to Southwestern Louisiana, this time by a score of 37–7. The Yellow Jackets next defeated the Mississippi College freshman team 12–6 before closing out the season with losses to Marion Military Institute, Copiah-Lincoln Junior College, and Clarke Memorial College. A huge crowd witnessed the game against Clarke, which was led by Walker (Cornbread) Wilson, whose brother, Irie (Biscuit) Wilson, was STC's star. In addition to Hackney, the Hattiesburg native and team captain whom the *Neka Camon,* the school yearbook, called "one of the best athletes STC has ever had" and who received the 1928 award for "best boy athlete," the Yellow Jackets featured Fred E. (Tiny) Davis, who would receive the award the following year. The team's 4–5 record represented a solid accomplishment for Saunders, especially after the Mississippi College debacle.

1929 SEASON

Saunders announced STC's 1929 football schedule late in 1928, and it was the toughest schedule that he could arrange. Releasing and publishing the schedule well in advance of the 1929 season, plus the news that the college had signed home-and-home contracts with two opponents for the 1929 and 1930 seasons, provided proof that Yellow Jacket football was becoming more organized. The coach also announced that the school would strictly adhere to the SIAA's player-eligibility rules. Both developments represented the continuation of STC's campaign to impress the SIAA and gain admission to the conference. For six weeks beginning in February, STC held its first spring football practice under the direction of William Childress, head football coach of the Demonstration High School, and assistants Homer McMahon and Noonie Hackney. Saunders was busy coaching the STC basketball and baseball teams.

In September, the team began preseason practices, with 18 lettermen returning from the 1928 squad. Coach Saunders and Assistant Coach Simpson Jackson were joined on the staff by Gerald Walker, a former star back at Ole Miss who had recently signed a contract with the Detroit Tigers. In another attempt to enhance the Yellow Jackets' status, the 1929 team would enjoy the privilege of traveling to and from away games in a white, tourist-style bus that the school had purchased for the athletic department's use.

The first two weekends of the 1929 season saw the Yellow Jackets lose games but win moral victories. The Yellow Jackets opened on the road at Southwestern Louisiana and lost 7–0, a much closer score than in previous seasons. Many newspaper accounts of the game indicated that Saunders was pleased with his team's showing against one of the premier teams in the SIAA, which Southwestern Louisiana had joined in 1925. In one of the most anticipated games in STC's history, the Yellow Jackets traveled to Mississippi College on October 5, hoping to avenge the previous season's embarrassing 83–0 pasting. Mississippi College refused to play the contest if several of STC's new recruits were allowed to play, arguing that SIAA rules prohibited the players' participation. Irie (Biscuit) Wilson, J. W. (Peck)

Davis, and Frank A. McClendon thus were held out of the lineup in the Yellow Jackets' 20–0 loss.

The Yellow Jackets tasted their first victory of the season on October 12, soundly defeating Marion Military Institute 31–0. Although the pregame press had featured Biscuit Wilson, the star of the Yellow Jacket backfield, Ellis Bilbo stole the show by scoring a touchdown, doing a brilliant job on punt coverage, and leading the STC defense. Lewis (Maggie) McGeehee, who had previously been known for his prowess as a receiver, became one of the Yellow Jackets' greatest defensive weapons, averaging 55 yards per punt during the Marion game, with one punt traveling an incredible 70 yards.

On October 18, in what may have been a letdown after the Marion victory, the Yellow Jackets played poorly in a 6–6 tie with Southwest Mississippi Junior College at Kamper Park. The game foreshadowed STC's performance for the remainder of the season, during which STC suffered four straight losses. Spring Hill, the SIAA leaders, beat the Yellow Jackets 25–6 in Mobile on November 2, a contest that seemed to indicate that the team could hang in against a very good opponent. The buildup for the next game, against Pearl River Junior College, the Mississippi junior college state champs, was tremendous, but Pearl River stopped STC's two-year win streak by beating the Teachers 14–7 on November 9.

The next loss was to Louisiana College, another relatively new SIAA member, by the score of 12–6 in Pineville on November 16. Once again, STC had stayed close to the SIAA's best

(Top) Fred (Coon) Leech served as alternating captain of the 1929 State Teachers College team.

(Bottom) R. H. Tucker served as captain of the 1929 State Teachers College team.

STATE TEACHERS COLLEGE AND THE BOBO ERA

but still could not prevail. The game was the first STC contest broadcast over the radio. According to the November 20 *Student Printz,* "A special attraction for students will be offered this week, President Bennett stated, in a play-by-play report of the Louisiana College–State Teachers College game in Pineville next Saturday over wires of one of the local telegraph companies. Students who hear this report will pay an admission of ten cents to care for telegraphic tolls."

The Yellow Jackets next played a new opponent, Delta Teachers College, on November 22 in snow and ice in Cleveland, Mississippi, losing 14–6. The final contest of the 1929 season was played on Thanksgiving Day against longtime foe Clarke Memorial College. The Yellow Jackets came out on top, 12–7, to finish the season on a positive note despite their 2–6–1 record.

Soon after the season ended, STC put in a formal bid to join the SIAA, the major southern athletic conference. Acceptance into the conference offered some potential major benefits for the STC football program, but by February 1930 the college changed its mind, petitioning the conference for a one-year probation, after which the STC would become a full-fledged conference member. The STC sought the delay to allow the school time to develop a budget for travel and other expenses, to work on player eligibility, and to put together a solid coaching staff. The school had realized that it simply was not financially ready to move to the big time. The conference agreed to the delay, and STC began preparations for a year of growth and development.

1930 SEASON

As part of the transition to SIAA membership, STC athletic officials announced that the school's 1930 football schedule would include nine games, all of them against four-year colleges and seven of them against SIAA members. (The schedule was later changed to include a game against Pearl River Junior College.) Conference rules generally did not permit freshmen to play, but officials granted STC a waiver because the association's strict rules left the Yellow Jackets with only 10 upperclassmen eligible to play. Willie Saunders was replaced as coach by John Lumpkin, a former star at Pearl River and Ole Miss who had served in World War I before becoming coach at the Mississippi Industrial and Training School from 1919 to 1926. Prior to accepting the position at STC, he served as principal of the Pearl River Agricultural High School and represented that county as a state representative. William Clark of Jackson, who had played at Mississippi State, became the new backfield coach, and Biscuit Wilson was named coach of the freshman team. Despite the Yellow Jackets' lackluster history, joining the conference had brought an aura of excitement to STC football.

The first game of the season was supposed to be against archrival Pearl River Junior College on

John Lumpkin, a former Ole Miss lineman (1916) spent one full season as the Yellow Jackets head coach in 1930. He was then elected to serve in the State Senate for a four-year term.

September 27, but the contest was canceled when a 19-year-old Pearl River player, Leslie Landrum, died of Bright's disease. Traditional rival Clarke Memorial College was brought in as a replacement at the last moment and for its trouble received a sound 45–0 thrashing. The STC backfield of S. A. Clark, E. M. Bilbo, David Lossette, and Cornbread Wilson was especially effective, prompting the *Hattiesburg American* to designate the players the "four gazelles." Cornbread Wilson had left Clarke and was making his debut for STC.

The next two games were losses to SIAA opponents Millsaps on October 4 by a score of 26–0 and Mississippi College on October 11 by a score of 18–6. The *Jackson Daily News* devoted a lot of ink to the Teachers, focusing on the school's attempt to join the SIAA and how the team had improved and was no longer a pushover for conference's football juggernauts. Nevertheless, another disappointing 14–0 loss to Southwestern Louisiana followed on October 18.

The Teachers hosted their first home game of the year on October 25 against Louisiana College, and the Four Gazelles put on a show, with the offense scoring seven touchdowns. After such an impressive win, the team and its supporters eagerly turned to the November 1 contest at Kamper Park against Spring Hill College, which had finished second in the SIAA in 1929, beating the Yellow Jackets 25–6. Although STC dominated Spring Hill on the field, making 15 first downs and holding the visitors to only 2, the result was a 7–6 defeat for the Teachers, who could not cash in on their opportunities. Despite the great disappointment, the school and team were proud of their showing.

The next game was in Natchitoches, on November 14 against Louisiana State Normal College (later Northwestern State College). Perhaps the team was still smarting from the bitter loss to Spring Hill, or perhaps the absences of Lossette (skin infection), Clark (rib injury), and Tony Martello (leg injury) were too much to overcome, but the Yellow Jackets lost the game 32–12. A week later, the Yellow Jackets avenged their 1929 loss to Delta Teachers College by thoroughly whipping the Professors 46–0 behind the Four Gazelles and in particular Cornbread Wilson, who scored five times. (Wilson would finish the season second in the SIAA scoring race, trailing only Kentucky quarterback Carey Spicer.) On November 27, the Yellow Jackets closed out their season with a 0–0 tie with Union College in front of 2,000 fans, finishing at 3–5–1.

At season's end, Lumpkin was elected to a four-year term in the State Senate, and his political obligations forced him to relinquish his head coaching position at STC after just one season, although he was often at practice and with the team. The team he left was well on its way to becoming respectable. More important, the Yellow Jackets would start 1931 as a full SIAA member: on December 16, 1930, STC officials learned that the school had received full conference membership. The next decade of the institution's football program would prove to be even more fruitful than its architects had hoped.

THE TRANSITION ERA
1931–1941

After years of working to become a member of the Southern Intercollegiate Athletic Association (SIAA), Mississippi State Teachers College entered the 1931 season as a league member. Like other state-supported institutions then and now, however, the school continued to face the problem of inadequate financial support. STC had incurred debts amounting to between $25,000 and $40,000, and if the state did not step in to help, the school's existence might be in trouble.

In 1931, the Mississippi legislature created the Board of Trustees of State Institutions of Higher Learning to assist state-supported schools facing increasing debt and financial hardship. The board instituted a pay-as-you-go policy, prohibiting state institutions of higher education from spending money they did not have. STC officials consequently began to look for additional ways to generate funds and saw athletics as one way to gain exposure for the school. Thus, over the next decade, many changes occurred at State Teachers College, and many of them affected the football program.

1931 SEASON

John Lumpkin, who had led the team to a 3–5–1 record the previous year, was now back as an assistant to new head coach Allison (Pooley) Hubert, a former University of Alabama All-American who had played a key role in the Crimson Tide's 20–19 1926 Rose Bowl win over Washington and who had replaced William Clark as STC's backfield coach during the 1930 season.

STC opened the season on October 3, hosting Millsaps College at Kamper Park. A crowd of 2,000 fans, including Governor-elect Martin Sennett Conner and his wife, Alma Graham Conner, a former student at the school, watched the team lose 19–0 in its first game as a member of an established league. Conner was one of the first Mississippi officials to recognize the potential importance of collegiate athletic programs in promoting the state. A few weeks later, speaking in New Orleans, where he had gone to see the Tulane–Georgia Tech game, Conner declared that Mississippi's outstanding high school and junior college football players should stay at home and even declared in jest that he would try to make it unconstitutional for Mississippi athletes to attend out-of-state schools.

Former Alabama All-American Allison (Pooley) Hubert took over the STC football program in 1931. The Meridian, Mississippi, native coached six seasons before accepting a position at VMI following the 1936 season.

The season's second game took place in Clinton, Mississippi, on October 10 against Mississippi College. Early in the first half, STC fullback Ellis Bilbo, guard O. M. (Brownie) Thomas, center Brownie Finch, tackle Sankey Koen, and end Gayle Fairley left the game after becoming ill with ptomaine poisoning contracted from something they had eaten; the Choctaws went on to defeat the shorthanded teachers, 46–13.

The next week brought a road game at Mobile, Alabama, against Spring Hill College, the season's toughest opponent. The unlucky Finch had recovered from his bout with food poisoning but went down for the season when he broke his collarbone during the second quarter. In one of the year's best defensive games, STC players Thomas, end Tony Martello, tackle Lance Lumpkin (Coach Lumpkin's brother), and halfbacks Walker (Cornbread) Wilson and David Lossette frequently tackled the Badger players for losses. Nevertheless, Spring Hill won 12–0.

After an October 24 13–0 defeat at the hands of Louisiana College gave the Teachers their fourth straight loss, the team recorded its biggest victory. A home crowd of 2,000 watched the Teachers upset Memphis's Southwestern University 13–7 in a game in which the visitors had been picked to win by at least two touchdowns. Southwestern scored first, taking a 7–0 lead, but according to the *Hattiesburg American*, the Yellow Jackets then "seemed to melt into one great football machine," stopping the Lynx dead in their tracks on their next possession. With Bilbo, Wilson, and Lossette leading the charge, the Teachers moved down the field and scored on a 27-yard touchdown pass from Bilbo to Martello. Martello's extra-point kick tied the game at 7–7. With the Teacher defense playing brilliantly and Southwestern unable to move the ball, STC scored again in the second quarter when Bilbo ran in for the touchdown. Martello's extra-point kick was blocked, making the score 13–7 at the half. During halftime, hundreds of STC fans rushed onto the field and engaged in a snake dance, joined by some spectators who had been watching the game through the fence lining Hardy Street. The second half saw a tremendous defensive struggle, with neither team scoring, but the Lynx saved their best effort for the final few minutes, when they had a first-and-goal at the Teacher 5-yard line. The defense held, stopping the Lynx at the 1 a few seconds before the gun sounded, securing the upset.

Following the win over Southwestern, the Teachers roared back with their best offensive display of the season, recording their only shutout of the year with a 32–0 home win over Louisiana Normal College on November 14. Led by Lossette's four touchdowns, including one on a 55-yard run, the STC rushing attack was almost unstoppable. Students celebrated the win and the school's 2–4 conference record in its first year in the SIAA with a multitude of campus activities, including a bonfire.

But game attendance remained a problem. Of the 1,500 people who attended the Louisiana Normal game, 500 were students, who did not pay for admission; another 215 boys attending the Older Hi-Y Boys Conference were guests of the college. Box office receipts amounted to only $92.

College officials vowed to stop fans from crashing the gates and hoped that an on-campus football facility would help to eliminate the problem.

The final game of the year was a November 21 nonconference battle with Delta State in Cleveland, Mississippi, but a series of injuries and the strange disappearance of the previous week's star made things difficult for the Teachers. In addition to Finch, the Yellow Jackets were without Martello and guard Sankey Koen, who had injured shoulders; back Bernard (Reed) Green, who had a knee injury; and Lance Lumpkin, who was also hurt. For some reason, Lossette did not to travel with the team but instead chose to drive to Cleveland by car. He never arrived, however, leaving his coaches and teammates wondering what had happened. The depleted Teachers were no match for Delta State, which rolled to a 27–7 win.

Thomas, Lumpkin, Martello, Lossette, and fullback Leonard Burns won honorable mention on the Associated Press All-SIAA team, and Lumpkin, Martello, and Lossette were named to the All-Mississippi team.

Despite the team's 2–5 record, STC supporters had high hopes for the following year, with an excellent group of freshman and junior college players expected to join the program. Furthermore, President Claude Bennett announced that by the fall of 1932, the college would construct a new stadium, which he envisioned as a focal point for athletics in southern Mississippi. The financial losses of the 1931 football season, coupled with Kamper Park's lack of size and seating, had brought attention to STC's long-standing athletic facility problem, and under the direction of L. E. Faulkner, the head of the Central Relief Committee, preliminary grading for the new facility began in December 1931 on the spot where M. M. Roberts Stadium still stands today.

1932 SEASON

Lumpkin and Hubert served as co-head coaches during the 1932 season, but they would be joined and assisted by Dobie Holden from Louisiana State and E. M. Ward from Mississippi State. After the STC season began with a 49–0 drubbing by Ole Miss before an Oxford crowd of more than 4,000 on September 24 and a 27–0 loss to Millsaps in Jackson the following week, it became quickly apparent that the Teachers had not improved substantially over the preceding season, despite fans' expectations for the team's new players. While they may have had talent, the newcomers lacked experience, and only eight players, some of them backups, had returned from the 1931 team. Backs Ellis Bilbo, Clay (Goofus) Boyd, Leonard Burns, Nolan Taconi, and Cornbread Wilson played well in the defensive backfield in the team's first two games, but on offense the backs struggled to escape the speedy Rebel and Major defenders.

With a record of 0–2, Coach Hubert announced that he would make changes in the starters, particularly in the front line, which needed more weight. He boldly predicted that his players had the ability to win the rest of their games. Hubert's juggling of the lineup, paid off, and the Teachers won their next game, an SIAA contest against Southwestern

Faulkner Field, built in 1932, was the first on-campus football facility at State Teachers College. It was named after L. E. Faulkner.

Louisiana Institute played before a crowd of 5,000 in Lafayette on October 8, by a score of 12–7. Another road loss followed, a 19–0 defeat by Rhodes College on October 22 in which the Teachers lost three fumbles to set up two Rhodes touchdowns.

The next game, against Spring Hill College, was STC's home opener and marked the debut of the new stadium, which was dubbed Faulkner Field in honor of the project director, who had donated materials and equipment and recruited unemployed laborers to do the construction. The stadium was built at no cost to the college and was dedicated by Mississippi First Lady Alma Graham Conner, the seventy-eighth student to enroll at the college and a member of the first graduating class in 1914, as part of Hattiesburg's Golden Jubilee Day celebration on October 29. After the ceremony, which was amplified and broadcast throughout the stadium, a crowd of 4,000 saw the Teachers defeat Spring Hill 12–0 on a second-quarter touchdown by halfback Hunter Denson and a fourth-quarter touchdown by Boyd. During halftime, the Teacher band, dressed in white uniforms, put on a great show and spelled out MSTC, much to the delight of the crowd, and the students staged their snake dance on the field.

The next three weeks brought the Teachers a 12–0 home win over Louisiana College on November 5, a 31–6 road defeat at Louisiana Normal on November 12, and another home victory, this time against Delta State by a 33–25 score on November 19. One of the year's highlights occurred during the traditional Thanksgiving game, played against Union College of Tennessee. After an intense defensive contest for more than three quarters, Green, a future STC head football coach and Mississippi Southern/Southern Miss athletic director known as the Leakesville Express, raced 80 yards for a touchdown to score the game's only points and boost the team's record to 5–4 on the year.

Like many schools, STC had difficulty drawing support during the Great Depression years. In addition to the new stadium, the college sought to attract fans during the 1932 season by lowering the admission price for games to just 60 cents. These changes failed to dramatically increase attendance but did result in an early version of a booster club, formed in November when a group of businessmen, alumni, and other school supporters met to discuss STC's problems and the institution's impact on the Hattiesburg area's visibility and economy. Attendees conservatively estimated that over the preceding 20 years, STC had pumped approximately $20 million into the local economy.

1933 SEASON

The 1933 season saw the end of the co-head coaching position as Lumpkin was reelected to the State Senate and Hubert assumed sole control of the team. Assisted by Ellis M. Bilbo, who had played on and served as captain of the 1931 squad, the 1933 Teachers posted a 3–5–2 record.

The 1933 campaign got off to a horrible start with three straight road losses: 47–0 to Loyola of New Orleans on September 22, 45–0 to Ole Miss on September 30, and 33–7 to Mississippi College on October 7. An October 14 scoreless tie with Millsaps in Jackson followed. The team notched its first win the next week at home against Southwestern Louisiana by a 6–0 score and followed up with a 21–6 win at Louisiana College on October 28. STC recorded its second scoreless tie of the season at Spring Hill on November 4 before dropping the Homecoming game 13–0 against Louisiana Normal on November 11. The Teachers closed the season with an impressive 33–6 victory over Delta State at Faulkner Field on November 25 and a rare December game, a 30–0 whitewash at Murray State.

As Hubert began to turn the STC football program around and to make his name as a fair yet hard-nosed coach, rumors began to circulate that he was being considered for the vacant head coaching job at Auburn, but he opted to continue his work with the fledgling Teacher program. He believed that a team would play like it practiced. A typical training session for the Teachers began with calisthenics. Next, he placed nine linemen up and down the field and handed the ball to a back with instructions to get to the other end of the field, a drill repeated for the next half hour or so with the linemen rotating positions and the backs taking turns carrying the ball so that no man escaped tackling and running practice. Hubert then sent his backs to one end of the field to practice passing and receiving the ball while the linemen reviewed the fundamentals of blocking and tackling. An hour later, the team began a scrimmage that lasted until dark, practicing both its own offensive plays and those of the opposition to gain experience in defending against the other team's attack.

After the 1933 season, Hubert was joined on the STC staff by Reed Green, a Leakesville, Mississippi, native who had earned ten letters as a Yellow Jacket football, basketball, and baseball star. Hubert's hiring of Green marked the beginning of his 40-year tenure as a coach and administrator at the school.

1934 SEASON

The 1934 season represented yet another mediocre year for the Yellow Jackets, who finished with a 3–4–2 record. The season opened on a positive note on September 28 when STC defeated Pearl River Community College 20–12 in a battle at Faulkner Field in which Hubert faced his former teammate with the Alabama Crimson Tide, Joe Sharpe, now the coach at Pearl River. After a 12–0 loss the following week to tough Mississippi College, the Yellow Jackets traveled to Cleveland, Mississippi, to battle the Statesmen of Delta State on October 12. Trailing 13–6 with just minutes to go, sophomore fullback Roy (Pug) Williamson tossed a 20-yard touchdown pass to end Charlie Herring to make the game 13–12. Williamson then kicked the extra point to salvage the tie for STC.

The first night game at Faulkner Field occurred on October 20, when the Yellow Jackets hosted Southwestern Louisiana. Williamson and Herring once again teamed up to win the ball game in the closing minutes. With the score tied 6–6, STC had driven deep into Southwestern Louisiana territory, and Williamson lofted a lazy pass into the end zone. Although the pass had been intended for Herring, a defender appeared to have the best shot catching the ball. It ricocheted off his hands, however, and Herring pulled it in for the winning touchdown. After the ensuing kickoff, Herring intercepted a Southwestern Louisiana pass as the final whistle blew to preserve the 12–6 victory.

After STC played Millsaps to a 0–0 tie at home on October 27, Spring Hill College spoiled the Yellow Jacket Homecoming with a 7–0 win. The STC players followed up with their poorest effort of the season, mustering just 6 yards of total offense in a 31–0 loss to Louisiana Normal on November 9 in Natchitoches. Another defeat followed when Union University picked up a 26–6 victory at Faulkner Field on November 17 by capitalizing on the Yellow Jackets' mistakes.

When Southern hosted Murray State on Thanksgiving Day, Coach Hubert unveiled a new defensive scheme that befuddled both the spectators and the opposition's running game: only five men played on the line, with a guard pulled back into the secondary. Murray State took a 2–0 lead after J. D. Stonestreet recovered his own blocked punt in the end zone. The score remained 2–0 until early in the third quarter, when the Yellow Jackets took the lead with a touchdown. A second touchdown followed after 208-pound Otto (Hippo) Phillips, who had caused problems for Murray State's offense all day, caught a punt that one of his teammates had blocked and returned the ball to the Racers' 25-yard line. On the ensuing play, Stonestreet, playing halfback, made an acrobatic catch of a Williamson pass and fell into the end zone, giving the Teachers a 12–2 lead. The fourth quarter featured one of the year's strangest plays. After an STC punt, Murray State had the ball at midfield with darkness falling. The Racers ran the ball, but the head linesman, former STC star Goofus Boyd, called the play back and penalized Murray State half the distance to the goal line. The Racer left end, Woodrow Simmons, then called Boyd "a dirty, lying ———." Boyd, a trained boxer, punched Simmons in the face. Players and officials quickly conferred, Hubert took Boyd's horn and linesman's stick, and Boyd and Simmons left the field.

THE TRANSITION ERA

1935 SEASON

The Teachers continued their improvement during the 1935 season, their first winning campaign since 1920. The team's 6–4 record was the first in a string of 30 nonlosing seasons.

The '35 opener took place against the Jones County Junior College Bobcats on September 20. The Teachers had several scoring opportunities in the opening half thanks to Stonestreet's running and the play of halfback Malcolm Patrick, but STC committed several turnovers and the game was scoreless at halftime. The Teachers tallied the game's only touchdown in the third quarter when Stonestreet returned a punt 45 yards to put the ball deep in Jones County territory, setting up a touchdown by Patrick.

Pooley Hubert's club made it two wins in a row by knocking off Louisiana College two weeks later. The biggest play of the game came early in the second quarter. With the ball on the STC 37-yard line, Stonestreet dropped back and fired what the *Hattiesburg American* described as a "rifle shot" to halfback Pug Williamson in the back of the secondary. Williamson broke a tackle, raced to the sidelines, and outran three defenders to the end zone. After a missed extra point, the score stood at 6–0. Stonestreet scored the Yellow Jackets' final touchdown on a short run early in the fourth quarter, making the final score 12–0.

Nonconference foe Troy State came to Faulkner Field the following week. Troy State led 14–13 early in the fourth quarter after Stonestreet crossed the goal line, but Ernest Cox's extra-point kick was batted down. The Yellow Jackets penetrated deep into Troy State territory three more times, but the defense held, recovering a fumble in the end zone, batting down a pass in the end zone, and holding on downs at the 15-yard line.

STC stayed unbeaten in the SIAA with a 26–12 home win over Louisiana Normal on October 18. The two teams were tied 6–6 at halftime, but the second half belonged to the Teachers, who finished the game with 252 total yards against just 47 for the Demons. The Teachers put the game away with a brilliant offensive show. Stonestreet capped off a 58-yard drive with a 1-yard touchdown run to make it 13–6 in the final minutes of the third quarter, and fullback Roy Williamson rumbled 60 yards for a touchdown early in the fourth quarter to give the Teachers a 21–6 victory. Southern recorded its second shutout of the season on the road on October 26, defeating the Memphis State Tigers 12–0. The Teacher defense was superb that day, and the Tigers never threatened to score. A Stonestreet touchdown in the first quarter and another by Patrick in the fourth provided all the points the Yellow Jackets needed.

Having won four of its first five games, the Teachers were confident as they traveled to Mobile on November 1 to take on the Spring Hill College Badgers. The Spring Hill defense stifled the STC attack, keeping the talented duo of Stonestreet and Williamson in check. The Yellow Jacket defense, which had performed so effectively all season long, was powerless against the Badger offense, which rolled up more than 300 yards, much to the delight of the 1,500 fans on hand. But the Teachers rebounded the following week against Southwestern Louisiana in Lake Charles. After falling behind 7–0 early in the game, STC rallied to score the final 19 points on two touchdowns by Stonestreet, who also kicked an extra point, and a touchdown by I. B. Fletcher. The Teachers' season record stood at 5–2.

A record crowd on 4,300 was on hand the following week for STC's Homecoming game against Mississippi State. The Bulldogs rolled up 371 yards compared to just 125 for the Teachers, and Mississippi State won 27–0. The Jones County Junior College and Hattiesburg High School bands joined with the STC band to entertain the crowd, and about 150 STC coeds put on a halftime show under the direction of Mattie Perry of the Physical Education Department. The following week brought another 27–0 loss, this time at the hands of Louisiana Tech in Ruston on Thanksgiving Day. In both defeats, the Yellow Jackets had trailed by only 7 points at halftime but had given up 13 points during the third quarter, putting the games out of reach.

The season ended on December 7 at Faulkner Field against Union University. In 50-mile-an-hour winds, field position proved to be a big factor, and Union took advantage of having the wind at its back during the first quarter to grab a 6–0 lead. At the start of the second quarter, the teams switched directions, and so did the momentum. The Teachers pinned the Union squad deep in its own territory, forcing a punt out of the end zone that Leo Purvis caught at the 30-yard line and returned for a touchdown to even the score at 6. The Teachers again had the wind in the third quarter and again took advantage, putting together a 41-yard drive that culminated in a Stonestreet touchdown. With the lead at 12–6 late in the fourth quarter, Union was driving deep in STC territory, but Austin saved the game with a fourth-down interception near the Teacher goal line.

1936 SEASON

The Teachers followed up their 1935 success with another good year. After opening the season with a 7–0 road victory against Louisiana College on September 26, the Teachers traveled to Jackson, Tennessee, to take on Union University. Like the previous year's contest between the two teams, the game was a great defensive struggle, with Union scoring the game's only touchdown early in the second quarter. The Yellow Jackets put together their best drive of the day late in the fourth quarter, reaching the Union 2-yard line but failing to score, and Union gained revenge for its 1935 defeat.

STC played its home opener on October 9 against Millsaps before a crowd of about 3,000 fans at Faulkner Field. Five times, the Teachers drove deep into Major territory, only to turn the ball over each time. With just a few minutes to go, Chester Scalzo, a Teacher defensive tackle, blocked a Millsaps field goal attempt and then fell on the ball to give the Yellow Jackets a final chance. They reached the Majors' 7-yard line on a pass from Willie (the Kemper County Flash)

Back Willie Oubre was known as "The Kemper County Flash" during his career at State Teachers College from 1936 to 1938. Oubre was elected to the M-Club Alumni Association Sports Hall of Fame in 1979.

George Westerfield, an outstanding end at STC from 1936 to 1938, was charter member of the M-Club Alumni Association Sports Hall of Fame in 1965.

Oubre to Pug Williamson, but a pass into the end zone fell incomplete as time expired. The teams combined for 19 punts in the 0–0 tie. The Yellow Jackets picked up their second victory the following week, beating Louisiana Tech 12–7 in Ruston. Fullback Malcolm Patrick scored both STC touchdowns.

The Teachers began a four-game home stand with Memphis State on October 23, with STC rolling over the Tigers 25–0. Next up was Spring Hill College on October 29, with the STC players intent on avenging the previous year's 19–0 defeat. Early in the game, the Teachers drove inside the Badger 10-yard line, but halfback Pug Williamson scrambled and threw a pass that was intercepted at the 1-yard line by Spring Hill's Olaf Fink, who returned the ball 99 yards for a touchdown, stunning the 2,000 spectators. The score held until the third quarter, when the Teachers struck on a touchdown pass from fullback Archie Odom to end Bracie Smith, but Oubre's extra-point kick missed, and Spring Hill still led 7–6. The Yellow Jackets scored their second touchdown in the fourth quarter by using a bit of razzle-dazzle. Facing fourth-and-11 with the ball on the Spring Hill 25-yard line, quarterback Leo Purvis called an end around for George Westerfield, who carried the ball down to near the 14-yard line, gaining the first down by inches. A few plays later, Purvis pushed the ball into the end zone, and the Teachers had their third straight win, 12–7.

The Yellow Jackets next turned in their fourth shutout of the season, a 24–0 win over Troy State on November 6, and then began preparations for the Homecoming game against Southwestern Louisiana Institute. The STC gridders outgained Southwestern Louisiana 407 yards to 88 and rolled to a 44–14 win, their fifth in a row.

The winning streak ended on November 21 in Natchitoches against Louisiana Normal. After being almost unstoppable in preceding weeks, the Jackets could never get their offense going against the Demons, losing 13–0. STC recovered with a 13–6 victory against East Texas State in the annual Thanksgiving game at Faulkner Field.

The Teachers' first score came early in the game after Roy Williamson intercepted a pass at his own 15-yard line. On fourth down, with the ball on the STC 23, Oubre took the ball on a fake punt, slipped around left end, and raced 77 yards for a touchdown to give the Yellow Jackets a 6–0 lead after the extra-point kick failed. Late in the third quarter, the Teachers embarked on a beautiful 60-yard drive that produced the winning touchdown on Westerfield's end around from the 8-yard line. The victory gave the school a 7–2–1 record and its first seven-win season. After scoring only 7 points in their first three games, the Yellow Jackets scored 130 and allowed on 47 in the final seven contests.

The team's success with such limited resources continued to draw attention to Coach Hubert, and following the 1936 season he accepted the head coaching job at Virginia Military Institute of the Southern Conference. In his short time at STC, Hubert had begun to give substance to a program that had lacked direction and goals. He gave football fans in Hattiesburg and around the state some idea of what a solid college football program could bring. His skill, dedication, and professionalism had solidified the program and made it one to be reckoned with throughout the South. Hubert had made Green a full-time assistant varsity coach during the 1935 season and wanted his young protégé to accompany him to Virginia, but Green refused the offer, and Hubert then strongly recommended Green as STC's new head coach.

Some Mississippi observers believed that although Green was an excellent young coach with a bright future, he was not ready for a head coaching job. Some STC supporters wanted Green to remain at the school as an assistant to Edward (Goat) Hale, a former Mississippi College All-American and a member of the College Football Hall of Fame who had coached at every Mississippi school except Teachers College. With a tenacity and determination that would later characterize his tenure as coach and athletic director, Green fought to get hired, telling anyone who asked, "I want this job, I have this job and I'm going to keep this job." J. B. George, who had become STC's president in 1933, saw something special in the 26-year-old Green and enthusiastically named him to head the school's football program in spite of the fact that he had only a couple of years of coaching experience. One of the new coach's first moves was to hire as line coach Thad (Pie) Vann, the captain of and a standout player for the Ole Miss Rebels during the early 1930s who was coaching at Meridian High School. Although no one could have known it at the time, the combination of Green and Vann would control Southern Miss football until the late 1960s.

1937 SEASON

Green's first squad picked up right where Hubert's teams had left off, winning the first three games of the 1937 season by a combined score of 65–0 and going on to finish the year at 7–3. The season opened at home with a 19–0 win over Louisiana College that featured the debut of a new loudspeaker system donated by the Class of

THE TRANSITION ERA

Reed Green (left), who became the head coach at State Teachers College in 1937, was one of the youngest head coaches in the country. One of his first moves was to hire Thad (Pie) Vann as his line coach.

1937 and the staff of the *Student Printz* for use during games at Faulkner Field. The following week on the road at Spring Hill College, halfback A. C. (Mule) Massengale scored three touchdowns in a 33–0 Yellow Jacket win. After a 13–0 win at Southwestern Louisiana, the Teachers had won nine of their last ten games dating back to the 1936 season.

The team gave up its first points of the year during the next contest, a 7–0 loss at Louisiana Tech. The Teachers rebounded to win their next two games, crushing Alabama's Jacksonville State at Faulkner Field 58–0 and rolling over Troy State 53–0. With a 34–0 win over Union University on November 5, STC's record improved to 6–1, and the Teachers had outscored their opponents 210–7. The Jacket defense continued to play superbly in the next week's Homecoming game against Louisiana Normal, although the Demons kicked a short field goal with 10 minutes remaining and won 3–0. The Teachers finished the season with another close loss, going down 14–6 to East Texas State on Thanksgiving Day.

Over the course of the nine-game season, STC had surrendered just 24 points, and the team had lost three games by a total of 18 points, a spectacular performance that earned the school its first postseason bowl invitations. The Yellow Jackets were invited to play in Meridian and Greenwood, Mississippi, as well as Pensacola, Florida, but STC officials accepted an offer from Gulfport, Mississippi, to meet North Carolina's Appalachian State Teachers College, coached by Kidd Brewer, who had once coached at Gulfport High School. The Gulfport Young Men's Business Club sponsored the game as a fund-raiser for the group's doll and toy fund. Appalachian State had lost only once in the past three years, but when the two teams met on December 3, the Teachers walked away with a 7–0 victory, their seventh shutout of the year.

THE TRANSITION ERA [35]

The 1937 season marked several other milestones for STC's athletic program. For the first time, some games were broadcast over the radio by Hattiesburg's WFOR-AM, and the school's first true booster group, the 500 Club, was organized, with supporters paying $10 a year for the privilege of membership.

1938 SEASON

STC continued to dominate its foes during the 1938 season, although the team struggled during the first half of the season opener against Arkansas A&M on September 23, holding just a 7–0 lead at the break on a touchdown by halfback Luther Hollingsworth and a Jake Scott extra-point kick. The Teachers found their form in the second half, however, as George Westerfield, Bee Smith, Linn Walton, John Rich, and Leo Alessandri scored touchdowns in the 39–0 STC romp. Playing at Troy State the following week, Alessandri's 16-yard touchdown run put the Teachers ahead in the second quarter 6–0, and a fourth-quarter touchdown by quarterback Ace Guin and Sporty Dabbs's extra-point kick made the score 12–0. A Glover Freeman interception in the closing minutes set up John Rich's 1-yard touchdown plunge to give the Teachers a 19–0 win.

The Jackets next prepared for a intrastate battle with Ole Miss in Oxford on October 8. The STC players' early game nervousness may have been the difference in the contest, as Mule Massengale's fumble and a blocked punt set up a pair of first-quarter Rebel touchdowns. The Teachers scored on a 20-yard run by Willie Oubre, but the play was called back on an offside penalty, and Ole Miss won 14–0.

The next four games brought a return to STC's winning ways. In a 44–0 home victory over Delta State, the Teachers amassed 334 yards rushing and 47 yards passing while limiting the Statesmen to just 74 yards on the ground and 67 yards through

Fred Dickey was a valuable guard on offense and defense during the 1938 and 1939 seasons.

[36] THE TRANSITION ERA

A. D. (Sandy) Morgan was a powerful two-way tackle for Coach Reed Green in 1938 and 1939.

the air. After a week off, the Teachers played their annual Homecoming game against Millsaps on October 28. The Yellow Jacket defense forced eight turnovers and blocked a punt as STC rolled to a 47–0 win. After a 7–0 win at Louisiana College on November 5, the Teachers returned to Faulkner Field to defeat Southwestern Louisiana 15–0.

With a chance to tie for first place in the SIAA standings, the Teachers traveled to Natchitoches, Louisiana, on November 18 to play Louisiana Normal. The Teachers made a valiant effort but lost 6–0, continuing their futility on the Demons home field. The game's sole touchdown followed a blocked Teacher punt that Louisiana Normal recovered on the STC 16-yard line.

The Yellow Jackets finished the season at Faulkner Field against Union on Thanksgiving Day, winning 32–0. The STC defense was superb, allowing Union to cross midfield only twice. The game was marred by a fistfight between defensive back William (Bee) Smith and a Union offensive lineman after the lineman attempted to block Smith on a running play and Smith pushed the Union player to the turf. The lineman got up swinging, and both teams joined in the melee, with Union's players piling out of the bus where they had been sheltered from the cold. The referee finally broke up the fight and threw Smith, the Union lineman, and half a dozen other players out of the game.

STC had finished another successful season, losing just 2 games by a combined total of just 20 points. Five of the team's 7 victories had been shutouts, giving the Teachers 12 in their last 19 games. Green's record in his two seasons as head coach was 14–5, and in January 1939 he turned down an offer to become the backfield coach at a large midwestern university, promising instead to remain at STC for at least one more year.

The football team's success led to increased exposure for both the team and the school and to accompanying gains in attendance and gate receipts. The 1938 season marked the first time that STC received guaranteed income from some

The Rock (a combination of stadium and dormitory on the east side of Faulkner Field) was constructed during the winter of 1938–1939.

of its away games, including a $1,000 guarantee for the game against Ole Miss. This additional income enabled the school to increase the size of the football squad from 26 to 33, and in November 1938 President George announced plans to construct a combination stadium and dormitory on the east side of Faulkner Field, which had previously had only a set of wooden bleachers on the west side. The concrete stadium-dorm was built over the winter of 1938–39, with members of the football team earning extra money by working on the construction team, hauling concrete for about 19 cents an hour. Thus, the players both literally and figuratively built the stadium that became known as "the Rock." The origins of this nickname remain murky, but it may have come from the fact that the laborers joked that construction work was almost as hard as being imprisoned at Alcatraz, the San Francisco federal prison also dubbed "the Rock."

1939 SEASON

The 1939 season began on September 29 with a 13–6 STC win over Troy State at Faulkner Field. In their next game, against Sam Houston State, the Yellow Jackets held a 7–0 lead until the game's final minutes, when the Texans blocked a Leo Alessandri punt, fell on the ball in the end zone, and then kicked the extra point to gain the tie. The next week brought another tie, 0–0 against Millsaps at the state fairgrounds in Jackson. The Teachers' 5-3-2-1 defense kept the Majors' star passer, "Chunkin" Charlie Ward,

Reginald Switzer played guard and tackle for State Teachers College in 1939 and 1940 earning an All-American team honorable mention.

under control, and the Jacket line led by Reginald Switzer, Sandy Morgan, and Thomas (Scoop) Howard outplayed the Millsaps line all afternoon. The Teachers, too, had difficulty moving the ball, finding their best opportunity to score in the fourth quarter when Alessandri, playing halfback, was stopped at the 5-yard line on a fourth-down play. Southern went on to shut out its next two opponents, winning 21–0 at Delta State on October 20 and recording a 7–0 Homecoming victory over Louisiana College two weeks later to improve to 3–0–2.

STC's undefeated season came to an end on November 11, when Ole Miss came to Hattiesburg and posted a 27–7 win. A crowd of almost 8,000 saw the Teachers put up a valiant fight, staying even with the Rebels during the first half, but Yellow Jacket mistakes led to three Ole Miss touchdowns during the third quarter and put the game out of reach.

After traveling to Lafayette on November 18 and defeating Southwestern Louisiana for the ninth time in a row, 9–7, the Yellow Jackets, second in the SIAA with a 4–0 conference record, prepared for first-place Louisiana Normal (9–0 overall, 5–0 in conference) in a battle to decide the conference title. With a win, Louisiana Normal would gain the chance to meet Slippery Rock in the Brain Bowl, a postseason contest for outstanding teachers' colleges. The November 23 Thanksgiving game was scoreless with just over five minutes to go when Alessandri intercepted a pass on the Louisiana Normal 47 to give the Yellow Jackets one of their three true scoring opportunities during the game, but the Demons held, and Alessandri punted into the end zone for a touchback. After three running plays and an offside penalty, the Demons had the ball on their own 27-yard line. On the next play, substitute halfback Willie Black raced around left end 73 yards for the game's only touchdown and a 7–0 Demon victory.

The Yellow Jackets closed the season by tying St. Mary's of Texas 13–13 at Faulkner Field on December 1, giving STC a 4–2–3 record in Green's third season as head coach. The Associated Press gave honorable mention on its All-America team to guard Reginald Switzer, back A. C. (Mule) Massengale, and tackle Audice Morgan. The Associated Press All-SIAA team included Massengale and Morgan, with Switzer and center Melvin (Pel) Autry receiving honorable mention.

Joe Stringfellow was an end for Mississippi Southern College from 1939 to 1941. He would become one of the school's first players selected in the NFL draft when the Detroit Lions picked him in the twelfth round in 1942.

1940 SEASON

In the spring of 1940, Mississippi State Teachers College became Mississippi Southern College, and the student body voted to change the athletic teams' nickname to the Confederates, although most people referred to the athletic teams as the Southerners. The first game played under the new moniker occurred on September 27, when the Southerners hosted the Troy State Teachers, a team that Southern had defeated

13–6 the previous year. The rematch was no contest, as Southern rolled to a 25–0 win, gaining 369 yards rushing and 51 yards passing while holding Troy State to just 39 yards rushing and 210 yards through the air. Backs C. L. (Dipsey) Dews and M. C. (Tuffy) Johnson scored second-quarter touchdowns, while J. W. (Dagwood) Jones and Alessandri added touchdowns in the fourth quarter.

Despite predictions of an undefeated Confederate season after the easy victory against Troy State, Southern lost its next game 18–16 at home against Sam Houston State Teachers College. Before Southern had managed a first down, the Bearcats had scored three first-half touchdowns—on a 65-yard runback of an intercepted pass, a 35-yard pass, and a blocked punt. Late in the game, Harry Clark blocked a Bearcat punt, but before Southern could fall on it for the winning score, the ball went out of the end zone.

A 13–6 victory over Southeastern Louisiana in Hammond on October 11 improved the Confederates' record to 2–1, but once again a defeat followed a victory, this time a 14–7 loss at Millsaps. It was the only game of the season in which Southern was thoroughly outplayed. The win-lose pattern continued through the next two games, a 38–6 Homecoming victory over Spring Hill College on October 26 and a 7–0 road loss to Louisiana College the following week. In the Spring Hill game, the Badgers took a 6–0 lead in the first quarter on a blocked punt, but Joe Vetrano ran for a touchdown and connected with Dews for another before halftime. Art Van Tone scored on a blocked punt in the third quarter and Jones, Vetrano, and Johnson all ran for touchdowns in the final period. In the Louisiana College game, Southern outgained the Wildcats on the ground, 230 yards to 123, but the Confederates could not punch the ball into the end zone. The Confederates also lost the following week on the road 9–6 to Louisiana Normal to fall to 3–4 on the year.

Facing a losing record, Green rallied his troops. On November 15 the Southerners battled SIAA leader Southwestern Louisiana on a bitterly cold day at Faulkner Field. With the game tied 14–14 with two minutes to play, Alessandri, playing fullback, culminated an 84-yard drive with a 1-yard touchdown run for the winning score. The victory seemed to inspire Southern to a 41–0 victory over Delta State the following week. The regular season ended on December 5 with another win, 27–6 over St. Mary's of Texas in Corpus Christi. Southern jumped out to a lead in the first quarter on a safety and a 30-yard end around, gave up a touchdown in the second quarter, and then ran away with the game in the second half, when Jones, Armand Critty, and Dews scored touchdowns.

The Confederates played a postseason exhibition game against players from the U.S. Army's 37th Ohio Division, which was stationed at Camp Shelby, just south of Hattiesburg. The game, sponsored by the Hattiesburg Chamber of Commerce and played at Faulkner Field, drew a crowd of 8,000, many of them soldiers. Dressed in uniforms loaned by Ohio State University, the army club never really threatened to score, and South-

The 1941 Mississippi Southern College football team finished the year 9–0–1 with the only blemish on their record a 0–0 tie with Southwestern Louisiana.

Dick Thames was a standout guard for Mississippi Southern College in 1941 and again after World War II in 1946. The New York Giants of the NFL drafted him in 1947.

ern tallied two touchdowns in both the second and fourth quarters to win 26–0 and close the year at 7–4. Guard Reginald Switzer and tackle Peter (Jabo) Jones were both named honorable mention Little All-Americans.

1941

The 1941 season demonstrated that Mississippi Southern had just about completed the transition to major football power. The Confederates opened with seven straight victories, starting with an impressive 70–0 September 26 win at Faulkner Field over Georgia State Teachers College. The next two weeks brought a 19–7 October 3 win at Louisiana Tech and a 43–6 home victory against Southeastern Louisiana. On October 17, still stinging from the previous season's 14–7 loss to Millsaps, Southern rolled to a

[42] **THE TRANSITION ERA**

20–0 win over the Majors in front of 10,000 fans, the largest crowd in the history of Faulkner Field. A 26–7 victory over Spring Hill in Mobile, Alabama, a 13–6 Homecoming victory over Louisiana College, and a 21–7 home win over Louisiana Normal followed. The perfect season ended when Southwestern Louisiana, whose hopes of an SIAA championship Southern had ended in 1940, played the Confederates to a 0–0 tie in Lafayette, but Southern bounced back to defeat Delta State 27–7 and St. Mary's of Texas 7–0, both on the road, finishing 9–0–1. Following the Confederates' remarkable season, end Joe Stringfellow became the first Mississippi Southern player to be selected in the National Football League's annual draft when the Detroit Lions selected him in the twelfth round.

1942

The 1941 season was Mississippi's final full season of football until 1946. On December 7, 1941, eight days after the St. Mary's game, Japanese planes bombed Pearl Harbor, drawing the U.S. into World War II. The casualties on that day included Andy Webb, who had played center and linebacker at Mississippi State Teachers College in 1937 and 1938.

As American men began leaving for combat, several schools canceled games with the Confederates, including St. Mary's, Louisiana College, and Spring Hill College. Although just six games remained on the 1942 schedule, Southern officials elected to continue intercollegiate athletics and scheduled football spring practice to begin on February 23. But Vann, the Confederates' line coach and a lieutenant in the Army Reserve, was ordered to report for active duty in the late spring of 1942. By the summer, faced with problems of scheduling, travel, and lack of players, the school announced the termination of all intercollegiate sports. A makeshift Southern team went on to play four games against military and service teams during the fall of 1942, defeating the Mobile Shipbuilders twice along with the Sixth Service Squad and Brookley Field. The state's Board of Trustees of State Institutions of Higher Learning subsequently suspended athletics at all state schools for the duration of World War II.

Several MSC football players lost their lives while fighting in World War II, including Andy Webb (1937–1938), who died during the Japanese attack on Pearl Harbor, Hawaii, on December 7, 1941.

Vann served in Europe as a second lieutenant in the field artillery for three years during the war and at the end of the war served as a Special Service officer, responsible for organizing recreational, athletic, and educational services to boost soldiers' morale. The eight decorations he earned during his tenure in the army included a Bronze Star for his service during the invasion of Europe, and he reached the rank of lieutenant colonel before being discharged from active service in 1945.

Southern's Coach, Reed Green, also joined the military. He attended the University of North Carolina Naval Indoctrination School, where one of his classmates was baseball great Ted Williams. Green left North Carolina as a lieutenant junior grade and went to the University of Iowa, where he met future Oklahoma head football coach Bud Wilkinson, Missouri head football coach Don Faurot, and future Maryland head football coach Jim Tatum. While at Iowa, Green was involved with the V-5 and V-12 programs, which were responsible for officers' military and physical fitness training. Green was subsequently stationed on the USS *Intrepid* and overseas. Before he was officially discharged from the service in 1946 as a lieutenant commander, he also had been stationed in Manteo, North Carolina; Key West, Florida; and Corpus Christi, Texas.

Many former Southern players also served in the military. Melvin (Pel) Autry, Henry (Frenchie) Bolis, M. G. (Foots) Clements, Fred Dickey, J. P. (Noonie) Hackney, William (Mike) Katrishen, Jake Scott, Bracie Smith, and Joe Vetrano were just some of the gridiron stars who served their country during the war. Thirty-four former Mississippi Southern students lost their lives during the war, including Webb, Bolis, James Forte, Thomas Rivers King, Rufus McSwain, and Bishop Rockwell.

THE POSTWAR ERA
1946–1949

One of the major factors contributing to the survival of Mississippi Southern College and its athletic program during World War II was the establishment of the Army Administration Program on campus. Early in the 1940s, the school's football coach, Reed Green, and president, J. B. George, traveled to Washington, D.C., to inquire about possible funds to aid Southern during the war. They contacted one of Mississippi's U.S. congressmen, William Colmer, and the state's two U.S. senators, Theodore G. Bilbo and James O. Eastland, who helped to persuade the War Department to establish the program at Southern.

Southern's enrollment decreased tremendously during the war, but the Army Administration Program supplemented the school's overall budget through the

Robert Cecil Cook became president of Mississippi Southern College in 1946. His vision and leadership was greatly responsible for the school's football success after World War II.

Reconstruction Finance Corporation, which paid Southern to house participating soldiers in the stadium-dorm. Of these fees, President George earmarked $25,000 for the athletic program after the war. In 1946 Robert Cecil Cook became the school's new president. An enthusiastic proponent of the athletic program, Cook declared that "a well rounded program in physical education and athletics was important to any college." Cook and Green worked to raise money for sorely needed athletic equipment and supplies and advocated the reorganization of the 500 Club, a community group that supported the college's athletic program, into the Quarterback Club. In 1946, the club raised $12,927 for athletic scholarships, proving that Hattiesburg was ready to back the Southerners.

When Green returned from service in 1945, Southern had 350 enrolled students, only 23 of them men. Green and Cook began recruiting players, and by the fall of 1946, many ex-servicemen had returned to Southern Miss to resume their collegiate athletic careers. After four years of war, both the Confederates and their opponents faced a daunting task in returning to football after such a long layoff.

1946 SEASON

Both Coach Reed Green and Assistant Coach Pie Vann returned to Mississippi Southern College in 1946. They were joined on the school's football staff by Joe Stringfellow, who had been an outstanding player for the school and was a professional baseball player. The first postwar game was played on September 21, 1946, at Faulkner Field against Louisiana Tech in front of 7,600 fans who endured a steady downpour to watch the game. After giving up a first-period touchdown to the visitors, who missed the extra point, the Southerners scored what proved to be the winning touchdown when quarterback Vernon (Zipper) Wells crossed the goal line early in the final quarter on a 1-yard run and Sawyer Sims kicked the extra point. Tech missed a game-winning field goal in the game's final minutes. The game was dominated by line play, and Southern's defense was solid, holding the Bulldogs to 84 yards rushing and four first downs. According to the *Hattiesburg American,* Coach Green was satisfied with the win but was a little disappointed in certain aspects of the team's play.

MSC's next game was predicted to be the most difficult of the season, as the Southerners traveled to Montgomery, Alabama, to play heavily favored Auburn on September 27. Mississippi Southern played very well, losing 13–12 to the Tigers in what the *Student Printz* called "one of the most spectacular sports events of the South," witnessed by more than 12,000 people. Much of the first half was played in Southern's territory, and the defense, led by end Jay Smith, made several strong stops before finally allowing a touchdown about midway through the second quarter. Early in the third period, Southerner halfback Bennie Ray Nobles intercepted an Auburn pass and returned it 30 yards for the score, bringing MSC to within a point. But Auburn responded by scoring on its next possession, although the Tigers missed the extra point. In the fourth period, fullback Joe Latham broke through the Auburn defensive line for a 50-yard run to the Auburn 6-yard line, and Wells subsequently scored. But the extra point attempt failed, and the Southerners lost, although their efforts earned them some measure of respect nationally and some observers believed that the STC gridders had outplayed the Southeastern Conference team.

The next four weeks of the season saw Southern in the win column, improving the team's record to 5–1. A 65–0 victory over Jacksonville State on October 4 was followed by a 6–0 Homecoming win over Southwestern Louisiana. Southern defeated Oklahoma City 20–6 at home on October 25 and then shut out Stephen F. Austin 7–0 on the road. Southern allowed only one touchdown during the streak, demonstrating that defense was definitely the team's strength.

The Jacksonville State game was an easy victory for MSC, which scored twice in each of the first two quarters, four times in the third, and twice more in the final quarter despite the fact that reserves played for a large part of the game. The 10 touchdown runs included Nobles's 85-yard kickoff return and his 88-yard run from scrimmage; James Bell's 53-yard interception return; and runs of 45 yards by Bobby Campbell, 32 yards by John LeGros, and 20 yards by Wells. The Southern offense racked up 445 yards on the ground, while Jacksonville State managed just 18 yards rushing and 58 yards of total offense. The defense also recorded five interceptions.

In the win over Southwestern Louisiana, however, heavily favored MSC "floundered" offensively as each time the offense pushed itself into scoring territory "signal-flops and fumbles stymied their chances to score," as the *Student Printz* reported. Southern scored the game's only touchdown on a drive that started at the Confederate 46-yard line. Wells passed 8 yards to C. J. (Pete) Taylor and then connected with Nobles on a 42-yard pass to bring the ball to the Southwestern Louisiana 4-yard line. On the next play, with the Bulldogs looking for the Southerners to go up the middle, Nobles swung wide around left end on a reverse and scored. The game remained in doubt until the final whistle, as the Bulldogs threatened twice late in the game but came up empty.

Southern's victory over previously unbeaten and untied Oklahoma City University was

End C. J. (Pete) Taylor earned letters in 1941 and 1946 and went on to serve as an assistant football coach, track coach, assistant athletic director, and head baseball coach. The school's baseball park, which opened in 1984, bears his name.

THE POSTWAR ERA [47]

The 1946 Mississippi Southern College football team was the school's first post–World War II squad. First row (left to right): Joe Latham, Vernon Wells, Frank Brown, Fred Waites, Morris Brown, James Bell, Falco Carrozza, Fred Waters; second row: Jerry (Buster) Mullin, Buddy Watkins, Benny Ray Nobles, John LeGros, Sawyer Sims, Calvin Triplett, Frank Beam, Dick Thames, Jim Graham, Jack Ryan, Bobby Campbell, Robert Wells; third row: George Kelly, Harold Crane, Bruce Womack, Joe Borde, Lucius Robinson, Robert (Sonny) Jordan, Maxie Lambright, Louis Campbell, Glenn Cook, Robert (Curley) Dement, Bernie Wilkes, A. J. (Red) Mangum, Jim Owens; fourth row: C. J. (Pete) Taylor, Boots McCormick, Pat Patterson, Orville Foshee, Leroy (Hawk) Austin, Reed Bailey, Doug (Spot) Honaker, Johnny May, Ernest (Limbo) Limbaugh, Melvin (Bucky) Waters, William (Mike) Katrishen, Lavern (Cooter) Lewis, Roland Loper, Jay Smith.

arguably the team's greatest win of the 1946 season. The *Student Printz* described the team from Oklahoma as almost unbeatable and stated that "the whole sports minded nation has been set back on its heels by reports of this Midwestern team's power." The team was a scoring machine, having tallied 286 points to their opponents' 13. On offense, the Chiefs ran from the single wing, sending a 255-pound fullback behind tackles who weighed in at 285 and 265 pounds. In anticipation of a large crowd, student bleachers were built across the field from the Rock. Any student wanting to bring a friend to the game was required to purchase a ticket from Coach Green. The contest lived up to its pregame hype, with the Southern defense holding the fearsome Chief offense to only 115 yards. LeGros, playing quarterback, scored twice, and MSC fullback Buster Mullin turned in a spectacular 71-yard touchdown run. Oklahoma City's lone touchdown came in the third quarter with the help of two long penalties against the Southerners. "We're on the map!" exulted the *Student Printz* after the game, "We beat the Hell out of 'Em." The *Printz* went on to claim that the victory made MSC "the leading small college football team of the nation" and that the win was one of the biggest upsets of the football world. Science professor Spout Austin, the team's former head coach, even contended during chapel on the Monday following the victory that the Southerners were better than national major-college power Army. Although these claims may have been somewhat exaggerated, the game clearly represented a huge step in the right direction for the school's postwar football program.

Several Southerner players were hurt during the Oklahoma City game and were unable to participate in the next contest against Stephen F. Austin, which occurred amid rain and mud on a brand-

THE POSTWAR ERA

Tackle Melvin (Bucky) Waters starred for Southern in 1941 and returned to contribute again in 1946 and 1947 after serving in World War II.

new field in Nacogdoches. The crippled MSC footballers nevertheless managed to squeak out a 7–0 victory courtesy of Smith's end-around score in the first quarter. The mud was so deep and slippery and he was traveling so fast that his momentum carried him from the Stephen F. Austin 12-yard line back to near the 20-yard line before he turned upfield and headed for the end zone.

Mississippi Southern's four-game winning streak came to an end in a 7–6 defeat by Northwestern State College of Louisiana (formerly Louisiana State Normal College) on November 11 in Natchitoches. The game was considered an upset, but some of MSC's marquee players remained out with injuries incurred during the Oklahoma City game. Northwestern scored on a trick first-quarter play that resulted in a 69-yard touchdown run. MSC's Cooter Lewis blocked a punt in the third quarter, and the Southerners recovered the ball on the Demon 20, leading to Latham's 1-yard touchdown run. But Sims missed the extra point, and the Southerners fell to 5–2 on the year. MSC's hopes of winning the Southern Intercollegiate Athletic Association (SIAA) championship were dashed, although the school still received feelers from the Raisin Bowl, the fifth-largest bowl game in the country (following the Rose, Sugar, Orange, and Cotton Bowls).

MSC trounced Louisiana College 65–0 on November 15, with Morris (Lightin') Brown scoring three touchdowns. One of the game's highlights was an incredible block by guard Sonny Jordan, who took out three men in one lunge on a fourth-quarter punt return by Brown. The game also featured a fourth-quarter fight involving players from both benches as well as spectators. The Southern defense held the Wildcats to just two first downs and a net-17 yards rushing, while the Southerner offense rolled up 535 yards of total offense, including 400 yards on the ground. With a key game the following week against Southeastern Louisiana, the Southerners wore white jerseys with gold numerals that could not be read from the stands in hopes of confusing the Lion scouts.

THE POSTWAR ERA

The jersey scheme must not have fooled the Lions, because the Southerners lost to Southeastern Louisiana 20–0 at Faulkner Field on November 22. The Lions pushed across all of their points in the first half, while their defensive line, paced by brilliant end Pat Kenelly and Little All-American tackle Turk Campion, bottled up the Southern attack for -11 yards and no first downs. The Southerners tried a different tack after halftime, shifting from the single wing to the T. MSC took the opening kickoff and drove 62 yards to inside the Bulldog 10-yard line, where the drive stalled. The loss dropped the Southerners to 6–3.

For the final game of the year, the Southerners took their first plane flight, traveling to Cuba to play the University of Havana in a December 14 game dubbed the Tobacco Bowl, with a $300 silver loving cup to be presented to the winner. If the Americans won, the cup was scheduled to be returned to Havana the following year and presented to the victor in a game between Havana and another U.S. team. The game, to be played in the University of Havana's beautiful $1 million stadium-gymnasium, which seated 12,000, would be the first contest played by a U.S. college team outside the continental United States. MSC President Cook and 16 other supporters, most of them prominent Hattiesburg businessmen, accompanied the team, which was greeted on arrival by members of the Havana team; Jimmy Kendrigan, who had coached the Havana squad for 23 years; and Dr. Joaquin Cristofol, administrator of the stadium. Through William Powe, a former Hattiesburg denizen who had been in business in Havana for 26 years, Cook and Hattiesburg businessman C. C. Sullivan called on Durley Harwood, the U.S. ambassador to Cuba. Cook, Coach Green, Sullivan, and several others from the school's entourage made an official call on Dr. Clemente Inclan, Havana University's rector, and invited him and his team to make a return visit to Hattiesburg. The MSC party was treated well, staying at the Plaza Hotel and eating in a colorful Havana restaurant. The Southerners returned the hospitality by soundly defeating the Cubans, 55–0. Paced by halfbacks Mullin and Bell, each of whom scored twice, the Southerners tallied eight touchdowns. Havana athletic officials had expressed concern that the game might end in a fight because of the Cubans' "hot temperament," but the contest was unusually clean, with only two penalties, both for being offside. The victory gave the Southerners a 7–3 record on the year. They had scored 243 points and surrendered only 52.

The 1946 campaign went a long way toward rebuilding the foundation established by MSC's strong prewar teams. William (Mike) Katrishen, a 6-foot, 205-pound tackle from Hazleton, Pennsylvania, made second-team Little All-America. Dick Thames was drafted by the New York Giants in the twenty-third round of the National Football League draft but accepted an offer to play for the Buffalo Bisons of the All-American Football Conference. And 41 players from the 1946 team would return for the following season, which would include a game against Mississippi State that President Cook declared would be one of the sporting highlights of the fall quarter.

1947 SEASON

The 1947 season began with some changes at MSC. The school's enrollment reached 1,506, and Hattiesburg radio station WFOR announced that it would broadcast all of the Southerners' football games that season. But the gridders' football success did not change, as the team matched its 1946 record of 7–3.

First up on the schedule was national power Alabama on September 20 in Birmingham before a crowd of 30,000, the city's largest ever, in what was billed as the toughest game in MSC's history. The Crimson Tide had played in the 1946 Rose Bowl and the 1945 Sugar Bowl and returned a strong team in 1947. Trailing 13–0 midway through the third quarter, Southern thrilled its supporters when quarterback Joe Romo flipped a lateral to Nobles, who was lined up outside the right end as a flanker. Nobles started running forward, stopped suddenly, and fired a pass to Doug (Spot) Honaker, who took the ball to around the Southern 45-yard line before lateraling to Bubba Phillips, who was traveling at full speed and had no trouble outrunning the startled Tide secondary to complete the 72-yard touchdown play. When Carl (Chicken) Howard added the extra point, the Southerners had cut Alabama's lead to just 6 points. In the fourth quarter, however, Alabama pulled away, soundly defeating Southern 34–7. The game featured the college debut of John Melvin (Bubba) Phillips, who had come to Southern as the nation's premier high school scorer, throwing twelve touchdown passes and tallying 235 points for his Macon, Mississippi, high school team.

The following week brought no respite for the Southerners, who traveled to Montgomery, Alabama, for a September 26 rematch with Auburn. MSC end Henry (Hindu) Reynolds scored on a pass from Nobles in the first quarter, and Southern defensive end Glyn Slay returned an interception 20 yards for the team's second touchdown, giving the Southerners a 12–6 lead at the half. The MSC squad opened the third quarter with a long drive dominated by Phillips's running and capped by halfback Don Winstead's 23-yard scoring run. Chicken Howard added the extra point, and the score stood 19–6. Auburn added another touchdown, but Southern's defense stiffened and the game ended with MSC on top, 19–13. This win over a Southeastern Conference power clearly demonstrated that Southern could compete against any team in the nation.

Southern squeaked by a tough Louisiana Tech team two weeks later in Ruston, running the Southerners' record to 2–1. Tech scored first, but Smith and Slay blocked the extra point, and in the fourth period, Latham ran 52 yards to the Tech 2-yard line, setting up Vernon Wells's touchdown sneak. Howard split the uprights with his extra-point kick, giving the Southerners the 7–6 victory. On the way home from the game, tackle Bucky Waters became ill, and the team left him at Baptist Hospital in Jackson, where his appendix was removed, putting him on the shelf for the remainder of the season. Center Al (Apple) Sanders, who had been outstanding against

(Left) Robert (Curley) Dement was selected as the team's most valuable player for the 1947 season. Dement played guard at MSC in 1941 and again in 1946. He switched to tackle for the 1947 season.

(Right) Tackle William (Mike) Katrishen was one of the leaders of the 1947 Mississippi Southern football team earning second-team Little All-America honors.

Alabama and Auburn, missed the Louisiana Tech game because he had played at Louisiana State University during 1946 and was thus ineligible to play against SIAA teams until 1948.

MSC's record jumped to 3–1 with a dramatic come-from-behind victory over Southwestern Louisiana on October 18 in Lafayette. Southern was an underdog going into the contest, and it seemed as if the prognostication would hold true as the Bulldogs led 7–0 at the half. However, during the third quarter, Latham tackled a Bulldog back in his own end zone to narrow the margin to 7–2, and LeGros threw a 16-yard touchdown pass to Frank Brown to give MSC an 8–7 lead. In the final period, Morris Brown scored on a brilliant 74-yard drive, and Howard made the extra point to give the Southerners a 15–7 win.

The three-game win streak ceased when the Southerners played their fifth straight road game, against Oklahoma City University, losing in what the *Student Printz* called "a wide open, penalty packed fracas." The October 25 game started out well for the Southerners, who led 6–0 following Phillips's first-quarter touchdown pass to Wells. In a bit of trickery, Wells pitched the ball to Phillips, who turned and threw back against the grain to Wells, who took the ball the distance. The Chiefs responded by taking control with three consecutive touchdowns, including a 97-yard punt return, a long pass for a score, and a blocked punt, for the 21–6 win. After the game, Coach Green commented that his team did not "look like a good ball club . . . as a team we didn't have the spark we had shown in previous games, maybe the boys were just too road weary."

The Southerners must have been looking forward to their first home game of the 1947 season as they hosted Stephen F. Austin for Homecoming on November 1. Green promised to field a different team than the one that performed so poorly against Oklahoma City, and more than 10,000 spectators saw the Southerners back up Green's vow with a 20–7 victory over the Lumberjacks. The game was scoreless at the half, but Southern broke the drought on the first possession of the second half, marching down the field on a 72-yard scoring drive that finished with Phillips's 34-yard scamper. MSC put together another 72-yard drive that featured the running of Sonny Carr and Morris Brown and finished with Winstead's 2-yard run to make the score 13–0. The Lumberjacks blocked a punt and scored on a third-down pass play to tighten the game to 13–7, but Phillips answered with a 71-yard run for the game's final score.

On November 7 the Southerners faced the Northwestern State College of Louisiana Demons, a team that had won 9 of its previous 10 against the Southerners. Led by Phillips, however, the MSC squad shut out Northwestern Louisiana 20–0. On the second play from scrimmage,

Legendary Ole Miss head coach Johnny Vaught (standing) and his coaching staff made a preseason visit with the Mississippi Southern coaching staff. Seated: Happy Campbell, Red Drew, Reed Green, Thad (Pie) Vann.

THE POSTWAR ERA [53]

End Jay Smith of Brookhaven, Mississippi, served as the team's captain during the 1947 season. He was named to the Associated Press third-team Little All-America that year.

Phillips broke through the line off right tackle and raced 87 yards to put Southern up 7–0. In the second quarter, Fred Waites blocked a Northwestern punt, Robert (Curley) Dement fell on the ball deep in Demon territory, and Winstead scored on the next play to make the score 14–0. Morris Brown and Phillips carried the load on Southern's final scoring drive, with Brown crossing the goal line. Nobles continued his mastery of the kicking game, hitting a 59-yard punt that rolled dead at the 1-yard line. MSC's record stood at 5–2 overall, 3–0 in the SIAA.

Mississippi Southern hosted Union University, "one of the toughest small school teams in the Southeast," according to the *Student Printz,* in the season's last game at Faulkner Field. The game was played on November 14 amid what the paper described as "rain so hard that it was almost impossible to see from one side of the field to the other and on ground so slippery and groggy that Farmer Jones' hogs probably would have turned it down." The threat of drowning in the ankle-deep water seemed to trouble the Southerners more than the visitors from Tennessee did. Behind Nobles's continued stellar punting and Phillips's long runs, including a 65-yard touchdown gallop, MSC took an 18–0 win.

MSC traveled to Starkville the next week for the long-anticipated showdown with Mississippi State. In another game played in inclement weather on a muddy field, the Bulldogs dominated, scoring in the first and third periods to go up 14–0. Southern had opportunities to score but fumbled twice inside the Mississippi State 35-yard line. Only a late 2-yard touchdown pass from Wells to George Stevens avoided the shutout and made the game appear closer than it was.

A Thanksgiving Day battle with Southeastern Louisiana in Hammond on November 27 gave the Southerners a chance to complete their season unbeaten in the SIAA and thus claim the conference championship for the first time. Despite the fact that most of the team's players had returned from the 1946 season, during which the Lions had gone unbeaten and had won the SIAA title, Southeastern Louisiana had struggled throughout 1947. After a scoreless first quarter, Wells hit Smith, the Southerner captain, on an 11-yard

The 1948 Gulf States Conference Champions. First row (left to right): Glyn Slay, Frank Brown, Cal Butler, Fred Waters, A. J. (Red) Mangum, Fred Waites, Cliff Coggin; second row: Gus Miciotto, Frank Purnell, Reese Snell, Henry (Hindu) Reynolds, George Stevens, Maxie Lambright, Dick Strain, Boots McCormick, Jack Jenevein, Eddie Langford; third row: Robert (Sonny) Jordan, Doug Taylor, Phil (Moose) Musmeci, Ernest (Limbo) Limbaugh, Eugene Kemper, Vernon (Zipper) Wells, Johnny Yates, Carl (Chicken) Howard, Bill Nichols, Roy (Shiny) Smith, Jack (Pop) Warner, Don Winstead; fourth row: Bob Stevens, Chuck Borde, Vernon Bullock, Walter Stampley, Sherrard Shaw, Bill Stewart, Vaughn Ellender, Al (Apple) Sanders, Wayne Jackson, Morris (Lightnin') Brown, Benny Ray Nobles, Sonny Carr; fifth row: Carl Smith, Joe Morgan, Webb (Boots) Farrish, Bill Querner, Razor Sharp, John Melvin (Bubba) Phillips, Al Hanzo, Frank Spruiell, Tom LeGros, Doug (Spot) Honaker, Barney Moore, Lavern (Cooter) Lewis.

pass for the team's first touchdown, and the rout was on. Wells threw two more touchdown passes, including another one to Smith, before the Southerners' reserves came on to add a safety and two more touchdowns in the fourth quarter of the 35–0 win. The win allowed MSC to claim the SIAA crown with a 7–3 overall record and a 5–0 conference mark. Although bowl games had expressed interest in the Southerners prior to their win over Southeastern Louisiana, a postseason bid never materialized.

Smith was named to the second-team All-America squad by the Associated Press and was chosen in the fifth round of the NFL draft by the Chicago Cardinals and in the sixth round of the All-American Football Conference draft by the Brooklyn Dodgers. Dement and Katrishen were also selected in the NFL draft, with Dement going in the fifteenth round to the Los Angeles Rams and Katrishen going in the tenth round to the Washington Redskins.

1948 SEASON

More than 80 students came out for MSC's football team prior to the 1948 season, with 57 men making the squad. However, the Southerners had lost several key players, among them linemen Katrishen, Dement, and Waters and backs Latham and Campbell. Green continued as head coach, assisted by Vann and former players J. D. Stonestreet and Falco Carrozza. The 1948 campaign marked the inaugural season for the Gulf States Conference (GSC), which Green had been instrumental in creating and which included many

THE POSTWAR ERA [55]

of Southern's frequent competitors in football, basketball, and baseball—Southwestern Louisiana, Northwestern State College of Louisiana, Louisiana College, Southeastern Louisiana, and Louisiana Tech.

The season began with a game against Auburn in Montgomery on September 24. After splitting with Auburn the previous two seasons, the Southerners again fought hard but lost by a touchdown, 20–14, the largest margin of victory for either team in the series. Wells picked up where he left off the previous season, throwing touchdown passes to ends Slay and newcomer Cliff Coggin. Southern played without the services of superstar Bubba Phillips, who had been ruled ineligible for games against Southeastern Conference teams because he had signed a professional baseball contract and played professional baseball in the summer of 1948.

The following week, Phillips ran 79 yards for a touchdown the first time that he touched the ball against Stephen F. Austin College. The rest of the game was much the same as the Southerners thrashed the Lumberjacks 41–0. Sanders blocked 2 punts, Wells connected with Coggin for a touchdown, and Eddie Langford ran for a score. Phillips also threw a touchdown pass to Vaughn Ellender, and Spot Honaker added six of seven extra points. MSC was simply much better than Stephen F. Austin, beating the Lumberjacks in every statistical category.

The offensive output came to a screeching halt when an inspired Trinity University team soundly defeated MSC on October 8 at Faulkner Field. Once again, Bubba Phillips was not allowed to play because of eligibility problems, and the team obviously missed him in the 26–9 loss. The *Student Printz* reported that many players believed that the team was "overconfident" and was "not ready for Trinity's single wing" offensive attack. Trinity scored on its first series and led 19–2 at halftime. MSC closed to 19–9 early in the third period, when Maxie Lambright passed to Coggin, who was quickly becoming one of the best receivers MSC fans had ever seen. Trinity scored again late in the third quarter and dropped the Southerners to 1–2.

After the loss, MSC reeled off three straight victories. In the team's first GSC game, the Southerners met Southwestern Louisiana Institute on October 15 at Mobile's Ladd Stadium in front of 8,433 spectators. The Southerners scored three second-quarter touchdowns to take a 20–0 halftime lead. After the Bulldogs were stopped on their own 30-yard line and forced to punt, Carr gathered in the kick at the Southerner 26-yard line, faked a handoff, and raced down the sidelines to Southwestern Louisiana's 16-yard line. A clipping penalty moved the ball back to the 31-yard line, but Southern wasted no time in scoring. Phillips tore through a huge hole up the middle, twisted away from several defenders, and crossed the goal line to make the game 7–0. After Carr had returned another punt to the Bulldogs' 32-yard line, Bill Stewart scored. The extra-point kick failed, bringing the score to 13–0. On Southwestern Louisiana's next drive, Jack Jenevein intercepted a pass on the Bulldog 14-yard line and raced into the end zone to make the score 20–0. After a third-quarter Southwestern Louisiana touchdown, Phillips recorded his second pickoff

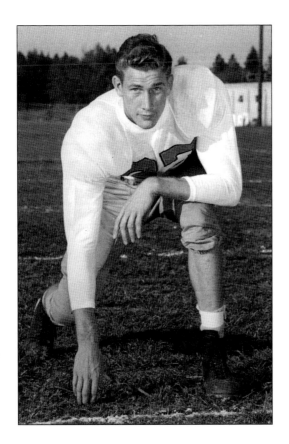

End Henry (Hindu) Reynolds (1947–1948) was once described by Coach Reed Green as "one of the best athletes who ever attended this institution."

23, 48, and 95 yards, and Wells and Lambright threw for four additional touchdowns.

The following week the Southerners traveled to Natchitoches to meet Northwestern State College of Louisiana in a GSC battle. Early in the game, with the ball at the Demon 15-yard line, quarterback Wells dropped back to pass, eluded a tackler, and fired a pass to Stevens deep in the end zone. Stevens leaped high to snare the ball and came straight down to avoid stepping out. MSC added two more touchdowns in the first quarter on a 4-yard pass from Wells to Coggin and a 6-yard run by Phillips. Phillips also threw a 30-yard touchdown pass to Reynolds early in the third quarter to stretch the lead to 26–0, but the Demons answered with a touchdown and then intercepted a Wells pass around midfield and returned it for a touchdown, closing the gap to 26–14. The Southerners came back with an impressive drive, scoring on an 8-yard run by Morris Brown to take a 32–14 lead. Frank Spruiell intercepted a Demon pass to set up the final Southern touchdown and seal the 38–14 victory. Coaches and players singled out tackle Charles Borde as lineman of the night as a reward for his numerous tackles and blocking prowess. Lambright was superb in the secondary, breaking up several Demon passes and intercepting one.

The Southerners were 4–2 going into their November 6 contest with Alabama in Tuscaloosa, but the Crimson Tide had little trouble with the Southerners, winning 27–0. Phillips was not allowed to play because Southeastern Conference rules prohibited a player from being a professional in one sport and remaining eligible in another on

of the night to set up another score. The Southern defense held Southwestern Louisiana's backs to just 42 yards rushing; although the Bulldogs had some success passing the ball, Southern intercepted six passes to take the 26–6 victory and move to 2–2 on the year and 1–0 in the GSC.

The October 23 road game against Oklahoma City University was especially gratifying to the team and coaching staff. With a 55–20 win, the Southerners knocked the Chiefs from the ranks of the unbeaten and untied for the second time in three years. Phillips ran wild, scoring on runs of

THE POSTWAR ERA

the collegiate level, but he would likely have made little difference, as the Crimson Tide completely outclassed the visitors from Hattiesburg.

MSC finished the 1948 football season with victories over Louisiana Tech, Southeastern Louisiana, and Union University. In the November 13 Homecoming contest against Louisiana Tech, the Southerners scored on the second play of the game when Spruiell took a pitch from Lambright and ran 65 yards for the touchdown. Phillips scored on a 22-yard run later in the first quarter, and Tech added a touchdown to cut the lead to 14–6 at halftime. Nobles found Coggin for a 55-yard third-quarter scoring pass, giving the Southerners a 20–6 victory and improving their overall record to 5–3 and their conference record to 3–0.

The Southerners had a chance to nail down the GSC's first championship when they hosted Southeastern Louisiana on November 19. Phillips added to his legendary status by returning the opening kickoff 103 yards for a touchdown. Spruiell passed 14 yards to Reynolds for a second-quarter touchdown and raced 51 yards for a touchdown in the third quarter. Frank Brown scored the game's final touchdown on a 9-yard run later in the quarter. Phillips rushed for 120 yards on 19 carries and had another 128 yards on kickoff and punt returns. Spruiell had 94 yards on just six carries. Southern had finished a perfect 4–0 in the league, winning the championship.

Union University was overmatched on November 24, losing 47–8 in a Thanksgiving night affair in which Southern's "meatballs" (Coach Green's term for his scout team) played extensively. A 13-yard touchdown pass from Spruiell to Reynolds on Southern's second possession of the night started the scoring and was followed by a Spruiell running touchdown a few minutes later after Slay had blocked a Union punt and recovered the ball at the 8-yard line. Phillips scored on a 46-yard touchdown run on the first play of the second quarter, and another partially blocked punt by Slay set up the fourth touchdown when quarterback LeGros lateraled to Morris Brown, who had difficulty getting a handle on the ball but recovered and raced into the end zone. Langford's 17-yard touchdown run gave Southern a 34–0 lead at halftime. Early in the fourth quarter, Southern's Gus Miciotto recovered a Union fumble at the 1-yard line, and Fred Waters scored on the next play. Southern added a final touchdown when Wayne Jackson passed to Coggin, who caught the ball around the Union 45-yard line and fought his way into the end zone.

With the GSC championship and an overall season record of 7–3, MSC was a candidate for a postseason game. Southern had signed before the season for a game at Mobile's Ladd Stadium, but the sponsor, the Mobile Touchdown Club, had difficulty in obtaining a suitable opponent for the Southerners. The possibility of bringing an outstanding team to Hattiesburg to play the Southerners in early December was considered but also came to naught. Sanders played in the Blue-Gray All-Star Classic and was drafted by the Pittsburgh Steelers in the eleventh round of the NFL draft and by the Baltimore Colts in the eighteenth round of the All-American Football Conference draft. Phillips had eligibility remaining but was taken in the eighteenth round of the All-

The 1948 coaching staff: (left to right) J. D. Stonestreet, Thad (Pie) Vann, Reed Green, Jess Thompson, and Falco Carrozza.

American Football Conference draft by the Chicago Hornets, although he chose to return to the Southerners, and the Los Angeles Rams selected Joe Morgan in the sixteenth round of the NFL draft.

In January 1949, Green resigned as MSC's football coach to become the school's full-time athletic director in what the *Student Printz* characterized as "an effort to keep the Southern athletic program moving ahead." Green's longtime assistant, Pie Vann, would take over the helm immediately. With a career record of 59–20–4, Green had personified Mississippi Southern football.

1949 SEASON

Despite the coaching change, the Mississippi Southern football team posted similar results during the 1949 season. The team's 7–3 record was significant not only because the season was Vann's first as head coach but also because the schedule was again considered the roughest in school history.

The season began on September 17 with Paul (Bear) Bryant's Kentucky team resoundingly defeating the Southerners 71–7, the worst loss in the history of MSC football. Of his squad's inaugural effort, Vann said, "We were outclassed, outmanned, outplayed and decisively beaten." Playing at home, Kentucky rolled up 26 first-quarter points behind Babe Parilli, whom Vann described as "one of the best T-formation quarterbacks that I have ever seen." Kentucky rushed for 362 yards and passed for 237 and, according to the *Southerner*, the school yearbook, might have scored even more points without the superlative defensive game turned in by Spruiell. Phillips again was not allowed to play because of eligibility problems. The only offensive highlight

THE POSTWAR ERA

for MSC was Coggin's touchdown on a pass from Tom LeGros.

The Southerners bounced back the next week to defeat an upset-minded Delta State squad 20–13 at Faulkner Field, where the best seats that season cost $2.60. Delta State led at the half 6–0, but MSC began its comeback midway through the third period. After a Delta State punt, the ball was about to roll dead on the Southern 35-yard line with a Delta State end hovering over the ball. Phillips suddenly scooped the ball up from under the opposing player's nose and raced 37 yards down the sideline to the Delta State 28. Fullback Jim Owen then scored to tie the game at 6–6. On Southern's next possession, Langford scored off left tackle on a 1-yard plunge. Delta State knotted the score at 13 on the next drive, but Southern responded with a 74-yard drive that ended with Phillips carrying the ball into the end zone untouched from 18 yards out to make the final score 20–13. After this lackluster win, the *Hattiesburg American* was somewhat apologetic about MSC's efforts under Vann: "With a new coaching staff and new men in several positions, it is not surprising that the Southerners are off to a slow start and it is reasonable to assume they are going to get better."

Homecoming took place on October 8 at Faulkner Field before a capacity crowd of more than 10,000. The game against McMurray College was preceded by a large Homecoming parade that included Governor Fielding Wright and what the *Hattiesburg American* described as "more than 40 attractive floats and festooned cars, . . . bands and [a] general air of festivity [that] drew what may have been a record breaking parade crowd. The route from Forrest Street down Main to Walnut Street was lined six deep, and spectators jammed windows of every office building." The Southerner offense responded by thumping McMurray 55–32. The *American* enthused that the team had "picked homecoming day to prove itself worthy of taking a place alongside any the school has ever produced." The Southerners' offensive output made it hard to believe that this was the same team that had played Delta State and Kentucky. Phillips rushed only five times but gained 60 yards and threw a touchdown pass, and Spruiell rushed seven times for 68 yards and returned a kickoff 78 yards. But although Vann was pleased with his offense, he and his coaching staff were worried about the MSC defense. McMurray halfback Brad Rowland, a Little All-America candidate, had rushed 19 times for 197 yards, and the Indians had rolled up more than 400 yards of total offense.

MSC rebounded with a formidable defensive effort on October 15, shutting out Southwestern Louisiana Institute 25–0 in Southerners' first GSC game of the year. The game was tied 0–0 at the half, but MSC scored on its first two series of the second half. The Southerners added two more touchdowns to gain an impressive victory, their third in a row.

Led by the Southerner offensive backfield, which the *Hattiesburg American* dubbed the Pony Express, MSC beat the University of Chattanooga Moccasins on the road on October 21. Southern scored first on an 80-yard, nine-play drive that was topped off by Bobby Holmes's 23-

yard touchdown pass to Coggin, who continued to play very well. Chattanooga responded by scoring 20 consecutive points, but MSC fought back with another drive highlighted by a Holmes-to-Coggin short pass that turned into a 50-yard gain and by Langford's 8-yard touchdown run. The Moccasins led 20–14 at intermission, but Vann and his staff made halftime adjustments, enabling the Southerners to tie the game on an impressive 81-yard drive on their first possession of the second half. Southern retook the lead on the first play of the fourth quarter as Phillips dove into the end zone from 4 yards out. The final

In 1949 Quarterback Bobby Holmes and record-setting end Cliff Coggin became one of the school's most prolific passing combinations.

Southern score came on a 98-yard drive that took just five plays and culminated in Holmes hitting Coggin with a 24-yard touchdown pass, his ninth catch of the night. According to the *American*, "When the smoke cleared, the Suthunuhs walked off the field with a well-earned 33 to 20 win over Scrappy Moore's Moccasins and a temporary claim to the best small college football team in the South. With Bubba Phillips, Frankie Spruiell and Eddie Langford striking viciously inside and out while the brilliant Bobby Holmes–Cliff Coggin passing combine kept the defense off balance, Coach Pie Vann's lads earned their win the hard way." Southern had now won four consecutive games to overcome its 0–1 start. After the season's fifth week, Phillips held the GSC rushing lead, having gained 667 yards in the four contests in which he had played. With the season only half over, Coggin had snared 27 passes for 562 yards, shattering the conference's single-season mark of 24 receptions for 475 yards.

MSC continued its winning ways during the next two weeks, beating Northwestern State College of Louisiana and Oklahoma City University. The Vannmen turned in a convincing 67–28 victory over Northwestern on October 29 at Faulkner Field, with the Pony Express once again controlling the game. The November 5 Oklahoma City game was much closer, but MSC won by a touchdown, 27–20, in a game that Phillips sat out as a result of a prior agreement between Vann and his Oklahoma City counterpart. Southern scored on its first possession of the game, driving 70 yards, and Morris Brown added the team's second score on a 63-yard run. But the Pony Express also helped the Chiefs to all three of their scores by fumbling deep in Southern territory and giving the Chiefs good field position. After once again making halftime adjustments, the Southerners scored on their first possession of the second half before adding another tally early in the fourth period that provided the margin of victory.

THE POSTWAR ERA [61]

Coggin caught 6 passes for 99 yards, giving him 39 receptions for 757 yards and leaving him only 64 yards shy of Arizona Wildcat Hank Stanton's 1941 national record of 820 yards on 50 pass receptions. Coggin was also closing in on the national record for receptions in a season, Barney Poole's 52 catches for Ole Miss in 1947. The Chiefs and the Southerners had developed a heated rivalry, with games that were usually explosive offensively and very physical, but the 1949 contest was the last between the two schools, as Oklahoma City administrators dropped football after the season. MSC had won more football games than it had lost against the Chiefs, something few schools could say.

The Southerners' six-game winning streak ended abruptly on November 12 in a 34–13 loss to Louisiana Tech in Ruston that gave Tech the GSC crown. The Bulldogs left little doubt about which team was better, executing their game plan to perfection and beating up on the Southerners in almost every aspect of the contest. With Spruiell sidelined because of a leg injury, Tech was able to stop Phillips and hold the Pony Express backs to 110 yards rushing. The only bright spot for the Southerners was Coggin's record-breaking night: he caught six passes for 173 yards, bringing his season total to 930 yards.

The heartbreaking GSC championship loss was followed by yet another loss to Alabama on November 19 in Tuscaloosa. In front of more than 15,000 fans, the Southerners made their best showing against the Tide but still went down 34–26. Langford fumbled on Southern's first drive of the game, with Alabama scoring soon thereafter to set the tone for the remainder of the contest. On MSC's next possession, the Tide blocked a punt and subsequently scored again, giving Alabama a 14–0 lead after only eight minutes. The Crimson Tide led 27–0 at the half, and the team's reserves added another touchdown early in the third quarter to seemingly put the game out of reach at 34–0. The Southerners rallied, however, reeling off four straight touchdowns, including two on long punt returns by Holmes. Although the Tide secondary was ranked No. 1 in the Southeastern Conference, Coggin amazed the fans with 2 acrobatic catches in the first half and a total of 5 receptions for the game, giving him 50 on the year.

Vann's first season as Southern's field general ended in a positive manner as more than 9,550 MSC supporters watched the Southerners record a 26–21 victory over Louisville on Thanksgiving Day, November 24. Most of the crowd had come to see Coggin break the record for catches in a season, and they were not disappointed, as he caught 3 passes to surpass Poole's mark: in the words of the *Hattiesburg American*, "Shackled for almost three full quarters Thursday night by a dogged defense which bumped him at every opportunity and had three men following him each time he crossed the line of scrimmage, Cliff hit his peak in the fourth quarter. Twice he made sensational catches of long touchdown passes to first tie and then break the national reception record and to give the Southerners their margin of victory." Coggin added 88 yards to his season total, giving him an average of 108.7 yards per game, far higher than Stanton's 1941 record of 82.0 yards per game.

Coggin played in the Senior Bowl and the Blue-Gray All-Star Classic and was selected by the Los Angeles Rams in the seventh round of the NFL draft. Despite the eligibility problems that had caused him to sit out the Kentucky and Alabama games, Phillips also received postseason accolades, as the United Press gave him an honorable mention on its All-America team.

Once again, there was speculation that MSC would play in a bowl game, but Green and other university officials turned down an invitation to the Paper Bowl in Pensacola, Florida, hoping to receive a bid to a more prestigious game, and although at least two other bowls expressed interest, no invitations were forthcoming. Nevertheless, Mississippi Southern had gone a long way toward establishing itself as a prominent football program, recording four 7–3 seasons in a row after football was resumed in 1946. The Southerners had dominated regional and small-college programs but continued to struggle against major college opponents, especially Southeastern Conference teams. As the 1950s dawned, Green and Vann had moved the program to the verge of great things.

THE FABULOUS FIFTIES
1950–1959

Football at Mississippi Southern College continued to flourish throughout the 1950s. In fact, the decade defined the football program. In addition to defeating Alabama for the first time, MSC also beat several other high-profile opponents. This unprecedented success against prominent opponents convinced school officials that the Southerners had outgrown the Gulf States Conference (GSC); consequently, the school attempted to affiliate with better, nationally recognized conferences. These attempts failed, however, thrusting the athletic program into independent status for the better part of four decades.

The Southerners' journey to big-time football received another boost in early 1950 when the Mississippi Legislature appropriated money for Delta State, Mississippi

The coaching staff of assistant Clyde (Heifer) Stuart (1949–1958), head coach Thad (Pie) Vann, and assistant H. A. (Bear) Smith (1949–1954) led Mississippi Southern College to some of the school's biggest victories in the early 1950s.

State, and MSC to construct stadium-dorms, although Southern officials would have preferred separate facilities. Southern received $350,000 for the dorm and a 7,500-seat addition on the west side of the stadium, resulting in a facility modeled on those at Louisiana State University in Baton Rouge.

1950 SEASON

The decade started rather inauspiciously for MSC, which opened the 1950 season on September 23 in Knoxville against the Tennessee Volunteers. General Robert Neyland's team, which the *Hattiesburg American* called one of the "top grid squads in the country" with a "savage running attack," smothered the Southerners 56–0. As in the 1949 loss to Kentucky, the beating indicated Southern's weakness relative to Southeastern Conference (SEC) teams. But Coach Vann's troops had responded well to the Kentucky thrashing and had salvaged a fine season, and MSC supporters expected the same type of turnaround in 1950, particularly since the Southerners' second opponent in both seasons was Delta State.

Delta State had different ideas, however, upsetting MSC 19–13 on September 30 before 7,500 fans at Faulkner Field. Southern held a 13–0 lead at the end of the first quarter on a 36-yard touchdown run by halfback Morris (Lightin') Brown and a 6-yard touchdown pass from quarterback Tom LeGros to end Bill Blackmon. The Statesmen rallied to tie the game with 13 third-quarter points and then scored the game-winning

THE FABULOUS FIFTIES

touchdown early in the fourth quarter when LeGros fumbled in his own end zone and a Delta State player pounced on the ball. The loss sent shock waves through the Hattiesburg community: losing to Tennessee was one thing, but losing to Delta State seemed to portend a miserable season for the Southerners. The *Hattiesburg American* predicted a "long, hard fall for the badly battered Mississippi Southern college football team." The stunning defeat also put some pressure on Coach Vann, whom supporters believed would have to "perform a minor miracle" to salvage the season. Furthermore, the Southerners had been badly bruised and battered in the Delta State game.

The third week of the season did little to remedy the situation as the Southerners suffered another convincing loss, this time by a score of 37–19 at the hands of McMurray College on October 7 in front of only 3,000 fans in Abilene, Texas. The MSC program was reeling after its longest losing streak in more than a decade. One of the Southerners' few bright spots was the play of superstar halfback Bubba Phillips, who rushed for 107 yards on 15 carries, passed once for 38 yards, caught a 35-yard touchdown pass, ran back two kicks for a total of 33 yards, and played most of the game on defense. Despite the terrible start, Southern's conference games were still

John Melvin (Bubba) Phillips (1947–1950) is still regarded as one of the most talented performers in school history.

ahead, providing a chance for the team to turn things around.

The team showed its character by beating Southwestern Louisiana 6–0 on October 14 in the Homecoming game at Faulkner Field. "Our boys played their hearts out to get in the win column," Vann commented. In front of more than 7,500 spectators, the Southerners reeled off a second-quarter, 76-yard, 17-play drive that culminated in a 1-yard run by quarterback David Lee Walker. Phillips added punting to his repertoire, averaging 38 yards per kick, and the Southern defense limited the Bulldogs to 69 yards of total offense. Despite their 1–3 start, the Southerners had won their first conference game, providing fans with renewed optimism regarding the football program.

Whatever momentum had been gained was lost the following week, however, when South-eastern Louisiana beat Southern 7–0 on October 21 in Hammond. The Southerners had chances to win the game, moving the ball inside the Lions' 30-yard line on three occasions but failing to score. Even compared to the season's earlier losses, the Southeastern Louisiana defeat was especially wrenching because it dealt a severe blow to the Southerners' league championship hopes. The *Hattiesburg American* was particularly pessimistic, saying that the loss "almost nullified" the Southerners' chances of winning the conference. To gain the crown, they needed some help from another league team.

Mississippi Southern notched its second win by squeezing past winless Chattanooga 14–13 at Ladd Memorial Stadium in Mobile on October 27. The *Hattiesburg American* reported that the

Athletic director Reed Green and halfback John Melvin (Bubba) Phillips led the Southerners into the 1950s.

Southerners had combined "breaks and alertness with grim determination to win." But luck also played a part, as the Moccasins dropped a touchdown pass, missed an extra point, and fumbled three times. Chattanooga had 15 first downs compared to just 8 for the Southerners, "but the Moccasins didn't have Bubber Phillips," the *American* wrote. The "brilliant" Phillips continued to carry the team on his shoulders, returning a Chattanooga punt 78 yards for the deciding touchdown.

THE FABULOUS FIFTIES

Southern won back-to-back games for the first time in 1950 by beating Northwestern State College of Louisiana the following week in Natchitoches in one of the most fantastic finishes in school history. The game was scoreless going into the final two minutes, but Phillips once again made a big play. With 70 seconds remaining, MSC had the ball on its own 20-yard line. LeGros, the Southern quarterback as well as a standout pitcher on the school's baseball team, dropped back to pass and threw what the *American* described as a "perfect, spiraling strike" 40 yards downfield. Phillips, who doubled as the baseball team's star outfielder, gathered in the pass like a long fly ball and raced the remaining 40 yards for the remarkable touchdown. The win kept alive MSC's conference title hopes, leaving them at 3–4 overall and 2–1 in the GSC.

But next up was Alabama in Tuscaloosa on November 11. Like the Tennessee Volunteers, the Crimson Tide players were simply much better than the Southerners, scoring early and often, shredding the MSC secondary, and administering a 53–0 thrashing.

Although the loss dropped Southern to 3–5 on the season, it did not affect the school's conference record, and the Southerners' GSC title hopes received a big boost when Louisiana College upset conference leader Southeastern Louisiana. This was the break that Southern had needed. For the third consecutive year, the conference championship would go to the winner of the Mississippi Southern–Louisiana Tech game. After great hype that left the Southerners "keyed higher than the proverbial kite," as the *Hattiesburg American* put it, the favored Techsters came to Faulkner Field on November 18. Phillips played well, but his fellow seniors, Morris Brown at halfback, Bobby Holmes at quarterback, and Ivan Rosamond at end also starred in the game. The 41–20 victory gave Southern a 3–1 GSC record and the conference championship despite the team's rather unexceptional 4–5 overall record.

The season finale occurred on November 25 when MSC hosted Louisville, with the Cardinals seeking revenge for the 1949 contest between the two teams. As in the previous year, MSC fell behind early, but the Southerners mounted what the *Hattiesburg American* termed "probably the greatest rally ever seen on Faulkner Field," using "team play, team spirit, alertness, and capitalization" to win 34–28. Phillips, Brown, and Holmes "closed out their collegiate careers with magnificent performances."

The first season of the decade ended with MSC finishing with a .500 record but still capturing the GSC championship to salvage a successful year. Vann was named GSC Coach of the Year, and Phillips was named to the Associated Press Little All-America team. Phillips represented MSC in the 1950 Senior Bowl at Mobile and was named captain and first-team All-GSC. Rosamond and Dave Allen also made first-team all-conference, and Holmes and Phil (Moose) Musmeci made the second team.

1951 SEASON

Mississippi Southern won its season opener for the first time since 1947 by beating East Carolina

40–0 on September 15 at Faulkner Field. There was little doubt that Southern was the stronger team, as many of the reserves played during the second half. Much of the *Hattiesburg American*'s coverage of the game focused on the scouts from Louisiana State University, who were watching to prepare for the following week, when the Southerners would travel to Baton Rouge.

With another chance to prove themselves against an SEC team, the Southerners "play[ed] the stripes off the LSU Tiger," as the *Hattiesburg American* wrote, but lost 13–0. Gaynell Tinsley, LSU's coach, spoke admiringly of the Southerners and told Coach Vann, "You've got a fine ball club, it was a tough game." Vann stated that he was pleased with his team's effort, but "we didn't score and that's why we are disappointed." Vann warned his team that the next opponent, Carswell Air Force Base, was "just as tough as LSU," an assessment that turned out to be right on the mark as Southern suffered its second straight shutout, 26–0. The Fort Worth team included several former college players, including two All-Americans, who were serving military assignments.

The next week brought a 54–7 thrashing of McMurray at Faulkner Field. The *American* contended that the victory showed "that there is nothing wrong with the Southern offense as long as it isn't pitted against a club of Southeastern Conference caliber or better." The win gave the team confidence as it headed into its conference schedule. The high offensive output continued as the Southerners crushed Southwestern Louisiana 41–0 and Southeastern Louisiana College 35–6 to open up 2–0 in GSC play. "Mississippi Southern looked like a major college powerhouse," Delbert Oliver of the *Lafayette Advertiser* remarked, "as they climbed over a fighting Southwestern Louisiana Institute." A week later, Vann stated, "We thought we did a creditable job and we're proud of" the team's effort against Southeastern. After six games, Southern was 4–2.

The Southerners' next opponent was the Chattanooga Moccasins, the "toughest small-college outfit in the nation," according to the *Hattiesburg American*. Despite the Southerners' efforts to prove otherwise, the Mocs won 19–7 behind the "smooth working" quarterbacking of Hal Ledyard. Ledyard, "one of the top T-formation quarterbacks in college football," was outstanding, completing 11 of 13 passes for 151 yards in front of 11,500 Homecoming fans in Chattanooga. The *American* said that Ledyard showed "as much poise as a ballet dancer at times and at other times as much power as the old 'choo choo' itself [and] was the main difference between the two struggling small college powers."

MSC rebounded to defeat Northwestern State College of Louisiana on November 3 at Faulkner Field by a score of 76–0, setting a post–World War II school record for points scored in a contest. The win left the Southerners in first place in the league with a 3–0 conference record, 5–3 overall.

The next week saw Southern lose once again to Alabama, 40–7. According to Alabama's head coach, Red Drew, the Crimson Tide played their "best ball game of the year" in defeating the Southerners. The sentiment provided little solace, and it was obvious to most observers that South-

Fullback Bucky McElroy (1951–1953) rushed for 2,560 yards in his career averaging 5.6 yards per carry.

ern was not on the same level as Alabama. Despite the Southerners' creditable showing against LSU earlier in the season, MSC was not faring well against SEC opponents.

The encounter between Louisiana Tech and Southern had regularly decided the GSC championship game, and the 1951 season was no exception. However, for the first time, defeating Southern would not give Louisiana Tech the title: if Southern lost, the crown would go to Southeastern Louisiana. With much more at stake for the Southerners, they soundly defeated the Bulldogs 33–7 to complete a perfect 4–0 conference season. Fullback Bucky McElroy broke the conference single-season rushing record with 856 yards, and the team set the conference mark for points scored in a season with 306.

For the 1951 finale, the MSC squad traveled to play Louisville on November 23. Following the pattern established during the two previous years, the Cardinals scored two first-quarter touchdowns. This time, however, the Southerners' comeback fell short, and they lost, 14–13. The game and the 6–5 season were disappointing, but Southern supporters still viewed the campaign as successful because the squad had won the conference yet again.

Coach Vann was named GSC Coach of the Year for the second straight season, and Southern dominated the All-GSC team, with 19 selections, including first-teamers Dick Caldwell, Granville (Scrappy) Hart, Eddie Kauchick, Walter Mann, Bucky McElroy, and Phil Musmeci; second-teamers Dave Allen, Jimmy Brashier, Jackson Brumfield, Ken Farris, Jack Fulkerson, Tom LeGros, Ed McDaniel, Bob McKellar, and Phil Muscarello; and honorable mentions Pat Ferlise, Elmer Kemper, Elmo Lang, and Herbert Nobles. McElroy was named to Paul Williamson's Mid-Bracket All-America team. Allen, Musmeci, and McElroy were named to the Associated Press Little All-America team. Hart played in the Senior Bowl, where he won the award for most outstanding defensive back. Musmeci was elected team captain, and LeGros received the team's Most Outstanding Player award.

THE FABULOUS FIFTIES

MSC's dissatisfaction with the GSC came to a head in 1951, after the league constitution was revised to require that a team had to schedule games against all other football-playing conference schools (Louisiana Tech, Southwestern Louisiana, Northwestern Louisiana, Louisiana College, Mississippi Southern, and Southeastern Louisiana) to be eligible for the conference title. MSC had not played Louisiana College since 1946 and did not play Louisiana Tech during 1951 because of scheduling conflicts. The rule would severely hamper MSC Athletic Director Reed Green's desire to schedule major opponents and thereby gain exposure for the school, and he remarked, "It may be that we are more ambitious than some of the other teams in the conference, but it is necessary that we continue our relationship with larger schools." Furthermore, by 1951 the Southern athletic program had expanded to include baseball, tennis, and golf, with plans to add track, but the GSC refused to encompass other sports to achieve equal status with other major conferences. Finally, Southern objected to the GSC's admission of McNeese State College and Northeast Louisiana, which had just received senior-college status. Consequently, Green announced in the spring of 1952 that Southern had withdrawn from the conference and would play as an independent. Southern would retain its affiliations with the Southern Intercollegiate Athletic Association (SIAA) and the National Association of Intercollegiate Basketball, and on February 1, 1952, the National Collegiate Athletic Association officially admitted Mississippi Southern College as a member.

1952 SEASON

School officials hoped that leaving the GSC and seeking affiliation with a stronger conference would be the first step along a path that would take Mississippi Southern football to a new level. The team responded to the move with a magnificent 10–2 record, a season that the *Southerner* predicted would seem "in retrospect [to be] the beginning of a new era in the athletic history of Mississippi Southern College."

The season did not get off to a promising start, however, when the Southerners traveled to the Crampton Bowl in Montgomery, Alabama, to play Alabama on September 19. Although Alabama fumbled an SEC record 12 times, Southern lost 20–6, scoring the lone touchdown on a first-quarter run by halfback Hugh Laurin Pepper after Alabama quarterback Clell Hobson had lost the ball on the Tide 13-yard line.

The first home game of the season was played against Memphis State in front of 10,000 fans on September 27. The Tigers led 14–13 at halftime, only to see Pepper return the second-half kickoff 85 yards for a touchdown. The game was an exciting back-and-forth contest that Southern finally won 27–20 on McElroy's second touchdown of the day. The Southern backfield of McElroy and Pepper scored all four of the team's touchdowns and gained an even 300 yards, with both men averaging more than 10 yards per carry.

Southern continued its offensive barrage the following week, beating the University of Tampa

THE FABULOUS FIFTIES

52–25 in front of more than 10,000 fans at Faulkner Field. The score was close throughout much of the game, with the teams tied after one quarter and the Southerners leading 26–19 at the half. One particularly strange play occurred during the first half when Southern lineman Ed McDaniel jumped off the bench to tackle a Tampa player as he ran back a kickoff for what it appeared would be a touchdown. After some debate, the officials decided to award a touchdown to Tampa. On the ensuing kickoff, Southern guard L. T. Herrmann was charged with a personal foul and ejected from the game, although the *Hattiesburg American* reported that Herrmann "was put out without committing a foul—but only because he didn't catch the man he was after." The rest of the contest belonged to MSC, and the team's record improved to 2–1.

As sports information director from 1951 to 1954, Jimmie (Mississippi Red) McDowell helped Mississippi Southern College earn a spot on the national stage in newspapers and on radio and television stations.

The running game remained one of the team's strongest attributes, racking up 421 yards in a 32–12 defeat of Southwestern Louisiana in Lafayette on October 11. After the contest, Southern was ranked third in rushing among small colleges nationwide, averaging more than 350 yards per game. Both Pepper and McElroy had rushed for nearly 500 yards in just four games.

Nevertheless, the Southerners "showed very little on offense" the following week, struggling to defeat Southeastern Louisiana College 20–12 on October 18 at Faulkner Field. Except for a long kickoff return by Pepper and a pair of touchdown passes by quarterback Billy Jarrell to ends Bob McKellar and Elmo Lang, the MSC offense performed uncharacteristically sluggishly. According to the *Hattiesburg American,* the Southerners had played only "one-fourth of their usual form" and were fortunate to have played a relatively weak team: "the sight of a Chattanooga Moccasin, much less the bite of one, would have been too much for Mississippi Southern," and the Moccasins "would have chased [the Southerners] off the field." Even Coach Vann admitted, "We looked our worst, didn't we?"

Like the *American,* the Southerners may have been looking ahead to the next week's matchup with the Chattanooga Moccasins and their returning quarterback, Hal Ledyard. The buildup to the contest with the Moccasins was enormous, and Vann felt that the matchup was so important that he closed practice to the public. Both teams had already played Memphis State, with Southern struggling for a close victory while the Mocs won 23–6. More than 12,000 "wildly-cheering, highly partisan Homecoming fans" packed Faulkner Field to see the October 25 contest, and the Southerners responded by posting a 27–14 victory that the *Hattiesburg American* called "without a doubt the best team effort" of the season.

After the huge win over Chattanooga, the 5–1 Southerners refused to let down at home against Northwestern State College Louisiana on Novem-

[72]   THE FABULOUS FIFTIES

Running back Hugh Laurin Pepper (#42) rushed for 1,191 yards during the 1952 season.

ber 1, defeating the Demons 39–13. McElroy, the "Black Knight," was injured on his fourth carry of the game, but halfback Bobby Posey ably filled McElroy's shoes, averaging 9.5 yards per carry in the victory.

The Southerners next traveled to Tallahassee for their first-ever contest against Florida State on November 8. Both teams had 6–1 records, and Joe Livingston, a scout for the Gator Bowl and sports editor of the *Jacksonville Journal,* watched the game. He must have been impressed with Southern's 50–21 whipping of the Seminoles, a victory made more impressive by the fact that Southern standouts McElroy, Posey, McDaniel, Brumfield, and Howard Lehman did not play because of injuries. The Southerners scored four times in the opening quarter and led 43–7 at the half. In something of an understatement, Livingston commented that he "was very much impressed with the Southerners' excellent offense."

The next contest occurred on November 15 when rival Louisiana Tech traveled to Hattiesburg. Southern scored three touchdowns during the game's first 10 minutes and never looked back, handily defeating the Bulldogs 52–0 before another capacity crowd at Faulkner Field. The *American*'s Robert (Ace) Cleveland increased the bowl fever sweeping Hattiesburg when he wrote in his November 17 weekly column, "Like a country lad feels when his Grade-A sweetnin' taters are kicked aside in favor of some Class-C city grown jobs, I'm a bit disgruntled today. Mississippi Southern isn't based in a huge city and neither is it blessed with a membership in a big-time conference but you can bet your collar button the Southerners have a crackerjack Grade-A

THE FABULOUS FIFTIES

football club. Yet, some of the better-known Bowl outfits are looking past this independent giant. Even the Orange Bowl committee would be wise to check the national rankings chart before it makes final arrangements. That also goes for the Gator and Sun Bowl matchmakers." The Southerners had scored 305 points on the season while holding their opponents to 137 and had gained an amazing 2,903 rushing yards, led by Pepper's 1,019 yards and McElroy's 803 yards. There was little doubt that the Southerners' ground attack—and arguably the entire offense—were as good as any in the country.

On November 22, MSC took on the University of Louisville in the fourth meeting between the two schools. Trailing 2–1 in the series, Louisville was supposed to host the 1952 game, but because the 1951 game had been played in Louisville, the following year's contest was switched to Jackson. The Southerners dominated and won 55–26, as Louisville star quarterback Johnny Unitas and running back Jim Williams were injured and playing at less than 100 percent.

After the Louisville game, MSC accepted a bid to participate in a true bowl game for the first time in school history. The school had played in the so-called Tobacco Bowl in Havana in 1947, but football authorities did not recognize that contest as a legitimate postseason bowl game. The Refrigerator Bowl, to be played in Evansville, Indiana, on December 7, had already extended an invitation to the Southerners, but on November 24, Athletic Director Green announced that the Southerners would play in the Sun Bowl on January 1, 1953, at Kidd Field in El Paso, Texas.

Gene Donohoe, chairman of the Sun Bowl selection committee, said that five teams were being considered for the other spot in the bowl—undefeated Miami of Ohio, Cincinnati, Dayton, New Mexico, and Utah—pending the outcome of the November 27 Cincinnati-Miami game, which would decide the Mid-American Conference championship. Vann cautioned, "While we consider it a great honor to be selected to play in the Sun Bowl, we cannot generate too much enthusiasm about the invitation" with one regular-season game remaining on the schedule. Senior offensive halfback Tony Rouchon said, "I think it's a big thing for us and a big thing for the school and I know we are all going to enjoy the trip."

The Southerners ended their regular season with a 42–0 shutout of the Stetson Hatters, described by Coach Vann as "the toughest of the three Florida schools we will play this year," on November 29 at Faulkner Field. Southern had posted one of the school's most successful seasons by reeling off 10 straight wins after the opening loss to Alabama.

In early December, the Southerners learned that their Sun Bowl opponent would be the College of the Pacific rather than one of the teams that had previously been mentioned. The Sun Bowl had first been played in 1936, a year before Dallas's Cotton Bowl, and paid $15,000 to each competing team. The Tigers played nine men on or near the line of scrimmage throughout the game, bottling up the Southerners' strong running game. The strategy was enhanced by the fact that "a strong wind made passing almost impossible," according to the *Hattiesburg American,* and by

McElroy's inability to play as a result of a lingering injury. Southern committed five fumbles, losing four, and the College of the Pacific notched a 26–6 victory. Tiger coach Ernie Jorge described the game as his team's "best effort of the season," and Vann concluded that the Southerners had "suffered from bowl-itis in the opening minutes of their first bowl appearance" and further attributed the defeat to the Tigers' ability to take "advantage of our numerous mistakes to win. Our team attack was certainly not as sharp as during the season with our star fullback out of action."

Nevertheless, with its 10–2 record, the 1952 season represented one of MSC's finest and seemed to indicate that the decision to leave the GSC had been a good one. In fact, school officials believed that the program had vaulted itself into the national picture. MSC began to explore the possibility of joining either the SEC or the Atlantic Coast Conference and applied unsuccessfully in September 1953 for ACC membership. Green explained that Southern was "interested in getting in[to] some conference that offers certain opportunities in athletic and academic standards." Conference membership would provide national recognition and would insulate MSC from charges that it was an "outlaw" school, using ineligible players and failing to abide by the rules and regulations to which conference schools were bound. Green also believed that Hattiesburg's proximity to New Orleans, Mobile, and Jackson would meet the demands of a conference.

In addition to the prospect of membership in an established conference, MSC also began to investigate the possibility of joining with some of the region's other major independents to form a new league. Several SIAA college presidents and athletic directors met in December 1953 in Memphis to discuss a the creation of a new southern conference. Mississippi Southern was especially interested in banding together with the University of Miami (Florida), Florida State, Memphis State, and Chattanooga and possibly with Tulane and Vanderbilt, which were struggling in the SEC. However, representatives from North Texas State, Arkansas State, and Abilene Christian also attended the meeting, causing some disagreement because the Florida schools objected to membership of institutions west of the Mississippi River, hoping to keep the members schools within the southeastern states and like Southern officials believing that affiliating with smaller schools would interfere with achieving major status. The five major schools located east of the Mississippi agreed to send representatives to the January 1953 NCAA meeting in Cincinnati to investigate the feasibility of forming a conference, but plans failed to materialize.

1953 SEASON

The 1953 season was another memorable one for MSC and did much to boost the school's case for becoming a member of a major athletic conference. The season opened with a landmark victory over mighty Alabama 25–19 in Montgomery on September 18. Southern entered the game a three- to five-touchdown underdog against the Crimson Tide, which were picked no lower than

fifth in the country and No. 1 in the SEC. Legendary sportswriter Grantland Rice selected the Crimson Tide as the nation's top-ranked team. Southern scored the winning touchdown when Jarrell found sophomore end Leonard Williams on the Alabama 2-yard line and halfback Jim (Brick) Mason scored a few plays later from the 1-yard line. Mason was subbing for Pepper, who had raced 65 yards for a touchdown early in the fourth quarter to pull Southern to within one at 19–18. Alabama threatened late in the game, but the Southern defense held, recording the biggest win in school history to that point.

A huge group of fans met the team bus on its way back from Montgomery. The bus was stopped in front of the Petal Stock Yard, about five miles outside of Hattiesburg, and the players climbed into 10 convertibles for the remainder of the journey into town. To the accompaniment of highway patrol and police sirens and the honking of car horns, the long string of cars crept down Buie and Gordon Streets and turned west on Pine Street. The Southern and Petal High School bands joined the parade at Market Street and led it through the throngs of people cheering and throwing confetti that jammed Pine, Main, and Front Streets on the route to City Hall, where Coach Vann was made honorary mayor and assistant coaches H. A. (Bear) Smith and Clyde Stuart were named honorary city commissioners. Said McElroy, "The victory celebration was the greatest thing I've ever seen since I've been playing." According to the *Hattiesburg American*, the college received "more free publicity than it could

(Left) End Leonard Williams makes the catch that sets up the winning touchdown in MSC's 25–19 upset of Alabama in 1953. Legendary sportswriter Grantland Rice had picked the Crimson Tide as the nation's top team.

(Right) Quarterback Billy Jarrell is carried off the field after the 1953 win over Alabama.

THE FABULOUS FIFTIES

have bought for a million dollars as a result of the victory." The New York headquarters of the Associated Press and other wire services urged their New Orleans offices to "give us all possible of Mississippi Southern." The UPI story, which, like the Associated Press account, appeared all over the nation, led, "Mississippi Southern, an overgrown teachers college, went shopping for a bowl bid and membership in either of two conferences Saturday with the hide of Alabama's Red Elephant as its talking point."

The next four weeks saw continued success as Southern beat the Parris Island Marines 40–0 in MSC's home opener, the University of Tampa 42–6 at home, Southwestern Louisiana Institute 41–14 on the road, and Southeastern Louisiana College 7–0 at home. After the rather easy Parris Island victory on September 26, Bill Keefe, the sports editor of the New Orleans Times Picayune, ranked Southern as the ninth-best team in the country. Paul B. Williamson, a New Orleans geologist and member of the Sugar Bowl Committee who had developed a power-rating system, ranked the team tenth in the nation. The University of Tampa, winners of the 1952 Cigar Bowl and boasting 22 returning lettermen, also proved no match for the vaunted Southern offense. The Southerners got off to a slow start against Southwestern Louisiana but came on furiously in the second half to record their fourteenth straight regular-season win over two seasons. More than 13,000 fans saw Southern pull out a tough win against Southeastern Louisiana College despite playing without both Pepper and Brashier, who had been injured in the Southwestern Louisiana game. Southern had scheduled an off week in preparation for the October 31 away game against Memphis State, and the open date could not have come at a better time.

The respite proved inadequate, however, as Memphis State upset MSC 27–13. The Southerners outplayed the Memphis State squad in almost all statistical categories but made too many mistakes to overcome an inspired Tiger team. Southern had five drives inside the Memphis State 10-yard line during the first half but fumbled three times and turned the ball over once on downs, managing only one touchdown. The loss sent shock waves through Hattiesburg. The *American* referred to the Southerners' "once-magnificent, now tainted football bubble" and said that the loss "had the same effect as a needle on a one-cent balloon." But, the paper reminded its readers, "the fact remains that five wins in six starts makes for a pretty fair record. One defeat doesn't spoil a good season. It's true that any thoughts of being invited to the Sugar Bowl, for instance, can be forgotten but it can't be said that failing to get such an invitation marks a disastrous year. As one local minister told his congregation Sunday: 'If I had their batting average, I'd be a Bishop.'"

In the wake of the shocking setback, the Southerners buckled down and returned to form, closing out the regular season with wins over Florida State, Louisiana Tech, Georgia, and Chattanooga. The November 7 game against Florida State was Homecoming at Faulkner Field, and more than 11,000 fans watched as end Hub Waters caught four balls for 111 yards in steady light rain, as the offense scored 21 points while the defense held the Seminoles scoreless.

Next up was a November 14 game at Louisiana Tech in which, in the eyes of the *Hattiesburg American,* the Southerners played "their best game since the opening 25–19 upset of Alabama," winning 30–0. Jarrell threw for two touchdowns, and Waters and Pepper each scored twice, while McElroy added all four extra points.

The Southerners turned in their finest defensive performance of the season in shutting out the mighty Georgia Bulldogs 14–0. The game was played on November 21 in front of 23,000 fans at Jackson's Memorial Stadium, the largest crowd in the arena's history. Toward the end of the first half, Pepper intercepted All-American candidate Zeke Bratkowski's pass on the Georgia 42-yard line and returned it for a touchdown, and McElroy added a second-half score.

The University of Chattanooga was the Thanksgiving Day opponent for the Southerners in their November 26 regular-season finale. Fans cheered as Southern scored two late touchdowns to break a 19–19 tie and win 33–19. The Southern offense notched its first 300-yard game of the season.

Two days after the Chattanooga victory, the Sun Bowl formally extended a bid to MSC, and on November 30 school officials announced that team members had voted to accept the invitation to face Texas Western, which was located in El Paso and would be the host team. Despite the Southerners' hopes for a better outcome than in the previous year, Texas Western soundly defeated MSC 37–14 on New Year's Day 1954. The game was effectively over by halftime, when the Miners led 30–7. The *Hattiesburg American* attributed the defeat largely to the play of Texas Western's star quarterback, Dick Shinaut, who "passed, ran and punted the Texas Western Miners" to victory. Shinaut "dominated the action all afternoon. His passing kept the Southerners off balance and paved the way for devastating sallies through the line by his backfield mates, Clovis Riley and Jesse Whittenton."

Although the 9–2 season had once again ended on a sour note, the Southerners could take a lot of pride in what they had accomplished in the preceding two years—a 19–4 record, two bowl appearances, and an impressive win over Alabama. Both McElroy and Pepper earned national recognition when the Helms Athletic Foundation (an organization established by Los Angeles sportsman and philanthropist Paul H. Helms that selected All-America teams and published a college football poll) named them first-team All-Americans.

1954 SEASON

The 1954 campaign again opened with a stunning 7–2 victory over Alabama in front of 21,000 fans at Montgomery's Crampton Bowl on September 17. While Alabama dominated the game statistically, racking up twice as many yards of offense and five times as many first downs as the MSC, the *Hattiesburg American* believed that the Tide could not match the "plain ole will to win of the Southerners." Southern scored the game's only points in the first quarter as halfback Brooks Tisdale rambled 18 yards for the touchdown. The Southern defense held tight, twice stopping

Alabama inside the 5-yard line. Although not as dramatic as MSC's 1953 victory over the Tide, the win still represented a major accomplishment.

Southern got its second win of the season the following week, shutting out Louisiana Tech 28–0 in front of a crowd of 11,000 at Faulkner Field on September 25. The Southerners took the lead late in the second quarter on a touchdown pass from quarterback Jim Davenport to end Curry Juneau. Coach Vann inserted four different players at quarterback and cleared his bench late in the game. In addition to the stellar defense, the Southerners were helped by Davenport; halfback Carl Bolt, a senior transfer from Washington and Lee who rushed for 61 yards; and halfback Fred Smallwood.

The third game of the 1954 campaign changed the tenor of the season, as the Mississippi Southern gridders, minus Herrmann, Al Tregle, and Jack Speracino, who did not make the trip because of injuries, played against North Texas State College in Denton on October 2. The already undermanned Southerners lost Davenport during the second quarter, while Waters suffered a painful hip injury, tackle Don Owens hurt his shoulder, and halfback Eddie Cardenas was limping when the game was over. The *Hattiesburg American* summed up the game under the headline "Listless Effort Results in 15–7 Upset." Vann admitted, "We have no excuses. They outblocked us and they out-tackled us all the way." The Texans scored two touchdowns through the air, while the Southern offense could muster only one score on a screen pass from quarterback George Herring to Smallwood.

Southern's next opponent was Abilene Christian, which was undefeated and had a win over Florida State and a tie with Memphis State. In the October 9 contest at Faulkner Field, the Southerner offense started slowly and led only 9–7 at the half. After the break, however, Southern scored twice to seal the 23–7 victory.

Southeastern Louisiana was the Southerners' next opponent, visiting Faulkner Field on October 16. The Lions came into the contest unbeaten, having held all of their opponents scoreless, and the two teams had become bitter rivals. Coach Vann described the series as "a very keen one and we know that they'll be ready for us. This is their big game of the year." A standing-room-only crowd saw a classic defensive battle between two evenly matched teams, with Southeastern winning 13–7 to snap Southern's 15-game home winning streak. Both teams scored on their first offensive possessions, the Lions also scored on their second possession, and the defenses stiffened and held for the rest of the game. Southern had a chance to win when Waters blocked a fourth-quarter punt and Dino Orphan recovered on the Southeastern Louisiana 20-yard line, but on the next play, Herring's pass was intercepted. Southern's record stood at 3–2.

Led by Smallwood, a hard-nosed senior from Laurel, Mississippi, who played with great heart that belied his relatively slight 166 pounds, the Southerners returned the following week to beat Chattanooga in the October 23 Homecoming game. The *Hattiesburg American* reported that the MSC squad "blocked and tackled better" than the previous week and "hustled all the way" to record the victory. Smallwood scored both Southern touchdowns "in rapid succession early in the third quarter. One was a 25-yard run and the other, the next time he carried the ball, on a 67-yard dash." The win marked the Southerners' fifteenth straight Homecoming win and their sixth win against Chattanooga in seven tries.

After a week off, Southern flew to Ohio to play the University of Dayton, coached by Hugh Devore, who had previously led Notre Dame, St. Bonaventure, and the Green Bay Packers. Dayton quarterback Ken Bockenstette led the Flyers to a 20–7 victory over Southern in front of more than 7,700 chilled spectators at the November 6 game. Carl Bolt scored Southern's lone touchdown on a 22-yard run as the Southern squad's penchant for fumbling continued.

The Southerners' roller-coaster ride continued with a 17–0 victory over Villanova before a crowd of more than 14,600 at Mobile's Ladd Stadium on November 13. Vann platooned Davenport, Herring, and Doug Barfield at quarterback, and the trio completed 13 of 24 passes for 210 yards, while the backfield ran for another 233 yards as MSC dominated despite the fact that many of the team's reserves played more than half the game.

Southern put together back-to-back wins for only the second time in the 1954 season with a 43–21 defeat of Memphis State on November 20 in Hattiesburg. Memphis had lost three previous games, but all were to SEC teams. More than 8,000 fans saw the Southerners gain some measure of revenge against the Tigers, who had ruined Southern's perfect 1953 season. The Southern players ran for 226 yards and gained 470 yards in total offense, by far the team's best effort of the season.

Guard Hamp Cook was the captain of the 1954 MSC team and was named first-team Little All-American by the Associated Press.

The Southerners' season came to a close with a 19–18 road loss to Florida State. After catching the ball 8 yards deep in the end zone, Bolt returned the opening kickoff to the Seminole 27-yard line, and Mississippi Southern quickly scored on Herring's 17-yard toss to Waters. Southern added another first-quarter touchdown, as did Florida State when halfback Lee Corso took a swing pass in for the Seminoles' first score. Turnovers and solid defensive play slowed the game down from that point, and Southern lost the game on a failed extra-point attempt.

Paul Williamson named tackle Jim (Coon Dog) Davis and guard Hamp Cook All-Americans and

[80] THE FABULOUS FIFTIES

gave honorable mentions to Bolt, Smallwood, Owens, and lineman P. W. Underwood. After two successive trips to the Sun Bowl, MSC supporters found the team's 6–4 record disappointing.

In March 1955 the Mississippi Senate considered a resolution that would have encouraged SEC members Mississippi State and Ole Miss to play Mississippi Southern, but the measure did not pass. Prior to the 1955 season, Southern formed a freshman football squad to further increase the school's ability to compete with the SEC institutions.

1955 SEASON

The inaugural game of the 1955 season set the tone for the rest of the campaign as the Southerners convincingly defeated Elon College 39–0 at Faulkner Field on September 17. Five different Southerners scored touchdowns against the overmatched Fighting Christians. The ever-cautious Vann commented after the win that he was happy to win the game, but the Southerners had "a lot to do to get ready for our other opponents."

The next week featured a close game against Louisiana Tech in Ruston. Neither team scored during the first quarter, but on MSC's second possession of the second period, Herring led the Southerners on a 10-play drive that mixed timely passing with effective running. Fullback Lawrence Meeks kicked the extra point, which eventually gave Mississippi Southern the win when Louisiana Tech scored on a pass play in the second half but botched the snap on the point after.

MSC played poorly during the next game, a road contest against the University of Chattanooga. The game was played on a Friday night, meaning that Southern had only three days of practice in Hattiesburg before traveling on Thursday and attempting to find a place to practice in Chattanooga. While Vann was less than pleased with the arrangements, he told the *Hattiesburg American,* "We knew it when we scheduled the game, so we're not going to cry about it." MSC was its own worst enemy in the 10–0 loss, fumbling four times deep in Southern territory and committing personal fouls that stifled potential scoring drives. The Southerners' ball-control offense could manage only one first down in the first half and gained a mere 69 yards for the game. Three wide-open receivers dropped passes, and Juneau fumbled in Chattanooga's end zone. The Southern defense played well, holding Chattanooga scoreless until right before the end of the first half and recovering three Moccasin fumbles to halt drives.

Southern came back on October 8 to defeat North Texas 26–0 at Faulkner Field and record the Southerners' second shutout of the season. MSC's outstanding line, led by Owens and Underwood, provided the difference in the contest, and the defense held North Texas to four first downs and 104 yards rushing for the game.

The Southerners may have played one of their best games of the season on October 15, when the squad traveled to Hammond and beat previously undefeated Southeastern Louisiana 33–0. The winners of 13 straight games, including an undefeated 1954 season, the Lions had allowed

Quarterbacks George Herring (left), Doug Barfield (center), and Bobby Hughes led the Southerners in 1955.

their previous 1955 opponents only two touchdowns. Southern rolled up 357 yards in total offense, while Southeastern Louisiana could muster merely 92 yards, never penetrating deeper than the Southern 43-yard line. The Southerners' dominance was so complete that Coach Vann played all 37 members of his traveling squad.

The team continued to roll with a 34–14 road defeat of Memphis State on October 21. Local newspapers reminded the Southerners that the Tigers had spoiled MSC's undefeated 1953 season, and Southern responded by scoring on its first possession as Herring hit halfback Dallas Whitfield with a 50-yard scoring pass. Memphis came back with the first rushing touchdown the Southerners had yielded all season and then added another on a quarterback sneak to gain the lead 14–7. Southern tied the game midway through the second period at 14–14. Just before halftime, a controversial play allowed the Southerners to score with no time remaining. According to the *Memphis Commercial Appeal*, "With

[82] **THE FABULOUS FIFTIES**

just nine seconds left in the first half and the score at 14–14, Southern halfback Ted Trenton fell to the ground after a play and grabbed his ankle. The clock stopped, enabling Southern to get in one more play, on which it scored and took a 21–14 lead that was still in force with just two minutes left in the game. Trenton was helped from the field, but he returned to action in the second half, making a great run to midfield with the second half kickoff." Neither Vann or Memphis State coach Ralph Hatley would comment on the play. Southern added two late scores despite committing an amazing six 15-yard penalties in the fourth period and despite the team's loss of Barfield, who suffered a broken nose and was hospitalized.

The next game provoked little controversy as many reserves once again played in Southern's 40–0 thrashing of Abilene Christian in Abilene. The offense notched its third 400-yard game of the season and improved its season average to 342 yards per game. The victory raised the Southerners' record to 6–1.

November 12 was Band Day at Faulkner Field. Thirty-eight high school bands performed with the MSC marching band, the Pride, and the Dixie Darlings, the school's dance line that performed at football games, in front of the 9,000 fans who had gathered to watch the footballers entertain North Dakota State. The pageantry was more exciting than the game, as the Southerner defense continued to pitch shutouts and the offense continued to amass huge numbers en route to a 58–0 victory. Nine players scored, including seven reserves, and Barfield performed exceptionally after missing the Abilene game because of his injury.

The Southerners' next opponent, the University of Dayton, provided one of the year's most difficult games in a contest held at Jackson's Hinds County Memorial Stadium. Many of Southern's players believed that Flyers, who had defeated MSC the previous year, were the best team the Southerners would face in 1955. Although Southern's 1953 games against Louisville and Georgia at the Jackson stadium had attracted large crowds, cold temperatures and a constant mist led only 6,500 hardy spectators to pay $3.00 per ticket to attend the Dayton contest. In the first quarter, Herring intercepted a pass and, following a great block by end Jerry Taylor, ran the ball back 75 yards for a touchdown. Trenton later took an option pitch from Herring and ran it in to stake the Southerners to a 13–0 lead. Turnovers were the story of the second half as Southern fumbled twice and Dayton once, with each mistake leading to a touchdown as MSC held on to win 19–13.

With a 21–6 win over Florida State on November 25 at Faulkner Field, MSC ran its final record to 9–1 and expected some serious bowl consideration. As Reed Green, the school's athletic director, commented, "I believe it's the best team we have ever had." After a series of miscommunications between Sun Bowl representatives and Southern officials, however, the bowl chose instead to invite Wyoming to play Texas Tech in the January 2 game, and the Southerners stayed home.

In the wake of Southern's continued success, the state legislature voted in 1955 to give the school authority to issue revenue bonds worth up to $750,000 to expand Faulkner Field. Southern had hoped gradually to expand the arena into a horseshoe or bowl-type stadium that would hold up to 40,000 fans, but inflation and the legislature's limited appropriations meant that only 16,000 seats were completed, raising the stadium's capacity by approximately 4,000. The revenue bonds issued were the general obligation not of the state of Mississippi but of the MSC athletic department, and a 20 percent stadium fee was added to ticket prices.

In another response to the Southern football team's success, the school announced that as of 1956, it would adhere to the SEC's player-eligibility rules. Mississippi State and Ole Miss had severely criticized the Southerners' lack of conference affiliation and lax standards for eligibility, and Southern officials made this decision partly to quiet such criticism.

1956 SEASON

MSC opened the 1956 campaign against longtime foe Louisiana Tech on September 22 at Faulkner Field. Southern recorded two first-half touchdowns on Harvey Seligman's 1-yard run and Barfield's 28-yard pass to halfback Joe Doggett and then rode the dominant defense to the 14–0 shutout. The second half was a little ragged, as both offenses committed turnovers and penalties.

Fullback Bo Dickinson scored a pair of touchdowns while displaying great running and kicked one extra point in a 23–6 road win over the previously undefeated University of Dayton on October 6. Quarterback Bobby Hughes accounted for the Southerners' other touchdown. The *Dayton Daily News* described the Southerners as "heavy of hand in the line and light of foot in the backfield," and Vann was pleasantly surprised as his team posted 414 yards of total offense despite the cold weather and wind.

MSC recorded its third win of the season on October 13 at Faulkner Field, coming from behind to defeat Southeastern Louisiana, 21–14. The 6-foot-5 Hughes threw for two touchdowns, including a 17-yard fourth-down pass to end Bob Yencho that delighted the 14,000 fans in attendance. With the game tied at 14 toward the end of the third quarter, Barfield led a 75-yard drive

Larry (Doc) Harrington became Mississippi Southern's athletic trainer in the mid-1950s and remained with the school over thirty years.

[84] THE FABULOUS FIFTIES

that culminated with him scoring the winning touchdown on an option run from 3 yards out. Among the Southerners' injuries in the contest was a painful bruise Coach Vann suffered when a Southeastern defender crashed into his leg.

Southern's October 20 game at Faulkner Field against Memphis State resulted in an uncharacteristically one-sided MSC win, 27–0. However, the victory was costly for the Southerners, who lost five key players: Owens, an All-America candidate; Doggett; Dickinson; Underwood; and guard Dave Fitzgerald. The game represented the Southerners' fourth straight win of the season and their eleventh in a row overall.

Next up was the University of Chattanooga, the team that had spoiled MSC's undefeated season in 1955, handing the Southerners' one of their most disappointing losses ever. The Southern team responded with a 33–0 shellacking of Chattanooga on October 27 at Faulkner Field. "Our boys had their minds made up to get revenge," said Vann. The outcome of the game was never in question as halfback J. C. Arban, end Jerry Taylor, and quarterback Willie Gene (Teenie) Coats scored touchdowns during the second period to help give MSC a 26–0 halftime lead. With less than 30 seconds left in the half and the Southerners facing fourth down, Coats scrambled to the 5-yard line and was hit by two defenders but managed to fall backward into the end zone.

MSC beat Abilene Christian 36–6 in front of a November 3 Homecoming crowd of more than 14,000. After Abilene fumbled on the game's first play from scrimmage, Southern needed only three plays to score, with Dickinson taking the ball in for the touchdown. Barfield scored on what many locals dubbed the Billy Jarrell play (after the quarterback who had so successfully used it in the past), faking to the two backs, hiding the ball on his hip, and then bootlegging the ball into the end zone. Abilene Christian's only score came on a Statue of Liberty play that caught the defense off guard.

The Southerners traveled to San Antonio, Texas, on November 10 to face Trinity University at the school's Homecoming. MSC ran its season mark to 7–0 with a 20–13 victory that was marred by numerous penalties and fumbles by both teams. Nevertheless, Vann was "exceptionally pleased with the manner in which our boys conducted themselves when hurt by penalties at crucial times." Furthermore, said the coach, "our fellows took the bad breaks in stride and won with a fine show of determination in the closing minutes," when Owens recovered a Trinity fumble on the 22-yard line to set up a Hughes-to-Taylor touchdown pass that gave Southern the victory.

The penalties and mistakes continued the next week, but this time Southern was unable to overcome them, suffering a 20–19 loss to the Florida State Seminoles on November 17 in Tallahassee. The Southerners' errors included a bad snap from the center on an extra point and an offside penalty that gave the Seminoles a first down on their final touchdown drive. In Vann's assessment, two first-half interceptions "were the two mistakes that hurt us the worst," helping to give the Seminoles a 13–0 lead. The game ended the

The Southerners battled West Texas State in the Tangerine Bowl on January 1, 1957 in Orlando, Florida. Despite out-gaining the Buffaloes 314–206, Southern lost the game 20–19.

Southerners' 14-game winning streak and may have cost them an invitation to the Gator Bowl.

After a one-year absence, the Alabama Crimson Tide reappeared on MSC's schedule in 1956. Although Alabama's coach, E. B. (Ears) Whitworth, stated that Southern had "played better football" than his team and had "definitely outplayed us," the game, played on November 24 in Tuscaloosa, ended in a 13–13 tie. Whitworth also complimented the play of Southern's backfield of Barfield, Dickinson, and Arban and stated that the Tide had "not faced a better tackle this year than Owens. He was an All-American."

After finishing the regular season with a 7–1–1 record, the 34 members of the Southern football team voted to accept a bowl bid if one was issued. On November 26, school and bowl officials announced that Southern would play West Texas State, a strong member of the Border Conference, the night of January 1, 1957, in the Tangerine Bowl in Orlando, Florida, in what Tangerine representatives stated was the strongest lineup ever scheduled for the bowl. Although Vann believed that his 1956 team was "the best all around club I've ever had" and Southern was favored by a touchdown, the game was disappointing in many respects. Organizers had expected a crowd of more than 15,000, but only 12,000 showed, and Southern supporters watched in dismay as their team jumped out to a

[86] THE FABULOUS FIFTIES

13–0 lead but lost control in the second half and suffered a 20–13 defeat. Mississippi Southern's bowl jinx continued. "It was my toughest loss ever," Vann commented after the game, "the other coaches feel the same way."

Longtime sports information director Ace Cleveland was a tradition at Southern Miss. Cleveland worked as the school's SID from 1955 to 1986. He was elected into the Mississippi Sports Hall of Fame in 1998. The press box at M. M. Roberts Stadium bears his name.

1957 SEASON

Mississippi Southern opened the 1957 campaign against Louisiana Tech on September 21 in Ruston and won the game 7–0 in what the *Student Printz* saw as "unimpressive" fashion. The Southerners did not perform well on either side of the ball and "were beaten in practically everything but score." The Bulldogs outgained the Southerners on the ground and had six more first downs. Quarterback Ollie Yates found Arban on a 39-yard touchdown pass early in the first quarter for the game's only score.

The defense recorded another shutout on September 28 in a 13–0 defeat of Trinity University in front of 8,000 cold, wet fans at Faulkner Field. George Sekul ran in a touchdown from 4 yards out in the second quarter and found Tommy Purvis for a touchdown in the third period. A 34–0 shutout of West Texas followed in Amarillo on October 5, extending Southern's streak of scoreless games and providing some measure of revenge for the 1956 Tangerine Bowl. Bobby Lance, Jack May, Yencho, Arban, and Doggett each scored touchdowns in the lopsided win. The string of shutouts reached four with Southern's October 12 road defeat of Southeastern Louisiana by a score of 14–0 on touchdowns by Dickinson and Meeks.

The team remained undefeated after beating Memphis State 14–6 in Memphis on October 19, but the shutout streak ended as the Tigers scored a second-quarter touchdown. Lance and May scored for the Southerners, but the game cost them their star halfback when Dickinson cracked three vertebrae.

The defense continued its stellar play, pitching another shutout in an October 26 away game against Chattanooga in front of 5,000 fans who had hoped to see a Homecoming win for their Mocs. Arban opened the scoring with a pass from Sekul, and then Meeks intercepted a Chattanooga pass and the MSC offense quickly turned the mistake into another touchdown. Buddy Supple bulled his way over from the 3-yard line on the opening drive of the second half to close out the scoring in the 20–0 victory.

The defense posted yet another 7–0 shutout against Abilene Christian at Faulkner Field on November 2. The game was a stalemate in the

THE FABULOUS FIFTIES

trenches, and Abilene played better on offense than MSC but could not score, as the Southerners won on a Sekul pass to Lance.

The Southerners may have had such trouble with Abilene because they had been looking ahead to their next game against the University of Houston, and the MSC squad's poor play continued in the 27–12 defeat at the hands of the Cougars. In surrendering almost five times as many points as it had given up during the earlier part of the season, the defense failed to corral former Vicksburg High School star Claude King, who came off the Cougar bench and ran wild.

The team rebounded by beating Florida State 20–0 in front of many alumni at Homecoming on November 16, paying the Seminoles back for their 1956 victory over the otherwise undefeated Southerners. The defense recorded yet another shutout and allowed only 85 yards rushing and 50 yards passing. Lance thrilled the crowd with a 57-yard jaunt in the second quarter after the defense had stopped Florida State on the 1-yard line, and Dickinson scored late in the second period to give Southern a comfortable lead, to which Sekul added later in the game. After winning this game, Southern once again accepted a bid to the Tangerine Bowl.

In the season's final week, the Southerners lost their second game of the year, 29–2, the most points they had yielded all season. The victory was Alabama's first win over Mississippi Southern in its past four attempts. The team had put together another fantastic year, finishing 8–2 in the regular season, largely on the strength of the defense, which allowed just one touchdown in the team's eight wins and surrendered only 62 points.

Southern's bowl misfortunes continued, however, as the team lost a 10–9 heartbreaker to East Texas in what could have been described as the wind bowl. After entering the second half tied at 7, MSC took a 9–7 lead on a safety when the Lion center snapped the ball over the punter's head. Late in the game, however, East Texas kicked a 31-yard wind-aided field goal that deflated the Southerners, who lost their second consecutive Tangerine Bowl. Despite its regional dominance and recognition on the national football scene, MSC had never won a bowl game.

1958 SEASON

The Southerners kicked off one of their greatest seasons on September 20, hosting Louisiana Tech in front of 7,500 fans at Faulkner Field. The first Southern touchdown of the season came late in the first quarter when halfback Tommy Morrow, a newcomer to the varsity, intercepted a Bulldog pass and returned it 26 yards for a touchdown and a 6–0 lead. With 16 seconds left in the half, Sekul hit Lance with a 12-yard pass to score the team's second touchdown and followed up by hitting end Homer Boyd for the 2-point conversion to give

All-American two-way end Bob Yencho was one of the leaders of the 1958 team.

the Southerners a 14–0 halftime lead. In a sloppy game played in mud and on a soggy field, Tech fumbled eight times but lost none, while Southern committed six fumbles, losing three. Neither team could score in the second half, and the Southerners had their first victory of the season as Sekul finished with 8 completions on 11 attempts for 119 yards. Later in the following week, the United Press International (UPI) announced its first-ever College Division poll, with the Southerners ranked No. 1.

Southern next traveled to San Antonio to play Trinity. Alamo Field was a sea of mud, with the middle barren of grass. Ten minutes after the game started, spectators had difficulty telling the players apart. Sekul threw a pair of second-half touchdown passes to Yencho to lead the Southerners to a 15–0 win. The game was marred by penalties, with Southern committing nine infractions for 105 yards and Trinity drawing eight for 90 yards. Furthermore, three Southern players were ejected.

The Southerners were 2–0 and still ranked No. 1 when they met Memphis State at Faulkner Field on October 4. Before a crowd of 11,000, the Southerners trailed Memphis 22–21 with about nine minutes left, and the situation quickly worsened for the home team. Sekul had to leave the game with a chipped bone in his left wrist, and Yates was already out with a chipped bone in his right hand. Vann had no choice but to call on little-used reserve quarterback Billy Larson. But with five minutes to go, Larson engineered a drive that stalled at the Tiger 15-yard line with 43 seconds remaining. Sophomore Hugh McInnis trotted on the field to try the first field goal of his college

Coach Thad (Pie) Vann is pictured with end Hugh McInnis. McInnis kicked the game-winning field goal against Memphis State in 1958.

THE FABULOUS FIFTIES [89]

career and calmly drilled the ball through the uprights to give Southern the 24–22 victory.

With the running game finally clicking into gear, the Southerners rolled to a 33–6 October 11 win over Southeastern Louisiana before 9,500 fans at Faulkner Field. The Southerners turned a close game into a rout in the second half with four touchdowns. With Sekul and Yates sidelined, Coats took over at quarterback and did a magnificent job, rushing for 91 yards on 14 carries to lead the team to 315 yards on the ground. Larson and freshman Morris Meador also contributed to the victory, which upped the Southerners' record to 4–0 and maintained their stranglehold on first place in the UPI rankings.

After a week off, Southern met West Texas State for Homecoming on October 25. With an overflow crowd of 14,000 on hand, the Southerners continued to run the ball with great success. Two fullbacks, Supple and Frank Broyles, led the ground game to 349 yards, with Supple running the ball 14 times for 97 yards and a touchdown and Broyles topping those numbers by rushing 11 times for 125 yards and a touchdown. Sekul returned to action to try to pass for a 2-point conversion and wound up running to make it. Yates also was back for the Southerners, playing well after his three-week layoff. Coats handled most of the quarterbacking duties, with Larson and Meador also seeing action.

Seeking their sixth straight victory, the Southerners traveled to Texas on November 1 to face Abilene Christian. An early 65-yard drive gave MSC a 7–0 lead, and the Southerners followed up with a 95-yard drive and 2-point conversion to stretch their edge to 15–0. Later in the game, Southern scored again to seal the 22–0 win that was marred by an ugly play after the third touchdown. Charley Ellzey kicked off for the Southerners, and the Wildcats sent two players after him to keep him out of the play. As he watched the flight of the ball, one Abilene player knocked him down, and as Ellzey returned to his feet, the other Wild-

Quarterback/defensive back George Sekul helped the Southerners to a perfect 9–0 record in 1958.

cat hit him. Ellzey stood up once again, but the first player again plowed into him. The kick was a touchback, so there was no return, and as the play ended, Coats sprang to Ellzey's aid, with the two Southerners fighting off their opponents. The official noticed the fracas, threw his flag, and ejected Ellzey and Coats from the game, although the official subsequently recognized his mistake and apologized to Vann after the game.

Playing in Mobile's Ladd Stadium on November 8, Southern's 6–0 squad played North Carolina State before a crowd of 18,987. Supple streaked 68 yards for a touchdown late in the first quarter to open up the scoring. After the Wolfpack tied the game at 7, Sekul scored on a 7-yard bootleg to make the score 13–7 at the half. A Wolfpack fumble early in the third quarter led to Sekul's 29-yard touchdown pass to McInnis for a 20–7 lead, but the Wolfpack rallied to cut the margin to 20–14 with 12 minutes left. Lance later added another Southern touchdown to give the team a 26–14 victory and maintain their top ranking.

On November 15 Southern rolled to a second straight win over a major opponent, routing Virginia Tech 41–0 before 11,000 at Faulkner Field. Tech's highly touted quarterback, Billy Holsclaw, entered the game as the nation's leader in total offense but was held to -5 yards rushing and two passes in three attempts for 10 yards. Tech netted just 80 yards and picked up just one first down. In stark contrast, the Southern offense churned out 502 yards on the ground, 28 yards passing, and 24 first downs. "That was the best blocking and tackling we've had in a long time,"

Jubilant Southern fans tear down the goal posts after the 20–13 win over Chattanooga in the 1958 finale.

Coach Pie Vann said. "I just hope we will get it again for Chattanooga. We know they will be pointing everything they have for us and they are a tough team."

That matchup occurred on November 27 on a chilly Thanksgiving afternoon in Chattanooga, with the Southerners' perfect season on the line. MSC President William D. McCain announced two days prior to the game that if the Southerners won, Thanksgiving break would be extended until the following Tuesday, and several hundred Southern supporters traveled to watch the game. They were rewarded with what Coach Vann later described "as one of the best examples of desire that I have ever seen." The Southerners were

THE FABULOUS FIFTIES

The Mississippi Southern College coaching staff is pictured with the 1958 UPI College Division national championship trophy. From left to right: end coach C. J. (Pete) Taylor, backfield coach Clyde (Heifer) Stuart, athletic director Reed Green, head coach Thad (Pie) Vann, and line coach Jack Thomas.

leading 20–13 when a punt by Moccasin John Green died inches from the Southern goal line. Sekul put the ball in play and fumbled, and the Mocs were in business. Facing first-and-goal from the 1-yard line, Southern defensive linemen McInnis, John Russell, Joe Battaglia, Richard Johnston, Jim Taylor, John Perkins, and Yencho staged a magnificent goal-line stand. Chattanooga's first play resulted in no gain, while the Mocs' second-down attempt lost a yard when the ball was bobbled. The third-down play regained that yard, but the defense held on fourth down. The line, backed up by Morrow, Sammy Broyles, Arban, and Sekul, had saved the school's perfect season. "They simply had what it takes to win," Vann said.

In the wake of the Southerners' 9–0 performance, supporters launched a campaign to secure their team a Sugar Bowl bid to face Louisiana State University, also coming off of an undefeated and untied season. Organizations and individuals in Mississippi, Louisiana, Alabama, and elsewhere sent hundreds of telegrams and letters to and telephoned bowl president Claude (Monk) Simons. Some telegrams were also directed at officials of the Blue Grass Classic in Louisville, Kentucky, but both bowls were reputed to be

THE FABULOUS FIFTIES

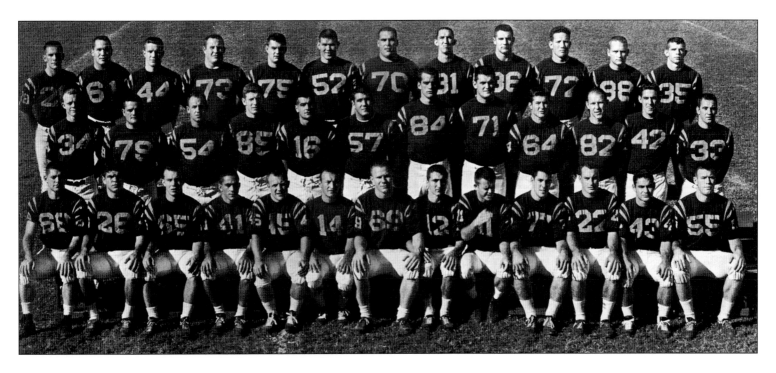

The 1958 UPI College Division national champions. Back row (left to right): Buddy Supple, Bobby Little, Joe Doggett, John Perkins, George Underwood, Richard Johnston, Sam Tuccio, Ted Crawford, Hugh McInnis, Vinson Sullivan, Tom Agner, Tommy Morrow; middle row: Arnold Spence, John Russell, Ray St. Pierre, Homer Boyd, Ollie Yates, Bob Rinehart, Butler (Sonny) Tucker, Charley Baetzman, Joe Battaglia, Bob Yencho, Rene Lorio, Charlie McArthur; front row: Jimmy Taylor, Sammy Broyles, Wilfred Spencer, J. C. Arban, Tommy Purvis, Billy Larsen, Eddie Godwin, George Sekul, Willie (Teenie) Coats, Cecil (Buddy) Long, Bill Weber, Bobby Lance, Charles Ellzey.

looking for big-name teams, a category that did not include Mississippi Southern College. Any chance that Southern would make a third straight appearance in the Tangerine Bowl or a third appearance in the Sun Bowl was eliminated by the fact that teams already chosen, Buffalo (Tangerine) and Wyoming (Sun), had black players. The political climate of the time prevented Mississippi Southern from playing against teams with African Americans.

Unfortunately for the Southerners, no bowl bid would be forthcoming. They did, however, earn the UPI College Division national championship, and on January 12, 1959, the school's alumni association honored the team with a banquet attended by coaches, players, school officials, their wives and dates, and members of the media. The evening was highlighted by the presentation of the UPI trophy by Chiles Coleman of Atlanta, the organization's southern division news manager. Before the delighted crowd, Coleman told Vann, "It is fitting that we honor a unique achievement with a unique award. This trophy is the first of its kind. In years to come others may say that they won it, but only you can say you won the first one." The banquet's other memorable moments included short talks by MSC President McCain, Athletic Director Green, and Coach Vann, who said, "It is wonderful to be appreciated. This is a tribute to the sacrifices the boys have made. It's not hard to coach when there are players like you, willing to give all. We'll never

THE FABULOUS FIFTIES

forget you 16 seniors. I think the things that made us better than average this year were our blocking and tackling. We're going to start right where we left off last year when spring training gets under way on February 2." "We take great pride in our undefeated, untied football team. Most schools never achieve a perfect season," McCain said. "You were undefeated, untied and uninvited, but . . . I am confident you could have beaten LSU in the Sugar Bowl. I wish you 16 seniors success wherever you go. The rest of you will face a tough schedule next year. I am looking for even bigger and better things from the finest in the land." The alumni association presented all the Southern players and coaches with a team photograph and plaque.

1959 SEASON

After the perfect 1958 campaign, the 1959 season was almost guaranteed to be a letdown, but the Southerners performed well below expectations, dropping more games in a season than they had lost since 1954. Southern opened on September 26 with a rather easy 21-point home win over Trinity University. More than 12,500 partisan fans saw McInnis and Morrow score first-quarter touchdowns, and just 20 seconds into the second period, Meador connected with Andin McLeod on a 16-yard scoring strike. McInnis added another touchdown after picking up a Trinity fumble in the third quarter. Trinity managed to push into the MSC end zone late in the final period to make the final score 29–8. Vann was "somewhat pleased" with the team's performance in the first period but added that his players had "made too many mistakes to keep winning."

MSC's second game occurred on October 3 in Mobile's Ladd Stadium, where the Southerners took on the Texas A & M Aggies in front of more than 26,000 fans. Although the game was close, A & M scored a touchdown in the final frame to win a hard-fought game, 7–3. McInnis and Supple played very well and Southern was better than A & M in almost every statistical category, outgaining the Aggies by almost 200 yards and recording five more first downs. A & M coach Jim Myers commented that with any breaks, Southern could have won the contest by two touchdowns, and he expressed his opinion that MSC would have a chance to defeat Auburn later in the season.

MSC rebounded with a 26–6 thrashing of Southeastern Louisiana before 12,200 at Faulkner Field on October 10. Southern used two third-quarter touchdowns to pull away from the Lions and break up a surprisingly tight contest. Supple once again starred for the Southerners: according to the *Hattiesburg American,*

> The little fullback who was acclaimed by one sportswriter as the "best in the country for his size" was a devil to the Southeasterners. Supple at one time during the game brought the entire stadium attendance to their feet when he out maneuvered a Southeastern defender; went high in the air, and snatched a pass from [Don] Fuell. [Supple] wasn't done though; when he came down he hesitated, picked up a blocker and headed for greener pastures. The little powerhouse proved it again in the third period when he churned through one group of defenders, gained speed, and plowed into three

more luckless Southeasterners. Two of the visitors didn't get up right away and one watched the rest of the scrap from the bench.

Southern continued its offensive production in defeating West Texas 37–6 on October 25 before a tiny crowd of 5,000 in West Texas's new 20,500-seat stadium. The game was never in doubt, and West Texas put points on the board only late in the contest. All members of MSC's traveling team played, with the reserves in for almost the entire second half. After the contest, West Texas Athletic Director Frank Kimbrough called the Southern backfield "the hardest running backs I've seen in years."

MSC yet again celebrated Homecoming with a victory, defeating Abilene Christian 30–10 the following week. Although the game remained close at the half, with Southern holding a 7–2 edge, Ellzey broke the game open with a third-quarter interception runback for a touchdown, and the Southerners added two more scores before surrendering a late touchdown.

Memphis State, still smarting from a bitter 1958 loss to Southern, beat the Southerners 21–6 in Memphis on October 31. Memphis never trailed in the game, and MSC committed several costly penalties as well as a fumble in the Tiger end zone when the Southerners had a chance to tie the game.

On November 7, Southern hosted North Carolina State at Ladd Stadium in Mobile. Going into the fourth quarter, Southern held a narrow 7–6 lead. MSC scored a touchdown but missed the extra point, stretching the lead to 13–6. With only 1:11 remaining, State back Don Podwika barreled over from the one to make the score 13–12. Rather than kicking the extra point, State decided to go for the win. Podwika, whom the *Southerner* called "one of the greatest backs Southern has faced in years," passed to a teammate in the end zone to give the Wolfpack their first lead of the game. In perhaps the biggest play of the season, Southerner Rene Lorio returned a short kickoff to the North Carolina State 37-yard line with only 50 seconds left on the clock. The next play may represent one of the best in the school's history: as the *Southerner* put it, "Meador, who had shown brilliantly all afternoon, dropped far back to pass. He spotted Lorio deep and let fly. Lorio grabbed the ball at the 9, juggled it momentarily, and then went into the end zone." The Southerners had won, 19–14. According to the *Hattiesburg American,* the win allowed Southern to "regain prestige" by beating a solid major-college opponent. Southern had snatched victory in dramatic fashion.

Southern posted another victory the following week, defeating Chattanooga 14–6 in front of 7,000 spectators at Faulkner Field who braved what the *Southerner* described as weather "as cold as the proverbial well digger." Supple ran in from the 1-yard line in the first quarter and Fuell passed to Leon Akins in the second period to account for the Southerners' two touchdowns, and MSC might have tallied more points had several penalties not thwarted promising drives. Chattanooga scored with only 33 seconds left to play to make the game appear closer than it was. The win was Southern's ninth in eleven tries against Chattanooga and improved MSC's season mark to 6–2.

The Southerners played their only game of the year against an SEC opponent on November 21, when they traveled to play Auburn. The game started well for MSC when the Tigers fumbled a punt and committed a pass-interference penalty and the Southerners capitalized on the mistakes to take a 7–0 lead on Meador's 1-yard scoring run. Auburn responded with a touchdown to tie the game in the first quarter and then crossed the goal line in each of the remaining quarters to win 28–7. Auburn's 21,000 spectators were delighted by the team's twenty-fifth straight home victory. The *Student Printz* lauded "Southern's try at an SEC team" and remarked that "MSC lost very little prestige" in the defeat. Both Ellzey and McInnis drew praise from Auburn coach Ralph (Shug) Jordan.

The Southerners closed out their 6–4 season with a disappointing 16–0 shutout at the hands of Louisiana Tech, the first time MSC's offense had been held scoreless since 1955 and Tech's first win over Southern in 10 years. Southern dominated during the first half, posting a 20–12 advantage in first downs and a 295–243 advantage in total yardage, but lost five fumbles to kill its chances. The star of the game was Louisiana Tech's 5-foot-9, 155-pound freshman quarterback, Johnny Hudson, who completed 9 of 11 passes for 179 yards and scored both touchdowns.

The decade began much as it had started, with a mediocre season by Southern standards. However, sandwiched between the 1950 and 1959 seasons were some of the most memorable campaigns in school history. In his 11 years at the helm, Vann had garnered an amazing 82–27–1 record. He and Green had put Mississippi Southern College on the national football map. But the failure to align with a conference left the school in a precarious position—too good to play against regional competition but unable to compete with the major football powers.

THE DECADE OF DEFENSE
1960–1969

Mississippi Southern College, fresh off its most successful football decade, entered the 1960s with unbridled enthusiasm for football. This enthusiasm was stoked by the announcement that the Football Writers Association of America had placed the Southerners in the group's major-college division for the 1960 season. The association determined prior to each season which teams would be classified "college division" and which schools would be "university division" based on the schedule of opponents. Efforts by the school administration and by friends of the school's athletic department as well as the team's consistent scheduling of high-quality opponents had led to the attainment of this long-sought-after goal, and according to the *Southerner,* supporters believed that the Southern gridders would

President William D. McCain, was an avid sports fan and great supporter of the school's athletic program. He is pictured here (standing, second from right, in front row) with the students during a football game in the early 1960s.

"soon be among the top clubs in the major college group." The school would play the 1960 season in the major-college division and return to the college division for 1961 and 1962 before gaining permanent major-college status in 1963.

The MSC football program's development into a major athletic program was paralleled by the school's development into a major educational institution, potentially the state's largest. In 1962, Southern's enrollment exceeded 5,000, while the faculty and staff numbered well over 200.

1960 SEASON

As the team prepared for his twenty-fourth season at MSC and his twelfth year at the helm, Coach Thad (Pie) Vann's squad had 56 men, most of them sophomores and only five weighing more than 210 pounds. George Hultz, at 230 pounds the team's biggest player, would have to fill the tackle spot vacated by the death of one of the team's best players, George Underwood, in a car accident. Vann was assisted by Jack Thomas, who coached the line; Maxie Lambright, who coached the backs; and C. J. (Pete) Taylor, who coached the ends.

Southern was a 10-point underdog going into the campaign's opening game on September 23 against Hardin-Simmons at Ladd Stadium in Mobile. The Texans were led by quarterback Harold (Hayseed) Stephens, an excellent passer, while MSC had an overabundance of quarterbacks, as Vann had to decide among four talented players. With outstanding running ability, Don Fuell, a transfer who had gotten Auburn in

[98]   THE DECADE OF DEFENSE

Mississippi Southern quarterback Don Fuell, a transfer from Auburn, led the team in passing in 1959, 1960, and 1961 and was the team's leading rusher in 1960 and 1961.

trouble with the National Collegiate Athletic Association for recruiting irregularities, won the starting job over Morris Meador, Val Keckin, and Billy Larson. Before the crowd of 8,112, MSC set the tone for the game by taking the opening kickoff and marching down the field on an impressive 88-yard scoring drive. Fuell justified his coach's decision, running for 93 yards on only five carries, including a fabulous 76-yard jaunt in the second quarter, to lead the Southerners to a decisive 27–0 whitewashing of the Texans. Although the Southerners had difficulty containing Stephens, who passed for 135 yards, they held the Texan running game to 13 yards.

The following week, the Southerners faced one of the country's top throwing quarterbacks in West Texas State's Jim Dawson, who came into the game ranked third in the nation in passing and tenth in total offense. Southern delighted the home crowd of 12,600 by driving 72 yards on its first possession of the game, with halfback Andin McLeod scoring the touchdown on a 2-yard plunge. Unlike Hardin-Simmons, however, West Texas answered on the next drive, tying the score. The seesaw battle continued as MSC put together an 81-yard scoring drive capped by fullback Dan Pugh's 19-yard run and the Buffaloes countered with a field goal with four seconds left in the half to make the score 13–10. Halfback Tommy Morrow scored a third-period touchdown and the Southerners completed the 2-point conversion to increase their lead to 21–10, ending the scoring until just over four minutes remained. MSC's Mike Olander intercepted a John Bryant pass and ran the ball back for a touchdown, and the Buffaloes responded with a late score to make the final 28–18.

The Southerners flew to San Antonio, Texas, to play Trinity on October 8. For the third straight week, MSC, led by Fuell, scored on its opening possession of the game to take a 7–0 lead. Southern added a safety in the third quarter when Trinity quarterback Dexter Butler fumbled a low snap in his own end zone, and Meador threw a 17-yard touchdown pass to halfback John Sklopan in the final period to seal the 16–0 win. The stellar defense held the Tigers to 69 total yards, a showing that actually increased the Southerners' season average. After three games, undefeated MSC was third in the nation in total offense, second in rushing offense, and third in rushing defense.

Southern's next contest was on October 15 against a tough Florida State team at Mobile's

THE DECADE OF DEFENSE

Ladd Stadium. MSC went into the game favored by a touchdown, and a crowd of 20,000 was expected to see the game, although about 5,000 fewer people showed. Morrow opened the scoring for MSC on a 19-yard touchdown run, and Larson kicked the extra point to make the score 7–0. After Fuell's touchdown on Southern's next possession and the 2-point conversion, the lead was up to 15. The Seminoles mounted a comeback in the second half, scoring two touchdowns but missing on a 2-point conversion to lose 15–13. Said Coach Vann, "Teamwork and desire to win was the difference."

The largest crowd ever at Faulkner Field, 16,100 fans, was on hand for the October 22 Homecoming game against the best team in the Atlantic Coast Conference, North Carolina State. The spectators were treated to a performance by one of the era's greatest college quarterbacks, North Carolina State's Roman Gabriel, whom Vann termed one of the finest players the Southerners had faced in many years. For the fourth time in five games, Southern scored on its opening possession, with Sklopan crossing the goal line on a 4-yard run and Larson kicking the extra point to give the home team a 7–0 lead. Gabriel responded with a 27-yard touchdown pass in the first quarter and a 1-yard quarterback sneak in the second quarter to enable the Wolfpack to forge ahead 14–7. Claude Gibson then intercepted a Southern pass at the Wolfpack 14-yard line, and Gabriel quickly drove his team down the field and threw another touchdown pass to make the score 20–7 at halftime. Southern scored on its first possession of the second half on a Meador-to-McLeod touchdown pass to close to within 7 points, but that was where the scoring ended, and the Southerners had suffered their first defeat of the season, 20–13. Gabriel completed 9 of 11 passes for 143 yards and two touchdowns on the day. "We knew from the start [that North Carolina State was] hungry for this one," Vann said after the game. "I'm proud of our kids for the desperate effort they made to come back in the last two quarters."

MSC bounced back on October 29 to soundly defeat Abilene Christian College 34–8 in front of 6,200 fans in Abilene, Texas. During the first half, Fuell, a surprise starter despite an ailing foot, both ran and threw for touchdowns, Larson threw a touchdown pass to end Don Hultz, and McLeod scored on a 1-yard run as the Southerners gained 300 yards and held a 27–0 lead at halftime. In the third period, Southern added another touchdown when Fuell connected with Morrow on a 76-yard scoring strike, the team's longest pass play of the year, and Coach Vann cleared the bench and played his entire travel squad.

On November 5 the Southerners traveled to Jonesboro, Arkansas, to play the Arkansas State Indians. Larson led MSC's second unit to a score in the second quarter, and the Southerners maintained the lead until the fourth period, when quarterback Jimmy McMurray and the Indians launched an aerial assault. After a disputed MSC fumble, McMurray and company took over on the Southern 43-yard line and reeled off a 12-play touchdown drive and added the 2-point conversion for an 8–7 lead. Morrow took the ball on the ensuing kickoff and raced 62 yards to the Indians' 28. Fuell took command and bulled his way over the goal line for the go-ahead touchdown, but his attempt at the 2-point conversion failed, making the score 13–8. Back came the Indians, who went 67 yards for a score that gave them the 14–13 victory, much to the delight of the 7,000 fans on hand for Homecoming. The Southerners fell to 5–2 on the year. Vann harshly criticized his team's performance: "We failed to take advantage of several scoring opportunities. We blocked during the game worse than we have all season. We also made numerous defensive mistakes that you just cannot overcome against an inspired opponent."

The Southerners lost for the third time in four tries when Louisiana Tech pulled off a 10–7 upset before just 4,000 fans at Faulkner Field on November 12. Southern drew first blood as Fuell hooked up with Morrow on a 21-yard scoring strike but followed with two costly mistakes—a second-quarter fumble and a third-quarter interception—that Tech turned into a touchdown and a field goal to give the visitors the win.

The Southerners' woes continued the following week with a 7–6 defeat courtesy of the Memphis State Tigers. Southern once again delighted the 12,500 fans at Faulkner Field by scoring early, taking a 6–0 lead on fullback Wendell Campbell's 1-yard scoring run. The lead held up until the fourth quarter, when Larson's field goal attempt sailed wide right and Memphis State took over on its own 18-yard line with 11:15 to go. Quarterback James Earl Wright dropped back to the 10-yard line and simply tossed the ball as far as he could. The pass landed in the hands of end Hal Sterling at the MSC 35-yard line, with no defender within 10 yards. After Sterling scooted into the end zone, the successful extra-point kick gave the Tigers the victory. After starting the season 4–0, the Southerners had fallen to 5–4, losing their last three games by a combined total of 5 points.

For the season's final game, MSC traveled to Chattanooga for a Thanksgiving Day encounter with the Moccasins. Southern scored in each quarter and held Chattanooga to just a second-period touchdown en route to a 30–6 win. Campbell, Morrow, Pugh, Olander, and Jack White crossed the Moc goal line for the Southerners, who rolled up 488 yards of total offense while limiting the Mocs to just 220 yards. Southern's first year of major-college football had ended with a 6–4 record, and Morrow had earned a slot in the Senior Bowl in Mobile.

In the springs of both 1961 and 1962, MSC President William D. McCain, Dean Porter Fortune, and Athletic Director Reed Green attended the annual meetings of the Southern Conference, which was considering expansion, but failed to persuade the league to invite the school to join. The Southern Conference had retained its appeal for Mississippi Southern because the conference members were for the most part segregated. Green's hopes for a new conference had waned because schools such as Florida State and Chattanooga that had formerly been interested were turning their attentions elsewhere.

THE DECADE OF DEFENSE

1961 SEASON

The 1961 season began at home on September 16 against Arlington State, which had just made the transition from a junior college to a four-year institution and major-college football. Vann was not overlooking the Rebels, however, telling the *Hattiesburg American* that the game would be MSC's toughest season opener since 1953, when the opponent was Alabama. Coach Vann utilized his "22-man" first string en route to a solid 30–7 victory in which the Southerners scored on their first position and Arlington never really got close. The Southerners gained 228 yards rushing and 261 yards through the air, with Campbell, Fuell, Sklopan, and Billy Coleman scoring touchdowns and Jerrel Wilson kicking a 34-yard field goal. "Overall, we were pleased with the impressive offensive showing and the spirit of the team," Vann said after the contest. "We were particularly well pleased with the improved passing of our quarterbacks. That was a phase of our game which had received special attention."

Southern had a week off before traveling to Lafayette to play the University of Southwestern Louisiana (formerly Southwestern Louisiana Institute) on September 30. Vann had never lost to the Bulldogs as either an assistant or head coach at Southern, and the string continued with a 22–6 victory on touchdowns by Sklopan, Coleman, and Charlie Dedwylder. Once again, MSC scored on its opening possession. The Southerners, who had dropped back to college-division status for the 1961 season, were ranked No. 1 in the first United Press International (UPI) poll of the year and ranked No. 7 in the Associated Press (AP) poll.

Both Chattanooga and Southern were undefeated going into their October 7 contest at Faulkner Field. Fuell excited the 13,000 spectators in attendance by scoring all of MSC's points—three touchdowns, three extra points, and a field goal—in the 24–7 victory. The Southern defense allowed the Mocs only a late-fourth-quarter touchdown to retain the top spot in UPI's rankings, although for some reason the AP did not rank the Southerners the following week.

Southern traveled to Tennessee to take on old nemesis Memphis State at Crump Stadium on October 14, with both teams perfect on the season. More than 22,000 fans witnessed the Memphis State Tigers beat the Southerners for the third straight year in what the *Hattiesburg American* termed another "vicious, hard-knocking" game. Southern spotted the Tigers two first-half touchdowns, failing to capitalize on opportunities to score. Fuell fought hard to bring the Southerners back in the second half, leading them to pay dirt on a 37-yard drive after a Meador interception midway through the third period to cut the Tiger lead to 14–7. But Memphis added a fourth-quarter touchdown to seal the 21–7 win and drop the Southerners to No. 2 in the UPI poll, behind Northern Michigan, and kept them out of the AP rankings. "We are making no alibis for losing this ball game," Vann said a few days later, but, he continued, "small injuries to key personnel such as John Ratesic, Dan Pugh, Don Fuell, Leon Akins, Sam Bella and Mike Olander had kept

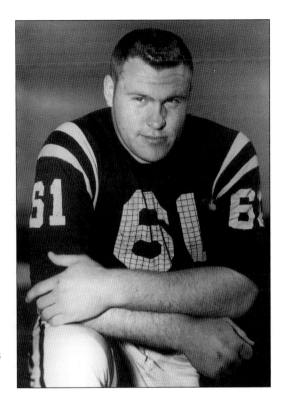

Freshman tackle Charlie Parker was touted early in his career as a star. He lettered in 1961, 1962, and 1963.

these boys out of contact work for the last week or so and it really showed on us in Memphis."

Southern returned to the win column at home on October 21 with a 20–0 shutout of Arkansas State, a team that had defeated the Southerners by a single point in 1960. Before only 7,000 supporters, linebacker Harold Hays intercepted an Indian pass and returned the ball to the one-foot line. On the next play, Fuell sneaked into the end zone for the touchdown. Later in the second quarter, Campbell scored to close out a 63-yard drive and give the Southerners a 13–0 halftime lead. End Roger Hicks returned another interception for MSC's final score. The victory improved the Southerners' record to 4–1, and they remained No. 2 in the UPI poll and were now ranked No. 10 in the AP poll.

Southern hosted Abilene Christian for Homecoming on October 28 and pummeled the Wildcats 33–6 in front of more than 11,000 fans. Vann used all four of his units in the contest. The game featured two touchdowns by Fuell, one each by Coleman and Campbell, and one on a 36-yard touchdown pass from quarterback James Berry to Dick Mates. Now 5–1 on the year, the Southerners returned to No. 1 in the UPI poll and were now ranked No. 8 by the AP.

North Carolina State had ruined the Southerners' 1960 Homecoming; this year's battle took place on November 4 at Mobile's Ladd Stadium. The 13,000 fans in attendance saw the Southerners do a better job of keeping Gabriel in check, holding him to four of eight passes for 41 yards, but the Wolfpack nevertheless won, 7–6. Southern halfback Jimmy Havard ran a punt back 82 yards for a touchdown in the first period, but Fuell missed the extra point. Later in the quarter, Southern fumbled, the Wolfpack recovered, and Gabriel led the Pack on a 38-yard scoring drive. Jake Shaffer's extra point gave N.C. State the lead and the win, as both defenses tightened and neither team scored for the final three quarters. Wolfpack Coach Earl Edwards described the game as "our finest team effort to date. Our blocking up front was the best of the season and this made a big difference in the contest." The defeat dropped the Southerners to 5–2 on the year and to No. 4 in the UPI poll, while they disappeared altogether from the AP rankings.

THE DECADE OF DEFENSE

Jerrel Wilson (1961–1962) was a fullback and kicker for the Southerners. He went on to become an all-pro punter with the Kansas City Chiefs.

MSC traveled to Ruston on November 11 to play Louisiana Tech. Despite the drenching rains, the Southerners followed their usual practice of scoring on their first possession when Ben Willoughby crossed the goal line on a 7-yard run with 5:51 left in the first quarter. Neither team threatened seriously the rest of the afternoon, and MSC had its first win over Tech in three years. The Southerners moved up to third in the UPI poll but remained out of the AP's Top 10.

Next up was a November 18 meeting with the Florida State Seminoles at Homecoming in Tallahassee. More than 17,000 Seminole fans were disappointed when Havard caught a pass from junior quarterback Billy Coleman and scored from 10 yards out after a fake field goal to give Southern a 6–0 lead. Midway through the fourth quarter, Fuell sneaked the ball in from inches out to give the Southerners the 12–0 upset. The Southern defense, led by Jim Payne, Charley Parker, Nick Kolinsky, Akins, and George Hultz, had been instrumental in the win, holding Florida State to 63 yards on the ground and forcing fumbles to set up both scores. "I thought this was a mighty fine team effort," an excited Vann said after the game. "Our tackles and ends played their best defensive game to date. This was definitely a ball game highlighted by defense." The final UPI poll released a few days later ranked the Southerners third, while the AP poll had them tied for tenth, and there were rumors that they might be in line for a Tangerine Bowl bid.

With so much talk about bowl games and rankings, the Southerners might have overlooked their regular-season finale against the Trinity Tigers on November 25. Although Southern was heavily favored, the game was surprisingly close, in part because the Southerners made numerous offensive mistakes, including fumbling the ball and overthrowing open receivers. The two teams were tied at 7 at halftime, and Trinity went ahead in the third period 14–7. Coleman took over in

The 1962 team won the UPI College Division national championship.

the fourth quarter, scoring on a 1-yard sneak and running in the 2-point conversion to put the Southerners ahead 15–14. A Billy Coleman–to–Dedwylder touchdown pass with seven seconds left iced the 22–14 win.

MSC finished the 1961 season with an 8–2 record but received no bowl bid, possibly because of the team's lackluster play against Trinity. Nevertheless, great excitement accompanied the Southerners' preparations for their last season as a small-college football program. As the team prepared to leave that designation behind, the school prepared to do the same. On February 22, 1962, the state legislature voted unanimously to change Mississippi Southern College into the University of Southern Mississippi. Powell Ogletree, secretary of the school's alumni association, was in Jackson with a group of students and reported the news to McCain at 3:15 that afternoon. Governor Ross Barnett signed the bill five days later, marking the triumphant end of McCain's seven-year drive to make "Southern a great University."

1962 SEASON

Building on the efforts of the 1961 team and the change in the institution's focus, the University of Southern Mississippi had arguably its best season ever. The school played its first game under its new moniker on September 15 on the road against Arlington State, winning by a score of 28–7. The game's opening minutes saw end Billy Lyons recover a Rebel fumble on the Arlington 20-yard line, setting up a touchdown pass from quarterback Billy Coleman to end Don Hultz to

THE DECADE OF DEFENSE

make it 6–0. Coleman's 9-yard touchdown pass to Lyons in the second quarter made it 12–0, and then the Southerners converted another fumble into a touchdown by Sklopan to take a 20–0 halftime advantage. Havard's 2-yard run closed out the scoring.

The following week Southern hosted the Richmond Spiders at Faulkner Field and rolled to an easy 29–8 victory. Sklopan, Havard, and halfback Jack White ran wild, setting up most of the Southern Miss scoring. The Southerners outgained the Spiders 428 yards to 239 and kept them out of the end zone until the final minute of play.

Southern Miss coasted to its third straight win with a 29–0 beating of Southwestern Louisiana at Faulkner Field on September 29. Coleman completed all six of his passes for 169 yards and three touchdowns, with Lyons on the receiving end of four of those balls, including two touchdowns. USM's reserves played most of the second half and held the Bulldogs scoreless. When UPI released its first college-division poll of the season, the Southerners were ranked No. 2, trailing only Florida A & M, while the AP ranked them No. 4.

USM's October 6 road game at Chattanooga promised to be tough and lived up to its promise. The Southerners scored first to go on top 6–0, but Chattanooga came back and took a 7–6 advantage at the end of the first quarter. Wilson's 38-yard field goal gave Southern a 9–7 halftime lead. With the seniors rallying the team in the second half, the Southerners scored three times to secure a 31–13 win, Vann's one hundredth victory as the school's head coach. Despite the happy outcome, Vann was not pleased about his

team's pass defense against the Mocs: "We never did get to their passer before he threw the ball. We must get better or we will be in trouble the rest of the way." The 4–0 Southerners were now ranked No. 2 in both the UPI and AP polls.

Southern Miss's next game was on October 13 at Crump Stadium against Memphis State. A Homecoming crowd of 11,500 watched as rain caused a great deal of poor ballhandling on both sides. The game was midway through the first quarter when Memphis State guard John Bramlett crashed through the Southern line and blocked a Wilson punt that bounced back through the end zone for a safety. Early in the second quarter, a poor Southern punt gave Memphis the ball at the USM 28-yard line, and the Tigers scored their only touchdown of the game a few plays later for

Sam Bella was a standout tackle for Southern Miss in 1962 and 1963.

Halfback Tommy Walters makes a catch during the 1962 season.

the 8–0 lead. The score stayed that way until early in the fourth quarter, when the Tigers could not handle Wilson's punt and Southern Miss center Larry Ecuyer pounced on the ball at the 1-yard line. After three unsuccessful running plays, fullback George Sekul dove over the top for the touchdown to make the score 8–6. But three defenders stopped Havard on the 2-point conversion, and the Tigers held on for the win. Now 4–1 on the year, the Southerners retained the No. 2 UPI ranking but fell to fifth in the AP poll.

Numerous USM supporters traveled to Mobile, Alabama, on October 20 to watch Southern play North Carolina State, no longer quarterbacked by Gabriel, at Ladd Stadium. A few plays after Ecuyer recovered a Wolfpack fumble at their 44-yard line, Wilson, playing fullback, scored on a 1-yard run, adding the extra-point kick to give Southern a 7–0 lead with 2:22 remaining in the first quarter. The score remained the same until the final quarter, when Wilson scored again, Coleman hit Lyons and halfback Tommy Walters with touchdown passes, and Wilson kicked a field goal to give the Southerners a 30–0 win. They remained second in the UPI poll and climbed to fourth in the AP rankings.

Another 30–0 shutout occurred the next week, this time against Abilene Christian at Faulkner Field. Like the N.C. State game, the Abilene contest was closer than the final score indicated, with the Southerners leading just 6–0 heading into the fourth quarter but adding several late scores to secure the win. Also as in the previous week, the Southerners, now 6–1, remained in second place in the UPI poll and climbed a spot in the AP poll, reaching third.

THE DECADE OF DEFENSE

As the calendar turned to November, the Southerners traveled to Jonesboro for a matchup against Arkansas State. After trailing 7–6 at halftime, the USM squad completely dominated the Indians during the second half, cashing in on mistakes as halfback Ben McLeod and Sekul scored touchdowns to give the Southerners a 20–7 win. USM's national rankings in both the UPI and AP polls remained unchanged.

Back home on November 10 to meet Trinity, Southern continued its drive for another national championship, rolling over the Tigers 33–6. Sklopan intercepted a pass and ran the ball back 48 yards for a touchdown in the first quarter to start the scoring, Coleman and White scored on 1-yard runs in the second and third quarters, and Sekul and fullback Kenny Martin scored on short fourth-quarter runs. Boasting a four-game winning streak and an 8–1 overall record, the Southerners climbed into the No. 1 slot in the UPI poll while remaining third in the AP poll.

The Southerners closed out the 1962 season at Faulkner Field on November 17, hosting Louisiana Tech for Homecoming. The spectators on hand included Governor Barnett and Lieutenant Governor Paul B. Johnson as well as several members of the state legislature. An inspired Bulldog team caused trouble early, but with a chance at another national championship, the Southerners rose to the occasion. Berry scored the Southerners' first touchdown with a 45-yard interception return, and Sklopan scored on a 37-yard run to give Southern a 15–6 edge at halftime. During the break, McCain presented Vann with a new 1963 Chrysler for his accomplishments, dedication, and contributions to Southern Miss football, and then play resumed. The Bulldogs closed to within 15–12 early in the third quarter. Southern then drove to Tech 1-yard line but fumbled the ball away, but the defense stopped the Bulldogs, forcing a punt. Tackle Danny Salmon blocked the kick, and the ball bounced back into the end zone, where Ben McLeod recovered for a touchdown and a 23–12 USM lead. Tech scored early in the fourth quarter to close to within 23–18, but a 1-yard run by Sklopan stretched the lead back to 29–18, where it remained when the final gun sounded.

When UPI released its final poll of the year, the 9–1 Southerners were crowned the college-division national champions for the second time. They had climbed as high as No. 2 in the AP poll during the season but wound up ranked fourth.

1963 SEASON

Southern Miss started the 1963 season by returning to major-college ranks. Former Southern standouts Billy Coleman and P. W. Underwood joined Taylor and Lambright as Vann's assistants, and the squad's largest member was Norman Ellis, who weighed in at 270 pounds. Twenty-four of the 57 team members were from Mississippi, with others hailing from as far away as Miami, Florida, and Patterson, New Jersey.

USM began the 1963 campaign in front of 24,000 fans in Jackson on September 14 against Memphis State. Behind the play of sophomore quarterbacks Oli Cordill and Billy Fletcher, the

(Top) Center/linebacker Harold Hays (1960–1962) was one of the leaders of the 1962 championship team.

(Bottom) P. W. Underwood (left) served as line coach at Southern Miss from 1963 to 1966. He is pictured with head coach Thad (Pie) Vann, the man Underwood would replace as head coach in 1969.

Tigers continued their mastery of the Southerners, soundly defeating them 28–7. The Southern offense struggled, managing to score only late in the game when halfback Robert (Rabbit) Brown did the honors. Mistakes proved costly for USM, which threw three interceptions and was penalized for 86 yards. The victory tied the bitter series between the two major-college independents at five wins each, but USM had not defeated Memphis since 1958.

Two weeks later, another series was evened at three when North Carolina State beat USM 14–0 at Faulkner Field, holding the Southerners scoreless for the first time since the 1959 contest against Louisiana Tech. USM outplayed the Wolfpack in most of the statistical categories, recording 14 first downs to 10 for N.C. State and rushing for an impressive 205 yards compared to the Wolfpack's 64, but USM could not muster much of a passing game. Although the USM defense had allowed only three touchdowns, the team was 0–2.

On October 12 the Richmond Spiders looked sluggish in the unseasonable 90-degree heat at Faulkner Field, losing to the Southerners 7–0 at Homecoming. The Southern defense continued to perform well, but the offense's scoring problems also persisted. Kolinsky, Parker, Tony DeFranco, Ecuyer, Ben McLeod, and Bill Gorney performed solidly on defense, with McLeod's fumble recovery allowing Herman Nall to score the game's only tally in the second quarter. Vic Purvis experienced his best day as a quarterback, passing for 35 yards, running for 51 yards, and providing excellent leadership on offense. "I was

THE DECADE OF DEFENSE

extremely pleased with our air game and also with the way we stopped their passing attack," said Vann. "[Harmon] Brannon had a good day and Nall did an excellent job for us, besides scoring the winning touchdown. But then he's done a good job for us all season. Coaches Underwood and Taylor had as much to do with our fine victory as anyone. Their scouting reports on Richmond were tremendous. Coach Lambright worked hard on our pass patterns during the week and it paid off."

USM was a 20-point underdog on October 19 against the Florida State Seminoles. The Mobile crowd of more than 11,000 was quite enthusiastic and was thrilled by a defensive battle. The Southerners outperformed the heavily favored Seminoles and had a chance to win the game late, but John Laird's 24-yard field goal attempt missed to the left as the game ended in a scoreless tie. "At that stage of the game, we felt that our best chance to score was on a field goal," Vann explained. "We knew Laird could kick that distance. Laird was heartbroken about missing the field goal." Four lost fumbles hurt the Southerners, but the defense once again was the story. "Boy, Southern hit us harder than anybody we've played this season," a Seminole lineman stated after the game. "They're tough." The Southerners held the Seminoles' sensational quarterback, Steve Tensi, to a mere 61 yards passing, in part because of the exceptional secondary play of Berry, who often blanketed receiver Fred Biletnikoff. Purvis provided the offensive fireworks, gaining 79 yards rushing and passing for another 55 yards.

The USM defense was ranked No. 9 in the nation when the Southerners hosted the Arkansas State Indians on October 26. The Southerners lived up to their billing, limiting the Indians to 39 yards and allowing Arkansas State to penetrate USM territory only twice. The Indians were held without a first down until 10 minutes remained in the game. Purvis continued to steal the show on offense, with 54 yards passing, 132 yards rushing, and one touchdown scored in the 25–0 victory. The *Hattiesburg American* said that Purvis "pitched, ran and plotted . . . to victory."

The Southerner defense moved up to third in the nation, trailing only Ole Miss and Princeton, after recording yet another shutout the following week. This time the victim was Southwestern Louisiana, which lost 28–0 in Lafayette. Vann was also pleased with his offense, which scored three touchdowns in the first half. Harmon (Bull) Brannon continued to perform well, with 142 yards on the ground and two touchdowns. Dooney Lippincott scored in the second quarter, and Gorney returned an interception 20 yards for the final USM score. With three wins in their past four games, the Southerners had climbed to 3–2–1.

After an open date, on November 16 the Southerners traveled to Ruston for their annual clash with the Louisiana Tech Bulldogs. Tech gave the Southerners a taste of their own medicine with a 10–0 shutout in which USM mustered only 41 yards rushing. The Southern defense continued to play well, limiting Tech to 99 yards rushing and 25 yards passing and holding the Bulldogs to a second-quarter field goal and a fourth-quarter punt return for a touchdown. Laird missed two

Kicker John Laird led the 1963 Southern Miss team in scoring with 33 points. He kicked six field goals that season and was a perfect 15 of 15 on extra points.

field goal attempts in the Southerners' only real scoring threats of the night. The Bulldog defense constantly harassed Purvis, who was sacked several times and recorded -35 yards rushing.

On Friday, November 22, 1963, President John F. Kennedy was assassinated in Dallas. NCAA Executive Secretary Walter Byars announced that individual schools could decide whether to cancel, postpone, or play their November 23 games: "Whereas the decision rests with your institution and your opponent, it is our view that you should plan to proceed with your contest with an appropriate, dignified opening ceremony and whatever other memorial tribute you might think appropriate at halftime," Byars said. Many of the country's major college football games, including the tradition-bound Harvard-Yale game, were canceled or postponed as the nation mourned, but most schools in the South chose to play. Southern Miss went ahead with its home game against the Citadel but, in keeping with the NCAA's suggestion, scheduled Band Day performances by more than 50 high school bands were replaced by ceremonies paying tribute to

THE DECADE OF DEFENSE

the late president. Before kickoff, USM's Pride marching band played the national anthem and "America the Beautiful," and a prayer was offered. There was a moment of silence at halftime with the band playing "This Is My Country." With most people's minds on the assassination, only an estimated 4,000 turned out to watch USM pummel the Citadel 37–12 in the Southerners' finest offensive performance of the year. The Southerners ran for 265 yards, 123 of them by Brannon, and scored two exciting second-quarter touchdowns when Joe Owen recovered a Citadel fumble in the end zone and Brown returned a punt 63 yards for a touchdown. The Citadel gained 74 yards rushing and 75 yards passing.

The USM defense saved the best for last, completely dominating the Chattanooga Moccasins 24–0 on Thanksgiving Day in Chattanooga in the season's final game. The Southerners held the Mocs to -24 yards rushing and 55 yards passing and never let them inside the Southerners' 40-yard line. Brown scored twice on passes from Purvis and Sid Atkins, Billy Atkins scored the other touchdown, and Laird kicked a school-record 50-yard field goal and three extra points. The Vannmen finished the 1963 season with a 5–3–1 record, and the coach's all-time record stood at an enviable 110–38–2.

1964 SEASON

The Southern Miss defense picked up where it had left off, beginning the 1964 season with a September 26 shutout of the University of Southwestern Louisiana at Faulkner Field. Southwestern Louisiana managed a meager 71 total yards for the day, while Purvis led the Southern offense to 503 yards of total offense. Nall scored two touchdowns in the first quarter and Laird kicked two field goals in the second quarter to make the score 19–0 at the half. Purvis ended a 57-yard drive with a 6-yard scoring run in the third quarter, and in the fourth, Laird kicked his third field goal for the 30–0 victory. Laird's trio of treys set a Southern Miss record. "I was especially pleased with the defense," said Vann after the game. "We were worried about it because of key losses from last year."

The Southerners traveled to Virginia to play the University of Richmond Spiders the next week. Neither team could score in the first period, but Purvis took over in the second quarter, scoring on runs of 71 and 34 yards in a game hampered by constant wind changes and wet grounds caused by Hurricane Hilda. Richmond got a safety in the second period and a touchdown in the third period after Joe Stromick ran a Purvis interception back for a touchdown, but the Spiders could get no closer and lost 14–9.

On October 10, the USM squad took on the Memphis State Tigers at Memphis's Crump Stadium. Brannan gained 114 yards rushing and scored three touchdowns to lead the Southerners to a 20–14 upset. Brannan's first touchdown came after Memphis opened the game with an incredible three consecutive fumbles, and the Southerners extended their lead to 14–0 on their next possession with a drive that culminated in Brannan's 10-yard run. Memphis responded with a 70-yard scoring drive on its next possession to cut the lead to 14–7, but USM countered with a fantastic 90-yard drive capped by Brannan's 9-yard scoring dash. Behind 20–7, Memphis went to the air in an attempt to mount a comeback, marshaling an 88-yard scoring drive against Southern's third string, but the Southern defense held on to preserve the school's first victory over Memphis State in five years. After the game, Vann and his troops spoke nicely about the Tigers, especially because the two teams were scheduled to play an unusual second game against each other at the end of the season. With both teams' success, scheduling major-college teams became more difficult, and in an effort to maintain their "university division" status, the two schools agreed to play each other again rather than facing smaller schools.

During the 1950s, Southeastern Conference (SEC) schools had shied away from playing Southern because of its success against league schools foolish enough to schedule the Southerners, but the 1964 season featured consecutive matchups at Mississippi State and at Auburn. USM was 3–0 going into the much-anticipated October 17 game in Starkville, the first meeting between the two schools since 1947. The Bulldogs had little to fear, however, scoring early and often in a 48–7 win. The Southerners' only bright spot came on Nall's incredible 100-yard kickoff return. "We didn't play a good game," a disappointed Vann related in the locker room following the loss. "Our pass defense was awful, our blocking bad and we didn't do a good job tackling in spots."

The next foe for Southern Miss was the Auburn Tigers, *Sports Illustrated*'s preseason No. 1 team and participants in the Orange Bowl at the end of the season. Southern drew first blood with a brilliant 71-yard pass from Purvis to Gorney. USM helped Auburn close the lead after the Tigers blocked Laird's punt and recovered the ball for a safety, and the score stood at 7–2 at the half. The Tigers roared back on their first possession of the second half with an 81-yard, 19-play drive that gave them an 8–7 lead and tacked on another touchdown on Doc Griffith's 2-yard run with a little over eight minutes remaining. The two teams engaged in a melee after Griffith's score, with officials, coaches, and police needed to restore calm before play could resume. The Tigers halted two more USM threats to win 14–7 and drop the Southerners to 3–2. "Our defense came to life and held us up. Although we lost, we had a chance to win down to the last," said Vann.

USM's schedule got no easier after the Auburn game, as the Southerners traveled to Florida State on October 31. Seminole quarterback Steve Tensi

The Pride of Mississippi Marching Band began to earn its reputation in the late 1950s and early 1960s as one of the best bands in the country.

THE DECADE OF DEFENSE [113]

electrified the 26,000-plus fans at Doak Campbell Stadium, completing 13 of 17 passes for two touchdowns and running for his first collegiate score to lead the Seminoles to a 34–0 victory. Fred Biletnikoff, who would become Florida State's first All-American, caught 10 of Tensi's passes for 170 yards and one touchdown. Southern could manage only 5 yards rushing. USM had lost three straight games during their "October Nightmare."

USM stopped the losing streak by thumping Chattanooga 31–0 on November 7 for Homecoming. The *Hattiesburg American* reported that the Southern pass defense "played a big part in the victory," and Purvis threw for 100 yards on six completions, including a 23-yard first-quarter scoring pass to end George Rodman. Laird added a 37-yard field goal early in the third quarter, Rusty Fry and Dooney Lippincott turned in short touchdown runs, and reserve quarterback Mike McClellan scored with 10 seconds left in the game to improve the team's mark to 4–3.

The winning continued the next week with a 14–7 home defeat of old nemesis Louisiana Tech, which came into the game with an 8–0 record and was ranked second in the country among small colleges. Lippincott ran 78 yards for a touchdown on the game's first play, but Tech tied the game at 7 later in the first quarter. The Southerners closed out the scoring in the second quarter with a 50-yard, 11-play drive capped by Purvis's 11-yard scoring pass to Gorney. However, the defense was the story of the game. Tech twice had the ball on the USM 1-yard line and penetrated the Southerner 30 on three other occasions but could not score on any of those drives.

Southern closed out its streaky 1964 season with another victory over rival Memphis State. Despite having defeated the Tigers earlier in the year, the Southerners were a touchdown underdog in the season finale. More than 9,000 fans braved temperatures in the 20s and a bone-chilling wind at Jackson's Memorial Stadium, but most spectators had departed before the Southerners secured the 20–18 victory. Billy Fletcher tossed a 30-yard scoring pass to Ron Higdon to cap off the Tigers' opening possession and make the score 7–0. USM answered with a 37-yard Laird field goal to close the gap to 7–3. After Ecuyer intercepted a Memphis pass, Purvis hit Troy Craft on a 21-yard pass play to the 2, and Nall scored to put Southern up 10–7 at the end of the first quarter. Purvis was sacked for a safety in the second period, and Memphis added a field goal to go ahead 12–10. USM fumbled again, opening the door for another Memphis touchdown, and trailed 18–10 at the half. But the Southerner defense shut down the Tigers in the second half. After Doug Satcher's third-quarter interception, Southern drove downfield and Laird kicked his second field goal to close the gap to 18–13. The game-winning drive ended late in the fourth quarter when Purvis connected with Rodman from 10 yards out, and USM's 6–3 season came to a close.

1965 SEASON

USM began the 1965 season on September 18 with a solid 15–0 win over Southeastern Louisiana at Faulkner Field. The defense, nick-

Quarterback Vic Purvis (#15) rushed for over 200 yards in two games during the 1965 season, gaining 238 yards against Memphis and 203 the following week against Richmond.

named the Vandals and under the able leadership of coordinator P. W. (Bear) Underwood, allowed the Lions a paltry 126 total yards of offense. Linebacker Ken Avery and defensive back Billy Devrow played exceptionally well for the defense, which set up two Southern Miss scores by causing fumbles. Purvis began his final year at USM in fine fashion, scoring from 4 yards out right before the first half ended to put USM up 6–0. Backup quarterback Glen Bynum hit Rabbit Brown in stride for a 33-yard touchdown pass late in the third quarter to make the score 12–0, and Julius (Poochie) Stringfellow recovered a fourth-quarter fumble to set up George Sumrall's field goal to close out the scoring.

USM continued its hard-hitting series with Memphis State in front of 22,000 at Jackson's

Memorial Stadium on September 25. Purvis entertained the crowd by rushing for an incredible 238 yards and one touchdown and throwing for 74 yards and another touchdown. Brannan gained 103 yards but committed two early fumbles that led to 9 Memphis points. The Southerners answered with a 70-yard, six-play drive, with Brannan redeeming himself with an 8-yard touchdown run. Defensive back Jimmy Bargar picked off a Memphis pass at the Southern Miss 41-yard line, and Purvis quickly connected with Brown for a touchdown that put USM on top 14–9 at the half. Devrow intercepted a Memphis pass at the 1-yard line to halt the Tigers' opening drive of the second half, and Southern marched 99 yards to score. Purvis ran the ball 10 times on the drive, including a nice 32-yard cutback run for the touchdown. Memphis answered with a third-quarter touchdown to end the scoring and give USM the 21–16 win. The Southerners compiled an impressive 449 yards of offense in the game.

Before the team's next game, a home contest against the University of Richmond, Coach Vann was hospitalized with what was initially thought to be a heart attack but turned out to be angina. Doctors stated that Vann would be okay and that their main concern was finding the proper medicine to treat his particular case. Vann had never missed a game and had rarely missed practice, but he listened to the Richmond game on the radio from his Hattiesburg home. Athletic Director Reed Green placed Lambright, the team's offensive coordinator, at the helm for Southern Miss. Despite the coaching change, the Purvis show continued against the Spiders. USM won the game 28–7 behind the All-America candidate's 203 rushing and 123 passing yards, three-quarters of the team's 438 total offensive yards. The Spiders' lone score came in the first quarter on a 73-yard, 15-play drive topped by Ron Gordon's touchdown. Purvis outran the Richmond defenders for a 66-yard touchdown to tie the game in the second quarter and passed the Southerners down the field for another touchdown with 40 seconds left to go in the half. USM added third- and fourth-quarter touchdowns set up by linebacker Doug Satcher's two interceptions to put the game out of reach.

The 3–0 Southerners traveled to Starkville to face Mississippi State, also undefeated and ranked No. 9 in the country, on October 9. Vann was still recovering from his illness, so Lambright remained in charge of the USM team. The Southerners spotted the Bulldogs 10 first-quarter points because of mistakes in the punting game and could not overcome those errors. Purvis brought the Southerners to within 3 points with an 84-yard, 15-play drive that included five passes to Brown and closed with Purvis's 10-yard run, but State responded by scoring 17 points and holding USM to only a safety for a 27–9 final.

The Vandals rebounded with another shutout in a 3–0 Homecoming win over Virginia Military Institute on October 16. With Vann back on the sidelines, the offense could muster only a 35-yard field goal by Sumrall, but the defense saved the day by limiting the Keydets to 60 yards of total offense. Punter Dickie Dunaway was also instrumental in the victory, consistently pinning the Keydets deep in their own territory. One of the reasons for the low offensive output was a second-quarter injury to Purvis, at the time the nation's second-leading rusher, and the ejection of Bull Brannan, who had a disagreement with Vann in the locker room at halftime and subsequently quit the team.

The Southerners' record stood at 4–1 as they looked ahead to their October 23 contest with Auburn, the leading team in the SEC. The star quarterback's injury and Brannan's absence did not bode well for USM, which was a two-touchdown underdog, but Sumrall's kicking and three pass interceptions by Tommy Brennan enabled Southern Miss to defeat the Tigers 3–0 and secure USM's first win over an SEC opponent since the 1954 Alabama contest. The highly regarded Southern defense intercepted four passes, recovered one fumble, and blocked a field goal to preserve the shutout and the victory.

For the third week in a row, the Southerners' game ended with a 3–0 score. But against William and Mary on October 30 in front of more than 25,000 fans in Norfolk, USM came out on the short end when Donnie McGuire kicked the first field goal of his college career with 39 seconds left in the first half and the Indian defense shut out the Southerners. The game featured numerous offensive errors, including a total of 11 fumbles between the two teams. But USM failed to retrieve any of William and Mary's miscues, and the punchless offense could not penetrate the Indian 40-yard line as Purvis, playing at less than 100 percent, completed just one pass. "William and Mary," Vann said later, "deserved to win, and apparently they wanted to because

Safety Billy Devrow (1964–1966) finished his career with fifteen interceptions, including eight in 1965.

they went after us like a bunch of wild Indians. They were the best team that day."

The defense continued to define USM's 1965 season, pitching a 17–0 shutout against Chattanooga on November 6. The Vandals held Chattanooga to 80 yards in total offense and only three first downs and scored a touchdown when Tommy Roussel blocked a punt and recovered the ball for a second-quarter touchdown. The Southerner offense got rolling again behind Purvis, who was at about 90 percent, according to the *Hattiesburg American,* and scored a first-quarter touchdown. Sumrall added a 38-yard field goal in the third period to round out the scoring.

Southern Miss closed out the season with a solid 31–7 win over rival Louisiana Tech in Ruston. Despite the Southerners' sound beating of the Bulldogs, the heretofore stellar defense surrendered 272 yards passing, far higher than the Vandals' 62 yard-per-game average to that point in the season. But the defensive front made up for the secondary, holding the Bulldogs to -57 yards rushing. Brennan started the scoring with a wild 59-yard punt return for a touchdown, Sumrall kicked a 13-yard field goal, and Lippincott scored on a 4-yard run to make the score 17–0 after one quarter. Late in the game, Bynum led USM on an 80-yard drive that ran the score to 24–0, and Brennan reeled off a 47-yard punt return for his second touchdown of the day. Tech added an inconsequential touchdown after Coach Vann had cleared the USM bench.

The 1965 season was the year that might have been. USM posted a fine 7–2 record, and the Vandals finished as the nation's top-ranked defense, but no bowl bid was forthcoming. The loss to William and Mary might have been avoided if the offense had been healthy or if the Southerners had received even one break. Purvis undoubtedly would have challenged for the national rushing title if he had not gotten hurt in the middle of the year.

1966 SEASON

USM began the 1966 season with another stellar defensive effort against Louisiana Tech on September 17 at Faulkner Field. The Vandals limited Tech to 7 yards rushing and 61 passing en route to a 14–0 victory. The offense, often called the Raiders, scored twice in the opening half, first on a 59-yard drive highlighted by Bynum's spectacular 44-yard run and capped by fullback Milo McCarthy's 10-yard run on a daring fourth-down play and again after Brennan intercepted a Terry Bradshaw pass and the Southern offense took over on the Tech 24-yard line and punched the ball in, with McCarthy doing the honors from 1 yard out. Elbert Trone, Gene Bachman, Avery, and Stringfellow were solid for USM on defense, while Bynum carried the ball 14 times for 103 yards and McCarthy recorded 91 yards rushing. "Our offense failed to jell in the second half although our defense came through about as we had hoped," Vann offered after the win. "We felt our rushing game was much improved with Earl King, Glen Bynum and Milo McCarthy handling most of the running."

Prior to the Southerners' September 24 road contest with Southeastern Louisiana, the Lions appeared to be somewhat of a mystery to the USM coaches. Southeastern had changed its entire offense and much of its defense from the previous season and had not yet played a game in 1966. Despite the changes, the Southerners defeated the Lions 15–13 on the strength of the defense, which limited Southeastern to 76 yards in total offense, including only 1 yard on the ground. USM put together a 12-play, 72-yard touchdown drive on its opening possession, with Bynum scoring on a sweep from 8 yards out. Bynum was injured on USM's next possession, however, and the Raiders struggled for the rest of the evening. The Lions went ahead 7–6 in the second period on a touchdown by Charles Whit-

[118] **THE DECADE OF DEFENSE**

ney, but Southern responded with a 40-yard field goal to take a 9–7 lead at the half. The Lions fumbled on the second play of the second half, and USM took advantage of the mistake to score again to stretch the lead to 8 points. The Lions quickly answered with a 64-yard drive, but the 2-point conversion failed, and the Southern defense, led by Art Gill, Bachman, and Stringfellow, pulled out the game.

USM was undefeated prior to its October 1 road game with Memphis State at Crump Stadium, but the season's toughest three games were just ahead. Vann was obviously worried about the Tigers, describing the 1966 squad as the "best team they have had in several seasons." Both defenses were superb in the Tigers' 6–0 win. Southern outplayed Memphis in almost every statistical category but could not manage to cross the goal line, and Sumrall missed three field goal attempts. After his third miss, midway through the third quarter, Memphis State took over on its 20-yard line. Led by quarterback Terry Padgett and aided by a Southerner holding penalty, the Tigers went the distance for the winning score. Southern had a late chance and took the ball to the Memphis State 19-yard line, only to have a fourth-down pass attempt intercepted. USM quarterback Terry McMillan, who had replaced Bynum, completed 14 passes for 174 yards, while Avery continued to lead a defense that limited the Tigers to 117 yards in total offense. "We thought our boys had their best team effort both on offense and defense against State but it wasn't our game to win," said Vann. "We had plenty of scoring opportunities but just could not get one across as the Memphis State defense rose to the occasion each time it was necessary."

The next week the Southerners faced Mississippi State in Starkville and once again outplayed their opponent statistically but could not find a way to win the game. The game started out badly for USM when State's Marcus Rhoden took the opening kickoff 95 yards for a touchdown. Undaunted, the Southerners responded with a long drive and a 34-yard Sumrall field goal to close the gap to 7–3. Devrow intercepted a State pass at the USM 14-yard line to begin the Southerners' only touchdown drive of the day. Quarterback Gary Bourgeois, playing for the first time in the 1966 season, guided the Raiders on an 86-yard second-quarter drive to put the Southerners ahead 9–7. Near the end of the first half, USM fumbled while attempting to run out the clock, and State recovered the ball and kicked a 34-yard field goal to go ahead 10–7 at the break. The score stood for the remainder of the game, although both teams had chances to put points on the board. Roussel recovered a fumble on State's 35-yard line with a little over five minutes left in the game, but USM returned the favor, fumbling the ball away on a controversial call. State managed a meager 85 yards rushing, while Devrow intercepted two passes and Dunaway remained a huge defensive weapon.

On October 15, USM met Ole Miss in Oxford, dominating the Rebels for three quarters and leading 7–0 with just over seven minutes left. The Vandals dominated the game, while the Raiders struggled: the USM defense repeatedly stifled the

Rebel offense, only to have to return to the field after a three-play offensive effort by the Southern offense. The defense even set up USM's first scoring effort when Craft blocked an Ole Miss punt in the first quarter and USM recovered the ball on the 4-yard line. The Southern offense was so anemic that day that Dunaway punted 17 times. With a little over seven minutes left, Ole Miss's Doug Cunningham ran a Dunaway kick back 57 yards to tie the game, and the Rebels later scored on a drive that began at their own 46 to win 14–7.

The October 29 home contest against the University of Richmond pitted the Southern defense against Larry Zunich, the reigning AP Back of the Week. Zunich had not seen a defense like the Vandals, which held him to 8 yards on 10 carries and limited the Spider team to -1 yard rushing. The USM offense came to life against Richmond. McCarthy scored the Southerners' first points on a 2-yard second-period run, and then the team broke loose in the third quarter. McClellan found end Clyde Dowd for a 62-yard touchdown on the opening drive of the second half, and on Southern's next possession, McCarthy outran Spider defenders 43 yards en route to his second touchdown to run the score to 20–0. Just before the end of the period, McClellan connected with tight end Stan Johnson on a 10-yard touchdown pass to give USM the 27–0 victory and end the three-game losing streak.

The offense continued to shine in the November 5 Homecoming game, scoring six touchdowns and racking up 447 total yards in a 42–6 win over an overmatched VMI team. The defense also did its part, allowing no passing yards and -4 yards on the ground in the first half. McClellan scored three touchdowns and threw a touchdown pass to halfback Robert Wells, while McCarthy added two touchdowns and led all rushers with 125 yards. After the game, Coach Vann complimented his players but had already turned his attention to the team's upcoming game against North Carolina State: "McClellan and McCarthy did outstanding jobs and the Vandals were again tough. However we will face the best offensive team we have met all season this Saturday in Norfolk and the Vandals will get their toughest test of the year. North Carolina State has been

Two legends of the game, Southern Miss head coach Pie Vann (left) and Ole Miss coach Johnny Vaught met after a game between the Southerners and the Rebels in the late 1960s.

coming fast since the season began and we will have to be at our best to stay with them." As Vann predicted, the game was tough, but with N.C. State holding a 6–0 lead with a little over three minutes remaining, McCarthy scored the tying touchdown and Sumrall kicked the extra point to give the Southerners the 7–6 victory.

The Southerners next game was in Greenville, North Carolina, on November 19 against East Carolina University in only the second meeting between the two schools. The Pirates presented the Vandals with an unusual challenge: "East Carolina is one of the few teams in the country that stuck with the single wing," Vann said. "They've modernized it. They split the ends some and run that off tackle with power. I'm trying to get ready for the single wing. And I don't know whether we're frightened of it or just getting so old we've forgotten about it." East Carolina scored first on a returned fumble recovery to make the score 7–0. USM tied the game early in the second period on McClellan's 19-yard pass to Dowd, but Sumrall missed the extra point. Devrow picked off a Pirate pass and returned the ball to the ECU 47-yard line, but the Southerners could not score, and the game went to the half with East Carolina holding a 7–6 lead. The Pirates threatened in the third quarter, but Avery once again came up big for the Southerners, blocking a field goal attempt. USM took advantage of the block and put together a fine 72-yard drive that ended with a 20-yard touchdown pass from McClellan to Jack McAlpin and gave the Southerners a 12–7 edge. Sumrall began the fourth period with a 26-yard field goal to increase the lead to 8 before McClellan and Dowd teamed up again for another touchdown that made the score 22–7. ECU responded with a touchdown to close the gap to 22–14, but John Johnson returned the ensuing kickoff 92 yards for a touchdown, and Bill Davis's interception return for another score made the final 35–14. As Vann predicted, ECU's offense had challenged his defense, amassing 241 total yards: in the coach's view, the Pirates "did an excellent job with their single wing and hurt us especially with their passing attack." But the Vandals had stiffened when it counted, and Southern Miss had notched its fourth win in a row to improve to 6–3.

On November 26, USM played the University of Alabama in Mobile for the season's final game. Ranked No. 3 by the AP, the Crimson Tide proved that they deserved their ranking by thrashing the Southerners 34–0 in front of 41,000 fans, the largest crowd ever to see a game at Ladd Stadium and the largest ever to see a USM contest. Led by quarterback Kenny (Snake) Stabler and end Ray Perkins, Bear Bryant's Tide gained 348 yards in total offense, jeopardizing USM's claim to having the nation's toughest defense. For all practical purposes the game was over by halftime, when Alabama held a 12–0 lead in part as a result of the play of Perkins, a native of Petal, Mississippi, who had caught 5 passes for 50 yards and a touchdown. USM, in contrast, had managed just 1 yard rushing, 12 yards passing, and one first down. Alabama added another 22 points in the second half, with Ed Morgan, a Hattiesburg native and later the city's mayor, playing an instrumental role in a couple of drives. Although the game ended in a 34–0 blowout, Bryant said, "We beat a fine, tough football team and don't you ever doubt it. Nobody has been able to run on Southern all year but we did get some good running on clutch downs and we thought we could throw on them, either deep or in front." The loss left USM with a respectable 6–4 season record "after playing the toughest schedule ever attempted by any USM team," according to the *Hattiesburg American*.

Prior to the 1967 season, the State Building Commission approved the construction of a new, privately financed dorm on the USM campus. Southern leased the $550,000 dorm from A. K. McInnis and Bobby Chain of Hattiesburg, with the school retaining the option to buy the facility, which would house about 160 athletes. Thad (Pie) Vann Hall officially opened in August 1967 and was dedicated to the coach on November 1, 1968.

1967 SEASON

Southern Miss opened the 1967 season on September 16 against the Citadel in Charleston, South Carolina, before a crowd of 11,407 that included more than 2,000 cadets who had come out to cheer on their Bulldogs. All the scoring took place early in the second period, with USM winning, 10–7, on a 41-yard field goal by Ihor (Mike) Kondrat with 5:43 to go in the quarter. USM had already scored a touchdown on the first play of the period when Johnson capped off a 62-yard drive with a 2-yard run. The Citadel took the kickoff and tied the game with a quick three-play drive. USM's next drive started at its own 28 and ended with the Kondrat field goal, which barely cleared the crossbar but nevertheless gave the Southerners the win as neither side could take advantage of further opportunities to score. The Southerners hurt themselves at times, committing nine penalties for 105 yards, but the Vandal defense continued to define the Southerners, holding the Bulldogs to 0 yards rushing and to 140 yards passing.

Steve Fore was the difference the following week at Faulkner Field against Southeastern Louisiana, reeling off two long punt returns, one for a touchdown, in USM's 20–7 win. After the Southerners took an early lead on Fore's first return, a dramatic 65-yard jaunt in which he broke several tackles, Southeastern came storming back to tie the score on its next possession. But USM answered with an 11-play, 66-yard drive that ended with Johnson scoring from 6 yards out. Fore's second return later gave the Southerners possession of the ball at the Lion 25-yard line, and six plays thereafter, quarterback Tommy Boutwell scored on a 1-yard sneak for USM's final touchdown.

USM's annual battle with Alabama took place on September 30 in Mobile. The Southerners trailed just 7–3 at halftime on Kondrat's 20-yard field goal, but the Tide recorded a third-quarter touchdown, a 2-point conversion, and a fourth-quarter field goal to win 25–3. USM was never really in the game offensively, but the Vandal defense managed to hold the Crimson Tide close. End Dennis Homan set a new Alabama record with 11 receptions for a total of 135 yards, breaking Perkins's mark of nine catches for 94 yards set the previous year against Ole Miss. The loss ran the Southerners' record to 2–1 on the young season.

USM rebounded to thump the University of Tampa 48–0 on October 7 at Faulkner Field. Tampa had the first scoring threat, but the Vandals held and subsequently settled down to allow the Spartans just 151 yards for the game. Johnson scored twice and speedster Tony Yelverton scored once to make the score 21–0 at the half, and Boutwell and Alan Isler scored in the third quarter to run the whitewashing to 34–0. The Southerners added two more touchdowns in the fourth quarter when Henry Quick ran the ball in from the 1-yard line and Rod Windham returned an interception 63 yards.

USM ran the gauntlet over its next three games, facing Mississippi State, Ole Miss, and Memphis State over a three-week span. On October 14, USM shocked Mississippi State's Homecoming crowd of 24,000 by recording USM's first victory against the Bulldogs in six tries dating back to 1935. USM struggled offensively in the first half, and State used a fumble recovery to take a 7–0 lead. After Kondrat missed on a field goal attempt, State took over on its 20-yard line with only four seconds left before the break. Incredibly, State fumbled, and USM took over with two seconds remaining. Vann elected to try for the touchdown instead of kicking the field goal, and Boutwell found Ronnie Channell in the end zone to tie the game at 7. The strange plays continued in the third quarter when USM punted and the ball went over the head of State's Tommy Garrison for what appeared to be a touchback. For some reason, however, Garrison moved into the end zone and touched the ball, and Wells alertly pounced on it. The officials discussed the play and ruled correctly that it was a Southern Miss touchdown. The Southerners kicked the extra point and had a 14–7 lead with about 12 minutes left in the period. State responded on the next possession with a brilliant 60-yard reverse that tied the score, but the Southerners put together a 10-play, 50-yard drive that resulted in the winning score at the beginning of the final period. In typical fashion, Southern kept the ball on the ground and scored on Yelverton's 14-yard scamper with just over 12 minutes left in the game. Vann proclaimed the game "the greatest squad victory in the history of football at Southern." Charley Shira, State's head coach, expressed his admiration for USM, saying, "You can't give a team like that a touchdown or two and win. Southern drove well for that winning touchdown and I can't say they didn't deserve it."

Now 4–1, the Southerners traveled to Oxford the following week to meet Ole Miss. USM's hopes of winning the mythical state championship appeared dashed as the Rebels took a 14–0 lead with two first-quarter touchdowns, one of them a 79-yard punt return by Tommy James. USM responded with a 76-yard scoring drive capped by Boutwell's 34-yard run to close the gap to 7, but Jimmy Keyes added a field goal to put the Rebels up 17–7 at the half. Late in the third period, backup quarterback Gary Rayburn led Southern Miss on a 45-yard, six-play drive, with McCarthy scoring to cut the lead to 17–14, but that was as close as the Southerners got. Keyes added two more field goals to ice the Rebels' 23–14 victory.

The Southerners' next foe was the Memphis State Tigers in a game to be played in Jackson. Southern totaled 19 first downs and gained 353 yards on offense but was held scoreless until late in the fourth period, when Rayburn threw the ball 42 yards to end Danny Haley, who made a beautiful over-the-shoulder catch between two Tiger defensive backs for the touchdown. The pass ended an impressive 99-yard scoring drive, but it was much too late as the Southerners lost 24–8.

USM hosted Richmond for Homecoming at Faulkner Field on November 4. The game was scoreless with 30 seconds remaining in the first half and Southern holding the ball on its own 40-yard line. A pass-interference call moved the ball to the Spider 34, and McMillan, the Southerners' third-string quarterback, ran the ball to the 25. McMillan then connected with Toby Vance at the 10, and Vance slashed through three defenders to the end zone with a couple of seconds left on the clock to give Southern a 7–0 lead. The Southerners took the second-half kickoff and put together an impressive 72-yard, 10-play drive that ended with McMillan's 14-yard touchdown pass to Channell. McCarthy added another touchdown to put the Southern Miss up 19–0, and the Spiders could add only a late touchdown to make the final score 19–7. The win improved the Southerners' record to 5–3.

USM traveled to Shreveport on Thanksgiving Day to play Louisiana Tech, a team coached by former Southern standout and assistant coach Maxie Lambright. The Southerners tallied 58 points, the team's highest scoring effort since 1951, when hapless Northwestern Louisiana had yielded 76 to the team from Hattiesburg. Bradshaw, the Tech quarterback, threw seven interceptions, four of them to Larry Ussery, who returned two of the balls for touchdowns. Fore again scored on a punt runback, this one for 72-yards, and Johnson, Boutwell, Channell, Vance, McMillan, and Yelverton all crossed the goal line for the Southerners. The 58–7 victory over Louisiana Tech gave Southern a 6–3 mark on the season.

1968 SEASON

USM won its September 21 season opener by defeating Southeastern Louisiana 27–15 in Hammond. Boutwell and Frank Johnston scored touchdowns in the first period to put the Southerners up 14–0, but the Lions responded with a 75-yard drive to cut the lead to 14–7. Boutwell then found Haley for a 44-yard reception that set up Johnston's second score as USM went up 21–7. The Lions again closed the gap after Boutwell threw an interception that led to a 45-yard, six-play scoring drive, but Boutwell then put the game out of reach with a third-quarter touchdown.

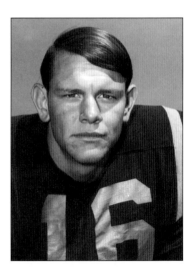

Quarterback Tommy Boutwell (1967–1968) passed for 1,583 yards and eight touchdowns during the 1968 season.

Quarterbacks for the 1968 season: (left to right) Terry McMillan, Gary Rayburn, Tommy Boutwell, Tommy Davis, Danny Palmer. Boutwell, a senior, earned the starting job.

USM's next opponent was Alabama. Of his team's performance, Vann said, "We played three fine quarters of football and let inconsistencies hurt us badly in the fourth period." Morgan scored from 9 yards out to put the Tide up 7–0 at the end of the first period, but the Southerners came back with a fury, putting together a 68-yard, six-play drive to tie the game. Boutwell-to-Haley passes accounted for 46 of the yards, and the touchdown came on fourth-and-goal from the 1-yard line with only 11 seconds left in the half when Boutwell found Vance open in the end zone. The second half began well for Southern as safety Doug Rouse intercepted a Scott Hunter

THE DECADE OF DEFENSE [125]

pass at the USM 18-yard line and the Southern offense took the ball down the field to score, with Larry Moulton doing the honors and giving the Southerners a 14–7 lead as the third period ended. But the final quarter belonged to the Tide. Bryant's troops kicked a field goal and added an outstanding 34-yard touchdown pass from Hunter to George Ranager that gave Alabama the 17–14 victory. In an unusual display of agitation, Vann publicly questioned "a couple of calls by the officials that we couldn't explain"—a pass-interference call that set up the field goal and some holding penalties.

USM, according to the *Hattiesburg American* "smarting from the loss to Alabama and wanting to win before the crowd at [the season's] first home game," put on an incredible display of offense against East Carolina on October 5, easily defeating the Pirates 65–0 in front of more than 12,500 spectators. The offense scored the first four times it had the ball and gained a total of 591 yards in offense. The Southern defense performed equally well, limiting the Pirates to no yards rushing, no first downs, and only 12 yards passing. Boutwell scored twice and threw a touchdown pass to Channell, and Johnson, Moulton, Tommy Davis, and Russell Miles ran for touchdowns. Yelverton scored on passes from McMillan and Miles, and John Hale kicked a field goal to round out the scoring.

On October 21, the Southerners took their 2–1 record to Starkville, where they would once again be Mississippi State's Homecoming foe. The Southerners spoiled the day for the 22,000 in attendance, routing the Bulldogs 47–14 and hammering home the point that USM had a solid football program. Moulton began the USM scoring blitz by taking a screen pass 55 yards for a first-quarter score. Hale added a 21-yard field goal to make the score 10–0 after one quarter. McMillan added another score to make the lead 17–0 before State got on the board when Tommy Pharr found Buddy Newson on a 58-yard pass early in the second quarter. Hale's second field goal of the day extended the USM lead to 20–7 at halftime, and Boutwell ran for two more touchdowns and threw for a third before the Bulldogs again found the end zone. Ussery, who had returned two interceptions for touchdowns in the 1967 Louisiana Tech game, ran back another pickoff for the Southerners' final score.

Playing Ole Miss on October 19 in Oxford, USM led 7–0 after three quarters, only to see the Rebels launch a couple of big plays and score three times in the fourth quarter. Boutwell and Vance combined for a first-quarter touchdown, and the lead held until a little over eight minutes remained in the game. First, Archie Manning scored on a 3-yard run to tie the game. Then, after the teams exchanged fumbles, Manning found Vernon Studdard for a 49-yard scoring bomb with only 4:41 left to give the Rebels their first lead. On USM's next possession, Danny Hooker intercepted a Boutwell pass on the Ole Miss 38-yard line and returned the ball for a touchdown and a 14-point lead. The Southerners refused to quit and quickly marched 76 yards down the field for a touchdown that cut the Rebel edge to 21–14 with 1:21 left to go, but the Rebels ran out the clock. A somber Vann blamed himself: "I would just like to let it go with the fact that [Ole Miss Coach Johnny] Vaught just out-coached me in that final quarter," Vann lamented after the loss.

Against Memphis State on October 26 in Memphis, the USM players made what the *Hattiesburg American* termed "crucial mistakes" that helped the Tigers defeat the Southerners 29–7. The Southern squad outperformed Memphis State in every statistical category, but four interceptions and four fumbles killed USM's chances. To make matters worse, USM was called for 10 penalties that cost the team almost 100 yards. The Southerners took a 7–0 lead by capitalizing on Doug Rouse's interception at the Memphis State 13-yard line, but the Tigers countered with 16 straight points before the half and 13 more after the break. Vann told the *American* that "both the players and coaches were bitterly disappointed over losing this one," but despite the team's sloppy performance, he commended the play of Bob Shepard, Kondrat, Hank Autry, Johnston, Lionel Fayard, Ussery, Mike Battles, Wayne Adkison, and Tommy Applewhite.

Vann had no excuses after the Southerners lost to Terry Bradshaw's Louisiana Tech team in front of more than 15,000 fans on November 2 at Faulkner Field. The Southerners' third consecutive loss left them with a 3–4 record on the season. As in the Memphis State game, USM scored first, only to see Bradshaw, whom Vann called "the best quarterback we will face this season," lead the Bulldogs to three straight touchdowns and a 21–7 lead early in the second quarter. USM responded by going 63 yards to close the gap to 21–14 at the half. Tech put up another touchdown during the fourth quarter to lead 27–14 with just under nine minutes left in the game, and Southern's next drive ended with a fumble at the Tech 2-yard line. A late Boutwell-to-Haley touchdown pass made the final score 27–20. Vann was dejected by his team's unfamiliar poor performance: "They out-blocked and out-tackled us and just seemed to want the game more than we did," the coach said. "I just can't say enough about how badly I feel. We have let the student body and other supporters down."

On November 9, the Southerners reached a new low when San Diego State crushed the USM squad 68–7 in San Diego. The game began poorly, with USM fumbling the opening kickoff and watching an Aztec lineman return the ball 28 yards for the score, but the Southerners' fortunes brightened when Boutwell led USM to a touchdown. Southern Miss trailed by only 6 points at the half. Then came the deluge. In the worst performance ever turned in by one of Vann's teams, the Southern defense surrendered 55 second-half points. "Let me say we were not only beaten but stunned and embarrassed as well," Vann reflected. "San Diego State has a real fine club, as good as any we have played, at least they were against us."

The next week was USM's Homecoming game against Richmond, a team that had never beaten the Southerners. But Richmond's quarterback, Buster O'Brien, completed 21 of 34 passes for a Southern Conference–record 366 yards in a 33–7 win that broke the Spiders' six-game losing streak against USM and constituted the Southerners' fifth straight loss. At 3–6 the Southerners were assured of their first losing campaign since 1934; it was Vann's first losing season as the Southerners' skipper. The Spiders jumped out to a 16–0 lead at the half, surrendered a touchdown on USM's opening possession of the second half, but victimized what the *Hattiesburg American* described as USM's "porous pass defense" for 17 more points before the final gun sounded.

Following the Richmond game, Vann requested permission to retire from active coaching at the conclusion of the season. USM President William D. McCain and Athletic Director Reed Green granted Vann's request "with regrets" and announced that they would ask the Board of Trustees of State Institutions of Higher Learning that Vann be retained in athletic public relations and recruiting for the duration of his contract. Concerning Vann's successor as head coach, Green said, "Coach Vann's request came as a shocking surprise and, naturally, we have not given any consideration to the matter of naming a successor. This will require a lot of thought and deliberation but you can rest assured it will be done with the utmost expediency." McCain and Green also revealed that Vann had previously asked to be relieved of active coaching duties in 1964, but according to Green, "Dr. McCain and I virtually talked Coach Vann out of leaving the field for another post until his retirement had reached its maximum."

The team still had to prepare for the final game of the season, a November 23 road contest against the University of Tampa, a team noted for its passing attack. Inspired by the impending departure of their longtime coach, who followed his 19 senior captains onto the field for the coin toss, the Southerners produced a 21–7 win over the seventh-ranked Spartans. USM's first score came on an 80-yard, 18-play drive engineered by Boutwell and climaxed by Moulton's 3-yard run. Tampa attempted an onside kick to begin the second half, but USM recovered on its own 43-yard line and scored on Boutwell's 1-yard sneak a few plays later to take a 14–0 lead. The Southerners put the game out of reach when Mike Harris intercepted a Jim Del Faizo pass at the Spartan 28 and returned the ball to the 3-yard line and Moulton scored on the next play and Boutwell ran in the 2-point conversion. Tampa put together a 77-yard scoring drive, but the day belonged to the Southerners and to Coach Vann.

Several of Vann's former players visited with him in the dressing room before and after the game and stayed around to celebrate his 139th career victory. At game's end, Vann's players carried him across the field on their shoulders, a trek that seemed, at least to those traveling on the long-awaited victory trip home, to consume as much time as the chartered airplane ride to the Hattiesburg airport, during which the passengers serenaded Vann with several choruses of "For He's a Jolly Good Fellow." When the team disembarked at midnight, they found that a sizable crowd of well-wishers had gathered to congratulate the legendary coach and his team.

On November 30, 1968, USM announced that former Southern Miss assistant football coach Roland Dale, who was completing his ninth season as an assistant at Ole Miss, his alma mater, had signed a four-year contract to return to Southern as head football coach. Green lauded Dale's "excellent record in high school and junior college ranks, as an assistant on three major college staffs, and as a professional," and stated, "I am positive he will do an outstanding job for us. I welcome his return to Southern." Dale returned the kind words, announcing, "It is a real challenge to follow Coach Vann and the outstanding record he has made." But, he continued, "I look forward with enthusiasm to joining the University and being a part of the amazing growth it has enjoyed under President McCain." Just three weeks later, however, on December 20, Green announced that Dale had asked to be released from the commitment. "This came as a surprise to us but certainly we won't try to alter his decision," Green said.

On January 9, 1969, McCain and Green announced that P. W. (Bear) Underwood, a former star player and assistant coach for the Southerners who had been an assistant at the University of Tennessee for the preceding two seasons, would become USM's new head football coach. "We are real pleased that Coach Underwood accepted the assignment as head football coach," Green said. "I've never known a more dedicated football man and I have never seen one more enthusiastic and eager than he is." Tennessee Coach Doug Dickey said that he hated to lose Underwood and wished him well in his new job: "He did an outstanding job for us, working with our linebackers and defensive ends. He was a valuable member of our staff and I believe he will make a good head coach." The Southern faithful were ecstatic about Underwood's selection. The Bear had a stellar reputation as a coach, and better still, he was one of USM's own.

The 1968 season had had two separate parts. The team that performed well early in the year against Mississippi State and Alabama was not the same squad that lost five straight. Despite the disappointing year, Pie Vann's retirement closed the book on the most successful era in USM football history. Over his 20-year tenure as head coach, Vann's teams had compiled a record of 139–59–2, winning 70 percent of their games. Very few coaches of any era at any institution have garnered such a winning percentage, especially while playing the types of formidable schedules that the Southerners faced. Green had built the foundation for USM football, and Vann had lifted the program to national respectability. No longer simply happy to schedule SEC opponents, USM expected to beat them.

1969 SEASON

In addition to the new coach, USM's 1969 squad faced another, more important, change: African American players. Following McCain's leadership, the school had integrated peacefully in September 1965, when a letter from the president to the school's students, faculty, and staff appeared in the *Student Printz*:

> Ladies and Gentlemen:
> Two Negro students have been admitted to this institution. These students will be participating in the various orientation activities on campus beginning Monday, September 6, 1965.

It is expected that all personnel connected with the University will go about their affairs in a business as usual manner. We are certain that the fine conduct and spirit of our people will manifest itself during these times of change and that the University community will continue to show that we are the biggest and the best.

Southern Miss had integrated without incident, but four years later, the football team remained all-white. Taking over the reins, however, Underwood realized that to compete on the national scene, the Southerners could no longer refuse to recruit African American athletes. And following the precedent set by the integration of the university as a whole, the integration of Southern Miss football occurred quite smoothly.

The first African American football player who signed with Southern Miss was Manuel Sullivan, a 6-foot-4, 200-pound end from Ocean Springs, Mississippi, who participated on the 1969 freshman squad but transferred to historically black Jackson State prior to the start of the 1970 season. Underwood's 1970 recruiting class included two African Americans, defensive back Eugene Bird of Kingston, Tennessee, and Willie Heidelburg, a 5-foot-6, 147-pound halfback from Purvis, Mississippi. Because freshmen were not eligible to play varsity football, Bird played on USM's freshman squad in 1970. Heidelburg had spent the two previous seasons at Pearl River Junior College in Poplarville, where he had starred for former Southern standout J. C. Arban. As a junior-college transfer, Heidelburg, now a member of the M-Club Alumni Association Sports Hall of Fame, was eligible to play on the USM varsity. On September 12, 1970, he became the first African American to play for the Southerners. He went on to play a key role in several victories during his two years with the team.

The Underwood era began on a positive note on September 20, 1969, when, according to the *Hattiesburg American*, a "vastly improved defense and a spotty offense" combined to defeat Southeastern Louisiana 14–6 before a crowd of 12,000 at Faulkner Field. After a Lion fumble on a first-

P. W. Underwood took over as head coach at Southern Miss in 1969. He returned to his alma mater from the University of Tennessee, where he was an assistant coach.

THE DECADE OF DEFENSE

period punt return, Southern was in business on the Lions 20-yard line. Quarterback Danny Palmer connected with end Billy Mikel, who outjumped two defenders in the end zone for the first touchdown. USM's second score came after Arnold Thomas returned a punt 39 yards to the Lions 24-yard line. Palmer completed a pass to Fayard that took the ball to the 1, and Moulton carried the ball into the end zone to put the Southerners up 14–0. Southeastern Louisiana scored late in the fourth quarter to make it 14–6. Coach Underwood praised the efforts of Palmer, who completed 11 of 22 passes for 119 yards, and of Southern defenders Radell Key and Henry Quick.

Unfortunately for USM, however, the win over the Lions did not prove to be a harbinger of good things. The vicious defense that had defined Southern Miss in the 1960s was nonexistent in the team's next four games, when Alabama, Idaho, Mississippi State, and Ole Miss combined to score 197 points against Underwood's charges while the offense managed only 62 points.

The losing skid started on September 27 in Tuscaloosa against a very good Alabama team that whipped Southern Miss 63–14. Behind quarterbacks Scott Hunter, Neb Hayden, and Benny Rippetoe, the Tide scored on nine out of their ten possessions. "Alabama didn't make any mistakes and we didn't produce any," Underwood summarized after the game, while Alabama's Bryant called his team's effort "the best offense I've seen since we played Nebraska in the 1967 Sugar Bowl." "We were whipped by a real good football team," Underwood stated, "they brought it to us and whipped us physically."

USM supporters hoped that their team would get back on the winning track the following week at Ladd Stadium in Mobile against the Idaho Vandals, but another night of porous defense combined with the throwing ability of Vandal quarterback Steve Olson to produce another defeat for Underwood's team. Olsen completed 33 passes in 57 attempts for 363 yards and three touchdowns as the Vandals shocked USM 31–21. Wide receiver Jerry Hendren caught 17 balls for 203 yards. Trailing 17–7 at the half, with their only score coming on Moulton's 43-yard jaunt, the Southerners surrendered two more touchdowns to dig themselves a 31–7 hole. The USM offense finally started to show some life when Palmer found Mikel for a 49-yard scoring pass that closed the gap to 31–14. After the Southern defense stopped the Vandals on the USM 7, Palmer threw the ball all over the field en route to a 93-yard drive, finishing with a 6-yard touchdown pass to Win Foshee that brought the Southerners to within 10. Hoping to continue the comeback on the team's next drive, Palmer threw an interception on the Idaho 4-yard line, one of three picks recorded by the Idaho defense, which also forced four fumbles.

The defensive woes continued on October 11 as Southern lost 34–20 to Mississippi State in Starkville. Like USM's previous opponents, State took advantage of the Southern secondary, as All-SEC quarterback Tommy Pharr completed 18 passes for 250 yards and three touchdowns. State led 7–0 at the half and scored two more touchdowns in the third period to go up 20–0 before Palmer got hurt. His replacement, Rick Donegan, engineered two late scoring drives, completing 11 passes for 144 yards, although the *Hattiesburg American* reported that the Southern offense was hampered by "illegal procedure penalties and blocking breakdowns" throughout the day. State added two more touchdowns, including one on Dickie Carpenter's 44-yard return of a Donegan interception, before Moulton closed out the scoring for the Southerners.

Things got even worse for the Southerners in Oxford on October 18, when Ole Miss crushed USM 69–7. USM's misfortunes included five interceptions, two lost fumbles, and the loss of Donegan with an injury. The Rebels took a 16–0 lead before Thomas scored on a 76-yard punt return to get the Southerners on the board, but USM trailed 29–7 at the half despite the fact that Ole Miss Coach Johnny Vaught had already pulled his starters in his belief that the "Rebels had a comfortable lead." In the *Hattiesburg American*'s view, USM "ran out of steam and was visibly exhausted, unable to hold the Rebels' second and third stringers" during the second-half scoring barrage. The Southerners' record stood at a dismal 1–4.

Underwood refused to let his troops quit, and the team ended the season with four wins in its last five games. In the October 25 Homecoming game against the favored University of Richmond, the Southerners pulled out a 31–28 victory. Richmond took a first-quarter 7–0 lead on a 40-yard touchdown pass from Charlie Richards to Walker Gillette, but the Southern offense charged back with 31 unanswered points. The first touchdown came on Donegan's pass to Mikel, and USM grabbed the lead on Moulton's 5-yard run before closing out the first-half scoring with Hale's 49-yard field goal for a 17–7 edge. Moulton added two more touchdowns, on a 4-yard run and a 27-yard screen pass, to give Southern Miss an apparently insurmountable 31–7 lead. The Spiders took to the air in the final quarter, however, scoring three late touchdowns to close the gap to 31–28 before time ran out. Gillette had a solid day for the visitors, catching 7 balls for 161 yards, and Jim Livesay caught another six of Richards's passes for 101 yards. Hattiesburg native Donegan returned from his injury to complete 18 of 32 passes for 259 yards.

The USM offense provided some more fireworks against Lambright's Louisiana Tech team on November 1 in Ruston. Donegan once again excelled as the Southerners came from behind to win 24–23 when Hale kicked a 36-yard field goal with 26 seconds remaining. A patchwork defense held Tech's superstar quarterback, Terry Bradshaw, in check, limiting him to 21 completions in 46 attempts for 278 yards and one interception. The Southerners' record stood at 3–4, and they had to win their remaining three games to salvage a winning season.

USM's next game was their annual contest against Memphis State. The Tigers dominated the November 8 game in Memphis, scoring 37 points before the Southerners managed their only touchdown of the day. The Southern Miss offense moved the football but made mistakes that prevented the team from scoring. Donegan had a good day, completing 21 of 31 passes for 163 yards, but was overshadowed by his Memphis State counterparts. Running the option, the Tiger quarterbacks shone, much to the dismay of Underwood, who, according to the *Hattiesburg American,* showed "extreme displeasure with the defense as it was cut apart by the Memphis State offensive line, opening the holes for the quarterbacks." The 37–7 win gave Memphis an 11–10 edge in the series and meant that the Southerners needed to win both of their final games to break even on the year.

The next game, a November 22 contest with East Carolina in Greenville, North Carolina, was one of the season's most exciting. Rayburn, starting his first game at quarterback for the Southerners since the season opener, threw touchdown passes to Mikel and Fayard to give the Southerners a 14–0 lead at halftime. The defense allowed Pirate fullback Butch Colson to amass 171 yards rushing but stiffened when the chips were down. ECU scored early in the third period when Colson fumbled on the goal line and the ball bounced into the end zone, where receiver Dwight Flanagan recovered for the touchdown. Trailing 14–7, the Pirates began a drive with a little over four minutes left but appeared to have been stopped when Southern's defense knocked down a fourth-and-15 pass from the USM 32-yard line. The officials called pass interference, however, giving the Pirates new life with 30 seconds remaining. First- and second-down passes fell incomplete, and on third down ECU's quarterback overthrew a wide-open receiver in the end zone. On fourth down, ECU's quarterback could not find an open receiver and ran the ball into the middle of the line, ending the game and allowing Southern to emerge with the 14–7 win.

The season ended on November 29 at Faulkner Field with a contest against West Texas State, led by running back Duane Thomas and tailback Olan Thompson. Despite being riddled with injuries, the Southern defense played well. After giving up a 71-yard pass that put the ball on the Southern 5-yard line, the defense held and forced the Buffaloes to settle for a field goal and a 3–0 lead. USM answered with a field goal of its own to knot the score at 3. In the third period, the Buffaloes intercepted a Donegan pass and subsequently scored on a quarterback sneak, but the extra point failed. West Texas threatened a couple more times during the period, but the Southern defense refused to yield. With less than two minutes left in the game and the ball on the USM 20-yard line, Donegan began an impressive seven-play drive, using five sideline passes and throwing the ball out of bounds to stop the clock as he led the team 80 yards to tie the game. Mikel scored the touchdown on a 27-yard pass, snatching "the ball from the hands of two West Texas State defenders," in the words of the *Hattiesburg American.* Hale then booted the extra point to give USM the 10–9 victory over the stunned Buffaloes. The *American* described the win as a "come-from-behind, one-point, last gasp victory . . . just short of being miraculous." Mikel's catch gave him nine touchdown receptions for the season, tying him with Cliff Coggin

THE DECADE OF DEFENSE [133]

for the USM record. Donegan, who completed 21 of 32 passes for 247 yards, tied a USM record with 13 passing first downs. The Southern defense checked the vaunted West Texas running attack, permitting Thomas only 41 yards rushing. The East Carolina and West Texas games represented a solid ending to the 5–5 season. Southern Miss football during the 1960s will be remembered for its defense, which consistently ranked highly in numerous categories. Led by that defense, Southern Miss football continued in its quest for national recognition and respectability, first under longtime coach Pie Vann and later under former Southern star Bear Underwood. During the 1970s, the school's football team finally began to achieve some of the goals for which it had been striving.

THE BEAR, BOBBY, THE EAGLES, AND ROBERTS STADIUM
1970–1979

Few people could have forecast the changes that would occur in football at the University of Southern Mississippi over the next ten years, as Coaches P. W. Underwood and Bobby Collins helped to elevate the program to new heights. In addition, the dream of a new stadium became a reality, and the team changed its longtime nickname from the Southerners to the Golden Eagles.

In April 1970, a firm of consulting engineers presented university officials with a stadium feasibility study. The 54-page document concluded that Faulkner Field had outlived its usefulness and looked at alternatives, providing suggestions on such matters as location, financing, and size. The engineers examined the possibility of enlarging Faulkner Field but agreed that with the growth of the university thereby providing easy stadium access for both opposing teams and spectators. Given USM's location in the most populated area of Mississippi and its proximity to the state's largest city, Jackson, the study recommended that the stadium initially be constructed to hold 40,000 fans, with foundations laid to accommodate expansion to 65,000 if a larger facility subsequently became necessary. The stadium would also include Astroturf, lights for night games, and a three-story press box with television and radio booths as well as booths for visiting dignitaries. The firm's engineers felt confident that the stadium would draw the big-name teams needed to catapult Southern's football program to the major-college status it deserved. USM Athletic Director Reed Green agreed "wholeheartedly and enthusiastically" with the study and planned to move quickly in that direction, and President William D. McCain concurred.

Halfback (Wee) Willie Heidelburg became the first African American to play on the varsity level for Southern Miss in 1970. He scored two touchdowns against Ole Miss in USM's 30–14 win over No. 4 Ole Miss that year.

and with increasing parking problems, revamping the old stadium would be unsuitable. Taking various factors into account, the engineers recommended the construction of a new stadium on a site located north of the university golf course and west of the I-59–Highway 49 intersection. The university already owned the land, thus eliminating the possibility that acquiring it would be prohibitively expensive, and the location was convenient to the major highways leading into Hattiesburg,

1970 SEASON

Coach Underwood and the Southerners opened the season on September 12 on the road against Southwestern Louisiana, defeating the Ragin' Cajuns 16–14. Southern scored the only points of the first half when kicker Ray Guy nailed a 24-yard field goal early in the first quarter. Southwestern Louisiana threatened to score midway through the second quarter, but Southern Miss linebacker Bill Davis, back after a two-year stint in the army, blocked a 36-yard field goal attempt. Guy's 31-yard field goal late in the third quarter made the score 6–0, and Southwestern Louisiana

Ray Guy was one of the most versatile players in Southern Miss history. In addition to establishing himself as one of the nation's finest punters and kickers, he was also one of the country's premier defensive backs.

fumbled three plays after the ensuing kickoff, leading to Larry Moulton's 18-yard touchdown run and a 13–0 USM lead. A Davis interception just before the end of the third quarter set up Guy's third field goal of the day, a 33-yarder, to put the Southerners up by 16 before Southwestern Louisiana rallied for a pair of fourth-quarter touchdowns. With 5:12 to go, the defense recorded a game-saving stop on fourth-and-goal from the Southern 1-yard line to preserve the win.

At Auburn on September 19, Southern Miss jumped out to an early 7–0 lead on Moulton's 20-yard touchdown run, but three touchdown passes by quarterback Pat Sullivan, who went on to win the 1971 Heisman Trophy, put Auburn up 19–7 at halftime, and the Tigers posted a 33–14 victory. Although the Southern offense rolled up 333 yards, the War Eagles had 456 to drop the Southerners to 1–1 on the year.

Playing at home at Faulkner Field for the first time September 26, Southern Miss defeated the University of Texas–Arlington 26–20. With the game tied at 20 after a Maverick touchdown pass with 6:37 to go, the Southern defense made a big play. After a Guy punt was downed on the 9-yard line, USM recovered a Texas–Arlington fumble on their 7-yard line. On the next play, quarterback Rick Donegan connected with Wayne Hatcher for the touchdown that gave the Southerners the win.

The Southerners hosted the Richmond Spiders on October 3 and improved to 3–1 with the 43–21 victory. Southern Miss jumped to a 29–14 halftime lead thanks to a pair of touchdown runs by Moulton—one for 61 yards—and touchdown passes from Donegan and quarterback Buddy Palazzo. "Our kids got after them real good physically," Underwood said after the game. "We made Richmond make some mistakes and of

THE BEAR, BOBBY, THE EAGLES, AND ROBERTS STADIUM

course we made some ourselves. Our young secondary shows improvement each week and did an overall good job against Richmond, but inexperience caused them to get beat a couple of times." The Southerner defense limited the Spiders to just 11 first downs and 255 yards and had four takeaways.

At San Diego State on October 10, the Southerners ran into one of the country's most explosive teams. The Aztecs led 27–14 at halftime and went on to win 41–14 behind the passing of quarterback Brian Sipe, who completed 26 of 46 passes for 318 yards and four touchdowns. The USM defense had three interceptions but nevertheless gave up 514 yards of total offense.

Off to an unremarkable 3–2 start, the Southerners traveled to Oxford on October 17 to face No. 4 Ole Miss and quarterback Archie Manning, a Heisman Trophy candidate. The Rebels were prohibitive favorites and started the game true to form with a 7–0 lead. Southern tied the game on a 44-yard touchdown run by fullback Bill Foley, but the Rebels regained the lead on a touchdown pass from Manning to tailback Randy Reed. Driving early in the second quarter, the Southerners had the ball on fourth-and-2 at the Rebel 11-yard line. Turning down the chance for a short field goal, Underwood called for a reverse by reserve tailback Willie Heidelburg, who raced around right end to tie the game. Guy's 47-yard field goal just before halftime gave the Southerners a 17–14 lead at the break. Early in the second half, Southern again drove to the Rebel 11-yard line, and Underwood again called for a Heidelburg reverse. The result was the same, and Southern held a

P. W. Underwood received national attention for leading Southern Miss to the 1970 victory over Ole Miss.

23–14 lead after Guy missed the extra-point kick. A few minutes later, Gerry Saggus returned a Rebel punt 60 yards for a touchdown, giving Southern a 30–14 lead with 5:45 left in the third quarter. Late in the period, an impressive drive had moved the Rebels to the Southern 1-yard line, where they faced fourth-and-goal. Manning ran left, but end Hugh Eggersman was looking for the Ole Miss quarterback all the way. Eggersman fought through two blockers and then hit Manning high on the shoulder pads, stopping him before he reached the end zone. And that was all she wrote: the Southerners had one of the biggest upsets of the young college football season.

THE BEAR, BOBBY, THE EAGLES, AND ROBERTS STADIUM

Three thousand fans were waiting for the Southerners when they arrived at Vann Hall later that night, and the victory celebration lasted long into the morning hours. Eggersman was named the Associated Press (AP) and United Press International (UPI) National Lineman of the Week for his part in the victory. The AP singled out Donegan, Heidelburg, and defensive back Craig Logan for their play, and UPI named Underwood the National Coach of the Week. Hattiesburg Mayor Paul Grady proclaimed the following week "Big Gold Week," named Underwood honorary mayor, and handed over the keys to the city to linebacker Bill Davis, Donegan, and Heidelburg. Governor John Bell Williams declared Hattiesburg to be the 1970 football capital of Mississippi, adding fuel to the ongoing discussion of the new USM football facility.

The bubble burst a week later when Mississippi State steamrolled the Southerners 51–15 in Starkville. Southern could manage only 7 net yards rushing and watched helplessly as the Bulldogs took a 27–7 halftime lead. "Mistakes played a major role in the lopsided score. When you play like that you have a hard time winning," reflected Underwood. "We made a lot of mistakes and State was always around to capitalize on them." The loss dropped the Southerners to 4–3 on the year.

A 33–0 Halloween shutout on the road at the hands of the Memphis State Tigers followed as the Southerner offense again struggled, managing only 258 yards. Memphis State was hitting on all cylinders, amassing 301 yards on the ground and 560 yards total. Now 4–4 on the year and losers of two straight games, the Southerners were searching for answers. Said a disappointed Underwood after the game, "We made more mistakes than I thought we would. We didn't make any mistakes against Ole Miss, but you can't get that kind of game out of your kids every week. The people we have played the last two weeks have been able to get up since we won that Ole Miss game. It's made things a lot tougher."

No answers were forthcoming during the following week's Homecoming game against Louisiana Tech, during which the Southern offense managed only 24 yards rushing and 142 total yards. With the offense hurting and the defense seemingly on the field all day long, the Bulldogs jumped out to a 21–0 halftime lead and never looked back in the 27–6 victory.

Trying to snap a three-game losing streak, the Southerners went to Canyon, Texas, on November 21 to meet West Texas State. Although the offense moved the ball much better than in the past few weeks, USM could manage only a 30-yard Guy field goal to trail 7–3 at halftime. After a scoreless third quarter, West Texas State scored midway through the fourth quarter to move ahead 14–3. The Southerners scored on Donegan's 10-yard pass to Steve Broussard with 2:45 left, and the 2-point conversion cut the lead to 14–11, but Southern Miss could get no closer.

The Southerners ended the season on a high note with an impressive 53–31 win over Trinity at Faulkner Field. Donegan completed 23 of 38 passes for 277 yards and three touchdowns as the offense piled up 448 yards. Trailing after the first quarter, the Southerners rallied to take a 26–21 lead at halftime. A third-quarter touchdown on a pass from Donegan to Hatcher made the score 32–21 before Southern Miss blew the game open with three unanswered touchdowns over the first eight minutes of the fourth quarter. The victory gave the Southerners a 5–6 record for the season.

With 685 yards, Moulton finished as the team's leading rusher for the second straight year, while Donegan again led the team in passing, completing 165 of 311 passes for 1,593 yards and eight touchdowns. Billy Mikel led the team in receiving, catching 26 balls for 299 yards and a touchdown. In his first year on the Southern Miss varsity, Guy kicked 59 punts for a school-record 45.3-yard average. Eggersman, Guy, and linebacker Dicky Surace were named to the All–South Independent team as well as honorable mention All-America.

In March 1971 the Mississippi State Legislature began to consider USM's proposal for a new football stadium. On March 30 President McCain announced that the legislature's $2 million construction appropriation for USM would be used for a football facility, but in McCain's words, "any final decision on the exact use of these funds will still have to come from Jackson." He continued, "The next step in determining the exact use of this money will now be with the State Building Commission. As this is primarily an engineering job I feel the Commission will appoint an engineering firm to study the situation to make recommendations and build the facility." Furthermore, "Only after such a study by qualified persons can any reasonable decision be made. Because this is an engineering problem I do not feel personally qualified to make any decisions without expert advice." Finally, the president concluded, "we are still optimistic about getting a new stadium." The *Hattiesburg American* expressed surprise at McCain's statement, which the newspaper took to indicate that after several months of campaigning for a new stadium, university officials were once again considering renovating Faulkner Field. The newspaper urged that plans for the new stadium proceed as outlined in the April 1970 report since the reasons for not modifying Faulkner remained valid. The editorial continued,

> We believe a long-range view is required. Whatever is built now is going to be there for many decades to come. If second best is accepted now, then that will be it down through the years while the University, the city, and the area continue to grow. There won't be any second chances.
>
> Once the stadium is under construction, we believe the Legislature will appropriate funds in the future for its completion without the kind of fight that has been required to get it started.

The project remained in limbo until early 1973, caught in political red tape as the university and legislature considered the best course of action.

1971 SEASON

The Southerners opened the 1971 season on September 11 at Ladd Memorial Stadium in Mobile against the Florida State Seminoles, falling by a score of 24–9. Southern got off to a good start when Bill Foley raced 34 yards for a touchdown late in the opening quarter, but FSU came back with 17 second-quarter points to take a lead it never gave up. Doyle Orange rushed for 100 yards on 16 carries for the Southerners, but the offense could manage only 252 yards total.

The season's second game occurred at Tuscaloosa's Denny Stadium on September 18, with No. 9 Alabama rolling to a 42–6 victory over USM. The Crimson Tide rushed for 276 yards and had 469 yards in total offense, while the Southerners struggled to move the ball all day and managed only 147 yards. "We didn't make the big mistakes and I don't think the score should have been so one-sided," Underwood said. "Our kids keep working and improving and they have got to get better."

Desperately in need of a victory, the Southerners hosted San Diego State in Jackson and won 10–0 on September 25, thereby gaining some revenge for the previous season's defeat by the Aztecs. The Southern defense held SDSU to just 19 yards rushing and 158 yards passing. Craig Logan and Kyle Gantt each had interceptions, while Donegan scored the game's only touchdown on a third-quarter quarterback sneak and Guy added a 22-yard field goal early in the fourth quarter. The Aztecs threatened late, driving to the Southern 3-yard line, but on fourth down, defensive end Fred Cook pressured Brian Sipe, the San Diego State quarterback, and Eugene Bird broke up the pass in the end zone. The victory put the Southerners' record at 1–2. "We played with

Defensive back Eugene Bird (1971–1973) was one of the defensive standouts for Coach P. W. Underwood in the early 1970s.

dedication tonight. We made the maximum effort. On any given day we can whip anybody. This was our day," Underwood shouted in the locker room.

After a week off, the Southerners traveled to face No. 4 Auburn on October 9, playing well but losing 27–14. After Auburn had scored midway through the first quarter to take a 7–0 lead, Southern answered with a pair of Orange 1-yard runs to take a 14–7 lead at halftime. Donegan completed 14 of 16 passes in the first half for

150 yards and at one stretch completed 12 straight throws. Auburn rallied behind Pat Sullivan's three touchdown passes to drop the Southerners to 1–3 on the season.

In Oxford on October 16, the Southerners hoped to repeat some of the previous year's magic against Ole Miss, but the Rebels also remembered the upset and stormed out with three first-quarter touchdowns to take a 20–0 lead. The Southerners were their own worst enemies, fumbling the ball away on their first three possessions and throwing an interception on their fourth. The USM offense never got going and mustered only a pair of Guy field goals, including a 51-yarder in the fourth quarter, as Ole Miss took a 20–6 win.

The Southerners tangled with the Memphis State Tigers on October 23, trying desperately to get back into the win column. The Tigers delighted their home crowd by taking a 6–0 lead on a couple of first-quarter field goals and added two second-quarter touchdowns to take a 20–0 edge at halftime. Memphis State added an early fourth quarter touchdown to go ahead 27–0 before the Southerners scored on 3-yard runs by Foley and Palazzo. But the USM squad did not score again, and the 27–12 loss dropped Southern to 1–5 on the year.

To record a winning season, the Southerners needed victories in their final five games, starting with the October 30 contest against the Richmond Spiders, USM's first home game of the season. The Southern offense, which had previously struggled, opened strongly against the Spiders when Palazzo connected with Heidelburg on an 81-yard screen pass for a touchdown on the Southerners' second possession of the day to make it 7–0. Richmond rallied early in the second quarter to take a 10–7 lead, but a 1-yard run by Orange gave USM a 14–10 advantage at halftime. The Spiders regained the lead at 17–14, but Guy kicked a 38-yard field goal in the third quarter to knot the game again. Richmond scored again to lead 24–17, but the Southerners answered with a 45-yard scoring pass from Palazzo to Broussard. Palazzo's run for a 2-point conversion failed, and the Southerners trailed by 1 point. After the ensuing kickoff, Richmond fumbled, and USM linebacker Johnny Herron recovered the ball at the Spiders' 19-yard line. A few plays later, Orange blasted over from the 3-yard line to give the Southerners the 31–24 win.

The Southerners made it two wins in a row when they defeated VMI 38–0 the next week at Faulkner Field. The Keydets managed only 103 yards in total offense, while Palazzo completed 19 of 34 passes for 234 yards and two touchdowns, one to Broussard and one to Harvey McGee. Foley and Orange had touchdown runs, and Guy added a 38-yard field goal. The victory improved the Southerners' record to 3–5.

The Southerners hit the road again to face Louisiana Tech in Ruston on November 13. With USM trailing 20–14 early in the fourth quarter, Guy nailed a 39-yard field goal to bring the Southerners within 4. After the Bulldogs failed to score on their next possession, the Southerners got the ball back with 3:26 remaining. Facing a fourth-and-1 at the USM 34-yard line, Donegan connected with Foley down the right side for 27 yards and a first down on the Bulldog 39. On the next play, Donegan connected with Broussard 25 yards downfield to move the ball to the Tech 14. A 13-yard run by Orange and his 1-yard touchdown plunge gave Southern the 24–20 lead. The Bulldogs drove to the Southern 36 with less than a minute to go, but Bird intercepted Ken Lantrip's pass to secure the win for Southern Miss.

The Southerners tried to win their fourth game in a row when they faced Virginia Tech in Blacksburg on November 20. By early in the fourth quarter, the Southerners held a 17–0 lead on a 7-yard run by Heidelburg, a 10-yard pass from Donegan to Broussard, and a 46-yard field goal by Guy. The Southern defense limited Hokie quarterback Don Strock to just 16 completions in 40 attempts for 173 yards. The 17–8 victory brought Southern Miss to .500 for the first time in the season, and Underwood complimented his players: "It was a real fine team effort by all our kids. I thought it was one of the best games the defense has played all year."

The last game of the season occurred on November 27, when Southern Miss hosted West Texas State. The game was not even close, as the Southerners notched an easy 35–0 win to end the year with five wins in a row and a 6–5 record, their first winning season since 1967. West Texas recorded only seven first downs, passed for just 37 yards, and had only 143 yards of total offense. Guy, playing at safety, had three of USM's six interceptions.

Orange led the team in rushing with 505 yards, while Donegan again was the team's top passer, completing 99 of 204 attempts. Broussard led the team with 26 receptions for 463 yards and three touchdowns. Gantt's 130 tackles were the highest on the squad. Guy, center Jimmy Haynes, and Herron were named All–South Independent and honorable mention All-America, with Haynes going on to play in the Senior Bowl.

1972 SEASON

The Southerners continued their winning ways when they opened the 1972 campaign at home on September 9 against the University of Texas–Arlington, rolling over the Mavericks 38–17. USM struck early when Gantt recovered a UTA fumble and Palazzo hit Plunkett with a 27-yard touchdown pass for a 7–0 lead. Southern made the score 14–0 when Palazzo directed a 92-yard, 15-play drive that ended with a touchdown run by Orange. Orange added three more touchdowns on the day, while Guy, a preseason All-American, intercepted a pair of passes and averaged 45.5 yards per punt.

At Faulkner Field on September 16 the Southerners faced Louisiana Tech, still led by Maxie Lambright, a former assistant coach at Southern Miss. Like Lambright's previous two visits to Faulkner Field with the Bulldogs, this one was a success for his team. Playing hard-nosed football and taking advantage of several breaks, Tech ended Southern's six-game winning streak with a stunning 33–14 victory. On the Southerners' first possession of the game, Orange fumbled at the Tech 22-yard line, and Tech cornerback Rodney

Wilburn snatched the ball out of the air and ran untouched into the Southern end zone. Southern never seemed to recover, falling behind 33–0 before scoring two late touchdowns.

Now 1–1 on the year, Southern met Ole Miss in Oxford on September 30. Trailing 9–6 late in the fourth quarter, the Rebels used 60 yards in penalties to put together an 80-yard scoring drive that gave Ole Miss the 13–9 victory. *Hattiesburg American* sports editor Mickey Edwards called the game "the Great Hemingway Stadium Football Robbery." The game turned on a interception by Southerner Doug White that would have killed the Rebels' hopes at the Southern 22-yard line. The back judge had thrown his flag on the play and called pass interference against Ole Miss, giving USM the ball. But as the Southern defense celebrated and made its way off the field, the field judge overruled the call, assessing pass interference against White and giving the Rebels new life. Four plays later, the Rebels' Greg Ainsworth scored, and his team escaped with the controversial victory. Underwood was outraged: "How can they call interference on him when [White] was in front of the boy? This hurts so bad, when your kids play well enough to win." Guy turned in another incredible performance, leading the Southerners with 10 tackles, kicking three field goals for all of Southern's points, and kicking seven punts—none of them returned—for an average of 54.9 yards. One of the punts had traveled a phenomenal 93 yards, the longest in school history and the longest in college football since 1955, when Kansas's John Hadl had ripped off a 94-yarder. Ole Miss Coach Billy Kinard called Guy's kick "the greatest punt I've ever seen" and called Guy "the greatest kicker I've ever seen."

Southern entertained West Texas State on October 7 and defeated the Buffaloes 14–7 before 11,500 fans. The West Texas wishbone offense had demolished its two previous opponents but managed only 140 yards of total offense against Southern, which amassed 299 yards. Led by Cook, Bird, Guy, and middle linebacker Mike Dennery, the Southern defense held West Texas to just eight first downs and 97 yards rushing. The victory evened Southern's record at 2–2.

The Southerners played the Richmond Spiders on the road on October 14 and had little trouble in the 34–9 win. The rushing attack produced 202 yards on 32 carries, with Orange rushing 21 times for 143 yards. Palazzo and reserve quarterback John Darling completed 15 of 29 passes, connecting with eight different receivers for 205 yards.

Riding a two-game winning streak, Underwood took the Southerners to Starkville on October 21 to meet Mississippi State. The Southerners capitalized on a bad snap on a Bulldog punt attempt to take a 7–0 lead six minutes into the game, but the Bulldogs shut out the Southerners the rest of the way. After the USM defense stopped the Bulldogs at the Southern 1-yard line, Palazzo fumbled in the end zone and was tackled for a safety to make the score 7–2, and State added 25 more points for a 27–7 victory. Palazzo completed 18 of 36 passes for 208 yards, while Guy and Bird each recorded an interception. The loss dropped Southern to 3–3 on the year.

Southern tried to bounce back the following week against No. 2 Alabama at Legion Field in

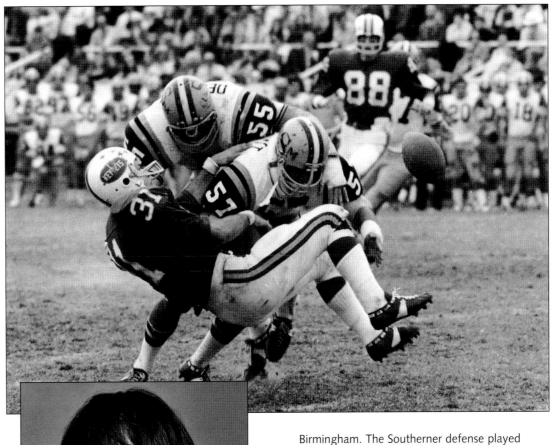

Linebacker Mike Dennery earned All-South Independent and honorable mention All-America honors in both 1972 and 1973. He finished his career with 431 tackles, including 185 in 1972.

Birmingham. The Southerner defense played superbly in the first half, holding the Tide to just a single touchdown, and USM's Ricky Palmer kicked a 32-yard field goal midway through the second quarter to keep Southern within 4 points at halftime. After the break, however, Alabama broke the game open with three third-quarter touchdowns, rolling to a 48–11 win. Southern Miss scored its only touchdown early in the fourth quarter when Palazzo completed a 12-yard touchdown pass to Marshall Veal. Alabama piled up 568 yards of total offense.

Southern Miss returned to play its second game of the season in Virginia, this time facing Virginia Tech in Blacksburg on November 4. The Hokies grabbed a 7–0 first-quarter lead, but a 64-yard punt return by Barry Gibson and an 11-yard touchdown pass from Palazzo to tight end John Sawyer gave Southern a 14–7 halftime edge. The Hokies shut out the Southerners the rest of the way, however, scoring 20 second-half points to win 27–14.

Trying to snap a three-game skid, the Southerners hosted the University of Tennessee–Chattanooga for Homecoming. The teams traded second-quarter field goals before the Moccasins scored the game's only touchdown midway through the third quarter to take a 10–3 lead. Guy's second field goal of the day brought USM to within 4 points heading into the fourth quarter. In the opening minutes of the final period, Southern drove to the Moc 7-yard line, but Palazzo's fourth-down pass to Johnny Dragg was overthrown, and the Southerners never threatened again. The 10–6 loss dropped the Southerners' record to 3–6.

During the Homecoming celebrations, Southern Miss officials announced the new nickname for the school's athletic teams. Over the preceding five months, alumni, students, and supporters had offered more than 400 suggestions for USM's athletic moniker, and an ad hoc committee had selected five finalists to appear on a ballot. Students, active members of the alumni association, faculty, and staff voted on whether to retain Southerners as the teams' nickname or to substitute Golden Eagles, Golden Raiders, Timber Wolves, or War Lords. No option received the required 60 percent of the total vote on the first ballot, and in a runoff, the old standby, Southerners, was defeated. Henceforth, USM's teams would be known as the Golden Eagles.

The team played its first game as the Golden Eagles on the road at Utah State on November 18 as snow fell. Late in the second quarter, Guy kicked a 61-yard field goal, breaking the National Collegiate Athletic Association record and helping Southern take an 18–11 lead into the locker room. Utah State rallied to tie the game at 21 with seven minutes left, and with Southern Miss facing a fourth down from its own 12-yard line with 10 seconds remaining, Guy dropped back in punt formation. Utah State blocked the kick and recovered the ball in the end zone for a heartbreaking 27–21 victory.

The final game of the season was in Jackson against Memphis State. The Tigers drove 60 yards to score on their opening possession and followed with a 68-yard drive to open up a 14–0 lead. The Southerner defense clamped down, but the offense was struggling. Plunkett scored on a 23-yard run early in the second quarter, and just after halftime, Orange reeled off a 36-yard run that set up a 14-yard touchdown pass from Palazzo to Dragg to tie the game. With just under four minutes remaining until halftime, however, the Golden Eagles lost their All-American punter, Guy, with a broken leg. The Southerners had a chance to win, but Palmer missed a 52-yard field goal with 1:33 to go. The 14–14 tie gave Southern Miss a 3–7–1 record for the year.

Orange once again led the team in rushing with 905 yards, while Palazzo was the top passer,

Defensive end Fred Cook (1971–1973) was a third-team All-America selection in 1973. The Baltimore Colts selected him in the second round of the 1974 NFL draft.

completing 160 of 291 passes for 1,888 yards and eight touchdowns. Flanker Doug Parker caught 41 passes for 534 yards, while Dennery set a school record with 185 tackles. Guy finished his career with a school-record average of 46.2 yards per punt and became the first Southern Miss player to be named a first-team All-America since the school made the move to Division I, as he was selected by the AP, the *Sporting News,* the Football Writers Association, Walter Camp, *Gridiron Football News,* and *Playboy,* among others. Cook and Dennery joined Guy on the All–South Independent team and earned honorable mention All-America honors. Although Guy could not play in the postseason college all-star games because of his broken leg, he became the first kicker ever taken in the first round of the NFL draft when the Oakland Raiders selected him with the twenty-third pick.

With plans to build a new football stadium apparently on the shelf, State Senator Ray Chatham of Hattiesburg said on January 5, 1973, that a joint study of the State House and Senate would recommend to the legislature a $2,886,000 appropriation to expand Faulkner Field. The expansion would not call for a bowl configuration but would entail making double decks on both sides, covering the same base areas now occupied by the single-deck facility and increasing the stadium's seating capacity from approximately 12,500 to 35,600. The legislature accepted the report's recommendation and appropriated the money, raising the project's total funding to approximately $4.8 million.

By late May 1973, after many stumbling blocks and much political red tape, the process of renovating Faulkner Field was finally under way. The original plans and drawings, done by Finch and Heery of Atlanta, Georgia, had been turned over to Hattiesburg architect Steve Blair for finalization. With seating for 36,000 fans, the new stadium would be slightly larger than the home fields of Ole Miss and Mississippi State and would have room for future expansion to 60,000 if needed. A modern press box would be constructed along the west side between the 20-yard lines and would have facilities for both print and broadcast media as well as scouting personnel. The Coca-Cola Company would construct a new scoreboard that would include a message board. And USM Athletic Director Reed Green wanted a

Golden Eagle perched on top. But no construction timetable yet existed. "Of course we'd like to get started on the reconstruction as soon as possible," Green said, "but this is such a tedious procedure that I couldn't hazard a guess as to when we can get started, much less finished." Furthermore, as Green pointed out, the 1974 football schedule was already set, with five games slated to be played at Faulkner Field: "We have these commitments, and we need to know something so we can reschedule the games in Jackson or elsewhere." Several months passed before the construction schedule was set, as the university had to overcome still more hurdles before the project could finally start.

1973 SEASON

Coach Underwood and his Golden Eagles began the season at home against East Carolina University on September 15 with a disappointing 13–0 loss. The Golden Eagle offense struggled, managing just 39 yards rushing and 177 total yards on the day. Even more devastating, however, were the three interceptions and the fumble USM surrendered.

The following week, Southern Miss traveled to Tampa to face the Florida Gators, turning in a much better performance. Palmer's 20-yard field goal on the Eagles' first possession gave them a 3–0 lead that held throughout the first quarter. The Gators rallied to take a 7–3 lead midway through the second quarter, but the Eagles battled back to regain the lead on a 10-yard touchdown pass from quarterback Jeff Bower to Sawyer. Florida answered quickly, however, scoring another touchdown just four seconds before halftime to lead 14–10. The Golden Eagles recorded the only score of the second half on a 26-yard field goal by Palmer, but 3 points were not enough, and USM fell to 0–2 on the year.

The Golden Eagles repeated the poor performance they turned in during the season's first game when they played at Ole Miss on September 29. The USM gridders fumbled seven times, losing three of them, and threw an interception in the 41–0 loss to the Rebels. "We did not play as good as we can," Underwood said after the game, "but playing good is tough in such an emotional contest when you lose your momentum early."

At Tennessee–Chattanooga on October 6, the Golden Eagles jumped out in front when Cook recovered a fumble and a few plays later Bower scored on a 5-yard run. The defense scored the next points when White intercepted a pass and rambled 40 yards for the score early in the second quarter. The Moccasins cut the lead to 14–7 early in the third quarter, but another Moc fumble led to another Bower touchdown run. Southern Miss blew things open in the fourth quarter when fullback Carlos Montgomery scored two touchdowns and wide receiver Barry Gibson added another to give the Eagles the 42–7 win.

Hoping to make it two in a row, the Eagles traveled to Richmond, Virginia, to meet the University of Richmond Spiders on October 13. Southern Miss fell behind 13–0 at the end of the first quarter. The Eagles got on the board early in

Jeff Bower (#7) was the team's starting quarterback from 1973 to 1975. His running and passing abilities were keys to the team's success. In 1990 he would become the school's head coach.

the second quarter when Bower hit McGee on a 37-yard touchdown pass, and both teams added additional scores to give Richmond a 20–14 halftime lead. The Spiders scored twice during the third quarter and coasted to the 42–20 victory. USM was now 1–4 on the year.

The Eagles rebounded on October 20 with a 41–14 road win over the University of Texas–Arlington. The Mavericks led 14–13 at halftime, but the Eagles roared back with one of their best halves of the year, scoring four times and holding UTA scoreless. Bower produced a school-record 376 yards of total offense, including 291 yards on 13 of 16 passing. The rest of the team contributed 200 yards rushing, and wide receiver Eddie Tate caught four balls for 149 yards, including a 76-yard touchdown pass. The Eagle defense forced five turnovers and limited the Mavericks to 249 yards of offense.

Next up was Mississippi State in Starkville on October 27. The Bulldogs led 3–0 early in the third quarter when Palmer kicked a 45-yard field goal to tie the game. In the fourth period, Mississippi State recovered a Chuck Clancy fumble and drove 22 yards to score, but the Eagles took the ensuing kickoff and drove 80 yards in nine plays, scoring on a 3-yard touchdown pass from Bower to tailback Terrance Wells. After Palmer's extra-

THE BEAR, BOBBY, THE EAGLES, AND ROBERTS STADIUM

point kick, the game was once again knotted at 10. The Bulldogs reached the Southern 24-yard line with under a minute to go, but safety Don Law intercepted a pass in the end zone to preserve the 10–10 tie.

The Eagles improved their season mark to 3-4-1 with a 28-7 Homecoming win over Weber State on November 3 at Faulkner Field. USM scored all of its points in the first half with touchdown runs by Plunkett and Montgomery, a 40-yard interception return for a touchdown by cornerback Norris Thomas, and a touchdown pass from Bower to Gibson.

The Golden Eagles met longtime rival Memphis State on November 10 at Liberty Bowl Memorial Stadium and escaped with a 13–10 win. Memphis scored first when Plunkett fumbled and the Tigers plucked the ball out of the air and returned it 95 yards for a touchdown. Palmer kicked second-quarter field goals of 32 and 36 yards to bring the Eagles to within 1 point, but the Tigers responded with a field goal just before halftime to take a 10–6 lead. Midway through the third quarter, USM's Dennery recovered a fumble at the Tiger 34-yard line, and Orange scored on a 7-yard run a few plays later to give the Eagles the 13–10 win and even their record at 4-4-1. "It's been a long time since we won against this club," said Underwood. "Our players did a good job."

In Canyon, Texas, the Eagles met West Texas State on November 17 and notched their third victory in a row, 28–0, USM's first shutout since 1971. Orange racked up 123 yards on the ground, including a 3-yard touchdown run, and Plunkett scored once to give the Eagles a 14–0 halftime lead. Wells added a 1-yard score in the third quarter, and split end Willie Thicklen caught a 15-yard pass from Bower in the fourth quarter to seal the victory.

The red-hot Golden Eagles hosted Utah State on Thanksgiving, November 22, and won 32–8. USM opened with a 73-yard scoring drive capped by Plunkett's 6-yard touchdown run and added another touchdown on Orange's 9-yard run to take a 14–0 lead early in the second quarter. Palmer added a 34-yard field goal before the Eagles blew the game open when Bower hit Palmer with a 19-yard touchdown pass and then added a 2-point conversion toss to Sawyer to make the score 25–0. Utah State scored to close to 25–8, but the Eagles answered with a 69-yard drive that ended with Orange's second touchdown of the day. After a 1–4 start, the Eagles had gone undefeated over their final six games to end the year with a 6-4-1 record.

Orange led the team in rushing with 539 yards on 109 carries, while Bower completed 116 of 199 passes for 1,495 yards and nine touchdowns. McGee was the team's leading receiver, with 28 catches for 359 yards and a touchdown. Dennery was the team's leading tackler for the second straight year, recording 117 tackles. Cook was named an AP third-team All-America as well as first-team All–South Independent, and he played in the Blue-Gray All-Star Classic in Montgomery, Alabama, and the Senior Bowl in Mobile. Dennery, Orange, Palmer, and offensive guard Clint Tapper joined Cook on the All–South Independent first team and earned honorable mention

Construction on the M. M. Roberts Stadium began in the early 1970s. The Golden Eagles spent all of the 1974 and 1975 seasons on the road, before playing the first game at the new stadium in 1976.

All-America honors. Cook (second round–Baltimore), Orange (sixth round–Atlanta), Dennery (thirteenth round–Oakland), Bird (eleventh round–New York Jets), and McGee (eleventh round–Dallas) were selected in the NFL draft.

The Utah State contest was USM's last home game in Hattiesburg until 1976, as the long-anticipated renovations to Faulkner Field finally commenced. Other major changes to the Southern Miss football program were also in the offing: at the end of the 1973 season, Reed Green began to plan his departure after nearly 25 years as the school's athletic director, and on December 20, 1973, USM President William D. McCain announced that Roland Dale would replace Green. Dale had served as line coach at Southern Miss for three years beginning in 1955 and had been a longtime assistant at Ole Miss before heading to Southeastern Louisiana, where he had spent the past two years as head football coach. Dale had accepted the USM head coaching position after the 1968 season but had changed his mind, a decision, ironically, that had been announced five years to the day before the

THE BEAR, BOBBY, THE EAGLES, AND ROBERTS STADIUM [151]

announcement that he would return as the school's athletic director. For the first year of his tenure, the 46-year old Dale would share the position with Green, the only full-time athletic director Southern had ever had. Green gave his successor his full support: "Coach Dale has been in athletics a long time and has been highly successful. I am fully confident he will do well in his new position. I believe the University is fortunate to have obtained the services of a man of his caliber." Dale returned the kind words: "I appreciate very much the confidence of Dr. McCain, Coach Green and the Athletic Continuity Committee. I have many pleasant memories of my coaching days at Southern and I look forward to rejoining the Athletic Department and being part of the tremendous program it now enjoys."

Just a few weeks after heralding Green's impending retirement, Mississippi newspapers carried the news that the State Building Commission would open bids for the remodeling of Faulkner Field on February 7. Plans for the stadium expansion were slowed, however, when all bids received surpassed the $4.8 million that the state legislature had appropriated for the work. School officials were unsure about their next move, but the State Senate provided an additional $1.3 million in early March, clearing the way for construction to proceed. Mississippi Governor Bill Waller signed the measure at 10:30 A.M. on March 5, and late that afternoon, the State Building Commission awarded the contract to Polk Construction Company of Columbia, Mississippi, which was the low bidder at $5,784,338.

The target date for completion was September 1975; all "home" football games during the 1974 season would be played in Jackson or Mobile. After several delays, groundbreaking ceremonies for the renovation project were held on April 16, 1974. McCain welcomed the various dignitaries in attendance, proclaiming, "This is a great day in the history of the University. It marks the end of a long and hard struggle." McCain thanked the legislature, governor, members of the Board of Trustees of State Institutions of Higher Learning, "and all of the many other friends who participated in the effort to make today possible." Green, now an assistant to President McCain, spoke next, showing great emotion as he too commended the efforts of all concerned: "It is a happy occasion for me to be a part of the ground breaking for a project that has been one of my fondest dreams for many a year."

1974 SEASON

The 1974 season began at Liberty Bowl Memorial Stadium against the Memphis State Tigers on September 14. Just before halftime, Southern Miss scored the game's only touchdown when Bower found Sawyer over the middle and the big tight end spun away from three tacklers and took the ball 38 yards for the score. The Eagle defense protected the 6–0 lead throughout the second half, but the Tiger defenders also played well, and neither team scored, although Memphis threatened late in the game, reaching the Golden Eagle

Jeff Bower and head coach P. W. Underwood discuss strategy along the sidelines during the 1974 season.

24-yard line before Law registered his second interception of the day to enable Southern Miss to hang on for the victory.

The following week the Golden Eagles traveled to Birmingham to meet fourth-ranked Alabama at Legion Field and were crushed 52–0. Alabama rushed for 502 yards and had 643 yards of total offense while holding Southern Miss to just 143 yards on the day. The game did not get completely out of hand until the fourth quarter, when the Crimson Tide exploded for 24 points.

The 1–1 Golden Eagles traveled to Oxford's Hemingway Stadium to meet Ole Miss on September 28 and lost a hard-fought 20–14 decision. The Rebels scored on a 70-yard touchdown run on their second play from scrimmage to lead 7–0. The Eagles drove to the Ole Miss 2-yard line early in the second quarter, but Bower was stopped on a quarterback sneak on fourth down. Southern fell behind 10–0 when the Rebels added a 37-yard field goal early in the third quarter. The Eagles once again marched deep into Rebel territory, but the Ole Miss defense turned in another excellent goal-line stand, stopping Montgomery at the 6-inch line on fourth down. The Eagles finally scored early in the fourth quarter when Bower connected with wide receiver Chris Pieper on a 4-yard touchdown pass to close the gap to 10–6, but Ole Miss responded with a field goal to make the score 13–6. Southern then took its first lead of the day on a 5-yard touchdown grab by Sawyer, who immediately caught another pass to give the Southerners the 2-point conversion and a 14–13 edge with 3:50 left. With time running out, Ole Miss drove 80 yards in 15 plays to score a touchdown with 31 seconds left and eke out the 20–14 win.

The Eagles endured another disappointing loss the following week at West Texas State. Before an announced crowd of just 5,074, the Buffaloes won 31–0 as nothing seemed to go right for the

THE BEAR, BOBBY, THE EAGLES, AND ROBERTS STADIUM

One of quarterback Jeff Bower's favorite targets was tight end John Sawyer who caught 26 passes for 390 yards and two touchdowns in 1974.

Golden Eagles, who managed only 154 yards of total offense while losing five fumbles and throwing two interceptions.

Next came an October 12 "home" game at Jackson's Memorial Stadium, and Southern bounced back with a 39–10 win over Texas–Arlington before a crowd of just 4,331. The Golden Eagles exploded for their best offensive performance of the year, rolling up 527 yards of total offense, while the defense held the Mavericks to just 247 yards. The Eagles rushed for 291 yards and four touchdowns, with Montgomery gaining 96 yards on just six carries. "We feel good this week, much better than a week ago," Underwood said. "I thought our backs ran well. It was the first time they ran as well as we thought they are capable of running. We will have to play this good every Saturday. We are not good enough to look past anybody like we did a week ago."

The Eagles heeded their coach's advice, again playing better against Virginia Military Institute at Ladd Stadium in Mobile. Trailing 6–0, Eagle safety Rick Gemmel intercepted a Keydet pass, and tailback Ben (Go-Go) Garry scored a few plays later to give USM a 7–6 lead. VMI regained the lead with a 70-yard touchdown drive and 2-point conversion with 6:34 left in the game, but Southern quickly found the end zone when quarterback Chris Speyrer hit Gibson on a 60-yard touchdown pass to pull the Eagles to within 1 point. Southern elected to go for the 2-point conversion and the win, and Speyrer dropped back to pass, found no one open, and ran the ball in with 5:53 remaining to give Southern the 15–14 victory and improve the team to 3–3.

The Golden Eagles saw their two-game winning streak snapped when they lost 10–7 at Lamar on October 26. The game was tied at 7 at halftime, and both teams subsequently had several opportunities to take the lead but could not capitalize. With just over a minute to go, Lamar missed a 54-yard field goal, and Southern Miss had the ball on its 20-yard line. After a first down and a quarterback sack, the ball was on the 18 when Speyrer threw a pass that was intercepted and returned down the left sideline to the Southern 7 with nine seconds left. Lamar's Jabo

Leonard came on and kicked the 24-yard field goal to give his team the 10–7 win.

On November 2 against Southwestern Louisiana in Lafayette, Southern won 41–7 behind a pair of touchdown runs by tailback Chuck (Fancy) Clancy and one by Curtis Dickey as well as Bower's three touchdown passes. The defense limited the Ragin' Cajuns to 209 yards of offense.

Now 4–4, the Golden Eagles traveled to Logan, Utah, to play Utah State on November 9. In a defensive struggle, Southern won 7–3 with Dickey scoring the game's only touchdown on a 1-yard run that ended a 13-play, 80-yard drive early in the third quarter.

Winners of four of their last five, the Golden Eagles took on Bowling Green at Mobile's Ladd Stadium on November 16 but went down to defeat, 38–20. The Eagles hurt themselves with a pair of fumbles, and the offense never really got going, managing only 53 yards on the ground and 207 yards through the air.

Back at .500, the Golden Eagles closed out the season on the road against the University of Tampa and future NFL standout Freddie Solomon. The Spartans jumped out to a 10–0 lead at halftime, as the Eagles managed only four first downs and 70 yards. During the fourth quarter, Tampa fumbled Palmer's punt, and the Eagles recovered the ball on the Spartan 15-yard line for their first true scoring opportunity of the game, which resulted in Palmer's 35-yard field goal to make the score 10–3. Later in the period, Bower drove the Eagles from their own 20 to the Tampa 12-yard line and connected with Montgomery on a touchdown pass to bring the Eagles to within 1 and then hit Sawyer for the 2-point conversion to give USM an 11–10 victory and a winning season at 6–5.

During the season, the student body elected Cook the first African American Mr. USM. Linebacker Ron Cheatham, Gemmel, and Sawyer were named All–South Independent and earned honorable mention All-America honors, and the Houston Oilers selected Sawyer in the eleventh round of the following spring's NFL draft. Bower, Thomas, and defensive tackle Mike Smith were named second-team All–South Independent.

A few weeks after the season ended, Coach Underwood announced that he was resigning his position effective December 31. Over his six seasons, the USM squad had amassed a record of 31–32–2. Regarding his departure, Underwood stated that the difficult decision to leave had been his alone and that "after a great deal of prayerful thought, I have decided that it is in the best interest of my family and the University." He continued, "As I resign, I am able to look with pride on the progress of the football program at the University. I trust that my contributions will mean something to the future, and will not be judged by the scoreboard alone."

Athletic Director Dale, who had coached Underwood at Southern in 1955 and 1956, accepted the resignation "with deep personal regret" and immediately launched the search for a new head coach. On December 21, less than three weeks later, Dale and Aubrey Lucas, who had become president of Southern Miss in 1975, officially announced that Laurel native Bobby

Former assistant coach Roland Dale (left) is congratulated by President William D. McCain (right) after being named the school's new athletic director in 1974, replacing the legendary Reed Green. Looking on are Hattiesburg attorney Paul (Bud) Holmes (second from left) and former football star C. L. (Dipsey) Dews (second from right).

Fiery head coach Bobby Collins, the former offensive coordinator at North Carolina, became the head coach at Southern Miss in 1975.

Collins would succeed Underwood. Collins, who had played college football at Mississippi State, came to Southern Miss from the University of North Carolina–Chapel Hill, where he had been assistant head coach in charge of defense. Said Collins, "I have always wanted to be a head coach, and I feel very fortunate that I am able to come back to my native state. The fact that I grew up in the shadows of USM and always had a great deal of respect for the school makes the opportunity even more appealing to me." North Carolina had used the I and wide slot offensive sets to rank among the nation's top 10 scoring teams, and Collins indicated that he would favor those schemes at USM. With only 14 of 30 scholarships committed, the new coach's first priority would be recruiting, and he noted, "I have a number of friends and contacts in Mississippi that should help us." Another important task would be the selection of assistant coaches. Said Collins, "I don't want to make a mistake, and I won't rush into it. Certainly members of the present staff will be contacted."

1975 SEASON

The Collins era started on September 13, 1975, in Ogden, Utah, against Weber State. The Wildcats fumbled on their first play from scrimmage, and Eagle defensive tackle Eddie Nunez recovered the ball at the 27-yard line. Six plays later, fullback David Hosemann scored from the 3, and Southern had an early 7–0 lead. Weber State answered with a 75-yard drive that tied the game, but Ben

(Go-Go) Garry raced 60 yards up the middle on Southern's next possession to make the score 14–7. The Golden Eagle defense limited the Wildcats to just a field goal the rest of the way, and USM had the 14–10 victory. Garry finished with 29 carries for 156 yards.

The following week the Golden Eagles traveled to Bowling Green, losing 16–14. Bowling Green had a 10–7 lead at halftime, but Bower scored on a 6-yard run early in the fourth quarter, and Southern took a 14–10 lead. Bowling Green running back Dave Preston scored on a 6-yard run with just 2:21 remaining, and even though the 2-point conversion failed, the Falcons sealed the victory by intercepting a Southern Miss pass in the final minutes. Garry recorded 116 yards rushing for his second straight 100-yard game.

The Golden Eagles met Ole Miss on September 27 at Hemingway Stadium. The Rebels scored all their points in the opening half on their way to a 24–8 win. USM's only score came on Bower's 3-yard run with just over a minute left in the game and his pass to Palmer for the 2-point conversion.

Collins's team dropped its third straight game on October 4 at Scott Field in Starkville. USM led Mississippi State 3–0 halftime on Mike Wright's 23-yard field goal just 34 seconds before the break, which had been set up by Cheatham's recovery of a Bulldog fumble. State went up 7–3 on its first possession of the third quarter when running back Walter Packer blasted 43 yards off right tackle for a touchdown, and that was enough to give the Bulldogs the win, as the Golden Eagles managed just 194 yards of total offense and Bower threw four interceptions.

The Golden Eagles improved to 2–3 on the year by beating the Memphis State Tigers in Memphis on October 11. With the game tied at 7 after three quarters, the Golden Eagles scored twice in the final quarter on short touchdown runs by Garry and Clancy and took a 21–7 victory. Memphis never got going against the Southern defense, gaining just 152 total yards.

USM notched its second win in a row with a 34–7 win at the University of Texas–Arlington. Montgomery ran for three touchdowns, and the Eagle defense was again superb, holding the Mavericks to 150 yards and 42 total plays.

The following week brought the Golden Eagles' third win in a row, a 24–14 defeat of Louisiana Tech in Ruston on October 25. Although the Eagles had staked themselves to a 10–0 lead, Tech battled back to take a 14–10 advantage early in the fourth quarter. But Bower took the Eagles on a 78-yard, 18-play drive that took 9:31 off the clock and ended with a 2-yard touchdown run by Montgomery with four minutes to go put Southern back ahead. Cheatham intercepted a screen pass and returned it to the Tech 21, and Garry added another touchdown to secure the victory and raise the Eagles' record to 4–3.

The Louisiana Superdome was the site of USM's November 1 "home" game against Lamar, and the Golden Eagles treated the 8,300 fans in attendance to an impressive 43–3 win over the Cardinals. All 48 players on the traveling squad saw action as Garry, Clancy, Montgomery, Pieper, and Bower turned in touchdown runs and Palmer added field goals of 49 and 38 yards. The Eagle offense rushed for 336 yards and had 419 total yards, while the defense dropped the Cardinals for a safety and held them to just 52 yards of total offense.

The Eagles rode a four-game winning streak into Bryant-Denny Stadium in Tuscaloosa to meet fifteenth-ranked Alabama on November 15. The Tide's All-American end, Ozzie Newsome, caught four passes for 112 yards and two touchdowns to lead the Tide to the 27–6 victory. The Golden Eagles did not help their cause by losing four fumbles and throwing two interceptions: "We knew before the game we couldn't make any mistakes, but we did," said Collins, "and we knew that if we got any scoring opportunities we would have to put points on the board, and we didn't."

The Golden Eagles' Homecoming game was held in Biloxi, Mississippi, where they faced Cal State–Fullerton in front of 9,300 fans. Southern scored on its first 8 possessions and on 10 of its first 11 on the way to a lopsided 70–0 win, the most points the team had scored since a 76–0 defeat of Northwestern Louisiana in 1951. Southern's players rolled up 468 yards on the ground, including 111 by Garry and 115 by Clancy, and scored nine touchdowns. The USM defense held Cal State–Fullerton to -11 yards rushing and 67 total yards.

At 6–4, the Golden Eagles faced Brigham Young University in Jackson on November 29. The contest was over almost before it started, as Southern roared to a 42–14 victory. A pair of Montgomery touchdown runs and a 51-yard Palmer field goal made the score 17–0 at the end of the first quarter, and Palmer added another field goal, this one from 33 yards out, in the second period to give USM a 20–7 edge at halftime. BYU closed to within 20–14 in the third quarter, but Bower scored on the first play of the fourth quarter, Cheatham intercepted a pass on BYU's next possession, and Bower quickly hit Pieper with a 29-yard touchdown pass to put the game out of reach at 35–14. Montgomery rushed for 104 yards on 17 carries, while Bower completed 6 of 12 passes for 113 yards. Collins and his team became the first Southern squad to win seven games in a season since 1965, and the Golden Eagles did it while playing all their games on the road for the second straight year. (Mississippi State would later forfeit its game against the Eagles, upping their official record for the season to 8–3.)

Offensive tackle Jerry Fremin, nose guard Randy Latta, and defensive back Norris Thomas earned All–South Independent and honorable mention All-America honors, and Thomas represented Southern Miss in the Senior Bowl. In the

(Top) Defensive back Norris Thomas (1972–1975) was an All–South Independent selection in 1975 and later starred for the Miami Dolphins and Tampa Bay Buccaneers of the NFL.

(Bottom) Cornerback Carl Allen (1974–1975) began his career as a walk-on but finished it as one of the best defensive backs in school history.

1976 NFL draft, Thomas went in the ninth round to the Miami Dolphins, cornerback Carl Allen went in the eleventh round to the Cincinnati Bengals, and safety Brad Bowman went in the thirteenth round to the Green Bay Packers.

1976 SEASON

With the team's success in 1975 and the opening of the new USM football stadium, USM supporters were excited about the upcoming season, which many people believed could be one of the best in school history. They were in for an unpleasant surprise.

The Eagles played their first game of 1976 on September 11 at East Carolina and were manhandled by the Pirates, who scored on six of their first seven possessions and rolled to a 48–0 win. ECU amassed 416 yards on the ground alone, while Southern produced just 173 yards total.

Collins hoped that his players could recover the following week when they faced Virginia Tech in Blacksburg, but the Hokies won 16–7. The Eagles racked up their first touchdown of the season midway through the third quarter when quarterback Kenny Alderman connected with Garry on a 48-yard touchdown pass that cut into Virginia Tech's 10–0 lead. In another highlight for the Eagles, Garry rushed for 143 yards to go with his touchdown grab.

Now 0–2, the Golden Eagles played in Hattiesburg for the first time since November 22, 1973, a span of 24 games. Before the September 25, 1976, game with Ole Miss, a sellout crowd of

Left to right: President Aubrey K. Lucas, M. M. Roberts, and Governor Cliff Finch take part in the dedication ceremonies of M. M. Roberts Stadium on September 25, 1976.

33,000 watched as Southern Miss dedicated its new stadium to Dr. M. M. Roberts, who had played football for the school during the 1915 and 1916 seasons and had been a dedicated supporter of the university and its athletic program for more than half a century. Roberts had served as president of the Board of Trustees, in which capacity he bore most of the responsibility for the creation of a formula that brought faculty and staff salaries into parity with those at USM's sister institutions, and a prominent Hattiesburg family had funded a scholarship program in his honor. He had been a member of and generous donor to the USM Foundation since its inception, and he had personally provided financial assistance to more than 500 undergraduate and graduate students at USM regardless of race, creed, or background. Roberts was also a member of the university's Century, Big Gold, and Hardwood Clubs, and in 1973 he had received the USM Department of Intercollegiate Athletics' annual Distinguished Service Award. The honor of the stadium name was fitting for someone who had devoted so much of his life to the university.

Unfortunately for Roberts and the other Golden Eagle fans, the Rebels rolled to a relatively easy 28–0 win. Ole Miss tailback Michael Sweet became the first player to score in the new stadium when he crossed the goal line on an 8-yard run midway through the first quarter. The Rebels had 338 yards of total offense despite losing four fumbles, while the Eagle offense mustered just 181 yards and committed six turnovers.

The Cincinnati Bearcats became the second opponent to play at Roberts Stadium when they came to town on October 2 to face the 0–3 Eagles. Garry's 14-yard touchdown run and Malachi Henry's 51-yard punt return for a score had the game knotted at 14–14 at halftime, but the Bearcats scored a touchdown early in the third quarter after Garry fumbled the ball away. The Bearcats added another touchdown to move ahead 28–14 and held on to win 28–21 despite a late Golden Eagle touchdown.

The Golden Eagles' skid continued against Alabama on October 9 at Birmingham's Legion Field with a 24–8 defeat. Alabama took a 21–0 lead and never looked back, while the Golden Eagles hurt their cause with four fumbles. One bright spot for Southern was the play of Garry, who carried 18 times for 109 yards and caught three passes.

The Golden Eagles dropped to 0–6 the next week in Provo, Utah, suffering a 63–19 crushing at the hands of Brigham Young. BYU piled up an astounding 713 yards of total offense, including 515 yards in the air. The game had started on a positive note, as the Eagles jumped to a 3–0 lead on Wright's field goal, and they trailed just 28–19 at halftime, but the Cougars ran off a devastating 35 straight points in the second half.

Mississippi State, tied for twentieth in the national rankings, came to Roberts Stadium on October 23 and left with a 14–6 win. With the Bulldogs leading 7–0, the Golden Eagles scored on Montgomery's 5-yard touchdown run early in the third quarter, although Wright's extra-point kick failed to leave State with a 1-point lead. Later in the quarter, the Eagles recovered a Mississippi State fumble and drove to the Bulldog 10-yard line, but USM fumbled the ball back to end the threat, and the Bulldogs added a late touchdown to produce the final margin of victory. "By far, this was the best effort we've had this season," Collins said. "I think we got the same kind of effort we got against Alabama. The fact that our offense was able to stay on the field and move the ball helped our defense out very much."

On November 6 in Tallahassee, the USM suffered its eighth straight loss, going down to

Florida State 30–27. Playing as well as they had all season, the Eagles opened up a 27–10 lead after three quarters, but the Seminoles rallied with a pair of touchdowns to close to within 27–23. When an Eagle punt pinned the Seminoles at their 8-yard line with just under five minutes to go, it looked as if Southern Miss might pull out the victory. Seminole quarterback Jimmy Black had other ideas, however, completing a screen pass to Rudy Thomas, who raced 95 yards for the winning touchdown.

The following week, the Eagles traveled to play Louisiana Tech on a cold, rainy day in Ruston. The Eagles were trailing late in the fourth quarter when Garry scored on a 1-yard run to give them a 20–16 lead. The USM defense held on the next series, forcing the Bulldogs to punt from their 23-yard line. End Reggie Odom blocked the kick, and the ball rolled out of the back of the end zone for a safety, increasing Southern's advantage to 6 points. After Tech's free kick, however, the Eagle offense could not run out the clock, and the Bulldogs had one final chance from their 29-yard line. A 42-yard completion from quarterback Steve Haynes to wide receiver Billy Ryckman put the ball at the Southern 29, and two plays later another pass play put the ball at the Southern 6-yard line with 1:15 to go. Southern was called for pass interference in the end zone, putting the ball at the 1, and Arry Moody crashed over to tie the game. With the successful extra-point kick, the Bulldogs had the 23–22 win and the Golden Eagles had suffered their ninth straight loss, this one in heartbreaking

Fullback David Hosemann (#22) was one of the leaders of the Golden Eagle offense during the mid-1970s. His all out, hard-nosed running style made him a favorite of Southern Miss fans.

THE BEAR, BOBBY, THE EAGLES, AND ROBERTS STADIUM

fashion. After the game, Coach Collins acknowledged the outstanding play of Ryckman, who was leading the nation in total pass receptions and total yards receiving: "He's tremendous, as good a receiver as we've been around."

Southern's season ended with a pair of home games against Memphis State and Texas–Arlington, two clubs battling for spots in postseason bowl games. On November 20, the Golden Eagles finally won their first game in Roberts Stadium, stunning the Tigers 14–12 behind first-time

Tailback Ben (Go-Go) Garry (1974–1977) rushed for over 100 yards in a game 17 times in his career, including 206 yards against Louisiana Tech in 1976.

starter Jeff Hammond, who had replaced Alderman at quarterback. Trailing by 6 midway through the third quarter, Clancy, playing halfback for the Eagles, threw a 5-yard touchdown pass to wide receiver John Pitts, and Mark Barhanovich added the extra point to give Southern a 7–6 lead. Clancy capped a 17-play, 83-yard drive with a 4-yard touchdown run to increase the Golden Eagle lead to 14–6, and although Memphis State scored late in the fourth quarter, Southern hung on to win its first of the year. Led by Don Law's three interceptions, the Southern defense yielded a meager 172 yards. "This was a great boost for a great bunch of kids who have hung through some bad times," said Collins. "The long drive was the real turning point."

Against the University of Texas–Arlington on November 27, the Golden Eagles fell behind 10–3 at halftime but exploded for 18 third-quarter points and a 21–10 victory. USM's first touchdown came after Henry's 44-yard punt return set up Garry's 1-yard touchdown run. The extra-point kick missed, but the Eagles took a 15–10 lead when Hammond scored on a 1-yard run. Southern Miss added its final touchdown when linebacker Ronald (Clump) Taylor recovered a fumble on the UTA 7-yard line and Garry ran the ball in on the next play. His 187 rushing yards in the game gave Garry a new Southern Miss single-season rushing record of 1,236 yards. "It wasn't pretty, but it was an important win for us," Collins remarked. "I don't think you can say enough about the jobs that Jeff Hammond and Ben Garry did. Our seniors stayed in there all season and played when they could have quit."

Despite the team's overall 2–9 record on the year (later improved to an official 3–8 after Mississippi State was once again forced to forfeit its victory), the season-ending wins had Collins and his players excited about the future: "The coaches are telling the players that we're 2–0 and we'll go from here. We've got to go out and recruit some players to fill in. Our juniors are excited. They're a good group and will provide good leadership next season."

Garry, offensive tackle Eric Smith, and defensive end Bobby Smithart were named to the All–South Independent team and earned honorable mention All-America honors. In the following spring's NFL draft, the Los Angeles Rams selected center Barry Caudill in the twelfth round.

1977 SEASON

The 1977 season opened on September 3 in Montgomery, Alabama, against Troy State. Benefiting from seven Trojan turnovers, USM rolled to an easy 42–19 win as Garry rushed for 126 yards and scored a pair of touchdowns, becoming the Golden Eagles' all-time leading rusher. Hosemann added two touchdown runs, while fullback Willie Corner also scored on a short run and cornerback Hanford Dixon ran an interception back for a score.

Facing the Florida State Seminoles at Roberts Stadium a week later, the Golden Eagles took a 3–0 lead on Randy Boyette's 26-yard field goal and held the edge until the Seminoles blocked Wright's punt and ran the ball in for a touchdown

55 seconds before halftime. Boyette nailed a 31-yard field goal on the final play of the first half to cut the margin to 7–6 at the break, but the Seminoles scored four second-half touchdowns to win 35–6. "The blocked punt was the play of the game," Florida State Coach Bobby Bowden said. "Until that point they had the momentum on their side and were winning the game. After that the entire game went in our favor, we controlled it."

The Golden Eagles bounced back with an impressive win against Auburn on September 17 at Jordan-Hare Stadium. The Tigers took a 6–0 lead in the opening minutes of the second quarter, but Southern Miss roared back, scoring on a 1-yard run by Garry, a 3-yard run by Hammond, and a 47-yard field goal by Wright to lead 17–6 midway through the game. Hammond added another short touchdown run in the third quarter to increase the lead to 24–6, and the defense surrendered only one more touchdown to record the 24–13 victory and improve the team's season mark to 2–1. Garry rushed for 110 yards, and David Odom and cornerback Emanuel Killingsworth had interceptions.

In Oxford on September 24, the Golden Eagles faced Ole Miss as well as the elements. With rain falling on Hemingway Stadium's artificial surface, the Eagles spotted the Rebels, riding high after the previous week's victory over Notre Dame, a 19–0 lead late in the first half before the USM defense completely stifled the Ole Miss attack. Garry got the Eagles on the board with a 26-yard touchdown run that cut the margin to 19–7 at halftime. Southern Miss took the second-half kickoff and drove 69 yards in 15 plays, with Garry charging in from the 1-yard line to make the score 19–13. Rebel quarterback Bobby Garner subsequently fumbled, and Smithart recovered the ball at the Ole Miss 23-yard line, giving the Eagles the chance to take the lead. The USM offense capitalized on the mistake as Hammond connected with Hosemann on a 5-yard touchdown pass and Boyette added the point after to put the Eagles up 20–19. The Rebels fumbled again on their next possession, and Odom's recovery set up another Hosemann touchdown and stretched the lead to 8. The Rebels drove deep into Southern Miss territory early in the fourth quarter but lost another fumble, and the Eagles held on for the 27–19 win. After back-to-back wins over Southeastern Conference teams, the Southern Miss record stood at 3–1.

On the road against the University of Cincinnati on October 1, the USM squad turned in a lackluster effort and went down 17–6. The Bearcats rolled up 455 yards, including 377 rushing, while holding the Golden Eagles to eight first downs and 179 total yards, 37 of them coming on the ground.

The Eagles returned to Roberts Stadium for their Homecoming contest against North Texas State on October 8. The Southern Miss defense gave up 471 yards to the Mean Green, while the offense again struggled, generating only 33 yards passing and 200 total yards in the 27–14 defeat. After the game, Collins assessed his team's anemic performance, telling reporters, "They're a good defensive team, but it is obvious that we have got problems offensively. We've got to iron

Five Golden Eagles who would earn postseason honors in 1977 clown for the cameras. Pictured from left to right are defensive end Bobby Smithart, offensive tackle Eric (Big E) Smith, tailback Ben (Go-Go) Garry, offensive guard Amos Fowler, and defensive tackle Anthony (Stoney) Parker.

out our problems in that respect if we are to finish the season on a winning note."

The following Saturday found the Golden Eagles at Aloha Stadium in Honolulu, playing the Hawaii Rainbows. Down 13–7 at halftime, the Golden Eagles seized the lead with three third-quarter touchdowns—tailback Raymond (Tiko) Beal's 1-yard run, tight end Marvin Harvey's 80-yard reception from quarterback Dane McDaniel, and McDaniel's 35-yard run. Two fourth-quarter touchdowns pulled Hawaii to within 28–26 with just under eight minutes to play. The Rainbows then drove to Eagle 10-yard line and attempted a 27-yard field goal to win the game, but Dixon blocked the kick, preserving the victory. The Eagles had apparently solved their offensive woes, rolling up 510 total yards, although they committed five turnovers.

THE BEAR, BOBBY, THE EAGLES, AND ROBERTS STADIUM

The Eagles returned from Hawaii to meet Mississippi State at Scott Field in Starkville on October 22 and won by a score of 14–7. With the game tied at 7 with 1:22 remaining, the Bulldogs took over at their own 28-yard line. Quarterback Dwayne Brown threw an incompletion on first down, and on the next play, Eagle safety Mike (Crazy) Crenshaw intercepted Brown's pass intended for wide receiver Mardye McDole and returned the ball 36 yards for the winning touchdown. The Bulldogs drove to the Southern 26-yard line, but time ran out before they could score, and the Eagles had the win.

The next game for the 5–3 Golden Eagles was at Liberty Bowl Memorial Stadium against the Memphis State Tigers on October 29. Southern Miss fell behind 20–0 at halftime and never recovered, eventually losing 42–14 in a contest in which the Tigers gained 488 yards of total offense.

Collins and the Eagles got back on the winning track on November 5 on the road against the University of Texas–Arlington. The Golden Eagle defense held the Mavericks to 196 yards and eight first downs, while Garry led the Southern offense with 140 yards in a 20–3 victory.

In contrast to the 1976 season, which had started dismally but ended with a pair of victories, the 1977 season began promisingly but ended with a couple of disappointing defeats. On November 12 at Roberts Stadium, the Golden Eagles lost 28–10 to Louisiana Tech. The lifeless Eagle offense managed just 183 yards, while the defense allowed the Bulldogs 324 yards through the air and 140 yards on the ground. "It was simple. We got out-coached, out-hit and outplayed," Collins fumed after the contest. "It was a good ole country whipping."

The final game of the 1977 season featured Arkansas State at Roberts Stadium. After Boyette kicked a 26-yard field goal midway through the first quarter, the Golden Eagles took a 3–0 lead into the third period, when the Indians scored to take a 7–3 edge. The Eagles answered with a 15-play, 75-yard drive that ended with Hosemann blasting over from the 1-yard line for a 10–7 USM advantage. But Arkansas State drove 80 yards and scored with 55 seconds to go, giving the Indians the 14–10 win and giving Southern Miss a 6–6 record on the year.

Garry, defensive tackle Stoney Parker, and offensive tackle Eric Smith were named first-team All–South Independent and earned honorable mention All-America honors, while offensive guard Amos Fowler and defensive end Bobby Smithart were named second-team All–South Independent. Fowler became the second Southern Miss player to appear in the East-West Shrine Game, following Don Owens in 1957, and Garry played in the Senior Bowl. Both players were taken in the 1978 NFL draft—Fowler in the fifth round by the Detroit Lions and Garry in the sixth round by the Baltimore Colts—as was Smith, who was chosen in the sixth round by the Buffalo Bills.

1978 SEASON

The 1978 campaign opened on the road against the Richmond Spiders. Trailing 7–3 midway through the third quarter, Parker blocked a third-down quick kick by the Spiders, and defensive end James Hale picked up the ball and ran it back for a touchdown that gave Southern Miss the 10–7 victory. The Golden Eagles accumulated just 166 yards of total offense, but the Eagle defense, known as the "Nasty Bunch," limited Richmond to 153 yards.

At War Memorial Stadium in Little Rock, the Golden Eagles met Arkansas State on September 9, rolling to a 21–6 win. After a scoreless first quarter, McDaniel connected with Harvey on a 19-yard touchdown pass and then ran 8 yards for a touchdown to give the Eagles a 14–0 halftime lead. Early in the third quarter, Crenshaw intercepted an Indian pass and raced 28 yards for a touchdown to put the game away.

Facing the University of Cincinnati on the road at Nippert Stadium, the Golden Eagles lost their first game of the season, 26–14. The Southern Miss offense performed terribly, eking out a mere four first downs and 92 total yards.

After an off week, Southern Miss played Ole Miss at Mississippi Memorial Stadium in Jackson on September 30. After falling behind 13–10 midway through the fourth quarter, the Rebels got a 32-yard field goal from Hoppy Langley to tie the game with 3:28 remaining. On the next series, Ole Miss safety Jon Fabris intercepted McDaniel's pass and was heading toward the Southern Miss end zone when he was tackled by defensive end James Hale at the Southern Miss 36-yard line with 1:27 to go. The problem, however, was that Hale was not in the game—he had come off the sidelines to make the stop. The Eagles were penalized 15 yards, moving the ball to the 21, and as the last seconds ticked off the clock, Langley booted a 29-yard field goal with just 16 seconds to go to give Ole Miss the 16–13 victory. Southern Miss fans watching the game had endured a devastating loss and had certainly seen a bizarre play, but most probably did not realize that they had also seen a turning point in the history of USM football. Prior to the contest, the Eagles had switched to the option attack, and the game marked the debut of tailback Sammy Winder, who carried four times for 5 yards.

The following week the Golden Eagles hosted Mississippi State at Roberts Stadium and put together a great comeback win. Trailing 17–7 at halftime, the Eagles cut the lead to just 3 points on a 1-yard run by Winder, who added another 1-yard touchdown gallop shortly thereafter to put his team in front 20–17. The snap for the extra-point kick was poor, and holder Joe Burckel had to pick up the football and scramble, buying himself enough time to find tight end Tom Jordan for the 2-point conversion. The Nasty Bunch kept the Bulldogs in check for the remainder of the game, and the 22–17 victory improved the Eagles' overall record to 3–2. "This football team has character," Collins said. "They came out here tonight and there was never any doubt in their mind they were going to come back and win. They don't know the word quit."

The Golden Eagles hosted the East Carolina Pirates on October 14 at Roberts Stadium and opened the game with a 65-yard touchdown drive, with tailback Chuck Cook doing the scoring honors on a 6-yard touchdown run. USM extended its lead to 14 points when Parker recovered an East Carolina fumble on the Pirates' first possession of the night, setting up a 51-yard Hammond-to-Harvey scoring pass. But the Pirates roared back with 16 second-quarter points to take a 16–14 halftime lead. Both defenses stiffened during the second half, with the Eagles scoring the winning points when Boyette knocked a 35-yard field goal through the uprights midway through the third quarter. Linebackers Cliff Lewis and Clump Taylor contributed two late interceptions to defuse East Carolina scoring threats, and the Eagles had the 17–16 victory. "Chalk that one up as another true team victory," Collins said afterward. "The offense carried us in the first half and when the offense bogged down in the second half the defense came through for us. There's no way to call it anything except another team win."

At Liberty Bowl Memorial Stadium in Memphis on October 21, the Eagles won their third game in a row, improving to 5–2 on the year with the 13–10 defeat of longtime foe Memphis State. On USM's first play from scrimmage, Hammond pitched the ball to tailback Ricky Floyd, a former high school quarterback who pulled up and threw downfield, hitting wide receiver Chuck Carr Brown for a 56-yard touchdown just 21 seconds into the game. Memphis State took advantage of a Southern Miss fumble to cut the lead to 7–3 at the end of the first quarter and then took the second-half kickoff and marched 96 yards downfield for a 10–7 lead, but Southern Miss battled back to tie the game on a 30-yard Boyette field goal in the opening minutes of the fourth quarter. Mid-

way through the fourth quarter, Southern Miss free safety Danny Jackson intercepted a long pass by Memphis State quarterback Lloyd Patterson, giving the Eagles the ball at their own 45-yard line. They drove to the Tiger 8, where Boyette kicked a 25-yard field goal with 2:43 left to give the Eagles the 13–10 win and improved their record to 5–2.

USM's winning streak ended with a 38–16 Homecoming loss to Florida State on October 28 at Roberts Stadium. With the Seminoles leading 10–0 early in the second quarter, Golden Eagle tailback Tiko Beal scored on a 1-yard run. FSU scored again to extend the lead back to 10 points, but Hammond connected with Brown on a 23-yard touchdown pass to close the gap to 17–14 at the half. The Seminoles dominated the second half, however, scoring 21 points and limiting the Golden Eagles to just a safety.

The following week, Southern Miss lost its second game in a row, falling to North Texas State 25–12 at Denton. Five Golden Eagle turnovers led to a 16–0 first-half deficit, and the USM squad never recovered. The Eagles rushed for 243 yards and had 355 total yards, but the turnovers negated that production. "Our team was extremely flat in the first half and I don't know why," Collins reflected. "We played as poorly as we have all year in the first half."

Now 5–4, the Eagles played their final two games at home. On November 11 Southern Miss hosted Bowling Green, and the Eagles turned in one of their best performances of the season in the 38–21 win. Although the Falcons led 21–14 at halftime, they fumbled on back-to-back possessions during the third quarter, mistakes that led to a pair of Southern Miss touchdowns that vaulted the Eagles into a lead they never relinquished. Against the Louisville Cardinals a week later, the Golden Eagles led 10–3 at halftime and broke the game open with a big third quarter. Lewis's fumble recovery led to a touchdown pass from McDaniel to Harvey, and McDaniel followed up with another touchdown pass, this time to tight end Larry Harrington, to extend the advantage to 24–3. McDaniel and Floyd added touchdown runs in the fourth quarter to give the Eagles the 37–3 win. The Nasty Bunch limited the Cardinals to 132 yards, while Southern compiled 351 yards of offense. The Eagles finished the year at 7–4, and Collins told the media, "I think all of our folks now should holler and whoop it up, and try to get us in a postseason game." No bowl bid was forthcoming, however.

Offensive tackle Randy Butler was named first-team All–South Independent and honorable mention All-America, and he represented Southern Miss in the Senior Bowl. Parker and Taylor also were named first-team All–South Independent and honorable mention All-America, while offensive tackle Greg Ahrens and defensive back David O'Dom were named to the All–South Independent second team.

1979 SEASON

Collins and the Golden Eagles opened the 1979 season on the road on September 8 in Tallahassee against the Florida State Seminoles. Few people

With victories over Ole Miss and Mississippi State in 1977 and 1979, Golden Eagle fans declared their team the Mississippi State champs.

had given Southern Miss much of a chance, but the Eagles held a 14–3 lead heading into the fourth quarter on two touchdowns by Floyd, the second one coming just after halftime when nose guard Albert Teague set up a drive by recovering an FSU fumble. Florida State closed the gap to 14–9 after blocking a punt by freshman Bruce Thompson. The next USM possession led to another Thompson punt, and Seminole Greg Henry returned this one for 65-yard touchdown. With the 2-point conversion, Florida State had a 17–14 win.

The following week, the Golden Eagles played their first home game of the season against the

Cincinnati Bearcats. A pair of short touchdown runs by Floyd gave Southern Miss a 15–6 lead at halftime, and a fourth-quarter field goal by Winston Walker and a touchdown pass from McDaniel to Harvey made the final score 24–6. The Golden Eagle defense held the Bearcats to just 196 total yards and registered a couple of interceptions in the victory. Despite the 1–1 start, Coach Collins was pleased with his team's performance in its first two games: "I've already said we have the best team we have had since I've been here. This team has balance both offensively and defensively."

Next up for the Eagles was a September 22 road contest against the Auburn Tigers, who were coached by former Southern Miss quarterback Doug Barfield. USM put up little resistance as Auburn cruised to an easy 31–9 win. The Golden Eagles rushed 56 times for 109 yards and completed 11 of 23 passes for 152 yards. "At times our poor execution hurt us as much as anything else. We felt that we would have to throw more and better than we had before," Collins said. "We had our offense going good until we fell behind and had to throw just about every down. I didn't see much wrong with our running game, however."

On September 29 at Jackson's Memorial Stadium, the Golden Eagles crushed the Ole Miss Rebels 38–8. The Eagles took the opening kickoff and went 80 yards in 11 plays, with Beal scoring on a 2-yard run to give USM a lead it never relinquished. Later in the opening quarter, McDaniel hooked up with Harvey on a 63-yard touchdown pass to extend the Eagle advantage to 14 points. Southern then shocked the Rebels with an onside kick, recovering the ball at the Ole Miss 42-yard line. The Eagles failed to score on that possession but subsequently recovered a fumbled punt at the Rebel 10, and Floyd quickly scored to give his squad a 21–0 lead at intermission. Walker punched through a 47-yard field goal in the third quarter, Floyd added a 15-yard touchdown run after the Eagles recovered another Ole Miss fumble, and Corner closed out the Eagle scoring with a 14-yard touchdown run. Southern Miss amassed 256 rushing yards—98 of them by Floyd—and passed six times for another 107 yards in picking up its second win of the year. Ole Miss Coach Steve Sloan was gracious in defeat, saying, "We just got beat very badly. Southern was better prepared and deserved to win. Coach Collins and his staff did a tremendous job and their players really played hard. They deserved everything they got."

Southern Miss made its first appearance on national television when the school hosted North Texas State on October 6 in a game that would be shown on a delayed basis on a new cable network, ESPN. The Golden Eagles treated the national audience to an impressive 30–10 win over the Mean Green. North Texas grabbed a 3–0 lead, but McDaniel hit Harvey on a 54-yard touchdown pass to give the Eagles a 7–3 edge at halftime. The Mean Green regained the lead 10–7 early in the third quarter, but Walker's 22-yard field goal tied the game before the Eagles added three more touchdowns for the win. Floyd finished the night with 19 carries for 128 yards and two touchdowns, and he threw for another touchdown on a halfback-option pass.

Located in New Orleans, just 100 miles from Hattiesburg, Tulane had never faced Southern Miss in football, although the two schools had played in virtually every other sport. That changed on October 13, 1979, when the Green Wave traveled to Roberts Stadium for what turned out to be a thrilling game. The Eagles took a 13–7 halftime lead on McDaniel's 1-yard touchdown run and Floyd's 64-yard punt return. The Green Wave's first possession of the second half ended with a punt, but Floyd fumbled the catch and Tulane recovered at the USM 16-yard line. Quarterback Roch Hontas immediately hit tight end Rodney Holman for the touchdown and the 14–13 advantage. The Eagles came back with a 12-play, 60-yard drive capped by another 1-yard touchdown run by McDaniel, but the 2-point conversion failed, leaving Southern up by 5 with 4:23 remaining. With under a minute to go, Hontas hit Robert Moses with a touchdown pass, putting the Green Wave ahead 20–19 after Hontas's 2-point conversion pass fell incomplete. Floyd took Eddie Murray's kickoff in the end zone and lateraled the ball to Harvey, who streaked up the sideline to the Green Wave 10-yard line. After a clipping penalty, however, the ball was brought back to the Eagle 30, and with time running out, McDaniel connected with split end Larry Taylor for 46 yards to the Tulane 24-yard line. With no timeouts and the clock ticking down, the Eagles rushed their field goal unit onto the field, but Walker's 41-yard kick just missed to the right, and the Green Wave escaped with the win.

Now at 3–3, the Golden Eagles entertained the Memphis State Tigers on October 20 and recorded USM's first shutout since 1975 and its first ever at Roberts Stadium. The Golden Eagle defense starred in the 22–0 victory, holding the Tigers to an average of .75 yards per carry on the ground and limiting them to 107 yards of offense. In addition, the Nasty Bunch recorded four interceptions and recovered three fumbles, never giving Memphis State a chance to get into the game.

At Mississippi State on October 27, the Golden Eagles fell behind 7–0 on halfback Michael Haddix's 98-yard touchdown run. USM tied the game when defensive tackle Gary Ivy intercepted Bulldog quarterback Tony Black's pass—the only pickoff of Ivy's career—and returned the ball to the Mississippi State 9-yard line, setting up a 1-yard touchdown run by Winder. The Eagles' next possession resulted in a five-play, 54-yard drive that ended with Floyd's 6-yard score to give USM a 14–7 advantage at halftime. The Eagles added another touchdown midway through the third quarter when Beal took the ball in from 3 yards out, and the Eagle defense kept the Bulldogs out of the end zone the rest of the way for the 21–7 win that improved USM's record to 5–3 on the year.

The Louisville Cardinals hosted the Eagles the following week, with Southern Miss scoring first on a 2-yard run by Floyd. The Cardinals returned the ensuing kickoff 89 yards for a touchdown to tie the game and kicked a field goal late in the second quarter to take a 10–7 advantage into the locker room. Walker's 22-yard field goal for the Eagles tied the game late in the third quarter, and neither team could record any further points.

Although the Eagle offense played poorly, committing seven turnovers, the Cardinals failed to capitalize on the mistakes as the Nasty Bunch limited the Louisville offense to 177 total yards.

On November 10, the Golden Eagles and the Bowling Green Falcons battled down to the wire before Southern Miss suffered its fourth loss of the season, 31–27 on the road. The Golden Eagles were leading 24–21 when Bowling Green got a field goal to tie the game with just over 12 minutes to go. Walker kicked a 37-yard field goal to give the Eagles a 27–24 lead with 5:02 remaining, but the Falcons responded with a 10-play, 82-yard drive capped by a 15-yard touchdown pass from quarterback Mike Wright to Kevin Browning with 1:26 left. Chuck Cook took the ensuing kickoff and lateraled the ball to Harvey, who returned it 88 yards to the Bowling Green 12. Trailing 31–27, the Eagles gained only a yard before McDaniel's pass was intercepted, giving the Falcons the victory. The Nasty Bunch failed to live up to their moniker, yielding 486 yards on the day.

The season finale occurred on November 17 at Roberts Stadium against Arkansas State, a contest that was scoreless after three quarters. Beal's 5-yard run gave Southern Miss a 7–0 advantage, and his 1-yard run increased the lead to 14 with 6:57 remaining. After Beal fumbled, the Indians scored with 23 seconds to go, but the Golden Eagles held on for the 14–6 win and finished the year at 6-4-1. More important than the victory or the season mark, however, was a second-quarter change by the coaching staff that revolutionized Golden Eagle football. After the first period, Collins replaced his veteran quarterback, McDaniel, with freshman Reggie Collier. Although Collier's numbers in the game—37 yards rushing and 8 completions in 12 attempts for 77 yards—were not particularly impressive, over the next few years he became one of the country's most dangerous threats.

Harvey, defensive tackle J. J. Stewart, and linebacker Clump Taylor were named first-team All–South Independent and honorable mention All-America, and Stewart appeared in the Senior Bowl.

As the 1970s came to an end, the Golden Eagles were on the verge of gaining the national spotlight. The next decade brought some of the greatest and most exciting moments in Southern Miss football history—but also some of the darkest.

Bobby Collins served as head coach of the Golden Eagles from 1975 to 1981. He led the team to postseason bowl games in 1980 and 1981, the first for the team since the late 1950s.

EAGLE FEVER AND I BELIEVE
1980–1989

During the 1980s, the football team at the University of Southern Mississippi got a new athletic director, had three head football coaches, appeared in three bowl games, and, for the first time since moving up to Division I, appeared in the Associated Press (AP) and United Press International (UPI) polls. The Golden Eagles established themselves as one of the country's best college football programs but also felt the sting of probation imposed by the National Collegiate Athletic Association as a result of rules violations. The decade also featured what might have

The dive for a touchdown by tailback Sammy Winder, perhaps the most famous play in school history, helped the Golden Eagles to a 28–22 win over the Ole Miss Rebels in 1980.

been the two best players ever to suit up for Southern Miss, quarterbacks Reggie Collier and Brett Favre, as well as the continuation of the Nasty Bunch defense, which placed the Golden Eagles among college football's elite defensive teams.

1980 SEASON

The Golden Eagles opened on September 6 in the Louisiana Superdome in New Orleans against the Tulane Green Wave. With the Green Wave's 20–19 win the previous year fresh in their minds, the Golden Eagles were determined to gain a bit of revenge before a crowd of more than 44,000 and an ABC-TV audience, USM's first appearance on over-the-air network television. Southern Miss spotted Tulane a 14–0 lead before rallying late in the game, with key plays including punt returns by Ricky (Sweet Pea) Floyd, several third-down conversions by quarterback Reggie Collier, and a pair of clutch catches by tight end Marvin Harvey. The stubborn defense contributed interceptions by safety Chuck Cook and defensive end George (Too-Tall) Tillman. And kicker Winston Walker atoned for missing a field goal at the buzzer during the teams' first meeting by splitting the uprights from 36 yards out with 31 seconds left to give Southern Miss a 17–14 victory. "When I kicked it, I didn't even have to look. I knew it was good. I've always dreamed about this. I feel so good it's unreal," Walker exulted.

Quarterback Reggie Collier (1979–1982) became the first player in NCAA Division I history to rush for 1,000 yards and pass for 1,000 yards in the same season.

Walk-on tailback Sammy Winder (1978–1981) eventually earned a scholarship and rushed for over 100 yards in a game nine times in his career. He finished his career with 3,114 yards rushing and 39 touchdowns.

"Coaches had told us during the week that we'd had a big game against Tulane and that a lot of people say we have a big game then we drop down," said Tillman. "That fired us up. There was no letdown tonight."

Southern Miss had not played at East Carolina since losing 48–0 in 1976, but the Golden Eagles returned to Greenville on September 27 and trounced the Pirates 35–7. Led by the running of Winder and Collier, the Golden Eagles were nearly unstoppable. Winder turned in the first of three three-touchdown games in a row, scoring from 19, 3, and 24 yards out. The Eagles added a late touchdown when defensive end Rhett Whitley blocked a punt and defensive end Robert Phillips scooped the ball up and ran 33 yards for a touchdown. East Carolina managed only 197 yards of total offense, including just 30 on the ground, and the Eagles improved their record to 3–0 on the year. "The momentum switched but our players reacted like we hoped they would," Coach Bobby Collins said. "The defense got us a turnover and we took it in for a touchdown, and we went right back to our knitting. I couldn't be prouder of our players."

Against Ole Miss in Jackson on October 4, the Golden Eagles again trailed 14–0, and again they overcame the deficit, winning 28–22. The Rebels

Southern Miss recorded the first of what would be three victories over Southland Conference foes by rolling to a 38–11 win over Louisiana Tech two weeks later in the Eagles' first game of the season at Roberts Stadium. Tailback Sammy Winder rushed for touchdowns of 2 and 4 yards, while Collier connected with Harvey and wide receiver Don Horn on a pair of touchdown passes. USM's Nasty Bunch also turned in another strong performance, limiting Louisiana Tech to 214 yards.

EAGLE FEVER AND I BELIEVE

scored in each of the first two quarters to open up a lead, but the Golden Eagles answered with a 1-yard touchdown run by Winder and a 62-yard scoring strike from Collier to Horn to tie the game at 14 at halftime. In the third quarter Winder gave his team the lead with a magnificent 11-yard scoring run on which he hurdled a Rebel defender at the 5-yard line and landed in the end zone. Winder added another rushing touchdown in the fourth quarter to stake his team to a 28–14 edge, but the Nasty Bunch allowed the Rebels to close to within 28–22 before slamming the door. Winder fumbled, and Ole Miss drove to the Golden Eagle 8-yard line, but Tillman sacked Ole Miss quarterback John Fourcade on three consecutive plays to end the threat. "We had been rushing three and dropping eight," Southern Miss defensive coordinator Jim Carmody recalled. "But you can do that just so much. Sooner or later, that guy [Fourcade] is going to scramble around and hurt you. We didn't feel like we could blitz when we went into the game, but we had to gamble." The Rebels managed only 208 yards against the Eagle defense, while the Eagles rolled up 428 yards.

Southern Miss went to 5–0 with a big 42–14 win over Mississippi State in Starkville on October 11 that locked up the mythical state title for the Golden Eagles, Collins's third state championship in his six seasons at the USM helm. A 26-yard touchdown pass from Collier to Floyd and a pair of touchdown runs by Winder gave Southern Miss a 21–0 lead early in the third quarter. The Bulldogs twice threatened to get back in the game, scoring on wide receiver Mardye McDole's 62-yard third-quarter run and running back George Wonsley's 30-yard fourth-quarter jaunt, but both times the Eagles answered. Fullback Mike Woodard turned in a 67-yard touchdown run of his own, and Collier produced a 53-yard touchdown gallop. "I can't say enough about this football team," Collins said of his team's fourth straight win over his alma mater. "We make the big plays. We beat a mighty good football team today on its home field at its Homecoming." "How many 5–0 teams are there?" asked linebacker Cliff Lewis in the Eagle locker room. "How many teams can beat Mississippi State like that? I definitely think we deserve a national ranking. Why not?"

Southern Miss improved to 6–0 for the first time in 22 years with an easy 35–0 shutout of the Arkansas State Indians at Roberts Stadium on October 18. The Nasty Bunch defense again dominated, holding the Indians to 19 yards of total offense (24 rushing and -5 through the air) and one first down (on a penalty). In contrast, the Eagle offense rolled up 496 yards, including 363 on the ground. The victory moved the Golden Eagles into the AP and UPI polls for the first time in their Division I history, with both organizations ranking USM at No. 20. Eagle Fever swept the state, with supporters sporting "I Believe" buttons and singing along to "Eagle Fever," a song by Jackson barber Bill Goodson.

The season's next contest, an October 25 matchup against the No. 1 Alabama Crimson Tide in Tuscaloosa, attracted considerable national attention. Alabama scored first, but the Eagles answered with a 75-yard drive that culminated in

Winder's 1-yard touchdown early in the second quarter. But it was all downhill from there for the Eagles, as the Tide proved that they deserved their ranking by crushing the USM squad 42–7 and knocking the Golden Eagles from the polls. The Eagles had contributed to their demise by losing three fumbles, and Collins acknowledged after the game, "We said all along, you can't win if you make mistakes and give them blood transfusions."

The Golden Eagles next cruised to a 36–10 home win against Lamar. The Golden Eagle defense allowed only 220 yards, while the offense put up 442 yards and Winder scored three touchdowns for the fourth time that season. Although the Eagles led just 7–3 at halftime, 29 second-half points put the game away. The Eagles upped their record to 7–1, their best start since 1962.

At Auburn on November 8, the Golden Eagles turned in a poor performance, throwing the ball an uncharacteristic 43 times, gaining only 232 yards while surrendering 471, and suffering a 31–0 defeat by the War Eagles. "We didn't move the ball, and we didn't score when we had the opportunity," Collins said after losing to former Southern Miss standout and Auburn Coach Doug Barfield. "We didn't play one of our better games defensively. I don't think we played well at all, period."

The Golden Eagles hosted the University of Richmond Spiders on November 15. The two teams traded field goals during the first half and had played to a 6–6 tie at the break, but Winder scored three times on 1-yard runs in the third quarter, and the Golden Eagles added a 20-yard touchdown pass from Floyd to wide receiver Mike Livings to secure a 33–12 victory.

With their team at 8–2, USM supporters began to talk about postseason bowl games, and Collins encouraged the discussion: "I will say this. There are teams that will be in bowl games with not as good a record as we have and that we have beaten." "I think we will get a bid," Athletic Director Roland Dale told the media after the Richmond game. "I believe this team is very deserving of a bid." Later in the week, the Independence Bowl invited the Eagles to face Southland Conference champion McNeese State, and USM officials accepted the offer.

Southern Miss closed out the regular season on November 22, a rainy, miserable night in Hattiesburg, against the University of Louisville, with both teams aware that mistakes would be costly. The Golden Eagles made one when the ball popped out of Collier's grasp with less than four minutes to go, and the Cardinals recovered and kicked a 38-yard field goal for a 6–3 win, giving Southern an 8–3 mark on the year.

The Golden Eagles' first postseason bowl appearance since the 1957 season occurred on December 13, when they played the McNeese State Cowboys in the Independence Bowl in Shreveport, Louisiana. Southern Miss had not won at four previous bowl appearances but jumped out to a 10–0 first-quarter lead on a 36-yard Walker field goal and a 14-yard touchdown run by fullback Clemon Terrell. Trailing 10–7 at halftime, McNeese State rallied to go ahead 14–10 late in the third quarter. With time running out in the fourth quarter, Collins decided to punt the ball and hope for a turnover or a quick stop. The Nasty Boys justified their coach's gamble by forcing a fumble, and linebacker Ron Brown recovered at the Cowboy 7-yard line with 2:24 left. Three plays moved the ball to the McNeese State 1, where the Eagles faced a fourth down. Woodard, usually a blocker in the goal-line offense, started in motion, and Collier faked to Winder up the middle before pitching to Woodard, who raced around left end to score with 1:17 to go. Walker missed the extra-point kick, leaving his team with a 16–14 advantage, but the USM defense again came up big: nose guard Jerald Baylis recorded a quarterback sack, and cornerback Hanford Dixon recovered a Cowboy fumble to ice the game. "The play was a zip sweep where I started in motion to the right and then came back to the left for the pitch," recalled Woodard. "Because Reggie waited until the last minute to pitch the ball, it sucked the defense up. First they went after Sammy going over the top, then they almost had Reggie, then when Reggie pitched the ball to me, nobody was around. I just took off for the goal line." The Golden Eagle defense had turned in a superb performance, recovering four fumbles and recording an interception. Baylis was named the game's Most Valuable Player. The postseason victory gave the Golden Eagles a final record of 9–3, their most wins since 1962.

Dixon, Harvey, Tillman, Winder, and center Jamey Watson were named to the All–South Independent team and also were named honorable mention All-Americans. Dixon earned first-team All-America honors from the *Sporting News,* and Harvey was a first-team selection by the Newspaper Enterprise Association. Both Dixon and Harvey appeared in the Senior Bowl, while Winder and Whitley played in the East-West Shrine Game. The Cleveland Browns selected Dixon in the first round of the 1981 NFL draft (twenty-second player overall), while Harvey went in the third round to the Kansas City Chiefs and Lewis went to the Green Bay Packers in the twelfth round.

1981 SEASON

The Golden Eagles opened the campaign at Roberts Stadium on September 5 against Southwestern Louisiana. Collier's 14-yard touchdown run gave Southern Miss a 7–0 edge, and Winder's 2-yard touchdown run upped the lead to 14. The Ragin' Cajuns cut the lead to 14–7, but Winder added another 2-yard touchdown run to put USM ahead 19–7 at halftime. With the Nasty Bunch limiting Southwestern Louisiana to 174 yards, the Golden Eagles rolled to an easy 33–7 win, accumulating 401 yards of total offense. Collier passed for 127 yards and rushed for 47 more. "I really felt this was what we needed," said Collins, "to play a game and see what we thought of our offensive line and our defensive secondary and

By the time Hanford Dixon (1977–1980) finished his career at Southern Miss, he had established himself as one of the school's best cornerbacks. He was a first-round draft pick of the Cleveland Browns in 1981.

our linebackers. We knew we had quality people in Winder and Floyd and Collier and those people. They took up where they left off last year."

After an open date, the Golden Eagles went after their second win of the season on September 19 at home against the Tulane Green Wave. Collier rushed for a touchdown and passed for another as the Eagles recorded a 21–3 victory. The Eagles opened the scoring in the first quarter when Collier hit tight end Jim Brown with a 7-yard touchdown pass and then extended the lead to 14–3 before halftime when Collier scored on a 3-yard run. Winder added USM's final touchdown early in the third quarter on a 1-yard run. The Nasty Bunch turned in another outstanding performance, limiting the Green Wave to just 109 yards rushing and snagging three interceptions, two of them by free safety Danny Jackson, who had missed the season opener.

The Golden Eagles hit the road for a September 26 matchup with the Richmond Spiders. The Eagles scored first when Collier hit Louis Lipps with a 16-yard scoring pass in the opening quarter. The Spiders came right back to tie the game at 7 when quarterback Napoleon DuBois connected with tight end Rich Scherer on a 71-yard scoring strike. The Eagles moved ahead 14–7 on Collier's 10-yard touchdown run in the second period, but Richmond kicked a 41-yard field goal as time expired in the first half to cut the lead to 4. The only points of the second half came on a 40-yard field goal by Golden Eagle kicker Steve Clark, and the 17–10 win improved the Eagles to 3–0. "I'm pleased with the win, but not satisfied with the play," said Collins. "The team made mental errors and the coaches made mental errors that indicate mental alertness wasn't what it should have been. I'm talking about being hyped up, ready to win."

On October 3, Southern Miss hosted the University of Texas–Arlington Mavericks for Homecoming, and the Golden Eagles rolled up a school-record 630 yards of total offense in a 52–9 rout. Collier turned in one of the greatest individual performances in school history, rushing for 186 yards, including touchdown runs of 80 and 84 yards, and throwing for an additional 112 yards, including a 62-yard scoring toss to Horn. The Nasty Bunch defense limited the Mavericks to 229 yards.

Before a crowd of 76,400 at Birmingham's Legion Field, Southern Miss met Alabama on October 10. With 2:57 left in the game, the Eagles were behind 13–10 with the ball on their own 20-yard line and no timeouts. On third-and-13 at the Alabama 48-yard line, Collier hit tight end Raymond Powell at the 21 with just eight seconds to go. With the Eagles scrambling to spike the ball to stop the clock and give their field goal unit a chance to tie the game, the Alabama defense inexplicably called a timeout. Alabama Coach Bear Bryant later said that he didn't know why his team had called the timeout: "I guess it was disorganization and confusion more than anything else." The timeout allowed the Eagles to regroup, and Clark drilled his second field goal of the day from 40 yards out to enable the Eagles to salvage the tie. Although he had already missed field goals of 34, 38 and 42 yards, Clark was calm with the game on the line: "This time I was thinking, 'Just kick the ball.' I was over there all by myself. I had thought that it might come

Placekicker Steve Clark (1981–1983) kicked 41 field goals in his career and 89 extra points for 212 points, more than any other Southern Miss kicker in history.

down to me kicking. But when it comes time to kick, you don't think about it. A field goal should be automatic, just like an extra point." Collier completed 14 of 25 passes for 202 yards and ran for a touchdown, and the Eagles remained undefeated on the season.

The Golden Eagles next battled Memphis State on October 17 at Liberty Bowl Stadium. Three inches of rain fell during the contest, with USM winning 10–0 on a 24-yard touchdown run by Collier and a 33-yard field goal by Clark. Winder rushed for a career-high 175 yards on 29 carries, while the Nasty Bunch limited the Tigers to just 178 yards. The victory ran the Golden Eagles' season record to 5–0–1.

Southern Miss played its second straight game in a driving rainstorm on October 31, defeating North Texas State 22–0. Collier scored the game's first two touchdowns on 54-yard and 13-yard runs, while Winder added a 1-yard touchdown run and the Nasty Bunch trapped the Mean Green quarterback in the end zone for the game's final points. The USM defense limited North Texas State, coached by former Mississippi State Coach Bob Tyler, to an average of only 0.9 yards per play, and Winder piled up 140 yards on 26 carries for his second straight 100-yard rushing game. "It wasn't tough playing in those conditions," said Baylis. "It got the offense slowed down. It made us the aggressors. We've been playing in it the last couple of weeks. It got us hyped up. It made us think shutout. We knew at the half we hadn't allowed them but one first down." The win vaulted the Golden Eagles to No. 20 in the AP poll and to No. 18 in the UPI poll, their first national rankings of the season.

On November 7, the Golden Eagles and the Mississippi State Bulldogs, ranked seventeenth in the AP poll, faced off at Jackson's Veterans Memorial Stadium before 64,112 excited spectators, the largest crowd ever for a sporting event in Mississippi, as well as an ABC-TV audience. The Bulldogs took a 6–0 lead on two field goals by Dana Moore, but Mississippi State fumbled a punt late in the second quarter, and the Golden Eagles recovered the ball at the Bulldog 14-yard line. Winder scored from the 1-yard line three plays later and Clark tacked on the extra point to give Southern Miss a 7–6 advantage at halftime. Defense dominated the second half, with the Nasty Bunch stopping the Bulldogs twice on fourth-and-1 to preserve the victory for the Eagles. The Bulldogs' explosive attack was held to 250 yards, while the USM offense managed only 195 yards. Now boasting a 7–0–1 record, the Golden Eagles moved up to fourteenth in the AP poll and tenth in the UPI rankings.

Again playing in front of the ABC-TV cameras as well as Tangerine Bowl officials, who indicated that they would be interested in the winner of the contest, the Golden Eagles met Florida State on November 14 in Tallahassee. The Eagles scored on their first seven possessions and trounced the Seminoles, who had beaten Ohio State and Notre Dame on the road and had been ranked twentieth by the AP, 58–14. USM rushed for 368 yards passed for an additional 128, while the Nasty Bunch limited the Seminoles to 290 total yards and held Florida State scoreless until the outcome had long since been decided. "It was a great effort from our football team," Collins said. "It seems like week after week we have got to prove something. They had to prove it again today, and they did." The AP rankings now had the Golden Eagles at No. 9, while the UPI poll had them at No. 8.

Undefeated and playing their sixth straight game away from Roberts Stadium, the Golden Eagles faced the Louisville Cardinals on November 21 in another game televised by ABC. With temperatures at or below freezing and with rain occasionally falling, the Eagles had a 3–0 halftime lead on Clark's 28-yard second-quarter field goal. But the Cardinals fought back and took a 6–3 lead when quarterback Dean May hit split end Keith Humphries with a 6-yard touchdown pass and the extra point failed. May extended the Cardinal lead to 13–3 with a 3-yard touchdown strike. The Eagles closed the gap to 13–10 on Winder's 1-yard touchdown run and had a chance to score in the game's final minutes, but the drive stalled deep in Cardinal territory and Louisville had the upset. Nevertheless, Tangerine Bowl officials invited Collins and his squad to play in their second straight postseason bowl game. The defeat dropped the Eagles to fifteenth in the UPI poll and seventeenth in the AP rankings.

The Golden Eagles rebounded from their first loss of the season with a record-setting 45–14 thrashing of Lamar on November 28 at Roberts Stadium. The game was tied at 14 at the end of the first period, but USM used 17 second-quarter points to run away with the contest. The Golden Eagles amassed 612 yards of total offense, and Collier became the first NCAA Division I quarterback to surpass 1,000 yards rushing and passing in a single season. Three USM players gained more than 100 yards in the game—Collier with 184 yards, Winder with 117 yards, and Floyd with 105 yards—and Winder added three touchdowns to finish his career as USM's career leader in touchdowns (39) and points scored (234). Collier recorded two touchdowns to bring him to 72 points scored on the season, tying Winder for the team lead. The AP ranked the Golden Eagles eighteenth during the following week.

The Golden Eagles played in the Tangerine Bowl in Orlando on December 19, facing the Missouri Tigers for the first time in the two schools' histories. The 50,450 fans in attendance as well as the players endured a bitterly cold night, with temperatures near freezing. The Eagles could manage only a 37-yard second-quarter field goal from Clark and trailed 13–3 at halftime but quickly cut the deficit to 13–10 when Winder scored on a 4-yard run early in the third quarter. A pair of short Tiger field goals gave Missouri a 19–10 lead late in the game, but with just 1:03 remaining, reserve quarterback Davy Sellers connected with Lipps on a 74-yard touchdown pass, and Clark added the extra point to bring the Eagles within 2. The Eagles attempted

During the weeklong activities at the Tangerine Bowl in Orlando in 1981, offensive lineman Dwayne Massey (right) represented the Golden Eagles against Missouri in a prime rib eating contest. Looking on are teammates Shane Gabourel (#28) and Mike Alford.

an onside kick, but the Tigers recovered the ball and ran out the clock to take the 19–17 win. USM cornerback Bruce (Juice) Miller had the game's only interception and was named the bowl's Most Valuable Defensive Player. The loss gave the Golden Eagles a 9–2–1 record on the year. They finished nineteenth in the final UPI rankings and were not ranked in the final AP poll.

Collier was named a third-team All-America by the AP and a first-team All–South Independent. Baylis, Tillman, and Winder were named honorable mention All-America as well as first-team All–South Independent. Safety Bud Brown, defensive end Rhett Whitley, and offensive tackle Glen Howe were named second-team All–South Independent. Winder played in the Senior Bowl and East-West Shrine Game, and the Denver Broncos selected him in the fifth round of the 1982 NFL draft. Floyd also was selected, going in the tenth round to Cleveland.

In early January 1982 Collins accepted the head coaching job at Southern Methodist Univer-

The Southern Miss cheerleaders of the 1960s were always on hand to cheer the Southerners on.

Art Newberry (left) and Danny Jackson (right) combine to break up an Ole Miss pass play during one of the many battles between the two schools in the late 1970s at Jackson's Memorial Stadium.

The Pride of Mississippi marching band travels to many Southern Miss road games. Here they perform at halftime at Mississippi State in the mid 1960s.

Head coach P. W. Underwood is pictured with the 1973 seniors. Front row (left to right): Gerry Saggus, Doyle Orange, Mike Dennery, Underwood, Terrence Wells, Wilson Plunkett, and Doug White; back row: Jim Montgomery, Eugene Bird, Harvey McGee, T. A. Ricks, Fred Cook, Mike Moon, Jim Boesch, and Dennis Malone.

Jim Carmody, who had served as defensive coordinator of the Golden Eagles under Bobby Collins, became head coach in January 1982 when Collins left for SMU.

Curley Hallman served as an assistant coach at Texas A&M before becoming the head coach at Southern Miss in 1988. He led the Golden Eagles to a 10–2 record and a berth in the Independence Bowl his first year.

Quarterback Brett Favre uncorks a long pass. From 1987 to 1990, he passed for 7,695 yards and 52 touchdowns and led the Golden Eagles to the 1988 Independence Bowl and the 1990 All-American Bowl.

Quarterback Brett Favre looks for an open receiver during the 1989 season opener against No. 6 Florida State in Jacksonville's Gator Bowl. The Eagles defeated the Seminoles 28–24 in the nationally televised game.

Offensive guard Chafan Marsh (1988–1991) provides the block for tailback Ricky Bradley (1987–1989).

Greg Dampeer (#45) and linebacker Greg Haeusler (#37) combine to cause a fumble. The two defensive standouts were leaders of the Nasty Bunch in the early 1980s.

Cedric Walthaw (left), Lytrel Pollard (middle) and T. J. Slaughter (right) formed one of the best linebacking groups in school history in the 1990s.

Middle linebacker Marchant Kenney (#43) was one of the leaders of the Golden Eagle defense during a career that spanned from 1994 to 1997.

Defensive end Jeff Posey closes in on the Louisiana-Lafayette quarterback to record a safety during a 52–27 Southern Miss win in 1996.

Running back Harold Shaw (#14) rushed for 32 touchdowns during his career, which spanned from 1994 to 1997. He led the 1997 team in rushing with 1,045 yards.

Bandit end Adalius Thomas (#97) was named a first-team All-American by the American Football Coaches Association in 1998.

Linebackers Michael Villalonga (#49) and T. J. Slaughter (#34) await the opening coin toss prior to the 1999 AXA Liberty Bowl in Memphis, where the Golden Eagles would defeat Colorado State 23–17.

Middle linebacker T. J. Slaughter (#34) causes a fumble against the Alabama Crimson Tide during one of the many battles between the two schools in the 1990s.

Quarterback Lee Roberts (1995–1998) helped lead the Golden Eagles to Conference USA championships in 1996 and 1997.

Cedric Scott (left) and DeQuincy Scott hold the championship trophy of the 2000 GMAC Mobile Alabama Bowl, where Southern Miss defeated TCU 28–21. Courtesy of Bert King Photography.

Golden Eagle cheerleader Brooke Bridges leads the crowd during a 2003 game at the Rock. Courtesy of Bert King Photography.

Tailback Derrick Nix rushed for over 1,000 yards in three separate seasons, including a career-high 1,194 yards as a senior in 2002. Courtesy of Bert King Photography.

Nix led the Golden Eagles to a 23–20 victory over defending Big Ten champion Illinois at the Rock in 2002.

Following the 2002 season, linebacker Rod Davis won the Conerly Trophy, which is awarded to Mississippi's top college football player. Courtesy of Bert King Photography.

When the Golden Eagles hosted TCU in a game broadcast by ESPN, the fans were confident Southern Miss would win the 2003 Conference USA championship. Courtesy of Bert King Photography.

Safety Etric Pruitt was one of the leaders of the Southern Miss defense during the 2003 season. Here he makes a tackle during a 40–28 win over TCU, a victory that earned the team a share of the Conference USA title. Courtesy of Bert King Photography.

Pruitt celebrates the win over TCU in 2003, a game televised nationally by ESPN. Courtesy of Bert King Photography.

Jeff Bower has been selected as the Conference USA Coach of the Year three times. Courtesy of Bert King Photography.

Southern Miss fans go all out to support the Golden Eagles. Courtesy of Bert King Photography.

Coach Bower is second in career victories at Southern Miss; only the legendary Thad "Pie" Vann has won more. Courtesy of Bert King Photography.

Wide receiver Marvin Young returns an 87-yard punt for a touchdown against Memphis during the 2003 season. Courtesy of Bert King Photography.

The Golden Eagle defense, ranked among the nation's leaders in 2003 season, celebrates another stop. Courtesy of Bert King Photography.

The Golden Eagles take the field. Courtesy of Bert King Photography.

The Golden Eagle flag is displayed by the cheerleaders during Southern Miss games. Courtesy of Bert King Photography.

Robby D'Angelo and other Golden Eagle players raise their helmets at the start of the fourth quarter of a 2003 game. Courtesy of Bert King Photography.

When Bobby Collins left to become head coach at Southern Methodist University, athletic director Roland Dale hired former defensive coordinator Jim Carmody, who had left to become defensive line coach of the Buffalo Bills of the NFL.

sity, leaving the Golden Eagles after seven seasons and a 48–30–2 record. Only Thad Vann and Reed Green had won more games as USM's head coach. Just a few hours after Collins announced his unexpected departure, Athletic Director Roland Dale appointed himself search, screening, and selection committee, and on January 18, Carmody, who had served as an assistant head coach and defensive coordinator under Collins from 1978 through 1980 before leaving to become the Buffalo Bills' defensive line coach, was named the new Southern Miss head coach at a press conference. In his previous stint at USM, Carmody, nicknamed "Big Nasty," had been the architect of the Nasty Bunch.

Another major offseason change was announced on July 27, when Metro Conference Commissioner Larry Albus told a large gathering of news media at the Hattiesburg Country Club that the Golden Eagles had become the league's newest member. For at least the past year, speculation regarding USM's entrance into the league had been rife, and discussions had finally come to fruition. "Obviously, this is a great day for the University of Southern Mississippi," said school president Dr. Aubrey K. Lucas. Dale concurred: "We think this is a move in the right direction for our athletic department. It is a plus day for USM." Southern Miss would compete for Metro Conference titles in men's and women's basketball, cross country, baseball, men's and women's tennis, indoor and outdoor track, and women's volleyball and tennis. Unfortunately for Southern Miss fans who had longed for the school to return to a football-playing conference, the Metro institutions did not compete in football. Although several schools, including USM, pushed for the addition of a football championship, it never occurred.

1982 SEASON

Although Carmody had built his coaching reputation on his work with defenders, the offense was on display when the Golden Eagles played their first game of the season at home on September 4 against the Northeast Louisiana Indians. With Auburn transfer Sam Dejarnette taking over for Winder as starting tailback and rushing for 171 yards and two touchdowns, the Golden Eagles rolled to a 45–27 win. Collier began his senior season by rushing for 106 yards and two touchdowns, and Lipps contributed a 50-yard punt return for a touchdown.

On September 11 at Ole Miss, the Rebels held on to defeat the Eagles 28–19 after jumping out to a 28–10 halftime lead. Collier rushed for 104 yards and completed 14 of 26 passes for 240 yards and one touchdown. Lipps caught five passes for 146 yards, including a 66-yard touchdown bomb from Collier, and Clark kicked field goals of 44 and 28 yards.

The Golden Eagles dropped to 1–2 with a 21–19 loss at Auburn. Southern Miss fell behind 21–6 in the third quarter but closed the gap on a 45-yard Clark field goal and a pair of 1-yard runs by Dejarnette, who had played at Auburn as a freshman in 1980, but time ran out as the Golden Eagles drove down the field hoping to set up a field goal attempt to win the game. The contest ended with a controversy when Collier completed a 5-yard pass to fullback Clemon Terrell that brought the Eagles to the Auburn 28-yard line with 13 seconds to go. The Golden Eagles had no timeouts remaining, but the Southern Miss coaches believed that they had enough time to stop the clock and get their kicking team on the field. "There were 13 seconds on the clock when we completed the pass," said Carmody.

"That's plenty long enough to get the ball out of bounds for a field goal. But the officials let their players lay on ours. I believe the clock should have been stopped as they were doing this."

Roberts Stadium was the site of an exciting September 25 game in which Florida State nipped the Golden Eagles 24–17 by scoring a touchdown on a fake field goal with just over five minutes left in the game. Dejarnette broke school records for rushing attempts and rushing yards in a single game, with 43 carries for 304 yards. FSU Coach

Tailback Sam Dejarnette (1982–1984) set a school record when he rushed for 304 yards against Florida State in 1982. He rushed for a school record 1,545 yards and scored 15 touchdowns that season.

Bobby Bowden had vowed before the game that Collier would not run wild against the Seminoles, as he had done in the Eagles' 58–14 win the previous year. Stationing defensive ends near the sidelines to keep Collier from getting outside, the Seminoles forced the Eagles to give the ball to Dejarnette, who produced the record-breaking night but could not propel his team to victory.

The Golden Eagles snapped the three-game losing streak with a 34–14 win over Memphis State on October 2 at Roberts Stadium. On the Tigers' first possession, USM free safety Scott Allen caused a fumble and Tillman recovered. Southern Miss scored three plays later to go ahead to stay. The Golden Eagles piled up an impressive 447 yards of total offense. "Seemed just like last year," said Collier. "I decided to go out and do things it takes to win. If it meant breaking an arm, or breaking a leg, I was ready to do it."

In a regionally televised October 9 game at Mississippi Memorial Stadium, 54,236 fans watched the Golden Eagles outduel the Mississippi State Bulldogs 20–14, to even USM's record at 3–3. Dejarnette rushed for 108 yards and scored the Eagles' two touchdowns, while Clark booted field goals of 40 and 17 yards. "This game really means a lot to the confidence of our defense," said Carmody. "They played like a true Nasty Bunch out there today."

The following Saturday, Dejarnette again scored two touchdowns, one on a dazzling 99-yard kickoff return, and Clark kicked three field goals as the Golden Eagles beat the Tulane Green Wave 22–10 at the Louisiana Superdome. Dejarnette carried the ball 40 times for 176 yards to lead the Eagles, while the Green Wave managed only 236 yards of total offense.

The Golden Eagles rolled up 500 yards of total offense, including 424 on the ground, on the way to a 48–0 whitewashing of the Louisville Cardinals on October 23. The defense held Louisville to 174 yards while forcing nine turnovers, including two interceptions each by linebacker Greg Haeusler and cornerback Eddie Ray Walker. The win was the team's fourth in a row and upped USM's record to 5–3. "They should have brought the cold weather and the rain if they expected to beat us," said Collier. "And even if they had brought bad weather they wouldn't have beat us." Added Baylis, "This was our chance to pay them back for what they did to us last year. They messed up what might have been a perfect season."

The Nasty Bunch recorded its second straight shutout and fifth consecutive win as the Eagles thumped Southwestern Louisiana 36–0 on October 30. Dejarnette rushed for 179 yards on 31 carries to give him 1,257 yards on the year and break Ben Garry's USM single-season record of 1,236 in 1977. The Ragin' Cajuns accumulated only 191 total yards, while the Eagle offense piled up 453 yards, including 380 on the ground. With the Eagle season mark at 6–3, Independence Bowl officials expressed interest in the team and attended the contest, but any chance of a postseason bowl game disappeared over the next few days.

In September 1981, the NCAA had notified Southern Miss of a preliminary inquiry into rules violations by the school, and in March 1982 it became an official investigation. Three months later, the NCAA announced that it had found 19 alleged violations over the previous three years. USM President Lucas hired Hattiesburg attorney Erik Lowery and attorney Dr. James Halsted of the university's criminal justice department and appointed an ad hoc committee to review the information compiled by the attorneys. The attorneys' investigation turned up 3 additional violations that the NCAA had missed, and the school had to defend itself against all 22 charges before the NCAA on August 22 at Hyannis Port, Massachusetts. The school admitted guilt to 8 of the violations, and the infractions committee found Southern Miss innocent of 8 more, leaving only 6 allegations disputed. On September 20, the NCAA informed Southern Miss that it had been found guilty of 14 violations, 4 of them serious—3 cases of improper recruiting inducements and 1 of unethical conduct by an assistant coach—and 10 less serious, including 2 cases of feeding illegal meals to recruits, 2 cases of improper recruiting visits, 2 cases of providing improper transportation to recruits, 1 case of obtaining an improper commitment to attend the university, 1 case of contacting a recruit after he had enrolled at another institution, 1 case of excessive off-campus visits, and 1 case of an assistant coach attending an athletic banquet outside of permissible dates. Dale, USM's athletic director, announced that university officials "felt that [the NCAA's] findings were a little more difficult or tougher than they should be" and that Southern Miss had "asked the committee if they could review their penalty." At a November 4 press conference, Dale broke the news that the NCAA "got back to us on October 11 and informed us that the infractions committee had reconsidered the penalty and let it stand." Lucas, Dale, and Carmody had decided against going over the NCAA infraction committee's head to appeal to the organization's executive committee, and the school accepted its punishment.

The penalties invoked by the NCAA included no bowl appearances in 1982 and 1983 and no television appearances in 1983 and 1984. The NCAA also ordered Southern Miss to keep three representatives of the university's athletic interests from any involvement in recruiting. An assistant coach, not identified by Dale or the NCAA, who knew about one of the incidents of monetary inducements would not be allowed to participate in any off-campus recruiting activities and would not receive any salary increases during the probation period unless such increases were given across the board as cost-of-living raises for all Southern Miss employees. "This case involved promises of significant financial benefits to prospective student-athletes who were recruited during the 1979–80, 1980–81 and 1981–82 academic years," read the official NCAA release, quoting Charles Alan Wright, the chairman of the Committee on Infractions. "The efforts of outside athletic representatives to circumvent NCAA legislation by making these offers and the committee's determination that an assistant football coach was aware of these promises heightened the seriousness of the case." According to the release, "The committee believed that the individuals who were directly involved in the case should be penalized and that significant institutional penalties also would be appropriate in the case to emphasize the university's responsibility to ensure that violations of NCAA legislation do not occur in the future."

The decision ended any chance that the Golden Eagles would appear in a postseason bowl. Instead, the team members turned their attention to the November 13 contest against No. 17 Alabama in Tuscaloosa, which they dubbed the "Bama Bowl." After exploding for three first-quarter touchdowns, the Eagles held a 28–14 advantage at halftime. The Crimson Tide rallied in the second half, but the Eagle defense and special teams came up with several big plays to preserve

Jim Carmody shakes hands with Alabama's legendary Paul "Bear" Bryant following USM's 38–29 win in 1982, the first loss in Tuscaloosa by the Crimson Tide since 1963.

the 38–29 upset, snapping the Tide's 57-game winning streak at Bryant-Denny Stadium, which dated back to October 12, 1963. Carmody became the first rookie head coach to defeat the legendary Bryant. "This is the greatest victory in Southern Miss history," declared Carmody. "There was a great deal of character on that field today." Said Bryant, "They are for real, no doubt about it. This was no fluke."

Southern Miss finished the 1982 season with a 7–4 mark after losing their final game of the year at home to Louisiana Tech 13–6. Playing in a steady drizzle, the Eagles committed three interceptions and three fumbles, although Dejarnette rushed for 136 yards, his eighth 100-yard performance of the season.

Baylis, Collier, Dejarnette, Howe, and Tillman were named honorable mention All-America and first-team All–South Independent, while Brown and Lipps were named to the second-team All–South Independent squad. Collier played in the Senior Bowl, while Baylis played in the Blue-Gray All-Star Classic. The Dallas Cowboys selected Collier in the sixth round of the NFL draft, but the quarterback had already signed with the Birmingham Stallions of the United States Football League.

1983 SEASON

The Golden Eagles opened at home on September 3 against the Richmond Spiders. Led by Dejarnette, who accumulated 150 of the Eagles' 378 yards on the ground, Southern Miss cruised to a 32–3 win. Collier's cousin, Robert Ducksworth, made his first start at quarterback for Southern Miss, completing six of seven passes for 89 yards. Lipps caught five of those tosses and returned three punts for 76 yards.

Quarterback Robert Ducksworth (#11) is seen here in a 27–7 Golden Eagle victory over the Ole Miss Rebels in Oxford in 1983.

The following week, USM dropped to 1–1 after a 24–3 loss to Sugar Bowl–bound Auburn at Jordan-Hare Stadium. The Tigers held the Eagles to 126 yards on the ground, limiting Dejarnette to 46 yards, and 98 yards in the air, while the Tigers piled up 352 yards against the Nasty Bunch. "We have no alibis or excuses," Carmody said. "Auburn makes very few mistakes and is very opportunistic. We gave them two touchdowns and a field goal. We can't make very many mistakes and have a chance against them."

The Golden Eagles bounced back on September 17 at Roberts Stadium with a 28–10 victory over Louisiana Tech. The USM defense recovered four fumbles and had an interception. Just after halftime, with the Eagles trailing 10–7, Southern Miss lost Ducksworth with an apparent broken nose. After sitting out the rest of the third quarter and the first series of the fourth quarter, the gritty quarterback returned and hit Lipps on a 68-yard touchdown pass to put USM up 14–10. After scoring two more touchdowns, the Eagles had improved to 2–1.

Against Ole Miss at Oxford's Vaught-Hemingway Stadium on October 1, USM led 17–7 at halftime, and although the Rebels threatened repeatedly in the second half, the Nasty Bunch stopped four Ole Miss advances into Southern Miss territory. During the fourth quarter, the Eagles added another Clark field goal and a 4-yard touchdown run by tailback Dejarnette to secure the 27–7 win. Dejarnette rushed for a game-high 106 yards, and Lipps recorded five receptions for 134 yards and scored on a 28-yard reverse. "Last year we took a low-key approach to the Ole Miss game," Carmody said amid the backslapping in the Eagle locker room. "It backfired and it was my fault. We can't play that way at Southern Miss. We don't have a Nebraska or Dallas Cowboys type team. We have to play with a lot of emotion. We have got to line up and get after folks."

A convincing 31–6 win over Mississippi State in Jackson on October 8 gave the Golden Eagles a three-game winning streak. A crowd of 58,311 watched the Eagles storm out to a 17–0 halftime lead with a beautiful 21-yard scoring pass from Ducksworth to tight end Mike Landrum, a 62-yard halfback-option pass from Tracy Gamble to split end Lyneal Alston, and the longest field goal of Clark's career, a 51-yarder. Dejarnette added a third-quarter touchdown run, and Terrell crossed the goal line for USM's final score before the Bulldogs scored their only points of the game. It was the Eagles seventh straight win over the Bulldogs and gave USM the unofficial state championship for the fourth time in seven years.

On October 15 at Memphis's Liberty Bowl Stadium, the Golden Eagles defeated the Memphis State Tigers 27–20. After two Clark field goals, rushing touchdowns by Ducksworth and Dejarnette, and a 38-yard touchdown pass from Ducksworth to Lipps, the Eagles took a 27–0 lead into the fourth quarter before Memphis State came roaring back. Jerry Harris took a kickoff back 98 yards for a touchdown, and quarterback Danny Sparkman contributed two touchdown passes for the Tigers, but they ran out of time as the Eagles held on for the victory. Dejarnette rushed for 135 yards, while Ducksworth connected on 11 of 14 passes for 182 yards. Lipps had another great game, catching seven passes for 143 yards. The Eagles' fourth win in a row made them 5–1 on the year.

The Golden Eagles endured a series of distractions over the next week as University of Oklahoma star running back Marcus Dupree, who had played high school football in Philadelphia, Mississippi, announced that he would be leaving Norman and transferring to either Mississippi State or Southern Miss. After changing his mind several times and briefly enrolling at USM, Dupree ultimately chose to forgo the remainder of his collegiate career rather than sit out until 1985, when he would be eligible to play for his new team. The hoopla surrounding Dupree may have diverted the Eagles' minds from their next game, at Roberts Stadium against Tulane, and Southern Miss went down 14–7. The contest got off to a good start for the Eagles when the Green Wave fumbled a punt deep in their own territory and a few plays later Dejarnette blasted over from a yard out for a 7–0 lead. Tulane kicked a second-quarter field goal to trail by just 4 points at halftime and added another field goal during the third quarter to make the score 7–6. Late in the fourth quarter, quarterback Wade Elmore connected with wide receiver Tyrone Vaughns on a 25-yard touchdown pass, and the 2-point conversion provided the final margin of victory. Although Tulane's defense limited Southern Miss to just 22 yards of offense, Lipps's five punt returns for 107 yards provided a bright spot for the Eagles, who dropped to 5–2.

The Eagles got back on the winning track with their October 29 Homecoming game against Southwestern Louisiana. USM rolled up 367 yards of total offense, including 250 yards on the ground, in the 31–3 win. Freshman tailback Vincent Alexander, subbing for the ailing Dejarnette, rushed for 153 yards on 23 carries and scored a touchdown to help his team to the victory.

Southern Miss won its seventh game of the year with a 27–3 defeat of the Louisville Cardinals on November 5 at Cardinal Stadium. Leading 6–0 at halftime, the Eagles broke the game open in the second half. Although Ducksworth was just three of six for 155 yards on the game, two of the completions were long touchdown passes to Lipps. Alexander had another good game, racking up 98 yards on 17 carries.

The Eagles fell to 7–3 after losing 28–16 to the Alabama Crimson Tide at Birmingham's Legion Field on November 12. Alexander took the game's opening kickoff 96 yards to the Alabama 4-yard line, but the Eagles could not score. The Crimson Tide moved out to a 14–10 halftime lead, and although USM closed to 14–13 on a 37-yard Clark field goal, Alabama scored a pair of touchdowns to ice the win. Lipps had another great game for the Eagles, catching four passes for 69 yards, returning seven punts for 91 yards, and running the ball twice for 36 yards.

USM's season came to an end at Roberts Stadium on November 19 against East Carolina in a driving thunderstorm. The Eagles opened up a 6–0 lead on 46- and 44-yard field goals by Clark, but the Pirates scored a touchdown and kicked a field goal in the third quarter for a 10–6 win. Lipps finished his brilliant career with three catches to give him 91 over his tenure at

One of the most talented and skilled wide receivers and kick returners in Southern Miss history was Louis Lipps (1980–1983), who caught 91 passes and returned 78 punts during his career.

Strong safety Bud Brown (1980–1983) earned All–South Independent and honorable mention All-America honors in 1983.

Southern Miss. As in 1982, the Eagles finished the season at 7–4.

Baylis, Brown, Howe, and Lipps were named first-team All–South Independent and honorable mention All-America, while defensive tackle Richard Byrd, center Steve Carmody (son of the head coach), and Dejarnette were second-team selections on the All–South Independent squad. Carmody, Howe, and Lipps played in the Senior Bowl, while Baylis and Howe appeared in the Blue-Gray All-Star Classic and Carmody went to the East-West Shrine Game. In the April 1984 NFL draft, Lipps went in the first round to the Pittsburgh Steelers, Terrell went in the eighth round to the New Orleans Saints, Howe was taken in the ninth round by the Atlanta Falcons, and Brown went in the eleventh round to the Miami Dolphins.

1984 SEASON

The Golden Eagles opened the season with a 26–19 road loss at the University of Georgia on September 8. Kicker Rex Banks set a new Southern Miss record by kicking four field goals and combined with Georgia's Kevin Butler, who also kicked four field goals, to set a new NCAA record for field goals in a game. Dejarnette rushed for 92 yards and Ducksworth connected on 12 of 19 passes for 155 yards to lead the Golden Eagle attack. Tailback Tracy Gamble had the only USM touchdown on an 11-yard second-quarter run.

Ducksworth rushed for 140 yards and a touchdown and passed for 127 yards, including a 59-yard touchdown strike, to lead the Golden Eagles to an easy 34–0 win over Louisiana Tech in USM's home opener the following week. The Golden Eagles piled up 455 yards of total offense, while the Nasty Bunch picked off four Bulldog passes and the special teams had a good night, including Andrew Mott's 59-yard punt return for a touchdown.

At Auburn on September 22, Dejarnette rushed for 93 yards and the Golden Eagles piled up 219 yards on the ground, but Southern Miss still dropped a 35–12 decision to the Tigers. The game was never close, with Auburn quarterback Pat Washington passing for 117 yards and rushing for 41 yards and a touchdown to pace the Tiger attack.

The Golden Eagles fell to 1–3 after Memphis State handed them a 23–13 defeat at Roberts Stadium on September 29. Running back Punkin Williams went 68 yards for a touchdown on the Tigers' first offensive snap of the night, but the Eagles rallied to go ahead 13–10 on Banks's 42-yard field goal and Alexander's 1-yard run. Jeff Womack turned in a 6-yard touchdown run early in the third period to give Memphis State a 17–13 lead that they did not relinquish.

Next up for Southern Miss was Mississippi State in Jackson. With the Bulldogs clinging to a 10–3 edge early in the third quarter, State quarterback Don Smith broke loose on an 84-yard scoring run and another of 56 yards to lead his team to a 27–18 win, ending the Bulldogs' seven-game losing streak against the Eagles. On that day, Smith rushed for 130 yards and the two touchdowns and passed for 68 yards and another score, while Alexander rushed for 119 yards and a touchdown and Ducksworth connected on 12 of 22 passes for 144 yards and a touchdown for Southern Miss.

Tulane scored three first-quarter touchdowns to open up a 21–0 lead and never looked back, stomping Southern Miss 35–7 at the Superdome on October 13. Quarterback Ken Karcher threw for 166 yards and two touchdowns to lead the Green Wave attack, while wide receiver Craig Harrison caught six passes for 77 yards and two touchdowns. Ducksworth scored the only Southern Miss touchdown on a 41-yard run in the third quarter, and the Eagles dropped to 1–5 on the year.

On October 20 at Jackson's Memorial Stadium, the Golden Eagles rallied from a 10–3 halftime deficit to defeat Ole Miss 13–10. Banks nailed a 32-yard field goal with 11:46 to go in the third quarter to bring Southern Miss within 4, and Ducksworth gave his team the lead for good with a 7-yard scoring run with 8:49 left in the quarter. Alexander rushed for 111 yards, while Ducksworth passed for 128 to lead the Eagles to victory and the defense held the Rebels to just 270 yards of total offense. "It was a real brutal defensive game out there," said Carmody. "We were finally able to come up with the big plays we'd been missing all year. We made things happen that haven't happened to us before." "We came out and took it to them," said Ducksworth. "We didn't make the mistakes we made the last few weeks. We played up to our ability."

With Timmy Byrd and Tommy Compton filling in for Ducksworth, who had suffered a deep thigh bruise in the Ole Miss game, the Golden Eagles traveled to Lafayette the next week to face Southwestern Louisiana. Ragin' Cajun kicker Patrick Broussard made fourth-quarter field goals of 21 and 29 yards to give his team the 13–7 victory, snapping Southwestern Louisiana's 17-game losing streak against Southern Miss. At 2–6 with just three games remaining, the Eagles were assured of their first losing season since 1976.

Again playing without Ducksworth, the Golden Eagles could manage only 128 yards in a 22–0 November 3 Homecoming loss to Northwestern State University of Louisiana. Alexander was also sidelined for the game, and the Demons held Dejarnette to 23 yards on 12 carries, piling up 319 yards on offense and capitalizing on two Golden Eagle turnovers to pull off the upset.

With Andrew Anderson quarterbacking the team, Southern Miss rallied for a 31–27 come-from-behind victory over East Carolina on November 10. Anderson passed for 104 yards and two touchdowns and rushed for another touchdown, Mott returned a punt 66 yards for a touchdown, and Alston caught five passes for 95 yards and two touchdowns. Although the Pirates outgained the Golden Eagles by almost 300 yards, the Nasty Bunch forced six Pirate turnovers. Carmody called it "one of the greatest comebacks in school history. Certainly since I have been associated with the program."

EAGLE FEVER AND I BELIEVE

Southern Miss became involved in yet another NCAA controversy after Brandon High School football star Don Palmer signed a letter of intent with the Golden Eagles in February 1984 but reneged on the agreement a few days later, claiming that his mother had pressured him into signing. In a July 18 letter to Dale, Palmer asked for a release so that he could attend Ole Miss and accused a Southern Miss assistant of having provided illegal recruiting inducements, among them clothing, money, and food. Palmer's letter closed with a thinly veiled threat: "I hope you prefer to release me based on the allegations made in this letter rather than take a chance on a ruling by the NCAA."

In keeping with Coach Carmody's policy of not releasing a signee to an opponent on USM's football schedule, the university did not release Palmer and began an investigation into the matter. On October 8, Southern Miss received an official inquiry from the NCAA that listed 11 allegations related to Palmer's recruitment. At a press conference on November 14, Southern Miss President Lucas announced that his internal committee's findings coincided with the NCAA's list of allegations, and he imposed four penalties on the football program: the release of Palmer from his letter of intent; the suspension of an unnamed football assistant from all association with the football program and nonrenewal of his contract, which expired at the end of the year; a freeze on Carmody's salary for the next year and the temporary cessation of any discussions of a contract extension; and the disassociation of four alumni and one other booster from the university's football program for two years. "We must realize that we cannot disobey the NCAA regulations and policies and survive," Lucas continued. "We just cannot do it. We do not have that option. We've done a fairly thorough job of informing ourselves about what we can and cannot do. What we have not been able to achieve at this point is a commitment from our people that we're going to abide by those dos and don'ts." Said Dale, "From an athletic standpoint, I'm not going to be remembered as a good athlete or pretty good coach and I might not have been good at either one of them. I'm going to be remembered as a cheater. And that doesn't appeal to me." Dale went on, "I was raised in Sullivan's Hollow in Magee, Mississippi, and in Zac's Pool Hall they might hit each other over the head with cue sticks and pull knives, but they didn't lie and they didn't cheat. And we're not going to cheat. We're going to run a good program."

The NCAA Committee on Infractions publicly reprimanded and censured the school, placed the team on probation for two years, and banned the team from appearing on television during the 1985 season. However, impressed by "the university's prompt disciplinary action in the case and its efforts to uncover complete information prior to the institution's appearance before the committee," the NCAA "determined that the television sanction and one year of the probationary period should be suspended."

The Eagle players returned their focus to football for the season's final game, posting their second come-from-behind victory in a row. This week's victim was the visiting Louisville Cardinals, who held an early 13–7 lead before the Golden Eagles turned the tables and won, 34–25. Anderson led the Eagles, passing for 101 yards and rushing for 38 and a touchdown. The Nasty Bunch intercepted four passes and recovered two fumbles, with safety Tim Smith returning one of the interceptions 26 yards for a touchdown. The win gave the Eagles a 4–7 record for the year.

Defensive tackle Richard Byrd was named to the All–South Independent team and was an honorable mention All-America, while offensive tackle Fred Richards was named second-team All–South Independent. Byrd played in the Senior Bowl, the Blue-Gray All-Star Classic, and the East-West Shrine Game and was selected in the second round of the NFL draft (thirty-sixth pick overall) by the Houston Oilers.

1985 SEASON

The Golden Eagles opened up the 1985 season at home on September 7 against the 1984 NCAA Division I-AA runner-up Louisiana Tech Bulldogs. Spurred by a defense that allowed only six first downs and 12 yards rushing, the Eagles recorded a 28–0 win. On their first possession of the season, the Golden Eagles marched 65 yards and scored on a 1-yard plunge by Alexander, who rolled up 125 yards on the day. The Eagles added a touchdown in each quarter thereafter, amassing 343 yards rushing. Ducksworth returned from the previous season's injury to rush for 109 yards, including a 61-yard touchdown run. "Our defense played outstanding," said Carmody, "just like our defense of last year, before we were decimated by injuries." "That's what we wanted to do, get the old defense back," said senior defensive tackle Fred Baskin. "And that's what we did."

After opening the scoring with a 37-yard Banks field goal in the second quarter during the next week's game, the Golden Eagles could not contain running back Bo Jackson and lost to the top-ranked Auburn Tigers 29–18 at Auburn. Jackson contributed 205 of Auburn's 274 yards on the ground, showing Golden Eagle fans why he deserved the Heisman Trophy. Ducksworth went down with 1:25 left in the first quarter with a knee injury that sidelined him for most of the year. The game was scoreless at the time, with the USM defense having held Jackson to one carry for 4 yards and Auburn to one first down. According to Coach Carmody, "When [Auburn] Coach [Pat] Dye ran off the field, he told me, 'If you don't lose your quarterback, you whip our butts.'"

At Jackson's Memorial Stadium on September 21, 90-degree heat and sunny skies greeted fans for the annual tilt between Southern Miss and Mississippi State. Bulldog quarterback Don Smith passed for 284 yards and three touchdowns, leading his squad to a 23–20 win. The Golden Eagles led 13–10 in the third quarter on a 51-yard touchdown pass from Anderson to Alston, but Smith came right back and threw a 52-yard touchdown pass to put Mississippi State back on top. Safety Tim Smith returned an interception 61 yards for a touchdown to pull Southern Miss to

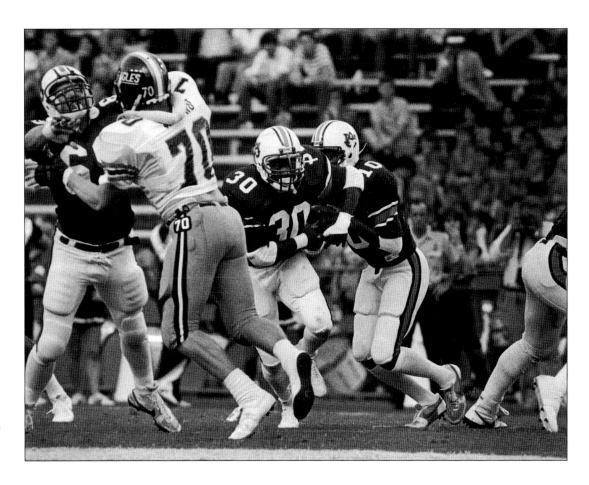

Defensive lineman Richard Byrd (#70) recorded 16 quarterback sacks in his career as one of the leaders of the Nasty Bunch from 1981 to 1984.

within 3 points in the fourth quarter, but the Eagles could get no closer, and the Bulldogs held on for the win.

The Golden Eagles got back in the win column the next Saturday by grinding out a 14–7 home victory over Northwestern State. The balanced Golden Eagle attack produced 209 yards rushing—98 of them by Alexander—and 141 yards passing. With his team down 7–0, Southern Miss fullback Randolph Brown scored on a 61-yard pass from Anderson to tie the game in the first quarter, and the Eagles opened the second half with an 11-play, 69-yard drive capped by Anderson's 3-yard touchdown run to close out the scoring. Cornerback James Cooper helped seal the win by intercepting a Demon pass at the Eagle goal line late in the third quarter.

Brown, Alexander, and tailback Shelton Gandy led the Golden Eagles to their second consecutive win, a 38–16 defeat of Southwestern Louisiana in

EAGLE FEVER AND I BELIEVE [195]

Lafayette on October 5. Safety Bobo Harris intercepted a Ragin' Cajun pass on the third play of the game to set up a 42-yard touchdown drive, and the Golden Eagles scored their first points on the way to a 28–3 halftime lead. Southern Miss added two more interceptions and controlled the ball to lock up the victory and improve to 3–2 on the year.

On the Golden Eagles' first possession against Louisville the next week, Anderson connected with Mott for an 83-yard bomb, setting the tone for a 42–14 pasting of the Cardinals on their home field. Brown and Alexander rushed for 130 and 121 yards, respectively, including an 80-yard touchdown run by Brown to open the second half, and Anderson passed for 170 yards as the Golden Eagles amassed 562 yards of offense. The Nasty Bunch recovered five Cardinal fumbles and held Louisville to 40 yards on the ground. "I've been saying all week if Southern Miss changed jerseys with a Top 20 team, you couldn't tell the difference," said Louisville coach Howard Schnellenberger. "I still believe it."

The Golden Eagles ran their win streak to four and improved their record to 5–2 on October 19 by hanging on for a 14–7 victory at Memphis State on the strength of 25- and 41-yard field goals by Banks in the first half and a 73-yard touchdown pass from Anderson to wide receiver Chris McGee in the third quarter. The Golden Eagle defense held Memphis State to 33 yards rushing and 219 total yards and recorded six sacks.

After an open date, Southern Miss rushed for 228 yards and had 129 yards passing from Anderson to shut out East Carolina 27–0 in USM's Homecoming game, played in a driving rainstorm. Paced by Gandy's 82-yard fourth-quarter sprint for a touchdown, six Golden Eagle rushers reached double figures, while seven Southern Miss players caught passes. The Nasty Bunch limited the Pirates to 1 completion in 17 passing attempts and to 132 yards rushing. Ducksworth played briefly in the first half, his first appearance in a game in nearly two months. With a 6–2 record and off of NCAA probation, the Golden Eagles and their fans began to think about a postseason bowl game. "It was a good win," said Carmody. "We've won five in a row now, eight of our last ten, and we're very pleased with the way we are playing."

When the Golden Eagles arrived in Fort Collins, Colorado, the day before their game against Colorado State, they were greeted by warm temperatures, blue skies, and sunshine, but the team awoke the next morning to near-freezing temperatures and blowing snow. After falling behind 14–0 in the first quarter, the Golden Eagles tied the game before halftime on Gandy's 18-yard run and Anderson's 5-yard pass to McGee. After intermission, however, the Rams dominated, adding a touchdown in the third quarter and two more in the fourth to take a 35–17 win. Gandy turned in his best game of the year with 125 yards rushing, while Anderson passed for 227 yards, but despite their efforts, the Eagles' bowl hopes diminished.

On November 16 in Tuscaloosa, Southern Miss led No. 20 Alabama at the beginning of the fourth quarter but could not hang on as the Crimson

Tide scored twice in the fourth quarter to win 24–13. Mott had 87 yards in kickoff returns, 97 yards in punt returns, and 68 yards in pass receptions for Southern Miss, but the Alabama defense held the Golden Eagles to just 104 yards on the ground. The Nasty Bunch was nearly as stingy, limiting the Tide to 122 yards rushing, but penalties made the difference, taking the Golden Eagles out of good field position on several occasions.

USM's 1985 season ended on November 23 with a 24–6 home victory over Tulane. The Golden Eagles limited the Green Wave to just 87 yards on the ground while rushing for 293 yards, led by Gandy, who had his second 100-yard game of the year. After sitting out most of the year, Ducksworth was 10 for 15 passing in his final game as a Golden Eagle, including three completions to Mott for 96 yards, and was selected by the New York Jets in the eighth round of the NFL draft. Southern Miss finished the year at 7–4.

On January 20, 1986, Southern Miss announced that Athletic Director Roland Dale had admitted himself to an alcohol-dependency unit for treatment of what he termed "multiple illnesses." Dale planned to return to work within six weeks, and the school's president, Aubrey K. Lucas, offered his "full support and understanding." Several weeks later, however, Dale held a press conference to declare that he would step down as athletic director effective July 1, and Lucas appointed a search committee to begin the process of finding a new athletic director.

In the spring of 1986, Southwestern Louisiana Athletic Director Terry Don Phillips accepted the post of USM athletic director but changed his mind a few days later. John Shaffer, assistant athletic director at the University of Georgia, was then announced as the choice but subsequently turned the job down.

On July 19, Lucas tried again, announcing the appointment of H. C. (Bill) McLellan, who had "literally worked miracles" at Clemson. "I don't have a magic wand," McLellan demurred, "but I do work hard and if we can get enough people involved, we can do anything that we want to do." The 54-year-old McLellan had served as Clemson's athletic director from 1971 to 1983 before resigning to take a job with Eastern Foods of Atlanta. McLellan signed a four-year contract with Southern Miss that paid him $70,000 per year; he would begin his duties on July 28.

1986 SEASON

USM's 1986 football season began on a tragic note when redshirt freshman running back Eric Sorey of Campbellton, Florida, collapsed with leg cramps while running during the team's first preseason practice on August 17. Sorey was treated on the field and taken to the USM Clinic between 11:00 and 11:30 A.M. At about 3:30 P.M. he was transferred to Methodist Hospital,

The 1986 season began tragically with the death of running back Eric Sorey following the first workout of the preseason.

where he was found to be in cardiac arrest. He was pronounced dead at 6:15 P.M.

"Our normal procedure for leg cramps is to cool the player down as quickly as possible, give them plenty of Gatorade to drink and make sure there is no dehydration," said Golden Eagle team physician Boyd Kellett. "We performed all of these initial tests on Eric and got him stabilized. At that time he had a nice pulse and his blood pressure was normal. He was alert, sitting up and talking. We really didn't think there was anything serious involved because he did not complain about anything but his legs hurting. We gave him a mild muscle relaxer. We kept him in bed and monitored his condition constantly." But while he was being transported to the hospital, Sorey went into cardiac arrest, and physicians were unable to revive him. The final autopsy showed that four related conditions caused Sorey's death: sickle-cell trait, an inherited condition; a breakdown of muscle cells; an anemia that caused blood cells to break down prematurely; and a slightly enlarged heart with a smaller-than-average left coronary artery. The report also showed scarring on the left side of the heart. The autopsy found no trace of drugs, including alcohol, in Sorey's system. According to Kellett, the sickle-cell trait and the breakdown of muscle cells had combined to create "the strain on his heart that led to the eventual congestive failure." Furthermore, the doctor said, "I don't think you can blame it on heat or exercise. The heat was not a problem. The physical exertion he went through wasn't unusual. It was minimal. He had been running for only six minutes and had no workout prior to that. That's not much exercise for an athlete."

With that cloud hanging over them, the Golden Eagles played their first game at home against Northeast Louisiana on September 6. The offense mustered only 36 yards passing but rushed for 300 yards in a 28–19 win. Alexander led the team with 149 yards on the ground as Southern Miss won its seventh consecutive home game.

Linebacker Onesimus Henry intercepted a Mike Shula pass and returned it 54 yards for a touchdown to give Southern Miss a 7–0 lead against No. 4 Alabama at Legion Field in Birmingham the next week. However, the Crimson Tide used a late-second-quarter touchdown to take a 14–10 lead and added 10 third-quarter points en route to a 31–17 win over the Golden Eagles, who dropped to 1–1. Alabama's powerful offense rolled up 515 yards against a paltry 206 for Southern Miss.

A 98-yard drive that left Southern Miss fans euphoric and Mississippi State fans drained highlighted another thrilling Golden Eagle–Bulldog game at Jackson's Memorial Stadium on September 20. Down 24–21 with the ball on the Southern Miss 2-yard line with just over four minutes remaining, Eagle offensive tackle Pat Ferrell looked at his teammates in the huddle and announced, "If there's anybody here who doesn't think we're gonna score and win this game, just leave. Get out of here. We don't need you because we are fixin' to score." The Eagles responded with a 15-play scoring drive capped by Gandy's 4-yard run with just 29 seconds to go, winning 28–24. Offensive coordinator Keith Daniels said that the game-winning drive "brought me to tears. That's what it did. You feel so much for the players. I tell you, it took some downright courage and character to do what they did out there today." The Golden Eagle offense rushed for 386 yards, while the Nasty Bunch limited the Bulldogs to 148 yards on the ground.

On September 27 in College Station, the Golden Eagles fought the powerful No. 14 Texas A & M squad to a 0–0 halftime standoff but surrendered a touchdown and three field goals in the second half to lose the game 16–7. The Eagles recorded their lowest offensive output of the season with 99 total yards—89 of them on the ground by tailback Craig Shackelford—yet managed to stay in the game. Eagle punter Billy Knighten also had a great game, averaging 43.5 yards for his 10 kicks.

With a 1–2 mark on the season, the Golden Eagles had what was probably their poorest outing of the season, failing to score against an aroused Kentucky Wildcat team playing before a capacity crowd in Lexington on October 4. Although the Golden Eagles trailed just 9–0 at halftime, 16 third-quarter points put the game away, and Kentucky won 32–0.

The Golden Eagles rebounded strongly to beat Memphis State 14–9 in USM's October 18 Homecoming game at Roberts Stadium. Trailing 9–0 in the third quarter, Southern Miss scored two touchdowns, one on a 30-yard pass from Anderson to Alston, to even their record at 3–3. The Golden Eagles picked up 168 yards rushing and 146 passing while limiting the visitors to 214 yards rushing and only 50 passing. Anderson connected on 9 of 12 passes, with Alston catching 5 balls.

Southern Miss caught the Tulane Green Wave the next week on perhaps their best day of the season and lost 35–20 at the Superdome in New Orleans. The Golden Eagles had trouble stopping Wave quarterback Terrance Jones, who hit on 13 of 18 passes for 166 yards and a pair of touchdowns. The Eagles grabbed a 17–14 halftime lead on a pair of touchdown runs by Shackelford and a 32-yard Banks field goal, but the second half belonged to the Green Wave, who took control with a couple of third-quarter touchdowns.

The Golden Eagles notched another improbable last-second win on November 1 in Greenville, North Carolina, against East Carolina. After the Pirates had scored on a 21-yard pass from Charlie Libretto to Walter Wilson and then passed for a 2-point conversion, they led 21–20. The ensuing kickoff gave Southern Miss the ball at their own 18-yard line with eight seconds left. Anderson dropped back and threw a pass as far as he could downfield, and Alston went up in a crowd of defenders near the Pirate 40-yard line and somehow caught the ball. Alston fought his way down near the Pirate 10-yard line, where he was tackled. But as he was going down, he lateraled the ball to fullback Randolph Brown, who raced into the end zone. But the officials ruled that the lateral had been a forward pass, and according to the rules, the defense had to take either the result of the play (touchdown) or the penalty, which would give Southern Miss the ball deep in East Carolina territory. After arguing that Alston had been down before he lateraled (as replays showed probably to be the case), the Pirates took the penalty. Time had run out, but the rules also stated that the game could not end on a penalty, so the Eagles had the opportunity to run one more play. Banks then kicked a 31-yard field goal to give Southern Miss the a 23–21 win. Anderson completed 14 of 30 passes for 240 yards, while Alston had seven catches for 135 yards. Carmody focused on Alston's big catch at the game's end rather than on the subsequent confusion: "I thought they had intercepted the ball Alston caught. I don't know how Lyneal caught it. They had two or three people up there with us. And all of a sudden Lyneal comes running out of there with it. I don't know how you could make a more spectacular comeback than that." Two days later, Jim Campbell, head of the Southern Independent Officials Association, announced that the officiating crew had erred by not ruling Alston down, but there was no provision for reversing the result of the game.

The Golden Eagles parlayed a stingy defense and a strong rushing game into a 17–0 home win over Southwestern Louisiana on November 8, putting together back-to-back wins for the first time in the season. The Nasty Bunch limited the Cajuns to 11 net rushing yards and 198 yards passing while recording an interception and five sacks. The Golden Eagle offense posted an impressive 316 yards on the ground to advance to 5–4 on the year.

A potent and improving Florida State team steamrolled the Golden Eagles 49–13 on November 15 in Tallahassee, scoring in every quarter. After falling behind 28–0 at halftime, the Eagles managed two third-quarter touchdowns but also gave up a couple to fall to 5–5.

Southern Miss won its tenth straight home game over two seasons with a 31–16 victory over Louisville the next week. With the game tied at 7 after the first quarter, the Eagles scored on a 56-yard pass from Anderson to Alston and a 73-yard punt return by Mott to lead 21–7 at halftime. Southern Miss added a 1-yard touchdown run by Gandy and a 44-yard field goal by Banks to secure the victory and finish at 6–5. The Eagles had gone two full seasons without losing a home contest.

Henry and Ferrell were All–South Independent first-team selections and honorable mention All-Americans, while Alexander and Knighten were named second-team All–South Independent. Alston played in the Senior Bowl.

1987 SEASON

The Golden Eagles opened on September 5 at Legion Field in Birmingham, with the offense struggling against the Alabama defense throughout the game. Southern Miss trailed 24–0 at halftime before scoring their only points of the day when quarterback Ailrick Young crossed the goal line from 2 yards out. The Tide tacked on a pair of second-half touchdowns to slam the Eagles 38–6. With Young and Simmie Carter ineffective at

H. C. "Bill" McLellan became the school's athletic director in 1987. The former Clemson AD set to work improving the facilities and the fund-raising arm of Golden Eagle athletics.

quarterback, Coach Carmody knew he needed to shake up the offense.

On September 19, the Tulane Green Wave rolled into Roberts Stadium. With the Eagles down 16–10 and the offense still having difficulty, Carmody inserted 17-year-old freshman quarterback Brett Favre from Kiln, Mississippi, with 5:48 left in the third quarter. Favre provided the spark the Golden Eagles needed, quickly driving the Eagles down the field and completing a 7-yard touchdown pass to wide receiver Chris McGee to put the Eagles up by 1. Tulane scored again to take a 24–17 lead, but Favre countered, taking the Eagles for one touchdown and then another, a 23-yard fourth-quarter scoring catch by wide receiver Alfred Williams that gave the Eagles a 31–24 decision. Favre finished 6 for 10 for 85 yards in his first appearance for the Golden Eagles. "When I went into the game, I was scared to death," he said. "I really didn't expect to get in the game. But after one series, I think the butterflies went away and I kinda got in the flow of the game." Another true freshman made a name for himself that afternoon: safety Kerry Valrie came off the Golden Eagle bench and recorded the first two interceptions of his career.

The Golden Eagles put a scare into No. 16 Texas A & M on September 26 in Jackson. The Aggies struck on a 69-yard touchdown pass in the first quarter, but Favre, making his first career start, hit wide receiver Darryl Tillman for a 52-yard touchdown to tie the game at halftime 7–7. The Eagles fell behind again 24–7 but cut the deficit to 10 when Favre and wide receiver Robbie Weeks hooked up for a 5-yard touchdown pass in the fourth quarter. Texas A & M proved to be too much for USM, however, taking a 27–14 victory and dropping the Eagles to 1–2 on the year.

On October 3 in Louisville, the Golden Eagles rolled up 519 yards of total offense, including 402 yards on the ground, en route to a 65–6 pasting of the Louisville Cardinals, one of the biggest margins of victory in USM history. Southern Miss scored in the opening quarter on tight end Preston Hansford's 5-yard touchdown pass from Favre, Eric Redd's return of a blocked punt for a touchdown, Gandy's 3-yard touchdown run, and Chris Seroka's 23-yard field goal. Favre and McGee combined for 22- and 38-yard touchdown passes in the second quarter to stake USM to a 37–0 halftime advantage. The Golden Eagles added four more touchdowns in the third quarter—a 1-yard run by Gandy; a 22-yard run by Shackelford; another blocked punt returned for a touchdown, this time by John Baylor; and a 20-yard run by tailback Ricky Bradley. The win evened the Eagles' record at 2–2.

Southern Miss had an October 10 Homecoming date with No. 6 Florida State, and the Seminoles jumped out to a 14–0 edge on the Golden Eagles before fullback Reginald Warnsley scored on a 69-yard touchdown run to cut the lead to 7. USM added only another field goal, while Florida State scored another 47 points to demolish the Eagles 61–10, their worst loss since 1969. "We were completely overwhelmed," Carmody said. "They're a great football team. And I still think they're the best team we've ever played at Roberts Stadium."

Trailing 14–3 heading into the fourth quarter, the Golden Eagles rallied, scoring 15 unanswered points to defeat Mississippi State 18–14 on October 17 in Jackson. Young replaced an ineffective Favre at quarterback and hit Tillman for a 14-yard touchdown pass and then for the 2-point conversion to cut the Mississippi State lead to 3. Tailback Eddie Ray Jackson provided the winning score with a 20-yard touchdown run. Young completed all six of his passing attempts for 75 yards, while Gandy romped for 113 yards, and Southern returned to the .500 mark for the season. "I'm a team player," said Young. "When I lost my job, that made me a better person. I kept my head up and kept working harder. I knew I'd get another chance. And today, [my teammates] made it easy for me. My line did a great job."

The October 24 meeting between Southern Miss and Memphis State was played at Liberty Bowl Memorial Stadium and typified the contests between the two teams, which were becoming known as the "Black-and-Blue Bowl." After a scoreless first quarter, Tillman caught a 44-yard pass from Favre to give the Golden Eagles a 7–0 halftime edge. The lead grew to 14 when Favre connected with Bill Schnider on a 20-yard touchdown pass, but the Tigers rallied to tie with a pair of fourth-quarter touchdown passes. With 5:22 to go, Seroka booted a 43-yard field that handed the Golden Eagles a 17–14 victory, their fourth of the season.

Southern Miss met Division I-AA Jackson State on October 31 before a crowd of 33,687 at Roberts Stadium, the first time that one of the state's three major football programs had played against a historically black school. The game was tied at the end of the first half, but the Golden Eagles took a 7–0 lead when James Henry returned a punt 72 yards for a touchdown during the third quarter. Gandy's 7-yard touchdown increased the margin to 14 early in the fourth quarter before Seroka booted a 44-yard field goal to make the score 17–0. The Tigers finally got on the scoreboard on a 1-yard run by All-America tailback Lewis Tillman but could get nothing more in the 17–7 defeat. "One thing ought to be clear," said Carmody. "Jackson State is as good or perhaps better than a lot of Division I teams that we play. They make few mistakes. They are sound fundamentally. They are well motivated and well coached. And when they tackle you, you stay tackled."

The eventual NCAA Division I-AA champion Indians of Northeast Louisiana University came to town to meet the 5–3 Eagles on November 7. After falling behind 10–0, USM scored 17 consecutive points to go ahead 17–10. The Indians tied the game at 17 before the half and increased their advantage to 34–17 before Henry returned a punt 89 yards for a touchdown for USM, but Northeast Louisiana held on for the 34–24 win.

The East Carolina Pirates visited the Eagles on November 14 for the final home game of the 1987 season, and Henry, one of the country's premiere punt returners, put the Golden Eagles on top by returning a Pirate punt 65 yards for a touchdown. The Eagles added another touchdown early in the second quarter when Favre connected with Tillman on a 26-yard touchdown pass, but the Pirates rallied to knot the game at 14 at half-

Cornerback James Henry (1986–1988) returned four punts for touchdowns in three consecutive games in 1987 setting an NCAA record.

time. Favre hit Hansford with an 11-yard touchdown pass, Henry returned another punt 81 yards for a touchdown, and the Eagles added another touchdown and a field goal to take a 38–20 fourth-quarter advantage, but the Pirates scored a pair of late touchdowns to make the game close. Bradley rushed for 119 yards to help lead the Golden Eagle attack, which rolled up 419 yards. The 38–34 victory improved the Eagles to 6–4 and guaranteed them a winning season.

The final game of the year came on November 28 at Southwestern Louisiana. The Eagles scored first in another wild offensive show, blocking a Southwestern Louisiana punt and recovering the ball in the end zone for a 6–0 lead. The Cajuns answered with three straight touchdowns to take a 21–6 lead midway through the second quarter, but Favre hit McGee with a 12-yard touchdown pass and Seroka knocked a 20-yard field goal through the uprights to cut the Cajun edge to 21–16 at halftime. The two teams traded touchdowns in the third quarter, but the Cajuns added a 2-point conversion and led 29–23 heading into the fourth quarter. Favre's 6-yard touchdown pass to McGee cut the margin to 37–30, but Southwestern Louisiana held on to pick up the win.

EAGLE FEVER AND I BELIEVE [203]

Favre threw for a school-record 295 yards but could not keep the Eagles from falling to 6–5.

Pat Ferrell was once again named to the All-South Independent first team, while linebacker Sidney Coleman, Gandy, Henry, and Knighten were named to the second team. Seroka played in the Senior Bowl, while Knighten played in the Blue-Gray All-Star Classic. The Indianapolis Colts took Baylor in the fifth round of the NFL draft.

Five days after the season ended, Carmody met with USM President Lucas and was asked to resign. Announcing his departure at a press conference, Carmody stated, "I did not see this coming." One of the reasons the university cited for making the change was the lack of attendance for home games. Carmody compiled an overall record of 37–29.

Southern Miss supporters quickly began discussing possibilities for Carmody's replacement, with the most popular candidates former USM quarterback and current Wake Forest offensive coordinator Jeff Bower and Northeast Louisiana head coach Pat Collins. Instead, on December 17, McLellan and Lucas named as the team's new head coach Curley Hallman, an assistant at Texas A & M whose coaching career had also included stops at Alabama, Memphis State, and Clemson, where he had worked with McLellan. "When the search committee report came to me," Lucas said at the press conference announcing Hallman's hiring, "Curley was the first choice of every member of the committee who was there and voted. He was the top candidate." According to McLellan, Hallman "did what he was supposed to do as a coach" when the two men worked together at Clemson. "Communication is his best asset. He's got a lot of energy, and we plan to use it." For his part, Hallman was eager to get going in his new position: "I'm at a point right now where it would be hard to go back and say when I have been

In three seasons as head coach Curley Hallman won 23 games and led the Golden Eagles to a pair of bowl games, the 1988 Independence Bowl and the 1990 All-American Bowl, although Hallman left for LSU before that game was played.

this excited. . . . I'm very, very excited to be a part of the Southern Miss Golden Eagle football program."

1988 SEASON

September 3, 1988, Hallman's forty-first birthday, was also the date of his first game in charge of the Golden Eagles. Playing at home against Division 1-AA Stephen F. Austin, Southern Miss got off to a slow start, giving up a 32-yard touchdown catch by running back Larry Centers for a 7–0 halftime deficit. But the Lumberjacks scored no more, while Bradley ran for two touchdowns and Gandy added another to give the Eagles a 21–7 victory. Bradley finished with 105 yards on 17 carries, and the Golden Eagle defense held Stephen F. Austin to 48 yards rushing and 206 overall. "It's my first win as a head coach," Hallman said, "and I've been waiting for this a long time."

At Doak Campbell Stadium in Tallahassee, the Golden Eagles met No. 10 Florida State on September 10. The Seminoles set the stage early when cornerback Deion Sanders intercepted a Favre pass and returned it 39 yards for a touchdown. Florida State surged to a 28–0 lead before the Eagles got on the board with a 33-yard pass from Favre to Bradley and a 45-yard Seroka field goal. But then it was all Seminoles again, as quarterback Chip Ferguson threw for 239 yards and three touchdowns, leading his team to a 49–13 win. The Seminoles piled up 495 yards of total offense, although the Eagle defense picked off four passes.

The Golden Eagles returned home on September 17 to face Virginia Tech, a fellow member of the Independence Bowl Football Association. Created the previous spring, the association was a loose coalition of Division I-A football schools that had an agreement under which the team with the best overall record would appear in the Independence Bowl. The Hokies took a 10–0 lead, but a strong second-half performance by the Eagle special teams ignited the team to a 35–13 win. Carter returned a blocked punt 60 yards for a score, while the ever-dangerous Henry returned another punt 44 yards for the fifth touchdown of his career. Favre's performance—11 completions in 17 attempts for 148 yards and three touchdowns—delighted former USM quarterback Jeff Bower, the Eagles' new offensive coordinator: "Brett did things I've never seen him do before. He's still got a lot of improving to do to get this offense where it needs to be, but I was very pleased at what I saw tonight."

At East Carolina on September 24, the Golden Eagles won a 45–42 shootout that spotlighted Favre's talents. The quarterback completed 17 passes for 301 yards and a touchdown as the Eagles racked up 592 yards of offense. Southern Miss scored the winning touchdown with 12 seconds remaining on a 5-yard pass from Young, USM's short-yardage quarterback, to Hansford. Favre set up the winning touchdown with a 40-yard line-drive pass that traveled the width of the field to wide receiver Alfred Williams near the Pirate 10-yard line. Favre later called it "the hardest ball I've ever thrown," and Williams recalled, "I swear the ball was never over my head. I heard the ball humming about 5 yards away from me. I mean I heard it coming. I swear I'm not joking, I heard it. I guess it was the laces whirring in the wind, but I heard it." Gandy had a career-high 188 yards on 27 carries, while Tillman caught seven passes for 148 yards. The two teams combined for 1,130 yards in the game.

Louisville jumped out to an early 10–0 lead against the Eagles at Roberts Stadium the next week, but Southern Miss got a pair of 3-yard touchdown runs from Gandy in the fourth quarter to pull out a 30–23 victory. Gandy romped for 110 yards on the ground and three touchdowns, while Favre threw for 275 yards. Louisville running back Deon Booker rushed for 106 yards, one of only two backs to break the 100-yard barrier against the Eagles in 1988. With its third win in a row, Southern Miss advanced to 4–1.

The Golden Eagle defense shone in a 38–13 rout of the Tulane Green Wave at the Superdome on October 8. The high-powered Green Wave offense gained just 236 yards, 68 on the ground, as the Eagles chased Jones, the Tulane quarterback, all over the artificial surface, holding him to 10 completions in 25 attempts. Favre threw for 179 yards and three touchdowns, and the Eagles rushed for a season-high 296 yards.

At Jackson's Mississippi Veterans Memorial Stadium on October 17, Southern Miss jumped to an early 21–0 lead against Mississippi State and never looked back, winning 38–21 to give them 10 victories in their last 12 games against the rivals from Starkville. Bradley slashed through the Bulldog defense for 167 yards and three touchdowns, while Henry had yet another punt return for a touchdown, this one for 73 yards. Five straight wins had brought Southern Miss to 6–1 on the year.

Against Southwestern Louisiana the next week, the game turned on the All-American arm of Favre, who was brilliant in the 27–14 victory. The 19-year-old quarterback completed 23 of 30 passes for 298 yards and three touchdowns. The Golden Eagle defense held the Ragin' Cajuns to just 98 yards rushing, as USM pushed its winning streak to six games.

A victory or a tie in their upcoming game with Memphis State would give the Eagles the host role in the Independence Bowl. The Homecoming crowd at Roberts Stadium watched in elation as Southern Miss came through in the clutch with a 34–27 win on October 29. After Memphis State had scored twice to take a 27–26 lead late in the game, Favre drove the Eagles down the field in the game's final minutes, throwing a 45-yard touchdown pass to wide receiver Eugene Rowell, who juggled the ball before pulling it in. Favre broke his own school record with 341 yards through the air, and the Eagle offense rolled up 498 yards. "We knew what a victory meant today," Coach Hallman said. "We closed the deal. We signed the check and we cashed it."

The 8–1 Golden Eagles found the ride a little rougher when they faced No. 9 Auburn on November 5 at Jordan-Hare Stadium. The Tigers held the Eagle offense to just 6 yards rushing and 218 yards overall while accumulating 462 yards in a 38–8 Tiger win.

Playing with a tornado warning, driving rain, and a thunderstorm hanging over Joe Aillet Stadium in Ruston, Louisiana, the Golden Eagles scored 26 points in the first half and held on for a 26–19 win over Louisiana Tech. Carter, playing cornerback, started the game on a positive note for Southern Miss, picking off a Tech pass and returning the ball 42 yards for a touchdown. Although the Eagle offense struggled in the second half, the defense held the Bulldogs to 10 points in the final two quarters to secure the victory and give Southern Miss a 9–2 final regular-season mark.

The Golden Eagles made their second appearance in the Independence Bowl in Shreveport, Louisiana, on December 23 when they met the University of Texas–El Paso Miners, who had been selected over Wake Forest and Kentucky. Southern led 10–7 at halftime before Henry dazzled the crowd at Independence Stadium with a pair of third-quarter punt returns for touchdowns to spark his team to an easy 38–18 victory, earning himself both the Offensive and Defensive Player of the Game awards. Gandy contributed 134 yards rushing and two touchdowns.

Hallman's first year as head coach of the Golden Eagles had been a success. The team became the first USM squad to win 10 games in a season since 1952. Punter Scott Bryant was an All–South Independent first-team selection and an honorable mention All-America pick, while Gandy, Henry, linebacker George Hill, and center Marty Williams were second-team All–South Independent. Henry and Seroka played in the Senior Bowl, and the Seattle Seahawks took Henry in the fourth round of the 1989 NFL draft.

1989 SEASON

The Golden Eagles' first contest of the 1989 campaign was a September 2 "home" game at the Gator Bowl in Jacksonville, Florida, against No. 6 Florida State. The contest had originally been scheduled for Hattiesburg, but the city of Jacksonville offered USM $500,000 for the privilege of hosting the season opener, which was televised nationwide by Atlanta-based Superstation TBS. The matchup against one of the nation's premier teams offered a chance for the Eagles to show viewers across the country how good Southern Miss was. The Seminoles seized a quick 10–0 lead and appeared poised to bury the Eagles, but Southern Miss scored on a 22-yard field goal from Chuck Davis with 17 seconds to go in the first quarter and added touchdowns on a 3-yard run by tailback Eddie Ray Jackson and a 4-yard pass from Favre to Williams to lead 17–10 after two periods. Florida State scored twice to move ahead 23–17 heading into the final quarter, but Southern Miss surged back in front with a 10-yard touchdown run by Bradley. The seesaw battle continued as Florida State kicked a field goal to go back ahead 26–24 with just under seven minutes to go, but the Golden Eagles responded with a 13-play drive that culminated in a 2-yard scoring pass from Favre to tight end Anthony Harris with 23 seconds left that gave Southern Miss the 30–26 win. Longtime USM sports information director Ace Cleveland told the *Jackson Clarion-Ledger* that he considered the win the biggest in school history: "I think the ramifications of this one could make this the best. It could lead to more television appearances, more financial gain, more exposure for our athletes."

The win over Florida State catapulted the Golden Eagles to No. 18 in the national rankings, with the Mississippi State Bulldogs the Eagles' next foes. For the first time since 1979, the game was played outside of Jackson, and a record Roberts Stadium crowd of 34,189 watched a close contest, with Mississippi State holding a 14–13 lead at intermission. The teams traded scores during the second half and the game was tied at 23 with 2:55 remaining. After an exchange of punts, Mississippi State had the ball at its own 37-yard line with 1:18 to go. Bulldog quarterback Eric Underwood hit receiver Kenny Roberts for a 38-yard gain, and two plays later, Joel Logan kicked a 34-yard field goal with to give Mississippi State the 26–23 win, dropping the Eagles to 1–1 and knocking them out of the polls.

The Golden Eagles came into their September 16 tilt on the road at fifth-ranked Auburn averaging 26.5 points per game, but the Tigers had one of the best defensive squads in the country. The Golden Eagle rushing attack managed just 31 yards, and the Tigers exploded for 273 yards on the ground in their 24–3 victory.

Traveling to Fort Worth, Texas, the Golden Eagles played Texas Christian for the first time on September 23. Both teams scored twice in the first half, but the Golden Eagles blocked a Horned Frog extra point for a 14–13 edge at halftime. Neither team produced much offense in the second half. TCU scored on a 1-yard run in the third quarter, but the 2-point conversion failed. Davis hit on a 23-yard field goal to make TCU's margin just 19–17, but the Horned Frogs ran out the clock, and the Golden Eagles fell to 1–3.

It was a homecoming of sorts for Coach Hallman when the Eagles battled No. 22 Texas A & M on September 30 in College Station. The Aggies did not make things easy for their former assistant coach, as Texas A & M rushed for 316 yards while winning 31–14. Favre was at the top of his game, throwing for 303 yards against normally stingy Aggie defense. Running back Dwayne Nelson had a 63-yard touchdown run for the Eagles in the third quarter, and first-year receiver Ron Baham caught an 80-yard scoring strike from Favre in the third quarter that pulled the Eagles to within 10, but Texas A & M shut the door and preserved the victory.

The Golden Eagles returned to Hattiesburg the following week to meet Tulane, recording their second win of the season, 30–21. Southern Miss led 30–9 early in the fourth quarter before two late Tulane scores made the final score look closer than the game really was. Favre threw for 216 yards and two touchdowns, while Tony Smith returned a kickoff 80 yards for a touchdown to set a Roberts Stadium record. Linebacker Thad McDowell was credited with 13 tackles, helping the Eagles to their seventh win in eleven tries against the Green Wave.

The Eagles next played at Louisville on October 14, striking first as Eddie Ray Jackson scored on a 5-yard run. Louisville countered with a second-quarter touchdown that evened the game at

Michael Jackson (1988–1989) began his career as a quarterback but finished it as one of the team's most feared wide receivers.

7. Southern Miss regained the lead early in the third quarter on a 32-yard field goal by Davis, but Louisville matched it in the fourth quarter, once again tying the game. With 23 seconds remaining, the Cardinals had the ball and attempted a 43-yard field goal, but true freshman Vernard Collins blocked the kick, giving USM the ball and one last opportunity to win the game. As the clock ticked down the game's final seconds, Favre rolled right and fought off Louisville defensive end Ted Washington before lofting a Hail Mary pass that was tipped by wide receiver Michael Jackson and caught behind the Louisville defenders by Tillman, who raced into the end zone to give the Eagles the 16–10 win as time expired. According to Bower, the play had worked exactly as it had been designed: "We put Alfred Williams, Michael Jackson and Tony Smith on the left side and Darryl [Tillman] by himself on the right. Michael is supposed to tip the ball up and hopefully one of our guys will catch it. Brett is supposed to spend a little time back there and throw it. He has to hesitate a little and throw it high."

Southwestern Louisiana spoiled USM's October 21 Homecoming by handing the hosts a 24–21 defeat. Southwestern Louisiana quarterback Brian Mitchell ran for 134 yards and passed for another 343 to lead his team. The Eagles ran out to a 14–0 lead, but the Ragin' Cajuns launched a comeback, scoring three consecutive touchdowns to forge ahead 21–14. The Eagles rallied to tie the game early in the fourth quarter, but with just 1:39 remaining, Southwestern Louisiana put together a 48-yard drive that ended with Greg Lemoine's 50-yard field goal for the win.

Upset over the last-second loss to Southwestern Louisiana, the 3–5 Eagles traveled to Memphis State on October 28 and put the squeeze on the Tigers. The Eagles ran up a commanding 24–0 lead on their way to a 31–7 triumph. The Golden Eagle defense played superbly, limiting Memphis to 133 yards through the air, registering four sacks, and forcing eight punts. Favre had one of the best games of his career, completing 24 of 41 passes for 345 yards and two touchdowns to Eugene Rowell, who caught 7 balls for 116 yards.

EAGLE FEVER AND I BELIEVE

After a two-week break, the Eagles struck first against No. 4 Alabama in Tuscaloosa when Favre connected with Rowell on a 47-yard touchdown strike. But the Tide scored 37 unanswered points before allowing another touchdown in the 37–14 win. Favre once again threw for 300 yards, including four completions to Rowell for 140 yards. The Eagles fell to 4–6.

The Golden Eagle offense clicked for 484 yards as Favre threw for 286 yards and three touchdowns in a 41–27 season-ending home win against East Carolina on November 25. One of the game's highlights was Smith's 82-yard kickoff return for a touchdown, which enabled him to finish as the NCAA leader with a 32.2-yard average. At 5–6, the Eagles recorded their first losing season since 1984.

Punter Scott Bryant, linebacker William Kirksey, offensive tackle Chris Ryals, and defensive back Kerry Valrie were named second-team All–South Independent, and offensive tackle Buddy King played in the Senior Bowl. In the 1990 NFL draft, Rowell was a ninth-round pick by the Cleveland Browns and fullback Reginald Warnsley an eleventh-round pick by the Detroit Lions.

The 1980s saw numerous highs and lows for the Southern Mississippi football program. For the first time, there had been some instability at the top, with three head coaches leading the program during the decade. But the program was continuing to grow and prosper, and some of its most exciting times lay ahead.

THE FINAL DAYS AS AN INDEPENDENT AND CONFERENCE USA

1990–2003

The 1990s and first years of the twenty-first century represented another successful era for the Golden Eagles of the University of Southern Mississippi. After another coaching change early in the decade, Jeff Bower settled in and provided the program with stable leadership for the rest of the period, and the formation of Conference USA in the spring of 1995 brought the Golden Eagle football team back into a conference for the first time since 1952. The team responded by winning or sharing four Conference USA championships and returning to postseason bowl play.

Quarterback Brett Favre finished his career (1987–1990) passing for a school record 7,695 yards and 52 touchdowns. He went on to star for the Green Bay Packers of the NFL and was named the league's most valuable player in 1995, 1996, and 1997.

1990 SEASON

USM's 1990 season opened at home at Roberts Stadium on September 1 against the Statesmen of Delta State, but the Eagles were without quarterback Brett Favre, who had been involved in a car accident during the summer. Favre had appeared to be all right when Southern Miss began preseason practice in August, but shortly thereafter he had to have emergency surgery to remove some of his small intestine. With John Whitcomb starting at quarterback, Coach Curley Hallman's troops held on for a 12–0 win. "I'm happy with the win. I don't care if it's two points, 10 or 16, the bottom line is, we won the game," Hallman said. "Our kids have worked hard in the preseason and I saw some good things out there."

Favre returned the following week to face No. 13 Alabama at Legion Field in Birmingham in Gene Stallings's debut as the Crimson Tide head coach. USM fell behind 10–3 early in the second quarter, but Golden Eagle safety Kerry Valrie intercepted a Gary Hollingsworth pass and returned it 75 yards for a touchdown to tie the game. With the Eagles again trailing 17–10 midway through the third quarter, tailback Tony Smith scored twice to give Southern its first lead, 24–17, but Alabama scored the tying touchdown late in the third quarter. The clock showed 7:22 remaining in the game when the Golden Eagles took over at their own 20-yard line, and Favre went to work, moving the Eagles to the Crimson Tide 35 with 3:35 to go. Jim (Stump) Taylor calmly booted a 52-yard field goal to give Southern Miss the 27–24 upset.

The team's next contest was against the Georgia Bulldogs between the hedges at Sanford Stadium in Athens. The Golden Eagles grabbed a 17–6 lead midway through the third quarter, but two Georgia touchdowns gave the hosts an 18–17 lead with 6:04 left in the game. Trapped deep in their own territory with just under two minutes left, the Bulldogs punted to Smith, who returned the kick to the Georgia 24-yard line to set the stage for Taylor's 42-yard field goal try. The kick had plenty of distance but hit the right upright, and the Bulldogs escaped with the narrow victory. "We lost a close one and that's tough," a disappointed Hallman told the media after the game. "I'll say this now, and this is important. I think we are a better football team. It didn't show early, but we came back and played well."

Before the fourth-largest crowd ever to assemble at Scott Field in Starkville, the Golden Eagles met Mississippi State on September 22. The teams traded field goals in the first quarter and touchdowns in the second, leaving the game knotted at 10 at halftime. The second half was a defensive stalemate, with the Bulldogs finally

Wide receiver Greg Reed played for the Golden Eagles from 1988 to 1991. He helped lead the team to postseason bowls in 1988 and 1990.

breaking the tie with 3:01 left on the clock when Joel Logan nailed a 41-yard field goal. The Golden Eagles drove to the Bulldog 30-yard line in the game's final minutes, but Taylor missed a field goal from 47 yards out, and Mississippi State had the 13–10 win. Favre said after the game, "It's tough to lose to them like that. It's tough to lose any but it's even tougher to lose to your big time rival. We had the opportunity to win the game but we didn't. We still have a long season ahead of us."

With a 2–2 record, Southern Miss hosted Louisville on September 29 at Roberts Stadium. In one of the year's weirdest games, the Eagles scored 22 points in the game's first 5:51 while running just two plays from scrimmage. Smith returned a Cardinal punt 45 yards for a touchdown barely a minute into the game, and the Eagles added the 2-point conversion for an 8–0 advantage. Running back Roland Johnson rumbled 47 yards for a touchdown on the Golden Eagles' second offensive snap of the night, and then Valrie scooped up a Louisville fumble and returned the ball 42 yards for a touchdown to give Southern the 22-point lead with just over nine minutes left in the first quarter. The Golden Eagles went on to win 25–13. After the game, Louisville coach Howard Schnellenberger, who had been burned several times over the years by miraculous Golden Eagle plays, credited the Southern win to "the moon over Hattiesburg." "It was a game of big plays," an elated Hallman shouted after the game. "I am very excited for our team, coaches and fans. This was an exciting game. Our crowd was really into the game."

The Golden Eagles defeated East Carolina on October 6 in Greenville, North Carolina, holding the Pirates to just 230 yards of total offense. Running backs Smith and Johnson combined for 170 yards to lead the Eagle attack, while Taylor added three field goals for the team's second straight win.

The 4–2 Golden Eagles traveled to the Superdome in New Orleans on October 13 to battle Tulane. Southern spotted the Green Wave a 14–0 lead but rallied to tie during the second half on a 23-yard touchdown pass from Favre to end Greg Reed and a 63-yard punt return by Smith. A pair of Taylor field goals in the fourth quarter sealed a 20–14 Golden Eagle victory.

Southern Miss won its fourth game in a row with a 23–7 Homecoming victory over Memphis State on October 20. Taylor again kicked three field goals, while Smith and tailback Quintus Casey turned in touchdown runs. The Eagle defense kept the Tigers out of the end zone until the final seconds and allowed just 191 yards as the team improved to 6–2 on the season.

The Eagles next squared off against Virginia Tech on the road in Blacksburg. The Eagles fell behind 20–0 at halftime, allowing the Hokies to amass 337 yards, but played much better after the break, limiting the Hokies to 134 yards and closing to within 20–14. With 2:27 remaining in the game, Smith returned a punt to the 50-yard line, and the Eagles drove to the Hokie 23-yard line before a fourth-down pass fell incomplete, giving Virginia Tech the win.

With a 6–3 record, Southern Miss supporters believed that the team needed to win its last two games to be considered for a postseason bowl game. But against Southwestern Louisiana at Lafayette the next week, Southern came out sluggishly and trailed 13–0 midway through the fourth quarter, although no one in the stands or the press box knew exactly how much time was left because the clock had malfunctioned early in the game and officials were keeping the time on the field. Smith ignited his team by returning a Ragin' Cajun punt to the Southwestern Louisiana 26, and Casey scored on the next play to bring the Eagles within 6. Then, with just 1:20 remaining, the Southern Miss defense forced a punt, and Smith once again came up big, returning the ball 25 yards to the Southwestern Louisiana 45. A few plays later,

THE FINAL DAYS AS AN INDEPENDENT AND CONFERENCE USA

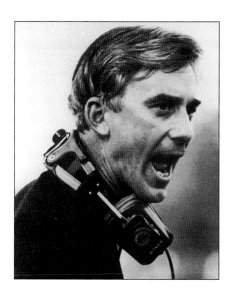

Former USM quarterback Jeff Bower became head coach of the Golden Eagles in December of 1990, replacing Curley Hallman. His first game as coach was in the 1990 All-American Bowl.

Favre found tailback Michael Welch, who outjumped a defender to catch the ball in the end zone and tie the game. The play turned out to be the last of the game, and with no time left, Taylor kicked the extra point that gave Southern Miss the 14–13 win.

The Eagles' regular-season finale occurred on November 10 at Jordan-Hare Stadium against No. 15 Auburn. The War Eagles drove deep into Southern Miss territory on four occasions, but the defense stiffened and limited Auburn to four Jim Von Wyl field goals and a 12–0 lead at the end of the third quarter. Early in the fourth period, Favre drove the Eagles 69 yards, capping the series with a 12-yard touchdown pass to Eddie Ray Jackson. Then, starting at the Auburn 42-yard line with 2:37 to go, the Eagles drove to the Tiger 10 and Favre hit Harris with a touchdown pass that enabled the Eagles to squeak out the 13–12 victory and finish the regular season at 8–3.

When the Independence Bowl was slow to extend a bid to Southern Miss, Athletic Director Bill McLellan opened talks with the All-American Bowl, located in Birmingham, Alabama. After Louisville, which had been slated to play in the All-American Bowl, chose instead to go to the Fiesta Bowl in Tempe, Arizona, the Golden Eagles took the spot in Birmingham. On November 27, however, the Eagle players learned that their coach would be leaving to replace Mike Archer as the head coach at Louisiana State University. Five days later, McLellan named 37-year-old former Golden Eagle quarterback Jeff Bower as Hallman's replacement. Bower had spent the past season as offensive coordinator at Oklahoma State after holding the same position under Hallman at USM during the 1989 and 1990 campaigns. Bower made his debut as the Golden Eagles' head coach against North Carolina State in the All-American Bowl on December 28. The 44,000 fans at Legion Field watched Favre throw for 341 yards, a Southern Miss bowl record, and two touchdowns, but the Wolfpack won 31–27. The Eagles finished the year at 8–4.

Offensive guard Chafan Marsh was named first-team All–South Independent and honorable mention All-America, while Favre, Smith, and linebacker Arnie Williams were named second-team All–South Independent. Both Favre and Valrie played in the Senior Bowl, and Favre also appeared in the East-West Shrine Game. In the April 1991 National Football League draft, Favre was taken in the second round (thirty-third pick) by the Atlanta Falcons, wide receiver Michael Jackson went in the sixth round to the Cleveland Browns, and cornerback Simmie Carter was selected in the seventh round by the New York Giants.

1991 SEASON

Bower coached his first game at Roberts Stadium on August 31 against the Delta State Statesmen. The Golden Eagles treated their new coach to a relatively easy 25–7 victory in the first game ever played by a Southern Miss team in the month of August.

The following week, the Golden Eagles traveled to Pittsburgh for their first meeting with the University of Pittsburgh Panthers. After falling behind 22–0 at halftime, Southern Miss scored twice in the third quarter on a pair of touchdown passes by quarterback Tommy Waters, but the Panthers went on to win 35–14.

Back home after a week off, the Golden Eagles hosted the Colorado State Rams on September 21. The Rams, who were not used to the September heat and humidity in southern Mississippi, suffered as the game wore on. The defense held the Rams to just 265 yards, and safeties Derrick Hoskins and Brian Wood and cornerback Vernard Collins intercepted passes as Southern Miss trounced Colorado State by a score of 39–7. In the third quarter, the Golden Eagles delighted their fans by executing the "fumblerooski" to perfection. Waters took the snap but laid the ball on the ground, where Marsh picked it up and rambled 17 yards for a touchdown. Bower said later that his team had practiced the play during the preceding week "and our players have had fun with it and I thought they deserved a good shot to run it."

USM's nine-game winning streak against the Louisville Cardinals ended on September 28 at Cardinal Stadium. The Golden Eagles took a 7–0 lead into the locker room at halftime, but the Cardinals came away with a 28–7 win that dropped Southern Miss to 2–2 for the year.

The Golden Eagles faced No. 16 Auburn at Jordan-Hare Stadium on October 5, scoring the first points of the game when tailback Roland Johnson capped a 77-yard drive with a 4-yard touchdown run that gave Southern Miss the 7–0 lead. A Tiger field goal late in the first quarter was matched by a 20-yard kick by Lance Nations early in the second quarter, and Southern Miss held a 10–3 lead at halftime. The second half remained scoreless until Auburn took over after a Golden Eagle punt with just over two minutes left in the game. Auburn then drove 58 yards, scoring on a 5-yard pass from quarterback Stan White to tight end Fred Baxter. The War Eagles went for the 2-point conversion and the win, but the pass fell incomplete, giving Bower and his Golden Eagles the 10–9 win.

In Memphis on October 12, the Memphis State Tigers jumped to a 17–3 halftime lead and held on to beat the Golden Eagles 17–12. The Eagle defense played well, holding the Tigers to 283 yards, but the Eagle offense produced only 228 yards.

The Golden Eagles rolled over the Tulane Green Wave 47–14 the following week. Smith raced 81 yards for a touchdown on the second play from scrimmage and then added an 11-yard scoring run late in the first quarter to give the Eagles a 14–0 lead. Smith finished the day with 190 yards on 18 carries, while Waters completed 14 of 20 passes for 162 yards and two touchdowns. The Golden Eagle defense held the Green Wave to 286 total yards, just 73 of them on the ground.

The Eagles played poorly on October 26 on the road against Cincinnati, losing 17–7. The Bearcats had 474 yards of total offense and held the Eagles to 12 first downs and 216 yards. Smith scored for Southern Miss on a 15-yard second-quarter run, but the Eagles were shut out in the second half to fall to 4–4 on the year.

A week later, the Golden Eagles traveled to Skelly Stadium to meet the University of Tulsa Golden Hurricane. With the temperature at 26 degrees and snow falling throughout the day, the Golden Eagles took a 10–0 lead at the end of three quarters. Tulsa scored early in the fourth quarter to cut the lead to 10–7 and tied the game on a 41-yard field goal with 3:50 to go. The Golden Eagles drove to the Tulsa 17-yard line with 16 seconds to play, but Nations missed a 35-yard field goal attempt, and it appeared that the game would end in a tie. But Tulsa quarterback T. J. Rubley completed a 65-yard pass that brought his team to the Southern Miss 25-yard line and called the team's final timeout with 1 second to go. The 32-yard field goal attempt missed; however, the Golden Eagles were penalized for having too many men on the field, giving Tulsa one last chance, and the Tulsa kicker split the uprights from 24 yards out for the 13–10 win.

Safety Derrick Hoskins (1989–1991) was a second-team All–South Independent selection in 1991, a season when he recorded three interceptions.

At 4–5 with a two-game losing streak, the Golden Eagles tried to bounce back for their November 9 Homecoming game against No. 16 East Carolina. Although an 86-yard punt return by Perry Carter kept the Golden Eagles in the game early, quarterback Jeff Blake led the Pirate offense to 551 yards and a 48–20 victory. "Turnovers killed us," a dejected Bower said after the game. "It's been that kind of season. We have another game left and we will hold our heads high and play well."

But the season ended with another loss, as Louisiana Tech thumped the Eagles 30–13 at Ruston. The Southern Miss defense again struggled, allowing the Bulldogs 402 yards. A 25-yard touchdown pass from Waters to wide receiver Ron Baham pulled the Eagles to within 7 points at 21–14 late in the third quarter, but the Bulldogs returned a Southern Miss fumble for a touchdown and added a safety to secure the victory. The Golden Eagles finished the year with a 4–7 record.

Smith was named to the All–South Independent team and was an honorable mention All-America, while Hoskins, Marcus Marsh, linebacker Thad McDowell, tackle Chris Ryals, and linebacker Arnie Williams were named second-team All–South Independent. Smith, Ryals, Williams, and defensive tackle Tim Roberts played in the Senior Bowl. The Atlanta Falcons selected Smith in the first round of the NFL draft (nineteenth pick overall), using a draft pick obtained by trading Favre to the Green Bay Packers. In the fifth round, Roberts went to the Houston Oilers and Hoskins went to the Los Angeles Raiders.

1992 SEASON

The Golden Eagles opened the 1992 campaign against longtime foe Memphis State at Roberts Stadium on September 4. Two fourth-quarter touchdowns gave the Tigers a 21–20 lead, and the Eagles had the ball with just under three minutes to go. Waters drove his squad to the Tiger 36-yard line, and Bower sent freshman placekicker Johnny Lomoro into the game to try the first field goal of his career. The strong-legged kicker drilled the ball 52 yards through the uprights, giving Southern Miss a 23–21 season-opening win.

At Birmingham's Legion Field the next week, the Golden Eagles fell behind No. 8 Alabama 7–0 at halftime. Southern Miss tied the game early in the third quarter when end James Singleton batted a Jay Barker pass into the air and tackle Bobby Hamilton snatched the ball out of the air and raced 18 yards for a touchdown. On the Crimson Tide's next possession, tailback Derrick Lassic fumbled, and Eagle safety Melvin Ratcliff recovered the ball at Alabama's 18-yard line. The turnover led to Nations's 33-yard field goal and a 10–7 Golden Eagle advantage. But the Crimson Tide, who won the national championship that season, rallied for the 17–10 victory, and USM dropped to 1–1 on the year.

Back home at Roberts Stadium on September 19, Lomoro's leg defeated Louisiana Tech 16–13. Nations, whom Bower used for short field goals, had nailed a 27-yarder with 3:42 left in the game to tie the score at 13. With 1:19 to go, Tech got possession of the ball and tried to go to the air, but Golden Eagle cornerback Terryl Ulmer intercepted a pass and returned the ball to the Bulldog 33-yard line. Lomoro then kicked another game-winning field goal, this time from 46 yards out, as time expired. "We never quit and I am very proud of the guys," Bower shouted over the celebration in the locker room. "At the timeout I told Johnny to do it just like practice. That's what I told him at the Memphis State game and so I said it again today."

The Golden Eagles lost 16–8 to Auburn on September 26, with the team's only points coming in the closing minutes on a 22-yard pass from backup quarterback Aaron Hightower to wide receiver Mark Montgomery and on Hightower's subsequent run for the 2-point conversion. The Eagle defense played well, limiting the War Eagles to 251 yards, but the Southern Miss offense managed only 165 yards.

The Golden Eagles faced Tulsa for Homecoming the following week. The Golden Eagles were hoping for avenge their last-second loss to the Golden Hurricane in 1991, but Tulsa jumped out to a 14–0 lead and appeared to be cruising to an easy victory. Midway through the second quarter, however, wide receiver Fred Brock got the Eagles back into the game with a 63-yard touchdown run on a reverse. Trailing 27–24 with time running out, the Golden Hurricane threw a pass that Ulmer intercepted at the Eagle 28-yard line. He returned the ball to the Tulsa 8 before being caught by a Hurricane player. As Ulmer was about to be tackled, he lateraled to linebacker Eugene Harmon, who dove into the end zone for a touchdown that gave Southern Miss the 33–24 victory and brought the Golden Eagles' season mark to 3–2. "We have told our players that the month of October is very important," Bower reflected. "We have five games in October and it was good to start off with a win. We now have to prove that we can win on the road."

But Bower's players failed their first test away from home, losing 23–10 to Northern Illinois on

THE FINAL DAYS AS AN INDEPENDENT AND CONFERENCE USA

October 10 in what was perhaps their worst game of the year. Waters and Hightower combined to complete just 18 of 42 passes for 206 yards, while Northern Illinois piled up 442 yards, including 188 on the ground by running back LaShon Johnson.

At the Superdome in New Orleans on the following Saturday, USM and Tulane were tied at 7 in the fourth quarter. Nations kicked a 29-yard field goal to give the Golden Eagles the lead, and Buckhalter added a 23-yard touchdown run with just over five minutes to go to give Southern Miss the 17–7 victory.

A 31–17 win at home over Cincinnati on October 24 gave the Eagles a 5–3 record. Two first-half touchdowns and tailback Myreon McKinney's 3-yard touchdown run early in the third quarter gave USM a 21–3 lead, and a late Bearcat rally fell short. The Golden Eagle defense produced three takeaways and three sacks to help secure the victory.

The next game for Southern Miss was a Thursday night showdown at East Carolina to be televised on ESPN. Leading 13–7 at halftime, the Golden Eagles put the game away during the third quarter, marching 58 yards in seven plays on the first possession of the second half and scoring on a 5-yard pass from quarterback Kevin Bentley to tight end Marcus Pope. Waters completed the 2-point conversion to Pope to give Southern Miss a 21–7 lead. Shortly thereafter, tailback Michael Welch picked up 50 of his 169 yards on the day on a touchdown run that upped the lead to 28–7. The Golden Eagle defense came up with big play after big play, including three interceptions by cornerback LaBarion Rankins, in the 38–21 victory.

The Golden Eagles took their 6–3 record and invaded the Swamp to play No. 14 Florida on November 7. The Gators jumped out to a early 17–3 lead, but the Eagles cut the gap to 7 when Carter intercepted a Shane Matthews pass and ran the ball back 52 yards for a touchdown. After Nations kicked a 40-yard field goal a few minutes later, the Eagles trailed by only 17–13. Southern Miss took the lead early in the fourth quarter on a 17-yard touchdown pass from Waters to wide receiver Mark Montgomery, who leaped high in the air to corral the ball. The Gators then took the kickoff and went 77 yards for a touchdown to surge back in front 24–20 with 9:36 remaining. Aided by a personal foul and a pass interference penalty against the Gators, Waters drove the Eagles to the Florida 17-yard line with 2:07 left. Facing a fourth-and-14, Waters dropped back to pass but lost control of the football, and Florida had the win.

The Golden Eagles closed the season on November 14 at Virginia Tech. The Hokies kicked a pair of field goals to grab a 12–3 edge late in the third quarter before Bower called a trick play: the flea-flicker. On third-and-inches with the ball on the Southern Miss 36-yard line, Bentley

Cornerback Perry Carter (1990–1993) was a double threat for the Golden Eagles as both a cornerback and kick returner. He had five interceptions in 1992, returning three of them for touchdowns, and averaged 10.8 yards per punt return in 1991.

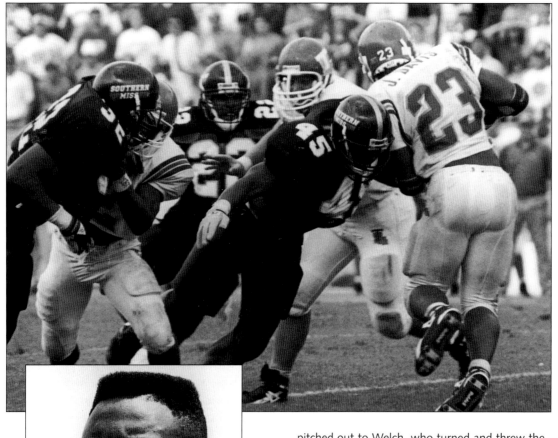

Tyrone Nix (#45) played middle linebacker for the Golden Eagles from 1990 to 1993. He would later become defensive coordinator under Coach Jeff Bower.

pitched out to Welch, who turned and threw the ball back to the quarterback, and Bentley raced 64 yards into the Tech end zone, stiff-arming several defenders as he ran down the sideline and bringing the Eagles to within 2 points. With 1:34 to go in the game, Nations connected on a 22-yard field goal that gave the Eagles a 13–12 victory and a 7–4 mark on the year.

Welch and Ulmer were named first-team All–South Independent and honorable mention All-America, as were offensive guard Leon Anderson and linebacker Tyrone Nix. Hamilton, Nations,

THE FINAL DAYS AS AN INDEPENDENT AND CONFERENCE USA

Pope, offensive guard George McReynolds, and defensive tackle Michael Tobias were named to the All-South Independent second team. Pope, deep snapper Mike Iosia, and defensive end James Singleton played in the Senior Bowl.

1993 SEASON

Playing at home, Southern Miss opened the 1993 season on September 2 against Coach Johnny Majors and the Pitt Panthers in a Thursday night game televised by ESPN. When Southern Miss fumbled on the game's second play from scrimmage, the Panthers quickly drove 60 yards for a touchdown and a 7–0 lead. The Golden Eagles tied the game at 7 on a 1-yard run by McKinney late in the first quarter and added 42-yard field goal by Lomoro for a 10–7 lead at the break. Pitt took a 14–10 lead late in the third quarter, and Waters threw three interceptions to kill any chance of a Golden Eagle comeback.

After a week off, the Golden Eagles outscored Northeast Louisiana Indians at Roberts Stadium 44–37, piling up 489 yards of total offense. A 27-point second quarter gave the Golden Eagles a 27–9 lead at halftime, but the Indians closed to within 37–30 with just over five minutes to play. L. T. Gulley returned a kickoff 51 yards to the Northeast Louisiana 29-yard line, and tailback Howard McGee took the ball on the next play and crossed the goal to put the game away.

The first road game of the year had the Golden Eagles facing the No. 25 Auburn Tigers on September 25. Auburn jumped out to a 21–7 halftime lead, but Southern Miss took a 24–21 lead by scoring 17 points within six minutes of the third quarter as Bentley hit tight end Anthony Owens with a 39-yard touchdown pass, Lomoro nailed a 30-yard field goal, and defensive tackle Kevin Jackson intercepted a Stan White pass and rumbled 11 yards into the end zone. Auburn recovered and scored a touchdown late in the third quarter and another midway through the fourth to take a 35–24 win.

The Golden Eagles lost 13–7 to Southwestern Louisiana on October 2 in Lafayette. Southern Miss scored first on a 14-yard second-quarter pass from Bentley to McKinney but could not register any more points, and Mike Shafer's two second-half field goals provided the margin of victory for the Ragin' Cajuns.

The 1–3 Golden Eagles next traveled to Athens on October 9 to meet the Georgia Bulldogs. Although the Golden Eagles trailed only 17–10 just before halftime, the Bulldogs subsequently caught fire, scoring just before halftime to go ahead 24–10 and adding 30 second-half points en route to a 54–24 pasting of the visitors. Georgia gained an incredible 667 yards of total offense, including 544 yards passing by quarterback Eric Zeier. Despite gaining 401 yards, Southern Miss lost its third game in a row. "The results were not what we wanted or expected," a dejected Bower said. "We did not do what it takes to win. We took a close game and let them break it open in the fourth quarter. I don't know why we haven't been a good fourth quarter team all year."

The following week the Golden Eagles took on No. 23 Louisville at Cardinal Stadium. USM held a

24–9 halftime lead but allowed the Cardinals to mount a second-half comeback for a 35–27 victory, their second in a row over Southern Miss, which fell to 1–5 on the year.

With a four-game losing streak, the Golden Eagles returned home on October 23 to host East Carolina. The Pirates grabbed a 10–3 halftime lead, but a 1-yard touchdown run by Chris Buckhalter early in the third quarter and a 31-yard run by tailback Barry Boyd late in the period put the Eagles on top for the first time, 17–10. McGee added an 8-yard touchdown run, and Southern Miss held on to win 24–16. "We knew we had to come up with a few big plays," safety L. T. Gulley said after the game. "We practiced hard all week. It was good to finish with a win." Bower said, "I am very proud of this team. We could have given up, but this week was one of our best at practice. These kids have character. We needed to dig ourselves out of a hole and we started that tonight."

No. 5 Alabama thrashed the Golden Eagles 40–0 on October 30 at Bryant-Denny Stadium in Tuscaloosa. The Crimson Tide offense recorded 550 total yards, while their defensive counterparts held the visitors to 72 yards on the ground and 104 yards through the air.

The Golden Eagles returned home to take on Tulane on November 6. After falling behind 10–0 in the game's first 10 minutes, the Golden Eagles pulled themselves to within 1 point on three Lomoro field goals. Midway through the third quarter, however, USM quarterback Ricky Carroll was hit and fumbled, and Tulane's Andre Goines ran the ball back 24 yards for a touchdown that increased the Green Wave lead to 17–9. Early in the fourth quarter, defensive tackle Reggie Elder intercepted a Tulane pass and returned the ball to the Tulane 9-yard line, and Boyd scored from 1 yard out three plays later to bring the Eagles to within 2 points at 17–15. But Southern Miss could get no closer, as the 2-point conversion failed and the Golden Eagles could not score on their last two possessions of the day.

Now 2–7 on the year, the Golden Eagles played Memphis State on November 13 at Liberty

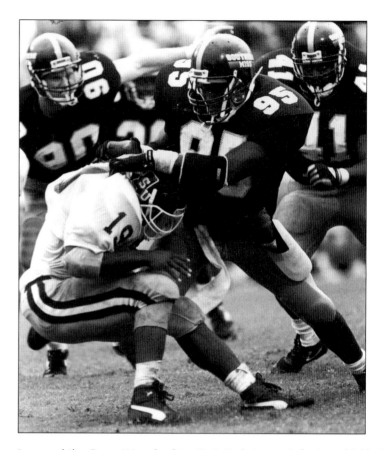

Defensive end Bobby Hamilton (#95) was one of the leaders of the Southern Miss defense from 1990 to 1993. He finished his career with 19 quarterback sacks. Also closing in to assist are defensive end James Singleton (#90) and linebacker Thad McDowell (#41).

[222] **THE FINAL DAYS AS AN INDEPENDENT AND CONFERENCE USA**

Bowl Memorial Stadium. When Gulley returned a Tiger pass 46 yards for a touchdown in the game's early minutes, Southern Miss had a 7–0 lead, but Memphis answered with a pair of touchdown passes to take a 14–7 halftime lead. The Tigers added a third quarter touchdown to take a 20–7 lead and then gave Southern Miss its only other points of the day by botching the extra-point snap and allowing Eagle linebacker Albert McRae get the ball and rumble 85 yards for 2 points, the first defensive extra points scored by the Eagles since the new rule permitting the play went into effect at the beginning of the season. The 20–9 Tiger victory dropped the Golden Eagles to 2–8.

The dismal 1993 season ended with a wild November 20 shootout at Skelly Stadium against the University of Tulsa Golden Hurricane. On Tulsa's first possession Carter intercepted a pass by quarterback Gus Frerotte and returned the ball 68 yards to the Hurricane end zone. Touchdown passes from Carroll to Ryan Pearson and Mark Montgomery put Southern up 20–3 early in the second quarter, and the lead grew to 27–9 at intermission. The Golden Eagles had a 30–16 edge, but Tulsa cut the gap to 7 on Frerotte's 78-yard touchdown pass to wide receiver Chris Penn. After a Hurricane touchdown run with 5:09 to go, the game was tied at 30, and that is where it ended as both teams missed field goals to win the game. USM's first tie since 1981 left the team with a 2–8–1 final record, although Alabama was subsequently forced to forfeit its victory over the Eagles, improving the team's official record to 3–7–1.

Offensive tackle Todd Beeching, Hamilton, Tobias, Nix, and Gulley were named first-team All–South Independent and honorable mention All-America. Carter played in the Senior Bowl.

1994 SEASON

The Golden Eagles opened the 1994 season on the road at the Louisiana Superdome against the Tulane Green Wave on September 3. A touchdown pass from Waters to wide receiver Kendrick Lee and a 1-yard touchdown run by fullback Brad Hamilton gave the Golden Eagles a 12–7 lead at halftime. The second half belonged to the Southern Miss defense, which held the Green Wave to 217 total yards in the game and 82 through the air. The Eagles added a pair of Lomoro field goals and a 60-yard touchdown run by McGee to take a 25–10 win.

The Golden Eagles next hosted No. 21 Virginia Tech in the season's first game at Roberts Stadium. Southern Miss took a 14–0 lead after a couple of punting miscues by the Hokies. First, Tech fumbled a punt, leading to a 3-yard scoring pass from Waters to wide receiver Adam Kennedy. Then the Hokies bobbled the snap on a punt, Southern Miss recovered the ball on the Tech 2-yard line, and Buckhalter took the ball in. But those were the Golden Eagles' only points of the night, as the Hokies scored twice to tie the game at halftime and then added 10 fourth-quarter points to take a 24–14 victory. Waters was complimentary in defeat: "I have great respect for Virginia Tech.

They were one of the most physical teams I have ever played. Hats off to the defense. They played a great game. The offense just could not make anything happen, especially in the red zone."

The University of Memphis came to Roberts Stadium on September 17 for the annual Black-and-Blue Bowl. The Golden Eagles scored on their second possession on the night when wide receiver Ryan Pearson caught a 12-yard touchdown pass from Waters to finish off a 52-yard drive, and Southern Miss carried a 7–3 lead into the locker room at halftime. Waters threw a 13-yard touchdown pass to wide receiver Fred Brock late in the third quarter to give the Eagles a 14–3 lead, and a 23-yard interception return for a touchdown by Gulley provided the final points in a 20–3 Eagle win.

The following week, Eagles took their 2–1 record to Kyle Field in College Station for a battle against No. 12 Texas A & M. The Aggies returned the opening kickoff 100 yards for a touchdown. The Eagles came back with a 27-yard Chris Pierce field goal to cut the lead to 7–3, but 20 second-quarter points by the Aggies helped them to a 27–10 halftime and a 41–17 victory.

The Golden Eagles' October 1 contest against East Carolina in Greenville, North Carolina, marked the changing of the guard at quarterback for Southern Miss. Although Waters started the game, USM's first three possessions ended with turnovers, and the Pirates capitalized for a 14–0 lead. In the second quarter, Bower replaced Waters with redshirt freshman Heath Graham, who drove his team to a 39-yard field goal before the Pirates added another touchdown for a 21–3 edge at the break. East Carolina cruised the rest of the way to a 31–10 victory, as the Golden Eagles committed an astounding eight turnovers—two fumbles, two Waters interceptions, and four Graham interceptions—and fell to 2–3 overall.

Graham made his first start the following week against No. 11 Alabama in Tuscaloosa, and although the Golden Eagles outgained the Crimson Tide 371–194, the Tide took a 14–6 win. All of the game's points came in the second quarter. Alabama scored first on a 10-yard pass from quarterback Jay Barker to Curtis Brown. On the Eagles' next possession, Graham was sacked and fumbled, and the Tide's Matt Parker scooped the ball up and ran 16 yards for a score that gave his team a 14–0 advantage. After defensive end Robert Brown recovered a Tide fumble, the Eagles got a 2-yard touchdown pass from Graham to Pearson, bringing the score to 14–6 when the extra point was blocked. The Golden Eagles held the Crimson Tide to 67 yards rushing and 10 first downs but could not score in the second half and lost the game.

At Roberts Stadium on October 15, Southern Miss posted a 43–20 victory over Southwestern Louisiana. The Golden Eagles broke open the game with 20 third-quarter points and finished with 455 yards of offense, holding the Ragin' Cajuns to 280.

A week later, the Golden Eagles hosted the Samford Bulldogs for Homecoming. Southern Miss struggled in the first half and led only 24–14 at halftime but exploded after the break for a 59–16 win, the most points recorded by the Eagles since 1987. Southern Miss piled up 502 yards of total offense, including 310 on the ground, and forced six Bulldog turnovers.

Now 4–4, the Golden Eagles hosted the University of Tulsa on October 29, and although the defense did not have one of its better days, it came up with big plays when they were needed. Defensive end Steve Latson ran a fumble in from 16 yards out to help the Eagles to a 17–15 halftime lead, and after the Golden Hurricane moved ahead 29–24 at the end of the third quarter, the defense held the explosive Tulsa offense scoreless, allowing Southern Miss to come back for a 47–29 win. Cornerback Derrick Hervey put the icing on the cake by intercepting a Hurricane pass and returning the ball 68 yards for a touchdown. "We have improved as a football team. We have gotten better each week and have played a lot of young players," Bower analyzed after the game. "We are a much better football team than we were earlier in the year. That's what you try to do, improve each week as a team."

USM's final two games of the year were against Southeastern Conference teams. The Eagles first journeyed to Florida's Swamp on November 5 to meet the No. 4 Gators and were trounced 55–17. A week later, the Eagles faced former coach Curley Hallman and the Louisiana State University Tigers in Baton Rouge. The Golden Eagles took a 7–0 lead when Graham hit Brock with a 77-yard touchdown pass, but LSU cut the margin to 4 points with a second-quarter field goal. Tailback Harold Shaw's dazzling 62-yard run early in the third quarter gave Southern Miss a 14–3 lead, but the Tigers connected on two touchdown passes to move on top 18–14 at the end of the third quarter. Pierce kicked a 30-yard field goal early in the fourth quarter to pull the Eagles to within one, and with 4:05 left in the game, freshman Patrick Surtain intercepted an LSU pass to give the Golden Eagles a final chance. On second-and-13 at the Tiger 33-yard line, Graham's pass was tipped and appeared to be falling to the ground incomplete, but tight end Scott Harper dove and made a fingertip catch at the LSU 12. A pair of sacks moved the ball back to the LSU 32, but Pierce came on and drilled a 52-yard field goal to give Southern Miss a 20–18 lead. LSU missed on a 50-yard field goal attempt as time ran out, and the Golden Eagles had a thrilling victory and a 6–5 mark for the year.

Michael Tobias was named to the All–South Independent first team and was an honorable mention All-America, while offensive guard Brent Duggins, Buckhalter, and Gulley were named to the All–South Independent second team. Tobias played in the Senior Bowl, and the Arizona Cardinals chose Carter in the fourth round of the NFL draft.

1995 SEASON

On April 24, 1995, the creation of Conference USA was announced at Harry Caray's Restaurant in Chicago, with Michael L. Slive the new conference's first commissioner. Conference USA would have 12 member institutions, 6 of which (the University of Southern Mississippi, the University of Houston, Tulane University, the University of

Memphis, the University of Cincinnati, and the University of Louisville) would compete for the league's first football championship in 1996, with the winner going to the St. Jude Liberty Bowl in Memphis. The league signed a five-year television contract for a conference game of the week on Fox Sports Net, with other games appearing on ESPN, ESPN2, ABC, and CBS. "This is the most important step that Southern Miss has ever taken in its athletic history," said Athletic Director Bill McLellan, who, along with President Aubrey K. Lucas, had been instrumental in making the school a part of the new league. "We now have a vehicle to push our programs to the next level. It will be exciting to begin play." Bower was equally excited, saying, "Players all want to compete for a championship, wear championship rings, play in bowl games and play on television."

Although league play would not begin for another year, eager Southern Miss officials began to spruce up Roberts Stadium, adding new scoreboards and "Attack Eagle" and Conference USA signs, making the end zones bolder, replacing the entrance gates, and transforming Stadium Drive into Eagle Walk, a painted replica of the Roberts Stadium field. Stadium handrails, exterior fences, and the south end zone speaker tower were painted black, while barbed wire was removed from most exterior fences. The bleachers were removed from the south end zone, opening that end of the field. According to USM Associate Athletic Director Nick Floyd, "Some of the things we're doing were suggested by our fans, and we think they will be well received." He continued by stating that the goal was "to make the stadium a fun place to come and enjoy ball games."

The first game in the refurbished stadium was the August 31 season opener against the Northern Illinois Huskies. To boost attendance and increase interest, the USM athletic administration enlisted supporters to sell blocks of tickets to local businesses and organizations in an effort called Sellout '95. The contest was moved from Saturday to Thursday evening to set it apart from all the other college football games that would occur that weekend. Before a capacity crowd of 33,092, the third-largest ever in Roberts Stadium, the Golden Eagles dominated the game in every way imaginable—through the air, on the ground, on defense, and with special teams. The star of the game was Brock, who started his senior season by amassing 204 all-purpose yards and turning in three big plays over a five-minute stretch to seal the Golden Eagle victory. Late in the first half, with Southern Miss already leading 24–7, Brock raced around the right side and blocked a punt, knocking the ball out of the end zone for a safety. After the free kick, Brock started a 54-yard Eagle march with a 15-yard catch and finished the drive with a 13-yard touchdown grab. Finally, Brock returned the second-half kickoff 95 yards for a touchdown, and the Golden Eagles went on to win 45–13.

Nine days later at Legion Field in Birmingham, the Golden Eagles suffered a heartbreaking defeat at the hands of No. 13 Alabama. With Southern Miss clinging to a 20–17 lead with just 17 seconds left and Alabama facing fourth-and-16, Crimson Tide quarterback Brian Burgdorf connected with end Toderick Malone on a 35-yard touchdown pass, enabling his squad to snatch the 24–20 win.

The 1–1 Golden Eagles traveled to Logan on September 16 to meet the Utah State Aggies. The Golden Eagles took an early 13–0 lead on a 35-yard touchdown pass from Graham to tight end Larry Norton and a pair of field goals by Pierce, but Utah State battled back to take a 14–13 lead early in the third quarter. An 80-yard drive late in the third quarter culminated in a 12-yard touchdown run by Buckhalter that put the Eagles back up 21–14. Linebacker Eugene Harmon recorded an interception that led to Pierce's third field goal of the day to make the score 24–14, but the Aggies came back with a touchdown to close to within 24–21 with eight minutes to go. Cornerback Rod Thomas intercepted an Aggie pass with 1:27 to go, ending Utah State's hopes for the win. Said Thomas in the aftermath of the victory, "Utah State is a very good team. They are actually a lot better than I think we may have expected them to be. They really came out to play tonight and they were ready for us. The altitude may have affected us a little but mostly we just played against a tough team tonight."

Lack of execution in the kicking game cost the Golden Eagles dearly the following week against Indiana University in Bloomington. Two failed extra points, a blocked field goal, and a fumbled kickoff that Indiana ran in for a touchdown made the difference in the 27–26 loss to the Hoosiers. Indiana running back Alex Smith rushed 41 times for 209 yards, both records for Golden Eagle opponents.

On a day when everything went well, the Golden Eagles notched a 45–0 home win against Tulane on September 30. The Golden Eagle defense set the tone early on, breaking Green Wave quarterback Aley Demarest's collarbone on Tulane's third offensive play and forcing Tulane to go with inexperienced freshman quarterback Shaun King. Thomas picked off King's third pass attempt and returned the ball 75 yards for a touchdown, opening the floodgates for the Golden Eagles. Kendrick Lee added a 74-yard punt return for a touchdown in another highlight for Southern Miss, which improved to 3–2 on the year.

Despite committing six turnovers, the Golden Eagle defense was superb against the Louisville Cardinals at Roberts Stadium on October 7. With the Cardinals leading 21–18 midway through the fourth quarter, Graham, who had already thrown three interceptions, moved the Golden Eagles down the field on an 80-yard drive that ended with Buckhalter's 4-yard touchdown plunge with just over two minutes left. As the Cardinals attempted their last-chance drive down the field, middle linebacker Marchant Kenney stripped the ball from wide receiver Robert Bates at the Golden Eagle 37-yard line, preserving the 25–21 win. "I thought Heath made some throws that were erratic, but on that last scoring drive, when they had to make the big plays, both Graham and Buckhalter made the plays," Bower said after the game. "That is just a great example of keeping your poise and positive attitude."

Nippert Stadium had never been a friendly place for Southern Miss, and 1995 was no different as the Golden Eagles faced the Cincinnati Bearcats on October 14. The Bearcats won 16–13 on Eric Richards's 20-yard field goal with two seconds left in the game. Less than two minutes earlier, Bower had gambled on a fourth-and-6 play at the Cincinnati 46-yard line, choosing to go for the first down rather than punt. But as Graham prepared to throw to a wide-open Eric Booth, Bearcat defensive end Darrius Felder hit the quarterback's arm, sending the ball straight up in the air before it fell incomplete and Cincinnati took over and drove for the game-winning kick. The loss dropped the Eagles to 4–3.

The East Carolina Pirates stole an October 28 Homecoming victory from the Golden Eagles, winning 38–34. After trailing the Pirates until less than a minute remained in the contest, Southern Miss took a 34–33 lead on a 19-yard touchdown pass from Graham to wide receiver Donald Cunningham with 51 seconds to go. As time ticked down, the Pirates quickly drove into field goal range. But East Carolina ran a fake on what would have been a 44-yard field goal attempt: instead of kicking, Chad Holcomb, who had already missed two field goals in the game, took a direct snap and launched a Hail Mary pass into the Golden Eagle end zone. The ball fell incomplete amid a trio of Southern Miss defenders, but the Golden Eagles were called for pass interference, giving the Pirates one final chance with 1 second remaining. This time, Holcomb drilled a 29-yard field goal, sending the Eagles to their fourth last-second loss of the year.

On November 4, the Golden Eagles traveled to Neyland Stadium in Knoxville to face No. 5 Tennessee, led by All-America quarterback Peyton Manning. The game was never close, as the Volunteers turned four of the six Golden Eagle turnovers into touchdowns on the way to a 42–0 win.

The following week the Golden Eagles were back in Tennessee, this time facing the University of Memphis Tigers on a bitter-cold day in Memphis. Once again, the Golden Eagle offense could not hold onto the ball, turning it over another six times, but the Southern Miss defense came through, limiting the Tigers to 138 yards of total offense and forcing five turnovers. Late in the third quarter, Southern Miss fumbled on the Tiger 1-yard line, giving Memphis the ball. Quarterback Qadry Anderson dropped back into the end zone to pass, but pressure from defensive end Tim Bell and linebacker Eugene Harmon forced Anderson to get rid of the ball early. Cornerback Derrick Hervey stepped in front of the intended receiver, made the interception, and went untouched into the end zone to give the Golden Eagles the 17–9 win and bring them to 5–5 on the year.

Southern Miss closed the 1995 season on the road against the Southwestern Louisiana Ragin' Cajuns on November 18. After an extremely physical contest marked by numerous injuries to players from both teams, the Eagles escaped with a 35–32 victory. Ending the year with consecutive road wins, the Golden Eagles finished at 6–5.

Bell, Brock, Pierce, and offensive lineman Darryl Terrell were named second-team All–South Independent. Although Conference USA would not officially begin play until the following year, an all-league team was selected, with Brock, Buckhalter, Pierce, Bell, and Thomas earning first-team honors and Terrell named to the second team. Buckhalter played in the Senior Bowl.

1996 SEASON

The Golden Eagles opened on the road on August 31 in Athens against the University of Georgia Bulldogs and their first-year head coach, Jim Donnan. Although the Southern Miss squad did not cross the goal line, Lomoro's three field goals and a defense that limited the Bulldogs to just 50 yards rushing and recorded a safety secured an 11–7 victory for the Eagles.

The Golden Eagles tangled with No. 13 Alabama the following week at Legion Field in Birmingham in another classic battle between the two teams. Alabama won the game 20–10, with 27 of the two teams' points scored in the first half.

On September 14 the Golden Eagles opened up a two-game homestand, taking on the Utah State Aggies. The visitors grabbed the lead on their first possession by driving 65 yards for a touchdown less than four minutes into the game, but the Golden Eagles used a 17-point second quarter to claim a lead they never gave up. Kenney led the USM defense with 12 tackles, 3 of them for losses, and a sack in the 31–24 victory.

Next up for Southern Miss was Southwestern Louisiana. The Ragin' Cajuns were riding high, coming off a 29–22 decision over No. 25 Texas A & M, Southwestern Louisiana's first-ever win over a ranked team. But behind backup quarterback Chris Windsor's four-touchdown performance, the Golden Eagles scored 29 unanswered points in the second period to take a 35–7 halftime lead and rolled to a 52–27 win that upped the squad's record to 3–1. The Cajuns passed for 343 yards but netted only 35 rushing yards on 30 carries.

Back on the road on September 28, Golden Eagles faced the Louisville Cardinals in USM's first Division I conference game. The Golden Eagles got out of the blocks quickly when defensive end Jeff Posey picked up a fumble by Louisville quarterback Chris Redman and returned the ball 27 yards to the Cardinal 14. A few plays later, a 33-yard Lomoro field goal gave Southern Miss a 3–0 edge. Later in the first quarter, special teams standout Karr Shannon blocked a Cardinal punt, and Chandler Smith returned the ball 13 yards for a touchdown and a 10–0 lead. While Louisville outgained Southern Miss 395–218 in total yardage, the Cardinals could manage only -5 yards rushing, and constant pressure by the Eagle defense resulted in seven Cardinal fumbles (four of them recovered by Southern Miss) and two Redman interceptions. The 24–7 win made Southern Miss 4–1 overall and 1–0 in Conference USA.

The Golden Eagles next played at East Carolina in a Thursday night game on ESPN2. With

Middle linebacker Marchant Kenney (1994–1997) had 141 tackles in 1996 and helped the Golden Eagles to a share of the first-ever Conference USA championship.

a three-game winning streak and a week off to prepare for the game, Bower surprised the Pirates by giving quarterback Lee Roberts the first start of his career. Roberts quickly made the most of the opportunity: after missing on his first pass, he completed 13 straight throws, finishing the game at 14 of 16 for 229 yards, one interception, and one touchdown. The 13 straight completions and his .875 completion percentage set new Southern Miss single-game records. The Golden Eagle defense also did its best to make life miserable for the East Carolina offense, coming up with three interceptions and a fumble recovery and holding the Pirates to 112 yards rushing. With the 28–7 win, the Eagles improved to 5–1 on the year. Bower told the media after the game that Roberts "has been our most consistent performer and that's why he started today." The coach was pleased with his team's effort: "We played one of our most balanced games and I also thought the kicking game was solid. We made the big plays at critical times."

In a defensive battle typical of the Black-and-Blue Bowl, Southern Miss held Memphis to 97 yards on the ground and pitched a shutout in the 16–0 victory on October 19. The Eagles posted their fifth straight win, improved their record to 6–1 overall and 2–0 in Conference USA, and moved themselves into the AP poll at No. 24, their first appearance in the rankings since 1989. According to Southern Miss defensive coordinator John Thompson, "The biggest reason we got a shutout was our offense. The offense really played well. We were unemotional on defense. I was disappointed in that aspect but it's hard to complain when you get a shutout."

The next week in the Louisiana Superdome in New Orleans, Southern Miss met Tulane in a Conference USA matchup. The Golden Eagles fell behind 21–7 early in the third quarter but rallied with a touchdown pass from Roberts to wide receiver Brandon Francis and a 20-yard field goal by Lomoro. Just before the end of the period, USM safety Jamaal Alexander intercepted an Xavier Salazar pass and returned the ball 50 yards for a touchdown to give the Eagles a 24–21 lead. Green Wave linebacker Derrick Singleton retaliated with his own interception return for a touchdown to give Tulane back the lead at 28–24 with just over 11 minutes to go. The Eagle defense dug in on its next series and forced Tulane to punt from deep in its own territory. Kendrick Lee returned the punt 29 yards to the Green Wave 14, and the Eagles were in business. Tailback Eric Booth scored from the 1-yard line with 6 minutes to go in the game, and Southern Miss had the 31–28 win.

Now 7–1 on the season and 3–0 in Conference USA, the Eagles moved up to No. 23 in the rankings before their Homecoming contest against conference foe Cincinnati, which had handed Southern Miss a 16–13 loss the previous year. The revenge-minded Golden Eagles scored 14 first-quarter points, limited the Bearcats to two third-period touchdowns and a field goal, and added a 29-yard touchdown pass from Roberts to Lee with five minutes remaining in the game to win 21–17. The victory moved USM to No. 20 in the AP poll.

The Golden Eagles traveled to Robertson Stadium to meet the Houston Cougars in a November

Quarterback Lee Roberts (1995–1998) threw for 6,289 yards and 52 touchdowns in his career, including 398 yards against Houston in 1996.

9 Conference USA contest. USM's string of strong defensive performances came to a sudden halt in a shootout in which the teams combined for 1,049 yards of total offense. The Eagles and Cougars traded points throughout the game, finishing the fourth quarter tied at 49 and setting the stage for the Golden Eagles' first sudden-death overtime game. The Cougars had the ball first in overtime and scored on a 12-yard run by Antowain Smith, his sixth touchdown of the day. The Eagles needed a touchdown to tie the game and force a second overtime, but Francis caught a swing pass in the left flat, was tripped up, and fell inches short of the end zone, leaving Houston with the 56–49 win. Roberts had an outstanding game, completing 22 of 36 passes for a school-record 398 yards and three touchdowns. Lee caught 10 passes for 260 yards, both USM records, and three touchdowns. Southern Miss finished its first season in Conference USA with a 4–1 record.

The loss dropped the Eagles out of the rankings before their season-ending contest in Tallahassee against No. 3 Florida State. The Golden Eagles could not repeat the impressive offensive performance they had turned in the previous week but stayed close for two quarters before going scoreless in the second half, yielding 31 unanswered points to give the Seminoles the 54–14 victory.

Despite finishing the year with an 8–3 record, the Golden Eagles did not receive a postseason bowl bid. Houston had finished its Conference USA season by beating Louisville, making the Cougars and Golden Eagles conference co-champions with 4–1 records. Having defeated Southern Miss, Houston received the league's berth in the Liberty Bowl. The first true All–Conference USA team included Southern Miss standouts Lee, Kenney, Surtain, running back Eric Booth, offensive lineman LeRoy DeWitt, and linebacker Cedric Walthaw. Terrell played in the Blue-Gray All-Star Classic and the East-West Shrine Game, while Lomoro played in the Senior Bowl.

1997 SEASON

In June 1997, USM's athletic department announced the return of the nickname "the Rock" for the school's football stadium: "In our quest to promote the tradition we have here, we figured this would be something for our people to tap into," said Paul Batchelder, USM athletic administrative assistant. A replica of Faulkner Field was placed on a pedestal at the northwest corner of the Roberts Stadium field, and "The Rock at Southern Miss" was painted on the wall below the press box on the west side of the stadium. The Golden Eagles opened the 1997 season on August 30 at the Swamp in Gainesville against the defending national champion University of Florida, but mistakes and missed opportunities cost Southern Miss a chance to knock off the Gators. Four times the Golden Eagles moved the ball deep into Gator territory with chances to score, but three of the four chances ended in turnovers and the fourth was brought to an end by a critical holding call. The Gators won the game, 21–6.

The following week the Golden Eagles traveled to Champaign to play the University of Illinois in the first meeting between the two schools. The Golden Eagles used a powerful running attack and a swarming defense to completely overwhelm the Illini by a score of 24–7. Tailback Harold Shaw ran for 127 yards for the first 100-plus rushing effort of his career, while the Golden Eagle defense held Illinois to 248 yards and safety Jamaal Alexander intercepted two passes, returning one of them 21 yards for a touchdown.

The Golden Eagles hosted the University of Nevada Wolfpack on September 20 in the first game played at the newly rechristened Rock. The USM players started a new tradition, touching the replica of Faulkner Field for good luck as they emerged from the tunnel prior to the opening kickoff. The Eagles had had a week off prior to the game, but the break had been tragic rather than restful: Coach Bower's daughter, Kristen, was killed in a car accident on September 12. The team, dressed in all black, dedicated the Nevada game to her and recorded a 35–19 win. Roberts set a stadium record with 346 yards through the air, while wide receiver Sherrod Gideon caught nine passes for 179 yards. After the game, Bower told reporters, "It was emotional walking through the Eagle Walk before the game, but after that, business was business. However," he continued, "this game meant a lot to me, I can tell you that."

The 2–1 Golden Eagles met the No. 21 Alabama Crimson Tide at Birmingham's Legion Field the next week, and turnovers made the difference in the game. The Eagles overcame some early mistakes to keep the score knotted at 10 at halftime, but after Southern Miss took a 13–10 lead on a 32-yard Tim Hardaway field goal, the Tide turned against the Golden Eagles. Roberts fumbled on the Southern Miss 14-yard line after being sacked from the blind side by Alabama's Kenny Smith, setting up a touchdown that gave the Crimson Tide a 17–13 lead. Two fourth-quarter interceptions sealed the Eagles' fate, as Alabama went on to win 27–13.

The Golden Eagles returned home to meet the Louisville Cardinals in USM's Conference USA season opener on October 4. Southern Miss turned in a complete effort, scoring on the ground, through the air, and on special teams, while the defense created three turnovers. The Golden Eagle defense even knocked Cardinal quarterback Chris Redman out of the game with one the worst performances of his career. The Cardinals scored twice the game's final minute to make the score 27–13, and Southern Miss improved to 3–2 on the year and 1–0 in conference.

The annual battle between the Golden Eagles and East Carolina took place in Greenville, North Carolina, the following week, but for the first time, the game was a conference contest, as East Carolina had joined Conference USA for football in the fall of 1996. A 15-second stretch changed the complexion of the game. Trailing 7–3, the Pirates had a first-and-goal at the Southern Miss 3-yard line with under a minute to go before halftime, but the Golden Eagle defense held, forcing the Pirates to kick a 19-yard field goal. With just a few seconds left on the clock, the Pirates elected to kick off deep to Eric Booth, who came into the game ranked No. 2 in the country in kickoff returns. Booth made the Pirates pay for the decision by returning the kick 59 yards and stepping out of bounds with time about to expire. Hardaway came on and nailed a career-best 49-yard field goal to give USM a 10–6 lead and all the momentum. Although the Pirates scored early in the third quarter to take the lead, two more Hardaway field goals and a touchdown run by Shaw gave Southern Miss a 23–13 win and another victory in Conference USA. After the game, Bower credited Hardaway for his performance: "That is by far the best he has kicked. To be honest, I had some doubt as to whether he had the leg to hit from 49, but he really hit them well and that was the key to the game."

The talk leading up to USM's October 25 game against Tulane at the Rock concerned the matchup of Tulane's league-leading offense against the Southern Miss defense, which was also the best in Conference USA. After building a 13–7 halftime lead, the Golden Eagles took control offensively with their rushing game, while the Eagle defense held Tulane quarterback Shaun King to a subpar day both rushing and passing and forced him to throw three interceptions, two of them to Surtain. The impressive 34–13 victory kept the Golden Eagles on top of the conference at 3–0 and improved their overall season mark to 5–2.

Now ranked No. 24 in the country, the Golden Eagles' next game was a road contest against the Cincinnati Bearcats at Nippert Stadium, where Southern Miss had never won. For two and half quarters the Golden Eagles appeared to be heading for another loss. Trailing 17–7, however, Southern Miss scored 17 unanswered points and the defense clamped down to produce a 24–17 win.

On November 8, the Golden Eagles played No. 7 Tennessee in a nonconference game before a crowd of 107,073 at Neyland Stadium. Peyton Manning, who went on to become the No. 1 pick in the next spring's NFL draft, led the Volunteers to a 44–20 win with a performance that won him the SEC Player of the Week award. Southern Miss opened the game by stopping a pair of Tennessee drives short of the end zone and forcing field goals and took a 13–6 lead early in the second quarter. But the Vols scored twice before halftime to take a 20–13 lead and then blew the game open with 21 third-quarter points. The only bright spot for the Golden Eagles in the second half was Booth's dazzling 96-yard kickoff return for a touchdown, and the Eagles fell to 6–3.

Throughout the season, the Golden Eagles had used the motto "Unfinished Business," referring to the previous season's loss to Houston, which had cost Southern Miss the outright Conference USA crown and the Liberty Bowl bid. On November 15, the Golden Eagles erased the bitter aftertaste of that defeat with a commanding 33–0 victory whose outcome was never really in doubt. The Cougars managed just 5 yards rushing and 147 yards total and did not get a first down until the three minutes before halftime. The victory gave the Golden Eagles a 5–0 Conference USA mark and guaranteed them at least a share of the league title. The executive director of the AXA Liberty Bowl, Steve Erhardt, extended an official invitation to Southern Miss during an on-field ceremony after the game. "The year's been good," said Bower amid the locker room celebration. "It's not over but I couldn't be happier about a bunch of guys that I think are really deserving of this opportunity to play an extra game this year. I've never had as much fun coaching."

USM's final regular-season game of the year also took place at Liberty Bowl Memorial Stadium. Against the Memphis Tigers, the Golden Eagles completed their perfect Conference USA season with a 42–18 win, finishing the regular season at 8–3 overall. Shaw rushed for a career-high 188 yards, the seventh-best total in school history, and finished the year with 1,045 yards, the first player since Shelton Gandy in 1987 to crack the 1,000-yard barrier. Gideon had six catches for 141 yards and three touchdowns, giving him 54 catches for the year to break Cliff Coggin's season mark of 53

Cornerback Patrick Surtain (1994–1997) finished his career with 16 interceptions and was the Conference USA Defensive Player of the Year in 1997.

set in 1949. Roberts had accumulated 2,249 yards passing and had thrown for 16 touchdowns, tying Brett Favre's 1988 single-season record. For the first time in Southern Miss history, a back and a receiver surpassed the 1,000-yard mark and a quarterback threw for more than 2,000 yards in the same season.

Southern Miss capped off the season by claiming a 41–7 victory over the University of Pittsburgh before a crowd of 50,209 in the December 31 AXA Liberty Bowl in Memphis. Both the Golden Eagle offense and the defense shone, with Gideon selected the game's Most Valuable Player after hauling in three touchdown passes from Roberts. Southern Miss also scored three defensive touchdowns courtesy of a fumble return by safety Perry Phenix and interception returns by defensive end Adalius Thomas and cornerback Terrance Parrish. The 34-point margin of victory was the widest in the bowl's history. The Eagles ended the season at 9–3 and ranked No. 22 in the nation. The *Sporting News* named Surtain a second-team All-America. Surtain, Gideon, Kenney, Phenix, Shaw, Thomas, defensive end Robert Brown, and offensive lineman Kasey Keith were named first-team All-Conference USA, while Alexander, Booth, Roberts, tight end Terry Hardy, and offensive lineman Henry McLendon were named to the second team. Surtain was selected as the league's defensive player of the year, with Bower receiving Coach of the Year honors. Defensive linemen John Nix and DeQuincy Scott were named to the conference's all-freshman team. Alexander and Surtain represented the school in the Senior Bowl. In the NFL draft, Miami selected Surtain in the second round, Arizona chose Hardy in the fifth round, Detroit took Alexander in the sixth round, and New England took Shaw in the sixth round.

1998 SEASON

On September 5, the No. 21 Golden Eagles started their season with a visit to No. 13 Penn State. Before an audience of millions watching the ABC telecast, the Nittany Lions thumped the Golden Eagles 34–6 while holding them to 9 yards rushing, the fewest yards Penn State had allowed since 1990. Gideon was one of the bright spots for Southern Miss, catching a school-record 13 passes for 176 yards to become USM's all-time leader in career receptions (100) and yards (1,684).

After a week off, the Golden Eagles hosted No. 17 Texas A & M on September 19. In early July, USM's athletic department had announced that Roberts Stadium would be getting a new, state-of-the-art, $1.3 million video display scoreboard. Just minutes before the kickoff of the Texas A & M game, the final components were lifted and dropped in place. Unfortunately for the 33,233 fans in attendance, however, Southern Miss produced few highlights to be shown on the new scoreboard, committing five turnovers in the 24–6 Aggie victory. Southern Miss outgained Texas A & M 176–171 yards, and only 2 of 16 Aggie possessions produced drives longer than 25 yards, but three of the Golden Eagle turnovers led to points for Texas A & M, and the Eagles started 0–2 for the first time since 1976.

The Eagle offense finally got on track against the Southwestern Louisiana Ragin' Cajuns, piling up 531 yards in a 55–0 win on September 26. Roberts completed 19 of 28 passes for 340 yards and a school-record five touchdowns, three of them caught by Gideon, who registered nine receptions on the night. The Golden Eagle defense limited the Cajuns to 181 yards.

With their first win under their belt, the Golden Eagles traveled to the Louisiana Superdome in New Orleans to meet No. 25 Tulane. In an early season matchup between the two favorites for the Conference USA title, turnovers again were costly for the Golden Eagles. Although Tulane quarterback Shaun King, the NCAA leader in passing efficiency, had a cast on his broken left (nonthrowing) hand and could take snaps only from the shotgun formation, the Green Wave won by a score of 21–7. The Golden Eagles had numerous scoring opportunities, but Roberts threw four interceptions and the Eagle offense fumbled twice, including once at the Tulane goal line. "We had a lot of penalties and played sloppy," Bower said. "We are not playing very well as a team right now. Tulane was a good football team and you have to give them credit. We have to pick it up and play better." The Eagles fell to 1–3 on the year, 0–1 in Conference USA.

The Golden Eagles took out their frustration about the Tulane loss with a dominating 56–21 win over the Louisville Cardinals at Roberts Stadium that evened their conference record at 1–1. Running backs Derrick Nix and Dawayne Woods, both freshmen, rushed for more than 100 yards each, and the Golden Eagle defense held Redman, who had thrown for 793 yards and nine touchdowns in his last two games, to 19 completions in 36 attempts for 207 yards, with four interceptions and no touchdowns.

On October 17, Southern Miss made its first trip to West Point to meet Army, which had joined Conference USA in March 1997 and was playing its first season of conference football. The game started well for the Cadets, who took a 10–0 lead as their triple-option attack confounded the Golden Eagle defense. Early in the second quarter, however, with Army ahead 10–7 and driving again, T. J. Slaughter dropped Cadet halfback Bobby Williams on a fourth-and-1 try at the Eagle 9. The Eagles embarked on a 91-yard scoring drive that ended with a 15-yard touchdown pass to wide receiver Kevin Heard. Southern Miss added a field goal before halftime to take a 17–10 lead and went on to win 37–13, improving the Eagles' conference mark to 2–1 and bringing their season record back to .500.

Back at the Rock seven days later, the Golden Eagles rolled to a relatively easy win over East Carolina in a series that had been marked by last-second victories. The Pirates took the opening kickoff and drove 76 yards for a score, but the Golden Eagle defense kept East Carolina out of the end zone for the rest of the day. Leading 13–7 in the second quarter, USM broke the game open when Parrish intercepted a pass by Pirate freshman quarterback David Garrard and raced 38 yards for a touchdown. The 2-point conversion put the Eagles up 21–7, and they never looked back, posting a 41–7 victory.

At Tuscaloosa's Bryant-Denny Stadium on October 31, the Golden Eagles trailed the Alabama Crimson Tide 27–10 midway through the third quarter. On their next possession, the Golden Eagles ran a fake punt and a fake field goal, and both gambles paid off. First, Michael Villalonga ran 24 yards out of punt formation on fourth-and-3, and then punter Jamie Purser, holding on a 31-yard field goal attempt, completed a shuttle pass to Nix that set up Nix's subsequent 1-yard touchdown run, bringing the Golden Eagles to within 10 points. Southern Miss faked another punt in the fourth quarter, resulting in big yardage when Purser connected with wide receiver Dannye Fowler on a 40-yard pass that took the Eagles to the Tide 27-yard line. But the Alabama defense forced the Eagles to settle for a 20-yard Hardaway field goal to cut the deficit to 27–20, and USM could get no closer in the 30–20 Crimson Tide victory.

At Houston's Robertson Stadium, Roberts threw his seventeenth, eighteenth, and nineteenth touchdown passes of the season, breaking Brett Favre's school record of 16 and leading the Golden Eagles to a 21–15 victory over the Cougars. With seven receptions in the game, Gideon had 55 on the year, bettering his own school mark. With the win, Southern Miss improved to 5–4 overall and 4–1 in Conference USA.

The final home game of the year took place on November 14 against the University of Memphis Tigers. After taking a 7–3 lead at the end of the first quarter, the Golden Eagles stormed to 24 second-quarter points and a 45–3 win. The Golden Eagles piled up 512 yards, including 271 through the air, while limiting the Tigers to 149 yards. Gideon had seven catches for 100 yards, extending his school-record season totals to 62 catches for 1,092 yards. The game gave the Golden Eagles a final conference record of 5–1 on the season and represented Roberts's final appearance in Hattiesburg. Bower reflected on his quarterback's contributions to the team: "He gave us so much consistency. That's one word that describes him. He's so accurate in throwing the football, knows what we're doing and he's a great person. He's one of our leaders. I can still remember thinking two years ago that we had this guy for two years. Now I look at it and realize that we only have him for two more games. That's a scary feeling. He'll be tough to replace and he's meant a lot to Southern Miss football."

On a chilly and windy day in Reno, Southern Miss closed out the regular season with a 55–28 win over the Nevada Wolfpack, clinching a berth in the Humanitarian Bowl. Roberts broke Favre's record for passing yards in a season with 2,680 and tied Favre's mark for career touchdown passes with 52. Nix rushed for 219 yards, the third-best single-game total in school history.

On December 30, Southern Miss faced off against the University of Idaho Vandals in the Humanitarian Bowl in Boise. In the second quarter, leading 21–7 and seemingly in control of the game, Purser passed the ball to Thomas on yet another fake punt, and USM had the ball at the Idaho 38-yard line. But the Eagles failed to score on that drive, and Idaho scored three touchdowns in the final 8:13 of the second quarter to take a 28–21 lead at halftime. The Vandals increased their lead by a touchdown in the third quarter before Southern Miss rallied to tie the game on a 7-yard Roberts-to-Gideon touchdown pass and a 15-yard touchdown run by Nix with

Linebacker T. J. Slaughter (1995–1999), one of the fiercest competitors in school history, was a two-time All–Conference USA selection and finished his career with 428 tackles.

6:37 left in the game. But the Vandals responded with a 68-yard scoring drive and won 42–35, and the Eagles finished the year at 7–5.

Nix, Gideon, Thomas, Slaughter, linebacker Ty Trahan, and offensive tackle Henry McClendon were named to the All–Conference USA team, with Thomas the Defensive Player of the Year and Nix earning Freshman of the Year honors. Defensive back DeShone Mallard played in the East-West Shrine Game.

After 13 years as athletic director at Southern Miss, the 66-year-old McLellan announced his retirement on January 15, 1999. The biggest accomplishment of McLellan's tenure had been getting Southern Miss into Conference USA, but he had also worked to extend the school's athletic budget, seeking ways to keep the Golden Eagles competitive with schools with larger fan bases and larger budgets. In addition, McLellan had overseen the construction of a track-soccer facility in 1997, and the renovation of the baseball stadium in 1990 as well as the addition of an administrative assistant for football, an all-sports strength and conditioning staff, the school's first full-time athletic equipment manager, and its first full-time men's and women's tennis and golf coaches and its first full-time women's volleyball coach. "We have come a long way from where we were when we first started [in 1986] and we still have many things on our plate that need to be accomplished," McLellan said. "The foundation we laid here for the athletic department is the important thing. The school's in a good position. The first thing was getting all the sports into a conference. Now we can build on that."

USM's 17-member search committee looked nationwide for a successor to McLellan, considering 50 applicants. In April, university officials announced that Richard Giannini, director of athletics at Northeast Louisiana, would assume the same position at Southern Miss on July 1. "My pledge to the Southern Miss family is that I will be tireless in my efforts to provide leadership to produce the best possible athletic program," said Giannini. "My family and I can't wait to move to Hattiesburg and get started with our new journey." In addition to his job at Northeast Louisiana, Giannini had previously served as sports information director and assistant athletic director at Duke University, as the NCAA's director of marketing, and as senior associate athletic director at the University of Florida, and he had also been co-owner, president, and CEO of the Raycom Management Group in Charlotte, North Carolina, and owner, president, and chief operating officer of GNI Sports, also in Charlotte.

Richard Giannini became director of athletics at Southern Miss in 1999. He began a drive to finish the new athletic center and expand Roberts Stadium.

1999 SEASON

On Labor Day Monday, September 6, the Golden Eagles opened the season against the defending

Wide receivers Todd Pinkston (#80) and Sherrod Gideon (#11) combined to catch 342 passes and 52 touchdowns from 1996 to 1999.

Conference USA champions, Tulane. Southern Miss players, coaches, and fans had been pointing to the rematch since the Green Wave had defeated the Golden Eagles the previous year. With Roberts Stadium nearly full and a national television audience watching, the Golden Eagles whipped the Green Wave 48–14. The Golden Eagles' surprise starter at quarterback was sophomore Jeff Kelly, who had beaten out junior college transfer Cable Davis in the final few days of the preseason. In his first career start, Kelly completed 13 of 19 passes for 248 yards and four touchdowns to wide receivers Sherrod Gideon, Todd Pinkston, and Leroy Handy and running back Derrick Nix. The Golden Eagle defense was superb, holding Tulane to just 15 yards rushing and 269 total yards.

Playing again just five days later, the host Golden Eagles stomped the Northwestern State Demons 40–6. Linebacker Roy Magee had a memorable night, running a blocked field goal back 48 yards for a touchdown and returning a blocked Demon extra point for 2 points. Senior bandit end Adalius Thomas had a 64-yard fumble recovery return for a touchdown.

The 2–0 Golden Eagles met No. 4 Nebraska in Lincoln on September 18 and turned in an impressive showing. The Golden Eagle defense dominated the powerful Cornhusker offense, holding Nebraska to eight first downs and just

THE FINAL DAYS AS AN INDEPENDENT AND CONFERENCE USA

Tailback Derrick Nix (#43) rushed for 3,584 yards and 30 touchdowns from 1998 to 2002. He finished his career just 12 yards from becoming the school's all-time leading rusher.

185 yards of offense, their lowest total since 1993. Kelly threw a pair of touchdown passes, one in the first quarter to Pinkston and another in the third quarter to Gideon, and the game was tied at 13 midway through the third. But Nebraska's Keyuo Craver deflected a Kelly pass into the air, and Husker linebacker Julius Jackson caught the ball and returned it 28 yards for a touchdown to give Nebraska the 20–13 win. The Golden Eagles had one last chance to score but came up short when Kelly threw an interception inside the Nebraska 10-yard line.

In their second consecutive contest against a highly ranked team, Southern Miss next faced No. 5 Texas A & M in College Station. The Golden Eagle defense turned in another spectacular performance, but turnovers again plagued the team, which lost 23–6 to fall to 2–2 on the year. After leading 9–0 at halftime, the Aggies returned two interceptions for touchdowns during the second half to secure the victory. In the two games against Nebraska and Texas A & M, the defense had allowed only one offensive touchdown, but Southern Miss had lost both contests.

The Golden Eagles took early command of the Conference USA race with a solid 39–22 win at No. 16 East Carolina on October 9. Nix set a Conference USA record with 42 carries, running for 171 yards and a touchdown, and Kelly threw three touchdown passes. Safety Leo Barnes turned in the defensive play of the game when he intercepted a David Garrard pass and ran 60 yards for a touchdown to put the game out of reach. The win moved the Golden Eagles into the AP poll at No. 25.

The Southern Miss defense had been one of the best in the country throughout the season, and the following Saturday at home, the Eagles posted a 24–0 shutout of Army, which had come into the game as the nation's top rushing team and was averaging more than 340 yards of offense per contest. The Golden Eagles held the Cadets to 172 yards, and Southern Miss improved to 4–2 overall and a perfect 3–0 in Conference USA.

Now ranked twenty-first in the country, the Golden Eagles roared to a 28–0 lead during their October 23 matchup against Cincinnati at Roberts Stadium but then surrendered 20 straight points to the Bearcats. With Cincinnati down by 8 and driving late in the game, safety Chad Williams nailed down the win by swatting down Deontey Kenner's pass at the Golden Eagle 8-yard line.

The following Saturday, No. 19 Southern Miss traveled to Tuscaloosa to meet the No. 14 Alabama Crimson Tide. In one of USM's best opportunities in several seasons to grab the national spotlight, the Golden Eagles came out flat and fell behind early to the Crimson Tide. Southern Miss never recovered, and 15 third-quarter points put the game away for Alabama, which won 35–14.

No. 25 Southern Miss hoped to clinch at least a share of the Conference USA title in a November 6 road contest against the University of Memphis. The Golden Eagles completely dominated, limiting the Tigers to just 227 yards in the 20–5 victory. Kelly opened the scoring by connecting with wide receiver Josh Gulley on a 25-yard touchdown pass, and Pinkston hauled in a 57-yard scoring strike early in the second quarter to make the score 14–0. Brant Hanna added a pair of second-half field goals to improve the Golden Eagles to 6–3 overall and 5–0 in Conference USA.

The next game was the No. 20 Golden Eagles' Homecoming, and they delighted the Roberts Stadium crowd with a resounding 48–0 victory over the University of Louisiana–Lafayette (formerly the University of Southwestern Louisiana). Southern Miss scored touchdowns on its first seven possessions, including Kelly-to-Pinkston touchdown passes of 28, 45, and 43 yards. The Southern Miss defense registered seven sacks and held the Cajuns to -26 yards rushing. The win sent the Golden Eagles to 7–3 on the season. The following Saturday brought a showdown at Louisville with Conference USA's berth in the AXA Liberty Bowl on the line. Redman kept the Golden Eagles on their heels throughout the first half, throwing for 278 yards and a pair of touchdowns to guide Louisville to a 24–17 lead. The Golden Eagle defense settled down in the second half, and Southern Miss outscored Louisville 13–3 after the break to take a 30–27 win. On fourth-and-5 from the Louisville 37-yard line, the Golden Eagles used a trick play to keep the drive alive. As Purser set up to punt, wide receiver Shawn Mills stood with his back to the ball near the USM sidelines, where Coach Bower appeared to be yelling at the player. In actuality, Mills was carefully positioned on the line of scrimmage, and he took off downfield when Bower told the receiver to go at the snap of the ball. Purser threw the ball 26 yards to Mills for the first down, and three plays later Hanna converted on his third field goal of the game, a 27-yarder with 1:07 remaining, to give Southern Miss the win. After surrendering 344 yards during the first half, the Golden Eagle defense forced a fumble and limited Louisville to 8 yards rushing and 67 yards passing after the break. The win gave Southern Miss another unblemished 6–0 Conference USA season and improved the Eagles' record to 21–2 since the league began football competition in 1996.

Ranked No. 16 in the country, the Golden Eagles capped off the season with a 23–17 victory over the Colorado State Rams in the 1999 AXA Liberty Bowl, played in Memphis on December 31. A crowd of 54,866 watched as the Golden Eagle defense scored the game's first touchdown on a 5-yard return of a fumble by Ram quarterback Matt Newton. After a Ram field goal had narrowed the gap to 7–3, John Floyd blocked a Ram punt and Brandon Francis fell on the ball in the end zone to give the Golden Eagles a 14–3 advantage. Colorado State rallied with a pair of touchdowns in the second quarter to take a 17–13 lead, but Nix crossed the goal line 26 seconds before halftime to put the Eagles back on top by a score of 20–17. Early in the third quarter, Hanna kicked a 25-yard field goal to increase USM's lead to 6, and the Golden Eagle defense took over, shutting out the Rams for the remainder of the game. Thomas was named the game's Most Valuable Player and the Golden Eagles'

Defensive end Adalius (A. D.) Thomas (1996–1999), the Conference USA Defensive Player of the Year in both 1998 and 1999, led the Golden Eagles to three C-USA championships.

Most Valuable Defensive Player after recording eight tackles, including three sacks.

The Golden Eagles finished the year at 9–3 and were ranked thirteenth in the USA Today/ESPN poll and fourteenth in the AP poll. Named to the All–Conference USA team and the honorable mention All-America team were offensive lineman Shederick Blackmon, defensive end Cedric Scott, linebacker T. J. Slaughter, and safety Leo Barnes. Thomas was Conference USA's Defensive Player of the Year and was a second-team AP All-America. Thomas, Slaughter, Parrish, Gideon, and Pinkston played in the Senior Bowl. In the 2000 NFL draft, the Philadelphia Eagles selected Pinkston in the second round, the Jacksonville Jaguars selected Slaughter in the third round, and Gideon and Thomas went in the sixth round to the New Orleans Saints and the Baltimore Ravens, respectively. Bower was named Conference USA Coach of the Year for the second time.

2000 SEASON

The No. 22 Golden Eagles opened the 2000 season on September 2 against No. 12 Tennessee before 108,064 at Knoxville's Neyland Stadium and millions more watching on ESPN. Tennessee led going into the fourth quarter, but Kelly hit tight end Bobby Garner with a 17-yard touchdown pass early in the period and then connected with Mills on a 7-yard touchdown pass with 55 seconds left to make the score 19–16, but the Volunteers recovered the onside kick to seal the victory.

Now ranked twenty-fifth in the country, the Golden Eagles traveled to Birmingham's Legion Field two weeks later to meet thirteenth-ranked Alabama. Cornerback Raymond Walls intercepted a halfback-option pass and returned the ball 54 yards for a touchdown midway through the first quarter to give the Golden Eagles an early 7–0 lead. Early in the second quarter, Kelly hit wide receiver Leroy Handy with a 5-yard touchdown pass to increase the lead to 14, and on the ensuing kickoff, Etric Pruitt stripped Alabama return man Michael James of the ball, and Joe Henley scooped it up and battled 18 yards into the end zone to make the score 21–0. Alabama's best scoring opportunity came in the fourth quarter, but linebacker Zaid Houston intercepted a Tide pass in the end zone to preserve USM's first shutout of Alabama.

Back at No. 22, the Eagles traveled to Stillwater on September 23 for their first faceoff against Oklahoma State. The game represented a homecoming of sorts for Bower, who had served as the Cowboys' offensive coordinator in 1990, and for Mills, who had signed with Southern Miss out of Northeastern Oklahoma A & M. The Golden Eagles took a 7–0 lead on their first possession when Kelly hit Mills with a 31-yard scoring strike, and Nix scored on a 1-yard run just before halftime to give the Eagles a 14–3 lead. Midway through the third quarter, Kelly and Mills connected again on a 9-yard scoring pass, and free safety Leo Barnes returned an interception 25 yards for the Eagles' final touchdown as they cruised to a 28–6 win and improved to 2–1 on the year.

USM's first Conference USA game of the season pitted the twenty-first-ranked Golden Eagles against the Memphis Tigers at the Rock on September 30. In a battle between two of the country's best defenses, the Golden Eagles got field goals of 37, 41, and 24 yards from Hanna while the Tigers got a 36-yard field goal from Ryan White, and Southern Miss led 9–3 heading into the fourth quarter. In the game's final minutes, Southern Miss tailback Dawayne Woods broke free for a 52-yard touchdown run and the Eagles added the 2-point conversion to go up by 14. On the next Memphis possession, Barnes intercepted a Tiger pass and took the ball 31 yards into the end zone to give the Eagles the 24–6 win.

The Golden Eagles climbed to No. 17 before their next contest, an October 7 home game against the University of South Florida, which would join Conference USA in 2003. The Golden Eagle defense limited the Bulls to just 18 yards rushing and 151 yards of total offense, while Kelly rushed for three touchdowns and threw for two more in USM's easy 41–7 win. The Golden Eagles improved their record to 4–1, had a four-game winning streak, and moved up to No. 16 in the national rankings.

Despite giving up a season-high 24 points, the Golden Eagle defense dominated during an October 14 game against Tulane in the Superdome. For its part, the Southern Miss offense turned in its best performance of the year, racking up 480 yards of total offense in the 56–24 thrashing of the Green Wave. Woods rushed for a career-high 143 yards on 20 carries and scored three touchdowns to lead the Eagle offense, while Magee returned a fumble for a touchdown and Barnes returned an interception 27 yards for a score to lead the defense. The victory improved the Eagles to 2–0 in conference, keeping them tied for the league lead.

Fourteenth-ranked Southern Miss met the University of Houston Cougars in a Conference USA matchup on October 28 at Houston's Robertson Stadium. In a defensive struggle, the Golden Eagles took a 6–3 victory, their sixth in a row. After falling behind 3–0 at halftime, the Eagles rallied with Hanna field goals of 31 and 27 yards, the latter with just under ten minutes to go. The Golden Eagle defense held the Cougars to 148 yards, including -2 yards rushing. The Eagles were now 6–1 overall and 3–0 in the league, and they moved up one spot in the rankings to No. 13.

In the Conference USA game of the year, Southern Miss hosted the University of Louisville at Roberts Stadium the next week. Trailing 21–14 at halftime, the Golden Eagles tied the game early in the third quarter on a 55-yard touchdown pass from Kelly to true freshman wide receiver Kenny Johnson. But the Cardinals exploded for four unanswered touchdowns before Southern Miss scored late in the game to make the final 49–28. The defeat was the Golden Eagles' first conference loss at home in the five years since the creation of Conference USA and dropped them to No. 25 in the polls.

USM's next game was the school's first against the University of Alabama–Birmingham, which had just joined Conference USA. Playing on the road, the Eagles fought the Blazers to a 20–20 standoff at the end of regulation, and both teams scored touchdowns in the first extra period to remain tied. In the second overtime, however, the Eagles won the toss, elected to defend, and held the Blazers to a 37-yard field goal for a 30–27 lead. The Eagles scored a touchdown on a 10-yard pass from Kelly to Woods and escaped with the 33–30 victory. Woods finished the game with 18 carries for 50 yards and a pair of touchdowns as well as five receptions for 42 yards and the winning score. He also contributed three kickoff returns for 102 yards, including a USM season-best 82-yarder that set up a score. Southern Miss improved to 7–2 overall and 4–2 in Conference USA.

The Golden Eagles moved up to No. 24 before taking on Cincinnati on November 18 at Nippert Stadium. After Southern Miss built a 24–7 lead at the end of three quarters, the bottom fell out for Bower's team. The Bearcats turned two Eagle fumbles into 14 points to close to within 3 and then added two field goals for the 27–24 win. The Eagles fell to 7–3 overall and 4–2 in the conference and dropped out of the national rankings for the first time since midway through the 1999 season.

In a rare Friday game, the Golden Eagles played the East Carolina Pirates in Hattiesburg on the day after Thanksgiving. Heavy rains saturated the Roberts Stadium field prior to kickoff, resulting in difficult playing conditions. Although the Golden Eagle defense held the potent Pirate offense to half of its average offensive output and although the Southern Miss offense amassed 371 yards in the game, the Pirates took a 14–9 victory. The Eagles finished the regular season at 7–4 overall and 4–3 in Conference USA.

The Golden Eagles secured a berth against thirteenth-ranked Texas Christian University in the GMAC Mobile Alabama Bowl to be played on December 20 at Ladd-Peebles Stadium. Trailing 21–14, the Eagles rallied to defeat the Horned Frogs 28–21. The Eagles tied the game with 7:24 remaining when Kelly connected with Handy on a 56-yard touchdown pass and had a chance to win the game with a 32-yard field goal two minutes later. Hanna missed his fourth field goal of the day, but the Eagle defense held on TCU's next possession, forcing a punt. Pruitt got a piece of the kick, and with eight seconds to go, Kelly hit Johnson with a 29-yard touchdown pass that gave Southern Miss the victory. Handy was named the Offensive Most Valuable Player and Barnes received the defensive award, while TCU's Heisman Trophy finalist, tailback LaDainian Tomlinson, won the game's Most Outstanding Player award despite being held to a season-low 118 yards by the Golden Eagle defense.

Barnes and defensive linemen Cedric Scott and DeQuincy Scott were named first-team All–Conference USA and honorable mention All-America, while offensive lineman Billy Clay and defensive backs Ray Walls and Chad Williams were second-team all–conference. Cedric Scott was also named the league's co-defensive player of the year with Houston linebacker Wayne Rogers. True freshman linebacker Rod Davis was named to several freshman All-America teams, including the one selected by the *Football News*. Four Southern Miss players were selected in the 2001 NFL draft:

THE FINAL DAYS AS AN INDEPENDENT AND CONFERENCE USA

Defensive end Cedric Scott, the Conference USA Co-Defensive Player of the Year in 2000, was named third-team All-America by the Associated Press.

the New York Giants picked Cedric Scott in the fourth round, the Indianapolis Colts chose Walls in the fifth round, and the Dallas Cowboys took defensive tackles Daleroy Stewart and John Nix in the sixth and seventh rounds, respectively.

2001 SEASON

The Golden Eagles had high expectations for the 2001 season, but a rash of injuries, including the preseason announcement that tailback Derrick Nix would sit out the entire year for medical reasons, decimated the team and resulted in a mediocre campaign.

The season began in the rain on September 1 with a 17–9 win over Oklahoma State at the Rock. Kelly completed 22 of 36 passes for 277 yards and a touchdown, while Woods rushed 25 times for 70 yards and another score. Johnson caught seven passes for 92 yards, and Handy had six catches for 82 yards. Oklahoma State could manage only three field goals against the Golden Eagle defense.

The Golden Eagles were next scheduled to face the Alabama Crimson Tide on September 15, but the September 11 attacks forced the postponement of that game until November 29. After a three-week layoff, the Golden Eagles returned to action on September 23 against the University of Louisiana–Lafayette at Cajun Field. Converted wide receiver Timmy Blackwell rushed for 78 yards and scored three touchdowns on 25 carries to lead Southern Miss to a 35–10 victory. The

Golden Eagle defense stymied the Ragin' Cajuns, limiting them to 144 yards, just 7 of them on the ground. The defense recorded three interceptions and four sacks in the Golden Eagles' sixth straight win over the Cajuns and thirty-seventh in forty-nine meetings.

When the Golden Eagles hosted the University of Alabama–Birmingham on September 28, the Southern Miss offense struggled to put points on the board, but the defense and special teams came up big in the 3–0 win. The game's only points came on Hanna's 25-yard field goal in the second quarter. The Blazers scored what appeared to be the go-ahead touchdown in the third quarter, but the play was called back because the Blazers had an ineligible receiver downfield. The Blazers attempted a 28-yard field goal, but Golden Eagle defensive tackle Rayshun Jones blocked the kick. Blackwell had another good game, rushing for 97 yards on 24 carries, while defensive backs Greg Brooks and Etric Pruitt had interceptions. The Eagles were now 3–0 overall and 1–0 in conference.

Despite throwing four interceptions and losing a fumble, Southern Miss had a shot at beating the University of Memphis for the eighth straight year. In the end, however, the turnovers proved too big an obstacle to overcome, and the Tigers won 22–17 at the Liberty Bowl on October 7. The Golden Eagle defense had held the Tigers without a touchdown in the teams' previous three meetings, but Memphis needed just under two minutes to cross the goal line this year as Blackwell fumbled on the first Southern Miss play from scrimmage and the Tigers recovered the ball and scored three plays later. The Eagles knotted the game at 7 in the second quarter after Pruitt blocked a punt that gave Southern Miss the ball at the Memphis 16-yard line and Kelly and Garner teamed up for a 7-yard touchdown pass. With the game tied again at 10, Greg Harper intercepted a Kelly pass and returned the ball 29 yards for a touchdown, and the Tigers added a safety early in the fourth quarter to make the score 19–10. Pruitt blocked another punt for the Eagles, who recovered the ball on the Memphis 3-yard line and quickly scored to get to within 2 points. Memphis added a 45-yard field goal midway through the fourth quarter, and the Eagles could not score on their final four possessions.

Playing on ESPN2 in the first Tuesday contest in Conference USA history, the Golden Eagles suffered a disappointing 24–14 road loss against Louisville on October 17. As had been the case against Memphis, turnovers played a major role in the game's outcome. Southern Miss led 7–6 at halftime after scoring on a 73-yard screen pass from Kelly to wide receiver Chris Johnson, while the Golden Eagle defense held the high-powered Cardinal offense to just a pair of field goals. The Golden Eagles increased their lead to 14–6 midway through the third quarter when a double reverse/flea-flicker resulted in a 6-yard touchdown pass from Garner to Kelly. The Cardinals subsequently drove 82 yards to the Eagle 9-yard line, but the Southern Miss defense held on fourth-and-1 and took over on downs. On the next play, however, the Golden Eagles mishandled the snap and the Cardinals recovered their second fumble of the day, quickly scoring a touchdown and adding the 2-point conversion to tie the game. The Cardinals took advantage of yet another Golden Eagle fumble and an interception to go on to the victory, the first time since 1980–81 that Louisville had defeated USM in back-to-back seasons. The Golden Eagles fell to 3–2 on the year, 1–2 in Conference USA.

The Southern Miss offense exploded for 469 yards in the October 27 Homecoming game against Houston, recording the team's highest point total since 1994 in the 58–14 win. Kelly completed 20 of 32 passes for 276 yards and four touchdowns, while Handy caught seven passes for 76 yards. The Eagles improved their overall record to 4–2 and their conference mark to 2–2.

Despite taking a 7–0 lead on an eight-play, 58-yard drive on its second possession of the day, Southern Miss could not find a way to stop Penn State freshman quarterback Zack Mills as the Nittany Lions reeled off 38 straight points en route to a 38–20 win at Beaver Stadium on November 3 in front of 106,158 fans, the third-largest crowd ever to watch a Golden Eagle game. Once again, mistakes cost the Golden Eagles, as Penn State turned an interception into 3 points and ran a blocked punt back 40 yards for another 7. The Southern Miss offense had 27 first downs, 1 more than Penn State, and accumulated 403 offensive yards to the Nittany Lions' 443. Handy caught 10 passes for 101 yards, but Southern Miss nonetheless fell to 4–3.

After another open date, the Golden Eagles equaled the record for points scored by a Southern Miss team at Roberts Stadium in a 59–6 Conference USA win over Tulane in the annual Battle for the Bell. Kelly set a new school record with 400 yards passing, completing 23 of 31 throws for three touchdowns, and added another score on the ground. Woods contributed four touchdowns—three rushing and one receiving—to aid the Southern Miss attack. The Golden Eagle offense scored on its first five possessions, including three in the first quarter, and took a 42–6 lead into the locker room at halftime, enabling the team's reserves to get their most extensive playing time of the year. Handy had five receptions for his second consecutive 100-yard game.

For the second year in a row, the Golden Eagles played East Carolina on the Friday after Thanksgiving, although this year the game was held at Dowdy-Ficklen Stadium in Greenville, North Carolina. The Pirates completely dominated the first quarter, rolling up 12 first downs to 1 for the Eagles, accumulating 162 yards of offense compared to 20 for Southern Miss, leading by 10:10 to 4:50 in time of possession, and taking a 10–0 lead. But before the second quarter had ended, the Golden Eagles had scored 25 points and led 25–18. After the exciting offensive show in the first half, both defenses took control, and each team could manage only a field goal during the final 30 minutes. The Golden Eagle offense played error-free ball, and the Southern Miss defense recovered four ECU fumbles and intercepted a David Garrard pass, with three of those takeaways coming in the second half. Kelly passed for 167 yards and became the first Golden Eagle quarterback to

Linebacker Rod Davis, a four-year starter at middle linebacker (2000–2003), was the Conference USA Defensive Player of the Year in 2003. He is the school's all-time leader in tackles with 526, including 60.5 tackles for losses and 18.5 quarterback sacks.

put together three straight 2,000-yard-plus seasons. The Eagles record stood at 6–3 overall and 4–2 in the conference, and the win had made them eligible to go to a postseason bowl.

Playing much of the game in high winds and driving rain, Southern Miss dropped a 28–15 decision to Alabama on November 29 at Legion Field in a game that had been postponed because of the September 11 tragedies. The Crimson Tide led 7–6 at halftime and increased their advantage to 22–8 in the third quarter, but the Eagles rallied to cut the gap to 22–15 at the end of the third quarter. The Crimson Tide put the game away with a 70-yard, nine-play drive early in the fourth quarter to score the game's final points.

Southern Miss had hoped to parlay a victory over Alabama into a second consecutive appearance in the GMAC Bowl; now, however, the Eagles would have to defeat conference foe Texas Christian on December 7 to salvage a bid to the

THE FINAL DAYS AS AN INDEPENDENT AND CONFERENCE USA [249]

galleryfurniture.com Bowl. In the rematch of the 2000 GMAC Bowl, the Horned Frogs edged the Eagles 14–12, sealing the victory with an interception in the final minute. The Golden Eagles finished the season 6–5 overall and 4–3 in Conference USA, missing out on a postseason bowl bid for the first time since 1996.

Linebacker Rod Davis, cornerback Greg Brooks, and safety Chad Williams were named first-team All–Conference USA, while offensive tackle Jeremy Bridges, bandit end Terrell Paul, and linebacker Roy Magee were second-team selections. Davis was also named a fourth-team All-America by the *Sporting News.* Defensive tackle Skylor Magee, wide receiver Chris Johnson, offensive linemen Jeremy Parquet and Myron Powe, and tailback James Walley were selected to the conference all-freshman team, and the *Sporting News* named Magee to its third-team all-freshman squad. In the April 2002 NFL draft, the Baltimore Ravens selected Williams in the sixth round, and the Seattle Seahawks selected Kelly in the seventh round.

Southern Miss opened the doors to its new Athletic Center, located at the north end of Roberts Stadium on the site of the old athletic field house, in July 2002, when the first floor of the new facility, which houses the football locker rooms, the training room, and the weight room, was put into use. The building's second floor, site of the athletic department's administrative offices and of coaches' offices, opened in March 2003. Twenty-five percent of the money for the 60,000-square-foot building came from a 1996 state appropriation, while the remainder of the funding was provided by private donations from the Circle of Champions, supporters who will donate $10,000 a year for 10 years.

Opened in 2003, the Southern Miss Athletic Center houses the football locker rooms, training rooms, weight room, meeting rooms, and offices for the Golden Eagle football coaching staff.

2002 SEASON

In a game billed as the "Rumble at the Rock," Southern Miss opened the 2002 season with a 55–7 victory over Jackson State on August 31. The Golden Eagle offense rolled up 478 yards before a crowd of 35,169, the largest in Roberts Stadium history. Redshirt sophomore quarterback Micky D'Angelo made his debut as a starter a good one, completing 13 of 23 passes for 273 yards and one touchdown. Senior running back Derrick Nix, making his first start in two seasons, ran the ball 16 times for 77 yards and three touchdowns. "Overall it was a pretty good performance for our first game," Bower said. "Offensively we made some good plays, and we really did a good job on our special teams."

After trailing for three quarters, Southern Miss rallied to score the go-ahead touchdown in the opening minutes of the fourth quarter and then held on for a 23–20 win over defending Big Ten champion Illinois at Roberts Stadium on September 7. Nix led the Golden Eagle offense with 201

Quarterback Micky D'Angelo passed for 1,647 yards and seven touchdowns during the 2002 season, leading the Golden Eagles to the Houston Bowl.

yards rushing and two touchdowns on 27 carries, including a 50-yard touchdown run that put the Golden Eagles ahead 23–17 with 12:55 remaining in the game. Defensively, Davis and Pruitt led the way with 14 and 12 tackles, respectively, and Pruitt also had two interceptions. "This was a good win for us, and I'm real proud of our football team," Bower said. "I thought we showed a lot of mental toughness in the game."

The Eagles went after their third straight win when they hosted longtime foe Memphis in USM's Conference USA opener on September 14. The Eagle offense had another big night, amassing 356 yards on the ground and 524 yards of total offense in the 33–14 victory over the Tigers. Nix gained 196 yards and scored two touchdowns, while redshirt freshman running back Anthony Harris had 27 carries for 127 yards, both career highs. The game marked the first time that two Golden Eagle running backs had rushed for more than 100 yards in a contest since Nix and Woods accomplished the feat against Louisville on October 10, 1998.

The Golden Eagles faced the University of Alabama on September 21 for their first road game of the year, but four lost fumbles and an interception created insurmountable obstacles, and the Crimson Tide rolled to a 20–7 victory. The Alabama defense limited the Golden Eagles to 35 yards on the ground, while the Tide rushed the ball 64 times for 351 yards, the first time a team had rushed for more than 300 yards against the Nasty Bunch, a nickname the school began to use and promote for the first time since the late 1980s, since Northern Illinois put up 303 in 1992.

Sophomore linebacker Michael Boley continued his fine play for the Eagles with 15 tackles, a 54-yard interception return for a touchdown, and a pass deflection.

The Golden Eagles traveled to West Point, New York, to meet Army on September 28. The Eagles notched a 27–6 victory for their fourth win of the year and second in Conference USA play. Army stayed close until well into the third quarter, when Cadet turnovers eventually turned the tide in favor of Southern Miss. Although the Eagles lost a pair of fumbles and threw an interception, Army quarterback Matt Silva threw six interceptions, three to Pruitt and one each to linebackers Davis and Joe Henley and cornerback John Eubanks.

After a week off, the Golden Eagles played their third consecutive road game, this time against the University of South Florida at Raymond James Stadium in Tampa on October 12. Redshirt freshman quarterback Dustin Almond saw his first extended action of the season for the Eagles, replacing D'Angelo early in the first quarter. Almond finished with 24 completions in 39 attempts for 258 yards and a touchdown, but Southern Miss lost the contest 16–13 to fall to 4–2 on the year. The Golden Eagles had a chance to force overtime, but senior placekicker Curt Jones missed a 43-yard field goal as time expired. Southern Miss had 412 yards of offense and South Florida had 464, but the teams could manage only a pair of touchdowns.

The Golden Eagles returned to the Rock for their Homecoming contest against Cincinnati, and although the Southern Miss defense surrendered more than 400 yards, it came up big when it needed to in a 23–14 win. Two Bearcat turnovers led to touchdowns, and the Nasty Bunch added a safety to help the Eagles improve to 5–2 overall and 3–0 in Conference USA. Southern Miss amassed just 211 yards of total offense, but Boley, Pruitt, and Davis each had 12 tackles, while Henley chipped in 10.

In a Wednesday night battle on ESPN2, Texas Christian produced a convincing 37–7 Conference USA victory over the Golden Eagles in Fort Worth, Texas, on October 30. Trailing 13–0 at halftime, Southern Miss scored on its first possession of the third quarter with a five-play, 72-yard drive capped by a 48-yard touchdown pass from Almond to wide receiver Marvin Young that cut the deficit to 6. But the Horned Frogs scored 24 unanswered points before the third quarter was over to drop the Eagles to 5–3 overall and 3–1 in conference. The Eagles managed just 185 yards of offense and were hampered by the loss of Nix, who departed with a leg injury late in the second quarter.

At Birmingham's Legion Field on November 9, the Golden Eagles bounced back with a 20–13 Conference USA victory over the University of Alabama–Birmingham. D'Angelo came off the Eagle bench in the second half to lead the team to 10 fourth-quarter points to erase a 13–10 UAB lead. The Nasty Bunch was superb, holding the Blazers to 88 yards rushing and 226 yards of total offense.

After two overtimes, the Louisville Cardinals were standing on top as Nate Smith's 27-yard field goal provided the margin of victory in a 20–17 win over the Eagles on November 14. Playing on Thursday night in a game televised by ESPN, the Golden Eagles jumped out to a 17–3 halftime lead on touchdown passes from D'Angelo to tight end Terrell Browden and wide receiver Chris Johnson, but the Cardinals tied the game with a pair of third-quarter touchdowns. Jones missed two fourth-quarter field goals that would have put Southern Miss ahead and was wide right on a 46-yard attempt during the first overtime, giving Louisville a chance to win the game. But the Southern Miss defense created the Cardinals' fourth turnover of the evening, sending the game into the second overtime. Louisville kicked a 27-yard field goal, but Jones missed yet again on a 32-yarder, and the Cardinals had the 20–17 win. The Eagles fell to 6–4 on the year and to 4–2 in Conference USA.

Tulane scored 18 points in the second half and kept Southern Miss off the scoreboard in a 31–10 Green Wave victory at the Louisiana Superdome in New Orleans on November 23. The Golden Eagles committed four turnovers and according to their coach "didn't play hard enough to win the football game." Bower told reporters after the game, "Tulane played a lot harder than us, and you have to give them credit for doing that. They must have wanted it a lot more than we did."

USM's strong defense limited East Carolina to 154 yards of total offense en route to a 24–7 victory on November 30 at the Rock. The Eagle offense also was impressive, putting up 414 total yards, including 139 on the ground by Nix, who was playing in his final game in Hattiesburg. His career total of 3,583 yards rushing left him 12 yards shy of Ben Garry's school record of 3,595. The season-ending victory over Conference USA member East Carolina upped the Eagles' league record to 5–3 and gave them an overall mark of 7–5.

A few days later, Southern Miss received and accepted its fifth bowl invitation in six years. The Eagles would face Oklahoma State in the Houston Bowl at Reliant Stadium on December 27. For three and a half quarters, Southern Miss challenged Oklahoma State, but the Cowboys overtook the Golden Eagles late in the game and won 33–23. Late in the third quarter, Southern Miss took its first lead at 23–20 when Jones connected on his third field goal of the game. But Oklahoma State quickly came back, tying the game on Luke Phillips's third field goal at the start of the final period. The Golden Eagles did not score on their next possession, but Brooks picked off an OSU pass at the Southern Miss 9-yard line to keep the score even. The Cowboys took a 30–23 lead on a drive on which they converted a fourth-and-1 at the Eagle 24-yard line with a quarterback sneak that took the ball to the 22 and then Tatum Bell carried the ball in on the next play. Phillips added another field goal with 5:15 remaining to ice the win. OSU's Rashaun Woods caught nine passes for 164 yards and a touchdown and collected the Most Valuable Player and Offensive Player of the Game honors. Almond came in at quarterback on the Golden Eagles' second drive of the game and completed 11 of 27 passes for 173 yards and rushed 17 times for 54 yards and one touchdown. "I was real proud of our team's effort," Bower said. "I thought we played hard, and you can't fault that. We played a physical game, but we gave up too many big plays."

On December 5, Davis made history by becoming the first Southern Miss player and the first defensive player to win the Conerly Trophy, given to the best player in the state of Mississippi as chosen by a panel of 60 media voters. The other finalists were Eli Manning, a junior quarterback from Ole Miss, and Robert Kent, a senior quarterback from Jackson State. CollegeFootball News.com and the All-American Football Foundation selected Davis as a first-team All-America, and the *Sporting News* and the Associated Press gave him third-team honors. Pruitt was named second-team All-America by CollegeFootball News.com. Nix, Boley, Davis, Pruitt, and offensive lineman Torrin Tucker were named first-team All–Conference USA, while offensive lineman Jason Jimenez and defensive end Terrell Paul were named to the second team. Eubanks was named to the league's all-freshman team. Bridges played in the Senior Bowl and the Rotary Gridiron Classic and was a sixth-round selection of the Philadelphia Eagles in the NFL draft. Tucker also played in the Senior Bowl, and Jimenez also appeared in the Gridiron Classic.

Although Nix finished the regular season within shouting distance of USM's career rushing record, he did not get the chance to break the mark. The senior's career at Southern Miss had been marred by medical problems since early in the 2000 season, when he sprained his ankle in the Memphis game. The injury was treated with anti-inflammatory medication, but the swelling did not decrease. Instead, Nix's body retained fluids, and he ballooned from 227 to 280 pounds. A kidney specialist diagnosed Nix with membranous glomerulonephritis, and he sat out much of the 2000 season. The next summer, Nix suffered chest pains when a potentially fatal blood clot traveled from his leg to his lung, but he recovered, received a medical redshirt for the 2001 season, and returned the next year to complete his collegiate career.

Nix had a stellar 2002 season for the Golden Eagles despite battling painful shoulder and ankle injuries and being treated for anemia. By the end of the season, however, he had begun to feel weaker, and he was again hospitalized. Doctors diagnosed focal glomerulosclerosis, a severe degenerative kidney disease. One of Nix's kidneys was not functioning, while the other was operating only at 10 percent. The disease was progressive and untreatable. He began to undergo dialysis three or four times a week, but a kidney transplant was the only long-term solution. The news stunned both Nix and the Southern Miss community: said Coach Bower, "You see this guy who does everything right and gets hit by something like this. It doesn't seem fair, but Derrick is a strong person who can overcome just about

Future expansion of Roberts Stadium will include the Touchdown Terrace, an addition that will contain 30 luxury suites.

anything. No question about it, he has been an inspiration to everybody. Everyone admires him for what he's accomplished and the way he has battled through all of this and hasn't let the illness change him. He's just been first class in the way that he has handled everything."

The university's athletic department established the Southern Miss Student Athlete Medical Fund in Nix's honor, and fans from across the country donated money to help pay his medical bills. On June 5, 2003, Nix received a kidney donated by his oldest brother. Nix was deeply grateful for the support of those around him, both his blood relatives and his USM family: "My family has really helped me through all of this. I couldn't have handled it by myself. With them, I never felt that I had to handle everything by myself. I was never alone in the situation."

In April 2003, Athletic Director Richard Giannini announced that the USM athletic department was embarking on a capital-improvement campaign called "Building Dominance" that represented the most comprehensive building endeavor in the department's history. In addition to improvements to Reed Green Coliseum, the home of the school's basketball teams, and the Olympic sport venues, the program would provide for the renovation and expansion of Roberts Stadium. The cornerstone of the Building Dominance campaign is the creation of premium football seating by enclosing the south end zone and creating the Touchdown Terrace, an addition that will include 30 luxury suites and more than 1,300 chair-back seats. Stadium capacity will be increased to 41,300. Other proposed improvements include installation of artificial turf, a renovated press box, and new dressing rooms for visiting teams.

2003 SEASON

The 2003 season opened on August 30 with the first meeting between Southern Miss and a Pac-10 team as the Golden Eagles traveled to Berkeley's Memorial Stadium to play the University of California. The game fell short of the Golden Eagles' hopes as the Golden Bears took an easy 34–2 win. Southern Miss got on the board early, recording a safety when the Bears fumbled the snap on their first punt of the game, but Cal scored four times in the second quarter en route to 34 unanswered points and 411 yards of total offense, including 260 yards rushing. D'Angelo threw for 163 yards on 16 of 26 passing and had one interception. Young had 90 yards on 6 catches, while sophomore wideout Antwon Courington grabbed a team-high 7 passes for 71 yards.

The Golden Eagles had little time to prepare for their next game, a Thursday night battle five days later against the University of Alabama–Birmingham. Playing on ESPN2 in front of more than 42,000 fans, the largest crowd to ever watch the Blazers play at Legion Field, Southern Miss won 17–12. The Southern Miss defense recovered four UAB fumbles, and the Golden Eagle offense put up 314 yards, led by D'Angelo, who completed 14 of 20 passes for 197 yards and one touchdown, and Blackwell, who rushed 20 times for a

In 2003, wide receiver Marvin Young led the team with 42 pass receptions for 703 yards and seven touchdowns. He also returned 33 punts for a 13.6-yard average.

game-high 88 yards and one touchdown. Defensively, Pruitt led all players with 17 tackles, while Davis finished with 13.

The annual Black-and-Blue Bowl between Southern Miss and the University of Memphis took place on September 13 before 29,233 fans at Roberts Stadium and once more lived up to its billing. The game was close until well into the fourth quarter, when Young returned a Tiger punt 87 yards for a touchdown and Blackwell added a 38-yard score to give Southern Miss the 23–6 victory. Blackwell led the team with 15 carries for 96 yards and one touchdown, while fellow running back James Walley rushed 24 times for 73 yards. The win improved Southern Miss to 36–17–1 all-time against Memphis and to 18–2 in games against the Tigers in Hattiesburg. Boley recorded 17 tackles and a sack and recovered a fumble, while Brooks added two interceptions.

Nebraska, ranked No. 11 in the ESPN/USA Today poll and No. 15 in the Associated Press poll, took advantage of three Southern Miss turnovers to score 21 points on the way to a 38–14 win on September 25 in front of a record 36,152 fans at the Rock. Late in the game, freshman quarterback Damion Carter saw his first action of the season, completing 10 of 13 passes on a 17-play, 92-yard drive to the end zone, with the touchdown coming on a 3-yard pass to freshman wide receiver Caleb Hendrix. The loss dropped the Golden Eagles to 2–2 on the year. "I thought our team played hard but you'll never win ballgames when you make that many mistakes," a disappointed Bower said following the game. "We've got to do things better if we are going to put ourselves in the position to win some ballgames."

Against Cincinnati on October 4 at Nippert Stadium, a strong fourth quarter gave Southern Miss the 22–20 win. The Bearcats took a 20–6 lead early in the second quarter, but the Golden Eagles brought themselves right back into the

THE FINAL DAYS AS AN INDEPENDENT AND CONFERENCE USA

game with Eubanks's 94-yard kickoff return for a touchdown. Carter made his first start at quarterback, completing 3 of 6 passes for 23 yards, an interception, and a touchdown before being replaced in the second quarter by Almond, who played the rest of the way, going 9 of 18 for 133 yards. Another freshman, Darren McCaleb, connected on three field goals, including a 26-yarder with 1:10 remaining, to push the Golden Eagles over the top. Davis had 22 tackles to lead the Southern Miss defense, while Boley added 18 tackles and a sack and forced a fumble. The victory made the Golden Eagles 3–0 in league play and 3–2 overall.

The Southern Miss defense held Alabama to 12 yards passing and 255 yards of total offense, but that was enough for the Crimson Tide to take a 17–3 victory in front of 82,818 spectators at Bryant-Denny Stadium on October 11. The Golden Eagle offense barely outgained the Tide, managing only 261 yards (17 of them on the ground), and failed to cross the goal line. Once again, Carter started but was replaced by Almond, who completed 16 of 28 passes for 196 yards. Boley finished the game with 14 tackles, while Pruitt had 13 tackles and an interception.

After an off week, the Golden Eagles returned to action against South Florida on October 25 at the Rock, and the first play from scrimmage proved to be a good omen for Southern Miss. Almond connected with Young for an 80-yard touchdown, and the Golden Eagles soared to a 27–6 victory. USM's new offensive system finally began to click, justifying the coaching staff's faith, and the Eagles accumulated 337 yards, including 155 on the ground, while the defense limited South Florida to two field goals. The special teams also contributed a touchdown for Southern Miss when Seth Cumbie blocked a Bull field goal attempt and Davis returned the ball 61 yards to the South Florida end zone. Almond finished the day 10 of 22 for 175 yards and two touchdowns. The Golden Eagles improved to a perfect 4–0 in Conference USA and once again crept above .500 on the year. "It was a good win for our football team. I thought we played hard. We got the big play early in the ballgame and started to execute some good things," a happy Bower told the media after the game. "I am real proud of our players and what they did. The game ball went to Derrick Nix."

Southern Miss turned in another strong offensive performance in a 48–3 Homecoming victory over Louisiana-Lafayette on November 1, amassing 264 yards rushing and 286 yards through the air and scoring six touchdowns. Almond threw for three touchdowns and ran for another, finishing with 187 yards on 11 completions in 15 attempts. Young caught 4 of those passes for 101 yards and two touchdowns, while Harris tallied a career-high 130 yards and a touchdown on 16 carries.

The Golden Eagles extended their winning streak to three games with a convincing 31–10 victory over Houston on November 8 at Robertson Stadium. The Cougars opened the game with a 14-play, 80-yard drive that gave them a 7–0 lead, but Southern Miss tied the game with a 7-play, 63-yard drive that ended with a 34-yard pass from Almond to Young. McCaleb then gave

Southern Miss the lead by kicking a 24-yard field goal, but Houston answered with its own three-pointer. The Golden Eagles surged in front for good on Almond's second touchdown pass of the game, a 25-yard completion to sophomore wide receiver Antwon Courington with 1:37 left in the first half. The defense was again solid, limiting the potent Houston offense to 363 yards and shutting out the Cougars in the second half. Senior cornerback Corey Yates recorded his second interception of the year, and Eubanks returned a fumble recovery 27 yards for a score. The Golden Eagles improved to 6–3 on the year and 5–0 in Conference USA.

A 28–14 home win over Tulane on November 15 gave Southern Miss its fourth victory in a row. Southern Miss took a 17–0 first-quarter lead, but the Green Wave hung tough, closing to within 6 points at 20–14 with 7:26 left in the game. The Golden Eagles iced the win with a 5:54 drive that culminated in Almond's 34-yard pass to freshman tight end Alan Whitney on a fake field goal. Davis led the Southern Miss defense with 13 tackles and forced a fumble. Pruitt had 11 tackles and forced a fumble.

Next up for the Golden Eagles were the Texas Christian University Horned Frogs, 7–0 in Conference USA and ranked ninth in the Associated Press poll. In front of a Hattiesburg crowd of 30,141 and a national ESPN audience, the Horned Frogs outgained the Eagles 429–278, but Southern Miss prevailed where it mattered, taking a 40–28 victory that clinched at least a share of the conference title for the Eagles. TCU went 87 yards in 16 plays on its first possession to take a 3–0 advantage, but that would prove to be the Horned Frogs' only lead, as Almond quickly completed a 50-yard touchdown pass to junior wide receiver Daron Lawrence for a 7–3 lead. Another TCU field goal cut the margin to 7–6 before Southern Miss reeled off 21 straight points to take a 31–6 edge late in the third quarter. TCU refused to throw in the towel and used a couple of onside kicks, two quick drives, and a pair of 2-point conversions to cut the lead to 31–28 with 6:55 remaining. Southern Miss gave itself a little breathing room with McCaleb's second field goal of the game and sealed the victory after Brooks forced a TCU fumble and Davis recovered the ball at the Horned Frogs' 11-yard line. Harris punched the ball into the end zone three plays later to give the Eagles their fifth straight win and improve their season mark to 8–3. Davis once again led the Nasty Bunch with 20 tackles, while Paul and Brooks combined to register three sacks.

Now 7–0 in Conference USA, the Eagles headed to East Carolina to nail down the outright league championship. The 38–21 win on November 29 earned USM a spot in the AXA Liberty Bowl and gave the Eagles a new league record for wins in a season. Southern Miss also became just the fourth team in league history to turn in a perfect season. Davis's 17 tackles against the Pirates gave him 510 for his career, making him Conference USA's all-time leader.

On December 31, Southern Miss faced off against Mountain West champion Utah in the 2003 AXA Liberty Bowl. Both defenses played well, with the teams combining to convert only 4 of 31 third-down attempts. Utah had averaged

381 yards a game but netted only 228 against the Golden Eagles, and Southern Miss managed just 213 yards, 121 fewer than the team's season average. Utah prevailed 17–0, recording the first shutout of Southern Miss since 1995. Davis ended his college career with a game-high 16 tackles, giving him 526 as a Golden Eagle and surpassing Clump Taylor for the school record.

Southern Miss placed a league-high 15 players on the All–Conference USA teams: Davis, Boley, Paul, Brooks, and Pruitt represented Golden Eagles' nationally ranked defense on the first-team squad, joined by offensive lineman Jeremy Parquet, and Eubanks and Young, who were honored as punt returner and kickoff returner, respectively. Senior center Jim Hicks and senior tight end Terrell Browden made the second team, while the third team featured Young, offensive lineman Chris White, defensive linemen Ronald Jones and Eric Scott, and defensive back Alex Ray. Three USM players made the league's all-freshman team: McCaleb, offensive lineman Travis Cooley, and defensive lineman Greg Casnave. The Associated Press named Davis to its third-team All-America squad, and CollegeFootballNews.com gave Young and Eubanks honorable mention as kick returners. Pruitt, Davis, and Brooks played in the Senior Bowl, while Jones played in the Rotary Gridiron Classic in Orlando, Florida. In the 2004 NFL draft, the Minnesota Vikings selected Davis in the fifth round, the Cincinnati Bengals selected Brooks in the sixth round, and the Atlanta Falcons selected Pruitt in the sixth round.

Southern Miss football has a rich and proud tradition of talented players, skillful coaches, and superb teams. Although no one knows what the future holds for Southern Miss football, the school and the athletic department have always exhibited a marvelous ability to adjust to changes, persevere, and move forward. Since its modest beginnings in 1912, Southern Miss football has always been Rock Solid.

A NOTE ON SOURCES

Most game summaries, especially for the early years of Southern Miss football, are taken from accounts published in contemporary newspapers, particularly the *Hattiesburg American,* the *Hattiesburg News,* the *Jackson Clarion-Ledger,* and the *Jackson Daily News.* In some cases, information about games was taken from newspapers from outside the state of Mississippi, including the *Memphis (Tennessee) Commercial Appeal* and the *Dayton (Ohio) Daily News.*

Also useful were the publications of what is now the University of Southern Mississippi, including school newspapers (the *Normal School News,* the *Teachers College News,* and the *Student Printz*) and yearbooks (the *Neka Camon* and the *Southerner*); in particular, the 1914 *Neka Camon* contains a section on "The Early History of Normal College" that furnished information for this volume. Beginning with the 1972 season, the *University of Southern Mississippi Football Media Guide* provided an invaluable resource. The collections of the William D. McCain Library at the University of Southern Mississippi contain several other important sources: William D. McCain and John Gonzales, *University of Southern Mississippi History,* vol. 2 (n.p., 19—); John P. Bacon, "A History of Intercollegiate Athletics at the University of Southern Mississippi, 1912–1949," master's thesis, University of Southern Mississippi, 1967; Siegfried W. Fagerberg, "A History of the Intercollegiate Athletic Program at the University of Southern Mississippi," dissertation, University of Southern Mississippi, 1970.

On the Internet, information was taken from Southern Miss.com, the official site of Southern Miss athletics, as well as from Conference USA's Web site, ConferenceUSA.com. For an exhaustive database of Southern Miss games, coaches' records, and other information, see the College Football Data Warehouse at cfbdatawarehouse.com.

The authors thank Coach P. W. Underwood, who agreed to be interviewed for this book, as well as Yvonne Arnold and the staffers in the McCain Library Archives for their willingness to help with this work, as well as Mike Montoro and Mike Martinez of the Southern Miss Athletics Media Relations office.

LETTERMEN

	YEAR	POSITION	HOMETOWN
A			
Abercrombie, Sonny	1977	DE	Roswell, Ga.
Achee, Buster	1933	G/C	Hattiesburg, Miss.
Adams, Deke	1992-93-94	LB	Meridian, Miss.
Adams, Drew	1989	C	Moss Point, Miss.
Adams, Henry	1914	—	Macon, Miss.
Adkison, Wayne	1966-67-68	E	Moss Point, Miss.
Agner, Tom	1959	E	Tunica, Miss.
Ahrens, Greg	1978-79	OT	St. Petersburg, Fla.
Ainsworth, J. W.	1925	E	Magnolia, Miss.
Akins, Leon	1959-60-61	E	Atmore, Ala.
Alderman, Ken	1975-76-77	QB	Radford, Va.
Alessandri, Leo	1938-39-40	B	Mishawaka, Ind.
Alexander, Jamaal	1994-95-96-97	S	New Orleans, La.
Alexander, Neal	1980-81-82-83	FB	Purvis, Miss.
Alexander, Otis	1984-85	NG	Covington, La.
Alexander, Vincent	1983-84-85-86	TB	Covington, La.
Alford, George	1934	—	Tylertown, Miss.
Alford, Larry	1979-80-81-82	NG	Foxworth, Miss.
Alford, Mike	1979-80-81	FS	Hattiesburg, Miss.
Alherimi, Ali	1999	WR	Navarre, Fla.
Allbritton, D. E.	1941	B	Farmville, La.
Allen, Carl	1974-75	CB	Hattiesburg, Miss.
Allen, Dave	1950-51	C	Meridian, Miss.
Allen, Edwin	1933-34-35	HB/FB	Bogue Chitto, Miss.
Allen, Moochie	1979-80-81-82	DT	McComb, Miss.

	YEAR	POSITION	HOMETOWN
Allen, Rickey	1976-77	LB	Houston, Miss.
Allen, Scott	1982-83-84	FS	Vicksburg, Miss.
Alley, Lehman	1981-82	OG	Birmingham, Ala.
Allums, J. F.	1929	——	Pachuta, Miss.
Allums, R. E.	1929	——	Petal, Miss.
Almond, Dustin	2002-03	QB	Orange Park, Fla.
Alonzo, Don	1950-51-52	G	Mobile, Ala.
Alston, Lyneal	1983-84-85-86	WR	Theodore, Ala.
Anderson, Alan	1988-89-90	DS/LB	Slidell, La.
Anderson, Andrew	1983-84-85-86	QB	Birmingham, Ala.
Anderson, G. D.	1912-13	QB	Hattiesburg, Miss.
Anderson, Leon	1989-90-91-92	OT	Grapeland, Tex.
Anderson, Terry	2001-02-03	LB	New Orleans, La.
Antoniou, Pete	1989-90-91	DT	Titusville, Fla.
Applewhite, A. H.	1922-23	T	Columbia, Miss.
Applewhite, Tommy	1967-68	E	Bassfield, Miss.
Applewhite, William	1940-41	E	Hattiesburg, Miss.
Arban, J. C.	1955-56-57-58	HB	Athens, Ala.
Archie, John	2003	DB	Canton, Miss.
Armond, Chuck	1963-64-65	T	Chalmette, La.
Armstrong, Andy	1965-66	G	Meridian, Miss.
Arnold, Clint	1949-50	HB	Pensacola, Fla.
Ates, Gwen	1929	——	Magee, Miss.
Austin, Leroy (Hawk)	1935-36	T/C	Grenada, Miss.
Autry, Melvin (Hank)	1966-67-68	C	Hattiesburg, Miss.
Autry, Melvin (Pel)	1939-40-41	C	Hattiesburg, Miss.
Avery, Ken	1964-65-66	C/LB	Miami, Fla.

B

	YEAR	POSITION	HOMETOWN
Bachman, Gene	1965-66-67	T	Parsippany, N.J.
Baetzman, Charley	1959	T	Leesburg, Fla.
Baham, Ron	1989-90-91	WR	Covington, La.
Bailey, Reed	1946	E	Sulphur, La.
Balazik, Brian	1997	QB	Homewood, Ala.
Ballard, Perry	1967	G	Opp, Ala.
Ballard, Wally	1974-75	TE	Norfolk, Va.
Banks, Derrick	1978	OT/OG	Lumberton, Miss.
Banks, Rex	1984-85-86	PK	Vancleave, Miss.
Banks, Seth (Shorty)	1938	G	Ruleville, Miss.
Bankston, Ronnie	1963	E	Hammond, La.
Barbaree, Jim	1960-61-62	E	Union Springs, Ala.
Barfield, Doug	1954-55-56	QB/DB	Grove Hill, Ala.
Barger, Jimmy	1964-65-66	S	Memphis, Tenn.
Barker, Patrick	2002	DS	Panama City, Fla.
Barlow, Jason	1994-95	OL	Savannah, Ga.
Barner, DeMarcus	2003	DE	Newnan, Ga.
Barnes, Leo	1997-98-99-2000	FS	Hattiesburg, Miss.
Barnes, Rex	1967-68-69	MG	Dadeville, Ala.
Barnett, W. C.	1915	——	Prentiss, Miss.

Name	YEAR	POSITION	HOMETOWN
Barney, Byron (Bye-Bye)	1983	FS	Gulfport, Miss.
Barr, Nevil	1972-73	FL/SE	Purvis, Miss.
Barrett, Howard	1935-36-37	B	Columbia, Miss.
Baskin, Fred	1982-83-84-85	DT	Meridian, Miss.
Basler, Randy	1973-74-75-76	DT	Clarksdale, Miss.
Bates, H. G.	1920-21-25-26	G/T	Purvis, Miss.
Batiste, George	2003	OG	Avondale, La.
Battaglia, Joe	1957-58	G	New Orleans, La.
Battles, Mike	1967-68-69	LB	Sylacauga, Ala.
Baylis, Jerald	1980-81-82-83	NG	Jackson, Miss.
Baylor, John	1984-85-86-87	CB	Meridian, Miss.
Baylot, Erwin	1950-51	FB	Vicksburg, Miss.
Beal, Raymond (Tiko)	1977-78-79	TB	Largo, Fla.
Beam, Frank	1946-47	G	McComb, Miss.
Beckwith, Mitch	1992-93	DT	Ochlocknee, Ga.
Beeching, Todd	1992-93	OT	Stockbridge, Ga.
Bell, A. D.	1936-37	E	Chalybeate, Miss.
Bell, Brian A.	1997-98	LB	Toomsuba, Miss.
Bell, Brian F.	1998-99	OL	Atmore, Ala.
Bell, James (Ding Dong)	1946	HB	Magee, Miss.
Bell, Royal	1996-97-98	LB	Greenville, Miss.
Bell, Tim	1994-95	DT	Gulfport, Miss.
Bella, Sam	1962-63	T	Arabi, La.
Benglis, Mike (Greek)	1937-38	B	Port Sulphur, La.
Bennett, Darrell	2001-02	WR/DB	Lake Charles, La.
Bentley, Kenny	1981-84-85	OT	Birmingham, Ala.
Bentley, Kevin	1992-93-94	QB	Mansfield, Tex.
Berry, James	1961-62-63	QB	Panama City, Fla.
Bethea, William	1925	E	Hattiesburg, Miss.
Bickerstaff, G. G.	1926	G	Tishomingo, Miss.
Bilbo, Ellis M.	1929-30-31-32	B	Hattiesburg, Miss.
Bird, Eugene	1971-72-73	DB	Waycross, Ga.
Bishop, G. J.	1929	FB	Hattiesburg, Miss.
Bishop, Jack	1930	C	Paragould, Ark.
Bishop, Jim (Bill)	1954	T	Memphis, Tenn.
Bishop, Ray	1934	B	Hattiesburg, Miss.
Black, Mitch L.	1929-30	G	Nettleton, Miss.
Blackman, Bill	1949-50	E	Montgomery, Ala.
Blackmon, Burnett	1956-57	G	Jackson, Miss.
Blackmon, Shederick	1996-97-98-99	OT	Pensacola, Fla.
Blackwell, A. B.	1924	T	Rawl Springs, Miss.
Blackwell, Clark	1973	LB	Tylertown, Miss.
Blackwell, Timmy	2000-01-03	WR/TB	Mize, Miss.
Blake, Gerald	1989-90-91	SS	Duluth, Ga.
Blakeney, Jack	1942	E	Crystal Springs, Miss.
Blanchard, Mike	1970-71	DT	Port Allen, La.
Blanks, Kevin	1999	TE	Meridian, Miss.
Boesch, Jim	1971-72-73	OT/OG	Long Beach, Miss.
Bohannon, Jarrod	1989	OL	Fairhope, Ala.

	YEAR	POSITION	HOMETOWN
Boleware, Tyrone	1994-95-96-97	FB	Panama City, Fla.
Boley, Michael	2001-02-03	LB	Athens, Ala.
Boling, Herman (Bill)	1951-52-53-54	E	Aliceville, Ala.
Bolis, Henry (Frenchie)	1938-39-40	B	Crystal Springs, Miss.
Bolt, Carl	1954	HB	Dublin, Va.
Bolt, Doug	1984-85-86	NG	Marietta, Ga.
Bolt, Karl	1988-89	OL	Marietta, Ga.
Bond, C. H.	1929	—	Wiggins, Miss.
Bonis, Mark	1999	LB	Slidell, La.
Booth, Eric	1994-95-96-97	TB	Bassfield, Miss.
Borde, Chuck	1946-47-48-49	T	Bogalusa, La.
Bourgeois, Gary	1966	QB	Gulfport, Miss.
Bourquard, Steve	1999	WR	New Orleans, La.
Boutwell, Tommy	1967-68	QB	Gulfport, Miss.
Bower, Jeff	1973-74-75	QB	Roswell, Ga.
Bowling, Don	1990-91-92	TE	Town Creek, Ala.
Bowman, Brad	1973-74-75	S	Baker, La.
Boyd, Barry	1993	TB	Waycross, Ga.
Boyd, Clay (Goofus)	1932-33	B	Scooba, Miss.
Boyd, Homer	1958-59	E	Raymond, Miss.
Boyd, Larry	1983	P	Columbus, Ga.
Boyett, Perry	1950	G	Starkville, Miss.
Boyette, Randy	1977-78	PK	Loranger, La.
Boyette, Steve	1975-76	OT	Loranger, La.
Boykin, Tony	1993	LB	Louisville, Ala.
Bradfute, Byron	1959	T	Beeville, Tex.
Bradley, Ricky	1987-88-89	TB	Bay Springs, Miss.
Braley, Lehman	1988-89-90-91	OL	Jefferson, Tex.
Bramlett, Doyle (Texas)	1939-40	G	Jefferson, Tex.
Brannon, Donnell	1989-90-91	OG	Florence, Ala.
Brannon, Harmon (Bull)	1963-64	FB	Rocky Creek, Miss.
Brantley, W. A. (Bulldog)	1926-27-28-29	G	Kilmichael, Tex.
Brasher, Buford	1939-40	E	Sarepta, Miss.
Brashier, Jimmy	1951-52-53	HB	El Dorado, Ark.
Brassfield, S. A.	1927-28	E	Hattiesburg, Miss.
Braud, Blanchard	1966-67-68	OG	Geismer, La.
Breazeale, Marvin	1961-62	T	Purvis, Miss.
Brechtel, Berengher	1963	T	New Orleans, La.
Brechtel, John	1963	C	New Orleans, La.
Breckner, Kevin	1976	OT	Endicott, N.Y.
Breeland	1925	—	
Brennan, Tommy	1965-66	CB	Savannah, Ga.
Brewer	1923	—	
Bridges, Donald Wayne	1972	S	Prentiss, Miss.
Bridges, Jeremy	1999-2000-01-02	OT	McComb, Miss.
Bridges, Wilbur	1940-41	E	Kossuth, Miss.
Brill, Charles	1947	—	McComb, Miss.
Britt, Harold	1932	G	
Broadus	1926	C	Purvis, Miss.

[266] LETTERMEN

	YEAR	POSITION	HOMETOWN
Brock, Fred	1992-93-94-95	WR	Montgomery, Ala.
Brock, Thomas Leon	1938-39	HB	Fayette, Ala.
Brock, Tom	1969-70-71	OG	Kenner, La.
Brooks, Greg	2000-01-02-03	CB	New Orleans, La.
Brooks, Jimmy	1923	—	—
Broughton, Jerry	1993	WR	Branson, Mo.
Broussard, Steve	1970-71	V	Biloxi, Miss.
Browden, Terrell	2000-01-02-03	TE	Baton Rouge, La.
Brown, Bud	1980-81-82-83	SS	De Kalb, Miss.
Brown, Charlie	1989	OT	Lucedale, Miss.
Brown, Chuck Carr	1976-77-78-79	WR	Roseland, La.
Brown, Eric	1994	FB	Petal, Miss.
Brown, Frank	1946-47-48	FB	Millry, Ala.
Brown, Hays	1934-35-36	E	Hattiesburg, Miss.
Brown, Jesse	1963-64-65	E	Georgiana, Ala.
Brown, Jim	1979-80-81-83	TE	Birmingham, Ala.
Brown, John	1990-91-92	DT	Clarksdale, Miss.
Brown, Marvin	1997-98-99	DE	Rolling Fork, Miss.
Brown, Morris (Lightin')	1947-48-49-50	HB	Millry, Ala.
Brown, Obie	1932-33	E	McLain, Miss.
Brown, Ralph	1941	B	Union, Miss.
Brown, Randolph	1984-85-86	FB	Natchez, Miss.
Brown, Robert (Rabbit)	1963-64-67	WB	Pensacola, Fla.
Brown, Robert	1994-95-96-97	DE	Niceville, Fla.
Brown, Ron	1978-79-80	LB	Brewton, Ala.
Brown, Ron	1987-88-89-90	NT	Starke, Fla.
Brown, Steve	1985-86-87-88	DE	Enterprise, Ala.
Brown, Terry	1976-77-78	OG	Brooksville, Fla.
Broyles, Sammy	1958-59	FB	Kentwood, La.
Brumfield, Jackson	1951-52-53	E	Franklinton, La.
Brutley, Daryon	1998-99-2000	DB	Eufaula, Ala.
Bryant, Joe	1974	C	Norfolk, Va.
Bryant, Scott	1988-89-90-91	P	Queen City, Tex.
Buckhalter, Chris	1992-93-94-95	TB	Collins, Miss.
Bullock, Vernon	1948	T	Tylertown, Miss.
Bunkley, Charlie	1932	G	Mobile, Ala.
Burckel, Joe	1978	QB	New Orleans, La.
Burge, Ken	1970-71	LB	Poplarville, Miss.
Burkett, John	1980	SS	Jackson, Miss.
Burnett, Blaine	1978-79-80	OT	Mobile, Ala.
Burnett, Ive	1984	CB	Brandon, Miss.
Burns, Bryan	1993-94-95-96	LB	Birmingham, Ala.
Burns, L. A.	1930-32	HB/FB/T	Satillo, Miss.
Burns, Robert	1934	—	—
Busby, A. E.	1920	—	New Orleans, La.
Busby, J. M.	1921	E	Dead, Miss.
Busby, J. R. (Black)	1919-20	HB/FB	McComb, Miss.
Busby, Leonard (Bubba)	1978-79	FS	Laurel, Miss.
Busby, W. Z. (Red)	1920	E	New Orleans, La.

	YEAR	POSITION	HOMETOWN
Busch, L.	1922	QB/HB	Mobile, Ala.
Butler, Cal	1947-48-49	C/T	Wesson, Miss.
Butler, Cassie	1987-88-89-90	DE	Dothan, Ala.
Butler, Randy	1976-77-78	OT	Hartford, Ala.
Byars, Don	1973	DE	Paris, Tenn.
Bynum, Glen	1965-66-67	QB	Baker, La.
Byrd, Mark	1995	OT	Alexandria, La.
Byrd, Richard	1981-82-83-84	DT	Jackson, Miss.
Byrd, Timmy	1984-85	QB	LaPlace, La.
Byrne, Brad	1972-73-74-75	DB	Brewton, Ala.

C

	YEAR	POSITION	HOMETOWN
Cagle, V. C.	1919-23	FB	Sumrall, Miss.
Caldwell, Richard	1951-52-53	E	Columbus, Miss.
Calhoun, Ben	1961	G	Hattiesburg, Miss.
Calhoun, C. C.	1930-32	—	Amory, Miss.
Callahan, Micheal	1987-88	OG	Birmingham, Ala.
Camhout, Jacques	1992	QB	Chalmette, La.
Campbell, Bobby	1946-47	HB	Forest Hill, Tenn.
Campbell, Claude (Cotton)	1937-38	G	Ocean Springs, Miss.
Campbell, Clifton C. (Mutt)	1915-16-19-20	T	Liberty, Miss.
Campbell, Jimmy	1971	QB	Fort Walton Beach, Fla.
Campbell, Louis	1946	QB	Columbus, Miss.
Campbell, Randy	1982-83-84-85	OT	Vicksburg, Miss.
Campbell, Windell	1960-61	FB/E	Pensacola, Fla.
Cannon, Carl	1991	WR	Mobile, Ala.
Cannon, John	1975-76-77-78	WR	Merion, Pa.
Cardenas, Eddie	1954-55	FB	Pensacola, Fla.
Carmichael, Mark	1979-80-81-82	LB	Mobile, Ala.
Carmody, Keith	1985-86	DT	Hattiesburg, Miss.
Carmody, Steve	1980-81-82-83	C	Hattiesburg, Miss.
Carpenter, Ken	1994	WR	Hattiesburg, Miss.
Carr, John	1939-40	T	Leeds, Ala.
Carr, Sonny	1947-48	HB	McComb, Miss.
Carroll, Ricky	1993-94	QB	Pensacola, Fla.
Carrozza, Falco	1941-42-46-47	B	McKeesport, Pa.
Carter	1924	—	—
Carter	1929	—	—
Carter, Charlie	1980-81-82	OT	Atlanta, Ga.
Carter, Damion	2003	QB	New Orleans, La.
Carter, Demetris	1992-93	DT	Waycross, Ga.
Carter, John	1934	—	Ellisville, Miss.
Carter, Lamar (Bubba)	1968-70	FB	Magee, Miss.
Carter, Perry	1990-91-92-93	CB	McComb, Miss.
Carter, Simmie	1987-88-89-90	CB/QB	Harvey, La.
Carter, Walter	1937	—	Scooba, Miss.
Carter, Woodrow	1934	—	Ellisville, Miss.
Casey, Quintus	1990	TB	Florence, Ala.
Cash, Antoine	2001-02-03	DB	Anguilla, Miss.

	YEAR	POSITION	HOMETOWN
Casnave, Greg	2003	DT	Lacombe, La.
Caton, Keith	1997-98	DS	Mobile, Ala.
Caudill, Barry	1974-75-76	C	Brandon, Miss.
Caughman, Donnie	1967-68-69	DB	Mendenhall, Miss.
Causcy, Nate	1997-98	OL	Tupelo, Miss.
Causey, Pedi	2002-03	WR	Franklinton, La.
Ceppenati, Larry	1970-71	OG	Godfrey, Ill.
Chambers, Tré	1988-99	OL	Forest, Miss.
Champagne, Karone	2000-01-02-03	DB	Hahnville, La.
Chancellor, James	1942	——	Hattiesburg, Miss.
Channell, Ronnie	1966-67-68	HB	Jackson, Miss.
Chapman, Anthony	1998-99-2000	LB	Gulfport, Miss.
Cheatham, Ronnie	1972-73-74-75	LB	Birmingham, Ala.
Childers, W. F.	1926-27-28	G/T	Vance, Miss.
Chisolm, Scott	1966-67-68	MG	Vero Beach, Fla.
Christmas, J. Y.	1935-36-37	HB	Laurel, Miss.
Clancy, Charles (Fancy)	1973-74-75-76	TB	Clarksdale, Miss.
Clark, Bish	1931	QB	Poplarville, Miss.
Clark, Brett	1992	PK	Tallahassee, Fla.
Clark, Harold	1955-56	E	Shubuta, Miss.
Clark, Harry	1939-40	C	Drew, Miss.
Clark, Lesley	1953-54-55	C	Belzoni, Miss.
Clark, S. A.	1930	HB	Poplarville, Miss.
Clark, Steve	1981-82-83	PK	Jonesboro, Ga.
Clark, Wesley (Buzzy)	1953-54-55	T	Belzoni, Miss.
Clay, Billy	1999-2000	OG/C	Longview, Tex.
Clayton, N. R.	1920-21	FB	Booneville, Miss.
Cleckler, Dillon	2001-02-03	LB	Pensacola, Fla.
Clements, M. G. (Foots)	1940-41	G	Greenwood, Miss.
Clinton, E. W.	1926	——	Hattiesburg, Miss.
Coats, Willie (Teenie)	1957-58	QB/DB	Stonewall, Miss.
Cochran, Linwood (Pete)	1934	FB	McLain, Miss.
Cockfield, Larry (Bo)	1972-73	LB	Lake City, S.C.
Coggin, Cliff	1948-49	E	Athens, Ala.
Colbert, Clevon	1991	DE	Columbus, Ga.
Coleman, Barrett	1982-83	DE	Marrero, La.
Coleman, Billy	1961-62	QB/DB	Chickasaw, Ala.
Coleman, F. M.	1915	——	Wallerville, Miss.
Coleman, John	1962	HB	Wildwood, Fla.
Coleman, Lee	1972	DT	Raleigh, N.C.
Coleman, Sidney	1984-85-86-87	LB	Gulfport, Miss.
Coley, Kevis	2002-03	LB	Palatka, Fla.
Coley, Trevis	2002-03	DB	Palatka, Fla.
Collier, I. A.	1925	G	Long Beach, Miss.
Collier, Reggie	1979-80-81-82	QB	Biloxi, Miss.
Collins, Kendrick	1988-89-90-91	NT	Decatur, Ga.
Collins, Vernard	1989-90-91-92	CB	Sumrall, Miss.
Colona, Darryl	1986-87	OT	Hammond, La.
Comacho, John	1989-90	C	Port Lavaca, Tex.

	YEAR	POSITION	HOMETOWN
Combest, Steve	1980	PK	Stonewall, Miss.
Conner, Walter	1925-26	QB/E	Hattiesburg, Miss.
Cook, Chuck	1977-78-79-80	TB/SS	Hattiesburg, Miss.
Cook, E. L.	1921	HB	Hattiesburg, Miss.
Cook, Ed	1925	FB	Hattiesburg, Miss.
Cook, Fred	1971-72-73	DE	Pascagoula, Miss.
Cook, Hamp	1952-53-54	G	Georgiana, Ala.
Cook, Harvey	1912	—	Hattiesburg, Miss.
Cook, Joe	1923-24	HB	Hattiesburg, Miss.
Cooley, Travis	2003	OG	Waynesboro, Miss.
Cooper, James	1982-83-84-85	CB	Raymond, Miss.
Cooper, Tim	1987	TE	Corinth, Miss.
Corbett, Patrick	2003	TE	Kosciusko, Miss.
Corley	1923	—	—
Corne, Charlie	1952-53	G	New Orleans, La.
Cornelison, Van	1940	G	Scottsboro, Ala.
Cornelius, N. H.	1919-20	E/C	Blue Springs, Miss.
Corner, Willie	1978-79	FB	Pensacola, Fla.
Coughlin, Walton	1924	—	—
Courington, Antwon	2002-03	WR	Jasper, Ala.
Cowart, Donivan	1933-34-35	G	McLain, Miss.
Cowart, O. E. (Cootie)	1922-23-24	T/FB/HB	Smithville, Miss.
Cowart, Roland	1914	—	Smithville, Miss.
Cox, Ernest	1935	G	Madison, Miss.
Cox, Luther M.	1912	—	Rawl Springs, Miss.
Crabb, A. B.	1916-20	E/T	Booneville, Miss.
Craft	1925	—	—
Craft, C. E.	1920-21	HB	Hattiesburg, Miss.
Craft, Mike	1968-69-70	DT/OT	Biloxi, Miss.
Craft, Troy	1964-65-66	E	Biloxi, Miss.
Crane, Losa	1924	B	—
Crawford, S. B.	1921	E	Ora, Miss.
Crenshaw, Mike	1976-77-78	SS	Mobile, Ala.
Crestman, J. H.	1928	G	Calhoun City, Miss.
Crimm, Ben	1988-89-90	DT	Pascagoula, Miss.
Critty, Armand	1939-40	B	Union City, N.J.
Croley, Scott	1998-99-2000-01	DS	Citronelle, Ala.
Crusoe, Carlos	2002	DE	Columbus, Miss.
Culliver, Grant (Mad Dog)	1978-79-80	DT	Brewton, Ala.
Cumbie, Seth	2001-02-03	DB	Pace, Fla.
Cunningham, Donald	1993-94-95-96	WR	Opelousas, La.

D

Dabbs, Fortner (Sporty)	1937-38	QB	Quitman, Miss.
Dabbs, J. V.	1916	FB	Amory, Miss.
Daigle, Stephen	2003	DS	Molino, Fla.
Dale, J. E.	1923-24-25-26	G	Hawthorne, Miss.
Dale, V. C.	1915	—	Prentiss, Miss.

	YEAR	POSITION	HOMETOWN
Dampeer, Greg	1982-83-84-85	DE	Mendenhall, Miss.
D'Angelo, Joey	1970-71	LB/WB	Gulfport, Miss.
D'Angelo, Mickey	2001-02-03	QB	Gulfport, Miss.
D'Angelo, Robby	2003	C	Gulfport, Miss.
Daniell, Steve	1974	DT	Carrollton, Ga.
Daniels, J. W. (Rabbit)	1929-30	HB	Hattiesburg, Miss.
Daniels, Terry	1976	CB/S	Satsuma, Ala.
Dantzler, Orlando (Pop)	1998-99-2000-01	TE	Purvis, Miss.
Darby, C. J.	1920	HB	Landon, Miss.
Davenport, Jim (Peanuts)	1952-53-54	QB/DB/PK	Siluria, Ala.
Davidson, Richie	1997-98	OL	Warner Robins, Ga.
Davis, Bill	1968-69-70	G/LB	Chickasaw, Ala.
Davis, Chuck	1989	PK	Martinez, Ga.
Davis, Fred E. (Tiny)	1926-27-28-29	T	Hamilton, Miss.
Davis, J. W. (Peck)	1928-29	HB/QB	De Kalb, Miss.
Davis, Jim (Coon Dawg)	1953-54	T	Ellijay, Ga.
Davis, Larry	1986-88	NT	New Orleans, La.
Davis, Rod	2000-01-02-03	LB	Gulfport, Miss.
Davis, Tommy	1969	DB	Semmes, Ala.
Davis, W. J. (Puny)	1916-1920	T	Covington, La.
Dawkins, David	1988-89	DB	Hattiesburg, Miss.
Dedwylder, Charley	1959-60-61	E	Quitman, Miss.
Deering	1932	G	—
Defranco, Tony	1961-62-63	G	Patterson, N.J.
Dejarnette, Sam	1982-83-84	TB	Selma, Ala.
Del Vaccario, Pat	1955	T	Brooklyn, N.Y.
Dement, Robert (Curley)	1941-46-47	G/T	Montevallo, Ala.
Dempsey, Alvin	1993	CB	Panama City, Fla.
Dennery, Mike	1971-72-73-74	LB	Philadelphia, Pa.
Dennis, Stacy	1989-90	QB	Baton Rouge, La.
Denson, Hunter	1932	FB	—
Deremer, Jeff	1988	OL	Port Richey, Fla.
DeVall, Les	1940-41	B	Ellisville, Miss.
Devrow, Billy	1964-65-66	S	Hattiesburg, Miss.
Dewitt, Leroy	1995-96	C	Bay City, Tex.
Dews, C. L. (Dipsey)	1940-41-42	B	Hattiesburg, Miss.
Dickerson, Harold	1941	B	Johnston Station, Miss.
Dickey, Curtis	1974-75-76	TB	Paris, Tenn.
Dickey, Fred	1938-39	L	Lucien, Miss.
Dickinson, Bo	1956-57	FB	Hattiesburg, Miss.
Dillard, Thad	1975-76-77-78	NG	Montgomery, Ala.
Dilworth, Billy	1985-86-87	OG	Corinth, Miss.
Dixon, Hanford	1977-78-79-80	CB	Theodore, Ala.
Doggett, Joe	1956-57	HB	Hattiesburg, Miss.
Donegan, Rick	1969-70-71	QB	Hattiesburg, Miss.
Dorsey, James	1994	OG	Luling, La.
Dorsey, Travis	1999-2000	DE	New Orleans, La.
Dowd, Clyde	1964-65-66	TB	Shelby, N.C.

	YEAR	POSITION	HOMETOWN
Doze, Mitch	1981-82	TB	Pascagoula, Miss.
Dragg, Johnny	1971-72	FL	Covington, La.
Draughn, Benny	1985	OT	Petal, Miss.
Drone, Mark	1989	LB	Jackson, Miss.
Ducksworth, Robert	1982-83-84-85	QB	Biloxi, Miss.
Duggins, Brent	1993-94	OT	Carrollton, Ga.
Dunaway, Dickie	1964-65-66	P	Gulfport, Miss.
Dunn, Kendall	1994-95-96-97	DT	Gulfport, Miss.
Dunn, Steve	1972-73-74	OG	Hampton, Va.
DuPont, Robert	1982	OG	Marrero, La.

E

	YEAR	POSITION	HOMETOWN
Earnest, Ryan	2003	TB	Laurel, Miss.
East, T. F.	1914	—	West Point, Miss.
Ector, Clemon	1974-75-76-77	LB	Griffin, Ga.
Ecuyer, Larry	1962-63-64	C	New Orleans, La.
Edgar, Frank	1942	—	—
Edwards, Addaryl	2003	OG	Amite, La.
Edwards, Elmer	1936	T	Bogue Chitto, Miss.
Edwards, W. G.	1912-15	—	Belfontaine, Miss.
Eggersman, Hugh	1969-70-71	DE/LB	North Augusta, S.C.
Elder, Reggie	1990-92-93	DT	Carrollton, Ga.
Ellender, Vaughn	1947-48	E	Sulphur, Ala.
Elliott, Roger	1967-68-69	TE/DE	Lumberton, Miss.
Ellis, Steve	1988	OG	Eupora, Miss.
Ellzey, Charles	1957-58-59	C/LB	Meridian, Miss.
Emerson, Ralph	1941-42	B	Oxford, Ala.
Eskridge, John	1998	DL	Riverview, Fla.
Estes, Eric	1992-93	QB/P	Northport, Ala.
Ethridge, Ron	1979	QB/DE	Birmingham, Ala.
Eubanks	1922	G	—
Eubanks, John	2002-03	CB	Mound Bayou, Miss.
Evans, Brian	2000-01	LB	Mobile, Ala.
Evans, Bruce	1950	T	Birmingham, Ala.
Evans, G. G.	1919	—	Poplarville, Miss.
Evans, George Worth	1933	FB	Cristobal, Canal Zone
Evans, Roy	1934	—	—
Evans, Russell	1932-33	HB	Leakesville, Miss.

F

	YEAR	POSITION	HOMETOWN
Fagan, Walter	1932	—	Hattiesburg, Miss.
Fairchild, Danny	1968-69	LB	Quitman, Miss.
Fairley, Gayle	1927-30-31	E	Gulfport, Miss.
Farrer, Pitt	1969-70-71	DE	Clinton, Miss.
Farris, Ken	1950-51	G	Corinth, Miss.
Farrish, Webb (Boots)	1950-51	HB/K	Waynesboro, Miss.
Faulk, Jasper	2003	DB	Lafayette, La.
Favre, Brett	1987-88-89-90	QB	Kiln, Miss.

	YEAR	POSITION	HOMETOWN
Favre, Jeff	1994-95	DB	Kiln, Miss.
Fayard, Lionel	1968-69-70	TE	Biloxi, Miss.
Fehrenbacher, Jim	1986-87	WR	Ocean Springs, Miss.
Felts, Nollie	1922-23-24-26	E/QB	Hattiesburg, Miss.
Ferlise, Pat	1951-52	G	Birmingham, Ala.
Ferrell, Hugh	1924-25	HB	Newton, Miss.
Ferrell, Jim	1984-85-86-87	OT	Huntsville, Ala.
Ferrell, Pat	1984-85-86-87	OT	Huntsville, Ala.
Fife, Dale	1978-79-80-81	OG	Fort Walton Beach, Fla.
Fillingim, Elmer	1940	B	Bay St. Louis, Miss.
Finch, Brownie	1930	——	——
Finch, Ray	1927	C	Hattiesburg, Miss.
Finch, Roy	1930-31-32	C	Hattiesburg, Miss.
Finch, W.	1920	G	Walthall, Miss.
Finlayson, John S.	1920	G/T	Hattiesburg, Miss.
Firestone, Frank	1997-98	C	Brenham, Tex.
Fisackerly, H. L.	1920	——	Winona, Miss.
Fisher	1932	——	——
Fitzgerald, Dave	1954-55-56	T/G	McKeesport, Pa.
Flanagan, P. P. (Pert)	1926-27-28-29	G	De Kalb, Miss.
Flanders, Bob	1970-71-72	OG/OT	Eau Gallie, Fla.
Fleming, A. B.	1927-28	G	Carmichael, Miss.
Fleming, Frank (Red)	1929	——	Coldwater, Kans.
Fleming, Joel	1978	OG	West, Miss.
Fleming, R.	1932	E	——
Fletcher, I. W.	1934-35	G	Perkinston, Miss.
Floyd, John	1999	WR	Monroe, La.
Floyd, Ricky	1978-79-80-81	TB	Gulfport, Miss.
Floyd, Stuart	2001-02	TE	Birmingham, Ala.
Flurry, Hubert	1920-21-25	G	Perkinston, Miss.
Flynt	1932	——	——
Foley, Bill	1970-71	FB	Huntington Valley, Pa.
Fooshee, Orville	1946	E	Purvis, Miss.
Ford, Terrance	2002-03	DL	Gheens, La.
Fore, Steve	1967-68-69	DB	Flomaton, Ala.
Forte, James (Pickle)	1939-40	C	Pensacola, Fla.
Foshee, Win	1969	E	Jackson, Miss.
Fowler, Amos	1975-76-77	OT	Pensacola, Fla.
Fowler, Dannye	1998-99-2000-01	WR	Birmingham, Ala.
Fox, E. E.	1915	——	Philadelphia, Miss.
Francis, Brandon	1996-97-98-99	TB/WR	Lafayette, La.
Franklin	1927	——	——
Franklin, Antonio	1998	OL	Water Valley, Miss.
Freeman, Bill	1961-62-63	T	Milton, Fla.
Freeman, Thomas Glover	1938-39	E	Artesia, Miss.
Fremin, Jerry	1973-74-75	OT	Ocean Springs, Miss.
Friedhoff, Gary	1966	FB	Philadelphia, Pa.
Fuell, Don	1959-60-61	QB/DB	Guntersville, Ala.

	YEAR	POSITION	HOMETOWN
Fulkerson, Jack	1950-51	T	Kingsport, Tenn.
Furlow, S. M.	1913-14-15	—	Wesson, Miss.
Fussell, Clifton	1972-73-74	C	Wray, Ga.

G

	YEAR	POSITION	HOMETOWN
Gabourel, Shane	1978-80-81	PK	Puertes Cortas, Honduras
Gabriel, Jack	1996-97-98	P	Ponchatoula, La.
Gafford, L. E.	1920-21-22-23	C/T/G	Etta, Miss.
Galloway, Tito	1995	TB	Ocean Springs, Miss.
Gamble, Shaun	1991-92-93-94	FS	Sweetwater, Ala.
Gamble, Tracy	1981-82-83-84	TB	Sandy Hook, Miss.
Gandy, Shelton	1985-86-87-88	TB	Waynesboro, Miss.
Ganse, Joe	1972-73-74	DT	Lancaster, Pa.
Gantt, Kyle	1970-71-72	LB	Andalusia, Ala.
Gardner, W. C. (Prep)	1928-29	HB	Wheeler, Miss.
Garner, Bobby	1999-2000-01-02	TE	Gulfport, Miss.
Garner, D.	1931	E	Fulton, Miss.
Garner, Terrel	1967	MG	Magee, Miss.
Garrett, Denton	1935-36	E	Meadville, Miss.
Garry, Ben (Go-Go)	1974-75-76-77	TB	Pascagoula, Miss.
Garton, Morris	1941	E	Millville, N.J.
Gates, Neil	1935-36	FB	Tolona, Ill.
Gatti, Dick	1952	—	Kenosha, Wis.
Gay, Jack	1927	QB	Hattiesburg, Miss.
Gemmel, Rick	1973-74-75	V	Catasauqua, Pa.
Gibson, Barry	1972-73-74-75	WR	Moss Point, Miss.
Gideon, Sherrod	1996-97-98-99	WR	Greenwood, Miss.
Gill, Art	1964-65-66	T	Biloxi, Miss.
Gill, Byron	1998-99-2000	DB	Baton Rouge, La.
Gillis, Malcolm	1934	B	Hattiesburg, Miss.
Glass, Tommie	1939-40	G	Biloxi, Miss.
Glover, Melton	1996	LB	Senatobia, Miss.
Godwin, Eddie	1958	G/T	Selma, Ala.
Golden, Wiley	1914	—	Taylorsville, Miss.
Gonzalez, Jose	1997-98	DB	Jacksonville, Fla.
Gordon, Anthony	1991	WR	Meridian, Miss.
Gordon, Derrick	1996	DL	Fort Lauderdale, Fla.
Gorney, Bill	1963-64-65	E	Orland Park, Ill.
Gowdy, Maurice	1996-97-98	TB	Pascagoula, Miss.
Grace, Nathan	2000-01	OT	Ocean Springs, Miss.
Graham	1916	—	—
Graham, Arthur	1925	HB	Seminary, Miss.
Graham, Greg	1978-79	WR	Corinth, Miss.
Graham, Heath	1994-95-96	QB	Stringer, Miss.
Graham, James	1946-47	G	—
Graham, Stanley	1941-42	E	Leakesville, Miss.
Graves, Otho	2003	TE	Bassfield, Miss.
Gray, Antonio	1998-99	DB	Trinity, Ala.
Gray, Tony	1983	OG	Magee, Miss.

	YEAR	POSITION	HOMETOWN
Grayson, Charles	1927-30	G	Hattiesburg, Miss.
Green, Cole	1994-95-96-97	OL	Lawrenceville, Ga.
Green, Jeff	1993	FB	Baton Rouge, La.
Green, Kwantell	2000-01	WR	New Orleans, La.
Green, Reed	1930-31-32-33	QB/HB	Leakesville, Miss.
Green, Richard	1988	OT	Troy, Ala.
Greene, Robert	1983	OG	Meridian, Miss.
Greer, George	1935-36	——	Potts Camp, Miss.
Gregory, J. E.	1921	HB	Bay Springs, Miss.
Griffin, Steven	2000-01	TB	Okolona, Miss.
Griffin, Terry	1969	DE	Salem, Miss.
Griffith, Cecil	1937	T	Waynesboro, Miss.
Grimes, Alton	1931-32	G	Union, Miss.
Grubbs, Gary	1969-70-71	SE	Prentiss, Miss.
Guin, Arlis (Ace)	1937-38	QB/HB	Lake Charles, La.
Gullette, A. T.	1925-26-27	HB	McLaurin, Miss.
Gulley, Josh	1998-99	TE/WR	Grand Prairie, Tex.
Gulley, Letorrance	1992-93-94-95	FS	Bay Minette, Ala.
Gunnell, Nick	1914	——	Bogue Chitto, Miss.
Guy, Ray	1970-71-72	P/PK/S	Thomson, Ga.
Guy, T. J.	1914-15	——	Macon, Miss.

H

	YEAR	POSITION	HOMETOWN
Haag, Chris R.	1982-83-84-85	OG	Chatom, Ala.
Haag, Chris	1973	OT	Danielsville, Ga.
Hackney, Joseph P. (Noonie)	1926-27-28-29	HB/QB	Hattiesburg, Miss.
Haeusler, Greg	1981-82-83-84	LB	Destin, Fla.
Hailey, Scooba	1930-31	T	Scooba, Miss.
Halbert, James	1932-33	E/HB	Artesia, Miss.
Hale, Ben	1975	DE	Sylacauga, Ala.
Hale, James	1978	DE	Montgomery, Ala.
Hale, John	1968-69	PK	Lucedale, Miss.
Hale, Ken	1969-70	WB	Wauchula, Fla.
Haley, Danny	1967-68	SE	Jackson, Miss.
Hall, Jason	1994-95-96	DT	Broken Arrow, Okla.
Hallman, Tim	1984-85-86-87	OG	Centrevillle, Ala.
Hambright, Brandon	1995-96-97	OL	Fort Lauderdale, Fla.
Hamilton, Bobby	1990-91-92-93	DE	Columbia, Miss.
Hammond, Jeff	1976-77-78	QB	Memphis, Tenn.
Hancock, Larry	1963	C	Gulfport, Miss.
Handy, Leroy	1999-2000-01-02	WR	Beaumont, Miss.
Hanna, Brant	1998-99-2000-01	PK	Natalbany, La.
Hansford, Preston	1986-87-88-89	TE	Maylene, Ala.
Hanzo, Al	1948	B	New Orleans, La.
Hardaway, Tim	1997-98	PK	Stone Mountain, Ga.
Hardman, Roger	1972-73-74	OG	Atlanta, Ga.
Hardy, Terry	1994-95-96-97	TE	Montgomery, Ala.
Hardy, Tom	1923	G	——
Hardy, Wayne	2003	FB	Monticello, Miss.

	YEAR	POSITION	HOMETOWN
Harmon, Eugene	1992-93-94-95	LB	Kosciusko, Miss.
Harper, Scott	1993-94	TE	Lawrenceville, Ga.
Harrell, Joe	1938	T	Dallas, Tex.
Harrington	1923	—	—
Harrington, Billy	1984	FB	Hattiesburg, Miss.
Harrington, Larry	1976-77-78	TE	Hattiesburg, Miss.
Harrington, Robert	1934	—	—
Harris, Anthony	1988-89-90	TE	Tuscaloosa, Ala.
Harris, Anthony	2002-03	RB	Demopolis, Ala.
Harris, Bobo	1982-83-84-85	CB	Vicksburg, Miss.
Harris, Don	1968	G	Mendenhall, Miss.
Harris, Jerry	1992-93-94-95	LB	Baxley, Ga.
Harris, Mike	1968-69-70	S	Jackson, Miss.
Harris, Orlando	1989	LB	Northport, Ala.
Harris, Ray	1933-34	G	Tylertown, Miss.
Harrison, Rocky	2001	WR	Tampa, Fla.
Hart, Granville (Scrappy)	1951	HB	Booneville, Miss.
Harvey, Marvin (Rock)	1977-78-79-80	TE	Marianna, Fla.
Hatcher, Wayne	1969-70-71	SE	Lucedale, Miss.
Hatchett, Marchenne	2000-01	DE	West Point, Miss.
Haulman, Mark	1999-2000-01-02	P	Vicksburg, Miss.
Havard, Jimmy	1960-61-62	HB	Lucedale, Miss.
Hayden, Charles	1969	OT	Hattiesburg, Miss
Haynes, Carmus	2001	DB	McComb, Miss.
Haynes, Jimmy	1969-70-71	C/OT	Gainesville, Fla.
Hays, Harold	1960-61-62	C/LB	Hattiesburg, Miss.
Heard, Kevin	1997-98	WR	Eupora, Miss.
Heath, Charles	1939-40	T	Grenada, Miss.
Heath, John	1935-36	G	Goodman, Miss.
Hefner, Reece	1956	E	Kingsport, Tenn.
Hegwood, Wayne	1947	T	Jackson, Miss.
Heidelburg, Willie	1970-71	HB	Lumberton, Miss.
Helms, Steve	1990	WR	New Orleans, La.
Henderson, Archie	1980-81-82	DE	Winona, Miss.
Henderson, Pat	1990-91	DT	Canton, Miss.
Henderson, Tom	1972-73-74	DE	Hampton, Va.
Hendrix	1919	—	—
Hendrix, Caleb	2003	WR	Jasper, Ala.
Hendrix, Joey	1979-80-81	OT	Columbus, Miss.
Hendrix, Steve	1983-84-85	NG	Plantersville, Miss.
Hendricks, Troy	1938-39	E	Percilla, Tex.
Henley, Joe	1999-2000-01-02	LB	Gainesville, Fla.
Henry, James	1986-87-88	CB	Poplarville, Miss.
Henry, Malachi	1974-75-76	CB	Starke, Fla.
Henry, Onesimus	1984-85-86-87	LB	Pensacola, Fla.
Herring, Charles	1933-34	E/T	Lake Providence, La.
Herring, George	1954-55	QB/DB	Hopes Bluff, Ala.
Herrington, Roland	1919	G	Wiggins, Miss.
Herrmann, Leo T.	1952-53-54	G	Mobile, Ala.

	YEAR	POSITION	HOMETOWN
Herron, Johnny	1969-70-71	NG/DT	Bay Minette, Ala.
Hervey, Derrick	1992-93-94-95	CB	Water Valley, Miss.
Hess, Collins	1984-85	SS	Huntsville, Ala.
Hester, E. W.	1922-23-24	E/QB	Amory, Miss.
Hicks, Jim	2000-01-02-03	C	Philadelphia, Miss.
Hicks, Roger	1960-61	E	Mulga, Ala.
Highstreet, Paul	1960	T	Bassfield, Miss.
Hightower, Aaron	1992	QB	Opp, Ala.
Hill, George	1985-86-87-88	LB	Eufaula, Ala.
Hillman	1929	——	
Hinton, Charles	1965	E	Hattiesburg, Miss.
Hinton, Jerry	1969-70-71	DT	Laurel, Miss.
Hinton, L. T.	1926	——	Liberty, Miss.
Hitt, Harold	1963-64	E	Mobile, Ala.
Hodges, Bill	1966-67	CB	Biloxi, Miss.
Holcomb	1931	G	Perkinston, Miss.
Holifield, G. E.	1936	B	Laurel, Miss.
Holleman, Clarence	1919	FB	Wiggins, Miss.
Hollingsworth, Luther (Holly)	1936-37-38	B	Piave, Miss.
Hollins, Raymond	1990-91	S	Mobile, Ala.
Holloway	1937		
Holloway, Jimmy	1998	LB	Eufaula, Ala.
Holmes, Bobby	1949-50	QB/DB	Tallassee, Ala.
Holmes, David Benton	1912	HB	Hattiesburg, Miss.
Holmes, Denton	1912	——	
Holmes, Ronnie	1971	DT	McComb, Miss.
Holmes, Sonny	1962	QB	Forest City, Ark.
Holt, Gary	1977-78	DB	Pensacola, Fla.
Honaker, Doug (Spot)	1946-47-48	E/PK	Bogalusa, La.
Hood, Richard	1968	OT	Richton, Miss.
Hopgood, Jeff	1995-97	OL	Bay St. Louis, Miss.
Horn, Don	1979-80-81-82	WR	Jackson, Miss.
Horton, Freeman	1975-76-77-78	LB	Lake, Miss.
Hosemann, David	1974-76-77	FB	Vicksburg, Miss.
Hosey, Corey	1999-2000-02-03	WR	Bay Springs, Miss.
Hoskins, Derrick	1989-90-91	FS	Philadelphia, Miss.
Houston, Zaid	1997-98-99-2000	LB	Bogalusa, La.
Howard, Carl (Chicken)	1947-48-49	HB/PK	Starkville, Miss.
Howard, Jackie	1951-52-53-54	HB	Purvis, Miss.
Howard, Thomas (Scoop)	1937-38-39	T	Albertville, Ala.
Howe, Glen (Big Dog)	1980-81-82	OT	New Albany, Miss.
Howell, Ronald	1987-88-89	FB	Duluth, Ga.
Howell, Tony	1980-81	CB	Pascagoula, Miss.
Howerton	1915	——	
Howington, Lee	1929	G	Purvis, Miss.
Huckabee, Cooper	1971-72	LB/DT	Mobile, Ala.
Huddleston, Fred	1982-84	TB	Plantersville, Miss.
Hudson, Ethridge	1932-35-36	G	Perkinston, Miss.
Hudson, Mickey	1970-71-72	DB	Bay Minette, Ala.

	YEAR	POSITION	HOMETOWN
Huelsbeck, Harry	1966-67	T	Pensacola, Fla.
Huesser, Huey	1954	E/C	Franklinton, La.
Huettel, Steve	1972-73-74	LB	Knoxville, Tenn.
Huff, Jim	1957	T	Jackson, Miss.
Huff, Robert	1920	HB	Taylorsville, Miss.
Huff, Scott	1981	NG	Brewton, Ala.
Hughes, Bobby	1955-56	QB	Fort Worth, Tex.
Hughes, Shane	1991	WR	Bogalusa, La.
Hultz, Don	1960-61-62	E	Grand Bay, Ala.
Hultz, George	1960-61	T	Grand Bay, Ala.
Hultz, Wilford	1963	E	Grand Bay, Ala.
Hunt, George	1970-71-72	FB/DB	Biloxi, Miss.
Hunter, George (Buddy)	1966-67	G/T	Pensacola, Fla.
Hurdle, Jesse	1933-34-35	G	Holly Springs, Miss.
Hurst, Adam	2003	WR	Mandeville, La.
Hutchins, Pierre	2001-02-03	DB	Tuscaloosa, Ala.

I

	YEAR	POSITION	HOMETOWN
Iosia, Mike	1991-92	DS	Oakland Park, Fla.
Isler, Alan	1967-68-69	HB	Theodore, Ala.
Ivy, Gary	1978-79	DT	Quitman, Miss.
Ivy, Jake	1939-40	T	Bruce, Miss.

J

	YEAR	POSITION	HOMETOWN
Jackson, Chris	1981-82-83-84	DE	Theodore, Ala.
Jackson, Danny	1978-79-80-81	FS	Picayune, Miss.
Jackson, Eddie Ray	1987-88-89-90	TB	Vidalia, La.
Jackson, Joe	1985	TE	Marrero, La.
Jackson, Kevin	1992-93	DT	Magee, Miss.
Jackson, Michael	1988-89-90	WR	Tangipahoa, La.
Jackson, Pat	1986-87-88-89	DE	Coaling, Ala.
Jackson, Quentin	1993-94-95-96	DT	Pensacola, Fla.
Jackson, T. A. (Simp)	1926-27-28-29	FB	Macon, Miss.
Jackson, Wayne	1948	QB	Purvis, Miss.
Jarrell, Billy	1952-53	QB/DB	Picayune, Miss.
Jeffries, Don	1986	DT	Milton, Fla.
Jenevein, Jack	1948-49	C	New Orleans, La.
Jenkins, Charlie (Teddy Bear)	1979-80-81-82	DT	Mendenhall, Miss.
Jimenez, Jason	2000-01-02	OT	Orlando, Fla.
Johnson, Arthur	1932-33	G	Carthage, Miss.
Johnson, Aubrey	1989-90-91-92	DE	Newnan, Ga.
Johnson, Chris	2001-02	WR	Gramercy, La.
Johnson, David Earl	1970-71	DE	Purvis, Miss.
Johnson, J. R.	1919	QB	Cohay, Miss.
Johnson, Johnny	1966-67-68	TB	Pensacola, Fla.
Johnson, Kenny	2000-01-02-03	WR	Gramercy, La.
Johnson, Leroy	2001-02	CB	Gulfport, Miss.
Johnson, Luke	2003	P/PK	Laurel, Miss.
Johnson, Marion C. (Tuffy)	1939-40	B	Lexington, Miss.

	YEAR	POSITION	HOMETOWN
Johnson, Mark	1978-79	C	Brooksville, Fla.
Johnson, Mel	1948	B	Lubbock, Tex.
Johnson, Nick (Doc)	1923-24-25	T/E	Scott County, Miss.
Johnson, Reggie	1985	OT	Collins, Miss.
Johnson, Roland	1990-91	TB	Hattiesburg, Miss.
Johnson, Sam	1973	OG	Andalusia, Ala.
Johnson, Stan	1968-69	TE	Baker, La.
Johnson, Tony	1989	WR	Birmingham, Ala.
Johnston, Frank	1967-68-69	FB/CB	Waynesboro, Miss.
Johnston, Richard	1956-57-58	C/LB	Biloxi, Miss.
Jones, Buster	1930	——	
Jones, Calvin	1977-78-79	FB	Pensacola, Fla.
Jones, Carl	1984-85-86-88	FB	Pensacola, Fla.
Jones, Coemba	1996	DB	Miami, Fla.
Jones, Coty	1993-94	OG	Brierfield, Ala.
Jones, Curt	2002	PK	Greenwood, Miss.
Jones, Dauvard (Dagwood)	1939-40	B	Indianola, Miss.
Jones, G. N.	1930	——	Waynesboro, Miss.
Jones, George W.	1959-60	G	Blakely, Ga.
Jones, Jimmy	1942	——	
Jones, John Wesley	1939-40	T	Lake, Miss.
Jones, Rayshun	2001-02	DT	Tuscaloosa, Ala.
Jones, Ronald	1992-93-94	FB	Birmingham, Ala.
Jones, Ronald	2002-03	DE	Gulfport, Miss.
Jones, Theodore	1938	C	Mangham, La.
Jones, Victor	1933-34	HB	Mize, Miss.
Jordan, Robert (Sonny)	1946-47-48-49	G	Carthage, Miss.
Jordan, Tom	1978	TE	Fort Walton Beach, Fla.
Jordan, Wilmer	1932-33	HB	Carthage, Miss.
Juneau, Curry	1954-55-56-57	E	New Orleans, La.
Junker, Milton	1978-79	OT	New Orleans, La.
Jussely, David	1968-69	DT/DE	Hattiesburg, Miss.
Justesen, Mike	1980-82	DT	Mobile, Ala.

K

Kaiser, Edward (Bubba)	1951-52	HB	Natchez, Miss.
Kaplan, Eddie	1974-75-76	OG	Miami, Fla.
Katrishen, William (Mike)	1941-42-46-47	T	Hazelton, Pa.
Kauchick, Eddie	1949-50-51	FB/LB	Gadsden, Ala.
Keckin, Val	1960	QB	Los Angeles, Calif.
Keith, David	1976	DT	Hattiesburg, Miss.
Keith, Kasey	1994-95-96-97	OL	Jesup, Ga.
Kelley, Greg	1979-80-81-82	LB	Biloxi, Miss.
Kelly, Adam	2003	DS	Hattiesburg, Miss.
Kelly, Jeff	1998-99-2000-01	QB	Deer Park, Ala.
Kemper, Elmer	1949-50-51	G	Blytheville, Ark.
Kemper, Eugene	1948	G	Blytheville, Ark.
Kemper, Robert	1947	——	
Kennedy, Adam	1992-93-94-95	WR	Panama City, Fla.

	YEAR	POSITION	HOMETOWN
Kennet, Ben	1936	—	—
Kenney, Marchant	1994-95-96-97	LB	New Orleans, La.
Kennington, Shelton	1982-83-84	PK	Grenada, Miss.
Key, Kendrick	2000-01	TE/OL	Batesville, Miss.
Key, Radell	1966-68-69	DT	Petal, Miss.
Keys, Correll	1992	WR	Seminary, Miss.
Killingsworth, Emanuel (Killer)	1977-78	CB	Cleveland, Miss.
King	1919	—	—
King, Buddy	1986-87-88-89	OT	Hueytown, Ala.
King, Earl	1965-66	TB	Biloxi, Miss.
King, James	1972	DE	Mullins, S.C.
King, Jim	1963-64	G	Adamsville, Ala.
King, Thomas Rivers	1940	T	Leland, Miss.
Kirke, John	1965	T	Picayune, Miss.
Kirker, George	1942	—	Nettleton, Miss.
Kirkland	1913	—	—
Kirksey, William	1986-87-88-89	LB	Leeds, Ala.
Kirsh, M.	1930	—	—
Kisner, Bernard	1933-34	G/C	Water Valley, Miss.
Kitchen, Jim	1994-95-96-97	TE	Baton Rouge, La.
Klein, Lee	1984	DE	Bay St. Louis, Miss.
Knight, Jake	1923	—	Hattiesburg, Miss.
Knighten, Billy	1985-86	P	Montgomery, Ala.
Knobloch, Donnie	1972	V	Jackson, Miss.
Knox, Bishop	1974-75-76-77	DT	Greenville, Miss.
Koen, Sankey	1930-31-32	G	Brooklyn, Miss.
Kolinsky, Nick	1961-62-63	G	McKees Rocks, Pa.
Kondrat, Ihor (Mike)	1966-67-68	G/PK	Mahwah, N.J.

L

Lacoste, Chris	1990-91	C	Bay St. Louis, Miss.
Ladner, A. R.	1927	G	Poplarville, Miss.
Ladner, Obie	1934-35	T/G	Poplarville, Miss.
Laird, John	1963-64	PK/C	Smithdale, Miss.
Lambert	1924	—	—
Lambright, Maxie	1946-47-48	QB/DB	Houston, Tex.
Lance, Bobby	1957-58	HB	Phillips, Miss.
Landers, Zeb	1999-01	C	Northport, Ala.
Landrum, Mike	1982-83	QB/TE	Columbia, Miss.
Landry, Darrell	1968-70	LB/DE	Bayou La Batre, Ala.
Lane, D. H.	1919	T	Hattiesburg, Miss.
Lang, Elmo	1951-52	E	Magnolia, Miss.
Langford, Eddie	1947-48-49	HB	Hattiesburg, Miss.
Langston, Chris	1999-2000-01-02	LB	Magee, Miss.
Larsen, Billy	1959-60	QB/S	Pascagoula, Miss.
Lasley, Martin	1952	G	Soddy, Tenn.
Latham, Joe	1941-46-47	B	Lawley, Ala.
Latson, Steve	1992-94	DE	Jesup, Ga.
Latta, Randy	1973-74-75	NG	Gardendale, Ala.

	YEAR	POSITION	HOMETOWN
Lauderdale, Keith	1985-86	TB	Jackson, Miss.
Law, Don	1973-74-75-76	CB	Pascagoula, Miss.
Lawrence, Daron	2001-02-03	WR	Orlando, Fla.
Leach, Andy	1935	—	—
Leach, William	1937-38	T	Fulton, Miss.
Lee, Kendrick	1994-95-96	WR	Jackson, La.
Lee, Zack	1919	E	—
Leech, Dewey C.	1923-24	E	Smithville, Miss.
Leech, F. S.	1921-22-23-24	G/E/C	Smithville, Miss.
LeFlore, Jessye	1921	—	Long, Miss.
LeGros, John	1946-47-48	QB/HB	Mobile, Ala.
LeGros, Tom	1948-49-50-51	QB	Mobile, Ala.
Lehman, Howard	1952	—	—
Lenore, Charles	1930	—	—
Letort, Henry	1968-69	DB	Biloxi, Miss.
Lever, John	1930-31-32	E	Macon, Miss.
Lewis, Cliff	1978-79-80	LB	Fort Walton Beach, Fla.
Lewis, L.	1925	—	Grove, La.
Lewis, Lavern (Cooter)	1946-47-48	C	Laurel, Miss.
Lilly, Sale	1948	B	Belzoni, Miss.
Limbaugh, Ernest (Limbo)	1942-46-47-48	T	Hattiesburg, Miss.
Lindley, Jeremy	1996-97	OL	Hueytown, Ala.
Lindsey, Chad	1994-95-96	DS	Liberty, Miss.
Lippincott, Dooney	1963-64-65	FB	Hattiesburg, Miss.
Lipps, Louis	1980-81-82-83	WR	Reserve, La.
Little, Bobby	1959	G	Enterprise, Ala.
Livings, Mike	1978-79-80-81	WR	Montgomery, Ala.
Lockett, Akeem	2002-03	DE	Ripley, Miss.
Lockley, Van	1941	—	Scooba, Miss.
Loescher, Keith	1989-90-91-92	LB	Lynn Haven, Fla.
Logan, Craig	1969-70-71	DB	Hattiesburg, Miss.
Lomoro, Johnny	1992-93-94-95	PK	Midfield, Ala.
Long, Cecil (Buddy)	1958-59-60	T	Ferriday, La.
Long, Larry	1972	E	Quitman, Miss.
Long, Richard	1979-80-81	DT	Toxey, Ala.
Long, Terry	1963	G/C	Carbon Hill, Ala.
Longest, H. B.	1912-13-14	C	Pontotoc, Miss.
Looman, Kevin	1972	DT	Canton, Ohio
Loper, O. B.	1929	—	New Augusta, Miss.
Loper, Roland	1940-41-46	T	Vossburg, Miss.
Lorio, Rene	1959	HB	New Orleans, La.
Lossette, David	1930-31	HB	Picayune, Miss.
Lott, H. V.	1921	G	Seminary, Miss.
Lovette, Vardaman	1939-40	B	Golden, Miss.
Lowe, C. A.	1915	—	Dossville, Miss.
Lumpkin, Lance	1930-31	T	Carriere, Miss.
Lundy, B. R.	1924	—	Poplarville, Miss.
Lynch, Rod	1988-90-91	LB	Meridian, Miss.
Lynch, Wade	1976-77-78	CB	Mobile, Ala.

	YEAR	POSITION	HOMETOWN
Lynn, Frank	1960	G	Moss Point, Miss.
Lyons, Billy	1961-62	E	Mobile, Ala.

M

	YEAR	POSITION	HOMETOWN
MacDonald, Don	1966-67	E	Memphis, Tenn.
Magee, Guy	1942	—	—
Magee, J. W.	1924	T	Prentiss, Miss.
Magee, Roy	1998-99-2000-01	LB	Mandeville, La.
Magee, Skylor	2001-02	DT	Poplarville, Miss.
Magers, Hugh	1936	—	Bentonia, Miss.
Magnum, Arthur J. (Red)	1946-47-48	G	Mendenhall, Miss.
Mahone, Mike	1964	G	Vicksburg, Miss.
Majure, Thomas	1941	C	Meridian, Miss.
Mallard, DeShone	1997-98	CB	Jackson, Miss.
Malone, Dennis	1971-72-73	C	Hattiesburg, Miss.
Malone, Sidney	1965	G	Hattiesburg, Miss.
Mangum, John	1964-65	T	Magee, Miss.
Mann, Bill	1979-80-81	C	Skene, Miss.
Mann, Walter	1951	T	Columbus, Miss.
Manning, J. E.	1926	—	Vance, Miss.
Mapes, Dick	1962	FB	Panama City, Fla.
Mapp, J. H.	1919	—	Hattiesburg, Miss.
Marlowe, Edmund	1942	—	Hattiesburg, Miss.
Marsh, Chafan	1988-89-90-91	G	Bagdad, Fla.
Marshall, William	1939	—	—
Marshall, Xearl (Earl)	1957	E	Greenville, Miss.
Martello, Tony	1929-30-31	FB/E	Hattiesburg, Miss.
Martin	1926	—	—
Martin, Bill	1955-56	C	Cullman, Ala.
Martin, Dawayne	1963	C	Albany, Ga.
Martin, J. H. (Abe)	1920	G	Quitman, Miss.
Martin, James	2001-02	DS	Bogue Chitto, Miss.
Marzula, Joey	1996	DB	Monroe, La.
Mason	1932	—	—
Mason, Bertis (Brick)	1934-35	G	Vossburg, Miss.
Mason, Jim (Brick)	1953-54	HB	Columbia, Miss.
Massengale, A. C. (Mule)	1937-38-39	HB	Hattiesburg, Miss.
Massey, Dwayne	1981-82-83	OT	Jackson, Miss.
Matlock, Jacob	2002-03	PK	Meridian, Miss.
May, George	1927	—	Hattiesburg, Miss.
May, George	1933	B	Decatur, Miss.
May, Jack	1956-57	HB	Milwaukee, Wis.
May, Johnny	1946	—	Liberty, Miss.
Mayfield, C. R.	1915	—	Kosciusko, Miss.
McAdams, Mike	1966-67-68	FB	Pascagoula, Miss.
McAllister, T. F.	1920-21	G	New Albany, Miss.
McAlpin, Jack	1965-66-67	E	Magee, Miss.
McArthur, Charlie	1957-58-59	HB	Laurel, Miss.
McCaleb, Darren	2003	PK	Biloxi, Miss.

	YEAR	POSITION	HOMETOWN
McCall, Tim	1977-78	OG	Montgomery, Ala.
McCarley, Howard	1938-39-40	HB	Baldwyn, Miss.
McCarthy, Milo	1965-66-67	FB	New Orleans, La.
McCarthy, Steve	1973-74-75	V	Olney, Md.
McClammy, Keith	1968-70	DE	East Brewton, Ala.
McClellan, Mike	1964-66	QB	Heidelberg, Miss.
McClendon, Henry	1997-98	OL	Killeen, Tex.
McCleskey, H. L., Jr.	1919-20-22-23	G/C	Hattiesburg, Miss.
McCleskey, J. Warren	1919-20-21-22	QB/E	Hattiesburg, Miss.
McCleskey, James Warren	1926	——	Pascagoula, Miss.
McCollough, Alan	1975-76-77	DT	Austell, Ga.
McCombs, Vic	1980	OG	Birmingham, Ala.
McCormick, Boots	1946-47-48-49	E	Meridian, Miss.
McCoy, Eddie	1978-79-80	OG	Hattiesburg, Miss.
McCrary, J. A. (Shorty)	1920-21	E	Hattiesburg, Miss.
McCrory, Patrick	1998-99-2000	DS	Petal, Miss.
McCullough, Paul	1949-50	G	Corinth, Miss.
McDaniel, Damon	1991-92-93	FB	Biloxi, Miss.
McDaniel, Dane	1977-78-79	QB	Fort Walton Beach, Fla.
McDaniel, Ed	1950-51-52	G	Kentwood, La.
McDay, Willie	1993	OT	Newnan, Ga.
McDonald, Jalce	1932-34-35	T	New Augusta, Miss.
McDonald, C. T.	1915-16	——	McLaurin, Miss.
McDonald, Jalce	1934	T	New Augusta, Miss.
McDowell, Thad	1988-89-90-91	LB	Huntsville, Ala.
McElroy, Bucky	1951-52-53	FB	Monroe, La.
McGee, Chris	1985-86-87	WR	Biloxi, Miss.
McGee, Harvey	1971-72-73	FL	Philadelphia, Pa.
McGee, Howard	1993-94	FB	Hattiesburg, Miss.
McGilvary, H. W.	1921	T	Collins, Miss.
McHenry, Leeman	1954	QB/S	Lucedale, Miss.
McIlwain, Ben	1998	WR	Richton, Miss.
McInnis	1927	——	——
McInnis, Hugh	1957-58-59	E	Leakesville, Miss.
McKay, John	1969-70	OG	Gulfport, Miss.
McKay, M. K.	1923	——	Hervey, Miss.
McKellar, Bob	1950-51-52	E	Plain Desling, La.
McKellar, Fats	1938	T	Locksburg, Ark.
McKenzie, Darrius	2000-01	LB	Dothan, Ala.
McKenzie, Mike	1977-79	LB	Laurel, Miss.
McKinney, Myreon	1992-93	TB	Tuscaloosa, Ala.
McKnight, O. A.	1926-27-28	E	Ringgold, La.
McLaughlin, Fred	1978-79-80	LB	Fort Walton Beach, Fla.
McLemore, Louis	1929-30-31	HB	Petal, Miss.
McLendon, Frank A. (Doc)	1928-29	HB/E	Quitman, Miss.
McLendon, R. D.	1925	C	Quitman, Miss.
McLeod, Andin	1959-60	HB	Leakesville, Miss.
McLeod, Ben	1961-62-63	E/HB	Leakesville, Miss.
McLeod, C. R.	1914-15	——	Mt. Olive, Miss.

	YEAR	POSITION	HOMETOWN
McLeod, Harry	1935	—	—
McLeod, I. M.	1915	—	Bexley, Miss.
McLeod, Mark	1987-88	NT	Hattiesburg, Miss.
McMahan, Brent	1967-68	G/LB	Hattiesburg, Miss.
McMahan, Homer	1926-27-28-29	C/T	Hattiesburg, Miss.
McMillan, Terry	1966-67-68	QB	Magee, Miss.
McPhail, Aubrey	1936-37	B	Mendenhall, Miss.
McPherson, Jamie	1993-94	DT	Grand Saline, Tex.
McRae, Albert	1992-93-94-95	LB	Mableton, Ga.
McRae, H. V.	1912	—	Increase, Miss.
McReynolds, George	1989-90-91	OG	Miami, Fla.
McSwain, Rufus	1941-42	G	Hattiesburg, Miss.
McWhorter	1927	—	—
Mead, Neal	2003	OT	Collins, Miss.
Meador, Claiborne G.	1912	—	Hattiesburg, Miss.
Meador, John	1967	T	Hattiesburg, Miss.
Meador, Morris	1959-60-61	QB/S	Butler, Ala.
Means, Marc	1979-80-81-82	WR	Jackson, Miss.
Medders, Bryant	1988-89	DE	Centreville, Ala.
Meeks, John	1951-52	C	Kossuth, Miss.
Meeks, Lawrence	1954-55-56-57	HB/PK	Kossuth, Miss.
Megehee, Lewis D. (Maggie)	1928-29	E	Picayune, Miss.
Melton, Davis	1949	HB	Tallassee, Ala.
Melton, John	1963-64-65	T	Baker, Fla.
Melton, Tommy	1964-65	T	Pascagoula, Miss.
Messer, Otho	1916	—	Sumrall, Miss.
Metevia, Tim	1994	OT	Port Allen, La.
Meyer, Fred	1970-71-72	V	Alice, Tex.
Miciotto, Buck	1999-2000-01-02	OG	Lafayette, La.
Miciotto, Gus	1948	G	Shreveport, La.
Mikel, Billy	1968-69-70	SE	Fort Walton Beach, Fla.
Miles, Russell	1969	QB	Wiggins, Miss.
Miller, Bruce	1980-81-82-83	CB	Ackerman, Miss.
Miller, Ray	1925	E	Foxworth, Miss.
Miller, Tim	1990-91	NG	Quitman, Miss.
Milling, Clarence L. (Red)	1923-24-25	E	Neshoba, Miss.
Milling, H. C.	1929	—	McLain, Miss.
Mills, Shawn	1999-2000	WR	Enid, Okla.
Mills, W. W.	1926	HB	New Augusta, Miss.
Millum	1923	—	—
Milner, Jay	1947	T	—
Milner, William W.	1912-13	—	Hattiesburg, Miss.
Mims, Doug	1952-53	—	Greenwood, Miss.
Mitchell, Gary	1974	FL	Conshohocken, Pa.
Mitchell, J. Hugh	1953-54	T	Picayune, Miss.
Mitchell, Landon	1939-40	G	Louisville, Miss.
Mitchell, Mike	1997	PK	Navarre, Fla.
Mitchell, Porter	1975-76	OT	Birmingham, Ala.
Mitchell, W. D.	1925	E	De Kalb, Miss.

	YEAR	POSITION	HOMETOWN
Mitcherson, Jim	1951	QB	Winfield, Ala.
Mize, Bobby	1991	NG	Meridian, Miss.
Moffett, Jackie	1980-81	TB/WR	Taylorsville, Miss.
Molden, Fred	1983	DT	Moss Point, Miss.
Monroe, Matt	1991-92	LB	Sanford, N.C.
Montague, Frank	1912	——	Hattiesburg, Miss.
Montgomery, Billy Hugh	1953	B	Hattiesburg, Miss.
Montgomery, Carlos	1973-74-75-76	FB	Bay Minette, Ala.
Montgomery, Jim	1972-73	FL	Croyden, Pa.
Montgomery, John	1919	HB	Hattiesburg, Miss.
Montgomery, Mark	1990-92-93-94	WR	Picayune, Miss.
Moon, Mike	1971-72-73	OT	Atlanta, Ga.
Moore, Barney	1947-48	C	McComb, Miss.
Moore, Ernie	1998	OL/TE	Slidell, La.
Moore, Keon	1998-99-2000	CB	Wiggins, Miss.
Moore, Red	1938	G	Carthage, Miss.
Moore, Sherron	2003	RB	Calhoun City, Miss.
Moore, Tom	1970-71-72	LB	Gulfport, Miss.
Moore, Willie B.	1981-82-83-84	DE	Noxapater, Miss.
Moorer, Carey	1990-91-92-93	OT	Vestavia, Ala.
Morgan, Audice D. (Sandy)	1937-38-39	T	Liberty, Miss.
Morgan, Earl (Harlow)	1936-37	T	Summitt, Miss.
Morgan, Fred	1923	——	Hattiesburg, Miss.
Morgan, Joe	1948	T	Meridian, Miss.
Morgan, Patrick	1996	DB	Samson, Ala.
Morrow, Tommy	1958-59-60	HB/S	Georgiana, Ala.
Mott, Andrew	1983-84-85-86	WR	Hattiesburg, Miss.
Moulton, Larry	1968-69-70	HB	Andalusia, Ala.
Moyer, Paul	1949-50	T	Columbus, Miss.
Mullin, Jerry (Buster)	1946-47	B	Bogalusa, La.
Mullis, Fred	1946	——	——
Mumford, Gerald	1997-98-99-2000	DE/DT	Jackson, Miss.
Murray, Lewis	1950	C	Purvis, Miss.
Muscarello, Phil	1950-52	C	Baton Rouge, La.
Musmeci, Phil (Moose)	1948-49-50-51	G	New Orleans, La.

N

	YEAR	POSITION	HOMETOWN
Nall, Herman	1962-63-64	TB	Alexandria, La.
Nance, Kelby	1997-98-99-2000	TB	Hattiesburg, Miss.
Naron, Braskel	1940-41	B	Cleveland, Miss.
Nathan, Boobie	1986	TB	Mobile, Ala.
Nations, Lance	1991-92	PK	Tampa, Fla.
Neill, John	1952-53	G/T	Philadelphia, Miss.
Nelson, Dwayne	1989-90-91-92	FB	Hattiesburg, Miss.
Neville, George	1947	——	Meridian, Miss.
Newberry, Art	1978-79-80	CB	Pensacola, Fla.
Newman, Kent	1976	S	Crystal Springs, Miss.
Nichols, John	1989-90-91	CB	Meridian, Miss.
Nichols, William	1947-48	E	Athens, Ala.

	YEAR	POSITION	HOMETOWN
Nix, A. L.	1926-27	E	Hamilton, Miss.
Nix, Derrick	1998-99-2000-02	TB	Attala, Ala.
Nix, John	1997-98-99-2000	DT	Lucedale, Miss.
Nix, Tyrone	1990-91-92-93	LB	Attala, Ala.
Nobles, Benny Ray	1946-47-48	HB	Hattiesburg, Miss.
Nobles, Herbert Ray	1951-52	T	Sumrall, Miss.
Nolan, Timirra	1997-98	TE	Brewton, Ala.
Norris, Jim	1957	G	Hattiesburg, Miss.
Norsworthy, Lamar	1930	—	Hattiesburg, Miss.
Northam, Ricky	1974-76-77	LB/DE	Meridian, Miss.
Norton	1922	B	—
Norton, Larry	1993-94-95-96	TE	Dothan, Ala.
Novak, Jeff	1992-93	OG	Fayette, Ala.
Nunez, Eddie	1974-75-76	DT	Lafayette, La.
Nunn, Terry	1993-94	LB	Mobile, Ala.
Nyers, Jim	1974-75	QB	Pascagoula, Miss.

O

	YEAR	POSITION	HOMETOWN
Oakes, Houston	1950-51	HB	Jackson, Miss.
Oakley, Tracy	1984-85	NG	Toledo, Ill.
O'Barr, Rod	1981-82-83	LB	Birmingham, Ala.
Odom, Archie	1935-36	FB	Brooklyn, Miss.
Odom, David	1977-78-79	SS	Miami, Fla.
Odom, Reggie	1974-75-76-77	DE	Deland, Fla.
Olander, Mike	1960-61	HB	McKees Rocks, Pa.
Oliver, Maurice	1985-86-87-88	DE	Bessemer, Ala.
Ollison, Rod	1993-94-95	OG	Greenville, Ala.
Olson, Billy	1972-73-74-75	V	Gulfport, Miss.
O'Mara, B. B. (Opp)	1919-20	C	—
O'Neal, Silas	1985-86-87	NG	Carthage, Miss.
Oradat, Larry	1972	OT	Marion, Ind.
Orange, Doyle	1971-72-73	HB	Waycross, Ga.
Orphan, Dino	1954-55	G	Montgomery, Ala.
Orrell, Sonny	1968	DB	Charleston, Miss.
Ott, A. D.	1932-33-34	C	Hattiesburg, Miss.
Ott, Sam	1930	E	Osyka, Miss.
Oubre, Willie (Kemper County Flash)	1936-37-38	B	Scooba, Miss.
Ovca, Joe	1939-40	B	Springfield, Ill.
Overby, A. H.	1929-30-31	T	Mize, Miss.
Overby, M. E.	1929-30-31	T/G	Mendenhall, Miss.
Owen, Jim Ray	1949	FB	Nowata, Okla.
Owen, Joe	1961-62-63	G	Blakely, Ga.
Owens, Anthony	1991-92-93	TE	Auburn, Ala.
Owens, Don	1953-54-55-56	T	St. Louis, Mo.
Owings, A. D.	1926	T	Hattiesburg, Miss.

P

	YEAR	POSITION	HOMETOWN
Pace, Chal	1981-83-84-85	LB/DE	New Orleans, La.
Palazzo, Buddy	1970-71-72	QB	Gulfport, Miss.

	YEAR	POSITION	HOMETOWN
Palmer, Danny	1969-70	QB	Tyler, Tex.
Palmer, Jonathan	2003	DE	Tyler, Tex.
Palmer, Ricky	1972-73-74-75	TE/P/PK	Tyler, Tex.
Parker, Anthony (Stoney)	1975-76-77-78	DT	Mt. Meigs, Ala.
Parker, Charles	1947	T	—
Parker, Charlie	1961-62-63	T	Chickasaw, Ala.
Parker, Doug	1970-71-72	FL	Collinsville, Miss.
Parker, W. L.	1921-22	FB	—
Parquet, Jeremy	2001-02-03	OT	Norco, La.
Parrish, David	1976-77	C	Savannah, Tenn.
Parrish, Terrance	1996-97-98-99	CB	Theodore, Ala.
Parsons, A. H.	1919-20	G	—
Patrick, Malcolm	1935-36-37	B	Alton, Ill.
Patterson	1928	—	—
Patterson, Pat	1946	E	Mobile, Ala.
Paul, Terrell	2000-01-02-03	DE	Troy, Ala.
Payne, Jim	1960-61	T	Pensacola, Fla.
Peacock, R. V.	1916	HB	Pinola, Miss.
Pears, LeVon	2001-02-03	DE	Mobile, Ala.
Pearson, Joe	1987	DB	Laurel, Miss.
Pearson, Ryan	1993-94-95	WR	Bainbridge, Ga.
Peck, Gabe	1988-89-90	SS	Mobile, Ala.
Pendarvis, Sylvester	1936-37	C	Hammond, La.
Pepper, Hugh Laurin	1952-53	HB	Benton, Miss.
Perine, Anthony	2003	WR	Lucedale, Miss.
Perkins, John	1957-58	T	Calhoun, Miss.
Pertero, J. T.	1920	E	—
Phenix, Perry	1996-97	DB	Dallas, Tex.
Phillips, Jerome	1936	—	Purvis, Miss.
Phillips, John Melvin (Bubba)	1947-48-49-50	HB	Macon, Miss.
Phillips, Ken	1970-71	DT	Manchester, Ga.
Phillips, Otto (Hippo)	1933-34-35	T	Hattiesburg, Miss.
Phillips, P. E.	1912	E	Rawl Springs, Miss.
Phillips, Quantrellis	1996-97	DL	Griffin, Ga.
Phillips, Ricky	1982	CB	Noxapater, Miss.
Phillips, Robert	1980-81	DE	Ellisville, Miss.
Pieper, Chris	1974-76	FL	Dunwoody, Ga.
Pieper, Greg	1974-75	FL	Dunwoody, Ga.
Pierce, Chris	1994-95	PK	Jackson, Miss.
Pigott	1922	HB	—
Pigott, Bud	1963	T	Picayune, Miss.
Pinkston, Joey	1999-2000	WR/FS	Forest, Miss.
Pinkston, Todd	1996-97-98-99	WR	Forest, Miss.
Pitts, John	1975-76-77	TE	Waynesboro, Miss.
Plunkett, Wilson	1971-72-73	FB	Aiken, S.C.
Pogue, Tony	1986-87-88-89	LB	Pearl, Miss.
Pollard, Lytrel	1994-95-96-97	LB	Bay Springs, Miss.
Pope, Marcus	1990-91	TE	Hattiesburg, Miss.
Pope, Moran	1912	—	Columbia, Miss.

	YEAR	POSITION	HOMETOWN
Pope, Moran	1942	—	Hattiesburg, Miss.
Pope, O'Lester	1995-96-97-98	OL	Utica, Miss.
Portis, Willie	1982-85	OG	Meridian, Miss.
Posey, Bobby	1951-52-53	HB	Philadelphia, Miss.
Posey, Jeff	1995-96	DE	Bassfield, Miss.
Poulin, Mike	1981-82-83-84	TE	Mobile, Ala.
Powe, Myron	2001-02-03	OL	Camden, Ala.
Powell	1937	—	—
Powell, Carlos	1985-86-87	TE	Lumberton, Miss.
Powell, Raymond	1979-80-81-82	TE	Columbia, Miss.
Powers, Carley	1973	LB	Memphis, Tenn.
Prestage, Aaron	1939-40	E	Golden, Miss.
Price	1932	—	—
Price, David	1968-69-70	OG	Clarkston, Ga.
Pruitt, Etric	2000-01-02-03	FS	Theodore, Ala.
Pugh, Dan	1959-60-61	FB	Yazoo City, Miss.
Pumphrey, Charles	1995-96	OL	Donalsonville, Ga.
Purnell, Frank	1948	G	Meridian, Miss.
Purser, Jamie	1996-97-98-99	P	Red Bay, Ala.
Purvis	1924	—	—
Purvis, Leo	1935-36	FB/QB	Puckett, Miss.
Purvis, Robert	1934	—	—
Purvis, Tommy	1958-59	HB	Ferriday, La.
Purvis, Vic	1963-64-65	QB	Puckett, Miss.

Q

	YEAR	POSITION	HOMETOWN
Querner, William	1948	T	Vernon, Tex.
Quick, Henry	1967-68-69	HB/DE	New Orleans, La.

R

	YEAR	POSITION	HOMETOWN
Randle, E. E.	1927	C	New Albany, Miss.
Rankin, Steve	1987-88	DT	Magee, Miss.
Rankins, LaBarion	1991-92-93	CB	Mobile, Ala.
Ratcliff, Melvin	1992-93-94-95	S	Hattiesburg, Miss.
Ratesic, John	1960-61	C	McKeesport, Pa.
Ray, Alex	2000-01-02-03	DB	Vicksburg, Miss.
Ray, Kenny	1992-93-94	C	Irondale, Ala.
Rayburn, Gary	1967-68-69	QB	Gulfport, Miss.
Rayman, Gerald	1940	—	Winter City, Miss.
Redd, Eric	1985-86	LB	Brandon, Miss.
Reed, Greg	1988-89-90-91	WR	Gulfport, Miss.
Reed, Rod	1988-89-90-91	DE	Eight Mile, Ala.
Reeves, Bryan	1997	PK	Moulton, Ala.
Reeves, John H.	1913	—	Bogue Chitto, Miss.
Reynolds	1913	—	—
Reynolds, Carl	1934-35	C	Ellisville, Miss.
Reynolds, Henry (Hindu)	1947-48	E	Starkville, Miss.
Reynolds, Marvin	1940	B	Springfield, Ill.
Rhed, Bobby	1951-52	T	McComb, Miss.

	YEAR	POSITION	HOMETOWN
Rial, Robbie	1986	SS	Tupelo, Miss.
Rice, Wiley	1962-63	E	Hemphill, Tex.
Rich, John	1937-38-39	B	Sumrall, Miss.
Rich, Larry	1954-55-56	G	Pell City, Ala.
Richards, Fred	1980-82-83-84	OG	Bessemer, Ala.
Richards, Mike	1985	WR/K	College Park, Ga.
Richardson, Eric	1983	DB	Birmingham, Ala.
Richardson, Milton	1983	WR	Gautier, Miss.
Ricks, Troy A.	1971-72-73	OT	Raymond, Miss.
Riley, E. J.	1912	G	Sumrall, Miss.
Riley, Karlin	2002	WR	Opelousas, La.
Rinehart, Bob	1957-58-59	G/FB	Brewton, Ala.
Roberts, Bill	1961	E/FB	Purvis, Miss.
Roberts, C. C.	1916	HB	Biloxi, Miss.
Roberts, Chris	1992-93	OT	Meridian, Miss.
Roberts, E. S.	1916	E	Arena, Miss.
Roberts, Gary	1972-73-74	LB	Sevierville, Tenn.
Roberts, Lee	1995-96-97-98	QB	Pace, Fla.
Roberts, M. M.	1916	E	Arena, Miss.
Roberts, Tim	1988-89-90-91	DT	Atlanta, Ga.
Roberts, Will	1990-91	WR	Pine Bluff, Ark.
Robertson	1937	——	
Robertson, Jonathan	1984-85-86	CB	Carriere, Miss.
Robinson, James	1992-93-94-95	DE	Mobile, Ala.
Robinson, Lucius (Roble)	1946	T	French Camp, Miss.
Rockwell, Ernest (Bishop)	1941	G	Selma, Ala.
Rodman, George	1964-65	E	Levittown, Pa.
Rodriguez, Tony	1971	OG	Belle Glade, Fla.
Rogers, Albert	1926-27	FB	Hattiesburg, Miss.
Rollins, Vincent	1985-86-87-88	SS	Slidell, La.
Romo, Joe	1947	QB/B	New York, N.Y.
Rosamond, Ivan	1949-50	E	Canton, Miss.
Rosello, Dennis	1974	QB	Bridgeton, N.J.
Rouchon, Tony	1950-51-52	HB	Pensacola, Fla.
Rouse, Doug	1968-69	DB	Hattiesburg, Miss.
Roussel, Tommy	1965-66-67	E/LB	Thibodeaux, La.
Rowan, T. J.	1913-14-15	——	Wesson, Miss.
Rowell, Eugene	1991-92-93	WR	Auburn, Ala.
Rowells	1922	T	——
Ruffin, Chad	2001-02-03	NT	New Orleans, La.
Russell, G. H.	1926-27	T	Hattiesburg, Miss.
Russell, John T.	1956-57-58	G	Monticello, Miss.
Russell, Reggie	1989-90-91	DT	Rolling Fork, Miss.
Rutherford, Rudy	1937	——	
Ryals, Chris	1988-89-90-91	OT	Purvis, Miss.

S

Sadler	1924	——	Hattiesburg, Miss.
Saggus, Gerry	1972-73	HB	North Augusta, S.C.

	YEAR	POSITION	HOMETOWN
Salmon, Dan	1960-61-62	T	Adamsville, Ala.
Salter	1932	—	—
Samples, Eual	1933	HB	—
Sanders, Al (Apple)	1947-48	C	Baton Rouge, La.
Sanders, George	1999	DB	Seattle, Wash.
Sanders, Stanley	1975-76	OG	Montgomery, Ala.
Satcher, Doug	1964-65-66	LB	Sandersville, Miss.
Saucier	1932	T/G	—
Sawyer, John	1972-73-74	TE	Baker, La.
Scalzo, Chester	1935-36	T	Long Branch, N.J.
Schiro, Mike	1980-81-82-83	SS	New Orleans, La.
Schnider, Billy	1987	TE	Fort Walton Beach, Fla.
Schoeneck, Joe	1967-68	OT	Jackson, Miss.
Schwartz, Bobby	1942	—	—
Scott, Cedric	1997-98-99-2000	DE	Gulfport, Miss.
Scott, DeQuincy	1997-98-99-2000	DT	LaPlace, La.
Scott, Deric	1997-98-99-2000	DT	Monroeville, Ala.
Scott, Eric	1998-99	LB	Monroeville, Ala.
Scott, Eric	2001-02-03	DT	Scottsboro, Ala.
Scott, Jake	1936-37-38	G	Scooba, Miss.
Scott, Maxie	1941	B	Forest, Miss.
Scott, P. C.	1921-23	E	Hattiesburg, Miss.
Sears, Corey	1998	LB	Montgomery, Ala.
Seay, Scott	1980-81-82	NG	Fort Walton Beach, Fla.
Seegars, James D.	1939-40	—	Winfield, Ala.
Sekul, George	1957-58	QB	Biloxi, Miss.
Sekul, George	1961-62-63	FB	Biloxi, Miss.
Seligman, Harvey	1955-56	FB	Brooklyn, N.Y.
Sellers, Davy	1979-80-81	QB	Lucedale, Miss.
Seroka, Chris	1986-87-88	PK	Slidell, La.
Seymour, Nicky	1993-94-95-96	WR/CB	Ocean Springs, Miss.
Shackelford, Craig	1986-87	TB	Decatur, Ala.
Shannon, Karr	1995-96-97	DB	Hammond, La.
Sharpe, Al (Razor)	1948-49	E	Tupelo, Miss.
Shattles, Otis	1953	T	Moss Point, Miss.
Shaw, Eddie	1995-96-97-98	WR	Magee, Miss.
Shaw, Harold	1994-95-96-97	TB	Magee, Miss.
Shaw, Sherrard	1947-48	FB	McComb, Miss.
Sheffield, Joe	1925	QB	Ratliff, Miss.
Shenk, Rodney	1959-60	G	Loxley, Ala.
Shepherd, Bob	1967-68-69	OT	Melbourne, Fla.
Shepherd, J. T.	1952-53	G	Moss Point, Miss.
Sherron, Jay	1985-86-87	DT	Bessemer, Ala.
Shields, Richard	1933-34-35	E	Pelahatchie, Miss.
Shirley, Lewis	1930	T	Hattiesburg, Miss.
Shoemake, Billy	1992	DB	Collins, Miss.
Short, Scott	1984-85-86	OT	Hueytown, Ala.
Shows, Carroll	1932-33	T	Moselle, Miss.
Shows, W. T.	1914	—	Hattiesburg, Miss.

	YEAR	POSITION	HOMETOWN
Silas, Melvin	1977-78-79	TE	Purvis, Miss.
Simmons, Edgar	1939	—	Magnolia, Miss.
Simmons, Gordon	1941-42	C	Alexandria, Ala.
Simmons, Jonathan	2002	TE	Jasper, Ala.
Sims, Chuck	1986-87-88-89	NT	Marianna, Fla.
Sims, Emmett	1938-39	E	DeQuincy, La.
Sims, Sawyer	1941	G/C	Frisco City, Ala.
Singleton, James	1989-90-91-92	DE	Wilmer, Ala.
Sizemore, Stacy	1991-92	LB	Vicksburg, Miss.
Sklopan, Johnny	1960-61-62	HB	Pittsburgh, Pa.
Slater, Rick	1985-86	OT	Mobile, Ala.
Slaughter, T. J.	1995-97-98-99	LB	Birmingham, Ala.
Slaughter, Ulysses	1984-85-86-87	NG	Jackson, Miss.
Slay, Glyn	1947-48	E	Hazelhurst, Miss.
Smallwood, Fred	1953-54-55	HB	Laurel, Miss.
Smith, Boo	1974-76	FL	Lancaster, Pa.
Smith, Bracie	1936-37	E	Brookhaven, Miss.
Smith, Butch	1977-78-79-80	OG	Starkville, Miss.
Smith, Carl	1947-48-49	G	Lubbock, Tex.
Smith, Chandler	1996-97	DB	Vicksburg, Miss.
Smith, Charles J.	1935-36	T	Lucedale, Miss.
Smith, Darian	1992-93	OG	Natchez, Miss.
Smith, Doug	1934-35	E/G	Duck Hill, Miss.
Smith, Eric	1974-75-76-77	OT	Orlando, Fla.
Smith, Eugene	1912-13	T	Raleigh, Miss.
Smith, Jay	1946-47	E	Brookhaven, Miss.
Smith, Mike	1973	DT	Brookhaven, Miss.
Smith, Roosevelt (Kip)	1983-84-85	DT	Vicksburg, Miss.
Smith, Roy (Shiney)	1946-47-48	QB	Mart, Tex.
Smith, Stacy	1991-92	FB	McComb, Miss.
Smith, Tim	1983-84-85-86	CB	Mendenhall, Miss.
Smith, Tony	1989-90-91	TB/WR	Vicksburg, Miss.
Smith, W. C.	1916-19-20	E/B	Perkinston, Miss.
Smith, William (Bee)	1937-38	B/QB	Brookhaven, Miss.
Smith, Willie	1931	HB	Poplarville, Miss.
Smithart, Bobby	1975-76-77	DE	Vicksburg, Miss.
Snell, Reese (Ape)	1947-48-49	G	Bonita, Miss.
Soberski, Ed	1969-70-71	HB	Clark Summit, Pa.
Spence, Arnold	1958-59-60	HB	Picayune, Miss.
Spence, William	1931	QB	Hattiesburg, Miss.
Spencer, Ken	1985-86	DE	Birmingham, Ala.
Speracino, Jack	1953-54	C	Monassen, Pa.
Speyrer, Mark	1974	QB	Lafayette, La.
Spigener, C. W.	1926	HB	Vance, Miss.
Spruiell, Frank	1948-49	QB/DB	Lawton, Okla.
St. Pierre, Ray	1959-60	G	New Orleans, La.
Stabler, Roy	1993-94-95	FS	Jackson, Ala.
Stallings, Robert Ray	1982-83-84-85	TE	Magnolia, Miss.
Stampley, Walter	1948	FB	Natchez, Miss.

	YEAR	POSITION	HOMETOWN
Stanley, George	1923	HB	—
Starnes, Joey	1977-79	TE	Largo, Fla.
Stephen, Marty	1975	LB	Huntington, Ind.
Stevens, Arnold	1941-42	T	Monroeville, Ala.
Stevens, Craig	1973-75-76	DT	Horsham, Pa.
Stevens, George	1947-48	T/E	Hogoton, Kan.
Stevens, Joe	1932	—	Itta Bena, Miss.
Stevens, Robert	1947-48	T	Hazelhurst, Miss.
Steward	1926	—	—
Stewart, Argile	1930	E	—
Stewart, Brunnus	1930-31	C/E	—
Stewart, Daleroy	1997-98-99-2000	DT	Vero Beach, Fla.
Stewart, J. J.	1976-77-78-79	DT	Hattiesburg, Miss.
Stewart, L.	1931	C	Lumberton, Miss.
Stewart, Lindy	1949-50-51	HB	Lakeland, Fla.
Stewart, Naton	2002-03	WR/LB	Vero Beach, Fla.
Stewart, William	1948	HB	McComb, Miss.
Stonestreet, J. D.	1934-35	HB	Goodman, Miss.
Strain, Richard	1948	E	Weatherford, Tex.
Stringer, Jim	1969	C	Madison, Miss.
Stringfellow, Joe	1939-40-41	E	Meridian, Miss.
Stringfellow, Julius (Poochie)	1964-65-66	G	Lucedale, Miss.
Stromas, Carsha	2001-02-03	DB	Cantonment, Fla.
Stuart, Claude	1926	QB	Hattiesburg, Miss.
Stubbs, Nevin	1935	—	Magee, Miss.
Sullivan, C. W.	1912	—	Hattiesburg, Miss.
Sullivan, Vinson	1957-58	T	Mt. Olive, Miss.
Summers, C. L.	1915	—	Marietta, Miss.
Sumrall, George	1965-66	PK/FB	Biloxi, Miss.
Sumrall, T. D.	1921-23	G	Laurel, Miss.
Supple, Buddy	1957-58-59	FB	Hope Hull, Ala.
Surace, Dicky	1968-69-70	OG/LB	Franklin, Va.
Surtain, Patrick	1994-95-96-97	CB	New Orleans, La.
Switzer, Reginald	1939-40	OL	Gulfport, Miss.
Symmes, Will	1993-94-95	C/DS	Gulfport, Miss.

T

	YEAR	POSITION	HOMETOWN
Taconi, Nolan	1932-33-34	HB	Bay St. Louis, Miss.
Tally, Paul	1924-25	—	Hattiesburg, Miss.
Tapper, Clinton	1971-72-73	OG	Biloxi, Miss.
Tapper, John T.	1971-72	DE	Biloxi, Miss.
Tate, Eddie	1973-74-75	SE	Roswell, Ga.
Tate, Fred (Chubby)	1995-96	DE	Hattiesburg, Miss.
Taylor	1925	—	—
Taylor, C. J. (Pete)	1941-46	E	New Orleans, La.
Taylor, Doug	1948-49	—	—
Taylor, E. S.	1915	—	Gulfport, Miss.
Taylor, Jerry	1954-55-56	E	Columbia, Miss.
Taylor, Jim (Stump)	1988-89-90-91	PK	Laurel, Miss.

	YEAR	POSITION	HOMETOWN
Taylor, Jimmy	1956-57-58	G	Biloxi, Miss.
Taylor, Larry	1979	SE	Pascagoula, Miss.
Taylor, Larry	1998	DB	Savannah, Ga.
Taylor, Ronald (Clump)	1976-77-78-79	LB	Jackson, Miss.
Teague, Albert	1977-78-79	NG	St. Petersburg, Fla.
Tenore, Jim	1927	E	Hattiesburg, Miss.
Terrell, Clemon	1980-81-82-83	FB	Hattiesburg, Miss.
Terrell, Darryl	1995-96	OL	Heidelburg, Miss.
Thames, Richard (Dick)	1941-46	G	Mendenhall, Miss.
Thatch, George	1912-13-14	T	Rawl Springs, Miss.
Thicklen, Willie	1973	SE	Fairhope, Ala.
Thigpen, Doug	1987-88-89	DB	Gulfport, Miss.
Thomas	1925	—	
Thomas, Adalius	1996-97-98-99	DE	Equality, Ala.
Thomas, Albert Pat	1939-40	E	Newton, Miss.
Thomas, Arnold	1968-69-70	HB/FL	Vicksburg, Miss.
Thomas, Brownie	1928-30-31	C	Lumberton, Miss.
Thomas, Jim	1960-61	G	E. McKeesport, Pa.
Thomas, Norris	1972-73-74-75	CB	Pascagoula, Miss.
Thomas, Percy	1929	—	Hattiesburg, Miss.
Thomas, Rod	1993-94-95	CB	Ridgeland, Miss.
Thomas, Sam	1986-87-88	DT	Jackson, Miss.
Thompson, Bruce	1979-80-81-82	P	Huntsville, Ala.
Thompson, D. D.	1981	TB	Biloxi, Miss.
Thompson, Jack	1912-13-14-15	G	Hattiesburg, Miss.
Thompson, Kevin	1999	WR	Dumas, Ark.
Thompson, Steve	1989-90	FB	Gulfport, Miss.
Thornton, Gordon	1952	G	Tunica, Miss.
Tillman, Darryl	1986-87-88-89	WR	Wiggins, Miss.
Tillman, George (Too-Tall)	1979-80-81-82	DE	Natchez, Miss.
Tisdale, Brooks	1953	HB	Moselle, Miss.
Tobias, Michael	1991-92-93-94	DT	Jefferson, La.
Tolbert, Larry	1966-67	T	Magee, Miss.
Tompkins, Clinton	1968-69	OG	Kilmichael, Miss.
Toomey, Erskine	1951-52-53	E	Hattiesburg, Miss.
Touchstone, G. R.	1913-14-15-16	G	Laurel, Miss.
Trahan, Tommy	1977-78	DB	Morgan City, La.
Trahan, Ty	1996-97-98-99	LB	Carriere, Miss.
Trantham, C. G. (Nub)	1923	C	Booneville, Miss.
Travis, Roy	1985	K	Purvis, Miss.
Tregle, Al	1954-55-56	G	Metairie, La.
Trimm, Ferrell	1999	QB	Amory, Miss.
Triplett, Calvin	1946	HB	Picayune, Miss.
Trone, Elbert	1966-67	LB	Biloxi, Miss.
Tuccio, Sam	1956-57-58	T	Vicksburg, Miss.
Tucker, Butler (Sonny)	1957-58-59	E	Columbus, Miss.
Tucker, Joe	1978	NG	Jackson, Miss.
Tucker, R. H.	1922-24-25	FB/HB	Laurel, Miss.
Tucker, Torrin	1999-2000-01-02	OL	Meridian, Miss.

	YEAR	POSITION	HOMETOWN
Tuggle, Joe	1968-69	C	Hattiesburg, Miss.
Tujaque, J. M., Jr.	1924	QB	Biloxi, Miss.
Tullis, Willie	1977	QB	Newville, Ala.
Turner, Claude	1912	B	Hattiesburg, Miss.
Turner, Louis	1937	—	
Tynes, John	1937	G	Louin, Miss.

U

	YEAR	POSITION	HOMETOWN
Ulmer, Terryl	1990-92	CB	Laurel, Miss.
Ulrich, Paul	1999	OL	Pearl, Miss.
Underwood, George	1958-59	T	Cordova, Ala.
Underwood, P. W.	1954-55-56	T	Cordova, Ala.
Urquhart, Don	1999-02	PK	Mobile, Ala.
Ussery, Larry	1966-67-68	CB	Shreveport, La.

V

	YEAR	POSITION	HOMETOWN
Valrie, Kerry	1987-88-89-90	SS	Loxley, Ala.
Van Hook, Cloyd	1937	B	Ruston, La.
Van Tone, Art	1939-40-41–42	B	Gary, Ind.
Vance, Toby	1967-68	TE	Ackerman, Miss.
Vaughn, Blake	1993	OG	Livingston, Ala.
Vaughn, Chris	1999-2000-01	LB	Marrero, La.
Veal, Marshall	1970-71-72	WB	Atlanta, Ga.
Venable, L. S.	1912	HB	Hattiesburg, Miss.
Verdell, David	1997-98	LB	Columbus, Miss.
Vetrano, Joe	1940-41–42	B	Neptune, N.J.
Vige, Maxie	1998	OL	Eunice, La.
Villalonga, Michael	1997-98-99	LB	Miami, Fla.
Vincent, Arno	1937-38	L/B	Meridian, Miss.
Vines, M. R.	1921-22	G	Smithville, Miss.
Vinson, James	1919	E	Biloxi, Miss.
Vracken, Van	1932	C	—

W

	YEAR	POSITION	HOMETOWN
Waites, Al	1923-25	HB	Louin, Miss.
Waites, Donnie	1956-57	E	Hattiesburg, Miss.
Waites, Edgar	1924-25	T	Louin, Miss.
Waites, Fred	1946-47-48	G	Billingsley, Ala.
Waites, Otis	1925-26	E	Louin, Miss.
Waldvogel, Perry	1941-42	B	Ellisville, Miss.
Walker, David Lee	1950-51-52	QB	Alexandria, La.
Walker, Eddie Ray	1979-80-81-82	FS	Pascagoula, Miss.
Walker, Harry	1930	—	
Walker, Ken	1959-60	E	Bourg, La.
Walker, Tracy	1935-36-37	G	Goodman, Miss.
Walker, W. H.	1923	—	
Walker, Winston	1979-80	PK	McComb, Miss.
Wallace, Charles	1942	—	Hattiesburg, Miss.
Wallace, William	1940	B	—

	YEAR	POSITION	HOMETOWN
Walley, James	2001-02-03	TB	State Line, Miss.
Walls, Raymond	1997-98-99-2000	CB	Kentwood, La.
Walters, Tommy	1962-63	HB	Petal, Miss.
Walthaw, Cedric	1993-94-95-96	LB	McCalla, Ala.
Walton, Linn	1938	FB	Bogalusa, La.
Ward, Bill	1953	C	Booneville, Miss.
Warner, Bill	1974-75-76-77	C	Miami, Fla.
Warner, Pop	1948	B	Louisville, Miss.
Warnsley, Reginald	1988-89	FB	Bay Springs, Miss.
Warren, Joey	1977	NG/DT	Panama City, Fla.
Washington, Ben	1987-88-89-90	CB	Jackson, Miss.
Waters, Fred	1946-47-48	HB	Benton, Miss.
Waters, Hub	1952-53-54	E	Benton, Miss.
Waters, Melvin (Bucky)	1941-46-47	T	Benton, Miss.
Waters, Tommy	1991-92-93-94	QB	Meridian, Miss.
Watkins, Buddy	1947	E	Hattiesburg, Miss.
Watkins, Warren	1946	——	Hattiesburg, Miss.
Watson, Clint	1984	FB	Enterprise, Ala.
Watson, Jamey	1977-78-79-80	C	Montgomery, Ala.
Watson, Milton	1942	——	Hattiesburg, Miss.
Watterson, Gerald	1992-93	DE	Baton Rouge, La.
Watts, Larry	1995-97-98	DB	Columbia, Miss.
Watts, Toby	1987-88-89	DT	Fort Worth, Texas
Watwood, Louis	1937-38	E	Goodwater, Ala.
Weakley, Bobby	2003	FB	Brandon, Miss.
Weathersby, Robert	1931-32	HB	Hattiesburg, Miss.
Webb, Andy	1937-38	C	Forest, Miss.
Webb, Bobby	1965-66-67	C	Panama City, Fla.
Weeks, Robbie	1985-86-87-88	WR	Indianola, Miss.
Welborn, J. P.	1912-13-14-15	E	Soso, Miss.
Welch, Michael	1990-91-92	TB	Douglasville, Ga.
Wells, Robert	1946	QB	Moss Point, Miss.
Wells, Robert	1966-67	HB/CB	Moss Point, Miss.
Wells, Terrence	1971-72-73	TB	Wade, Miss.
Wells, Vernon (Zipper)	1946-47-48	QB	Moss Point, Miss.
West, Walton	1934	——	Hattiesburg, Miss.
Westerfield, George	1936-37-38	E	Leakesville, Miss.
Wheat, Otis	1936-37	T/G	Poplarville, Miss.
Wheeler, Jimmie B.	1924-25	G	Fulton, Miss.
Wheeler, Tom	1956	——	
Whitcomb, John	1990	QB	Chipley, Fla.
White, Chris	2003	OT	Winona, Miss.
White, Doug	1971-72-73	DB	Gulfport, Miss.
White, Jack	1961-62-63	HB	Blakely, Ga.
White, Joe	1959-60	C	Griffin, Ga.
White, Joe	1992	OT	Ellenwood, Ga.
White, Milton	1951-52	HB	Columbiana, Ala.
White, Richard	1991-92	S	Enterprise, Ala.
White, Zac	2000	QB	Gardendale, Ala.

	YEAR	POSITION	HOMETOWN
Whitehead, Ray	1946	——	——
Whitfield, Dallas	1954-55-56	HB/PK	Picayune, Miss.
Whitley, Rhett	1978-79-80-81	DE	Birmingham, Ala.
Whitney, Alan	2003	TE	Fairhope, Ala.
Wiggins, C. H.	1923	——	Toomsuba, Miss.
Wilbanks, Mike	1976	DE	Savannah, Tenn.
Wiles, Willie Dee	1949-50	G	Kosciusko, Miss.
Wilkes	1929	——	——
Wilkes, Bernie	1946-47	P/RB	Petal, Miss.
Wilkes, Chuck	1966	CB	Biloxi, Miss.
Williams	1925	——	——
Williams, Alfred	1987-88-89	WR	Meridian, Miss.
Williams, Arnie	1988-89-90-91	LB	Bay Minette, Ala.
Williams, Chad	1998-99-2000-01	SS	Birmingham, Ala.
Williams, Darrell	1985-86-87	FS	Meridian, Miss.
Williams, Eric	1989-90-91	TE	Atlanta, Ga.
Williams, Gary	1982	LB	Magee, Miss.
Williams, Jackie	1950	T	Tallassee, Ala.
Williams, James	1998	LB	Arabi, La.
Williams, Kerry	1987-88-89	FS	Midfield, Ala.
Williams, Leonard	1953-54	E	Jacksonville, Fla.
Williams, Marty	1987-88-89	OG	Eufaula, Ala.
Williams, R. M.	1919	QB	Hattiesburg, Miss.
Williams, W. B.	1915	——	Sandersville, Miss.
Williams, Wendell	1979-80-81	DT/NG	Pensacola, Fla.
Williamson, D.	1932-33	T	Sontag, Miss.
Williamson, Roy	1934-35-36	HB	McLain, Miss.
Willoughby, Ben	1961-62	HB	Liberty, Miss.
Willoughby, Will	1964-65	T	Liberty, Miss.
Wilson, Bob	1973-74	DT	Horsham, Pa.
Wilson, Edward	1983-84-85	WR	Vicksburg, Miss.
Wilson, Fred	1985	DE	Panama City, Fla.
Wilson, Henry	1998	WR	Vicksburg, Miss.
Wilson, Irie (Biscuit)	1929	HB	Louisville, Miss.
Wilson, Jack	1942	——	——
Wilson, Jerrel	1961-62	C/FB/P	Brookhaven, Miss.
Wilson, Richard	1938-39-40	E	Monticello, Miss.
Wilson, Walker (Cornbread)	1930-31-32	FB	Louisville, Miss.
Wimberly, Donald	1939	—-	
Winchester, Gayle	1960	E	Cantonment, Fla.
Winder, Sammy	1978-79-80-81	TB	Pocahontas, Miss.
Windham, Rod	1966-67-68	S	Jackson, Miss.
Windham, Rusty	1969	CB	Jackson, Miss.
Windsor, Chris	1995-96	QB	Bessemer, Ala.
Winn, Melvin	1995-96-97	DT	Pearl, Miss.
Winstead, Don	1947-48	HB	Jackson, Miss.
Witt, Robert	1941-46	E	Elkmont, Ala.
Womack, Bruce	1946	G	Bogalusa, La.
Wood, Brian	1989-90-91	SS	Tallahassee, Fla.

	YEAR	POSITION	HOMETOWN
Wood, R. L.	1926-27-28	E/HB	Phoenix, Miss.
Wood, Richard	1969	CB	Meraux, La.
Wood, Tommy	1952-53	B	Laurel, Miss.
Wood, W. H.	1919-20	HB	Wallerville, Miss.
Woodard, Mike	1980	FB	Prichard, Ala.
Woods, Dawayne	1998-99-2000-01	TB	Slidell, Miss.
Woodward, D. M.	1923-24	HB	Ovett, Miss.
Worthington, Brad	2002	OL	Highland Home, Ala.
Wright, Curtis	1986	LB	Dallas, Tex.
Wright, James	1964	C	Oxford, Miss.
Wright, Jerry	1969-70	OT	Northport, Ala.
Wright, Larry	1966	E	Homestead, Fla.
Wright, Mike	1976-77-78	P/PK	Mobile, Ala.
Wright, Robert	1966-67-68	T	Jackson, Miss.
Wright, Tim	1991-93	S	Meridian, Miss.
Wright, William	1967-68	OT	Jackson, Miss.
Wynn, Pat	1989-90-91	CB	Huntsville, Tex.

Y

Yates, Corey	1999-2000-01-03	CB	Holly Springs, Miss.
Yates, Johnny	1948	E	Hamilton, Tex.
Yates, Ollie	1957-58	QB	Hattiesburg, Miss.
Yelverton, Tony	1967-68	HB/CB	Madison-Ridgeland, Miss.
Yencho, Bob	1955-56-57-58	E	McKeesport, Pa.
Yenni, Joe	1939	HB	Kenner, La.
Youmans, Tommy	1963-64-65	TB	Quitman, Ga.
Young, Ailrick	1987-88	QB	New Orleans, La.
Young, Marvin	2001-02-03	WR	Clarksdale, Miss.

Z

Ziegler, Curtis	1978	TB	Elmore, Ala.

ABBREVIATIONS USED

B	back	HB	halfback	RB	running back
C	center	LB	linebacker	S	safety
CB	cornerback	MG	middle guard	SE	split end
DE	defensive end	NG	nose guard	SS	strong safety
DS	deep snapper	OG	offensive guard	T	tackle
DT	defensive tackle	OL	offensive lineman	TB	tailback
E	end	OT	offensive tackle	TE	tight end
FB	fullback	P	punter	V	vandal
FL	flanker	PK	placekicker	WR	wide receiver
FS	free safety	QB	quarterback		
G	guard	R	rover		

STARTING LINEUPS

1912
- E   P. E. Phillips
- E   J. P. Welborn
- G   E. J. Riley
- G   Jack Thompson
- C   H. B. Longest
- T   George Thatch
- T   Eugene Smith
- QB   G. B. Anderson
- HB   Benton Holmes
- HB   L. S. Venable
- FB   Claude Turner

1913
- E   J. P. Welborn
- G   Jack Thompson
- C   H. B. Longest
- T   George Thatch
- T   Eugene Smith
- QB   G. B. Anderson

1914
- E   J. P. Welborn
- G   Jack Thompson
- C   H. B. Longest
- T   George Thatch

1915
- E   J. P. Welborn

1916
- E   M. M. Roberts
- T   C. C. Campbell
- G   C. T. McDonald
- C   Dunahoo
- G   G. R. Touchstone
- T   A. B. Crabb/W. J. Davis
- E   E. S. Roberts
- QB   W. C. Smith
- HB   C. C. Roberts
- HB   R. V. Peacock
- FB   J. V. Dabbs

1919
- E   Zack Lee
- E   James Vinson
- G   A. H. Parsons
- G   Roland Herrington
- C   B. B. O'Mara
- T   D. H. Lane
- T   C. C. Campbell
- QB   R. M. Williams
- HB   John Montgomery
- HB   J. R. Busby
- FB   Clarence Holleman

1920
- E   J. T. Pertero
- E   W. Z. Busby
- G   G. E. Gafford
- G   Hubert Flurry
- C   H. L. McCleskey
- T   C. C. Campbell
- T   W. J. Davis
- QB   J. W. McCleskey
- HB   Bob Huff
- HB   W. C. Smith
- FB   J. R. Busby

1921
- E   J. M. Busby
- E   S. B. Crawford
- G   H. G. Bates
- G   Fred Leech
- C   T. D. Sumrall
- T   H. W. McGilvary
- T   G. E. Gafford
- QB   J. W. McCleskey
- HB   J. E. Gregory
- HB   E. L. Cook
- FB   W. L. Parker

1922
- E   E. W. Hester
- E   Nollie Felts
- G   Fred Leech
- G   M. R. Vines
- C   L. E. Gafford

T	O. E. Cowart
T	Rowells
QB	L. Busch
HB	Pigott
HB	R. H. Tucker
FB	W. L. Parker
PK	R. H. Tucker

1923
E	E. W. Hester
E	D. C. Leech
G	Fred Leech
G	Nick Johnson
C	C. G. Trantham
T	A. H. Applewhite
T	L. E. Gafford
QB	Nollie Felts
HB	George Stanley
HB	Al Waites/Joe Cook
FB	O. E. Cowart
PK	Nollie Felts
P	Nollie Felts

1924
E	E. W. Hester
E	Nollie Felts
G	J. E. Dale
G	Jimmie Wheeler
C	Fred Leech
T	Nick Johnson
T	O. E. Cowart
QB	J. M. Tujaque Jr.
HB	Hugh Ferrell
HB	Paul Tally
FB	R. H. Tucker
PK	R. H. Tucker

1925
E	W. D. Mitchell
E	J. W. Ainsworth/ William Bethea
G	Jimmie B. Wheeler
G	H. G. Bates
C	Kenneth McRae
T	Fred E. Davis
T	J. E. Dale/E. Waite
QB	Walter Conner
HB	Hugh Ferrell
HB	A. T. Gullette

FB	R. H. Tucker

1926
E	Walter Conner
E	Otis Waites
G	J. E. Dale
G	H. G. Bates
C	Broadus
T	G. H. Russell
T	Homer McMahan
QB	Nollie Felts
HB	C. W. Spigener
HB	A. T. Gullette
FB	J. P. Hackney

1927
E	R. L. Wood
E	Fred E. Davis
G	W. A. Brantley
G	P. P. Flanagan
C	Ray Finch
T	G. H. Russell
T	W. F. Childers
QB	Jack Gay
HB	J. P. Hackney
HB	A. T. Gullette
FB	Albert Rogers

1928
E	Lewis McGehee
E	S. A. Brasfield
G	P. P. Flanigan
G	J. H. Crestman
C	Homer McMahan
T	Fred E. Davis
T	W. F. Childers
QB	Ellis Bilbo
HB	J. W. Davis
HB	G. J. Bishop
FB	Frank A. McLendon

1929
E	Lewis McGehee
E	Tony Martello
G	M. E. Overby
G	W. A. Brantley
C	G. J. Bishop
T	R. R. Dunagin
T	A. H. Overby

QB	J. P. Hackney
HB	Ellis Bilbo
HB	Irie Wilson
FB	J. W. Davis

1930
E	Argile Stewart
E	A. H. Overby
G	M. E. Overby
G	Brownie Thomas
C	Brunnus Stewart
T	R. R. Dunagin
T	Lance Lumpkin
QB	S. A. Clark
HB	Ellis Bilbo
HB	David Lossette
FB	Walker Wilson

1931
E	John Lever
E	Tony Martello
G	M. E. Overby
G	Sankey Koen/ Brownie Thomas
C	Brunnus Stewart
T	Lance Lumpkin
T	A. H Overby
QB	Reed Green
HB	Ellis Bilbo
HB	Walker Wilson
FB	L. A. Burns

1932
E	John Lever
E	Obie Brown
G	Arthur Johnson
G	Alton Grimes
C	A. D. Ott
T	Saucier/D. Williamson
T	Carroll Shows
QB	Ellis Bilbo
HB	Reed Green
HB	L. A. Burns
FB	Hunter Denson

1933
E	Obie Brown
E	James Halbert
G	Bernard Kisner

G	Arthur Johnson/Don Cowart	
C	A. D. Ott	
T	Otto Phillips	
T	Carroll Shows	
QB	Nolan Taconi	
HB	Vernon Boyd	
HB	Russell Evans	
FB	Edwin Allen	
PK	Vernon Boyd	

1934

E	Richard Shields
E	Hays Brown
G	Ray Harris/I. W. Fletcher
G	Bernard Kisner/ Donivan Cowart
C	Carl Reynolds
T	Otto Phillips
T	Obie Ladner
QB	Edwin Allen
HB	Nolan Taconi
HB	Victor Jones/J. D. Stonestreet
FB	Pete Cochran

1935

E	Doug Smith
E	Richard Shields
G	Ethridge Hudson
G	Tracy Walker
C	Carl Reynolds
T	Otto Phillips
T	Obie Ladner
QB	Edwin Allen
HB	Roy Williamson
HB	J. D. Stonestreet
FB	Leo Purvis

1936

E	Denton Garrett
E	A. D. Bell
G	John Heath
G	Hays Brown/Tracy Walker
C	Leroy Austin
T	Charles Smith
T	Chester Scalzo
QB	Leo Purvis
HB	Roy Williamson
HB	Malcolm Patrick
FB	Archie Odom

1937

E	Bracey Smith
E	A. D. Bell/George Westerfield
G	Cotton Campbell
G	Arno Vincent
C	Andy Webb
T	Red Downing
T	Earl Morgan
QB	Sporty Dabbs
HB	Mule Massengale
HB	Malcolm Patrick
FB	Mike Benglis
PK	Jake Scott/Sporty Dabbs
P	Mule Massengale

1938

E	Louis Watwood
E	George Westerfield
G	Cotton Campbell
G	Arno Vincent
C	Andy Webb
T	Bill Leach
T	Sandy Morgan
QB	Bee Smith
HB	Mule Massengale
HB	Willie Oubre
FB	Sporty Dabbs/Mike Benglis
PK	Sporty Dabbs/Linn Walton
P	Mule Massengale

1939

E	Joe Stringfellow
E	Troy Hendricks/ Thomas Glover Freeman
G	Fred Dickey/ Doyle Bramlett
G	Reginald Switzer
C	Pel Autry/Dagwood Jones
T	Sandy Morgan
T	Scoop Howard
QB	Joe Ovca
HB	Mule Massengale/ Leo Alessandri
HB	Joe Yenni
FB	Armand Critty
PK	Joe Stringfellow/ Pel Autry
P	Mule Massengale/ Leo Alessandri

1940

E	Joe Stringfellow
E	Buford Brasher
G	Doyle Bramlette
G	Reginald Switzer
C	Pel Autry/Harry Clark
T	John Carr
T	John Wesley Jones
QB	Joe Ovca
HB	D. Jones/Joe Vetrano
HB	Art Van Tone
FB	Leo Alessandri

1941

E	Joe Stringfellow
E	Bob Witt
G	Dick Thames
G	M. G. Clements
C	Pel Autry
T	Arnold Stevens
T	Roland Loper
QB	Les DeVall
HB	Joe Vetrano/Dipsey Dews
HB	Art Van Tone
FB	Joe Latham
PK	Joe Stringfellow/Joe Vetrano
P	Joe Stringfellow

1942

E	Stanley Graham
T	Arnold Stevens
G	Rufus McSwain
C	Gordon Simmons
G	Dick Thames
T	Mike Katrishen
E	Jack Blakeney
QB	Dipsey Dews
HB	Joe Vetrano
HB	Perry Waldvogel
FB	Art Van Tone/Falco Carrozza
PK	Joe Vetrano
P	Joe Vetrano

1946

E	Jay Smith
E	Doug Honaker
G	Curley Dement
G	Dick Thames
C	Cooter Lewis

STARTING LINEUPS

T	Roland Loper	T	Chuck Borde	HB	Hugh Laurin Pepper
T	Mike Katrishen	QB	Bobby Holmes	HB	Tony Rouchon
QB	Bobby Campbell	HB	Bubba Phillips	FB	Bucky McElroy
HB	John LeGros/Vernon Wells	HB	Frank Spruiell	PK	Jim Davenport/
HB	Buster Mullin/	FB	Jim Ray Owen		Bucky McElroy
	Benny Ray Nobles	PK	Carl Howard		
FB	Joe Latham	P	Clint Arnold		
PK	Sawyer Sims				
P	Benny Ray Nobles				

1947

E	Jay Smith
E	Hindu Reynolds
G	Sonny Jordan
G	Red Mangum
C	Cal Butler/Apple Sanders/Cooter Lewis
T	Curley Dement
T	Mike Katrishen
QB	Vernon Wells
HB	Bubba Phillips
HB	Benny Ray Nobles
FB	Joe Latham
PK	Carl Howard/ Doug Honaker
P	Benny Ray Noble

1950

E	Ken Walker
E	Ivan Rosamond
G	Willie D. Wiles
G	Ken Farris
C	Lewis Murray
T	Moose Musmeci
T	Paul Moyer
QB	Bobby Holmes
HB	Bubba Phillips
HB	Morris Brown
FB	Clint Arnold
PK	Webb Farrish
P	Clint Arnold

(Defense)

E	Dick Caldwell
E	Jackson Brumfield
T	Herbert R. Nobles
T	Bobby Rhed
G	Ed McDaniel
G	Pat Ferlise
LB	Dick Gatti
LB	Phil Muscarello
HB	Jackie Howard
HB	Jimmy Brashier
S	Milton White
P	Bucky McElroy

1948

E	Hindu Reynolds
E	Cliff Coggin
G	Sonny Jordan
G	Red Mangum
C	Apple Sanders
T	Chuck Borde
T	Doug Taylor
QB	Vernon Wells
HB	Bubba Phillips
HB	Benny Ray Nobles
FB	William Stewart
PK	Doug Honaker
P	Benny Ray Nobles

1951

E	Bob McKellar
E	Elmo Lang
G	Elmer Kemper
G	Ken Farris
C	Dave Allen
T	Moose Musmeci
T	Jack Fulkerson/ Bobby Rhed
QB	Tom LeGros
HB	Scrappy Hart
HB	Lindy Stewart
FB	Bucky McElroy
PK	Webb Farrish
P	Scrappy Hart

1953

E	Dick Caldwell
E	Jackson Brumfield
G	J. T. Shepherd
G	L. T. Hermann
C	Les Clark
T	Buzzy Clark
T	Don Owens
QB	Billy Jarrell
HB	Hugh Laurin Pepper
HB	Jimmy Brashier
FB	Bucky McElroy
PK	Bucky McElroy
P	Bucky McElroy

1949

E	Boots McCormick
E	Cliff Coggin
G	Carl Smith
G	Sonny Jordan
C	Dick Jenevein
T	Doug Taylor

1952

(Offense)

E	Bob McKellar
E	Elmo Lang
G	Martin Lasley
G	L. T. Hermann
C	John Meeks
T	Howard Lehman
T	John Neill
QB	Billy Jarrell

1954

E	Hub Waters
T	Don Owens
G	L. T. Hermann
C	Les Clark
G	Hamp Cook
T	Jim Davis
E	Leonard Williams
QB	Jim Davenport
HB	Ted Trenton
HB	Brooks Tisdale
FB	Fred Smallwood
PK	Brooks Tisdale
P	George Herring

STARTING LINEUPS

1955

E	Jerry Taylor
T	Don Owens
G	P. W. Underwood
C	Les Clark
G	Al Tregle
T	Buzzy Clark
E	Curry Juneau
QB	George Herring
HB	Ted Trenton
HB	Fred Smallwood
FB	Leo Cardenas
PK	Lawrence Meeks/ Dallas Whitfield
P	George Herring

1956

E	Jerry Taylor
T	Don Owens
G	Dave Fitzgerald
C	Bill Martin
G	Al Tregle
T	P. W. Underwood
E	Curry Juneau
QB	Bobby Hughes
HB	J. C. Arban
HB	Dallas Whitfield
FB	Bo Dickinson
PK	Dallas Whitfield
P	Bo Dickinson

1957

E	Bob Yencho
T	John T. Russell
G	Burnett Blackmon
C	Richard Johnston
G	Jimmy Taylor
T	John Perkins
E	Curry Juneau
QB	George Sekul
HB	Jack May
HB	Lawrence Meeks
FB	Bo Dickinson
PK	Ollie Yates
P	Jack May/Ollie Yates

1958

E	Bob Yencho
T	Sam Tuccio
G	Bob Rinehart
C	Richard Johnston
G	Jimmy Taylor
T	John Perkins
E	Hugh McInnis
QB	George Sekul
HB	Bobby Lance
HB	J. C. Arban
FB	Buddy Supple
PK	Bobby Lance/Hugh McInnis
P	George Sekul

1959

E	Hugh McInnis
T	George Underwood
G	Bob Rinehart
C	Charley Ellzey
G	Buddy Long
T	Byron Bradfute
E	Butler Tucker
QB	Don Fuell
HB	Arnold Spence
HB	Charley McArthur
FB	Buddy Supple
PK	Hugh McInnis
P	Morris Meador

1960

E	Leon Akins
T	Buddy Long/Jim Payne
G	Ray St. Pierre
C	Joe White
G	George Jones
T	George Hultz
E	Charley Dedwylder
QB	Don Fuell/Morris Meador
HB	Andin McLeod
FB	Dan Pugh/ Windell Campbell
HB	Arnold Spence
P	Morris Meador
PK	Billy Larson

1961

E	Leon Akins
T	Jim Payne
G	Charley Parker
C	Harold Hays
G	Nick Kolinsky
T	George Hultz
E	Charley Dedwylder
QB	Don Fuell
HB	Jimmy Havard
FB	Wendell Campbell
HB	Johnny Sklopan
PK	Don Fuell
P	Jerrel Wilson

1962

E	Billy Lyons
T	Bill Freeman
G	Charley Parker
C	Harold Hays
G	Nick Kolinsky
T	Marvin Breazeale
E	Don Hultz
QB	Billy Coleman
HB	Jimmy Havard
FB	George Sekul
HB	Johnny Sklopan
PK	Jerrel Wilson
P	Jerrel Wilson

1963

E	Bill Gorney
T	Sam Bella
G	Tony DeFranco
C	Larry Ecuyer
G	Nick Kolinsky
T	Charley Parker
E	Ben McLeod
QB	Vic Purvis
HB	Tommy Walters
FB	Harmon Brannan
HB	Herman Nall
PK	John Laird
P	John Laird

1964

E	Troy Craft
T	Chuck Armond
G	Jim King
C	Larry Ecuyer
G	Doug Satcher

T	John Melton
E	Bill Gorney
QB	Vic Purvis
TB	Herman Nall
FB	Harmon Brannan
WB	Rabbit Brown
PK	John Laird
P	John Laird

1965
(Offense)

SE	Bill Gorney
T	Chuck Armond
G	Andy Armstrong
C	Robert Webb
G	Tom Melton
T	John Melton
TE	George Rodman
QB	Vic Purvis
TB	Henry Letort
FB	Harmon Brannan
WB	Rabbit Brown
PK	George Sumrall

(Defense)

E	Troy Craft
T	John Mangum
MG	Poochie Stringfellow
T	Art Gill
E	Jesse Brown
LB	Doug Satcher
LB	Ken Avery
CB	Tommy Brennan
S	Billy Devrow
S	Jimmy Barger
CB	Tommy Youmans
P	Dickie Dunaway

1966
(Offense)

SE	Clyde Dowd
T	Buddy Hunter
G	Andy Armstrong
C	Bobby Webb
G	Blanchard Braud
T	Larry Tolbert
TE	Larry Wright
QB	Mike McClellan

HB	Ronnie Channell
FB	Milo McCarthy
WB	Robert Wells
PK	John Laird

(Defense)

E	Tommy Roussel
T	Art Gill
MG	Poochie Stringfellow
T	Gene Bachman
E	Troy Craft
LB	Elbert Trone
LB	Ken Avery
CB	Tommy Brennan
S	Billy Devrow
S	Jimmy Barger
CB	Larry Ussery
P	Dickie Dunaway

1967
(Offense)

SE	Danny Haley
T	Buddy Hunter
G	Blanchard Braud
C	Bobby Webb
G	Mike Kondrat
T	Larry Tolbert
TE	Robert Wells
QB	Tommy Boutwell
HB	Johnny Johnson
FB	Milo McCarthy
HB	Ronnie Channell
PK	Mike Kondrat

(Defense)

E	Tommy Roussel
T	Harry Huelsbeck
MG	Rex Barnes
T	Gene Bachman
E	Jack McAlpin
LB	Elbert Trone
LB	Larry Heflin
CB	Mike McAdams
S	Donnie Caughman
S	Steve Fore
CB	Larry Ussery
P	Dickie Dunaway

1968
(Offense)

SE	Billy Mikel
T	Bob Shepherd
G	Mike Kondrat
C	Hank Autry
G	Joe Schoeneck
T	Blanchard Braud
TE	Toby Vance
QB	Tommy Boutwell
HB	Johnny Johnson
FB	Frank Johnston
HB	Larry Moulton
PK	John Hale

(Defense)

E	Tommy Applewhite
T	Radell Key
MG	Rex Barnes
T	Mike Craft
E	Wayne Adkison
LB	Mike Battles
LB	Brent McMahan
CB	Donnie Caughman
S	Mike McAdams
S	Steve Fore
CB	Larry Ussery
P	Sonny Orrell

1969
(Offense)

SE	Billy Mikel
T	Bob Shepherd
G	Clinton Tompkins
C	Joe Tuggle
G	David Price
T	Jimmy Haynes
TE	Toby Vance
QB	Rick Donegan
TB	Larry Moulton
FB	Frank Johnston
WB	Wayne Hatcher
PK	John Hale

(Defense)

E	Henry Quick
T	Radell Key
MG	Rex Barnes

T	Mike Craft
E	Terry Griffin
LB	Mike Battles
LB	Dicky Surace
MM	Henry Letort
HB	Donnie Caughman
HB	Steve Fore
S	Mike Harris
P	John Hale

1970
(Offense)

SE	Lionel Fayard
T	Bob Flanders
G	David Price
C	Joe Tuggle
G	Larry Ceppenati
T	Jimmy Haynes
FL	Billy Mikel
QB	Rick Donegan
HB	Larry Moulton
FB	Ed Soberoski
WB	Wayne Hatcher
PK	Ray Guy

(Defense)

E	Pitt Farrar
T	Johnny Herron
T	Mike Blanchard
E	Hugh Eggersman
LB	Ken Burge
LB	Bill Davis
LB	Dicky Surace
V	Fred Meyer
HB	George Hunt
HB	Craig Logan
S	Ray Guy
P	Ray Guy

1971
(Offense)

SE	Gary Grubbs
T	Troy Ricks
G	Tom Brock
C	Jimmy Haynes
G	Larry Ceppenati
T	Bob Flanders
FL	Doug Parker
QB	Rick Donegan
HB	Doyle Orange
FB	Bill Foley
WB	Marshall Veal
PK	Ray Guy

(Defense)

E	Fred Cook
T	Ken Phillips
T	Johnny Herron
E	Hugh Eggersman
LB	Kyle Gantt
LB	Mike Dennery
LB	Ken Burge
V	Fred Meyer
HB	Ray Guy
HB	Mickey Hudson
S	Craig Logan
P	Ray Guy

1972
(Offense)

SE	Doug Parker
T	Mike Moon
G	Bob Flanders
C	Dennis Malone
G	Clint Tapper
T	Jim Boesch
FL	John Dragg
QB	Buddy Palazzo
TB	Doyle Orange
FB	Wilson Plunkett
WB	Marshall Veal
PK	Ray Guy

(Defense)

E	Fred Cook
T	Lee Coleman
T	John Tapper
E	Tom Henderson
LB	Kyle Gantt
LB	Mike Dennery
LB	Gary Roberts
V	Fred Meyer
HB	Eugene Bird
HB	Doug White
S	Ray Guy
P	Ray Guy

1973
(Offense)

SE	Eddie Tate
T	Jerry Fremin
G	Steve Dunn
C	Dennis Malone
G	Clint Tapper
T	Mike Moon
TE	John Sawyer
QB	Jeff Bower
HB	Doyle Orange
FB	Wilson Plunkett
FL	Harvey McGee
PK	Ricky Palmer

(Defense)

E	Fred Cook
T	Mike Smith
T	Kevin Looman
E	Craig Stevens
LB	Gary Roberts
LB	Mike Dennery
LB	Steve Huettel
V	Billy Olson
HB	Eugene Bird
HB	Norris Thomas
S	Doug White
P	Ricky Palmer

1974
(Offense)

SE	Eddie Tate
T	Jerry Fremin
G	Steve Dunn
C	Clifton Fussell
G	Roger Hardman
G	David Keith
TE	John Sawyer
QB	Jeff Bower
TB	Ben Garry
FB	Chris Pieper
FL	Greg Pieper
PK	Ricky Palmer

(Defense)

E	Craig Stevens
T	Joe Ganse
NG	Randy Latta

T	Mike Smith
E	Don Byars
LB	Steve Huettel
LB	Ron Cheatham
V	Rick Gemmel
CB	Brad Byrne
CB	Norris Thomas
S	Billy Olson
P	Ricky Palmer

1975
(Offense)
SE	Greg Pieper
T	Jerry Fremin
G	Stan Sanders
C	Bill Warner
G	Eddie Kaplan
T	Eric Smith
TE	Wally Ballard
QB	Jeff Bower
TB	Ben Garry
FB	Carlos Montgomery
FL	Eddie Tate
PK	Ricky Palmer

(Defense)
E	Reggie Odom
T	Stoney Parker
NG	Randy Latta
T	Eddie Nunez
E	Craig Stevens
LB	Clemon Ector
LB	Ron Cheatham
CB	Carl Allen
S	Brad Bowman
V	Rick Gemmel
CB	Norris Thomas
P	Ricky Palmer

1976
(Offense)
SE	John Cannon
T	Amos Fowler
G	Steve Boyette
C	Barry Caudill
G	Porter Mitchell
T	Eric Smith
TE	John Pitts
QB	Ken Alderman
TB	Ben Garry
FB	Curtis Dickey
FL	Chuck Carr Brown
PK	Mike Wright

(Defense)
E	Bobby Smithart
T	Stoney Parker
NG	Thad Dillard
T	Craig Stevens
E	Reggie Odom
LB	Freeman Horton
LB	Ricky Allen
CB	Carl Allen
S	Terry Daniels
V	Mike Crenshaw
CB	Don Law
P	Mike Wright

1977
(Offense)
SE	John Cannon
T	Randy Butler
G	Terry Brown
C	Bill Warner
G	Amos Fowler
T	Eric Smith
TE	Marvin Harvey
QB	Jeff Hammond
TB	Ben Garry
FB	David Hosemann
FL	Chuck Carr Brown
PK	Randy Boyette

(Defense)
E	Bobby Smithart
T	Stoney Parker
NG	Thad Dillard
T	Alan McCollough
E	Reggie Odom
LB	Freeman Horton
LB	Clump Taylor
CB	Terry Daniels
V	Mike Crenshaw
S	Randy McDonald
CB	Emanuel Killingsworth
P	Mike Wright

1978
(Offense)
SE	John Cannon
T	Randy Butler
G	Terry Brown
C	David Parrish
G	Butch Smith
T	Greg Ahrens
TE	Marvin Harvey
QB	Jeff Hammond/ Dane McDaniel
TB	Tiko Beal
FB	Calvin Jones
FL	Chuck Carr Brown
PK	Randy Boyette

(Defense)
E	James Hale
T	Stoney Parker
NG	Thad Dillard
T	J. J. Stewart
E	Mike McKinzie
LB	Freeman Horton
LB	Clump Taylor
CB	Hanford Dixon
FS	Bubba Busby
SS	Mike Crenshaw
CB	Gary Holt
P	Mike Wright

1979
(Offense)
SE	Larry Taylor
T	Joey Hendrix
G	Dale Fife
C	Mark Johnson
G	Butch Smith
T	Greg Ahrens
TE	Marvin Harvey
QB	Dane McDaniel
TB	Tiko Beal
FB	Calvin Jones
FL	Chuck Carr Brown
PK	Winston Walker

(Defense)
| E | Rhett Whitley |
| T | J. J. Stewart |

NG	Albert Teague	
T	Gary Ivy	
E	Mike McKinzie	
LB	Cliff Lewis	
LB	Clump Taylor	
CB	Hanford Dixon	
FS	Bubba Busby	
SS	Chuck Cook	
CB	Art Newberry	
P	Bruce Thompson	

1980

(Offense)

SE	Don Horn
T	Blaine Burnett
G	Eddie McCoy
C	Jamey Watson
G	Butch Smith
T	Glen Howe
TE	Marvin Harvey
QB	Reggie Collier
TB	Sammy Winder
FB	Neal Alexander
FL	Louis Lipps
PK	Winston Walker

(Defense)

E	Rhett Whitley
T	Charley Jenkins
NG	Jerald Baylis
T	Moochie Allen
E	George Tillman
LB	Ron Brown
LB	Cliff Lewis
CB	Hanford Dixon
FS	Danny Jackson
SS	Chuck Cook
CB	Eddie Ray Walker
P	Bruce Thompson

1981

(Offense)

SE	Don Horn
T	Joe Hendrix
G	Dale Fife
C	Bill Mann
G	Fred Richards
T	Glen Howe
TE	Jim Brown
QB	Reggie Collier
TB	Sammy Winder
FB	Neal Alexander
FL	Mike Livings
PK	Steve Clark

(Defense)

E	Rhett Whitley
T	Charley Jenkins
NG	Jerald Baylis
T	Moochie Allen
E	George Tillman
LB	Ron Brown
LB	Greg Kelley
CB	Bruce Miller
FS	Danny Jackson
SS	Bud Brown
CB	Eddie Ray Walker
P	Bruce Thompson

1982

(Offense)

SE	Marc Means
T	Dwayne Massey
G	Randy Campbell
C	Steve Carmody
G	Fred Richards
T	Glen Howe
TE	Raymond Powell
QB	Reggie Collier
TB	Sam Dejarnette
FB	Clemon Terrell
FL	Louis Lipps
PK	Steve Clark

(Defense)

E	Richard Byrd
T	Charlie Jenkins
NG	Jerald Baylis
T	Larry Alford
E	George Tillman
LB	Greg Kelley
LB	Mark Carmichael
CB	Bruce Miller
FS	Scott Allen
SS	Bud Brown
CB	Eddie Ray Walker
P	Bruce Thompson

1983

(Offense)

SE	Edward Wilson
T	Dwayne Massey
G	Randy Campbell
C	Steve Carmody
G	Fred Richards
T	Glen Howe
TE	Jim Brown
QB	Robert Ducksworth
TB	Sam Dejarnette
FB	Clemon Terrell
FL	Louis Lipps
PK	Steve Clark

(Defense)

E	Willie B. Moore
T	Richard Byrd
NG	Jerald Baylis
T	Kip Smith
E	Chris Jackson
LB	Greg Kelley
LB	Greg Haeusler
CB	Bruce Miller
FS	Scott Allen
SS	Bud Brown
CB	Bobo Harris
P	Larry Boyd

1984

(Offense)

SE	Andrew Mott
T	Randy Campbell
G	Ken Bentley
C	Fred Richards
G	Tony Gray
T	Chris Haag
TE	Robert R. Stallings
QB	Robert Ducksworth
TB	Sam Dejarnette
FB	Tracy Gamble
FL	Lionel Alston
PK	Rex Banks

(Defense)

E	Willie B. Moore
T	Richard Byrd
NG	Tracy Oakley
T	Kip Smith

E	Chris Jackson
LB	Greg Dampeer
LB	Greg Haeusler
CB	James Cooper
FS	Scott Allen
SS	Collins Hess
CB	Bobo Harris
P	Billy Knighten

1985
(Offense)

SE	Chris McGee
T	Rick Slater
G	Ken Bentley
C	Jim Ferrell
G	Tim Hallman
T	Benny Draughn
TE	Carlos Powell
QB	Robert Ducksworth
TB	Vincent Alexander
FB	Randolph Brown
FL	Andrew Mott
PK	Rex Banks

(Defense)

E	Greg Dampeer
T	Doug Bolt
NG	Tracy Oakley
T	Kip Smith
E	Steve Brown
LB	Eric Redd
LB	Onesimus Henry
CB	James Cooper
FS	Tim Smith
SS	Vincent Rollins
CB	Bobo Harris
P	Billy Knighten

1986
(Offense)

SE	Chris McGee
T	Rick Slater
G	Billy Dilworth
C	Jim Ferrell
G	Tim Hallman
T	Pat Ferrell
TE	Carlos Powell
QB	Andrew Anderson
TB	Vincent Alexander
FB	Randolph Brown
FL	Lionel Alston
PK	Rex Banks

(Defense)

E	Steve Brown
T	Don Jeffries
NG	Ulysses Slaughter
T	Doug Bolt
E	Maurice Oliver
LB	Sidney Coleman
LB	Onesimus Henry
CB	Tim Smith
FS	Collins Hess
SS	Vincent Rollins
CB	Jonathan Robertson
P	Billy Knighten

1987
(Offense)

SE	Robbie Weeks
T	Darryl Colona
G	Jay Sherron
C	Jim Ferrell
G	Tim Hallman
T	Pat Ferrell
TE	Carlos Powell
QB	Brett Favre
TB	Shelton Gandy
FB	Carl Jones
FL	Chris McGee
PK	Chris Seroka

(Defense)

E	Maurice Oliver
T	Ulysses Slaughter
NG	Larry Davis
T	Steve Rankin
E	Steve Brown
LB	Sidney Coleman
LB	Onesimus Henry
CB	John Baylor
FS	Darrell Williams
SS	Vincent Rollins
CB	Jonathan Robertson
P	Billy Knighten

1988
(Offense)

SE	Darryl Tillman
T	Buddy King
G	Michael Callahan
C	Marty Williams
G	Chafan Marsh
T	Chris Ryals
TE	Carlos Powell
QB	Brett Favre
TB	Shelton Gandy
FB	Reggie Warnsley
FL	Eugene Rowell
PK	Chris Seroka

(Defense)

E	Steve Brown
T	Toby Watts
NG	Chuck Sims
T	Sam Thomas
E	Maurice Oliver
LB	Tony Pogue
LB	George Hill
CB	Simmie Carter
FS	Kerry Valrie
SS	Vincent Rollins
CB	James Henry
P	Scott Bryant

1989
(Offense)

SE	Darryl Tillman
T	Buddy King
G	Ben Crimm
C	Lehman Braley
G	Chafan Marsh
T	Chris Ryals
TE	Preston Hansford
QB	Brett Favre
TB	Ricky Bradley
FB	Reggie Warnsley
FL	Eugene Rowell
PK	Chuck Davis

(Defense)

E	Pat Jackson
T	Toby Watts
NG	Chuck Sims
T	Kendrick Collins
E	Bryant Medders
LB	William Kirksey
LB	Tony Pogue

CB	Simmie Carter		*(Defense)*		G	Coty Jones
FS	Kerry Valrie		LB	James Singleton	T	Carey Moorer
SS	Gabe Peck		T	Tim Roberts	TE	Anthony Owens
CB	Ben Washington		NG	Tim Miller	QB	Tommy Waters
P	Scott Bryant		T	Pete Antoniou	TB	Barry Boyd
			LB	Gerald Blake	FB	Howard McGee

1990
(Offense)

SE	Ron Baham
T	Ben Crimm
G	Lehman Braley
C	John Camacho
G	Chafan Marsh
T	Chris Ryals
TE	Eric Williams
QB	Brett Favre
TB	Eddie Ray Jackson
FB	Dwayne Nelson
FL	Michael Jackson
PK	Jim Taylor

(Defense)

E	James Singleton
T	Kendrick Collins
NG	Ron Brown
T	Pete Antoniou
E	Rod Reed
LB	Arnie Williams
LB	Thad McDowell
CB	Simmie Carter
FS	Kerry Valrie
SS	Brian Wood
CB	Ben Washington
P	Scott Bryant

1991
(Offense)

SE	Ron Baham
T	Reggie Russell
G	Lehman Braley
C	Chris LaCoste
G	Chafan Marsh
T	Chris Ryals
TE	Eric Williams
QB	Tommy Waters
TB	Tony Smith
FB	Dwayne Nelson
FL	Greg Reed
PK	Lance Nations

LB	Arnie Williams
LB	Thad McDowell
CB	John Nichols
FS	Derrick Hoskins
SS	Brian Wood
CB	Pat Wynn
P	Scott Bryant

1992
(Offense)

SE	Mark Montgomery
T	Carey Moorer
G	George McReynolds
C	Kenny Ray
G	Leon Anderson
T	Todd Beeching
TE	Anthony Owens
QB	Tommy Waters
TB	Michael Welch
FB	Dwayne Nelson
FL	Greg Reed
PK	Lance Nations

(Defense)

E	James Singleton
T	Kevin Jackson
T	Michael Tobias
E	Bobby Hamilton
LB	Eugene Harmon
LB	Tyrone Nix
LB	Albert McRae
CB	Perry Carter
FS	Terryl Ulmer
SS	Melvin Ratcliff
CB	LaBarion Rankins
P	Eric Estes

1993
(Offense)

SE	Mark Montgomery
T	Todd Beeching
G	Darian Smith
C	Kenny Ray

G	Coty Jones
T	Carey Moorer
TE	Anthony Owens
QB	Tommy Waters
TB	Barry Boyd
FB	Howard McGee
FL	Fred Brock
PK	Johnny Lomoro

(Defense)

E	James Robinson
T	Kevin Jackson
T	Michael Tobias
E	Bobby Hamilton
LB	Eugene Harmon
LB	Tyrone Nix
LB	Albert McRae
CB	Perry Carter
FS	Shaun Gamble
SS	Melvin Ratcliff
CB	Derrick Hervey
P	Eric Estes

1994
(Offense)

WR	Ryan Pearson
T	Brent Duggins
G	Rod Ollison
C	Kenny Ray
G	Jason Barlow
T	Coty Jones
TE	Scott Harper
QB	Heath Graham
TB	Chris Buckhalter
FB	Ronald Jones
WR	Adam Kennedy
PK	Chris Pierce

(Defense)

E	Steve Latson
T	Quentin Jackson
T	Michael Tobias
E	Robert Brown
LB	Eugene Harmon
LB	Cedric Walthaw
LB	Albert McRae
CB	Derrick Hervey
FS	L. T. Gulley
SS	Roy Stabler

| CB | Rod Thomas |
| P | Chris Pierce |

1995
(Offense)

SE	Fred Brock
T	Darryl Terrell
G	Rod Ollison
C	Will Symmes
G	Jason Barlow
T	Brandon Hambright
TE	Terry Hardy
QB	Heath Graham
TB	Chris Buckhalter
FB	Brad Hamilton
FL	Ryan Pearson
PK	Chris Pierce

(Defense)

E	Tim Bell
T	Quentin Jackson
T	Kendall Dunn
E	Robert Brown
LB	Eugene Harmon
LB	Marchant Kenney
LB	Albert McRae
CB	Derrick Hervey
FS	L. T. Gulley
R	Melvin Ratcliff
CB	Rod Thomas
P	Chris Pierce

1996
(Offense)

WR	Eddie Shaw
T	Darryl Terrell
G	Shederick Blackmon
C	Leroy DeWitt
G	Kasey Keith
T	O'Lester Pope
TE	Terry Hardy
QB	Lee Roberts
TB	Eric Booth
FB	Tyrone Boleware
FL	Kendrick Lee
PK	Johnny Lomoro

(Defense)

E	Jeff Posey
T	Jason Hall
T	Quentin Jackson
E	Cedric Walthaw
LB	Lytrel Pollard
LB	Marchant Kenney
LB	T. J. Slaughter
CB	Patrick Surtain
FS	Perry Phenix
R	Jamaal Alexander
CB	Nicky Seymour
P	Jamie Purser/ Jack Gabriel

1997
(Offense)

WR	Sherrod Gideon
T	Henry McLendon
G	Shederick Blackmon
C	Frank Firestone
G	Kasey Keith
T	O'Lester Pope
TE	Terry Hardy
QB	Lee Roberts
RB	Harold Shaw
WR	Todd Pinkston
WR	Eddie Shaw
PK	Tim Hardaway

(Defense)

E	Robert Brown
T	John Nix
T	DeQuincy Scott
E	Adalius Thomas
LB	Lytrel Pollard
LB	Marchant Kenney
LB	Brian A. Bell
CB	Patrick Surtain
FS	Perry Phenix
R	Jamaal Alexander
CB	DeShone Mallard
P	Jack Gabriel

1998
(Offense)

WR	Sherrod Gideon
T	Henry McLendon
G	Jeff Hopgood
C	Frank Firestone
G	Shederick Blackmon
T	O'Lester Pope
TE	Antonio Franklin
QB	Lee Roberts
RB	Derrick Nix
WR	Todd Pinkston
WR	Eddie Shaw
PK	Brant Hanna

(Defense)

E	Cedric Scott
T	John Nix
T	DeQuincy Scott
E	Adalius Thomas
LB	Ty Trahan
LB	T. J. Slaughter
LB	Brian A. Bell
CB	Terrance Parrish
FS	Jose Gonzalez
R	Leo Barnes
CB	DeShone Mallard
P	Jamie Purser

1999
(Offense)

WR	Sherrod Gideon
T	Jeremy Bridges
G	Billy Clay
C	Zeb Landers
G	Shederick Blackmon
T	Torrin Tucker
TE	Buck Miciotto
QB	Jeff Kelly
RB	Derrick Nix
WR	Todd Pinkston
FL	Dannye Fowler
PK	Brant Hanna

(Defense)

E	Cedric Scott
T	Daleroy Stewart
T	DeQuincy Scott
E	Adalius Thomas
LB	Ty Trahan
LB	T. J. Slaughter
LB	Roy Magee
CB	Terrance Parrish
FS	Leo Barnes
R	Chad Williams

CB	Raymond Walls		TE	Bobby Garner		E	Terrell Paul
P	Jamie Purser		QB	Jeff Kelly		LB	Michael Boley
			RB	Dawayne Woods		LB	Rod Davis

2000
(Offense)

			WR	Rocky Harrison		LB	Joe Henley
			FL	LeRoy Handy		CB	Greg Brooks
SE	Dannye Fowler		PK	Brant Hanna		FS	Etric Pruitt
T	Jeremy Bridges					SS	Alex Ray
G	Kendrick Key					CB	Leroy Johnson
C	Billy Clay		*(Defense)*			P	Mark Haulman
G	Torrin Tucker		E	Brian Evans			
T	Jason Jimenez		T	Rayshun Jones			

2003
(Offense)

TE	Bobby Garner		T	Skylor Magee			
QB	Jeff Kelly		E	Terrell Paul		WR	Marvin Young
RB	Dawayne Woods		LB	Roy Magee		T	Chris White
WR	Shawn Mills		LB	Rod Davis		G	T. Cooley/Addaryl Edwards
FL	Kenny Johnson		LB	Joe Henley		C	Jim Hicks
PK	Brant Hanna		CB	Greg Brooks		G	George Batiste
			FS	Etric Pruitt		T	Jeremy Parquet
(Defense)			R	Chad Williams		TE	Terrell Browden
E	Cedric Scott		CB	Leroy Johnson		QB	Dustin Almond
T	John Nix		P	Mark Haulman		RB	Anthony Harris
T	DeQuincy Scott					WR	Antwon Courington
E	Terrell Paul					WR	DaRon Lawrence

2002
(Offense)

LB	Chris Langston		WR	Marvin Young		PK	Darren McCaleb
LB	Rod Davis		T	Jason Jimenez			
LB	Roy Magee		G	Jeremy Bridges		*(Defense)*	
CB	Keon Moore		C	Jim Hicks		E	Ronald Jones
FS	Chad Williams		G	Torrin Tucker		T	Chad Ruffin
R	Leo Barnes		T	Jeremy Parquet		T	Eric Scott
CB	Raymond Walls		TE	Bobby Garner		E	Terrell Paul
P	Mark Haulman		QB	Micky D'Angelo		LB	Antoine Cash
			RB	Derrick Nix		LB	Rod Davis

2001
(Offense)

			WR	LeRoy Handy		LB	Michael Boley
			WR	Chris Johnson		CB	Corey Yates
SE	Chris Johnson		PK	Curt Jones		FS	Etric Pruitt
T	Jeremy Bridges					SS	Alex Ray
G	Kendrick Key		*(Defense)*			CB	Greg Brooks
C	Jim Hicks		E	Ronald Jones		P	Luke Johnson
G	Torrin Tucker		T	Rayshun Jones			
T	Jason Jimenez		T	Eric Scott			

Abbreviations Used

B	back	LB	linebacker	RB	running back
C	center	MG	middle guard	S	safety
CB	cornerback	MM	monster man	SE	split end
DE	defensive end	NG	nose guard	SS	strong safety
DT	defensive tackle	OG	offensive guard	T	tackle
E	end	OL	offensive lineman	TB	tailback
FB	fullback	OT	offensive tackle	TE	tight end
FL	flanker	P	punter	V	vandal
FS	free safety	PK	placekicker	WB	wingback
G	guard	QB	quarterback	WR	wide receiver
HB	halfback	R	rover		

SCORES

1912 (2–1)
Coach Ronald J. Slay *Game Captains*

Day	Date	Opponent	Score	Site	Day/Night
Sunday	10/13	Hattiesburg Boy Scouts	W/30–0	Hattiesburg	Day
Saturday	10/19	Gulf Coast Military Acad.	L/0–6	Hattiesburg	Day
Tuesday	11/05	Mobile Military Acad.	W/6–0	Hattiesburg	Day

1913 (1–5–1)
Coach M. J. Williams *Game Captains*

Day	Date	Opponent	Score	Site	Day/Night
Saturday	09/27	Poplarville HS	L/0–25	Poplarville, Miss	Day
Saturday	10/11	Gulf Coast Military Acad.	L/0–19	Gulfport, Miss.	Day
Saturday	10/18	Mobile Military Acad.	W/11–0	Hattiesburg	Day
Saturday	10/25	Gulf Coast Military Acad.	L/6–11	Hattiesburg	Day
Saturday	11/08	Mobile Military Acad.	L/0–14	Mobile, Ala.	Day
Saturday	11/22	Poplarville HS	T/0–0	Hattiesburg	Day
Thursday	11/27	Mississippi	L/7–13	Hattiesburg	Day

1914 (2–3–1)
Coach A. B. Dillie *Game Captains*

Day	Date	Opponent	Score	Site	Day/Night
Friday	10/02	Mississippi College	L/0–39	Clinton, Miss.	Day
Saturday	10/17	Spring Hill	L/13–24	Mobile, Ala.	Day
Saturday	10/24	Mobile Military Acad.	W/24–0	Hattiesburg	Day
Saturday	10/31	Gulf Coast Military Acad.	L/0–22	Gulfport, Miss.	Day
Saturday	11/07	Perkinston HS	W/9–0	Hattiesburg	Day
Saturday	11/14	Poplarville HS	T/0–0	Hattiesburg	Day

1915 (4–4)
Coach A. B. Dillie *Captain: Jack Thompson*

Day	Date	Opponent	Score	Site	Day/Night
Saturday	10/09	Poplarville HS	L/0–6	Hattiesburg	Day
Saturday	10/16	Gulf Coast Military Acad.	L/0–3	Gulfport, Miss.	Day
Saturday	10/23	Mississippi College	L/7–55	Jackson, Miss.	Day
Saturday	10/30	Perkinston HS	W/26–0	Hattiesburg	Day
Saturday	11/06	Spring Hill	L/7–33	Mobile, Ala.	Day
Saturday	11/13	Copiah-Lincoln HS	W/55–0	Hattiesburg	Day
Saturday	11/20	Poplarville HS	W/12–0	Hattiesburg	Day
Thursday	11/25	Gulf Coast Military Acad.	W/7–6	Hattiesburg	Day

1916 (0–3)
Coach A. B. Dillie *Game Captains*

Day	Date	Opponent	Score	Site	Day/Night
Saturday	10/07	Poplarville HS		Hattiesburg	Day
Saturday	10/14	Meridian High School	L/0–31	Meridian, Miss.	Day
Saturday	10/28	Chamberlain Hunt Acad.		Hattiesburg	Day
Tuesday	11/07	Mississippi College	L/0–75	Hattiesburg	Day
Saturday	11/11	Spring Hill College	L/0–87	Mobile, Ala.	Day
Saturday	11/18	Poplarville HS		Poplarville, Miss.	Day
Friday	11/24	Meridian High School		Hattiesburg	Day
Thursday	11/30	Gulf Coast Military Acad.		Hattiesburg	Day

1917–18
No team due to World War I

1919 (4–1–2)
Coach Cephus Anderson *Captain: B. B. O'Mara*

Day	Date	Opponent	Score	Site	Day/Night
Saturday	10/04	Perkinston AHS	W/12–0	Hattiesburg	Day
Saturday	10/18	Poplarville AHS	W/2–0	Hattiesburg	Day
Saturday	10/25	Meridian College	T/6–6	Meridian, Miss.	Day
Saturday	11/01	Gulf Coast Military Acad.	T/6–6	Hattiesburg	Day
Saturday	11/08	Chamberlain Hunt Acad.	W/20–0	Hattiesburg	Day
Monday	11/17	Mississippi College	L/7–19	Hattiesburg	Day
Thursday	11/27	Meridian College	W/47–0	Hattiesburg	Day

1920 (5–2–1)
Coach B. B. O'Mara *Captain: C. C. (Mutt) Campbell*

Day	Date	Opponent	Score	Site	Day/Night
Saturday	10/02	Perkinston HS	W/64–0	Hattiesburg	Day
Saturday	10/09	Mississippi	L/54–0	Hattiesburg	Day
Saturday	10/16	Millsaps	T/7–7	Hattiesburg	Day
Saturday	10/23	Spring Hill College	W/12–2	Mobile, Ala.	Day
Saturday	11/06	Spring Hill College	W/32–0	Hattiesburg	Day

Day	Date	Opponent	Score	Site	Day/Night
Thursday	11/11	Tulane Freshman	L/0–19	Hattiesburg	Day
Saturday	11/20	Miss. Industrial Training School of Columbia	W/27–0	Hattiesburg	Day
Thursday	11/25	Gulf Coast Military Acad.	W40–0	Hattiesburg	Day

1921 (3–4)
Coach O. V. Austin *Captain: H. V. McGilvary*

Day	Date	Opponent	Score	Site	Day/Night
Friday	10/07	Ellisville HS	W/20–0	Ellisville, Miss.	Day
Saturday	10/15	Smith County HS	W/113–0	Hattiesburg	Day
Friday	10/21	Millsaps	L/0–27	Jackson, Miss.	Day
Saturday	10/29	Jones County HS	W/37–0	Hattiesburg	Day
Saturday	11/05	St. Stanislaus College	L/0–49	Bay St. Louis, Miss.	Day
Friday	11/11	Poplarville HS	L/0–40	Hattiesburg	Day
Thursday	11/24	Loyola University	L/13–25	Hattiesburg	Day

1922 (2–6)
Coach O. V. Austin *Captain: L. E. Gafford*

Day	Date	Opponent	Score	Site	Day/Night
Friday	09/29	Jones County HS	W/31–0	Ellisville, Miss.	Day
Saturday	10/07	Purvis HS	L/0–6	Hattiesburg	Day
Thursday	10/12	Millsaps College	L/7–10	Jackson, Miss.	Day
Saturday	10/28	St. Stanislaus College	L/0–10	Bay St. Louis, Miss.	Day
Saturday	11/04	Gulf Coast Military Acad.	L/0–20	Hattiesburg	Day
Saturday	11/11	Loyola University	L/6–20	New Orleans, La.	Day
Saturday	11/18	Marion Military Institute	L/0–44	Marion, Ala.	Day
Thursday	11/23	Miss. State Freshman	W/19–12	Hattiesburg	Day

1923 (3–3)
Coach O. V. Austin *Captain: Nollie C. Felts*

Day	Date	Opponent	Score	Site	Day/Night
Friday	10/05	Purvis HS	W/26–0	Hattiesburg	Day
Friday	10/12	Millsaps	L/0–31	Jackson, Miss.	Day
Saturday	11/03	Seashore Camp Ground	W/52–0	Hattiesburg	Day
Saturday	11/10	Gulf Coast Military Acad.	L/6–7	Hattiesburg	Day
Saturday	11/17	Louisiana-Lafayette	L/0–66	Lafayette, La.	Day
Friday	11/23	Miss. Coll. Freshman	W/6–0	Hattiesburg	Day

1924 (3–3–2)
Coach Herschel Bobo *Captain: R. H. Tucker; Alternate Captain: F. S. Leech*

Day	Date	Opponent	Score	Site	Day/Night
Saturday	10/04	Clarke Memorial College	W/27–0	Hattiesburg, Miss	Day
Friday	10/17	Loyola College	L/7–32	New Orleans, La.	Day
Friday	10/24	Gulf Coast Military Acad.	T/14–14	Gulfport, Miss.	Day
Saturday	11/01	Pearl River CC	L/6–26	Hattiesburg	Day
Friday	11/07	Miss. State Freshman	T/14–14	Starkville, Miss.	Day
Saturday	11/15	Stetson	L/6–48	DeLand, Fla.	Day

Day	Date	Opponent	Score	Site	Day/Night
Saturday	11/22	Marion Military Institute	W/7–6	Hattiesburg	Day
Thursday	11/27	Louisiana College	W/13–12	Hattiesburg	Day

1925 (0–6)

Coach Herschel Bobo *Captain: F. S. Leech*

Day	Date	Opponent	Score	Site	Day/Night
Friday	10/02	Clarke Mem. College	L/32–0	Hattiesburg	Day
Saturday	10/10	Mississippi Freshman	L/6–38	Hattiesburg	Day
Saturday	10/17	All-Navy Service Team	L/6–32	Pensacola, Fla.	Day
Saturday	10/24	Louisiana-Lafayette	L/0–40	Lafayette, La.	Day
Friday	11/07	Pearl River CC	L/7–13	Poplarville, Miss.	Day
Saturday	11/15	Spring Hill	L/0–40	Mobile, Ala.	Day
Thursday	11/25	Gulf Coast Military Acad.	W/40–0	Hattiesburg	Day

1926 (3–4–1)

Coach Herschel Bobo *Captain: H. T. Ferrell; Alternate Captain: R. H. Tucker*

Day	Date	Opponent	Score	Site	Day/Night
Saturday	09/25	Louisiana-Lafayette	L/6–33	Lafayette, La.	Day
Saturday	10/02	Clarke Mem. College	W/12–7	Hattiesburg	Day
Saturday	10/09	Spring Hill College	L/6–27	Mobile, Ala.	Day
Saturday	10/16	Louisiana College	W/14–7	Hattiesburg	Day
Friday	10/22	Gulf Coast CC	W/26–3	Perkinston, Miss.	Day
Saturday	10/30	Gulf Coast Military Acad.	T/6–6	Hattiesburg	Day
Saturday	11/13	Pearl River CC	L/0–20	Hattiesburg	Day
Saturday	11/27	Miss. St. Freshman	L/7–26	Starkville, Miss.	Day

1927 (3–4–1)

Coach Herschel Bobo *Captain: A. T. Gullette; Alternate Captain: Nollie Felts*

Day	Date	Opponent	Score	Site	Day/Night
Saturday	09/24	Louisiana-Lafayette	L/0–6	Lafayette, La.	Day
Saturday	10/01	Gulf Coast CC	T/0–0	Hattiesburg	Day
Saturday	10/08	Hinds Junior College	W/12–0	Hattiesburg	Day
Friday	10/21	Miss. St. Freshman	L/0–24	Hattiesburg	Day
Saturday	10/29	Clarke Mem. College	L/0–18	Newton, Miss.	Day
Saturday	11/05	Spring Hill College	L/0–37	Mobile, Ala.	Day
Friday	11/11	Pearl River CC	W/15–0	Hattiesburg	Day
Saturday	11/18	St. Stanislaus College	W/25–13	Bay St. Louis, Miss.	Day

1928 (4–5)

Coach W. B. Saunders *Captain: Albert Rogers; Alternate Captain: Joseph P. (Noonie) Hackney*

Day	Date	Opponent	Score	Site	Day/Night
Saturday	09/29	Mississippi College	L/0–83	Clinton, Miss.	Day
Friday	10/05	Gulf Coast CC	W/12–2	Perkinston, Miss.	Day
Saturday	10/13	Newton JC	W/7–0	Hattiesburg	Day
Wednesday	10/17	Pearl River CC	W/6–0	Hattiesburg	Day
Saturday	10/27	Louisiana-Lafayette	L/7–37	Lafayette, La.	Day

Day	Date	Opponent	Score	Site	Day/Night
Saturday	11/10	Miss. College Freshmen	W/12–6	Hattiesburg	Day
Friday	11/16	Marion Military Institute	L/6–53	Selma, Ala.	Day
Friday	11/23	Copiah-Lincoln CC	L/6–13	Hattiesburg	Day
Thursday	11/29	Clarke Mem. College	L/6–40	Hattiesburg	Day

1929 (2–6–1)
Coach W. B. Saunders   Captain: Joseph P. (Noonie) Hackney

Day	Date	Opponent	Score	Site	Day/Night
Saturday	09/28	Louisiana-Lafayette	L/0–7	Lafayette, La.	Day
Saturday	10/05	Mississippi College	L/0–20	Clinton, Miss.	Day
Saturday	10/12	Marion Military Institute	W/31–0	Hattiesburg	Day
Friday	10/18	Southwest Miss. JC	T/6–6	Hattiesburg	Day
Saturday	11/02	Spring Hill College	L/6–25	Mobile, Ala.	Day
Saturday	11/09	Pearl River CC	L/7–14	Hattiesburg	Day
Saturday	11/16	Louisiana College	L/6–12	Pineville, La.	Day
Saturday	11/22	Delta State	L/6–14	Cleveland, Miss.	Day
Saturday	11/29	Clarke Mem. College	W/12–7	Hattiesburg	Day

1930 (3–5–1)
Coach John Lumpkin   Captain: Homer McMahan

Day	Date	Opponent	Score	Site	Day/Night
Friday	09/27	Clarke Mem. College	W/45–0	Hattiesburg	Day
Friday	10/04	Millsaps	L/0–26	Jackson, Miss.	Day
Saturday	10/12	Mississippi College	L/6–18	Clinton, Miss.	Day
Saturday	10/18	Louisiana-Lafayette	L/0–14	Lafayette, La.	Day
Saturday	10/25	Louisiana College	W/47–20	Hattiesburg	Day
Saturday	11/01	Spring Hill	L/6–7	Hattiesburg	Day
Friday	11/14	NW Louisiana	L/12–32	Natchitoches, La.	Day
Saturday	11/22	Delta State	W/46–0	Hattiesburg	Day
Thursday	11/27	Union College	T/0–0	Hattiesburg	Day

1931 (2–5, SIAA: 2–4)
Coach Pooley Hubert   Captain: Ellis Bilbo; Alternate Captain: Jack Bishop

Day	Date	Opponent	Score	Site	Day/Night
Saturday	10/03	*Millsaps	L/0–19	Hattiesburg	Night
Saturday	10/10	*Mississippi College	L/13–46	Clinton, Miss.	Day
Saturday	10/17	*Spring Hill	L/2–12	Mobile, Ala.	Day
Saturday	10/24	*Louisiana College	L/0–13	Pineville, La.	Night
Saturday	11/07	*Southwestern Univ.	W/13–7	Hattiesburg	Day
Saturday	11/14	*NW Louisiana	W/32–0	Hattiesburg	Day
Saturday	11/21	Delta State	L/7–27	Cleveland, Miss.	Day

*SIAA game

1932 (5–4, SIAA: 3–3)
Coach Pooley Hubert   Captain: Brownie Thomas; Alternate Captain: Walker Wilson

Day	Date	Opponent	Score	Site	Day/Night
Saturday	09/24	Mississippi	L/0–49	Oxford, Miss.	Day

Day	Date	Opponent	Score	Site	Day/Night
Saturday	10/01	*Millsaps	L/0–27	Jackson, Miss.	Night
Friday	10/07	*Louisiana-Lafayette	L/0–19	Lafayette, La.	Night
Saturday	10/22	*Southwestern Univ.	L/0–19	Memphis, Tenn.	Day
Saturday	10/29	Spring Hill (HC)	W/12–0	Hattiesburg	Day
Saturday	11/05	*Louisiana College	W/12–0	Hattiesburg	Day
Friday	11/11	*NW Louisiana	L/6–31	Natchitoches, La.	Day
Saturday	11/19	Delta State	W/33–25	Hattiesburg	Day
Thursday	11/24	*Union University	W/6–0	Hattiesburg	Day

*SIAA game

1933 (3-5-2, SIAA: 2-4-1)
Coach Pooley Hubert   *Captain: Nolan Taconi*

Day	Date	Opponent	Score	Site	Day/Night
Friday	09/22	*Loyola of the South	L/0–47	New Orleans, La.	Night
Saturday	09/30	Mississippi	L/0–45	Oxford, Miss.	Day
Saturday	10/07	*Mississippi College	L/7–33	Clinton, Miss.	Day
Saturday	10/14	*Millsaps	T/0–0	Jackson, Miss.	Night
Saturday	10/21	*Louisiana-Lafayette	W/6–0	Hattiesburg	Day
Saturday	10/28	*Louisiana College	W/21–6	Pineville, La.	Day
Saturday	11/04	Spring Hill	T/0–0	Mobile, Ala.	Day
Saturday	11/11	*NW Louisiana (HC)	L/0–13	Hattiesburg	Day
Saturday	11/25	Delta State	W/33–6	Hattiesburg	Day
Friday	12/01	*Murray State	L/0–30	Murray, Ky.	Night

*SIAA game

1934 (3-4-2; SIAA: 2-2-1)
Coach Pooley Hubert   *Captain: Bernard Kisner*

Day	Date	Opponent	Score	Site	Day/Night
Friday	09/28	Poplarville CC	W/20–12	Hattiesburg	Day
Saturday	10/06	*Mississippi College	L/0–12	Clinton, Miss.	Day
Friday	10/12	Delta State	T/13–13	Cleveland, Miss.	Night
Friday	10/19	*Louisiana-Lafayette	W/12–6	Hattiesburg	Night
Saturday	10/27	*Millsaps	T/0–0	Hattiesburg	Night
Friday	11/02	Spring Hill (HC)	L/0–7	Hattiesburg	Night
Friday	11/09	*NW Louisiana	L/0–31	Natchitoches, La.	Night
Saturday	11/17	Union University	L/6–26	Hattiesburg	Night
Thursday	11/29	*Murray State	W/12–2	Hattiesburg	Day

*SIAA game

1935 (6-4, SIAA: 5-1)
Coach Pooley Hubert   *Captain: J. D. Stonestreet*

Day	Date	Opponent	Score	Site	Day/Night
Friday	09/20	Jones County JC	W/7–0	Ellisville, Miss.	Night
Saturday	10/05	*Louisiana College	W/12–0	Hattiesburg	Night
Saturday	10/12	Troy State	L/13–14	Hattiesburg	Night
Friday	10/18	*NW Louisiana	W/26–12	Hattiesburg	Night
Saturday	10/26	*Memphis	W/12–0	Memphis, Tenn.	Day
Friday	11/01	Spring Hill	L/0–19	Mobile, Ala.	Night

Day	Date	Opponent	Score	Site	Day/Night
Friday	11/08	*Louisiana-Lafayette	W/19–7	Lake Charles, La.	Night
Friday	11/15	Mississippi State (HC)	L/0–27	Hattiesburg	Night
Thursday	11/28	*Louisiana Tech	L/0–27	Ruston, La.	Day
Saturday	12/07	*Union	W/12–6	Hattiesburg	Day

*SIAA game

1936 (7-2-1, SIAA: 4-2-1)
Coach Pooley Hubert   *Captain: Leroy Austin*

Day	Date	Opponent	Score	Site	Day/Night
Saturday	09/26	*Louisiana College	W/7–0	Pineville, La.	Night
Saturday	10/03	*Union	L/0–7	Jackson, Tenn.	Night
Friday	10/09	*Millsaps	T/0–0	Hattiesburg	Night
Friday	10/16	*Louisiana Tech	W/12–7	Ruston, La.	Night
Friday	10/23	*Memphis	W/25–0	Hattiesburg	Night
Thursday	10/29	Spring Hill	W/12–7	Hattiesburg	Night
Friday	11/06	Troy State	W/24–0	Hattiesburg	Night
Friday	11/13	*Louisiana-Lafayette (HC)	W/44–14	Hattiesburg	Night
Saturday	11/21	*NW Louisiana	L/0–13	Natchitoches, La.	Night
Thursday	11/26	East Texas State	W/13–6	Hattiesburg	Day

*SIAA game

1937 (7-3, SIAA: 5-2)
Coach Reed Green   *Game Captains*

Day	Date	Opponent	Score	Site	Day/Night
Friday	09/24	*Louisiana College	W/19–0	Hattiesburg	Night
Friday	10/01	Spring Hill	W/33–0	Mobile, Ala.	Night
Friday	10/08	*Louisiana-Lafayette	W/13–0	Lafayette, La.	Night
Friday	10/15	*Louisiana Tech	L/0–7	Ruston, La.	Night
Friday	10/22	*Jacksonville St.	W/58–0	Hattiesburg	Night
Friday	10/29	*Troy State	W/53–0	Hattiesburg	Night
Friday	11/05	*Union	W/34–0	Hattiesburg	Night
Saturday	11/13	*NW Louisiana (HC)	L/0–3	Hattiesburg	Day
Thursday	11/25	East Texas State	L/6–14	Commerce, Tex.	Day
Wednesday	12/01	Appalachian State	W/7–0	Gulfport, Miss.	Night

*SIAA game

1938 (7-2, SIAA: 6-1)
Coach Reed Green   *Game Captains*

Day	Date	Opponent	Score	Site	Day/Night
Friday	09/23	Arkansas-Monticello	W/39–0	Hattiesburg	Night
Friday	09/30	*Troy State	W/19–0	Dothan, Ala.	Night
Saturday	10/08	Mississippi	L/0–14	Oxford, Miss.	Day
Saturday	10/15	*Delta State	W/44–0	Hattiesburg	Night
Friday	10/28	*Millsaps (HC)	W/47–0	Hattiesburg	Night
Saturday	11/05	*Louisiana College	W/7–0	Pineville, La.	Night
Friday	11/11	*Louisiana-Lafayette	W/7–0	Hattiesburg	Night
Saturday	11/19	*NW Louisiana	L/0–6	Natchitoches, La.	Day

Day	Date	Opponent	Score	Site	Day/Night
Thursday	11/24	*Union	W/32–0	Hattiesburg	Day

*SIAA game

1939 (4-2-3, SIAA: 4-1)
Coach Reed Green *Game Captains*

Day	Date	Opponent	Score	Site	Day/Night
Friday	09/29	*Troy State	W/13–6	Hattiesburg	Night
Friday	10/06	Sam Houston State	T/7–7	Huntsville, Tex.	Night
Saturday	10/13	Millsaps	T/0–0	Jackson, Miss.	Day
Saturday	10/20	*Delta State	W/21–0	Cleveland, Miss.	Night
Saturday	11/04	*Louisiana College (HC)	W/7–0	Hattiesburg	Day
Saturday	11/11	Mississippi	L/7–27	Hattiesburg	Day
Saturday	11/18	*Louisiana-Lafayette	W/9–7	Lafayette, La.	Day
Thursday	11/23	*NW Louisiana	L/0–7	Hattiesburg	Night
Friday	12/01	Saint Mary's (Tex.)	T/13–13	Hattiesburg	Night

*SIAA game

1940 (7-4, SIAA: 3-2)
Coach Reed Green *Game Captains*

Day	Date	Opponent	Score	Site	Day/Night
Friday	09/27	*Troy State	W/25–0	Hattiesburg	Night
Friday	10/04	Sam Houston State	L/16–18	Hattiesburg	Night
Friday	10/11	SE Louisiana	W/13–6	Hammond, La.	Night
Saturday	10/19	Millsaps	L/7–14	Jackson, Miss.	Day
Saturday	10/26	Spring Hill (HC)	W/38–6	Hattiesburg	Night
Saturday	11/01	*Louisiana College	L/0–7	Pineville, La.	Night
Saturday	11/08	*NW Louisiana	L/6–9	Natchitoches, La.	Day
Friday	11/15	*Louisiana-Lafayette	W/21–14	Hattiesburg	Night
Friday	11/22	*Delta State	W/41–0	Hattiesburg	Night
Thursday	12/05	Saint Mary's (Tex.)	W/27–6	Corpus Christi, Tex.	Night
Saturday	12/14	37th Division	W/26–0	Hattiesburg	Day

*SIAA game

1941 (9-0-1, SIAA: 4-0-1)
Coach Reed Green *Game Captains*

Day	Date	Opponent	Score	Site	Day/Night
Friday	09/26	Georgia St. Teachers	W/70–0	Hattiesburg	Night
Friday	10/03	*Louisiana Tech	W/19–7	Ruston, La.	Night
Friday	10/10	SE Louisiana	W/43–6	Hattiesburg	Night
Friday	10/17	Millsaps	W/20–0	Hattiesburg	Night
Friday	10/24	Spring Hill	W/26–7	Mobile, Ala.	Night
Saturday	11/01	*Louisiana College (HC)	W/13–6	Hattiesburg	Day
Friday	11/07	*NW Louisiana	W/21–7	Hattiesburg	Day
Friday	11/14	*Louisiana-Lafayette	T/0–0	Lafayette, La.	Night
Friday	11/21	*Delta State	W/27–7	Cleveland, Miss.	Day
Saturday	11/29	Saint Mary's (Tex.)	W/7–0	San Antonio, Tex.	Night

*SIAA game

1942 (4–0)

Coach Reed Green *Game Captains*

Day	Date	Opponent	Score	Site	Day/Night
Friday	10/23	6th Service Squad	W/41–0	Hattiesburg	Night
Saturday	10/31	Mobile Shipbuilders	W/26–7	Mobile, Ala.	Night
Friday	11/20	Mobile Shipbuilders	W/42–0	Hattiesburg	Night
Friday	12/04	Brookley Field	W/33–0	Hattiesburg	Night

1943–45
No team due to World War II

1946 (7–3)

Coach Reed Green *Game Captains*

Day	Date	Opponent	Score	Site	Attendance	Day/Night
Saturday	09/21	Louisiana Tech	W/7–6	Hattiesburg	7,000	Night
Friday	09/27	Auburn	L/12–13	Montgomery, Ala.	12,000	Night
Friday	10/04	Jacksonville State	W/65–0	Hattiesburg	6,500	Night
Friday	10/18	Louisiana-Lafayette (HC)	W/6–0	Hattiesburg	8,000	Night
Friday	10/25	Oklahoma City	W/20–6	Hattiesburg		Night
Saturday	11/02	Stephen F. Austin	W/7–0	Nacogdoches, Tex.		Night
Friday	11/08	NW Louisiana	L/6–7	Natchitoches, La.		Day
Friday	11/15	Louisiana College	W/65–0	Hattiesburg	5,000	Night
Friday	11/22	SE Louisiana	L/0–20	Hattiesburg		Night

Cigar Bowl

| Saturday | 12/07 | Havana | W/55–0 | Havana, Cuba | | Night |

1947 (7–3)

Coach Reed Green *Captain: Jay Smith; Alternate Captain: Bucky Waters*

Day	Date	Opponent	Score	Site	Attendance	Day/Night
Saturday	09/20	Alabama	L/7–34	Birmingham, Ala.	30,000	Night
Friday	09/26	Auburn	W/19–13	Montgomery, Ala.	15,000	Night
Saturday	10/11	Louisiana Tech	W/7–6	Ruston, La.		Night
Saturday	10/18	Louisiana-Lafayette	W/15–7	Lafayette, La.		Night
Saturday	10/25	Oklahoma City	L/6–21	Oklahoma City, Okla.		Night
Saturday	11/01	Stephen F. Austin (HC)	W/20–7	Hattiesburg	9,500	Night
Friday	11/07	NW Louisiana	W/20–0	Hattiesburg		Night
Friday	11/14	Union	W/18–0	Hattiesburg		Night
Saturday	11/22	Mississippi State	L/7–14	Starkville, Miss.	24,000	Day
Thursday	11/27	SE Louisiana	W/35–0	Hammond, La.		Day

1948 (7–3, GSC: 4–0)

Gulf States Conference Champions

Coach Reed Green *Captain: Cooter Lewis; Co-Captain: Cliff Coggin*

Day	Date	Opponent	Score	Site	Attendance	Day/Night
Friday	09/24	Auburn	L/14–20	Montgomery, Ala.	16,000	Night
Friday	10/01	Stephen F. Austin	W/41–0	Hattiesburg	8,000	Night

Day	Date	Opponent	Score	Site	Attendance	Day/Night
Friday	10/08	Trinity	L/9–26	Hattiesburg		Night
Friday	10/15	*Louisiana-Lafayette	W/26–6	Hattiesburg	8,433	Night
Saturday	10/23	Oklahoma City	W/55–20	Oklahoma City, Okla.		Night
Saturday	10/30	*NW Louisiana	W/38–14	Natchitoches, La.		Night
Saturday	11/06	Alabama	L/0–27	Tuscaloosa, Ala.	20,000	Day
Saturday	11/13	*Louisiana Tech (HC)	W/20–6	Hattiesburg	8,000	Night
Friday	11/19	*SE Louisiana	W/27–0	Hattiesburg		Night
Wednesday	11/24	Union	W/47–8	Hattiesburg		Night

*Gulf States Conference game

1949 (7-3, GSC: 3-0)

Coach Thad Vann *Captains: Bobby Holmes, Cliff Coggin*

Day	Date	Opponent	Score	Site	Attendance	Day/Night
Saturday	09/17	Kentucky	L/7–71	Lexington		Day
Saturday	09/24	Delta State	W/20–13	Hattiesburg		Night
Saturday	10/08	McMurray (HC)	W/55–32	Hattiesburg		Night
Saturday	10/15	*Louisiana-Lafayette	W/25–0	Lafayette, La,		Night
Friday	10/21	Tenn.-Chattanooga	W/33–20	Chattanooga, Tenn.	7,500	Night
Saturday	10/29	*NW Louisiana	W/67–28	Hattiesburg		Night
Saturday	11/05	Oklahoma City	W/27–21	Hattiesburg		Night
Saturday	11/12	*Louisiana Tech	L/13–34	Ruston, La.		Night
Saturday	11/19	Alabama	L/26–34	Tuscaloosa, Ala.		Day
Thursday	11/24	Louisville	W/26–21	Hattiesburg		Night

*Gulf States Conference game

1950 (5-5, GSC: 3-1)

Gulf States Conference Champions

Coach Thad Vann *Captain: Bubba Phillips; Alternate Captain: Ivan Rosamond*

Day	Date	Opponent	Score	Site	Attendance	Day/Night
Saturday	09/23	Tennessee	L/0–56	Knoxville, Tenn.		Day
Saturday	09/30	Delta State	L/13–19	Hattiesburg	7,500	Night
Saturday	10/07	McMurray	L/19–37	Abilene, Tex.	3,000	Night
Saturday	10/14	*Louisiana-Lafayette (HC)	W/6–0	Hattiesburg		Night
Saturday	10/21	*SE Louisiana	L/0–7	Hammond, La.		Night
Friday	10/27	Tenn.-Chattanooga	W/14–13	Mobile, Ala.	5,000	Night
Saturday	11/04	*NW Louisiana	W/7–0	Natchitoches, La.		Night
Saturday	11/11	Alabama	L/0–53	Tuscaloosa, Ala.	15,000	Day
Saturday	11/18	*Louisiana Tech	W/41–20	Hattiesburg		Night
Saturday	11/25	Louisville	W/34–28	Hattiesburg	3,000	Night

*Gulf States Conference game

1951 (6-5; GSC:4-0)

Gulf States Conference Champions

Coach Thad Vann *Captain: Phil Musmeci; Alternate Captain: Tom LeGros*

Day	Date	Opponent	Score	Site	Attendance	Day/Night
Saturday	09/15	East Carolina	W/40–0	Hattiesburg		Night

Day	Date	Opponent	Score	Site	Attendance	Day/Night
Saturday	09/22	Louisiana State	L/0–13	Baton Rouge, La.		Night
Saturday	09/29	Carswell AFB	L/0–26	Hattiesburg		Night
Saturday	10/06	McMurray	W/54–7	Hattiesburg	6,000	Night
Saturday	10/13	*Louisiana-Lafayette	W/41–0	Lafayette, La.		Night
Saturday	10/20	*SE Louisiana	W/35–6	Hattiesburg		Night
Friday	10/26	Tenn.-Chattanooga	L/7–19	Chattanooga, Tenn.	11,500	Night
Saturday	11/03	*NW Louisiana (HC)	W/76–0	Hattiesburg	6,500	Night
Saturday	11/10	Alabama	L/7–40	Tuscaloosa, Ala.		Day
Saturday	11/17	*Louisiana Tech	W/33–7	Ruston, La.		Night
Friday	11/23	Louisville	L/13–14	Louisville, Ky.		Day

*Gulf States Conference game

1952 (10–2)

Coach Thad Vann   *Captain: Bob McKellar; Alternate Captain: Milton White*

Day	Date	Opponent	Score	Site	Day/Night
Friday	09/19	Alabama	L/6–20	Montgomery, Ala.	Night
Saturday	09/27	Memphis	W/27–20	Hattiesburg	Night
Saturday	10/04	Tampa	W/52–25	Tampa, Fla.	Night
Saturday	10/11	Louisiana-Lafayette	W/32–12	Lafayette, La.	Night
Saturday	10/18	SE Louisiana	W/20–12	Hattiesburg	Night
Saturday	10/25	Tenn.-Chattanooga (HC)	W/27–14	Hattiesburg	Night
Saturday	11/01	NW Louisiana	W/39–13	Natchitoches, La.	Night
Saturday	11/08	Florida State	W/50–21	Tallahassee, Fla.	Day
Saturday	11/15	Louisiana Tech	W/52–0	Hattiesburg	Night
Saturday	11/22	Louisville	W/55–26	Jackson, Miss.	Day
Saturday	11/29	Stetson	W/42–0	Hattiesburg	Night

Sun Bowl

Day	Date	Opponent	Score	Site	Day/Night
Thursday	1/01	Pacific	L/7–26	El Paso, Tex.	Day

1953 (9–2)

Coach Thad Vann   *Captain: Jackson Brumfield; Alternate Captain: J. T. Shepherd*

Day	Date	Opponent	Score	Site	Attendance	Day/Night
Friday	09/18	Alabama	W/25–19	Montgomery, Ala.	14,500	Night
Saturday	09/26	Parris Island Marines	W/40–0	Hattiesburg		Night
Saturday	10/03	Tampa	W/42–6	Hattiesburg		Night
Saturday	10/10	Louisiana-Lafayette	W/41–14	Lafayette, La.		Night
Saturday	10/17	SE Louisiana	W/7–0	Hattiesburg	13,000	Night
Saturday	10/31	Memphis	L/27–13	Memphis, Tenn.		Night
Saturday	11/07	Florida State (HC)	W/21–0	Hattiesburg		Night
Saturday	11/14	Louisiana Tech	W/30–0	Ruston, La.	7,000	Night
Saturday	11/21	Georgia	W/14–0	Jackson, Miss.	25,000	Day
Thursday	11/26	Tenn.-Chattanooga	W/33–19	Chattanooga, Tenn.		Day

Sun Bowl

Day	Date	Opponent	Score	Site	Day/Night
Friday	1/01	Texas Western	L/14–37	El Paso, Tex.	Day

1954 (6–4)
Coach Thad Vann   Captain: Hamp Cook; Alternate Captain: Brooks Tisdale

Day	Date	Opponent	Score	Site	Attendance	Day/Night
Friday	09/17	Alabama	W/7–2	Montgomery, Ala.	21,000	Night
Saturday	09/25	Louisiana Tech	W/28–0	Hattiesburg		Night
Saturday	10/02	North Texas State	L/7–15	Denton, Tex.		Night
Saturday	10/09	Abilene Christian	W/23–7	Hattiesburg		Night
Saturday	10/16	SE Louisiana	L/7–13	Hattiesburg		Night
Saturday	10/23	Tenn.-Chattanooga (HC)	W/14–7	Hattiesburg	10,000	Night
Saturday	11/06	Dayton	L/7–20	Dayton, Ohio		Night
Saturday	11/13	Villanova	W/27–0	Mobile, Ala.	14,617	Night
Saturday	11/20	Memphis	W/34–21	Hattiesburg	8,000	Night
Saturday	11/27	Florida State	L/18–19	Tallahassee, Fla.		Day

1955 (9–1)
Coach Thad Vann   Captain: George Herring; Alternate Captain: Fred Smallwood

Day	Date	Opponent	Score	Site	Attendance	Day/Night
Saturday	09/17	Elon	W/39–0	Hattiesburg	8,000	Night
Saturday	09/24	Louisiana Tech	W/7–6	Ruston, La.	7,500	Night
Friday	09/30	Tenn.-Chattanooga	L/0–10	Chattanooga, Tenn.	6,800	Night
Saturday	10/08	North Texas St. (HC)	W/26–0	Hattiesburg	12,500	Night
Saturday	10/15	SE Louisiana	W/33–0	Hammond, La.	8,000	Night
Friday	10/21	Memphis	W/34–14	Memphis, Tenn.	9,189	Night
Saturday	11/05	Abilene Christian	W/40–0	Abilene, Tex.	7,000	Day
Saturday	11/12	North Dakota State	W/58–0	Hattiesburg	10,000	Night
Saturday	11/19	Dayton	W/19–13	Jackson, Miss.	6,500	Night
Friday	11/25	Florida State	W/21–6	Hattiesburg	7,000	Night

1956 (7–2–1)
Coach Thad Vann   Captain: Doug Barfield; Alternate Captain: Al Tregle

Day	Date	Opponent	Score	Site	Attendance	Day/Night
Saturday	09/22	Louisiana Tech	W/14–0	Hattiesburg	10,000	Night
Saturday	10/06	Dayton	W/23–6	Dayton, Ohio	7,895	Night
Saturday	10/13	SE Louisiana	W/21–14	Hattiesburg	12,500	Night
Saturday	10/20	Memphis	W/27–0	Hattiesburg	6,500	Night
Saturday	10/27	Tenn.-Chattanooga	W/33–0	Hattiesburg	6,500	Night
Saturday	11/03	Abilene Christian (HC)	W/36–6	Hattiesburg	15,000	Night
Saturday	11/10	Trinity	W/20–13	San Antonio, Tex.	6,081	Day
Saturday	11/17	Florida State	L/19–20	Tallahassee, Fla.	12,200	Day
Saturday	11/24	Alabama	T/13–13	Tuscaloosa, Ala.	16,000	Day

Tangerine Bowl

Day	Date	Opponent	Score	Site	Attendance	Day/Night
Tuesday	1/01	West Texas State	L/13–20	Orlando, Fla.	12,000	Night

1957 (8–3)
Coach Thad Vann   Captains: Lawrence Meeks, Curry Juneau

Day	Date	Opponent	Score	Site	Attendance	Day/Night
Saturday	09/21	Louisiana Tech	W/7–0	Ruston, La.	7,500	Night

Day	Date	Opponent	Score	Site	Attendance	Day/Night
Saturday	09/28	Trinity	W/13–0	Hattiesburg	7,000	Night
Saturday	10/05	West Texas State	W/34–0	Amarillo, Tex.	10,000	Night
Saturday	10/12	SE Louisiana	W/14–0	Hammond, La.	5,000	Night
Saturday	10/19	Memphis	W/14–6	Memphis, Tenn.	10,614	Night
Friday	10/25	Tenn.-Chattanooga	W/20–0	Chattanooga, Tenn.	6,500	Night
Saturday	11/02	Abilene Christian	W/7–0	Hattiesburg	11,000	Night
Saturday	11/09	Houston	L/12–27	Jackson, Miss.	11,000	Night
Saturday	11/16	Florida State (HC)	W/20–0	Hattiesburg	12,500	Night
Saturday	11/23	Alabama	L/2–29	Tuscaloosa, Ala.	18,500	Day

Tangerine Bowl

Day	Date	Opponent	Score	Site	Attendance	Day/Night
Wednesday	01/01	East Texas State	L/9–10	Orlando, Fla.	12,000	Night

1958 (9–0)
UPI College Division National Champions
Coach Thad Vann   Captain: Richard Johnston; Co-Captain: Jimmy Taylor

Day	Date	Opponent	Score	Site	Attendance	Day/Night
Saturday	09/20	Louisiana Tech	W/14–0	Hattiesburg	7,500	Night
Saturday	09/27	Trinity	W/15–0	San Antonio, Tex.	7,058	Night
Saturday	10/04	Memphis	W/24–22	Hattiesburg	11,000	Night
Saturday	10/11	SE Louisiana	W/33–6	Hattiesburg	9,500	Night
Saturday	10/25	West Texas St. (HC)	W/15–0	Hattiesburg	14,000	Night
Saturday	11/01	Abilene Christian	W/22–0	Abilene, Tex.	7,000	Day
Saturday	11/08	North Carolina State	W/26–14	Mobile. Ala.	18,987	Night
Saturday	11/15	Virginia Tech	W/41–0	Hattiesburg	11,000	Night
Thursday	11/27	Tenn.-Chattanooga	W/20–13	Chattanooga, Tenn.	9,500	Day

1959 (6–4)
Coach Thad Vann   Captain: Buddy Supple; Alternate Caption: Bob Rinehart

Day	Date	Opponent	Score	Site	Attendance	Day/Night
Saturday	09/26	Trinity	W/29–8	Hattiesburg	12,500	Night
Saturday	10/03	Texas A & M	L/3–7	Mobile, Ala.	25,781	Night
Saturday	10/10	SE Louisiana	W/26–6	Hattiesburg	12,200	Night
Saturday	10/17	West Texas State	W/37–6	Canyon, Tex.	5,000	Night
Saturday	10/24	Abilene Christian (HC)	W/30–10	Hattiesburg	14,200	Night
Saturday	10/31	Memphis	L/6–21	Memphis, Tenn.	9,262	Night
Saturday	11/07	North Carolina State	W/19–14	Mobile, Ala.	18,987	Day
Saturday	11/14	Tenn.-Chattanooga	W/14–6	Hattiesburg	7,100	Night
Saturday	11/21	Auburn	L/7–28	Auburn, Ala.	20,300	Day
Saturday	11/28	Louisiana Tech	L/0–16	Ruston, La.	7,000	Day

1960 (6–4)
Coach Thad Vann   Captain: Billy Larsen; Co-Captain: Ray St. Pierre

Day	Date	Opponent	Score	Site	Attendance	Day/Night
Friday	09/23	Hardin-Simmons	W/27–0	Mobile, Ala.	8,112	Night
Saturday	10/01	West Texas State	W/28–18	Hattiesburg	12,600	Night
Saturday	10/08	Trinity	W/16–0	San Antonio, Tex.	6,000	Night

Day	Date	Opponent	Score	Site	Attendance	Day/Night
Saturday	10/15	Florida State	W/15–13	Mobile, Ala.	15,207	Night
Saturday	10/22	N. Carolina St. (HC)	L/13–20	Hattiesburg	16,100	Night
Saturday	10/29	Abilene Christian	W/34–8	Abilene, Tex.	6,200	Day
Saturday	11/05	Arkansas State	L/13–14	Jonesboro, Ark.	7,000	Day
Saturday	11/12	Louisiana Tech	L/7–10	Hattiesburg	4,000	Night
Friday	11/18	Memphis	L/6–7	Hattiesburg	12,500	Night
Thursday	11/24	Tenn.-Chattanooga	W/30–6	Chattanooga, Tenn.	7,367	Day

1961 (8–2)

Coach Thad Vann *Captains: Don Fuell, Morris Meador*

Day	Date	Opponent	Score	Site	Attendance	Day/Night
Saturday	09/16	Arlington State	W/30–7	Hattiesburg	8,000	Night
Saturday	09/30	Louisiana-Lafayette	W/22–6	Lafayette, La.	3,500	Night
Saturday	10/07	Tenn.-Chattanooga	W/24–7	Hattiesburg	13,000	Night
Saturday	10/14	Memphis	L/7–21	Memphis, Tenn.	22,119	Night
Saturday	10/21	Arkansas State	W/20–0	Hattiesburg	6,100	Night
Saturday	10/28	Abilene Christian (HC)	W/33–6	Hattiesburg	11,000	Night
Saturday	11/04	North Carolina State	L/6–7	Mobile, Ala.	13,000	Night
Saturday	11/11	Louisiana Tech	W/7–0	Ruston, La.	2,500	Night
Saturday	11/18	Florida State	W/12–0	Tallahassee, Fla.	18,700	Day
Saturday	11/25	Trinity	W/22–14	Hattiesburg	5,000	Night

1962 (9–1)

UPI College Division National Champions
Coach Thad Vann *Captains: Harold Hays, Johnny Sklopan*

Day	Date	Opponent	Score	Site	Attendance	Day/Night
Saturday	09/15	Arlington State	W/28–7	Arlington, Tex.	9,800	Night
Saturday	09/22	Richmond	W/29–8	Hattiesburg	8,200	Night
Saturday	09/29	Louisiana-Lafayette	W/29–0	Hattiesburg	8,000	Night
Saturday	10/06	Tenn.-Chattanooga	W/31–13	Chattanooga, Tenn.	8,000	Night
Saturday	10/13	Memphis	L/6–8	Memphis, Tenn.	11,500	Night
Saturday	10/20	North Carolina State	W/30–0	Mobile, Ala.	10,522	Night
Saturday	10/27	Abilene Christian	W/30–0	Hattiesburg	12,000	Night
Saturday	11/03	Arkansas State	W/20–7	Jonesboro, Ark.	8,000	Night
Saturday	11/10	Trinity	W/33–6	Hattiesburg	10,500	Night
Saturday	11/17	Louisiana Tech (HC)	W/29–18	Hattiesburg	11,800	Day

1963 (5–3–1)

Coach Thad Vann *Captain: James Berry; Co-Captain: Nick Kolinsky*

Day	Date	Opponent	Score	Site	Attendance	Day/Night
Saturday	09/14	Memphis	L/7–28	Jackson, Miss.	24,000	Night
Saturday	09/28	North Carolina State	L/0–14	Hattiesburg	11,500	Night
Saturday	10/12	Richmond (HC)	W/7–0	Hattiesburg	10,000	Day
Saturday	10/19	Florida State	T/0–0	Mobile, Ala.	1,353	Day
Saturday	10/26	Arkansas State	W/25–0	Hattiesburg	7,500	Night
Saturday	11/02	Louisiana-Lafayette	W/28–0	Lafayette, La.	4,500	Night
Saturday	11/16	Louisiana Tech	L/0–10	Ruston, La.	7,000	Night

Day	Date	Opponent	Score	Site	Attendance	Day/Night
Saturday	11/23	The Citadel	W/37–12	Hattiesburg	4,000	Night
Thursday	11/28	Tenn.-Chattanooga	W/24–0	Chattanooga, Tenn.	7,000	Day

1964 (6–3)

Coach Thad Vann   *Captains: Jim King, Larry Ecuyer*

Day	Date	Opponent	Score	Site	Attendance	Day/Night
Saturday	09/26	Louisiana-Lafayette	W/30–0	Hattiesburg	9,500	Night
Saturday	10/03	Richmond	W/14–9	Hattiesburg	7,500	Night
Saturday	10/10	Memphis	W/20–14	Memphis, Tenn.	18,005	Night
Saturday	10/17	Mississippi State	L/7–48	Starkville, Miss.	19,000	Day
Saturday	10/24	Auburn	L/7–14	Auburn, Ala.	22,000	Day
Saturday	10/31	Florida State	L/0–34	Tallahassee, Fla.	26,132	Day
Saturday	11/07	Tenn.-Chattanooga (HC)	W/31–0	Hattiesburg	9,500	Day
Saturday	11/14	Louisiana Tech	W/14–7	Hattiesburg	9,000	Night
Saturday	11/21	Memphis	W/20–18	Jackson, Miss.	9,000	Night

1965

Coach Thad Vann   *Captains: Vic Purvis, Robert Brown*

Day	Date	Opponent	Score	Site	Attendance	Day/Night
Saturday	09/18	SE Louisiana	W/15–0	Hattiesburg	11,000	Night
Saturday	09/25	Memphis	W/21–16	Jackson, Miss.	22,500	Night
Saturday	10/02	Richmond	W/28–7	Hattiesburg	10,000	Night
Saturday	10/09	Mississippi State	L/9–27	Starkville, Miss.	25,000	Day
Saturday	10/16	Virginia Military Inst. (HC)	W/3–0	Hattiesburg	13,000	Day
Saturday	10/23	Auburn	W/3–0	Auburn, Ala.	25,000	Day
Saturday	10/30	William and Mary	L/0–3	Norfolk, Va.	24,000	Day
Saturday	11/06	Tenn.-Chattanooga	W/17–0	Chattanooga, Tenn.	6,400	Night
Saturday	11/13	Louisiana Tech	W/31–7	Ruston, La.	7,500	Night

1966 (6–4)

Coach Thad Vann   *Captain: Ken Avery*

Day	Date	Opponent	Score	Site	Attendance	Day/Night
Saturday	09/17	Louisiana Tech	W/14–0	Hattiesburg	10,000	Night
Saturday	09/24	SE Louisiana	W/15–13	Hammond, La.	8,000	Night
Saturday	10/01	Memphis	L/0–6	Memphis, Tenn.	21,213	Night
Saturday	10/08	Mississippi State	L/9–10	Starkville, Miss.	23,000	Day
Saturday	10/15	Mississippi	L/7–14	Oxford, Miss.	25,000	Day
Saturday	10/29	Richmond	W/27–0	Hattiesburg	8,600	Night
Saturday	11/05	Virginia Military Inst. (HC)	W/42–6	Hattiesburg	13,000	Day
Saturday	11/12	North Carolina State	W/7–6	Norfolk, Va.	22,000	Day
Saturday	11/19	East Carolina	W/35–14	Greenville, N.C.	12,811	Day
Saturday	11/26	Alabama	L/0–34	Mobile, Ala.	41,010	Day

1967 (6–3)

Coach Thad Vann   *Captains: Gene Bachman, Buddy Hunter*

Day	Date	Opponent	Score	Site	Attendance	Day/Night
Saturday	09/16	The Citadel	W/10–7	Charleston, S.C.	11,407	Night

Day	Date	Opponent	Score	Site	Attendance	Day/Night
Saturday	09/23	SE Louisiana	W/20–7	Hattiesburg	14,000	Night
Saturday	09/30	Alabama	L/3–25	Mobile, Ala.	38,785	Night
Saturday	10/07	Tampa	W/48–0	Hattiesburg	9,000	Night
Saturday	10/14	Mississippi State	W/21–14	Starkville, Miss.	24,000	Day
Saturday	10/21	Mississippi	L/7–14	Oxford, Miss.	25,000	Day
Saturday	10/28	Memphis	L/8–24	Jackson, Miss.	16,000	Night
Saturday	11/04	Richmond (HC)	W/19–7	Hattiesburg	12,000	Day
Thursday	11/23	Louisiana Tech	W/58–7	Shreveport, La.	4,500	Day

1968 (4–6)
Coach Thad Vann   *Captains: Blanchard Braud, Tommy Applewhite*

Day	Date	Opponent	Score	Site	Attendance	Day/Night
Saturday	09/21	SE Louisiana	W/27–15	Hammond	7,000	Night
Saturday	09/28	Alabama	L/14–17	Mobile, Ala.	38,051	Day
Saturday	10/05	East Carolina	W/65–0	Hattiesburg	17,500	Night
Saturday	10/12	Mississippi State	W/47–14	Starkville, Miss.	22,000	Day
Saturday	10/19	Mississippi	L/13–21	Oxford, Miss.	28,000	Day
Saturday	10/26	Memphis	L/7–29	Memphis, Tenn.	30,080	Night
Saturday	11/02	Louisiana Tech (HC)	L/20–27	Hattiesburg	15,000	Day
Saturday	11/09	San Diego State	L/7–68	San Diego, Calif.	43,766	Night
Saturday	11/16	Richmond	L/7–33	Hattiesburg	7,500	Night
Saturday	11/23	Tampa	W/21–7	Tampa, Fla.	20,890	Night

1969 (5–5)
Coach P. W. Underwood   *Captains: Frank Johnston, Donnie Caughman*

Day	Date	Opponent	Score	Site	Attendance	Day/Night
Saturday	09/20	SE Louisiana	W/14–6	Hattiesburg	12,200	Night
Saturday	09/27	Alabama	L/14–63	Tuscaloosa, Ala.	50,035	Night
Friday	10/03	Idaho	L/21–31	Mobile, Ala.	7,132	Night
Saturday	10/11	Mississippi State	L/20–34	Starkville, Miss.	21,000	Day
Saturday	10/18	Mississippi	L/7–69	Oxford, Miss.	25,283	Day
Saturday	10/25	Richmond (HC)	W/31–28	Hattiesburg	11,000	Day
Saturday	11/01	Louisiana Tech	W/24–23	Ruston, La.	20,000	Day
Saturday	11/08	Memphis	L/7–37	Memphis, Tenn.	18,808	Night
Saturday	11/22	East Carolina	W/14–7	Greenville, N.C.	3,500	Day
Saturday	11/29	West Texas State	W/10–9	Hattiesburg	11,600	Night

1970 (5–6)
Coach P. W. Underwood   *Captains: Larry Moulton, Bill Davis*

Day	Date	Opponent	Score	Site	Attendance	Day/Night
Saturday	09/12	Louisiana-Lafayette	W/16–14	Lafayette, La.	11,000	Night
Saturday	09/19	Auburn	L/14–33	Auburn, Ala.	48,500	Day
Saturday	09/26	Texas-Arlington	W/26–20	Hattiesburg	9,074	Night
Saturday	10/03	Richmond	W/43–21	Hattiesburg	9,422	Day
Saturday	10/10	San Diego State	L/14–41	San Diego, Calif.	32,968	Night
Saturday	10/17	Mississippi	W/30–14	Oxford, Miss.	27,200	Day
Saturday	10/24	Mississippi State	L/15–51	Starkville, Miss.	33,000	Day
Saturday	10/31	Memphis	L/0–33	Memphis, Tenn.	24,468	Night

Day	Date	Opponent	Score	Site	Attendance	Day/Night
Saturday	11/14	Louisiana Tech (HC)	L/6–27	Hattiesburg	12,800	Day
Saturday	11/21	West Texas State	L/11–14	Canyon, Tex.	5,291	Day
Saturday	11/28	Trinity	W/53–31	Hattiesburg	5,000	Day

1971 (6–5)
Coach P. W. Underwood *Captains: Wayne Hatcher, Johnny Herron*

Day	Date	Opponent	Score	Site	Attendance	Day/Night
Saturday	09/11	Florida State	L/9–24	Mobile, Ala.	12,133	Night
Saturday	09/18	Alabama	L/6–42	Tuscaloosa, Ala.	52,701	Day
Saturday	09/25	San Diego State	W/10–0	Jackson. Miss.	11,157	Night
Saturday	10/09	Auburn	L/14–27	Auburn, Ala.	42,000	Day
Saturday	10/16	Mississippi	L/6–20	Oxford, MIss.	23,200	Day
Saturday	10/23	Memphis	L/12–27	Memphis, Tenn.	19,484	Night
Saturday	10/30	Richmond	W/31–24	Hattiesburg	10,000	Night
Saturday	11/06	Virginia Military Inst. (HC)	W/38–0	Hattiesburg	12,400	Day
Saturday	11/13	Louisiana Tech	W/24–20	Ruston, La.	16,000	Day
Saturday	11/20	Virginia Tech	W/17–8	Blacksburg, Va.	22,000	Day
Saturday	11/27	West Texas State	W/35–0	Hattiesburg	5,300	Day

1972 (3–7–1)
Coach P. W. Underwood *Captains: Kyle Gantt, Buddy Palazzo*

Day	Date	Opponent	Score	Site	Attendance	Day/Night
Saturday	09/09	Texas-Arlington	W/38–17	Hattiesburg	12,500	Night
Saturday	09/16	Louisiana Tech	L/14–33	Hattiesburg	11,600	Night
Saturday	09/30	Mississippi	L/9–13	Oxford, Miss.	27,200	Day
Saturday	10/07	West Texas State	W/14–7	Hattiesburg	11,500	Night
Saturday	10/14	Richmond	W/34–9	Richmond, Va.	7,500	Day
Saturday	10/21	Mississippi State	L/7–26	Starkville, Miss.	26,000	Day
Saturday	10/28	Alabama	L/11–48	Birmingham, Ala.	57,090	Night
Saturday	11/04	Virginia Tech	L/14–27	Blacksburg, Va.	25,000	Day
Saturday	11/11	Tenn.-Chattanooga (HC)	L/6–10	Hattiesburg	14,200	Day
Saturday	11/18	Utah State	L/21–27	Logan, Utah	8,805	Day
Saturday	12/02	Memphis	T/14–14	Jackson, Miss.	15,000	Day

1973 (6–4–1)
Coach P. W. Underwood *Captain: Fred Cook*

Day	Date	Opponent	Score	Site	Attendance	Day/Night
Saturday	09/15	East Carolina	L/0–13	Hattiesburg	10,800	Night
Saturday	09/22	Florida	L/13–14	Tampa, Fla.	38,377	Night
Saturday	09/29	Mississippi	L/0–41	Oxford, Miss.	31,500	Day
Saturday	10/06	Tenn.-Chattanooga	W/42–7	Chattanooga, Tenn.	10,000	Day
Saturday	10/13	Richmond	L/20–42	Richmond, Va.	20,000	Day
Saturday	10/20	Texas-Arlington	W/41–14	Arlington, Tex.	4,000	Night
Saturday	10/27	Mississippi State	T/10–10	Starkville, MIss.	33,500	Day
Saturday	11/03	Weber State (HC)	W/28–7	Hattiesburg	10,100	Day
Saturday	11/10	Memphis	W/13–10	Memphis, Tenn.	23,399	Night

Day	Date	Opponent	Score	Site	Attendance	Day/Night
Saturday	11/17	West Texas State	W/28–0	Canyon, Tex.	5,800	Night
Thursday	11/22	Utah State	W/32–8	Hattiesburg	6,000	Day

1974 (6–5)
Coach P. W. Underwood *Captain: John Sawyer*

Day	Date	Opponent	Score	Site	Attendance	Day/Night
Saturday	09/14	Memphis	W/6–0	Memphis, Tenn.	26,608	Night
Saturday	09/21	Alabama	L/0–52	Birmingham, Ala.	62,000	Night
Saturday	09/28	Mississippi	L/14–20	Oxford, Miss.	29,000	Day
Saturday	10/05	West Texas State	L/0–31	Canyon, Tex.	5,074	Night
Saturday	10/12	Texas-Arlington	W/39–10	Jackson, Miss.	4,025	Night
Saturday	10/19	Virginia Military Inst.	W/15–14	Mobile, Ala.	4,331	Night
Saturday	10/26	Lamar	L/7–10	Beaumont, Tex.	14,106	Night
Saturday	11/02	Louisiana-Lafayette	W/41–7	Lafayette, La.	10,360	Day
Saturday	11/09	Utah State	W/7–3	Logan, Utah	10,046	Day
Saturday	11/16	Bowling Green	L/20–38	Mobile, Ala.	3,571	Day
Saturday	11/23	Tampa	W/11–10	Tampa, Fla.	14,083	Night

1975 (8–3)
Coach Bobby Collins *Captains: Jeff Bower, Ron Cheatham*

Day	Date	Opponent	Score	Site	Attendance	Day/Night
Saturday	09/13	Weber State	W/14–10	Ogden, Utah	9,396	Night
Saturday	09/20	Bowling Green	L/14–16	Bowling Green, Ohio	14,369	Day
Saturday	09/27	Mississippi	L/8–24	Oxford, Miss.	26,700	Day
Saturday	10/04	Mississippi State #	L/3–7	Starkville, Miss.	29,000	Day
Saturday	10/11	Memphis	W/21–7	Memphis, Tenn.	17,337	Night
Saturday	10/18	Texas-Arlington	W/34–7	Arlington, Tex.	4,750	Night
Saturday	10/25	Louisiana Tech	W/24–14	Ruston, La.	8,300	Night
Saturday	11/01	Lamar	W/43–3	New Orleans, La.	8,700	Night
Saturday	11/15	Alabama	L/6–27	Tuscaloosa, Ala.	58,000	Day
Saturday	11/22	Cal St.-Fullerton (HC)	W/70–0	Biloxi, Miss.	9,300	Night
Saturday	11/29	Brigham Young	W/42–14	Jackson, Miss.	9,262	Day

Mississippi State later forfeited the game

1976 (3–8)
Coach Bobby Collins *Captains: Barry Caudill, Carl Allen*

Day	Date	Opponent	Score	Site	Attendance	Day/Night
Saturday	09/11	East Carolina	L/0–48	Greenville, N.C.	17,400	Night
Saturday	09/18	Virginia Tech	L/7–16	Blacksburg, Va.	35,000	Day
Saturday	09/25	Mississippi	L/0–28	Hattiesburg	33,000	Night
Saturday	10/02	Cincinnati	L/21–28	Hattiesburg	13,500	Night
Saturday	10/09	Alabama	L/8–24	Birmingham, Ala.	42,202	Day
Saturday	10/16	Brigham Young	L/19–63	Provo, Utah	23,029	Day
Saturday	10/23	Mississippi State # (HC)	L/6–14	Hattiesburg	31,225	Night
Saturday	11/06	Florida State	L/27–30	Tallahassee, Fla.	29,173	Night
Saturday	11/13	Louisiana Tech	L/22–23	Ruston, La.	11,258	Day

Day	Date	Opponent	Score	Site	Attendance	Day/Night
Saturday	11/20	Memphis	W/14–12	Hattiesburg	12,154	Night
Saturday	11/27	Texas-Arlington	W/21–10	Hattiesburg	9,665	Day

Mississippi State later forfeited the game

1977 (6–6)
Coach Bobby Collins   *Captains: Ben Garry, David Hosemann, Stoney Parker*

Day	Date	Opponent	Score	Site	Attendance	Day/Night
Saturday	09/03	Troy State	W/42–19	Montgomery, Ala.	12,550	Night
Saturday	09/10	Florida State	L/6–35	Hattiesburg	19,376	Night
Saturday	09/17	Auburn	W/24–13	Auburn, Ala.	42,000	Day
Saturday	09/24	Mississippi	W/27–19	Oxford, Miss.	20,000	Day
Saturday	10/01	Cincinnati	L/6–17	Cincinnati, Ohio	13,392	Night
Saturday	10/08	N. Texas State (HC)	L/14–27	Hattiesburg	22,432	Night
Saturday	10/15	Hawaii	W/28–26	Honolulu, Hawaii	26,474	Night
Saturday	10/22	Mississippi State	W/14–7	Starkville, Miss.	36,000	Day
Saturday	10/29	Memphis	L/14–42	Memphis, Tenn.	28,420	Night
Saturday	11/05	Texas-Arlington	W/20–3	Arlington, Tex.	5,200	Day
Saturday	11/12	Louisiana Tech	L/10–28	Hattiesburg	16,431	Night
Saturday	11/19	Arkansas State	L/10–14	Hattiesburg	9,216	Night

1978 (7–4)
Coach Bobby Collins   *Captains: Jeff Hammond, Freeman Horton*

Day	Date	Opponent	Score	Site	Attendance	Day/Night
Saturday	09/02	Richmond	W/10–7	Richmond, Va.	15,000	Day
Saturday	09/09	Arkansas State	W/21–6	Little Rock, Ark.	16,848	Night
Saturday	09/16	Cincinnati	L/14–26	Cincinnati, Ohio	10,500	Night
Saturday	09/30	Mississippi	L/13–16	Jackson, Miss.	42,756	Night
Saturday	10/07	Mississippi State	W/22–17	Hattiesburg	31,720	Night
Saturday	10/14	East Carolina	W/17–16	Hattiesburg	15,632	Night
Saturday	10/21	Memphis	W/13–10	Memphis, Tenn.	22,630	Night
Saturday	10/28	Florida State (HC)	L/16–38	Hattiesburg	23,248	Day
Saturday	11/04	North Texas State	L/12–25	Denton, Tex.	18,400	Night
Saturday	11/11	Bowling Green	W/38–21	Hattiesburg	16,846	Night
Saturday	11/18	Louisville	W/37–3	Hattiesburg	16,219	Night

1979 (6–4–1)
Coach Bobby Collins   *Captains: Dane McDaniel, Clump Taylor, Tiko Beal*

Day	Date	Opponent	Score	Site	Attendance	Day/Night
Saturday	09/08	Florida State	L/14–17	Tallahassee, Fla.	45,467	Night
Saturday	09/15	Cincinnati	W/24–6	Hattiesburg	23,750	Night
Saturday	09/22	Auburn	L/9–31	Auburn, Ala.	45,226	Day
Saturday	09/29	Mississippi	W/38–8	Jackson, Miss.	46,720	Night
Saturday	10/06	North Texas State	W/30–10	Hattiesburg	24,810	Night
Saturday	10/13	Tulane	L/19–20	Hattiesburg	30,028	Night
Saturday	10/20	Memphis (HC)	W/22–0	Hattiesburg	27,286	Day
Saturday	10/27	Mississippi State	W/21–7	Starkville, Miss.	35,500	Day

Day	Date	Opponent	Score	Site	Attendance	Day/Night
Saturday	11/03	Louisville	T/10–10	Louisville, Ky.	13,085	Day
Saturday	11/10	Bowling Green	L/27–31	Bowling Green, Ohio	10,556	Day
Saturday	11/17	Arkansas State	W/14–6	Hattiesburg	16,340	Day

1980 (9–3)

Coach Bobby Collins   *Captains: Jamey Watson, Marvin Harvey, Chuck Cook*

Day	Date	Opponent	Score	Site	Attendance	Day/Night
Saturday	09/06	Tulane	W/17–14	New Orleans, La.	44,698	Day
Saturday	09/20	Louisiana Tech	W/38–11	Hattiesburg	24,640	Night
Saturday	09/27	East Carolina	W/35–7	Greenville, N.C.	20,037	Night
Saturday	10/04	Mississippi	W/28–22	Jackson, Miss.	47,211	Day
Saturday	10/11	Mississippi State	W/42–14	Starkville, Miss.	36,211	Day
Saturday	10/18	Arkansas State	W/35–0	Hattiesburg	21,915	Night
Saturday	10/25	Alabama	L/7–42	Tuscaloosa, Ala.	60,210	Day
Saturday	11/01	Lamar (HC)	W/36–10	Hattiesburg	30,485	Night
Saturday	11/08	Auburn	L/0–31	Auburn, Ala.	56,800	Day
Saturday	11/15	Richmond	W/33–12	Hattiesburg	17,320	Night
Saturday	11/22	Louisville	L/3–6	Hattiesburg	21,210	Night

Independence Bowl

Day	Date	Opponent	Score	Site	Attendance	Day/Night
Saturday	12/13	McNeese State	W/16–14	Shreveport, La.	42,600	Night

1981 (9–2–1)

Coach Bobby Collins   *Captains: Sammy Winder, Rhett Whitley*

Day	Date	Opponent	Score	Site	Attendance	Day/Night
Saturday	09/05	Louisiana-Lafayette	W/33–7	Hattiesburg	23,576	Night
Saturday	09/19	Tulane	W/21–3	Hattiesburg	32,756	Night
Saturday	09/26	Richmond	W/17–10	Richmond, Va.	12,500	Day
Saturday	10/03	Texas-Arlington (HC)	W/52–9	Hattiesburg	24,348	Night
Saturday	10/10	Alabama	T/13–13	Birmingham, Ala.	76,400	Day
Saturday	10/17	Memphis	W/10–0	Memphis, Tenn.	14,252	Night
Saturday	10/31	North Texas State	W/22–0	Denton, Tex.	3,156	Day
Saturday	11/07	Mississippi State	W/7–6	Jackson, Miss.	64,112	Day
Saturday	11/14	Florida State	W/58–14	Tallahassee, Fla.	51,819	Night
Saturday	11/21	Louisville	L/0–13	Louisville, Ky.	12,940	Day
Saturday	11/28	Lamar	W/45–14	Hattiesburg	31,842	Day

Tangerine Bowl

Day	Date	Opponent	Score	Site	Attendance	Day/Night
Saturday	12/19	Missouri	L/17–19	Orlando, Fla.	56,450	Night

1982 (7–4)

Coach Jim Carmody   *Captains: Reggie Collier, Greg Kelley, Bruce Thompson*

Day	Date	Opponent	Score	Site	Attendance	Day/Night
Saturday	09/04	Louisiana-Monroe	W/45–27	Hattiesburg	30,767	Night
Saturday	09/11	Mississippi	L/19–28	Oxford, Miss.	40,954	Day
Saturday	09/18	Auburn	L/19–21	Auburn, Ala.	55,000	Night

Day	Date	Opponent	Score	Site	Attendance	Day/Night
Saturday	09/25	Florida State	L/17–24	Hattiesburg	32,591	Night
Saturday	10/02	Memphis	W/34–14	Hattiesburg	21,674	Night
Saturday	10/09	Mississippi State	W/20–14	Jackson, Miss.	54,236	Day
Saturday	10/16	Tulane	W/22–10	New Orleans, La.	39,685	Night
Saturday	10/23	Louisville (HC)	W/48–0	Hattiesburg	28,642	Night
Saturday	10/30	Louisiana-Lafayette	W/36–0	Hattiesburg	22,416	Night
Saturday	11/13	Alabama	W/38–29	Tuscaloosa, Ala.	60,210	Day
Saturday	11/20	Louisiana Tech	L/6–13	Hattiesburg	31,256	Night

1983 (7-4)

Coach Jim Carmody   *Captains: Louis Lipps, Jerald Baylis, Bud Brown*

Day	Date	Opponent	Score	Site	Attendance	Day/Night
Saturday	09/03	Richmond	W/32–3	Hattiesburg	27,351	Night
Saturday	09/10	Auburn	L/3–24	Auburn, Ala.	73,500	Night
Saturday	09/17	Louisiana Tech	W/28–10	Hattiesburg	28,342	Night
Saturday	10/01	Mississippi	W/27–7	Oxford, Miss.	36,015	Day
Saturday	10/08	Mississippi State	W/31–6	Jackson, Miss.	58,311	Day
Saturday	10/15	Memphis	W/27–20	Memphis, Tenn.	35,323	Night
Saturday	10/22	Tulane	L/7–14	Hattiesburg	31,257	Night
Saturday	10/29	Louisiana-Lafayette (HC)	W/31–3	Hattiesburg	28,837	Night
Saturday	11/05	Louisville	W/27–3	Louisville, Ky.	17,064	Day
Saturday	11/12	Alabama	L/16–28	Birmingham, Ala.	78,424	Day
Saturday	11/19	East Carolina	L/6–10	Hattiesburg	21,000	Night

1984 (4-7)

Coach Jim Carmody   *Captains: Sam Dejarnette, Richard Byrd, Greg Haeusler*

Day	Date	Opponent	Score	Site	Attendance	Day/Night
Saturday	09/08	Georgia	L/19–26	Athens, Ga.	81,421	Day
Saturday	09/15	Louisiana Tech	W/34–0	Hattiesburg	28,842	Night
Saturday	09/22	Auburn	L/12–35	Auburn, Ala.	24,841	Night
Saturday	09/29	Memphis	L/13–23	Hattiesburg	26,831	Night
Saturday	10/06	Mississippi State	L/18–27	Jackson, Miss.	50,136	Day
Saturday	10/13	Tulane	L/7–35	New Orleans, La.	30,764	Night
Saturday	10/20	Mississippi	W/13–10	Jackson, Miss.	57,000	Day
Saturday	10/27	Louisiana-Lafayette	L/7–13	Lafayette, La.	19,605	Night
Saturday	11/03	NW Louisiana (HC)	L/0–22	Hattiesburg	24,682	Night
Saturday	11/10	East Carolina	W/31–27	Greenville, N.C.	21,237	Day
Saturday	11/17	Louisville	W/34–27	Hattiesburg	15,904	Night

1985 (7-4)

Coach Jim Carmody   *Captains: Robert Ducksworth, Kip Smith, Steve Hendrix*

Day	Date	Opponent	Score	Site	Attendance	Day/Night
Saturday	09/07	Louisiana Tech	W/28–0	Hattiesburg	23,432	Night
Saturday	09/14	Auburn	L/18–29	Auburn, Ala.	68,000	Day
Saturday	09/21	Mississippi State	L/20–23	Jackson, Miss.	54,300	Day
Saturday	09/28	NW Louisiana	W/14–7	Hattiesburg	18,216	Night

Day	Date	Opponent	Score	Site	Attendance	Day/Night
Saturday	10/05	Louisiana-Lafayette	W/38–16	Hattiesburg	17,344	Night
Saturday	10/12	Louisville	W/42–12	Louisville, Ky.	25,843	Night
Saturday	10/19	Memphis	W/14–7	Memphis, Tenn.	21,033	Night
Saturday	11/02	East Carolina (HC)	W/27–0	Hattiesburg	23,496	Night
Saturday	11/09	Colorado State	L/17–35	Fort Collins, Colo.	3,812	Day
Saturday	11/16	Alabama	L/13–24	Tuscaloosa, Ala.	58,714	Day
Saturday	11/23	Tulane	W/24–6	Hattiesburg	21,753	Night

1986 (6–5)

Coach Jim Carmody *Captains: Andrew Anderson, Tim Smith, Rex Banks*

Day	Date	Opponent	Score	Site	Attendance	Day/Night
Saturday	09/06	Louisiana-Monroe	W/28–19	Hattiesburg	21,364	Night
Saturday	09/13	Alabama	L/17–31	Birmingham, Ala.	73,687	Day
Saturday	09/20	Mississippi State	W/28–24	Jackson, Miss.	50,000	Day
Saturday	09/27	Texas A & M	L/7–16	College Station, Tex.	54,938	Night
Saturday	10/04	Kentucky	L/0–32	Lexington, Ky.	58,102	Night
Saturday	10/18	Memphis (HC)	W/14–9	Hattiesburg	25,853	Night
Saturday	10/25	Tulane	L/20–35	New Orleans, La.	28,417	Night
Saturday	11/01	East Carolina	W/23–21	Greenville, N.C.	18,127	Day
Saturday	11/08	Louisiana-Lafayette	W/17–0	Hattiesburg	14,512	Night
Saturday	11/15	Florida State	L/13–49	Tallahassee, Fla.	60,103	Day
Saturday	11/22	Louisville	W/31–16	Hattiesburg	11,231	Night

1987 (6–5)

Coach Jim Carmody *Captains: Tim Hallman, Onesimus Henry, Billy Knighten, Chris McGee*

Day	Date	Opponent	Score	Site	Attendance	Day/Night
Saturday	09/05	Alabama	L/6–38	Birmingham, Ala.	75,808	Day
Saturday	09/19	Tulane	W/31–24	Hattiesburg	16,023	Day
Saturday	09/26	Texas A & M	L/14–27	Jackson, Miss.	22,150	Day
Saturday	10/03	Louisville	W/65–6	Louisville, Ky.	20,687	Night
Saturday	10/10	Florida State (HC)	L/10–61	Hattiesburg	25,853	Day
Saturday	10/17	Mississippi State	W/18–14	Jackson, Miss.	40,000	Day
Saturday	10/24	Memphis	W/17–14	Memphis, Tenn.	27,448	Night
Saturday	10/31	Jackson State	W/17–7	Hattiesburg	33,687	Day
Saturday	11/07	Louisiana-Monroe	L/24–34	Hattiesburg	10,123	Day
Saturday	11/14	East Carolina	W/38–34	Hattiesburg	11,023	Day
Saturday	11/28	Louisiana-Lafayette	L/30–37	Lafayette, La.	17,500	Day

1988 (10–2)

Coach Curley Hallman *Captains: Marty Williams, Maurice Oliver, James Henry*

Day	Date	Opponent	Score	Site	Attendance	Day/Night
Saturday	09/03	Stephen F. Austin	W/21–7	Hattiesburg	15,032	Night
Saturday	09/10	Florida State	L/13–29	Tallahassee, Fla.	53,129	Night
Saturday	09/17	Virginia Tech	W/35–13	Hattiesburg	17,135	Night
Saturday	09/24	East Carolina	W/45–42	Greenville, N.C.	28,240	Day
Saturday	10/01	Louisville	W/30–23	Hattiesburg	17,584	Night

Day	Date	Opponent	Score	Site	Attendance	Day/Night
Saturday	10/08	Tulane	W/38–13	New Orleans, La.	22,704	Day
Saturday	10/15	Mississippi State	W/38–21	Jackson, Miss.	38,542	Day
Saturday	10/22	Louisiana-Lafayette	W/27–14	Lafayette, La.	23,599	Night
Saturday	10/29	Memphis (HC)	W/34–27	Hattiesburg	25,594	Day
Saturday	11/05	Auburn	L/8–38	Auburn, Ala.	73,787	Day
Saturday	11/12	Louisiana Tech	W/26–19	Ruston, La.	7,500	Day

Independence Bowl

Day	Date	Opponent	Score	Site	Attendance	Day/Night
Thursday	12/23	Texas–El Paso	W/38–18	Shreveport, La.	20,242	Night

1989 (5–6)
Coach Curley Hallman   *Captains: Darryl Tillman, Pat Jackson, William Kirksey*

Day	Date	Opponent	Score	Site	Attendance	Day/Night
Saturday	09/02	Florida State	W/30–26	Jacksonville, Fla.	48,746	Day
Saturday	09/09	Mississippi State	L/23–26	Hattiesburg	34,189	Night
Saturday	09/16	Auburn	L/3–24	Auburn, Ala.	83,465	Night
Saturday	09/23	Texas Christian	L/17–19	Fort Worth, Tex.	15,839	Night
Saturday	09/30	Texas A & M	L/14–31	College Station, Tex.	58,843	Night
Saturday	10/07	Tulane	W/30–21	Hattiesburg	18,891	Night
Saturday	10/14	Louisville	W/16–10	Louisville, Ky.	38,484	Day
Saturday	10/21	Louisiana-Lafayette (HC)	L/21–24	Hattiesburg	20,732	Day
Saturday	10/28	Memphis	W/31–7	Memphis, Tenn.	18,572	Day
Saturday	11/18	Alabama	L/14–37	Tuscaloosa, Ala.	70,123	Day
Saturday	11/25	East Carolina	W/41–27	Hattiesburg	11,189	Day

1990 (8–4)
Coach Curley Hallman   *Captains: Brett Favre, Kerry Valrie, Steve Thompson*

Day	Date	Opponent	Score	Site	Attendance	Day/Night
Saturday	09/01	Delta State	W/12–0	Hattiesburg	17,590	Night
Saturday	09/08	Alabama	W/27–24	Birmingham, Ala.	75,962	Day
Saturday	09/15	Georgia	L/17–18	Athens, Ga.	79,812	Day
Saturday	09/22	Mississippi State	L/10–13	Starkville, Miss.	40,115	Night
Saturday	09/29	Louisville	W/25–13	Hattiesburg	20,545	Night
Saturday	10/06	East Carolina	W/16–7	Greenville, N.C.	31,305	Day
Saturday	10/13	Tulane	W/20–14	New Orleans, La.	26,662	Night
Saturday	10/20	Memphis (HC)	W/23–7	Hattiesburg	24,520	Day
Saturday	10/27	Virginia Tech	L/16–20	Blacksburg, Va.	37,462	Day
Saturday	11/03	Louisiana-Lafayette	W/14–13	Lafayette, La.	17,860	Day
Saturday	11/10	Auburn	W/13–12	Auburn, Ala.	85,214	Day

All-American Bowl*

Day	Date	Opponent	Score	Site	Attendance	Day/Night
Saturday	12/28	North Carolina State	L/27–31	Birmingham, Ala.	44,000	Night

* Hallman did not coach in the All-American Bowl; Jeff Bower coached that game

1991 (4–7)
Coach Jeff Bower Captains: Pete Antoniou, Derrick Hoskins, Chafan Marsh, Tony Smith

Day	Date	Opponent	Score	Site	Attendance	Day/Night
Saturday	08/31	Delta State	W/25–7	Hattiesburg	17,191	Day
Saturday	09/07	Pittsburgh	L/14–35	Pittsburgh, Pa.	34,756	Day
Saturday	09/21	Colorado State	W/39–7	Hattiesburg	20,154	Day
Saturday	09/28	Louisville	L/14–28	Louisville, Ky.	38,231	Day
Saturday	10/05	Auburn	W/10–9	Auburn, Ala.	79,790	Day
Saturday	10/12	Memphis	L/12–17	Memphis, Tenn.	19,162	Day
Saturday	10/19	Tulane	W/47–14	Hattiesburg	16,558	Day
Saturday	10/26	Cincinnati	L/7–17	Cincinnati, Ohio	15,899	Day
Saturday	11/02	Tulsa	L/10–13	Tulsa, Okla.	27,284	Day
Saturday	11/09	East Carolina (HC)	L/20–48	Hattiesburg	18,117	Day
Saturday	11/16	Louisiana Tech	L/14–30	Ruston, La.	11,200	Night

1992 (7–4)
Coach Jeff Bower Captains: Greg Reed, James Singleton, Michael Welch

Day	Date	Opponent	Score	Site	Attendance	Day/Night
Saturday	09/05	Memphis	W/23–21	Hattiesburg	16,059	Day
Saturday	09/12	Alabama	L/10–17	Birmingham, Ala.	83,091	Day
Saturday	09/19	Louisiana Tech	W/16–13	Hattiesburg	15,168	Day
Saturday	09/26	Auburn	L/8–16	Auburn, Ala.	72,296	Day
Saturday	10/03	Tulsa (HC)	W/33–24	Hattiesburg	18,253	Day
Saturday	10/10	Northern Illinois	L/10–23	De Kalb, Ill.	14,246	Day
Saturday	10/17	Tulane	W/17–7	New Orleans, La.	21,760	Night
Saturday	10/24	Cincinnati	W/31–17	Hattiesburg	17,298	Day
Thursday	10/29	East Carolina	W/38–21	Greenville, N.C.	33,249	Night
Saturday	11/07	Florida	L/20–24	Gainesville, Fla.	82,882	Day
Saturday	11/14	Virginia Tech	W/13–12	Blacksburg, Va.	27,342	Day

1993 (3–7–1)
Coach Jeff Bower Captains: Jerry Broughton, Bobby Hamilton, Tyrone Nix

Day	Date	Opponent	Score	Site	Attendance	Day/Night
Thursday	09/02	Pittsburgh	L/10–14	Hattiesburg	25,516	Night
Saturday	09/18	Louisiana-Monroe	W/44–37	Hattiesburg	20,384	Night
Saturday	09/25	Auburn	L/24–35	Auburn, Ala.	83,476	Day
Saturday	10/02	Louisiana-Lafayette	L/7–13	Lafayette, La.	22,853	Night
Saturday	10/09	Georgia	L/24–54	Athens, Ga.	68,458	Day
Saturday	10/16	Louisville	L/27–35	Louisville, Ky.	36,322	Day
Saturday	10/23	East Carolina	W/24–16	Hattiesburg	15,227	Night
Saturday	10/30	Alabama #	L/0–40	Tuscaloosa, Ala.	70,123	Day
Saturday	11/06	Tulane (HC)	L/15–17	Hattiesburg	16,397	Night
Saturday	11/13	Memphis	L/9–20	Memphis, Tenn.	13,042	Day
Saturday	11/20	Tulsa	T/30–30	Tulsa, Okla.	21,783	Day

Alabama later forfeited the game

1994 (6–5)

Coach Jeff Bower *Captains: Ronald Jones, Mark Montgomery, Michael Tobias*

Day	Date	Opponent	Score	Site	Attendance	Day/Night
Saturday	09/03	Tulane	W/25–10	New Orleans, La.	24,786	Night
Saturday	09/10	Virginia Tech	L/14–24	Hattiesburg	17,381	Night
Saturday	09/17	Memphis	W/20–3	Hattiesburg	17,563	Night
Saturday	09/24	Texas A & M	L/17–41	College Station, Tex.	56,006	Day
Saturday	10/01	East Carolina	L/10–31	Greenville, N.C.	32,867	Day
Saturday	10/08	Alabama	L/6–14	Tuscaloosa, Ala.	70,123	Day
Saturday	10/15	Louisiana-Lafayette	W/43–20	Hattiesburg	14,592	Night
Saturday	10/22	Samford (HC)	W/59–16	Hattiesburg	15,514	Day
Saturday	10/29	Tulsa	W/47–29	Hattiesburg	13,473	Night
Saturday	11/05	Florida	L/17–55	Gainesville, Fla.	85,448	Day
Saturday	11/12	Louisiana State	W/20–18	Baton Rouge, La.	51,710	Night

1995 (6–5)

Coach Jeff Bower *Captains: Chris Buckhalter, Jerry Harris, Albert McRae*

Day	Date	Opponent	Score	Site	Attendance	Day/Night
Thursday	08/31	Northern Illinois	W/45–13	Hattiesburg	33,092	Night
Saturday	09/09	Alabama	L/20–24	Birmingham, Ala.	83,081	Day
Saturday	09/16	Utah State	W/24–21	Logan, Utah	15,227	Night
Saturday	09/23	Indiana	L/26–27	Bloomington, Ind.	31,216	Day
Saturday	09/30	Tulane	W/45–0	Hattiesburg	27,141	Night
Saturday	10/07	Louisville	W/25–21	Hattiesburg	21,079	Night
Saturday	10/14	Cincinnati	L/13–16	Cincinnati, Ohio	18,522	Night
Saturday	10/28	East Carolina	L/34–36	Hattiesburg	21,293	Night
Saturday	11/04	Tennessee	L/0–42	Knoxville, Tenn.	93,433	Day
Saturday	11/11	Memphis	W/17–9	Memphis, Tenn.	11,503	Day
Saturday	11/18	Louisiana-Lafayette	W/35–32	Lafayette, La.	19,341	Night

1996 (8–3, CUSA: 4–1)

Conference USA Co-Champions
Coach Jeff Bower *Captains: Kendrick Lee, Jeff Posey, Cedric Walthaw*

Day	Date	Opponent	Score	Site	Attendance	Day/Night
Saturday	08/31	Georgia	W/11–7	Athens, Ga.	81,076	Day
Saturday	09/07	Alabama	L/10–20	Birmingham, Ala.	82,338	Day
Saturday	09/14	Utah State	W/31–24	Hattiesburg	24,307	Night
Saturday	09/21	Louisiana-Lafayette	W/52–27	Hattiesburg	23,169	Night
Saturday	09/28	*Louisville	W/24–7	Louisville, Ky.	36,482	Day
Thursday	10/10	East Carolina	W/28–7	Greenville, N.C.	34,480	Night
Saturday	10/19	*Memphis	W/16–0	Hattiesburg	25,601	Day
Saturday	10/26	*Tulane	W/31–28	New Orleans, La.	20,384	Night
Saturday	11/02	*Cincinnati (HC)	W/21–17	Hattiesburg	25,241	Day
Saturday	11/09	*Houston (OT)	L/49–56	Houston, Tex.	18,107	Night
Saturday	11/16	Florida State	L/14–54	Tallahassee, Fla.	72,280	Night

*Conference USA game

1997 (9-3, CUSA: 6-0)
Conference USA Champions
Coach Jeff Bower   Captains: Tyrone Boleware, Marchant Kenney, Lytrel Pollard, Patrick Surtain

Day	Date	Opponent	Score	Site	Attendance	Day/Night
Saturday	08/30	Florida	L/6–21	Gainesville, Fla.	85,439	Night
Saturday	09/06	Illinois	W/24–7	Champaign, Ill.	44,519	Night
Saturday	09/20	Nevada	W/35–19	Hattiesburg	26,481	Night
Saturday	09/27	Alabama	L/13–27	Birmingham, Ala.	83,091	Day
Saturday	10/04	*Louisville	W/42–14	Hattiesburg	23,028	Night
Saturday	10/11	*East Carolina	W/23–13	Greenville, N.C.	33,904	Day
Saturday	10/25	*Tulane	W/34–13	Hattiesburg	26,092	Day
Saturday	11/01	*Cincinnati	W/24–17	Cincinnati, Ohio	23,799	Day
Saturday	11/08	Tennessee	L/20–44	Knoxville, Tenn.	107,073	Day
Saturday	11/15	*Houston	W/33–0	Hattiesburg	20,091	Day
Saturday	11/22	*Memphis	W/42–18	Memphis, Tenn.	17,243	Day

AXA Liberty Bowl
Day	Date	Opponent	Score	Site	Attendance	Day/Night
Wednesday	12/31	Pittsburgh	W/41–7	Memphis, Tenn.	50,209	Day

*Conference USA game

1998 (7-5, CUSA: 5-1)
Coach Jeff Bower   Captains: Frank Firestone, Jose Gonzalez, Lee Roberts, Larry Watts

Day	Date	Opponent	Score	Site	Attendance	Day/Night
Saturday	09/05	Penn State	L/6–34	State College, Pa.	96,617	Day
Saturday	09/19	Texas A & M	L/6–24	Hattiesburg	33,233	Day
Saturday	09/26	Louisiana-Lafayette	W/55–0	Hattiesburg	24,379	Night
Saturday	10/03	*Tulane	L/7–21	New Orleans, La.	32,527	Day
Saturday	10/10	*Louisville	W/56–21	Hattiesburg	22,043	Night
Saturday	10/17	*Army	W/37–13	West Point, N.Y.	40,395	Day
Saturday	10/24	*East Carolina	W/41–7	Hattiesburg	24,020	Day
Saturday	10/31	Alabama	L/20–30	Tuscaloosa, Ala.	83,818	Day
Saturday	11/07	*Houston	W/21–15	Houston, Tex.	16,260	Day
Saturday	11/14	*Memphis	W/45–3	Hattiesburg	19,132	Night
Saturday	11/21	Nevada	W/55–28	Reno, Nev.	18,336	Day

Humanitarian Bowl
Day	Date	Opponent	Score	Site	Attendance	Day/Night
Wednesday	12/30	Idaho	L/35–42	Boise, Idaho	19,664	Day

*Conference USA game

1999 (9-3, CUSA: 6-0)
Conference USA Champions
Coach Jeff Bower   Captains: Todd Pinkston, T. J. Slaughter, Adalius Thomas, Michael Villalonga

Day	Date	Opponent	Score	Site	Attendance	Day/Night
Monday	09/06	*Tulane	W/48–14	Hattiesburg	30,098	Day
Saturday	09/11	NW Louisiana	W/40–6	Hattiesburg	24,871	Night
Saturday	09/18	Nebraska	L/13–20	Lincoln, Neb.	77,826	Day

Day	Date	Opponent	Score	Site	Attendance	Day/Night
Saturday	09/25	Texas A & M	L/6–23	College Station, Tex.	65,264	Day
Saturday	10/09	*East Carolina	W/39–22	Greenville, N.C.	39,418	Day
Saturday	10/16	*Army	W/24–0	Hattiesburg	26,054	Day
Saturday	10/23	*Cincinnati	W/28–20	Hattiesburg	24,012	Day
Saturday	10/30	Alabama	L/14–35	Tuscaloosa, Ala.	83,818	Day
Saturday	11/06	*Memphis	W/20–5	Memphis, Tenn.	23,635	Day
Saturday	11/13	Louisiana-Lafayette	W/48–0	Hattiesburg	24,133	Day
Saturday	11/20	*Louisville	W/30–27	Louisville, Ky.	41,826	Day

AXA Liberty Bowl

Day	Date	Opponent	Score	Site	Attendance	Day/Night
Friday	12/31	Colorado State	W/23–17	Memphis, Tenn.	54,866	Day

*Conference USA game

2000 (8-4, CUSA: 4-3)

Coach Jeff Bower   Captains: Leo Barnes, Billy Clay, Cedric Scott, DeQuincy Scott

Day	Date	Opponent	Score	Site	Attendance	Day/Night
Saturday	09/02	Tennessee	L/16–19	Knoxville, Tenn.	108,064	Night
Saturday	09/16	Alabama	W/21–0	Birmingham, Ala.	83,091	Night
Saturday	09/23	Oklahoma State	W/28–6	Stillwater, Okla.	41,205	Night
Saturday	09/30	*Memphis	W/24–3	Hattiesburg	30,658	Night
Saturday	10/07	South Florida	W/41–7	Hattiesburg	26,559	Night
Saturday	10/14	*Tulane	W/56–24	New Orleans, La.	27,645	Day
Saturday	10/28	*Houston	W/6–3	Houston, Tex.	17,565	Day
Saturday	11/04	*Louisville	L/28–49	Hattiesburg	31,667	Day
Saturday	11/11	*Alabama-Birmingham	W/33–30	Birmingham, Ala.	25,000	Day
Saturday	11/18	*Cincinnati	L/24–27	Cincinnati, Ohio	21,958	Day
Friday	11/24	*East Carolina	L/9–14	Hattiesburg	25,152	Day

GMAC Mobile Alabama Bowl

Day	Date	Opponent	Score	Site	Attendance	Day/Night
Thursday	12/20	Texas Christian	W/28–21	Mobile, Ala.	40,300	Night

*Conference USA game

2001 (6-5, CUSA: 4-3)

Coach Jeff Bower   Captains: Jeff Kelly, Chad Williams, Dannye Fowler, Roy Magee

Day	Date	Opponent	Score	Site	Attendance	Day/Night
Saturday	09/01	Oklahoma State	W/17–9	Hattiesburg	25,134	Day
Saturday	9/22	Louisiana-Lafayette	W/35–10	Lafayette, La.	14,132	Night
Saturday	9/29	*Alabama-Birmingham	W/3–0	Hattiesburg	29,782	Night
Saturday	10/06	*Memphis	L/17–22	Memphis, Tenn.	28,668	Night
Tuesday	10/16	*Louisville	L/14–24	Louisville, Ky.	33,627	Night
Saturday	10/27	*Houston	W/58–14	Hattiesburg	26,162	Day
Saturday	11/3	Penn State	L/20–38	State College, Pa.	106,158	Day
Saturday	11/17	*Tulane	W/59–6	Hattiesburg	24,054	Day
Friday	11/23	*East Carolina	W/28–21	Greenville, N.C.	30,127	Day
Thursday	11/29	Alabama	L/15–28	Birmingham, Ala.	79,947	Night
Friday	12/7	*Texas Christian	L/12–14	Hattiesburg	23,114	Night

*Conference USA game

2002 (7-6, CUSA: 5-3)

Coach Jeff Bower   Captains: Rod Davis, Derrick Nix, Terrell Paul, Torrin Tucker

Day	Date	Opponent	Score	Site	Attendance	Day/Night
Saturday	8/31	Jackson State	W/55-7	Hattiesburg	35,169	Night
Saturday	9/7	Illinois	W/23-20	Hattiesburg.	22,183	Day
Saturday	9/14	*Memphis	W/33-14	Hattiesburg	28,419	Night
Saturday	9/21	Alabama	L/7-20	Tuscaloosa, Ala.	83,818	Night
Saturday	9/28	*Army	W/27-6	West Point, N.Y.	31,402	Day
Saturday	10/12	South Florida	L/13-16	Tampa, Fla.	28,181	Night
Saturday	10/19	*Cincinnati (HC)	W/23-14	Hattiesburg	28,031	Day
Wednesday	10/30	*Texas Christian	L/7-37	Fort Worth, Tex.	26,612	Night
Saturday	11/9	*Alabama-Birmingham	W/20-13	Birmingham, Ala.	19.698	Day
Thursday	11/14	*Louisville	L/17-20 (2OT)	Hattiesburg	28,076	Night
Saturday	11/23	*Tulane	L/10-31	New Orleans, La.	21,832	Day
Saturday	11/30	*East Carolina	W/24-7	Hattiesburg	19,888	Day

Houston Bowl

Friday	12/27	Oklahoma State	L/23-33	Houston, Tex.	44,687	Day

*Conference USA game

2003 (9-4, CUSA: 8-0)

Conference USA Champions

Coach Jeff Bower   Captains: Rod Davis, Terrell Paul, Etric Pruitt, Terrell Browden, Jeremy Parquet

Day	Date	Opponent	Score	Site	Attendance	Day/Night
Saturday	8/30	California	L/2-34	Berkeley, Calif.	33,552	Day
Thursday	9/4	*Alabama-Birmingham	W/17-12	Birmingham, Ala.	42,000	Night
Saturday	9/13	*Memphis	W/23-6	Hattiesburg	29,233	Night
Thursday	9/25	Nebraska	L/14-38	Hattiesburg	36,152	Night
Saturday	10/4	*Cincinnati	W/22-20	Cincinnati, Ohio	24,522	Night
Saturday	10/11	Alabama	L/3-17	Tuscaloosa, Ala.	82,818	Day
Saturday	10/25	*South Florida	W/27-6	Hattiesburg	23,708	Day
Saturday	11/1	Louisiana-Lafayette (HC)	W/48-3	Hattiesburg	25,649	Day
Saturday	11/8	*Houston	W/31-10	Houston, Tex.	20,377	Day
Saturday	11/15	*Tulane	W/28-14	Hattiesburg	26,987	Day
Thursday	11/20	*Texas Christian	W/40-28	Hattiesburg	30,141	Night
Saturday	11/29	*East Carolina	W/38-21	Greenville, N.C.	24,175	Day

AXA Liberty Bowl

Wednesday	12/31	Utah	L/0-17	Memphis, Tenn.	55,989	Day

*Conference USA game

BOWL HISTORY

Southern Miss has participated in the following bowl games sanctioned by the National Collegiate Athletic Association:

Sun Bowl, El Paso, Texas, January 1, 1953
    Mississippi Southern 7, College of the Pacific 26
Sun Bowl, El Paso, Texas, January 1, 1954
    Mississippi Southern 14, Texas Western 37
Tangerine Bowl, Orlando, Florida, January 1, 1957
    Mississippi Southern 13, West Texas State 20
Tangerine Bowl, Orlando, Florida, January 1, 1958
    Mississippi Southern 9, East Texas State 10
Independence Bowl, Shreveport, Louisiana,
    December 13, 1980
    Southern Miss 16, McNeese State 14
Tangerine Bowl, Orlando, Florida, December 19, 1981
    Southern Miss 19, Missouri 20
Independence Bowl, Shreveport, Louisiana,
    December 23, 1988
    Southern Miss 38, Texas–El Paso 18

All-American Bowl, Birmingham, Alabama,
    December 28, 1990
    Southern Miss 27, North Carolina State 31
Liberty Bowl, Memphis, Tennessee, December 31, 1997
    Southern Miss 41, Pittsburgh 7
Humanitarian Bowl, Boise, Idaho, December 30, 1998
    Southern Miss 35, Idaho 42
Liberty Bowl, Memphis, Tennessee, December 31, 1999
    Southern Miss 23, Colorado State 17
Mobile, Alabama Bowl, Mobile, Alabama,
    December 20, 2000
    Southern Miss 28, Texas Christian University 21
Houston Bowl, Houston, Texas, December 27, 2002
    Southern Miss 23, Oklahoma State 33
Liberty Bowl, Memphis, Tennessee, December 31, 2003
    Southern Miss 0, Utah State 17

COACHING RECORDS

By Chronology

Coach	Years	Win	Loss	Tie	Percent
Ronald J. Slay (1912)	1	2	1	0	.667
M. J. (Blondie) Williams (1913)	1	1	5	1	.231
A. B. Dillie (1914–16)	3	6	10	1	.382
Cephus Anderson (1919)	1	4	1	2	.714
B. B. (Opp) O'Mara (1920)	1	5	2	1	.733
O. V. (Spout) Austin (1921–23)	3	8	13	0	.381
William Herschel Bobo (1924–27)	4	9	17	4	.367
William B. Saunders (1928–29)	2	6	11	1	.371
John Lumpkin (1930)	1	3	5	1	.375
Allison (Pooley) Hubert (1931–36)	6	26	24	5	.480
Reed Green (1937–42, 46–48)	9	59	20	4	.735
Thad (Pie) Vann (1949–68)	20	139	59	2	.700
P. W. (Bear) Underwood (1969–74)	6	31	32	2	.492
Bobby Collins (1975–81)	7	48	30	2	.613
Jim Carmody (1982–87)	6	37	29	0	.561
Curley Hallman (1988–90)	3	23	11	0	.676
Jeff Bower (1991–2003) *	13	89	62	1	.589
Totals	87	496	332	27	.596

By Percentage

Coach	Years	Win	Loss	Tie	Percent
Reed Green (1937–42, 46–48)	9	59	20	4	.735
B. B. (Opp) O'Mara (1920)	1	5	2	1	.733

Coach	Years	Win	Loss	Tie	Percent
Cephus Anderson (1919)	1	4	1	2	.714
Thad (Pie) Vann (1949–68)	20	139	59	2	.700
Curley Hallman (1988–90)	3	23	11	0	.676
Ronald J. Slay (1912)	1	2	1	0	.667
Bobby Collins (1975–81)	7	48	30	2	.613
Jeff Bower (1991–02) *	13	89	62	1	.589
Jim Carmody (1982–87)	6	37	29	0	.561
Allison (Pooley) Hubert (1931–36)	6	26	24	5	.543
P. W. Underwood (1969–74)	6	31	32	2	.492
John Lumpkin (1930)	1	3	5	1	.412
A. B. Dillie (1914–16)	3	6	10	1	.382
O. V. (Spout) Austin (1921–23)	3	8	13	0	.381
William B. Saunders (1928–29)	2	6	11	1	.371
William Herschel Bobo (1924–27)	4	9	17	4	.367
M. J. (Blondie) Williams (1913)	1	1	5	1	.231
Totals	87	496	332	27	.596

* Bower coached the 1990 All-American Bowl.

SERIES RECORDS VERSUS OPPONENTS

Opponent	First Meeting	Last Meeting	Total Games	Won	Lost	Tied	Percent
Abilene Christian	1954	1962	9	9	0	0	100.0
Alabama*	1947	2003	40	6	32	2	17.5
Alabama-Birmingham	2000	2003	4	4	0	0	100.0
Alabama State Teachers	1937	1937	1	1	0	0	100.0
All-Navy Service Team	1925	1925	1	0	1	0	0.0
Appalachian State	1937	1937	1	1	0	0	100.0
Arkansas-Monticello	1938	1938	1	1	0	0	100.0
Arkansas State	1962	1980	8	6	2	0	75.0
Army	1998	2002	3	3	0	0	100.0
Auburn	1946	1993	21	5	16	0	23.8
Bowling Green	1974	1979	4	1	3	0	25.0
Brigham Young	1975	1976	2	1	1	0	50.0
Brookley Field	1942	1942	1	1	0	0	100.0
California	2003	2003	1	0	1	0	0.0
Carswell Air Base	1951	1951	1	0	1	0	0.0
Chamberlain Hunt Academy	1919	1919	1	1	0	0	100.0
Cincinnati	1976	2003	13	7	6	0	53.8
The Citadel	1963	1967	2	2	0	0	100.0
Clarke Memorial College	1924	1930	7	4	3	0	57.1
Colorado State	1985	1999	3	2	1	0	66.7
Copiah-Lincoln High School	1915	1915	1	1	0	0	100.0
Copiah-Lincoln CC	1928	1928	1	0	1	0	00.0
Dayton	1954	1956	3	2	1	0	66.7
Delta State	1929	1991	14	10	3	1	76.9
East Carolina	1951	2003	29	22	7	0	75.9
East Texas State	1936	1957	3	1	2	0	33.3
Ellisville High School	1921	1921	1	1	0	0	100.0
Elon College	1955	1955	1	1	0	0	100.0
Florida	1973	1997	4	0	4	0	0.0

Opponent	First Meeting	Last Meeting	Total Games	Won	Lost	Tied	Percent
Florida State	1952	1996	22	8	13	1	36.4
Fullerton State	1975	1975	1	1	0	0	100.0
Georgia	1953	1996	5	2	3	0	40.0
Georgia State Teachers	1941	1941	1	1	0	0	100.0
Gulf Coast CC	1926	1928	3	2	0	1	50.0
Gulf Coast Military Acad.	1913	1926	12	2	7	3	29.2
Hardin-Simmons	1960	1960	1	1	0	0	100.0
Hattiesburg Boy Scouts	1912	1912	1	1	0	0	100.0
Havana (Cuba)	1946	1946	1	1	0	0	100.0
Hawaii	1977	1977	1	1	0	0	100.0
Hinds CC	1927	1927	1	1	0	0	100.0
Houston	1957	2003	7	5	2	0	71.4
Idaho	1969	1998	2	0	2	0	0.0
Illinois	1997	2002	2	2	0	0	100.0
Indiana	1995	1995	1	0	1	0	0.0
Jackson State	1987	2002	2	2	0	0	100.0
Jacksonville State	1946	1946	1	1	0	0	100.0
Jones County High School	1921	1922	2	2	0	0	100.0
Jones County Junior Coll.	1935	1935	1	1	0	0	100.0
Kentucky	1949	1986	2	0	2	0	0.0
Lamar	1974	1981	4	3	1	0	75.0
Louisiana College	1924	1946	15	12	3	0	80.0
Louisiana-Lafayette	1923	2003	49	37	11	1	76.5
Louisiana-Monroe	1982	1993	4	3	1	0	75.0
Louisiana State	1951	1994	2	1	1	0	50.0
Louisiana Tech	1935	1992	42	29	13	0	69.0
Louisville	1949	2002	27	18	8	1	68.5
Loyola University	1921	1933	4	0	4	0	0.0
Marion Military	1922	1929	4	2	2	0	50.0
McMurray College	1949	1951	3	2	1	0	66.7
McNeese State	1980	1980	1	1	0	0	100.0
Memphis	1935	2003	54	36	17	1	67.6
Meridian High School	1916	1916	1	0	1	0	0.0
Meridian College	1919	1919	2	1	0	1	75.0
Millsaps College	1920	1941	14	2	7	5	22.2
Mississippi	1913	1984	24	6	18	0	25.0
Mississippi Freshmen	1925	1925	1	0	1	0	0.0
Miss. Ind. Training School	1920	1920	1	1	0	0	100.0
Mississippi State**	1935	1990	27	14	12	1	53.8
Mississippi State Freshmen	1924	1927	4	1	2	1	16.7
Mississippi College	1914	1934	10	0	10	0	0.0
Mississippi Coll. Freshmen	1923	1928	2	2	0	0	100.0
Missouri	1981	1981	1	0	1	0	0.0
Mobile Military Academy	1912	1914	4	3	1	0	75.0
Mobile Shipbuilders	1942	1942	2	2	0	0	100.0
Murray State	1933	1934	2	1	1	0	50.0
Nebraska	1999	2003	2	0	2	0	00.0
Nevada	1997	1998	2	2	0	0	100.0
Newton Junior College	1928	1928	1	1	0	0	100.0

Opponent	First Meeting	Last Meeting	Total Games	Won	Lost	Tied	Percent
North Carolina State	1958	1990	8	4	4	0	50.0
North Dakota State	1955	1955	1	1	0	0	100.0
North Texas	1954	1981	6	3	3	0	50.0
Northern Illinois	1992	1995	2	1	1	0	50.0
Northwestern State	1930	1999	22	11	11	0	50.0
Oklahoma City	1946	1949	4	3	1	0	75.0
Oklahoma State	2000	2002	3	2	1	0	66.7
Pacific	1952	1952	1	0	1	0	0.0
Parris Island Marines	1953	1953	1	1	0	0	100.0
Pearl River CC	1924	1934	7	3	4	0	42.9
Penn State	1998	2001	2	0	2	0	0.0
Perkinston High School	1915	1920	4	4	0	0	100.0
Pittsburgh	1991	1997	3	1	2	0	33.3
Poplarville High School	1913	1921	7	2	3	2	42.9
Purvis High School	1922	1923	2	1	1	0	50.0
Richmond	1962	1983	16	14	2	0	87.5
St. Mary's	1939	1941	3	2	0	1	83.3
St. Stanislaus College	1921	1927	3	1	2	0	33.3
Sam Houston State	1939	1940	2	0	1	1	25.0
Samford	1994	1994	1	1	0	0	100.0
San Diego State	1968	1971	3	1	2	0	33.3
Seashore Camp Ground	1923	1923	1	1	0	0	100.0
Sixth Service Squadron	1942	1942	1	1	0	0	100.0
Southeastern Louisiana	1940	1969	20	17	3	0	85.0
Southwestern (Memphis)	1931	1932	2	1	1	0	50.0
Southwest CC	1929	1929	1	0	0	1	00.0
Smith County High School	1921	1921	1	1	0	0	100.0
South Florida	2000	2003	3	2	1	0	66.7
Spring Hill	1914	1941	19	7	11	1	44.5
Stephen F. Austin	1946	1988	4	4	0	0	100.0
Stetson	1924	1952	2	1	1	0	50.0
TCU	1989	2003	5	2	3	0	40.0
Tampa	1952	1974	5	5	0	0	100.0
Tennessee	1950	2000	4	0	4	0	0.0
Tennessee-Chattanooga	1949	1973	19	16	3	0	84.2
Texas A & M	1959	1999	7	0	7	0	0.0
Texas-Arlington	1961	1981	10	10	0	0	100.0
Texas–El Paso	1953	1988	2	1	1	0	50.0
Thirty-seventh Division	1940	1940	1	1	0	0	100.0
Trinity	1948	1970	9	8	1	0	88.9
Troy State	1935	1977	7	6	1	0	85.7
Tulane	1979	2003	25	18	7	0	72.0
Tulane Freshmen	1920	1920	1	0	1	0	0.0
Tulsa	1991	1994	4	2	1	1	50.0
Union	1930	1948	9	6	2	1	72.2
Utah	2003	2003	1	0	1	0	0.0
Utah State	1972	1996	5	4	1	0	80.0
Villanova	1954	1954	1	1	0	0	100.0
Virginia Military Inst.	1965	1974	4	4	0	0	100.0

Opponent	First Meeting	Last Meeting	Total Games	Won	Lost	Tied	Percent
Virginia Tech	1958	1994	8	4	4	0	50.0
Weber State	1973	1975	2	2	0	0	100.0
West Texas State	1957	1974	11	8	3	0	72.7
William and Mary	1965	1965	1	0	1	0	0.0
Totals			855	496	332	27	59.6

*Includes one forfeit
**Includes two forfeits

AWARD WINNERS AND HONORS

All-Americans
First Team
1972 Ray Guy, punter: *Sporting News,* Football Writers Association, Walter Camp, Gridiron, *Football News, Playboy,* Associated Press
1980 Hanford Dixon, defensive back: *Sporting News;* Marvin Harvey, tight end: Newspaper Enterprise
1988 James Henry, punt returner: *Sporting News*
1998 Adalius Thomas, defensive end: American Football Coaches Association
1999 Adalius Thomas, defensive end: *College Football News*
2002 Rod Davis, linebacker: CollegeFootballNews.com, All-American Football Foundation
2003 Rod Davis, linebacker: All-Amercian Football Foundation, *Playboy*

Second Team
1997 Patrick Surtain, defensive back: *Sporting News*
1999 Adalius Thomas, defensive end: CBS Sportsline, *Sporting News,* Associated Press, BCS Online
2000 Leo Barnes, defensive back: *Football News*
2002 Etric Pruitt, free safety: CollegeFootballNews.com, CNNSI.com
2003 Michael Boley, linebacker: CollegeFootballNews.com; Rod Davis, linebacker: *Sporting News*

Third Team
1973 Fred Cook, defensive end: Associated Press
1981 Reggie Collier, quarterback: Associated Press
1990 Kerry Valrie, defensive back: Associated Press
1998 Adalius Thomas, defensive end: *Football News,* Associated Press, *College Sports News*
1999 Adalius Thomas, defensive end: *Football News*
2000 Cedric Scott, defensive end: *Football News,* Associated Press
2002 Rod Davis, linebacker: *Sporting News,* Associated Press
2003 Rod Davis, linebacker: Associated Press; CollegeFootballNews.com

Fourth Team
2001 Rod Davis, linebacker: *Sporting News*
2002 Etric Pruitt, free safety: *Sporting News*

National Defensive Player of the Year
1999 Adalius Thomas: SportsRampage.com

Little All-Americans
First Team
1938 George Westerfield, end: International News Service
1946 Jay Smith, end: Paul Williamson's Mid-Bracket
1951 Bucky McElroy, fullback: Paul Williamson's Mid-Bracket, Associated Press; Phil Musmeci, tackle: Associated Press
1952 Bucky McElroy, fullback: Paul Williamson's Mid-Bracket
1953 Bucky McElroy, fullback: Helms Foundation; Hugh Lauren Pepper, halfback: Helms Foundation
1954 Hamp Cook, guard: Associated Press

1955	Les Clark, center: Helms Foundation
1956	Don Owens, tackle: Helms Foundation
1958	Hugh McInnis, end: Associated Press; Bob Yencho, end: Associated Press

Second Team

1946	Mike Katrishen, tackle: Associated Press
1947	Jay Smith, end: Associated Press
1950	Bubba Phillips, halfback: Associated Press
1954	Jim Davis, tackle: Paul Williamson's Mid-Bracket; Hamp Cook, guard: Paul Williamson's Mid-Bracket

Third Team

1951	Phil Musmeci, tackle: Paul Williamson's Mid-Bracket

Honorable Mention

1935	Richard Shields, end: Associated Press; J. D. Stonestreet, back: Associated Press
1938	A. D. Morgan, tackle: Associated Press; A. C. (Mule) Massengale, back: Associated Press
1939	Reginald Switzer, guard: Associated Press; Peter (Jabo) Jones, tackle: Associated Press
1941	Joe Stringfellow, back: Associated Press; Melvin (Pel) Autry, center: Associated Press; C. L. (Dipsey) Dews, back: Associated Press
1952	Hugh Lauren Pepper, back: Paul Williamson's Mid-Bracket; Jackson Brumfield, end: Paul Williamson's Mid-Bracket
1953	Hugh Lauren Pepper, halfback: UPI
1954	Don Owens, tackle: Paul Williamson's Mid-Bracket; P. W. Underwood, tackle: Paul Williamson's Mid-Bracket; Carl Bolt, back: Paul Williamson's Mid-Bracket; Fred Smallwood, back: Paul Williamson's Mid-Bracket

All-South Independent—Associated Press

First Team

1968	Melvin Autrey, center; Rex Barnes, nose tackle; Radell Key, defensive tackle; Ihor Kondrat, offensive guard
1969	Radell Key, defensive tackle; Billy Mikel, wide receiver; Bob Shepherd, offensive tackle
1970	Hugh Eggersman, defensive end; Ray Guy, defensive back/punter; Dickey Surace, linebacker
1971	Ray Guy, punter; Jimmy Haynes, center; Johnny Herron, defensive tackle
1972	Fred Cook, defensive end; Mike Dennery, linebacker; Ray Guy, defensive back/punter
1973	Fred Cook, defensive end; Mike Dennery, linebacker; Doyle Orange, tailback; Ricky Palmer, punter; Clint Tapper, offensive guard
1974	Ron Cheatham, linebacker; Rick Gemmel, defensive back; John Sawyer, tight end
1975	Jerry Fremin, offensive tackle; Randy Latta, nose guard; Norris Thomas, defensive back
1976	Ben Garry, tailback; Eric Smith, offensive tackle; Bobby Smithart, defensive end
1977	Ben Garry, tailback; Stoney Parker, defensive tackle; Eric Smith, offensive tackle
1978	Randy Butler, offensive tackle; Stoney Parker, defensive tackle; Clump Taylor, linebacker
1979	Marvin Harvey, tight end; J. J. Stewart, defensive end; Clump Taylor, linebacker
1980	Hanford Dixon, defensive back; Marvin Harvey, tight end; George Tillman, defensive end; Jamey Watson, center; Sammy Winder, tailback
1981	Jerald Baylis, nose guard; Reggie Collier, quarterback; George Tillman, defensive end; Sammy Winder, tailback
1982	Jerald Baylis, nose guard; Reggie Collier, quarterback; Sam Dejarnette, tailback; Glen Howe, offensive tackle; George Tillman, defensive end
1983	Jerald Baylis, nose guard; Bud Brown, safety; Glen Howe, offensive tackle; Louis Lipps, wide receiver
1984	Richard Byrd, defensive tackle
1986	Pat Ferrell, offensive tackle; Onesimus Henry, linebacker
1987	Pat Ferrell, offensive tackle
1988	Scott Bryant, punter
1990	Chafan Marsh, offensive guard
1991	Tony Smith, tailback
1992	Leon Anderson, offensive guard; Tyrone Nix, linebacker; Terryl Ulmer, defensive back; Michael Welch, running back
1993	Todd Beeching, offensive tackle; Letorrance Gulley, defensive back; Bobby Hamilton, defensive end; Tyrone Nix, linebacker; Michael Tobias, defensive tackle
1994	Michael Tobias, defensive tackle

Second Team

1974	Jeff Bower, quarterback; Mike Smith, defensive tackle; Norris Thomas, defensive back
1977	Amos Fowler, offensive guard; Bobby Smithart, defensive end
1978	Greg Ahrens, offensive tackle; David Odom, defensive back
1981	Bud Brown, defensive back; Glen Howe, offensive tackle; Rhett Whitley, defensive end
1982	Bud Brown, defensive back; Louis Lipps, wide receiver

1983 Richard Byrd, defensive tackle; Steve Carmody, center; Sam Dejarnette, tailback
1984 Fred Richards, tackle
1986 Vincent Alexander, tailback; Billy Knighten, punter
1988 Shelton Gandy, tailback; James Henry, defensive back; George Hill, linebacker; Marty Williams, center
1989 Scott Bryant, punter; William Kirksey, linebacker; Chris Ryals, tackle; Kerry Valrie, defensive back
1990 Brett Favre, quarterback; Tony Smith, tailback; Arnie Williams, linebacker
1991 Derrick Hoskins, defensive back; Chafan Marsh, guard; Thad McDowell, linebacker; Marcus Pope, tight end; Chris Ryals, tackle; Arnie Williams, linebacker
1992 Bobby Hamilton, defensive end; George McReynolds, guard; Lance Nations, placekicker; Marcus Pope, tight end; Michael Tobias, defensive tackle
1994 Brent Duggins, offensive guard; Letorrance Gulley, defensive back
1995 Tim Bell, defensive lineman; Fred Brock, wide receiver; Chris Pierce, placekicker; Daryl Terrell, offensive lineman

Third Team
1995 Robert Brown, defensive lineman; Eugene Harmon, linebacker; Derrick Hervey, defensive back; Chris Pierce, punter

Honorable Mention
1995 Fred Brock, returner; Albert McRae, linebacker; Rod Thomas, defensive back

College Football Association All-Academic Team
1991 James Singleton, defensive end
1992 James Singleton, defensive end

Conerly Trophy
(Best Player in the State of Mississippi)
2002 Rod Davis, linebacker

College Football Chronicle Unsung Hero All-America
1996 Karr Shannon, defensive back

National Football Foundation and College Hall of Fame Scholar-Athlete
2001 Jeff Kelly, quarterback

Woody Hayes NCAA Division I National Scholar-Athlete
2001 Jeff Kelly, quarterback

Verizon Academic All-America
First Team
1992 James Singleton, defensive end
1997 Jeremy Lindley, offensive lineman

Second Team
1991 James Singleton, defensive end
2000 Jeff Kelly, quarterback

Sporting News Freshman All-Americans
1996 Adalius Thomas, defensive end
1997 John Nix, defensive tackle
1998 Derrick Nix, running back (first team)
2000 Rod Davis, linebacker (second team)
2001 Skylor Magee, defensive lineman (third team)
2003 Darren McCaleb, kicker (third team)

All–Independent Football Alliance
1992 Leon Anderson, guard; Perry Carter, defensive back; Tyrone Nix, linebacker; James Singleton, defensive end; Terryl Ulmer, defensive back; Michael Welch, tailback
1993 Todd Beeching, tackle; Perry Carter, defensive back; Eric Estes, punter; Letorrance Gulley, defensive back; Bobby Hamilton, defensive end; Michael Tobias, defensive tackle

Liberty Bowl Alliance All-Star Team
1994 Robert Brown, defensive end; Eugene Harmon, linebacker; Derrick Hervey, defensive back; Mark Montgomery, wide receiver; Michael Tobias, defensive tackle
1995 Tim Bell, defensive lineman; Fred Brock, wide receiver; Eugene Harmon, linebacker; Chris Pierce, placekicker/punter; Darryl Terrell, offensive lineman

All-Southern Intercollegiate Athletic Association
Second Team
1938 George Westerfield, end: Associated Press
1939 A. D. Morgan, tackle: Associated Press; A. C. (Mule) Massengale, back: Associated Press

Honorable Mention
1931 Brownie Thomas, guard: Associated Press; Leonard

Burns, back: Associated Press; Lance Lumpkin, tackle: Associated Press
1939 Reginald Switzer, guard: Associated Press; Melvin (Pel) Autry, center: Associated Press
1940 Reginald Switzer, guard: Associated Press; Peter (Jabo) Jones, tackle: Associated Press

All–Gulf States Conference
First Team
1950 Dave Allen, center; Bubba Phillips, halfback; Ivan Rosamond, end
1951 Dick Caldwell, end; Scrappy Hart, halfback; Eddie Kauchick, linebacker; Walter Mann, tackle; Bucky McElroy, halfback; Phil Musmeci, tackle

Second Team
1950 Bobby Holmes, quarterback; Phil Musmeci, tackle
1951 Dave Allen, center; Jimmy Brashier, halfback; Jackson Brumfield, end; Ken Farris, guard; Jack Fulkerson, tackle; Tom LeGros, quarterback; Ed McDaniel, guard; Bob McKellar, end; Phil Muscarello, linebacker

All-Conference USA
First Team
1996 Eric Booth, running back; Leroy Dewitt, offensive lineman; Marchant Kenney, linebacker; Patrick Surtain, defensive back; Cedric Walthaw, linebacker
1997 Robert Brown, defensive end; Sherrod Gideon, wide receiver; Kasey Keith, offensive lineman; Marchant Kenney, linebacker; Perry Phenix, defensive back; Harold Shaw, running back; Patrick Surtain, defensive back; Adalius Thomas, defensive end
1998 Sherrod Gideon, wide receiver; Henry McLendon, offensive lineman; Derrick Nix, running back; T. J. Slaughter, linebacker; Adalius Thomas, defensive end; Ty Trahan, linebacker
1999 Leo Barnes, defensive back; Shedrick Blackmon, offensive lineman; Cedric Scott, defensive lineman; T. J. Slaughter, linebacker; Adalius Thomas, defensive end
2000 Leo Barnes, defensive back; Cedric Scott, defensive lineman; DeQuincy Scott, defensive lineman
2001 Greg Brooks, defensive back; Rod Davis, linebacker; Chad Williams, defensive back
2002 Michael Boley, linebacker; Rod Davis, linebacker; Derrick Nix, running back; Etric Pruitt, defensive back; Torrin Tucker, offensive lineman
2003 Michael Boley, linebacker; Greg Brooks, defensive back; Rod Davis, linebacker; John Eubanks, punt returner; Jeremy Parquet, offensive tackle; Terrell Paul, defensive end; Etric Pruitt, defensive back; Marvin Young, kickoff returner

Second Team
1996 Terry Hardy, tight end; Perry Phenix, defensive back; Lee Roberts, quarterback; Darryl Terrell, offensive lineman
1997 Jamaal Alexander, defensive back; Eric Booth, kick-off returner; Terry Hardy, tight end; Henry McLendon, offensive lineman; Lee Roberts, quarterback
1998 Jose Gonzalez, defensive back; DeShone Mallard, defensive back; O'Lester Pope, offensive lineman; Cedric Scott, defensive lineman
1999 Sherrod Gideon, wide receiver; Derrick Nix, running back; Terrance Parrish, defensive back; Todd Pinkston, wide receiver; DeQuincy Scott, defensive lineman; Ty Trahan, linebacker
2000 Billy Clay, offensive lineman; Raymond Walls, defensive back; Chad Williams, defensive back
2001 Jeremy Bridges, offensive lineman; Roy Magee, linebacker; Terrell Paul, defensive lineman
2002 Jason Jimenez, offensive lineman; Terrell Paul, defensive lineman
2003 Terrell Browden, tight end; Jim Hicks, offensive lineman

Third Team
2003 Ronald Jones, defensive end; Alex Ray, defensive back; Eric Scott, defensive lineman; Chris White, offensive lineman; Marvin Young, wide receiver

Freshman Team
1996 Shedrick Blackmon, offensive lineman; Sherrod Gideon, wide receiver; Jamie Purser, punter; Adalius Thomas, defensive end
1997 John Nix, defensive lineman; DeQuincy Scott, defensive lineman
1998 Derrick Nix, running back
1999 Jeremy Bridges, offensive lineman; Joe Henley, linebacker; Zeb Landers, offensive lineman; Buck Miciotto, tight end; Torrin Tucker, offensive lineman
2000 Greg Brooks, defensive back; Rod Davis, linebacker; Jim Hicks, offensive lineman; Kenneth Johnson, wide receiver/return specialist; Terrell Paul, defensive end

2001 Chris Johnson, wide receiver; Skylor Magee, defensive lineman; Jeremy Parquet, offensive lineman; Myron Powe, offensive lineman; James Walley, running back
2002 John Eubanks, defensive back
2003 Greg Casnave, defensive lineman; Travis Cooley, offensive lineman; Darren McCaleb, kicker

Defensive Player of the Year
1997 Patrick Surtain, defensive back
1998 Adalius Thomas, defensive end
1999 Adalius Thomas, defensive end
2003 Rod Davis, linebacker

Coach of the Year
1997 Jeff Bower
1999 Jeff Bower
2003 Jeff Bower

Freshman of the Year
1998 Derrick Nix, running back

Postseason All-Star Games
Blue-Gray All-Star Classic
1948 Albert Sanders, center
1949 Cliff Coggin, wide receiver
1961 Don Fuell, quarterback
1962 Billy Coleman, quarterback
1965 John Mangum, tackle
1966 Ken Avery, linebacker; Troy Craft, end
1967 Tommy Roussel, linebacker
1974 Fred Cook, defensive end; Mike Dennery, linebacker
1980 Hanford Dixon, defensive back; Marvin Harvey, tight end; Jamey Watson, offensive lineman
1982 Reggie Collier, quarterback
1983 Jerald Baylis, nose guard; Glen Howe, offensive lineman
1984 Richard Byrd, defensive lineman
1986 Vincent Alexander, tailback; Collins Hess, defensive back
1987 Billy Knighten, punter
1989 Buddy King, tackle
1991 Derrick Hoskins, defensive back; Tim Roberts, defensive tackle
1992 Chris Pierce, placekicker; Marcus Pope, tight end
1996 Daryl Terrell, offensive lineman
2000 Daleroy Stewart, defensive tackle
2001 Roy Magee, linebacker; Chad Williams, defensive back

Senior Bowl
1950 Cliff Coggin, end
1951 Bubba Phillips, halfback
1952 Scrappy Hart, halfback
1954 Bucky McElroy, fullback
1955 Hamp Cook, guard
1956 George Herring, quarterback/punter
1957 Don Owens, tackle
1958 Curry Juneau, end
1959 Richard Johnston, center; George Sekul, quarterback
1960 Hugh McInnis, end; Johnny Sklopan, halfback
1961 Tommy Morrow, linebacker
1962 Don Fuell, quarterback
1963 Harold Hays, center
1967 Ken Avery, linebacker
1968 Tommy Roussel, linebacker
1969 Melvin Autrey, center
1970 Henry Quick, defensive end
1972 Jimmy Haynes, center
1974 Fred Cook, defensive end; Harvey McGee, wide receiver
1975 John Sawyer, tight end
1976 Norris Thomas, defensive back
1978 Ben Garry, tailback
1979 Randy Butler, tackle
1980 J. J. Stewart, defensive end
1981 Hanford Dixon, defensive back
1982 Sammy Winder, tailback
1983 Reggie Collier, quarterback
1984 Steve Carmody, center; Glen Howe, tackle; Louis Lipps, wide receiver
1985 Richard Byrd, defensive tackle
1986 Lyneal Alston, wide receiver
1987 Sidney Coleman, linebacker
1988 Chris Seroka, placekicker
1989 James Henry, defensive back
1990 Brett Favre, quarterback; Kerry Valrie, defensive back
1991 Tim Roberts, defensive tackle; Chris Ryals, tackle; Tony Smith, tailback; Arnie Williams, linebacker
1992 Mike Iosia, deep snapper; Marcus Pope, tight end; James Singleton, linebacker
1993 Perry Carter, defensive back
1994 Michael Tobias, defensive tackle
1996 Johnny Lomoro, placekicker
1997 Jamaal Alexander, defensive back; Patrick Surtain, defensive back
1999 Sherrod Gideon, wide receiver; Terrance Parrish,

defensive back; Todd Pinkston, wide receiver; T. J. Slaughter, linebacker; Adalius Thomas, defensive end
2000   John Nix, defensive tackle; Cedric Scott, defensive end; Raymond Walls, defensive back
2002   Jeremy Bridges, offensive lineman; Torrin Tucker, offensive lineman
2003   Greg Brooks, defensive back; Rod Davis, linebacker; Etric Pruitt, defensive back

East-West Shrine Game
1956   Don Owens, tackle
1977   Amos Fowler, guard
1979   Randy Butler, offensive guard
1982   Rhett Whitley, defensive end; Sammy Winder, running back
1983   Eddie Ray Walker, defensive back
1984   Steve Carmody, center
1985   Richard Byrd, defensive tackle
1991   Brett Favre, quarterback
1997   Daryl Terrell, offensive lineman
1999   DeShone Mallard, defensive back
2000   Sherrod Gideon, wide receiver
2001   Leo Barnes, defensive back
2003   Etric Pruitt, defensive back

Japan Bowl
1987   Collins Hess, defensive back
1988   Billy Knighten, punter

All-America Bowl
1958   Bob Yencho, end

Rotary Gridiron Classic
2000   John Nix, defensive lineman; Daleroy Stewart, defensive lineman
2002   Jeremy Bridges, offensive lineman; Jason Jimenez, offensive lineman
2003   Ronald Jones, defensive end

College All-Star Game
1954   Bucky McElroy, halfback
1957   Don Owens, tackle
1960   Charles Ellzey, center; Hugh McInnis, end
1962   Don Fuell, quarterback
1968   Tommy Roussel, linebacker
1973   Ray Guy, punter

PLAYERS IN THE PROS

Players Selected in the All-American Football Conference Draft
1948 Jay Smith, sixth round, Brooklyn Dodgers
1949 Al Sanders, eighteenth round, Baltimore Colts; Bubba Phillips, eighteenth round, Chicago Hornets

Players Selected in the American Football League Draft
1960 Byron Bradfute, Los Angeles Chargers; Hugh McInnis, Houston Oilers
1961 Don Fuell, twenty-sixth round, Houston Oilers; George Hultz, thirtieth round, Boston Patriots
1962 Harold Hays, twenty-sixth round, Houston Oilers
1963 Jerrel Wilson, eleventh round, Dallas Texans; Bill Freeman, eighteenth round, Dallas Texans
1964 Charlie Parker, thirteenth round, Denver Broncos
1966 Ken Avery, second round, Boston Patriots; John Mangum, fifth round, Boston Patriots

Players Selected in the National Football League Draft
1942 Joe Stringfellow, twelfth round, Detroit Lions
1947 Dick Thames, twenty-fifth round, New York Giants
1948 Jay Smith, fifth round, Chicago Cardinals; Mike Katrishen, tenth round, Washington Redskins; Bob Dement, fifteenth round, Los Angeles Rams
1949 Al Sanders, eleventh round, Pittsburgh Steelers; Joe Morgan, sixteenth round, Los Angeles Rams
1950 Cliff Coggin, seventh round, Los Angeles Rams
1951 Bubba Phillips, nineteenth round, San Francisco 49ers
1952 Bucky McElroy, twenty-sixth round, Chicago Bears; Scrappy Hart, twenty-eighth round, Los Angeles Rams; Jack Fulkerson, thirtieth round, Green Bay Packers
1953 Bucky McElroy, seventh round, Chicago Bears; Howard Lehman, nineteenth round, New York Giants; Hugh Laurin Pepper, twenty-eighth round, Detroit Lions
1954 Hugh Laurin Pepper, sixth round, Pittsburgh Steelers; P. W. Underwood, twenty-eighth round, Chicago Bears
1955 Wes Clark, seventeenth round, Baltimore Colts; Carl Bolt, twentieth round, Green Bay Packers
1956 George Herring, sixteenth round, San Francisco 49ers; Pat Del Vaccario, twenty-second round, Baltimore Colts; Bob Hughes, twenty-ninth round, Philadelphia Eagles
1957 Don Owens, third round, Pittsburgh Steelers; Bo Dickinson, sixth round, Chicago Bears; Curry Juneau, twenty-first round, Cleveland Browns
1958 Richard Johnston, fifteenth round, Los Angeles Rams; John Perkins, sixteenth round, Pittsburgh Steelers

1959 Sam Tuccio, tenth round, Green Bay Packers; Rene Lorio, twenty-sixth round, Baltimore Colts
1960 Charles Ellzey, third round, Chicago Cardinals; Hugh McInnis, third round, Chicago Cardinals
1961 George Hultz, seventh round, St. Louis Cardinals; Val Kecklin, eleventh round, Green Bay Packers
1962 Harold Hays, fourteenth round, Dallas Cowboys
1963 Bill Freeman, ninth round, Green Bay Packers; John Sklopan, twelfth round, Minnesota Vikings; Jerrel Wilson, seventeenth round, Los Angeles Rams
1964 Charlie Parker, thirteenth round, Baltimore Colts; Tommy Walters, sixteenth round, Washington Redskins
1966 Ken Avery, twelfth round, New York Giants
1967 Billy Devrow, eighth round, Cleveland Browns
1968 Tom Roussel, second round, Washington Redskins; Bobby Webb, sixth round, Los Angeles Rams
1969 Tommy Boutwell, thirteenth round, Cleveland Browns; Hank Autry, seventeenth round, Houston Oilers
1973 Ray Guy, first round, Oakland Raiders
1974 Fred Cook, second round, Baltimore Colts; Mike Dennery, thirteenth round, Oakland Raiders; Eugene Bird, eleventh round, New York Jets; Harvey McGee, eleventh round, Dallas Cowboys; Doyle Orange, sixth round, Atlanta Falcons
1975 John Sawyer, eleventh round, Houston Oilers
1976 Norris Thomas, ninth round, Miami Dolphins; Brad Bowman, thirteenth round, Green Bay Packers
1977 Carl Allen, eleventh round, Cincinnati Bengals; Barry Caudill, twelfth round, Los Angeles Rams
1978 Amos Fowler, fifth round, Detroit Lions; Eric Smith, sixth round, Buffalo Bills; Ben Garry, sixth round, Baltimore Colts
1981 Hanford Dixon, first round, Cleveland Browns; Marvin Harvey, third round, Kansas City Chiefs; Cliff Lewis, twelfth round, Green Bay Packers
1982 Sammy Winder, fifth round, Denver Broncos; Ricky Floyd, tenth round, Cleveland Browns
1983 Reggie Collier, sixth round, Dallas Cowboys
1984 Louis Lipps, first round, Pittsburgh Steelers; Clemon Terrell, eighth round, New Orleans; Glen Howe, ninth round, Atlanta Falcons; Bud Brown, eleventh round, Miami Dolphins
1985 Richard Byrd, second round, Houston Oilers
1986 Robert Ducksworth, eighth round, New York Jets
1988 John Baylor, fifth round, Indianapolis Colts
1989 James Henry, fourth round, Seattle Seahawks
1990 Eugene Rowell, ninth round, Cleveland Browns; Reginald Warnsley, eleventh round, Detroit Lions
1991 Brett Favre, second round, Atlanta Falcons; Michael Jackson, sixth round, Cleveland Browns; Simmie Carter, seventh round, New York Giants
1992 Tony Smith, first round, Atlanta Falcons; Derrick Hoskins, fifth round, Los Angeles Raiders; Tim Roberts, fifth round, Houston Oilers
1994 Perry Carter, fourth round, Arizona Cardinals
1998 Patrick Surtain, second round, Miami Dolphins; Terry Hardy, fifth round, Arizona Cardinals; Jamaal Alexander, sixth round, Detroit Lions; Harold Shaw, sixth round, New England Patriots
2000 Todd Pinkston, second round, Philadelphia Eagles; T. J. Slaughter, third round, Jacksonville Jaguars; Sherrod Gideon, sixth round, New Orleans Saints; Adalius Thomas, sixth round, Baltimore Ravens
2001 Cedric Scott, fourth round, New York Giants; Raymond Walls, fifth round, Indianapolis Colts; Daleroy Stewart, sixth round, Dallas Cowboys; John Nix, seventh round, Dallas Cowboys
2002 Chad Williams, sixth round, Baltimore Ravens; Jeff Kelly, seventh round, Seattle Seahawks
2003 Jeremy Bridges, sixth round, Philadelphia Eagles
2004 Rod Davis, fifth round, Minnesota Vikings; Greg Brooks, sixth round, Cincinnati Bengals; Etric Pruitt, sixth round, Atlanta Falcons

Players Selected in the United States Football League Draft
1983 Reggie Collier, first round, Birmingham Stallions; Eddie Ray Walker, nineteenth round, Birmingham Stallions; George Tillman, twentieth round, Birmingham Stallions; Moochie Allen, twenty-second round, Birmingham Stallions
1985 Richard Byrd, territorial pick, Portland Breakers; Sam Dejarnette, territorial pick, Portland Breakers; Greg Haeusler, territorial pick, Portland Breakers

Players with Professional Careers
All teams are NFL teams unless otherwise noted.

Allen, Carl (1974–75)
    St. Louis Cardinals   1977–82
    Chicago Blitz (USFL)   1983
    Arizona Wranglers (USFL)   1984
    Arizona Outlaws (USFL)   1985
Allen, Moochie (1979–82)
    Birmingham Stallions (USFL)   1983
Alexander, Jamaal (1994–97)
    St. Louis Rams   1998

Alexander, Vincent (1983–86)			Montreal Alouettes (CFL)	2002
New Orleans Saints	1987		Carter, Simmie (1987–90)	
Alston, Lyneal (1983–86)			Birmingham Fire (WLAF)	1992
Pittsburgh Steelers	1987		Coleman, Sidney (1984–87)	
Autry, Hank (1966–68)			Tampa Bay Buccaneers	1988–90
Houston Oilers	1969–70		Phoenix Cardinals	1991
Avery, Ken (1964–66)			Collier, Reggie (1979–82)	
New York Giants	1967–68		Birmingham Stallions (USFL)	1983
Cincinnati Bengals	1969–74		Washington Federals (USFL)	1984
Kansas City Chiefs	1975		Orlando Renegades (USFL)	1985
Barnes, Leo (1997–2000)			Dallas Cowboys	1986
Frankfurt Galaxy (NFL–Europe)	2002		Pittsburgh Steelers	1987
Baylis, Jerald (1980–83)			Cook, Fred (1971–73)	
New Orleans Breakers (USFL)	1984		Baltimore Colts	1974–80
Portland Breakers (USFL)	1985		Dennery, Mike (1971–73)	
Toronto Argonauts (CFL)	1986–89		Oakland Raiders	1974–75
British Columbia Lions (CFL)	1991		Miami Dolphins	1976
Saskatchewan Roughriders (CFL)	1992–93		Devrow, Billy (1964–66)	
Baltimore Colts (CFL)	1994		Cleveland Browns	1967
Baylor, John (1984–87)			Dickinson, Bo (1956–57)	
Indianapolis Colts	1989–93		Kansas City Chiefs	1960–61
Boutwell, Tommy (1967–68)			Denver Broncos	1962–63
Miami Dolphins	1969		Houston Oilers	1963
Bradfute, Byron (1959)			Oakland Raiders	1964
Dallas Cowboys	1960–61		Dixon, Hanford (1977–80)	
Bridges, Jeremy (1999–2002)			Cleveland Browns	1981–89
Philadelphia Eagles	2003		Duggins, Brent (1993–94)	
Brock, Fred (1992–95)			Indianapolis Colts	1995
Arizona Cardinals	1996–98		Ellzey, Charles (1957–59)	
Broussard, Steve (1970–71)			St. Louis Cardinals	1960–61
Green Bay Packers	1975		Favre, Brett (1987–90)	
Brown, Bud (1980–83)			Atlanta Falcons	1991
Miami Dolphins	1984–88		Green Bay Packers	1992–2003
Brown, Jim (1979–83)			Fowler, Amos (1975–77)	
Birmingham Stallions (USFL)	1984–85		Detroit Lions	1978–79
Brown, Robert (1994–97)			Fuell, Don (1959–61)	
Edmonton Eskimos (CFL)	1998–2001		Toronto Argonauts (CFL)	1963–65
Montreal Alouettes (CFL)	2002–2004		Montreal Alouettes (CFL)	1965
Brumfield, Jackson (1951–53)			Garry, Ben (1974–77)	
San Francisco 49ers	1954		Baltimore Colts	1979–80
Bryant, Tim (1983)			Gideon, Sherrod (1996–99)	
Minnesota Vikings	1987		Miami Dolphins `	2000
Byrd, Richard (1981–84)			St. Louis Rams	2001
Houston Oilers	1985–89		Ottawa Renegades (CFL)	2003–2004
Carter, Perry (1990–93)			Guy, Ray (1970–72)	
Kansas City Chiefs	1994–95		Oakland Raiders	1973–86
Oakland Raiders	1996–98		Hamilton, Bobby (1990–93)	
Edmonton Eskimos (CFL)	2000–2001		Seattle Seahawks	1994

London Monarchs (WLAF)	1994–95	Pittsburgh Steelers	1984–91
New York Jets	1997–99	New Orleans Saints	1992
New England Patriots	2000–2003	Magnum, John (1964–65)	
Hardy, Terry (1994–97)		New England Patriots	1966–67
Arizona Cardinals	1998–2001	McElroy, Bucky (1951–53)	
Harvey, Marvin (1977–80)		Hamilton Tiger Cats (CFL)	1954–55
Kansas City Chiefs	1981–82	McGee, Howard (1993–94)	
Tampa Bay Bandits (USFL)	1984–86	Birmingham Barracudas (CFL)	1995
Hays, Harold (1960–62)		McInnis, Hugh (1957–59)	
Dallas Cowboys	1963–67	St. Louis Cardinals	1960–62
San Francisco 49ers	1968–69	Detroit Lions	1964
Henry, James (1986–88)		Atlanta Falcons	1966
Birmingham Fire (WLAF)	1991–92	Miller, Bruce (1980–83)	
Herring, George (1954–55)		New Orleans Breakers (USFL)	1984
Denver, Broncos	1960–61	Portland Breakers (USFL)	1985
Hoskins, Derrick (1988–91)		Saskatchewan Roughriders (CFL)	1986
Oakland Raiders	1992–97	Mills, Shawn (1999–2000)	
Howe, Glen (1980–83)		Atlanta Falcons	2001–2002
Pittsburgh Steelers	1985	Morgan, Joe (1948)	
Atlanta Falcons	1985–86	San Francisco 49ers	1949
Hultz, Don (1960–62)		Morrow, Tommy (1958–60)	
Minnesota Vikings	1963	Oakland Raiders	1962–64
Philadelphia Eagles	1964–73	Nix, John (1997–2000)	
Chicago Bears	1974	Dallas Cowboys	2001–2002
Hultz, George (1960–61)		Cleveland Browns	2003
St. Louis Cardinals	1962	Amsterdam Admirals (NFL Europe)	2004
Jackson, Michael (1987–90)		Oliver, Maurice (1985–88)	
Cleveland Browns	1991–95	Tampa Bay Buccaneers	1991
Baltimore Ravens	1996–98	Birmingham Fire (WLAF)	1991–92
Jimenez, Jason (2000–2002)		Orange, Doyle (1971–73)	
Green Bay Packers	2003	Toronto Argonauts (CFL)	1974
Frankfurt Galaxy (NFL Europe)	2004	Owens, Don (1953–56)	
Katrishen, Mike (1941, 1946–47)		Washington Redskins	1957
Washington Redskins	1948–49	Philadelphia Eagles	1958–60
Kecklin, Val (1960)		St. Louis Cardinals	1960–63
San Diego Chargers	1962	Parker, Charlie (1961–63)	
Kelly, Jeff (1998–2001)		Denver Broncos	1965
Seattle Seahawks	2002	Parker, Stoney (1975–78)	
King, Buddy (1986–89)		Saskatchewan Roughriders (CFL)	1979
Birmingham Fire (WLAF)	1991–92	Parrish, Terrance (1996–99)	
Kirksey, William (1986–89)		Ottawa Renegades (CFL)	2002
Minnesota Vikings	1990	Phenix, Perry (1996–97)	
London Monarchs (WLAF)	1992	Tennessee Titans	1998–2001
Montreal Alouettes	1996	Carolina Panthers	2001
Landrum, Mike (1982–83)		Pinkston, Todd (1996–2000)	
Atlanta Falcons	1984	Philadelphia Eagles	2000–2003
Lewis, Cliff (1978–80)		Pope, O'Lester (1995–98)	
Green Bay Packers	1981–84	Miami Dolphins	1999
Lipps, Louis (1980–83)		Barcelona Dragons (NFL Europe)	2000–2001

Calgary Stampeders (CFL)	2002
British Columbia Lions (CFL)	2003

Posey, Jeff (1995–96)
- San Francisco 49ers — 1997–2001
- Carolina Panthers — 2001
- Houston Texans — 2002
- Buffalo Bills — 2003

Purvis, Vic (1963–65)
- New England Patriots — 1966–67

Reed, Rod (1988–91)
- Las Vegas Posse (CFL) — 1994

Roberts, Tim (1988–91)
- Houston Oilers — 1992–94
- New England Patriots — 1995

Roussel, Tommy (1965–67)
- Washington Redskins — 1968–70
- New Orleans Saints — 1971–72
- Philadelphia Eagles — 1973

Rowell, Eugene (1988–89)
- Cleveland Browns — 1990
- Birmingham Fire (WLAF) — 1992

Satcher, Doug (1963–65)
- New England Patriots — 1966–68

Sawyer, John (1972–74)
- Houston Oilers — 1975–76
- Seattle Seahawks — 1977–82
- Washington Redskins — 1983
- Denver Broncos — 1983–84

Scott, Cedric (1996–2000)
- New York Giants — 2001
- Cleveland Browns — 2002
- Scottish Claymores (NFL Europe) — 2004

Scott, DeQuincy (1996–2000)
- San Diego Chargers — 2001–2003

Shaw, Harold (1994–97)
- New England Patriots — 1998–2000

Sklopan, John (1960–62)
- Denver Broncos — 1963

Slaughter, T. J. (1995–99)
- Jacksonville Jaguars — 2000–2003
- Green Bay Packers — 2003
- Baltimore Ravens — 2003

Smith, Tony (1989–91)
- Atlanta Falcons — 1992–94
- Carolina Panthers — 1995
- Toronto Argonauts (CFL) — 1998

Stallings, Robert Ray (1982–85)
- St. Louis Cardinals — 1986
- Raleigh-Durham (WLAF) — 1991

Stewart, Daleroy (1996–2000)
- Dallas Cowboys — 2001–2003

Stringfellow, Joe (1941)
- Detroit Lions — 1942

Surtain, Patrick (1994–97)
- Miami Dolphins — 1998–2003

Terrell, Daryl (1995–96)
- New Orleans Saints — 1999–2001
- Jacksonville Jaguars — 2002
- Washington Redskins — 2003

Thomas, Adalius (1996–99)
- Baltimore Ravens — 2000–2003

Thomas, Norris (1972–75)
- Miami Dolphins — 1977–79
- Tampa Bay Buccaneers — 1980–84

Tucker, Torrin (1999–2002)
- Dallas Cowboys — 2003

Ulmer, Terryl (1990, 1992)
- Saskatchewan Roughriders (CFL) — 1993–98, 2000

Underwood, P. W. (1954–56)
- Hamilton Tiger Cats (CFL) — 1957–58

Van Tone, Art (1939–42)
- Detroit Lions — 1943–45

Vetrano, Joe (1940–42)
- San Francisco 49ers — 1946–49

Walker, Eddie Ray (1979–82)
- Arizona Wranglers (USFL) — 1983
- Saskatchewan Roughriders (CFL) — 1985–88

Walls, Raymond (1996–2000)
- Indianapolis Colts — 2001–2002
- Cleveland Browns — 2002
- Baltimore Ravens — 2003

Walters, Tommy (1962–63)
- Washington Redskins — 1964–67

Wells, Terrance (1971–73)
- Houston Oilers — 1974
- Green Bay Packers — 1975

Williams, Arnie (1988–91)
- British Columbia Lion (CFL) — 1994

Williams, Chad (1999–2002)
- Baltimore Ravens — 2002–2003

Wilson, Jerrel (1961–62)
- Kansas City Chiefs — 1963–77
- New England Patriots — 1978

Windsor, Chris (1995–96)
- Edmonton Eskimos (CFL) — 1997

Winder, Sammy (1979–81)
- Denver Broncos — 1982–90

INDEX

ABC-TV, first appearance on, 174
Abilene Christian, 75, 79, 83, 85–87, 90, 95, 100, 103, 107
Adkison, Wayne, 127
Ahrens, Greg, 169
Ainsworth, Greg, 144
Akins, Leon, 95, 102, 104
Alabama, University of, 51, 57, 62, 68, 69, 71, 75, 78, 88, 121, 122, 125, 131, 141, 145, 153, 158, 160, 176, 179, 187, 190, 196, 198, 200, 210, 212, 218, 222, 224, 226, 229, 232, 236, 241, 243, 246, 249, 252, 258
Alabama–Birmingham, University of. *See* UAB
Albus, Larry, 183
Alderman, Kenny, 159
Alessandri, Leo, 36, 39–41
Alexander, Jamaal, 230, 232, 235
Alexander, Vincent, 190–92, 194–96, 198, 200
All-American Bowl, 215
Allen, Carl, 159
Allen, Dave, 68, 70
Allen, Scott, 185
All-Navy Service Team, 16
Almond, Dustin, 252–54, 258, 259
Alston, Lyneal, 189, 192, 194, 199–200
Anderson, Andrew, 192, 194–96, 199–200
Anderson, Cephus, 8
Anderson, G. B. (Blink), 4
Anderson, Leon, 220
Anderson, Qadry, 228
Appalachian State, 35
Applewhite, Tommy, 127
Arban, J. C., 85, 86–87, 92, 130
Arkansas State, 36, 75, 100, 103, 107, 110, 166–67, 172, 176
Arlington State. *See* Texas–Arlington, University of
Army (West Point), 236, 241, 252
Army Administration Program, 45
Army 37th Division, 41
Athletic Center, opening of new, 250
Atkins, Billy, 112
Atkins, Sid, 112
Auburn University, 46, 51, 56, 95, 113, 117, 137, 141, 164, 170, 177, 184, 188, 191, 194, 206, 208, 215–16, 218, 221
Austin, Leroy (Hawk), 32
Austin, O. V. (Spout), 10–11, 16, 48
Autry, Hank, 127
Autry, Melvin (Pel), 40, 44
Avery, Ken, 115, 118–19, 121
AXA Liberty Bowl, 234, 242, 259

Bachman, Gene, 118–19
Baham, Ron, 208, 217
Bama Bowl, 187
Banks, Rex, 191–92, 194, 196, 199–200
Barfield, Doug, 80, 83–86, 170, 177
Barger, Jimmy, 116
Barhanovich, Mark, 163
Barker, Jay, 218, 224
Barnes, Leo, 241, 243–45
Barnett, Governor Ross, 105, 108
Baskin, Fred, 194
Batchelder, Paul, 232
Bates, Robert, 227
Battaglia, Joe, 92

Battles, Mike, 127
Baxter, Fred, 216
Baylis, Jerald, 178, 180, 182, 185, 187, 191
Baylor, John, 201, 204
Beal, Raymond (Tiko), 165, 168, 170–72
Beeching, Todd, 223
Bell, James (Ding Dong), 47, 50
Bell, Tatum, 254
Bell, Tim, 228
Bella, Sam, 102
Bennett, Claude, 18, 22, 27
Bentley, Kevin, 219–21
Berry, James, 103, 108
Bilbo, Ellis, 21, 23, 26–27, 29
Bilbo, Senator Theodore, 45
Biletnikoff, Fred, 110, 114
Bird, Eugene, 130, 141, 143–44, 151
Black, Jimmy, 161
Black, Tony, 171
Black, Willie, 40
Blackmon, Bill, 65
Blackmon, Shederick, 243
Blackwell, Timmy, 246–47, 256–57
Blake, Jeff, 217
Blue Grass Classic, 92
Bobo, William Herschel, 14
Bockenstette, Ken, 80
Boley, Michael, 252–54, 257–58, 260
Bolis, Henry (Frenchie), 44
Bolt, Carl, 79–81
Booker, Deon, 206
Booth, Eric, 228, 230–31, 233, 235
Borde, Charles, 57
Bourgeois, Gary, 119
Boutwell, Tommy, 122–28
Bowden, Bobby, 164, 185
Bower, Jeff, 148–50, 152–53, 155, 157–58, 204–5, 209, 211, 215, 224, 226, 230, 232, 235, 243
Bower, Kristen, 232
Bowling Green State University, 155, 157, 168, 172

Bowman, Brad, 158
Boyd, Barry, 222
Boyd, Clay (Goofus), 27–28, 30
Boyd, Homer, 88
Boyette, Randy, 163–64, 166, 168
Bradley, Ricky, 201, 203, 205–7
Bradshaw, Terry, 118, 124, 127, 132
Bramlett, John, 106
Brannan, Herman (Bull), 110, 112–13, 116, 117
Brasfield, S. A., 17
Brashier, Jimmy, 70, 77
Bratkowski, Zeke, 78
Brennan, Tommy, 117–18
Brewer, Kidd, 35
Bridges, Jeremy, 250, 254
Brigham Young University, 158, 160
Brock, Fred, 218, 224–26, 228
Brookley Field, 43
Brooks, Greg, 247, 250, 254, 257, 259–60
Broussard, Patrick, 192
Broussard, Steve, 139, 142–43
Browden, Terrell, 253, 260
Brown, Bud, 182, 187, 191
Brown, Chuck Carr, 168
Brown, Curtis, 224
Brown, Dwayne, 166
Brown, Frank, 52, 58
Brown, Jim, 179
Brown, Morris (Lightin'), 49, 52–54, 57, 58, 61, 65, 68
Brown, Randolph, 195, 196, 199
Brown, Robert, 224, 235
Brown, Robert (Rabbitt), 109, 112, 115–16
Brown, Ron, 178
Browning, Kevin, 172
Broyles, Sammy, 90, 92
Brumfield, Jackson, 70, 73
Bryant, John, 99
Bryant, Paul (Bear), 59, 122, 126, 131, 179
Bryant, Scott, 207, 210
Buckhalter, Chris, 219, 222–23, 225, 227–29

Building Dominance Campaign, 256
Burckel, Joe, 167
Burgdorf, Brian, 226
Burns, Leonard, 27
Busby, J. M. (Red), 11
Busby, J. R. (Black), 11
Butler, Dexter, 99
Butler, Kevin, 191
Butler, Randy, 169
Bynum, Glen, 115, 118–19
Byrd, Richard, 191, 194
Byrd, Timmy, 192

Caldwell, Dick, 70
California, University of, 256
California State–Fullerton, University of, 158
Campbell, Bobby, 47, 55
Campbell, Clifton C. (Mutt), 6, 8, 10–11
Campbell, Jim, 200
Campbell, Wendell, 101–3
Campion, Turk, 50
Cardenas, Eddie, 79
Carmody, Jim, 176, 183, 186, 193, 204
Carmody, Steve, 191
Carpenter, Dickie, 132
Carr, Sonny, 53, 56
Carroll, Ricky, 222–23
Carrozza, Falco, 55
Carswell Air Force Base, 69
Carter, Damion, 257–58
Carter, Perry, 217, 219, 223, 225
Carter, Simmie, 200, 205, 207, 215
Casey, Quintus, 214
Casnave, Greg, 260
Caudill, Barry, 163
Centers, Larry, 205
Chamberlain Hunt Academy, 7, 9
Channell, Ronnie, 123–24, 126
Chatham, Senator Ray, 147
Chattanooga, University of. See Tennessee–Chattanooga, University of
Cheatham, Ron, 155, 157–58

Childress, William, 20
Cincinnati, University of, 160, 164, 167, 170, 216, 219, 228, 230, 233, 241, 245, 252, 257
Citadel, The, 16, 111, 122
Clancy, Chuck (Fancy), 149, 155, 157–58, 163
Clark, Harry, 41
Clark, S. A., 23
Clark, Steve, 179, 181, 184–85, 189–90
Clark, William, 22
Clarke Memorial College, 15–19, 22–23
Clay, Billy, 245
Clements, M. G. (Foots), 44
Cleveland, Robert (Ace), 73, 207
Coats, Willie Gene (Teenie), 85, 90–91
Coggin, Cliff, 56–59, 61–63, 133, 234
Coleman, Billy, 102–7
Coleman, Chiles, 93
Coleman, Sidney, 204
Collier, Reggie, 172, 174–77, 179–82, 184–85, 187
Collins, Bobby, 135, 156, 158, 177, 182–83
Collins, Pat, 204
Collins, Vernard, 209, 216
Colmer, Congressman William, 45
Colorado State, 196, 216, 242
Colson, Butch, 133
Compton, Tommy, 192
Conerly Trophy, 254
Conference USA, formation of, 225–26
Conner, Alma Graham, 25, 28
Conner, Governor Martin Sennett, 25
Cook, Chuck, 167, 172, 174
Cook, Fred, 141, 144, 147–48, 150–51, 155
Cook, Hamp, 80
Cook, Joe, 9, 18
Cook, Robert Cecil, 46, 50

Cooley, Travis, 260
Cooper, James, 195
Copiah-Lincoln High School, 6
Copiah-Lincoln Junior College, 19
Cordill, Oli, 108
Corner, Willie, 163, 170
Corso, Lee, 80
Courington, Antwon, 256, 259
Cowpert, Roland, 6
Cox, Ernest, 31
Craft, Troy, 114, 120
Crane, Losa, 14
Craver, Keyuo, 240
Crenshaw, Mike (Crazy), 166–67
Cristofol, Dr. Joaquin, 50
Critty, Armand, 41
Cumbie, Seth, 258
Cunningham, Donald, 228
Cunningham, Doug, 120

Dabbs, Fortner (Sporty), 36
Dale, Roland, 128, 151–52, 155, 177, 183, 186, 193, 197
D'Angelo, Micky, 251–53, 256
Daniels, Keith, 199
Darling, John, 144
Davenport, Jim (Peanut), 79–80
Davis, Bill, 121, 136–37, 139
Davis, Cable, 239
Davis, Chuck, 207–9
Davis, Fred (Tiny), 19
Davis, J. W. (Peck), 21
Davis, Jim (Coon Dog), 80
Davis, Rod, 245, 250, 252–54, 257–60
Davis, Tommy, 126
Davis, W. J. (Puny), 7, 10
Dawson, Jim, 99
Dayton, University of, 80, 83–84
Dedwylder, Charlie, 102, 105
DeFranco, Tony, 109
Dejarnette, Sam, 184–85, 187–92
Del Faizo, Jim, 128
Delta State University, 22–23, 27–30, 36, 39, 41, 43, 60, 65, 212, 216

Dement, Robert (Curley), 54–55
Demerest, Aley, 227
Dennery, Mike, 144, 147, 150–51
Denson, Hunter, 28
Devore, Hugh, 80
Devrow, Billy, 115–16, 119, 121
DeWitt, Leroy, 231
Dews, C. L. (Dipsey), 41
Dickey, Curtis, 155
Dickey, Doug, 128
Dickey, Fred, 44
Dickinson, Bo, 84–88
Dillie, A. B., 6
Dixon, Hanford, 163, 165, 178
Doggett, Joe, 84–85, 87
Donahoe, Gene, 74
Donahoe, Tom, 7
Donegan, Rick, 132–34, 137, 139–43
Donnan, Jim, 229
Dowd, Clyde, 120–21
Dragg, Johnny, 146
Drew, Red, 69
Drive, The, 198–99
DuBois, Napolean, 179
Ducksworth, Robert, 187–92, 194, 196–97
Duggins, Brent, 225
Dunaway, Dickie, 116, 119–20
Dupree, Marcus, 189
Dye, Pat, 194

Eagle Fever, song, 176
East Carolina University, 69, 121, 126, 133, 148, 159, 167, 175, 190, 196, 199, 202, 205, 210, 214, 217, 219, 222, 224, 228, 229, 233, 236, 241, 245, 248, 253, 259
East Texas State, 33, 88
Eastland, Senator James O., 45
Ecuyer, Larry, 107, 109, 114
Edwards, Earl, 103
Edwards, Mickey, 144
Edwards, W. G., 4
Eggersman, Hugh, 138–40

Elder, Reggie, 222
Ellender, Vaughn, 56
Ellis, Norman, 108
Ellisville High School, 10
Ellzey, Charley, 90, 95–96
Elmore, Wade, 190
Elon College, 81
Erhardt, Steve, 23
ESPN, first telecast, 170
Eubanks, John, 252, 254, 258–60

Fabris, Jon, 167
Fairley, Gayle, 26
Farris, Ken, 70
Faulkner, L. E., 27
Faulkner Field, 27–28; expansion of, 135–36; final game, 151; first night game, 30; loudspeaker system added, 35; renovation of, 147; renovation bids opened, 152
Favre, Brett, 174, 201–10, 212–15, 234, 237
Fayard, Lionel, 127, 130, 133
Felder, Darrius, 228
Felts, Nollie, 12
Ferguson, Chip, 205
Ferlise, Pat, 70
Ferrell, Hugh (Hi), 15–16
Ferrell, Pat, 198, 200, 204
Finch, Brownie, 26
Fink, Olaf, 33
Fitzgerald, Dave, 85
Five Hundred Club, 46
Flanagan, Dwight, 133
Fletcher, Billy, 108, 114
Fletcher, I. B., 32
Florida, University of, 148, 219, 225, 232
Florida State University, 73, 75, 77, 80, 83, 85, 88, 99, 104, 110, 113, 141, 161, 163, 168, 170, 180, 184, 200, 201, 205, 207, 231
Floyd, John, 242
Floyd, Nick, 226

Floyd, Ricky, 168–71, 174, 176–77, 179, 181–82
Foley, Bill, 138, 141–43
Football Writers Association of America, 97
Fore, Steve, 122
Forte, James (Pickle), 44
Fortune, Dr. Porter, 101
Forward Lateral Game vs. East Carolina, 199–200
Foshee, Win, 131
Fourcade, John, 176
Fowler, Amos, 166
Fowler, Dannye, 237
Francis, Brandon, 230–31, 242
Freeman, Glover, 36
Fremin, Jerry, 158
Frerotte, Gus, 223
Fry, Rusty, 114
Fuell, Don, 94, 98, 100–4
Fulkerson, Jack, 70
Fumblerooski, 216
Furlow, Spicer, 6

Gabriel, Roman, 100, 103
Galleryfurniture.com Bowl, 249–50
Gamble, Tracy, 189, 191
Gandy, Shelton, 195–98, 200, 201–2, 204–7, 234
Gantt, Kyle, 141, 143
Garner, Bobby, 243, 247
Garner, Bobby (Ole Miss), 164
Garrard, David, 236, 241, 248
Garrison, Tommy, 123
Garry, Ben (Go-Go), 154, 157–61, 163–64, 166, 185, 254
Gay, Jack, 17
Gemmel, Rick, 154–55
George, President J. B., 34, 39, 45
Georgia, University of, 77–78, 191, 213, 221, 229
Georgia State, 42
Giannini, Richard, 238, 256
Gibson, Barry, 146, 148, 150, 154
Gibson, Claude, 100

Gideon, Sherrod, 232, 234–35, 237–40, 243
Gill, Art, 119
Gillette, Walker, 132
GMAC Mobile Alabama Bowl, 245, 249
Goines, Andre, 222
Golden, Wiley, 6
Golden Eagles, name changed to, 146
Goodson, Bill, 176
Gordon, Ron, 116
Gorney, Bill, 109–10, 113–14
Grady, Paul, 139
Graham, Heath, 224–25, 227–28
Great Hemingway Stadium Football Robbery, 144
Green, Bernard (Reed), 27–29, 34, 37, 44–46, 59, 71, 83, 93, 96, 101, 116, 128, 129, 147–48, 151–52
Green, John, 92
Griffith, Doc, 113
Guin, Ace, 36
Gulf Coast (Perkinston) Junior College, 17, 19
Gulf Coast Military Academy, 5–7, 9–12, 15–17
Gulf States Conference: departure from, 71; formed, 55
Gullette, A. T., 17–18
Gulley, Josh, 241
Gulley, L. T., 221–25
Guy, Ray, 136–44, 146–47

Hackney, J. P. (Noonie), 17–20, 44
Haddix, Michael, 171
Hadl, John, 144
Haeusler, Greg, 185
Hale, James, 167
Hale, John, 126, 132
Haley, Danny, 124–25, 127
Hallman, Curley, 204, 225
Halstead, Dr. James, 186
Hamilton, Bobby, 218, 220, 223

Hamilton, Brad, 223
Hammond, Jeff, 163–64, 168
Handy, Leroy, 239, 243, 245–46, 248
Hanna, Brant, 241–42, 244–45, 247
Hansford, Preston, 201, 203, 205
Hardaway, Tim, 232–33, 237
Hardin-Simmons, 98
Hardy, Terry, 235
Harmon, Eugene, 218, 227–28
Harper, Greg, 247
Harper, Scott, 225
Harrington, Larry, 169
Harris, Anthony, 207, 215
Harris, Anthony (RB), 252, 258–59
Harris, Bobo, 196
Harris, Jerry, 189
Harris, Mike, 128
Harrison, Craig, 192
Hart, Granville (Scrappy), 70
Harvey, Marvin, 165, 167–70, 172, 174, 178
Harwood, Durley, 50
Hatcher, Wayne, 137, 140
Hatley, Ralph, 83
Havana, University of (Cuba), 50
Havard, Jimmy, 103, 106
Hawaii, University of, 165
Hayden, Neb, 131
Haynes, Jimmy, 143
Haynes, Steve, 161
Hays, Harold, 103
Heard, Kevin, 236
Heidelburg, (Wee) Willie, 130, 138–39, 142
Helms, Paul H., 78
Hendren, Jimmy, 131
Hendrix, Caleb, 257
Henley, Joe, 243, 252
Henry, Greg, 169
Henry, James, 202–7
Henry, Malachi, 160, 163
Henry, Onesimus, 198, 200
Herring, Charlie, 30
Herring, George, 79–81, 83

Herrmann, L. T., 72, 79
Herron, Johnny, 142–43
Hervey, Derrick, 225, 228
Hicks, Jim, 260
Hicks, Roger, 103
Higdon, Ron, 114
Hightower, Aaron, 218–19
Hill, George, 207
Hinds Junior College, 17
Hobson, Clell, 71
Holcomb, Chad, 228
Holden, Dobie, 27
Hollingsworth, Gary, 212
Hollingsworth, Luther, 36
Holman, Rodney, 171
Holmes, Benton, 4
Holmes, Bobby, 60–62, 68
Holsclaw, Billy, 91
Homan, Dennis, 122
Homecoming, in Biloxi, 157
Honaker, Doug (Spot), 51, 56
Hontas, Roch, 171
Hooker, Danny, 126
Horn, Don, 175–76, 179
Hosemann, David, 156, 163–65
Hoskins, Derrick, 216–17
Houston, University of, 88, 230–31, 234, 237, 244, 248, 258
Houston, Zaid, 243
Houston Bowl, 254
Howard, Carl (Chicken), 51–52
Howard, Thomas (Scoop), 39
Howard College. *See* Samford University
Howe, Glen, 182, 187, 191
Hubert, Allison (Pooley), 25, 27, 34
Hudson, Johnny, 96
Huff, Bob, 10–11
Hughes, Bobby, 84–85
Hultz, Don, 100, 105
Hultz, George, 98, 104
Humanitarian Bowl, 237
Humphries, Keith, 181
Hunter, Scott, 125–26, 131
Hurricane Hilda, 112

Idaho, University of, 131, 237
Illinois, University of, 232, 251
Inclan, Dr. Clemente, 50
Independence Bowl, 177, 207, 214
Independence Bowl Football Association, 205
Indiana, University of, 227
Integration, of the football program, 129
Iosia, Mike, 221
Isler, Alan, 123
Ivy, Gary, 171

Jackson, Bo, 194
Jackson, Danny, 168, 179
Jackson, Eddie Ray, 202, 207–8, 215
Jackson, Julius, 240
Jackson, Kevin, 221
Jackson, Michael, 209, 215
Jackson, Simpson, 20
Jackson, Wayne, 58
Jackson State University, 202
Jacksonville, Florida "home game," 207
Jacksonville (Ala.) State, 35, 46
James, Michael, 243
James, Tommy, 123
Jarrell, Billy, 72, 76, 78, 85
Jimenez, Jason, 254
Johnson, Chris, 247, 250, 253
Johnson, John, 121–24, 126
Johnson, Kenny, 244–46
Johnson, LaShon, 219
Johnson, M. C. (Tuffy), 41
Johnson, Paul B., 108
Johnson, Roland, 214, 216
Johnson, Stan, 120
Johnston, Frank, 124, 127
Johnston, Richard, 92
Jones, Curt, 252–54
Jones, J. W. (Dagwood), 41
Jones, Peter (Jabo), 42
Jones, Rayshun, 247
Jones, Ronald, 260
Jones, Terrance, 199, 206

Jones County High School, 11
Jones Junior College, 31
Jordan, Ralph (Shug), 96
Jordan, Sonny, 49
Jordan, Tom, 167
Jorge, Ernie, 74
Juneau, Curry, 79, 81

Kamper Park, 4
Karcher, Ken, 192
Katrishen, William (Mike), 44, 50, 55
Kauchick, Eddie, 70
Keckin, Val, 99
Keefe, Bill, 77
Keith, Kasey, 235
Kellett, Dr. Boyd, 198
Kelly, Jeff, 239–41, 243–48, 250
Kemper, Elmer, 70
Kendrigan, Jimmy, 50
Kennedy, Adam, 223
Kennedy, President John F., assassinated, 111
Kennelly, Pat, 50
Kenner, Deontey, 241
Kenney, Marchant, 227, 229, 231, 235
Kent, Robert, 254
Kentucky, University of, 59, 199
Key, Radell, 130
Keyes, Jimmy, 123–24
Killingsworth, Emanuel, 164
Kimbrough, Frank, 95
Kinard, Billy, 144
King, Buddy, 210
King, Claude, 88
King, Earl, 118
King, Shaun, 227, 233, 236
King, Thomas Rivers, 44
Kirksey, William, 210
Knighten, Billy, 199–200, 204
Koen, Sankey, 26–27
Kolinsky, Nick, 104, 109
Kondrat, Ihor (Mike), 122–23, 127

Ladd Stadium, 67, 80, 94–95, 98–99, 103, 107, 122, 131, 140, 154–55, 245
Laird, John, 110, 112–14
Lamar University, 154, 157, 177, 181
Lambright, Maxie, 56–58, 98, 108, 110, 116, 124, 132, 143
Lance, Bobby, 87–88, 91
Landrum, Leslie, 23
Landrum, Mike, 189
Lang, Elmo, 70, 72
Langford, Eddie, 56, 58, 60–62
Langley, Hoppy, 167
Lantrip, Ken, 143
Larson, Billy, 89–90, 99–101
Lassic, Derrick, 218
Latham, Joe, 47, 49, 51–52, 55
Latson, Steve, 225
Latta, Randy, 158
Law, Don, 153, 163
Lawrence, DaRon, 259
Ledyard, Hal, 69, 72
Lee, Kendrick, 223, 227, 230–31
Legion Field, 144–45, 153, 160, 179, 190, 218, 226, 229, 232, 243, 253
LeGros, John, 47–48, 52, 58, 59
LeGros, Tom, 65, 68, 70
Lehman, Howard, 73
Lemoine, Greg, 209
Leonard, Jabo, 155
Lewis, Cliff, 168–69, 176–77
Lewis, Cooter, 49
Libretto, Charlie, 199
Lippincott, Dooney, 110, 114, 118
Lipps, Louis, 179, 181, 184, 187–91
Livesay, Jim, 312
Livings, Mike, 177
Livingston, Joe, 73
Logan, Craig, 139, 141
Logan, Joel, 208, 213
Lomoro, Johnny, 218, 221, 223, 229–31

Longest, H. B., 4, 6
Lorio, Rene, 95
Lossette, David, 23, 26–27
Louisiana College, 15, 17, 21–23, 26, 28–29, 31–32, 34, 37, 39, 41, 49, 56
Louisiana State Normal College. *See* Northwestern State
Louisiana State University, 69, 92, 225
Louisiana Superdome, 157, 174, 185, 199, 206, 214, 219, 223, 230, 235, 244
Louisiana Tech University, 32, 33, 35, 42, 46, 51, 56, 58, 62, 68, 70, 73, 77, 78, 79, 81, 84, 87, 88, 96, 101, 104, 108, 110, 114, 117, 118, 124, 127, 132, 139, 142, 143, 157, 161, 166, 175, 187, 188, 191, 194, 207, 217, 218
Louisiana–Lafayette, University of, 12, 16, 17, 19, 20, 23, 28, 29, 32, 33, 37, 40, 41, 42, 43, 47, 52, 56, 60, 67, 69, 72, 77, 102, 106, 110, 112, 136, 155, 178, 185, 190, 192, 195, 200, 203, 206, 209, 214, 221, 224, 228, 229, 235, 241, 246, 258
Louisiana–Monroe, University of, 184, 198, 202, 221
Louisville, University of, 62, 68, 70, 74, 169, 171, 177, 181, 185, 190, 194, 196, 200, 201, 206, 208, 213, 216, 221, 227, 229, 232, 236, 241, 244, 247, 253
Love, Ernest, 4
Lowery, Erik, 186
Loyola of the South, 11, 15, 29
Lucas, Dr. Aubrey K., 155, 183, 186, 193, 197, 204, 226
Lumpkin, John, 22, 27
Lumpkin, Lance, 26–27
Lyons, Billy, 106–7

[364] INDEX

Magee, Roy, 239, 244, 250
Magee, Skylor, 250
Majors, Johnny, 221
Mallard, DeShone, 238
Malone, Toderick, 227
Mann, Walter, 70
Manning, Archie, 126, 138
Manning, Eli, 254
Manning, Peyton, 228, 233
Marion Military Institute, 11, 15, 19, 21
Marsh, Chafan, 215–17
Martello, Tony, 23, 26–27
Martin, Kenny, 108
Mason, Jim (Brick), 76
Massengale, A. C. (Mule), 35–36, 40
Mates, Dick, 103
Mathews, Shane, 219
May, Dean, 181
May, Jack, 87
McAlpin, Jack, 121
McCain, William D., 91, 93–94, 101, 105, 108, 128–29, 140, 151–52
McCaleb, Darren, 258–60
McCaleb, Maude, 4
McCarthy, Milo, 118, 120–21, 123
McClellan, Mike, 114, 120–21
McClendon, Frank, 21
McCleskey, Lynn, 11
McDaniel, Dane, 165, 167, 169–70, 172
McDaniel, Ed, 70, 72–73, 171
McDole, Mardye, 166, 176
McDowell, Thad, 208, 217
McElroy, Bucky, 70–76, 78
McGee, Chris, 196, 201, 203
McGee, Harvey, 142, 148, 150–51
McGee, Howard, 221–23
McGeehee, Lewis (Maggie), 21
McGuire, Donnie, 117
McInnis, Hugh, 89, 91–92, 94–95
McKellar, Bob, 70, 72
McKinney, Myreon, 219, 221
McLaurin, Stella, 4
McLellan, H. C. (Bill), 197, 215, 226, 238
McLendon, Henry, 235, 238
McLeod, Andin, 94, 99–100, 108
McLeod, Ben, 108–9
McLeod, C. R. (Tall), 6
McLeod, Carl, 6
McMahon, Homer, 20
McMillan, Terry, 119, 124, 126
McMurray, Jimmy, 100
McMurray College, 60, 66, 69
McNeese State University, 177
McRae, Albert, 223
McRae, H. V., 4
McReynolds, George, 221
McSwain, Rufus, 44
Meador, Morris, 90, 94–96, 99–100, 102
Meeks, Lawrence, 81, 87
Memorial Stadium, Jackson, Miss., 74, 78, 83, 108, 115, 124, 141, 146, 154, 170, 180, 185, 192, 194, 198, 201, 206
Memphis, University of (Memphis State), 31, 32, 71, 75, 77, 80, 82, 85, 87, 89, 95, 101, 102, 106, 112, 114, 115, 119, 123, 124, 127, 132, 139, 142, 146, 150, 152, 157, 162, 166, 168, 171, 180, 185, 189, 191, 196, 199, 202, 206, 209, 214, 216, 217, 222, 224, 228, 230, 234, 237, 241, 244, 247, 252, 257
Meridian College, 8
Meridian High School, 7
Metro Conference, gain admission to, 183
Miami (Florida), University of, 75
Miciotto, Gus, 58
Mikel, Billy, 130–33, 140
Miles, Russell, 126
Miller, Bruce (Juice), 181
Mills, Shawn, 242–43
Mills, Zack, 248
Mills Kills play, 242
Millsaps College, 10–12, 16, 23, 25, 27, 29–30, 32, 37, 39, 41–42
Miracle of Louisville, 208–9
Mississippi, University of, 5–7, 10, 27, 29, 36, 39, 119, 123, 126, 132, 138, 142, 144, 148, 153, 157, 159, 164, 167, 170, 175, 184, 188, 192; freshmen, 16
Mississippi College, 6–7, 9, 16, 19–20, 23, 26, 29–30; freshmen, 12, 19
Mississippi Industrial Training School, 10
Mississippi Normal College, 4
Mississippi Southern College, name changed to, 40; stadium dorm, 64–65
Mississippi State University, 32, 54, 113, 116, 119, 123, 126, 131, 139, 144, 149, 157, 160, 166, 167, 171, 176, 180, 185, 189, 191, 194, 198, 202, 206, 208, 213; freshmen, 11, 15, 16, 17
Missouri, University of, 181
Mitchell, Brian, 209
Mize (Smith County) High School, 10
Mobile Military Academy, 5–6
Mobile Shipbuilders, 43
Montgomery, Carlos, 148, 150, 153–55, 157–58, 160
Montgomery, Johnnie, 8, 11
Montgomery, Mark, 218, 223
Moody, Ary, 161
"Moon over Hattiesburg" game vs. Louisville, 214
Moore, Dana, 180
Moore, Scrappy, 61
Morgan, A. D. (Sandy), 39, 402
Morgan, Ed, 121, 125
Morgan, Joe, 59
Morrison, Ray, 9

Morrow, Tommy, 88, 92, 94, 99–101
Moses, Robert, 171
Mott, Andrew, 191–92, 196–97, 200
Moulton, Larry, 125–26, 128, 130–32, 137, 140
Mullin, Buster, 48, 50
Murray, Eddie, 171
Murray State University, 29–30
Muscarello, Phil, 70
Musmeci, Phil (Moose), 68, 70
Myers, Jim, 94

Nall, Herman, 109, 110, 112–14
Nasty Bunch, 167
National Collegiate Athletic Association: admitted into, 71; on probation with, 185–87, 193
Nations, Lance, 216–20
Nebraska, University of, 239, 257
Nelson, Dwayne, 208
Nevada, University of, 232, 237
Newsom, Buddy, 126
Newsome, Ozzie, 158
Newton Aggies, 19
Newton, Matt, 242
Nix, Derrick, 236–39, 241–43, 246, 251–56
Nix, John, 235, 246
Nix, Tyrone, 220, 223
Nobles, Bennie Ray, 47, 51, 54, 58
Nobles, Herbert, 70
North Carolina State University, 91, 100, 103, 107, 109, 121, 215
North Dakota State University, 83
North Texas State University, 75, 79, 81, 95, 164, 168, 170, 180
Northeast Louisiana. *See* Louisiana–Monroe, University of
Northern Illinois, 218, 226
Northwestern State University (Louisiana Normal College), 23, 26, 28–31, 33, 35, 37, 40–41, 43, 49, 53, 56–57, 61, 68–69, 73, 158, 192, 195, 239
Norton, Larry, 227
Nunez, Eddie, 156

O'Brien, Buster, 127
Odom, Archie, 33
Odom, David, 164, 169
Odom, Reggie, 161
Ogletree, Powell, 105
Oklahoma, University of, 189
Oklahoma City University, 47, 52, 57, 61
Oklahoma State University, 243, 246, 254
Olander, Mike, 99, 101–2
Olson, Steve, 131
O'Mara, B. B., 8, 10–11
Orange, Doyle, 141–44, 146, 150–51
Orphan, Dino, 79
Oubre, Willie (Kemper County Flash), 32–34, 36
Owen, Jim, 60
Owen, Joe, 112
Owens, Anthony, 221
Owens, Don, 79, 81, 85–86

Pacific, College of, 74
Packer, Walter, 157
Padgett, Terry, 119
Palazzo, Buddy, 137, 142–46
Palmer, Danny, 130, 131
Palmer, Don, 193
Palmer, Ricky, 145–46, 148–50, 155, 157–58
Paper Bowl, 63
Parilli, Babe, 59
Parker, Charley, 104, 109
Parker, Doug, 147
Parker, Matt, 224
Parker, Stoney, 166, 168–69
Parquet, Jeremy, 250, 260
Parris Island Marines, 77

Parrish, Terrance, 235–36, 242
Patrick, Malcolm, 31–32
Patterson, Lloyd, 168
Paul, Terrell, 250, 254, 259–60
Payne, Jim, 104
Peacock, R. V., 7
Pearl Harbor, effects of, 43
Pearl River Junior College, 15–19, 21–22, 30
Pearson, Ryan, 223–24
Penn, Chris, 223
Penn State University, 235, 248
Pepper, Hugh Laurin, 71–72, 74, 76–78
Perkins, John, 92
Perkins, Ray, 121–22
Perkinston AHS, 8, 10
Perkinston High School, 6
Pharr, Tommy, 126, 131
Phenix, Perry, 235
Phillips, Bubba, 51–54, 56–63, 66–68
Phillips, Luke, 254
Phillips, Otto (Hippo), 30
Phillips, P. E., 4
Phillips, Robert, 175
Phillips, Terry Don, 197
Pieper, Chris, 153, 157–58
Pierce, Chris, 224–25, 227–28
Pinkston, Todd, 239–41, 243
Pitts, John, 163
Pittsburgh, University of, 216, 221, 234
Plunkett, Wilson, 143, 146, 150
Podwika, Don, 95
Poole, Barney, 62
Pope, Marcus, 217, 219, 221
Poplarville AHS, 8
Poplarville High School, 5–7, 11
Posey, Bobby, 73
Posey, Jeff, 229
Potero, Johnnie, 11
Powe, Myron, 250
Powe, William, 50

Powell, Raymond, 179
Preston, Dave, 157
Pruitt, Etric, 243, 245, 247, 252–54, 257–60
Pugh, Dan, 99, 101–2
Purser, Jamie, 236–37, 242
Purvis, Leo, 32–33
Purvis, Tommy, 87
Purvis, Vic, 109–18
Purvis High School, 11–12

Quarterback Club, 46
Quick, Henry, 123, 131

Radio broadcast, first, 22
Raisin Bowl, 49
Ranager, George, 126
Rankins, LaBarion, 219
Ratcliff, Melvin, 218
Ratesic, John, 102
Ray, Alex, 260
Rayburn, Gary, 123–24, 133
Recontruction Finance Corporation, 46
Redd, Eric, 201
Redman, Chris, 229, 232, 236, 241
Reed, Greg, 214
Reed, Randy, 138
Refrigerator Bowl, 74
Reynolds, Henry (Hindu), 51, 57–58
Rhoden, Marcus, 119
Rice, Grantland, 76
Rich, John, 36
Richards, Charlie, 132
Richards, Eric, 228
Richards, Fred, 194
Richmond, University of, 106, 109, 112, 116, 120, 124, 127, 132, 137, 142, 144, 148, 166, 177, 179, 187
Riley, Clovis, 78
Riley, E. J., 4
Rippetoe, Benny, 131
Roberts, C. C., 7

Roberts, Kenny, 208
Roberts, Lee, 230–32, 234–37
Roberts, M. M., 7, 159–60
Roberts, Tim, 217
Roberts Stadium: dedication and opening, 159; facelift, 226; new scoreboard, 235
Rock, The, 39; players touching, 232; replica of pedestal, 232; use of name returns, 231–32
Rockwell, Bishop, 44
Rodman, George, 114
Rogers, Albert, 17, 18
Rogers, Wayne, 245
Romo, Joe, 51
Rosamond, Ivan, 68
Rouchon, Tony, 74
Rouse, Doug, 125–26
Roussel, Tommy, 117, 119
Rowan, Tommy, 6
Rowell, Eugene, 206, 209–10
Rowland, Brad, 60
Rubley, T. J., 217
"Rumble at the Rock" game, 251
Russell, G. H., 17
Russell, John, 92
Ryals, Chris, 210, 217
Ryckman, Billy, 161–62

Saggus, Gerry, 138
Salazar, Xavier, 230
Salmon, Danny, 108
Sam Houston State, 39, 41
Samford University, 16, 224
San Diego State, 127, 137, 141
Sanders, Al (Apple), 51, 56, 58
Sanders, Deion, 205
Satcher, Doug, 114, 116
Saunders, William (Willie) B., 19
Sawyer, John, 146, 148, 150, 152–53, 155
Scalzo, Chester, 32
Scherer, Rich, 179
Schnellenberger, Howard, 196, 214

Scott, Cedric, 243, 245–46
Scott, DeQuincy, 235, 245
Scott, Eric, 260
Scott, Jake, 36, 44
Seashore Camp Ground, 12
Sekul, George (FB), 107–8
Sekul, George (QB), 87–92
Seligman, Harvey, 84
Sellers, Davy, 181
Sellout '95, 226
September 11 attack, 246
Seroka, Chris, 201–3, 205, 207
Shackelford, Craig, 199, 201
Shaffer, Jake, 103
Shaffer, John, 197
Shaffer, Mike, 221
Shannon, Karr, 229
Shaw, Harold, 225, 232–35
Shepard, Bob, 127
Shinaut, Dick, 78
Shira, Charley, 123
Shula, Mike, 198
Silva, Matt, 252
Simmons, Woodrow, 30
Simons, Claude (Monk), 92
Sims, Sawyer, 46, 49
Singleton, Derrick, 230
Singleton, James, 218, 221
Sipe, Brian, 138, 141
Sixth Service Squadron, 43
Sklopan, John, 99–100, 102, 106, 108
Slaughter, T. J., 236, 238, 243
Slay, Glyn, 51, 56, 58
Slay, Ronald J., 4, 8
Slive, Michael, 225
Sloan, Steve, 170
Smallwood, Fred, 79–81
Smith, Alex, 227
Smith, Antowain, 231
Smith, Bracie, 33, 44
Smith, Chandler, 229
Smith, Don, 192, 194
Smith, Eric, 163, 166

Smith, Eugene, 4
Smith, H. A. (Bear), 76
Smith, Jay, 47, 49, 51, 54–55
Smith, Kenney, 232
Smith, Mike, 155
Smith, Nate, 253
Smith, Tim, 194
Smith, Tony, 208–10, 213–17
Smith, W. C. (Red), 7
Smith, William (Bee), 36–37
Smithart, Bobby, 163–64, 166
Solomon, Freddie, 155
Sorey, Eric, 197
South Florida, University of, 244, 252, 258
Southeastern Louisiana University, 41, 50, 54, 56, 58, 67, 69, 72, 77, 79, 81, 84, 87, 90, 94, 114, 118, 124, 130
Southern Conference Meetings, 101
Southern Independent Officials Association, 200
Southern Intercollegiate Athletic Association (SIAA), 16, 18, 22–23; eligibility, 20
Southern Mississippi, University of: name changed to, 105; return to major college ranks, 108; stadium construction appropriation, 140, 147; stadium feasibility study, 135–36
Southwest Mississippi Junior College, 21
Southwestern Louisiana, University of. *See* Louisiana–Lafayette, University of
Southwestern University of Memphis (Rhodes College), 26, 28
Sparkman, Danny, 189
Speracino, Jack, 79
Speyrer, Chris, 154
Spring Hill College, 6–7, 10, 16–18, 21, 23, 26, 28–32, 35, 41, 43
Spruiell, Frank, 57–59, 61, 62

St. Mary's (Texas), 40–41, 43
St. Stanislaus, 11, 18
Stabler, Kenny (Snake), 121
Stallings, Gene, 212
Stanton, Hank, 62
State Teachers College, name changed to, 12
Stephen F. Austin, 47, 48, 53, 56, 205
Stephens, Harold (Hayseed), 98
Sterling, Hal, 101
Stetson, 15, 74
Stevens, George, 54, 57
Stewart, Bill, 56
Stewart, Daleroy, 246
Stewart, J. J., 172
Stonestreet, J. D., 30–32, 55
Stringfellow, Joe, 43, 46
Stringfellow, Julius (Poochie), 115, 118–19
Strock, Don, 143
Stromick, Joe, 112
Stuart, Clyde (Heifer), 76
Studdard, Vernon, 126
Student Athlete Medical Fund, establishment of, 256
Sugar Bowl, 92
Sullivan, C. C., 50
Sullivan, Manuel, 130
Sullivan, Pat, 137, 142
Sumrall, George, 115–19, 121
Sun Bowl, 74, 78, 93
Supple, Buddy, 87, 90–91, 94–95
Surace, Dicky, 140
Surtain, Patrick, 225, 231, 233, 235
Sweet, Michael, 160
Switzer, Reginald, 39–40, 42

Taconi, Nolan, 27
Talley, Paul (Bull), 14–16
Tampa, University of, 72, 77, 122, 128, 155
Tangerine Bowl, 86, 88, 93, 181
Tapper, Clint, 150

Tate, Eddie, 149
Taylor, C. J. (Pete), 47, 98, 108, 110
Taylor, Jerry, 83, 85
Taylor, Jim, 92
Taylor, Jim (Stump), 213–15
Taylor, Larry, 171
Taylor, Ronald (Clump), 163, 168–69, 172
Teague, Albert, 169
Tennessee, University of, 65, 228, 233, 243
Tennessee–Chattanooga, University of, 16, 60, 67, 69, 72, 75, 77, 78–79, 81, 85, 87, 91, 95, 101, 102, 106, 112–14, 117, 146, 148
Tensi, Steve, 110, 113
Terrell, Clemon, 177, 184, 189, 191
Terrell, Daryl, 228–29, 231
Texas A&M, 94, 199, 201, 208, 224, 235, 240
Texas Christian University, 208, 245, 249, 253, 259
Texas Western. *See* Texas–El Paso, University of
Texas–Arlington, University of (Arlington State), 102, 105, 137, 143, 149, 154, 157, 163, 166, 179
Texas–El Paso, University of, 78, 207
Thames, Richard (Dick), 50
Thatch, G. C., 4
Thicklen, Willie, 150
Thomas, Adalius, 235, 237–39, 242–43
Thomas, Arnold, 130, 132
Thomas, Duane, 133–34
Thomas, Jack, 98
Thomas, Norris, 150, 155, 158
Thomas, O. M. (Brownie), 26–27
Thomas, Rod, 227–28
Thomas, Rudy, 161
Thompson, Bruce, 169
Thompson, Jack, 4, 6
Thompson, John, 230

Thompson, Olan, 133
Tillman, Darryl, 201–2, 206, 209
Tillman, George (Too-Tall), 174–77, 182, 185, 187
Tillman, Lewis, 202
Tisdale, Brooks, 78
Tobacco Bowl, 50, 74
Tobias, Michael, 221, 223, 225
Tomlinson, LaDainian, 245
Touchstone, G. R., 6
Trahan, Ty, 238
Training table concept, 9
Tregle, Al, 79
Trenton, Ted, 83
Trinity University, 56, 85, 87, 89, 94, 99, 104, 108, 139
Trone, Elbert, 118
Troy State University, 31, 33, 35–36, 39–40, 163
Tucker, R. H. (Herman), 16
Tucker, Torrin, 254
Tujaque, J. M., Jr., 15
Tulane University, 75, 171, 174, 179, 185, 189, 192, 197, 199, 201, 206, 208, 214, 216, 219, 222, 223, 227, 230, 233, 235, 239, 244, 248, 253, 259; freshmen, 10
Tulsa, University of, 217, 218, 223, 225
Turner, Claude, 4
Tyler, Bob, 180

UAB, 244, 247, 253, 256
Ulmer, Terryl, 218, 220
Underwood, Eric, 208
Underwood, George, 98
Underwood, P. W., 81, 85, 108, 110, 115, 128, 133, 139, 155
"Unfinished Business," 234
Union College, 23, 28, 30, 32, 35, 37, 54, 58
Unitas, Johnny, 74
UPI College Division Championship, 93

UPI College Division Poll, 89, 102
Ussery, Larry, 124, 126–27
Utah, University of, 259
Utah State, 146, 150, 155, 227, 229

Valrie, Kerry, 210, 212, 214–15
Van Tone, Art, 41
Vance, Toby, 124–25
Vanderbilt, 75
Vann, Thad (Pie), 34, 43, 46, 59, 70, 76, 91, 93, 96, 106, 108, 116, 128
Vann Hall, approval of, 122
Vaughns, Tyrone, 90
Vaught, Johnny, 127, 132
Veal, Marshall, 145
Venable, L. S., 4
Vetrano, Joe, 41, 44
Villalonga, Michael, 236
Villanova University, 80
Virginia Military Institute (VMI), 116, 120, 142, 154
Virginia Tech, 91, 143, 146, 159, 205, 214, 219, 223
Von Wyl, Jim, 215

Waites, Fred, 54
Walker, David Lee, 67
Walker, Eddie Ray, 185
Walker, Gerald, 20
Walker, Winston, 170–72, 174, 178
Waller, Governor William, 152
Walley, James, 250, 257
Walls, Raymond, 243, 245–46
Walters, Tommy, 107
Walthaw, Cedric, 231
Walton, Lin, 36
Ward, "Chunkin" Charlie, 39
Ward, E. M., 27
Warnsley, Reginald, 201, 210
Washington, Pat, 191
Washington, Ted, 209
Waters, Fred, 58
Waters, Herbert (Hub), 77–79

Waters, Melvin (Bucky), 51, 55
Waters, Tommy, 216–17, 219, 221, 223–24
Watson, Jamey, 178
Webb, Andy, 43–44
Weber State, 150, 156
Weeks, Robbie, 201
Welborn, J. P. (Shorty), 4
Welch, Michael, 215, 219–20
Wells, Robert, 120, 123
Wells, Terrance, 149
Wells, Vernon (Zipper), 46–47, 51–52, 54–57
West Texas State University, 86–87, 90, 95, 99, 133, 139, 143, 144, 150, 153
Westerfield, George, 33–34, 36
Whitcomb, John, 212
White, Chris, 260
White, Doug, 143, 148
White, Jack, 101, 106, 108
White, Ryan, 244
White, Stan, 216, 221
Whitfield, Dallas, 82
Whitley, Rhett, 175, 177, 182
Whitney, Alan, 259
Whitney, Charles, 118
Whittenton, Jesse, 78
Whitworth, E. B. (Ears), 86
Wilburn, Rodney, 144
William & Mary, College of, 117
Williams, Alfred, 201, 205, 207, 209
Williams, Arnie, 215, 217
Williams, Bobby, 236
Williams, Chad, 241, 245, 250
Williams, Jim, 74
Williams, John Bell, 139
Williams, Leonard, 76
Williams, Marty, 207
Williams, M. J. (Blondie), 5
Williams, Punkin, 191
Williams, R. M., 8
Williamson, Paul, 77, 80
Williamson, Roy (Pug), 30–34

Willoughby, Ben, 104
Wilson, Irie (Biscuit), 19–22
Wilson, Jerrel, 102, 106–7
Wilson, Walker (Cornbread), 19, 23, 26–27
Wilson, Walter, 199
Winder, Sammy, 167, 171, 175–76, 178–82
Windham, Rod, 123
Windsor, Chris, 229
Winstead, Don, 51, 53–54
Womack, Jeff, 191
Wonsley, George, 176
Wood, Bill, 11
Wood, Brian, 216
Woodard, Mike, 176, 178
Woods, Dawayne, 236, 244–46, 248, 252
Woods, Rashaun, 254
World War I, suspension of football during, 7
World War II, suspension of football during, 43
Wright, Charles Alan, 186
Wright, Governor Fielding, 60
Wright, James Earl, 101
Wright, Mike, 172
Wright, Mike (USM), 157, 160, 163–64
WTBS-TV, 207

Yates, Corey, 259
Yates, Ollie, 87, 89–90
Yellow jackets, 14
Yelverton, Tony, 123–24, 126
Yencho, Bob, 84, 87, 89, 92
Young, Ailrick, 200, 202, 205
Young, Marvin, 253, 256–58, 260

Zeier, Eric, 221
Zunich, Larry, 120